London in the Twentieth Century

A City and Its People

JERRY WHITE

VIKING

VIKING

Published by the Penguin Group
Penguin Books Ltd, 27 Wrights Lane, London w8 5TZ, England
Penguin Putnam Inc., 375 Hudson Street, New York, New York 10014, USA
Penguin Books Australia Ltd, Ringwood, Victoria, Australia
Penguin Books Canada Ltd, 10 Alcorn Avenue, Toronto, Ontario, Canada M4V 3B2
Penguin Books India (P) Ltd, 11 Community Centre,
Panchsheel Park, New Delhi – 110 017, India
Penguin Books (NZ) Ltd, Cnr Rosedale and Airborne Roads,
Albany, Auckland, New Zealand
Penguin Books (South Africa) (Pty) Ltd, 5 Watkins Street,
Denver Ext 4, Johannesburg 2094, South Africa

Penguin Books Ltd, Registered Offices: Harmondsworth, Middlesex, England

First published 2001
1

Set in 11/13.25 pt Monotype Bembo
Typeset by Rowland Phototypesetting Ltd, Bury St Edmunds, Suffolk
Printed in Great Britain by Clays Ltd, St Ives plc

A CIP catalogue record for this book is available from the British Library

ISBN 0–670–89139–8

In memoriam
RAPHAEL SAMUEL

And for
Rosie, Duncan, Thomas,
Jennifer and Catherine

Contents

List of Illustrations

PICTURE ACKNOWLEDGEMENTS

Guildhall Library, Corporation of London: 1, 16; Hulton Getty: 2, 4, 6, 18, 19; London Metropolitan Archives: 3, 5; Tower Hamlets Local History Library & Archives: 7; Museum of London, Docklands Collections: 8, 22; Source Unknown. All Rights Reserved: 9, 11, 12; © Bill Brandt/Bill Brandt Archives Ltd; 'Our Homes, Our Streets', North Kensington Community History Series, No. 2, 1987: 13; Laszlo Moholy-Nagy © DACS 2001: 14, 15; Topham Picturepoint: 17; © Roger Mayne: 20; 'Multi-Racial North Kensington', North Kensington Community History Series, No. 2, 1986: 21; Courtesy of the Museum of London: 23; © Don McCullin: 24; The *Illustrated London News* Picture Library: 25; William Whiffin Collection at the Tower Hamlets Local History Library & Archives: 26; © Michael Kirkland: 27; © John R. J. Taylor. Photo: courtesy of the Museum of London: 28; PA Photos: 29, 31; © *The Times*: 30, 32; © Nick Danziger/ Contact Press Images/Colorific

Every effort has been made to contact the copyright holders. The publishers will be glad to correct any errors or omissions in future editions.

Preface

London is a giant subject. 'The Great World of London' was how Henry Mayhew described it in the 1850s and 100 years on it had roughly tripled in size and population. At some time during that monstrous expansion London became literally unknowable. There could never be a definitive history or biography of the city and its people. Every aspect of life there can fill a book, or several. Famous districts, fashionable neighbourhoods, aristocratic estates, single streets or a single house have all been the subject of literary endeavour, whether the work of a lifetime or passing fancy. There are shelves full of books on London pubs and restaurants, London buses and trams, London statues and memorials, parks and gardens, guilds and trades, its business houses and literary associations, its rivers on and below ground, its graveyards and public conveniences, even a book on London's seagulls. Everything about it has fascinated and intrigued. It is inexhaustible.

So yet another book on London needs no justification, because there will always be more to say. On the other hand, some of the choices I've made in writing this particular book at least call for explanation.

London is an old city. If we believe the archaeologists, who can find no evidence for a significant pre-Roman settlement, it has lasted almost 2,000 years. At some time in the future it may well be proved older still. Given such a past, there is no reason to suppose that London won't go on to enjoy another two millennia or more beyond this. In a longer view of the city's story just what mark will the twentieth century have left on London and the Londoner?

In choosing what to include and what to discard, I've tried to bear this question in mind. Some things demand inclusion. The doubling in size of London on the ground, the evaporation of its manufacturing industry and closure of its working river have been changes of historic importance even in this long view of London. But this is a book as much – maybe more – about Londoners as about London, about the shaping of people by city and city by people. And so most important, positive and creative of all have been the changes wrought on the Londoner in the last fifty years or so by the creation of a multiracial city. All this and more will make up the twentieth century's endowment. These were transcendental events that will determine to some extent the shape of life in London in the twenty-first century and beyond.

So these are unavoidable themes. But in making further choices I've been bound as much by personal inclination as by overarching design. I would defend filling pages on policing and housing, to take two examples, because these things have been generally important in the lives of Londoners – even those who have been law-abiding and well housed. And I think I can justify giving space to those more 'marginal' Londoners who have eked a living in the byways of London life, on its streets, in its clubs and outside the law, for I believe their significance to be an abiding truth about London and the Londoner. But I know I could reasonably have taken just as much space for education or organized religion or shopping or popular music. No doubt there are other examples. At the end, I've kept with the things I know best or am most moved by, for this has had to be one man's selection. And in any event there will be others who bring their own interpretation after mine, as no one will ever have the last word on London and Londoners in the twentieth century.

There could be different but valid points of view on structure as well as content. I have chosen to divide the book into themes while adhering more or less strictly to chronology within each thematic section. It would have been perfectly possible to begin with 'Edwardian London' and then move to 'Inter-war', 'Post-war' and so on. There are gains and losses in both these approaches. But I found it more graspable to consider each theme as having its own narrative dynamic, even though there may need to be some cross-referencing. In the end, I hope the reader will find it easier this way, too.

If choice of material is at the mercy of personal inclination, then personal preference in turn depends on biography. No doubt my own experiences as a Londoner will have shaped this book definitively. I have tried to correct for any north London bias that might creep in through having lived only in Highbury, Earls Court, Wood Green, Clapton, Stamford Hill and Stoke Newington. I have tried to suppress my bourgeois enthusiasm for the London Symphony Orchestra and say something about London's pop music industry (with the patient assistance of family and friends). I have tried to be fair to the achievements of London government though acknowledging its failures, all the while harbouring the guilty secret of having been chief executive of the London Borough of Hackney from 1989 to 1995. Despite having written two previous books on the minutiae of London life, I know just how important it is to hold on to a vision of the city's skeletal structures and seismic movements. As an adopted son of London – I arrived from Dorset in 1970 at the age of twenty-one – I have not been able to rid myself of the idea that 'coming to London' remains one of the great themes in the city's history. As an instinctive (though not limitless) libertarian, so reprehensible in these retributive times, I have retained some enduring sympathy for disaffected and opportunistic Londoners. And I have no time for puritans and puritanism. All this, no doubt, will have left its mark.

Many people have helped and supported me through this delightful task. It wouldn't have been written without the prompting, against my more cautious instincts, of Maggie Hanbury and Andrew Franklin; or without the faith of Andrew Kidd, who commissioned the book and has proved an exemplary editor. My thanks, too, to his colleagues at Penguin Books. I have many other debts. The Nuffield Foundation and the British Academy's Thank-Offering to Britain Fellowship supported my researches financially in the late 1980s; it is only now (after busy years which left no time for scholarly indulgence) that their investment can claim any proper reward. The London Library has been my indispensable first resort for elusive texts, the British Library my last; but I have used material gleaned over the years at the British Library of Political and Economic Science (at the London School of Economics), the local history libraries of Tower Hamlets and Hackney (with special thanks to David Mander of the latter), the Greater London Record Office (with special thanks to the London Labour Party for permission to access its archive there) and Warwick University, who kindly (through the good offices of Carolyn Steedman) granted me an Associate Research Fellowship, which allowed me invaluable use of their library. The Commissioner of Police of the Metropolis, the Port of London Authority, the London Tourist Board, the London Research Centre and Toby Taper of MORI have all responded most generously to my requests for information. And Dan Weinbren gave me enormous help in charting the rise of Labour in outer London between 1919 and 1945.

I am most grateful to the holders of various literary copyrights for their kind permission to quote from texts they own: to Curtis Brown for a quote from Elizabeth Bowen's *The Heat of the Day* (1949); to the Society of Authors as the Literary Representative of the Estate of Compton Mackenzie for a quote from *Sinister Street* (1913–14); and to Pearson Education for a quote from Sam Selvon's *The Lonely Londoners* (1956).

I have also benefited from the selfless sacrifice of friends who have read the whole of the text in draft, namely Sally Alexander, Andrew Williams and Ken Worpole. I'd love to hold them responsible for the errors that I know will have crept into a book that necessarily relies on a multitude of facts and figures, but all sins of omission and commission are inescapably mine.

One of the secret delights of being a lonely researcher, grubbing about in the spare hours left by day job and family, has been the gathering together of my own London library. I know I'm lucky to have been able to do it, even if it has had to take me twenty-five years or more. But I couldn't have done it at all without the restless enterprise of the second-hand book-selling fraternity, whose scholarship and significant role in the nation's intellectual life has gone largely unacknowledged by the writers who exploit it and the reading public who finally benefit from it. So let me pay one small compliment to the antiquarian booksellers of Great Britain and my own special thanks to John Hodgkins, John Coombes, Nick Spurrier, Martyn Davies and Mr Sperr.

Throughout, I have had huge support and encouragement from Rosie and my long-suffering family, who have (almost always) shown forbearance and have (generally) tempered exasperation with tolerant bemusement.

Finally, I have dedicated the book to them and to Raphael Samuel, my mentor as a historian from 1975 until his too early death in 1996. When he was alive he was the person for whom I always imagined myself writing. Even now, he's been my silent interlocutor. I, and so many others, miss him deeply.

Jerry White
Leamington Spa/Reform Club, January 2001

A Note on Areas

Until 1964 Greater London is the Metropolitan Police District; from 1965 it is the modern boundary, including the City, the London Boroughs, the former Greater London Council and (from 2000) the Greater London Authority. Population figures are generally adjusted for the modern boundary (the old Metropolitan Police District was slightly larger). When I refer to 'the city', I mean Greater London. But the City is the City of London or the Square Mile, whose boundaries changed hardly at all in the twentieth century. Inner London is the area covered before 1964 by the Administrative County of London, or the City and the twenty-eight Metropolitan Boroughs. I sometimes refer to it before 1964 as 'the County'. Outer London is the rest of Greater London. This is shown on the maps on pp. xvi–xvii.

1. Acton
2. Barking
3. Barnes
4. Barnet
5. Battersea
6. Beckenham
7. Beddington and Wallington
8. Bermondsey
9. Bethnal Green
10. Bexley
11. Brentford and Chiswick
12. Bromley
13. Camberwell
14. Carshalton
15. Chelsea
16. Chingford
17. Chislehurst and Sidcup
18. City of London
19. City of Westminster
20. Coulsdon and Purley
21. Crayford
22. Croydon
23. Dagenham
24. Deptford
25. Ealing
26. East Barnet
27. East Ham
28. Edmonton
29. Enfield
30. Erith
31. Feltham
32. Finchley
33. Finsbury
34. Friern Barnet
35. Fulham
36. Greenwich
37. Hackney
38. Hammersmith
39. Hampstead
40. Harrow
41. Hayes and Harlington
42. Hendon

43. Heston and Isleworth
44. Holborn
45. Hornsey
46. Ilford
47. Islington
48. Kensington
49. Kingston-upon-Thames
50. Lambeth
51. Lewisham
52. Leyton
53. Malden and Coombe
54. Merton
55. Mitcham
56. Orpington
57. Paddington
58. Penge
59. Poplar
60. Richmond
61. Ruislip-Northwood
62. St Marylebone
63. St Pancras
64. Shoreditch
65. Southall
66. Southgate
67. Southwark
68. Stepney
69. Stoke Newington
70. Surbiton
71. Sutton and Cheam
72. Tottenham
73. Twickenham
74. Uxbridge
75. Walthamstow
76. Wandsworth
77. Wanstead and Woodford
78. Wembley
79. West Ham
80. Willesden
81. Wimbledon
82. Wood Green
83. Woolwich
84. Yiewsley and West Drayton

—— County of London

London administrative areas 1900–1964

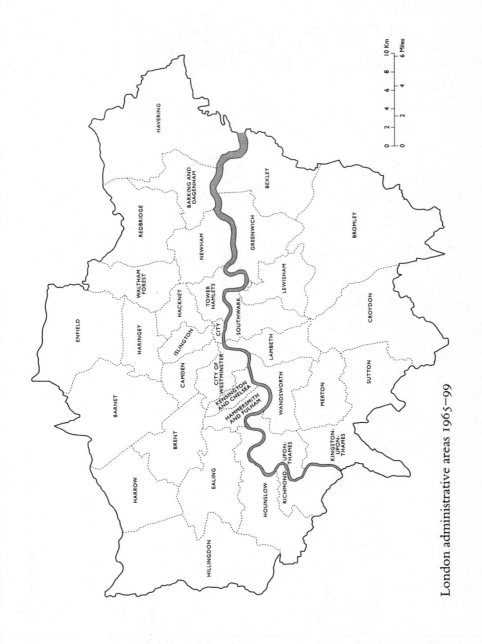

London administrative areas 1965–99

PART ONE

City

1. London Growing: 1900–1950

It started at the Mansion House. At 9.20 that Friday evening the Lord Mayor ordered a placard to be posted announcing the news. It spread 'with astonishing rapidity from mouth to mouth'. Within minutes the streets and pavements of the City were choked 'by a mass of people waving flags and shouting themselves hoarse'. By ten the West End was in uproar. Young women balanced precariously on the roofs of hansom cabs, four-wheeled growlers were chartered by men who clambered on top or hung from the windows, crowds packed the top decks of horse-buses, all – or it seemed like all – frantically sporting Union Jacks. As the theatres emptied, Piccadilly Circus 'was jammed with people', 'motionless among them the blocked streams of omnibuses and cabs all crowded with persons waving flags, hats, umbrellas, and anything they could lay their hands on'. Men in silk toppers and tails emptied 'squirts' into a sea of faces, society women in evening dresses waggled peacock-feather 'ticklers', City men threw handfuls of sovereigns and half-crowns into the air, tobacconists ripped open boxes of cigars and handed them out, publicans refused to take money for beer, 'ragged urchins' beat time on empty biscuit tins, young men turned rattles and blew on 'bull-roarers' and cornets and 'pink and white tuppenny trumpets' and 'squeakers' and 'buzzers' and 'corncrakes'. 'Donahs from the East End' with 'bounteous bosoms' did 'Lottie Collins' high-kicks arm in arm with 'white-fronted Johnnies, town bucks in capes and canes'. At midnight crowds were still streaming across London, Southwark and West-minster bridges from south of the river to join the exultant uproar that could be heard for miles. From 3 a.m. they were swollen by porters and costers and vanmen interrupted on their way to work at Covent Garden, Smithfield and Billingsgate. At 10 a.m. 'traffic was stopped around the Mansion House', 'again the centre of the manifestations'. The streets around were 'packed with people singing and cheering and throwing up their hats in the air. Those who had lost their own hats removed those of their neighbours' and 'hats of all descriptions were to be seen flying up two storeys high . . . in a continuous shower'. Apart from Mayfair and Park Lane – where 'scarcely a flag was to be seen' – the whole of London now seemed to be on the streets, in 'the suburbs, and in Bloomsbury and Camden-town, in Southwark and

Whitechapel – but above all in the City and thence to the Strand and Trafalgar Square. It was here that scenes were witnessed which have never been seen in the history of this country. Perhaps a Roman triumph was like this . . .'[1]

London, 18–19 May 1900. The news of the relief of Mafeking from the Boers seemed to bring on to London's streets every one of its 6.5 million citizens who could crawl from their cots or hobble from their beds. All this to celebrate a passing moment in the annals of war and Empire. It was a fitting opening to a century of extraordinary drama for London in which war would continue to cast a shadow over the first fifty years, and in which the unanticipated legacies of Empire would dominate the fortunes of the second.

It was a fitting end, too, to the nineteenth century, which had incongruously thrust Whitechapel donahs and Pall Mall Johnnies to the very pinnacle of modern civilization. Of the many centuries since the Roman walls first defined the city's boundaries, the nineteenth was the greatest of all in terms of London's growth and its accumulation of wealth and world power.

The first half of the eighteenth century had been years of stagnation. The next fifty years saw a rising tide of expansion, prosperity and civic grandeur. The population of what was later to become the County of London rose from around 677,000 in 1750 to 960,000 in 1801; Greater London, with its dormitory suburbs for the merchant class, reached about 1.1 million.[2] London's built-up area at the beginning of the nineteenth century was contained within a walkable rectangle: five miles or so west to east (from Edgware Road to Limehouse) and less than three miles north to south (from Euston Road to Elephant and Castle).

London of the Napoleonic Wars was a sapling compared to the great oak of Boer War imperial London in the closing year of Victoria's reign. This was a city with a population six times greater than a century before – 6.5 million, or one in five of the people of England and Wales. They lived in a built-up area some sixteen miles west to east (from Acton to Plumstead) and around the same north to south (from Edmonton to Croydon). The growth of their 'monster city' seemed to be accelerating out of control: the 1890s alone produced an increase of almost a million Londoners. The insatiable metropolis was shooting tentacles deep into the Home Counties along the ancient roadways from London, grasping at Waltham Abbey in Hertfordshire, at Loughton and Ilford in Essex, at Chislehurst and Sidcup in Kent, at Sutton and Surbiton in Surrey, at Hounslow and Harrow in Middlesex.

By 1900 London was unquestionably 'the richest, largest, most populous city' that the world had ever seen; the imperial city, 'Immense . . . vast! . . . endless!' to H. G. Wells, 'illimitable' to Ford Madox Ford. Its population was greater than those of Paris, Berlin, St Petersburg and Moscow combined, greater than those of twenty-two of the next largest British cities and towns put together, very much greater than those of Canada or Australia or South Africa.[3]

Essentially, too, London was a modern city. Despite its antique lineage, around two-thirds of its built-up area was just fifty years old or younger in 1900. Even much of the ancient core was in modern dress, for the Victorians were rapacious modernizers. Under the banner of 'improvement' the past was swept away for new roads, for railway lines and stations, for warehouses, offices, museums, town halls, model dwellings, board schools, prisons and art galleries: 'for London, even more than most cities, is ever changing, ever, year by year, improving, reforming, innovating . . .'[4] In the process, London's famous galleried coaching inns all but disappeared, made obsolete by railway mania; twenty City churches were demolished for office development, including seventeen of Wren's; and virtually all of London's pre-Great Fire timbered and half-timbered streets and buildings had been 'improved' away by 1900, many medieval treasures among them. The Victorians' modernizing zeal was to be a legacy actively pursued by their successors-in-title for around seventy years to come.

Many of the products of the Victorian age still bound London together at the beginning of the twenty-first century: a sewerage system to protect the Thames from human waste; a road and rail transport system (including the great termini) which, though added to, had never been replaced; the London parks, those in the centre already there by 1830 but the rest of inner London's largely in place by 1900; the great public institutions of Victorian London – prisons, hospitals, museums, schools, town halls, galleries, meeting halls – an intriguing mix of family silver and embarrassed liabilities 100 years after they were bequeathed to the twentieth century; and then, perhaps most surprising of all, the sprawling legacy of Victorian terraced housing, which looked at one stage as though it was destined all to be replaced but at the century's end looked set to last another century at least, worry without end to their owners, profit without end to the jobbing builders and plumbers of London town.[5]

The Victorians continued to influence modern London in less obvious ways. They, more than people in any preceding era, provided the mental and physical map by which London was still read and understood by Londoners, a map more concerned with divisions and barriers than links and bridges.

The classic division between West End and East End had been inherent in the separation between the court with its suburbs and the ancient port below London Bridge. But it was the Victorians who built the separation into a mystic divide between good and evil, civilization and savagery. In between these two extremes was an infinitely variegated identification of class or function with neighbourhood, the distinctions so finely nuanced as to be almost invisible to the naked eye but real enough to Londoners all the same. Some of these functional distinctions were of long standing, like Holborn's identification with the law, or Soho's with eating out and indulgence more generally. Others were Victorian creations, like the clubland of St James's, the medical district around Harley Street, the zone of learning around the British Museum, the kasbah of consumption around Oxford and Regent Streets. Others still grew out of the process of absorption by which Victorian London spread, retaining original village or town nuclei and taking something of their old character into the new streets of stucco which were to surround them. However the identity of an area was fixed, the contours of class were no less palpable for being endlessly redrawn as street or area lost caste or won credit. The unpredictable social value attaching to each of London's uncountable neighbourhoods was to become an endlessly fascinating plaything for twentieth-century London. It is, indeed, one of the most treasured characteristics of the present-day city.

Even the fears and obsessions and imaginative world of the Victorians continued to play on the minds and imaginations of Londoners throughout the twentieth century. The potent image of the Whitechapel murders of 1888 retained a deathless fascination. Charles Dickens continued to haunt the idea of London in the popular mind a century and a half after *Oliver Twist* or *Bleak House*, and more than a century after the London he described had largely disappeared from the ground. Resurrected in film and television, his books devoured by succeeding generations, Dickens and his illustrators went on shaping and colouring London and Londoners in the mind's eye. All the major genres of twentieth-century imaginative writing had at least some roots in Victorian London: crime, detective and spy fiction; children's romances; horror and the macabre; erotica and pornography; science fiction, utopias and dystopias; feminist, socialist, even environmentalist fictions. Wells's Martians first landed in the London hinterland at Weybridge, Mr Hyde stalked the gaslit streets of Soho, Peter Pan swooped over the roofs of Kensington, Sherlock Holmes injected cocaine in Baker Street, insatiable Walter plied his pego north of Oxford Street, Richard Jefferies saw nature fighting back in *After London*. It seemed as though every byway of the literary imagination had been trod first by the Victorians and first in London.

So there was never yet quite such a century as the nineteenth since the Romans left London. Its influence was likely to be felt well into the twenty-first century and maybe beyond. Yet not all its legacy proved fixed property or real estate. Despite the appearance of permanence in 1900, much that the Victorians handed on had a limited life. That included, of course, the idea of the 'imperial city', the Empire itself disappearing within about fifty years or so of Victoria's death; and 'the greatest city in the world' was overtaken by metropolitan New York in the 1920s and by many others by the end of the century (some of them virtually unheard of, or uninvented, in 1900).[6] The 'greatest port in the world', and indeed the Thames as a working river, also lasted less than a lifetime from 1900. So did most of the wholesale markets; so did smoky air and the deathly yellow fogs christened by Sam Weller 'London Particulars'; so did a skyline dominated by St Paul's, the Monument and Wren's church spires; and so (until reinvented in the twenty-first century) did a self-governing 'voice for London'.

Most important of all, perhaps, was the evaporation of Victorian London's industrial inheritance, strengthened to apparently unassailable proportions during the 1930s. Printing, furniture, leather, shoes and boots, scientific instruments, pianos, musical instruments and many other trades – supporting local economies in Finsbury, Bethnal Green, Bermondsey, Shoreditch, Clerkenwell, Camden Town and elsewhere – all going in 1900 to make up the world-famous boast 'Made in London', and all gone to speak of within a lifetime.

Yet even these more transient of the Victorians' gifts to posterity survived intact for half a century and frequently longer. The Victorian shadow was cast long and deep over London. It was at its deepest in the London contained within the County boundary. Effectively, for the first fifty years of the century the Victorian legacy produced two Londons. The first was inner London, essentially Victorian, changing certainly but in ways foretold and ordained by the nineteenth century. The second was a vast suburban girdle formed largely in the twenty years between the end of the First World War and the beginning of the Second – brighter, less crowded, with new building forms and new industries with which to manufacture a new way of life.

It was not until the 1950s that the twentieth century firmly began to impose its will on the recalcitrant legacy of the nineteenth. In the process it made its own version of London, absorbing the old in the new and making the division between the two a battleground on which London's identity was still being forged as the twentieth century came to an end.

Inner London: 1900–1940

The Edwardians carried on with zeal the modernizing agenda of the Victorians, most of all in a taste for grandiose architecture and technological innovation in transport. Both had big effects, the first on the redevelopment of central London, mainly through the transformation of residential into commercial districts, and the second on the suburban impulse which continued to draw Londoners from the crowded inner areas to the city's periphery. In and around these major changes lay the constantly shifting social geography of the city's neighbourhoods, endowed with new meanings as the winds of fashion veered round all points of the London compass.

It was Edwardian London's merchants, rentiers and entrepreneurs who pushed forward the capital's modernization, rather than the civic patriarchs who had taken the lead in Victoria's day. The municipal self-confidence of the 1850s, 1860s and 1870s had largely evaporated by the century's end. The widening of the Archway Road, completed in 1901, with its new bridge a symbolic gateway to London from the north, still had something of that grandeur about it. But other schemes of the time proved less imposing. Right from the start of the twentieth century, public efforts to make London better were marred by Treasury and ratepayer penny-pinching and bureaucratic indecision: the Greenwich foot tunnel opened without lifts from 1902–4 because there was insufficient electrical current to power them; the new Vauxhall Bridge, approved by Parliament in 1895, did not open until 1906 after years of legal wrangles and a complete redesign from stone to steel; the replacement of Lambeth Bridge, subject to traffic restrictions from the turn of the century, did not finally take place until 1932.[7]

Even the London County Council's (LCC's) new County Hall, a genuinely Edwardian project, had been mooted since 1889, was not begun until 1909, didn't open for business until 1922, wasn't completed until 1933 and was never big enough for the Council's needs. It swept away old wharves and warehouses along Pedlar's Acre, typical of a shabby South Bank that shamed the twentieth century's lack of enterprise when faced across the river with Sir Joseph Bazalgette's 1860s Victoria Embankment. Despite Ralph Knott's grand design for County Hall and its embankment, little more attention was paid to the rest of the riverside until post-war redevelopment for the Festival of Britain in 1951.[8]

This chronic half-heartedness was all too visible in the most ambitious redevelopment scheme of the Edwardian era. The 'Holborn to Strand Improvement' presented London with Kingsway, Aldwych and a wider Strand. Argued over for more than sixty years before it was finally approved by Parliament in 1899, Kingsway and Aldwych were opened by the King and Queen in October 1905. Yet the frontages were not fully built on until the 1930s with the completion of Bush House and India House. For some years, empty building sites on the Strand were hidden from view by the biggest advertising hoarding ever seen in London before or even, probably, since.

The formation of Kingsway and Aldwych unequivocally continued into the twentieth century the Victorians' passion for the new at the expense of the old. In pulling down dozens of streets, in evicting 3,700 people and in clearing some of the worst slums in London around Clare Market, the scheme destroyed the largest remaining intact quarter of pre-Great Fire London. Holywell and Wych Streets were 'the most picturesque streets in London' at the turn of the century. Lined with tall buildings whose jutting gabled fronts overhung the narrow carriageway, they were an antiquarian's delight. Holywell Street, known popularly as 'Bookseller's Row', had by 1900 recovered some respectability from the days when it had been the centre of Victorian London's pornographic book trade. Wych Street still retained Elizabethan inns and, in the popular memory, its connections with the notorious thief, highwayman and gaolbreaker of eighteenth-century London, Jack Sheppard. Hardly a voice was raised to forestall the destruction of these unique streets, made necessary to build the eastern segment of Aldwych and its junction with the Strand. A few were sounded in lament once they had gone. But the passing of Holywell and Wych Streets deprived a later London of jewels it would have treasured almost beyond compare.[9]

What took their place became typical of the grand manner of commercial developments in Edwardian London – and, indeed, the remainder of the first half of the century. Here, in all its starch-fronted complacency, was the most extensive example of 'Edwardian Baroque' in London. Eclectic in its borrowings from classical architecture, and from Wren and the French Baroque, as grandiose as the LCC's height restrictions would permit, with a buttoned-up pomposity of bearing which the odd flutter of decorative fancy did little to relieve, making offices look like rich men's mansions and calling them, with false modesty, 'Houses', these great Portland stone buildings dominated significant parts of central London even at the end of the century, not only Holborn around Aldwych and Kingsway but especially the north-western part of the City, Whitehall and the West End.

The Edwardian neoclassical revival provided a common style for an extraordinary range of building functions, so that it was impossible to tell from the outside whether a new building was a bank or a hotel, a government office or a department store, a company headquarters or a Corner House restaurant. It was a style that captured the imagination of governments and capitalists alike, who found they had to have, for the honour of their enterprises, street-front showcases on the new pattern. And it was a style that outlived the era that gave it a name, fixed in the minds of post-Edwardian architects, developers and commercial tenants until modernism at last became truly fashionable in London in the 1950s.

Between 1900 and 1914 large portions of central London were reconstructed in the new 'Grand Manner'. In the north of the City, Finsbury

Square, Finsbury Pavement and Finsbury Circus, Moorgate and London Wall were largely rebuilt in these years. East of Mansion House, the Baltic Exchange was opened in 1903, Fenchurch and Leadenhall Streets were widened, and the Port of London Authority, established in 1909, knocked down the beautiful old houses of Seething Lane and Trinity Square for its headquarters close to the Tower of London; Gracechurch Street was remodelled around 1912 for a hoard of banks and King William Street for a caution of insurance companies. A 'palatial' Lyons Corner House found itself in strange company in Throgmorton Street in 1907. West of Mansion House, George Dance the Younger's Newgate Prison was demolished and replaced by the Old Bailey from 1903, Fleet Street was widened and Holborn redeveloped with a red-brick fairytale castle for the Prudential Assurance Company (1899–1906).[10]

Two other quarters of London were transformed by rebuilding during this period: Whitehall and the West End. Whitehall, the Tudor and Stuart seat of royal power, still largely contained seventeenth- and eighteenth-century buildings in 1900. The old houses and mansions had become government offices as leases fell in during the second half of the nineteenth century. From the 1860s, an era of imperial government and bureaucratic inflatus, some of the old buildings had been demolished to make way for a succession of immense palaces of paper. This process quickened beyond all precedent with the 'Wrenaissance' of the 1890s and the Edwardian years.[11] The Admiralty (1895) was first off the ground, followed by a huge Parliament Street office block for the Board of Trade, Ministry of Health and Education Department (1900–1915), Sir Aston Webb's Admiralty Arch (1906–11) and the Office of Woods and Forests (1908). And the 1,000-roomed War Office (William Young, 1899–1906) was ready in good time to plan the slaughters commemorated in Sir Edwin Lutyens's nearby Cenotaph of 1920.

But the changes that affected most Londoners in these years were to the swirling rapids of London life around Piccadilly Circus and Oxford Street. This was the era of the great London hotels, restaurants, gentlemen's clubs and department stores. Of the hotels and restaurants, the most prestigious were Norman Shaw's Piccadilly Hotel (1904–8), his final London work and considered among the best buildings of its time; the Ritz Restaurant and Hotel, Piccadilly (1903–6, by Mewès and Davis, the architects of the Paris Ritz a few years earlier); the Regent Palace Hotel (1912–15), famous for showing officers a good time in the First World War; and the hugely popular Lyons Corner Houses, the first opened in Piccadilly (1904), followed by veritable palaces of pastry in Coventry Street (Leicester Square, 1908) and Oxford Street (1915). Of the new clubs, the most important Edwardian example was the 'French Renaissance' Royal Automobile Club

(1908–11), its spectacular swimming pool 'carved out of the marble floor'.

The department stores were even more important for the future of London's West End. The American Gordon Selfridge's store, straight from the drawing boards of Chicago, significantly extended Oxford Street's retail use westwards from 1907. It joined an already thriving shopping environment boosted by new stores from Waring and Gillow (1901–5) and Mappin and Webb (1906), and new extensions and modernizations of nineteenth-century enterprises like John Lewis, Peter Robinson, Marshall and Snelgrove, and Bourne and Hollingsworth. And Oxford Street itself faced new competition from superstores elsewhere in London, like Harrod's immense Knightsbridge development of 1901–5, Gamage's at High Holborn from 1904, and Whiteley's at Queensway and Swan and Edgar's at Piccadilly Circus, both 1908–12.

All this splendour, much of it of recent flowering, was enough to convince W. D. Howells, a New Yorker, that there was nowhere in the world like London:

we have as yet nothing to compare with at least a half of London's magnificence . . . The sky-scrapers, Brooklyn Bridge, Madison Square Garden, and some vast rocketing hotels offer themselves rather shrinkingly for the contrast with those miles of imperial and municipal architecture which in London make you forget the leagues of mean little houses, and remember the palaces, the law-courts, the great private mansions, the dignified and shapely flats, the great department stores, the immense hotels, the bridges, the monuments of every kind.[12]

This luxurious ostentation undoubtedly worked on the imagination of middle-class Londoners in these years. Working, dining and shopping in these 'stately pleasure domes', it was difficult not to be conscious of the limitations of a home environment still largely dependent on coal for heat and gas for light, and still largely in thrall to the tyranny of stairs, inconvenience and truculent servants. The passion for middle-class flats in this period – no stairs, electric lighting, gas heating – was given a push by commercial extravagance. It led to the destruction of many an old mansion in Mayfair and St John's Wood and their replacement with blocks of luxury apartments, which were 'coming more and more into vogue', a German visitor noted in 1904.[13] And it helped push a desire for modern labour-saving housing wherever it could be had.

So the Edwardian Grand Manner added its considerable weight to the middle-class movement away from central London to the suburbs, where most up-to-date homes were being built. There were other pressures, too. In and around the great new edifices making their six- or eight-storey mark on the centre's streetscapes and skyline there was a general movement from residential to commercial land use in central London. 'The City becomes more and more a collection of office buildings', losing a quarter of its population in the process between 1901 and 1911. That trend was apparent, too, in all the districts close to the City that had developed from the sixteenth to the eighteenth centuries, with old buildings demolished to make way for new: in Holborn, for example, where demolition for warehouses and factories around 1902–6 largely displaced 'the Italian colony' from the Warner Street area near Saffron Hill; or in Shoreditch and the inner East End, where, between 1899 and 1908, 'It is astonishing to note, even in this short time, how much has changed and how much has been swept away.' The novelist E. M. Forster watched London's 'bricks and mortar rising and falling with the restlessness of the water in a fountain'. And Philip Norman, artist and antiquarian, complained in 1905 that 'soon perhaps it will be as difficult to find an old house within the four mile radius as to light upon an unrestored church – or to flush a snipe in Eaton Square'.[14]

London's private-sector dynamism in these years, its restlessness, its urge for change and newness, its Wellsian 'whoosh and go', were greased and oiled by an historic transport revolution that took place between 1900 and 1914. These were years without parallel in the history of public transport in London. The phenomenon was unique to the metropolis in its scope and complexity, although its technologies – electric traction and the petrol engine – had worldwide significance. Indeed, there was a strong international component, at least in the expansion of the city's underground railways: financed by American and European capital, driven largely by US electrical engineering know-how and masterminded by a rogue entrepreneur from Philadelphia. This was Charles Tyson Yerkes – playboy, ex-banker, ex-convict, literally the stuff that novels are made of.[15]

London has never satisfactorily resolved its traffic problems sufficient to enable road users to travel with reasonable speed from one part of the city to another or to enable pedestrians to enjoy its streets in reasonable safety and comfort. Traffic was one of the enduring problems of the nineteenth century – a 'lock' of carriages and carts had blocked the young Thomas de Quincey's progress into London in 1800 – and so it remained throughout the twentieth.

A Royal Commission on London traffic in 1903–5 put faith in the better coordination of the various bodies influencing transport in the capital, but its proposal for a Traffic Board for Greater London was not pursued. In those innocent years at the beginning of the century it looked as though technical advances in transportation might also have the answers to London's problems. Most hope was pinned on electrification, of railways, especially underground railways, but also trams.

Horse-drawn trams had begun to be ousted by electric trams in American cities from 1888. Britain had been slow to exploit the new technology and London was even behind more adventurous cities like Bristol, Glasgow and Dublin. The new trams did not reach London until 1901, first in East Ham, then in Croydon, then west London from Hammersmith to Kew Bridge. But it was not until the LCC, the monopoly provider of tramways in inner London, began its electrification programme in 1903 that electric trams began comprehensively displacing their horse-drawn originals. The city's main roads endured years of disruption as they were torn up for the complex network of conduit and track to be laid. There were endless difficulties for passengers transferring from LCC trams to other council or private services at the County boundary; long-running disputes between Metropolitan Boroughs, which could veto the LCC's plans to run trams in their areas (Hampstead steadfastly refused to allow trams to carry the 'great unwashed' up Haverstock Hill, for instance); and fierce vendettas between the LCC and the owners of motor buses, potentially deadly competition for the capital-intensive tramways. Even so, by 1914 electric trams had penetrated most main roads in the north, south, and east of London; but bourgeois west London, probably because the tram was classed as an essentially proletarian form of transport, largely resisted its invasion to the end.[16]

Electrification of the railways, especially the tubes, moved faster. London's underground dated from the 1860s – the first in the world. But it did not keep pace with the growth of the city. At the end of the nineteenth century it was largely confined to the inner portions of what became the Circle, Metropolitan and District Lines and a small part of the Northern Line south of the river. Virtually all of it was powered by sulphurous and suffocating steam engines.

The first electrification breakthrough of the new century was the Central Line Railway, opened by the Prince of Wales in June 1900. It ran from Shepherd's Bush to the Bank and was financed by a share issue which had many European bankers and American investors as subscribers of capital. In the same year, the small City and South London Railway, electrified from 1890, extended northwards from the Borough to Moorgate and south from Stockwell to Clapham. Other small electrification schemes took place shortly after.

But the real power behind the modernization of London's underground system was Yerkes. He was active in London from 1900 and busy forming underground railway development companies from 1901. He combined brilliant deal-making abilities (putting in place the complex land assembly, finance and construction partnerships needed for expensive tunnelling under built-up areas) with the political skills to steer private bills through the arcane parliamentary processes which seemed more designed to prevent development than permit it. This slippery buccaneer died early in 1906, before trains had even begun to run on the lines he made possible. His achievements were remarkable none the less. They included the Bakerloo Line, opened from Baker Street to Lambeth North via Waterloo in March 1906 and extended south to the Elephant and Castle and north to Edgware a year or so later; the Piccadilly Line from Baron's Court to Gillespie Road (now Arsenal), opened in December 1906; and the Hampstead (later Northern) Line from Charing Cross to Golders Green and Highgate (June 1907). Simultaneously, and in response to Yerkes's competition, the rest of the network was electrified by the beginning of 1906.

Close on the heels of the underground transformation a similar wand was waved at street level. Despite a few pioneers at the beginning of the century and a boom in 1905, the era of the London motor bus did not really get under way until the all-powerful London General Omnibus Company (LGOC) introduced them in 1907. Even then there was no immediate switch from horses to motors and both worked the London streets side by side for some uncomfortable years to come. The turning point arrived in 1910, when 'the General' put on the road the Vanguard B-type bus, made in Walthamstow. The last LGOC horse-drawn service ended the following year; and on the day the First World War was declared the last horse bus in London, one of Tilling's, trod its final route from Peckham Rye Station to the Honor Oak Tavern. The war was to demonstrate the final triumph of mechanization over the horse. In the Boer War, London's omnibus horses had been shipped out to pull siege guns across the veldt. Now a fleet of London motor buses ferried troops from port to trenches.

The hansom cab waged a longer battle with the motor taxi, 'and up to 1918 it was not such a rarity on the streets as to be pointed out and looked at'.[17] Even so, the displacement of horse power by the petrol engine was complete for all practical purposes in passenger transport by 1914. This was the beginning of the end of the horse as a means of locomotion on London's streets, changing for ever their sight, smell and sound. It removed, too, the characteristic cloying London mud from roads, pavements and ladies' skirts. This was the first step of the century towards a cleaner, brighter London.

Not all this change was for the better. London became a noisier city, at least outside the main thoroughfares, where traffic had always been deafening. And street accidents accelerated with traffic speeds: 15,851 Londoners injured (222 fatally) in 1906, 25,822 (625 killed) in 1913, with motor buses the main culprits. (For comparison, in 1997 there were 276 deaths on London's roads.) Seven people were killed in one six-week period trying to cross the busy junction of Gray's Inn Road and Theobald's Road.[18] But the technological revolution brought with it a revolution in habit, with more Londoners travelling greater distances round their city than ever before in history. Journeys on public transport in Greater London numbered 935 million, or 142 per head of population, in 1901. They nearly doubled to 1,813 million, or 250 per head, in 1911. By 1921, on a public transport system largely in place by 1914, they had risen to 2,689 million, 364 per person.

No change in the last generation [it was said in 1930] has had more far-reaching effects upon the life of the whole community in London than the improvement in transport facilities. It has influenced almost every Londoner, both in his work and in his play. It has extended the urbanized area, increased the mobility of labour, offered a partial solution of the problems of housing and overcrowding, assisted in standardizing wages and prices, and increased opportunities for culture, recreation and amusement, and even crime.[19]

Ease of moving around inner London helped some move out altogether. Inner London reached its greatest ever population in 1901 – 4.54 million. It fell away slightly, probably the first decline since the 1660s, to 4.52 million by 1911. But this small drop disguised enormous migration out of inner London. Once the natural increase of births over deaths is taken out of the figures, it is clear that inner London experienced a net loss of over 550,000 people (12 per cent) by migration between 1901 and 1911. For the next seventy years and more the population of inner London fell steadily to a low of just over half the 1901 figure in the mid-1980s.[20]

The volume of emigration from Edwardian inner London had no precedent. Of course, London's outer suburbs had attracted people from the centre for some generations. A trend among the rich to leave the West End for the balmy air of villages like Barnet or Blackheath was well established by 1870. This was a trend which had spread extensively to the middle classes, and even artisans, by the 1890s. Within inner London, the movement out of middle-class households freed up some single-family houses for multiple occupation by working-class families renting a floor, or a room, at a time. 'We find to-day [1905] thousands of empty houses in almost every borough; there is a steady exodus of the middle classes, the mainstay of a neighbourhood . . . In fact, London is in a state of progressive dissolution.'[21] Similarly the demolition of houses in the oldest districts of London to make way for commerce squeezed manual workers out of their old domain close to the City. Charles Booth, the great social investigator of late-nineteenth-century London, noted slum populations moving out from the centre of London, so that (as in St Pancras) 'the best streets tend downwards . . . while the worst streets tend upward'.[22]

Almost all moved outward. In the Edwardian period all twenty-eight
Metropolitan Boroughs of inner London showed net emigration, except
suburban Lewisham and Wandsworth, where house-building was still
actively covering the ground. The greatest losers were a mixture of especially
middle-class districts (Holborn, Westminster, St Marylebone) and working-
class ones (Finsbury, Stepney, Shoreditch). What they had in common was
a border with the City or West End and their voraciously expanding
commercial life, shifting people before it whether rich or poor.

Even so, it is unlikely that London felt any less crowded in 1914 than in
1900. On the contrary, the development of office and retail space in the
City and West End brought people to London's centre as never before.
Cannon Street and King Street were considered the busiest streets in the
world and the rush-hour traffic at the junction of Cheapside and
Threadneedle Street 'a curiosity of world-wide interest'. The day population
of the City (employers and employees) rose from 301,000 in 1891 to 364,000
in 1911, up 2 per cent (there was no day census in 1901). If 'visitors' to the
City are added to its workforce, then over a million people every day moved
in and out of the square mile. Despite the revolution in London's transport
capacity, no fewer than 426,662 of them were on foot – a reminder that the
pre-industrial days of shanks's pony lasted well into the century that saw the
birth of a post-industrial capital city.[23]

The Londoners among these City workers and visitors would have left
and returned to homes in districts sharply differentiated from one another
by class, tradition, reputation, history – districts at the mercy of changing
fashion or market whim, where loss of caste might lead to one sort of people
moving out and another moving in within the space of a couple of years.
Just as the City's walk-on players wore a myriad faces, so the backdrops
to the great theatre of London changed appearance and character with
bewildering speed. This enduring and endearing feature of twentieth-
century London was no less apparent at the beginning than at the end.

The critics of every generation lined up to appraise each performance in
turn. Bloomsbury, in 1902, is 'a city of cheap boarding-houses . . . chiefly
frequented by Americans and Germans . . . through the late summer and
autumn', its 'modern unfashionableness' awaiting rehabilitation by the
Woolfs and their pack after 1911.[24] Edwardian Soho was still 'a French
colony', as it had been for much of the nineteenth century, 'grubby' by day
but after 7 p.m. London's premier district for eating out.[25] 'The little villagery
of Chelsea' retained its late-Victorian reputation as a bohemia of writers,
theatrical people and especially painters – 'long-haired Chelsea', E. M.
Forster called it in 1910 – but was less prosperous than it had been: the
King's Road is 'now shabby and mediocre enough'.[26] St John's Wood, or

'the "Wood"', is a 'city of refuge for those who fled Philistinism [and the] intolerable respectability of more conventional London', just as it had been for George Eliot in the 1860s and 1870s.[27] Hampstead had 'only lately become an integral part of London' and was 'a stronghold of "the literary life"'. Despite its many allures, it gets a bad review from the young Arthur Ransome as 'the home of people who have had trivial successes . . . Painters who can no longer paint, poets whose fame has penetrated the suburban wildernesses and become no more than notoriety, journalists who have never had their day . . . The place has the feeling of a half-way house between this world and the next.'[28]

The West End, rather than one homogeneous quarter, was divided into districts nuanced by class and wealth. 'Park Lane! Surely this is the centre of the universe', according to Clarence Rook, the grub-street chronicler of hooliganism; he meant the universe of ostentatious wealth, whether old money or the new riches of the South African gold and diamond mines.[29] Aristocratic Mayfair could be identified at a glance by 'its sleek carriage-horses, and also by the very superior maids and butlers you meet in its silent streets'. In Bayswater, 'Even the side-streets breathe prosperity.'[30] But the price of prosperity was eternal vigilance. South Kensington might well be the district

where no self-respecting lady or gentleman of the professional or 'middle classes' can really help living. He, or she, must, nevertheless, beware lest they stray too far from the sacred precincts. For, on the west, South Kensington degenerates into Earl's Court; on the south, a belt of 'mean streets' divides it from equally select Chelsea (and, in London, the difference of but one street may divide the green enclosure of the elect from the dusty Sahara of the vulgar); while on the east, its glories fade into the dull, unlovely streets of Pimlico, brighten into the red-brick of the Cadogan Estate, or solidify into the gloomy pomp of Belgravia.[31]

Similar stratifications were found right across London, with the fault-lines always on the move. In south London, Blackheath in 1902 'has been fashionable, but is losing status'; Clapham is '"fashion though faded"'; Brixton Hill and Angell Town are home to 'the servant-keeping middle class'; next-door Balham is even more prosperous, but next to that Tooting is losing caste – 'why is Tooting always so abused?' it was asked in 1908.[32]

Constantly shifting as these neighbourhoods were, it was difficult to fix a label accurately or for long. In addition, labels inevitably misled by smoothing away the niceties of class within a district: even Mayfair had its back-mews slums, at least until the 1920s. The smart label attaching to Kensington belied its reality as the most divided of the London boroughs. The fashionable south was separated by the High Street from the unevenly dilapidated north, where the Bangor Street area of Notting Dale 'is so notorious as a guilt garden that it has been called the London Avernus'. Nowhere was the juxtaposition of classes so marked as Westminster, around the Abbey and the Houses of Parliament. Here George Sims – as a Tory journalist and a campaigner for better housing in London, an odd juxtaposition himself – found streets which 'are slums on one side and palaces on the other. At the bottom of foul courts are picturesque little houses with trailing creepers and fruit trees in bloom. The common lodging-house and the fashionable flat face each other.'[33] Most inappropriate of all was the opprobrium attaching to the label 'East End' for a mosaic of districts with class allegiances almost as wide as anywhere in London outside the West End. Here the reputation of two small neighbourhoods in particular had overshadowed much of the rest: Whitechapel – 'unjustifiably . . . connected with crime' since the murder of Harriet Lane by Henry Wainwright in 1874 and then the terrible Jack the Ripper murders of 1888; and Hoxton, notorious for its pickpockets, shoplifters, warehouse-breakers and safe-crackers.[34]

Edwardian inner London, then, on the eve of the First World War was a shifting kaleidoscope of districts. All were changing in some way. The main agents of change were depopulation, especially by the middle classes, and redevelopment, especially in the areas closest to the City and West End. Change was greatly facilitated by London's transport revolution of 1900–1914, which made movement in and around and out of it easier than ever before. And on 4 August 1914 London was to confront a new agent that would also help change it irreversibly: world war.

At the time, however, it seemed as though the impact of the war on the physical character of inner London was insignificant. Indeed, beneath the froth of illicit shebeens and gambling dens, an epidemic of prostitution and the new cocaine habit, physical change in London marked time. Shortages of supplies and labour hit building projects very quickly. By 1916, with war bleeding the nation white, large construction projects were in direct competition with resources needed for the Western Front: Cornish granite for County Hall, for instance, just could not get to London because of the military demand for rail transport. Under the Defence of the Realm Acts (DORA), all building was ordered to cease in 1916. County Hall and other projects remained half-built for the duration and beyond, as restrictions were not lifted until the spring of 1919.[35] House-building virtually ceased, too, although conversion of housing to commercial uses continued. In 1918 more housing accommodation was destroyed in London than new accommodation provided, probably for the first time since the Great Fire of 1666.

The damming effect of this terrible four-year pause in London's development was to be breached in the 1920s, with tremendous impact on the growth of outer London. In inner London, the restoration of peace meant picking up the pieces. Edwardian Baroque would live out a grand old age right through the 1920s and 1930s, monuments in Portland stone to the 'hard-faced men' who had done well from the war. It was gradually stripped down into a sparer neo-Georgian style, for offices, stores, hotels and blocks of flats. Apart from some isolated examples, architectural modernism had to wait for the politically charged 1930s to make a shy appearance on London's crowded streets.

Redevelopment in the City quickly regained its pre-war impetus after 1919. If insurance companies had dominated the Edwardian scene, in the 1920s it was the turn of the banks. They were as sumptuous as international hotels, as extravagant as palaces. The Midland and the National Provincial headquarters jostled one another for pride of place in Poultry; the rebuilt Bank of England (from 1921) did its best to put the new Lloyds Bank and London City and Westminster firmly in the shade: all were ready just in time to fortify the moneymen as the Great Depression began to bite. The banks were joined by a host of company headquarters, insurance companies still prominent among them but now joined by industrial giants like Unilever, Spiller and the great newspaper proprietors. It was in Fleet Street that metropolitan modernism first bore commercial fruit, with Sir Owen Williams's black-glass *Daily Express* building (1930–33). But there were to be few imitators for almost the next twenty-five years. By the late 1920s some parts, especially around Finsbury Circus, were so entirely remodelled as to be called 'the "new City"'.[36]

The West End was similarly affected. Indeed, the most ambitious redevelopment scheme between the wars took place in the very heart of London. The redevelopment of Regent Street was to George V's reign what Kingsway had been to his father's. Like Kingsway, it had been mooted for decades before building began. Like Kingsway, too, it had exercised the nation's top decision-makers. Sir Reginald Blomfield's designs for the street's new frontages were approved only after the Cabinet itself, in the second year of world war, had found time to consider and reject an earlier scheme as too costly and unsympathetic to trade: the shopkeepers of Regent Street had been vociferous and influential in their opposition. Building eventually began in 1921. From then until 1927, when the King and Queen marked the new street's 'opening' with a drive-through, Regent Street 'resembled the devastated regions of France and Belgium' or 'the aftermath of some disastrous fire or earthquake . . .'[37] Little thought, if any, seems to have been given to the fate of John Nash's Regency façades, the greatest town-planning scheme attempted in London between the Great Fire and the 1860s. Indeed, rebuilding at the south end of the Quadrant turned Piccadilly Circus into a square; there was for a time a plan to rename it King Edward VII Square, replacing Eros with an equestrian statue of the great philanderer.[38]

That came to nought. But redevelopment spread outwards from Regent Street through every part of the West End. There was clearance and rebuilding for offices and restaurants in Piccadilly Circus, for hotels in Bloomsbury, for cinemas around Leicester Square and Haymarket, and for 'probably the largest restaurant in the world', seating 4,500 diners, at the extended Lyons Corner House in Coventry Street (1923). Much of Piccadilly was rebuilt from 1921, with glitzy motor-car showrooms a prominent new feature. Oxford Street's shopping area was extended west of Selfridge's to Marble Arch. The Regency houses of Park Lane were demolished to make way for hotels, shops and flats, mainly in the 1930s. Flats invaded Mayfair, taking down hundreds of eighteenth-century houses in the process, and so did offices, transforming Berkeley Square, Bruton Street and others into commercial areas. Further north, the Marylebone and Euston Roads were largely lined with new office buildings between 1921 and 1939. Offices spread, too, along the north bank of the river. Most striking were the gigantic Adelaide House (1921–5) at London Bridge and Shell-Mex House (1931) on the Victoria Embankment. This last required the demolition of the Hotel Cecil, the most magnificent hotel in Europe as the century opened; it was just thirty-four years old when it was pulled down.

All in all, the four decades after 1900 'witnessed the greatest amount of rebuilding all over the metropolis that has ever taken place within so short a period of time since the Great Fire of London'.[39] In these years inner London was essentially remade in a new commercial image. Little was allowed to stand in its way. 'London cares nothing about its past,' remarked H. J. Massingham in 1933. Even so, the first skirmishes of what a generation later would be a battle for London's soul were detectable even in these rapacious times. Nineteen City churches, by Wren, Hawksmoor, Inigo Jones and others, were scheduled for clearance in 1920 to make way for offices, but a campaign saved almost all. From 1900 the LCC had begun to buy up the gardens of squares in the East End to stop them being built on for factories and in 1904 the picturesque Edwardes Square garden just south of Kensington High Street was put up for sale for residential development. A local outcry grew to London-wide proportions and the LCC sought parliamentary powers to safeguard all metropolitan squares as open spaces. This failed, but Edwardes Square was eventually saved through legal action by the leaseholders. And in 1906 the gardens of sixty-four London squares were protected by Act of Parliament where freeholders agreed to waive their development rights in perpetuity. But after the First World War developers renewed their assault on the London squares and with more success. In the late 1920s the open space in Endsleigh Gardens on the Euston Road was built over for Friends' House, and Mornington Crescent for the giant Carreras cigarette factory. Agitation by the London Society and the LCC led in 1928 to a Royal Commission on London Squares, which recommended almost universal protection of London's 461 squares and other enclosures. This was delivered by Parliament in 1931.[40]

In these same years, London grew 'upwards generally speaking by two storeys'. Four-storey Georgian or Regency buildings were replaced by at least six storeys in the modern office block, hotel or department store. Yet even the tallest buildings in London at the end of the 1930s had still to keep their street fronts at no more than eighty feet, although a further two floors were allowed in the roof as long as this was raked back from the façade. No floors could be occupied more than 100 feet from the ground. Some – notably the Malet Street headquarters of London University (1932–7) – exploited the provision in the London Building Acts that allowed unoccupied towers to exceed the 100-foot limit. Its empty 210-foot tower made Charles Holden's Senate House the tallest secular building in London for the first half of the century. Still 150 feet short of the dome of St Paul's, it was dubbed 'the dummy skyscraper' when first built.[41]

These grand schemes were merely the tip of the development iceberg. Commerce continued to eat up run-down residential areas near the City. There were riots in the Brick Lane area when 135 people were evicted to make way for a cinema in 1919 and protests that same year when 100 Marylebone families were displaced for a new factory. The expansion of Spitalfields market in the 1920s destroyed the notorious Dorset Street area where Jack the Ripper had claimed his last victim; the enlargement of Waterloo Station to become the biggest railway terminus in Europe took down eight north Lambeth streets in the process; warehousing had 'almost' cleared the Italians from the whole of Holborn by 1934; south Hackney was increasingly depopulated by the expansion of industry north from Shoreditch and Bethnal Green, and so was Finsbury by warehousing from the City. These were merely the leading edges of an accelerating process that was changing living space into work space across inner London.[42]

Demolition of older housing was also occasioned by council housing programmes. The LCC pulled down the homes of over 127,000 people in inner London in the 1920s and 1930s, and the Metropolitan Borough Councils a further 55,000. In twenty years, a population as big, say, as Bolton's was displaced, and not many returned to occupy the new flats that had replaced their old neighbourhoods.

All this rebuilding pushed people out of central London. It combined with a pull from the suburbs to produce a flood-tide away from the London of Victoria, especially during the 1930s. From 1921 to 1939, inner London's population declined by 471,000, a net loss of 11 per cent. Loss by migration alone would have been far higher, so that around 650,000 moved away from inner London.[43] Over 80 per cent of this reduction took place in the years between 1931 and 1939. Once again it was the central areas which were losing the largest share of their people during the 1930s. But all boroughs lost population apart from Woolwich and Lewisham (where there were still green fields for suburban building) and Hampstead (where middle-class flats were being developed on the sites of old mansions or fashioned from large houses).

Just who was moving out of inner London? There were two main trends. Commercial redevelopment was pushing working-class people out of areas like Finsbury, Shoreditch, Bethnal Green, north Lambeth and Southwark. The suburbs were pulling middle-class people out of areas like Islington, St Pancras, Paddington, Hammersmith, south Lambeth and Camberwell. The place of the middle-class leavers was taken by workers displaced from the centre or migrating in from other parts of the country.

This brought about a change in the class balance of inner London which had major implications for London from the early 1930s until the 1970s and beyond. The middle-class areas of inner London tended to shrink into embattled enclaves. In St Pancras in 1930 'the number of tenement houses' was said to be 'steadily increasing' as middle-class family houses were let out in rooms to working-class households. Stoke Newington had started the century as one of the most solidly middle-class areas of inner London; by 1932, 'The better-class houses are now more and more confined to the quiet streets near the New River reservoirs.' In Brixton, the boxes at the Brixton Empress theatre were torn out in 1931 to make way for cheaper seats because 'the neighbourhood had become hardly the place for social graces'. In Paddington, 'many streets . . . have degenerated' close to the Harrow Road. The area west of Eastbourne Terrace, by Paddington Station, became known for its 'sleazy hotels' where prostitutes lived and took their clients – Graham Greene was a punter there in the late 1930s and 1940s; he knew Eastbourne Terrace as 'Arbuckle Avenue' after the lubricious American movie star. Highbury, one of the few remaining middle-class districts of Islington in 1930, had surrendered street after street of five-storey houses to working-class tenants renting by the floor or room by 1938. In Hampstead, 'the fashionable and the intellectual' retreated 'up the hill'. 'Behind them a tide of multi-occupation swept in across the low ground', like some cloud of poison gas ('social deterioration') across the trenches.[44]

But it was not all one way. At the margins there was early evidence in the 1920s and 1930s of what forty years later became notorious as 'gentrification'. Thirty streets near Buckingham Palace Road were turned over to 'million-aires' around 1927 though just recently occupied by 'poor people'. In Hampstead, by 1934, 'several old cottages have been converted in recent years into middle-class residences'. Bloomsbury saw 'fashion flowing back-wards' from west to east, so that 'Bloomsbury is to-day [1935] to a very great extent what Chelsea was in the '90s.' And Chelsea itself, faded flower of bohemia that it had become by the 1910s, can stand as the first battle-site of contested class change in twentieth-century London. The 1920s saw many of its working-class streets demolished for expensive flats, and its mews stables converted for 'the intelligenzia': 'perverted coachmen's homes', H. G. Wells called them in 1925, at 'a quite aristocratic rent'. In 1930, some Chelsea streets were 'turned into an armed camp' by tenants resisting eviction to make way for luxury flats: 'I have about 40 men in the area. They have thick sticks, clappers, bells, and whistles. They are properly posted to cover the district,' said one organizer of the resisters. They were eventually dis-lodged by foot and mounted police and a small army of bailiffs. And the rich moved in behind.[45]

None of this change undermined what was called at the time London's 'town within a town' feel. On the contrary, instability and perceptible change for the 'worse', with chaos apparently lurking round every street corner, prob-ably intensified the identification of people with areas. As Jan and Cora Gordon – arty, travelled, self-conscious bohemians looking for a flat around 1932 – wryly observed, middle-class London had become colonized by 'sets':

Thus Bloomsbury will tempt you to the higher-aesthetic set; Gower Street to the regenerate-England-by-the-intellect set; Fitzroy Square and its environs to the middle-aesthetic set; St John's Wood to the 'What-do-you-think-of-Komisarjefsky?' set; South Kensington to the bridge-or-be-damned set; Ham-mersmith to the own-your-own-boat set; Chelsea to the lower-aesthetic, the good-ole-booze, and the get-rid-of-your-complexes set; Balham and Tooting to the short-pants-and-hobnails-for-holidays set; Mayfair to the Royalty-to-tea-if-you-can set; and so on.[46]

They settled for Bayswater.

So, by 1939 inner London, the Victorian city inherited by the twentieth century, exhibited one of those paradoxes which make the metropolis at once so fascinating and so elusive. Central London – the City, the West End and their hinterland – had never been more prosperous, confident, thrusting and up to date. Around it most of the rest of the Victorian city was palpably in decline: the well-off were moving out, backstreet industry was squeezing out living space, the streets of the great building boom of the 1860s and 1870s were looking their age and worse. And the life-blood of inner London seemed sapped to exhaustion by a new twentieth-century London that had grown up within a generation on its outer edge.

Suburban London: 1900–1940

On a sunny autumn morning around 1907, Clarence Rook set out to discover where London began in the west and ended in the east. He boarded his first tramcar in Hanwell High Street. 'This, surely, must be the limit; for there was a slope, with a vista of trees, and if you stood carefully on the proper spot, there was no house visible.' Ominously, though, tramcars still travelled west to somewhere beyond Uxbridge. By tram and motor bus he journeyed eastwards to Wanstead Flats, arriving at lighting-up time. Here he gave up. In front of him lay a 'road upon which I could see houses all the way to Romford' and possibly beyond. 'I never found the end of London.' He had travelled, he calculated, twenty-five miles, but it was only seventeen – as the rook flies. There were doubtless other ways of reckoning where London ended. In the 1990s, the ever-seeping south-east dialect dubbed 'estuary English' became one fashionable indicator. In 1905, Ford Madox Ford identified another: 'London begins where the tree trunks commence to be black.'[47]

In Ford's day the population of outer London was just under 2 million, less than a third of the capital's total. The greatest clusters of people on the boundaries of London County were to the east. The oldest and biggest of these settlements was West Ham, 267,000 people in 1901, mainly workers and clerks in the docks, railways and gas manufacture. To the north and east of West Ham were huge swathes of lower-middle-class and skilled-working-class housing in red-brick terraces running mile after mile across Waltham-stow, Leyton and East Ham.

On the north of the County boundary Tottenham, a town of 100,000, was close in age and character to Walthamstow and Leyton. It was connected in the north to Edmonton and Enfield, industrial townships in their own right, the latter world-renowned for its small-arms factories, one more link to the Empire that London helped conquer as well as rule. To the west, Hornsey was more middle-class and suburban, with red-brick terraced villas straddling the 'Northern Heights' of Muswell Hill and Crouch End at the foot of Alexandra Palace. Then, on the borders of Highgate and Hampstead, more or less open countryside ran in an arc to Willesden, a huge railway and industrial town of 115,000 people, the most populous in Middlesex. To its south-west, and similar in character, lay Acton, famous for its laundries, and to the west again was Ealing, the Hornsey of west London.

Around three-quarters of outer London's population lived north of the river. Of the half-million or so in Surrey and Kentish London, Croydon alone could claim 134,000. Fiercely independent and only loosely connected to the metropolis by an isthmus of built-up land, it was to be many years before Croydon would allow itself to be considered part of 'London'. The other major settlements south of the river were Kingston-upon-Thames, Richmond and Wimbledon, ancient boroughs in their own right finding themselves attached ever more tightly to London as building encroached outwards. In the south-east, Kentish London had no settlement with more than 30,000 people in 1901.

The Edwardian suburbs that filled and grew out from these areas had a transitional feel about them. Many were locked into a Victorian way of doing things. Building land was maximized for profit in straight streets, with long terraces, cramped back gardens, a dusty front patch for privet or shrubs, and dark back-addition kitchens. But even here the twentieth century flexed its muscles in a cautious flamboyance – in fancy details to roofs, in balconies more decorative than functional, and with the promiscuity of terraced life broken into smaller groups or semi-detached pairs, like dignified married couples.

A few of the new suburbs were affected even more by a self-conscious modernity and by the ideals of the emerging town-planning movement. Here 'beauty' required curves, broken lines, individuality of design, air and light, space and greensward. Design was dominated by an English vernacular architecture which imported the cottage into town. This reached its fullest expression in the garden city or garden suburb movement inspired by Ebenezer Howard around the turn of the century. His vision demanded neo-villagery not only in the house but in the community as well, attempting to create societies with an organic balance between the classes. Outside London, Howard's model community was attempted at Letchworth in Hertfordshire, from 1903. Inside, Henrietta Barnett's suburban variation on the theme was laid down east of Golders Green from 1906, with streets and houses designed by Raymond Unwin and Barry Parker. But her ambition 'to house all classes in attractive surroundings at the Hampstead Garden Suburb' was quickly frustrated by the middle classes finding it just too attractive to let anyone else live there.[48]

Indeed, the general character of the Edwardian suburbs was decisively more middle-class than their outer London Victorian forebears. They were altogether more Hornsey and Ealing than Walthamstow and Willesden, less for artisans and clerks than for managers, brokers, accountants, lawyers and others of the servant-keeping classes. It was thus largely a middle-class influx that added another quarter of a million people to London-in-Essex before the First World War, mainly in Ilford Garden Suburb, East Ham, Wanstead Park and Woodford; another third of a million to Middlesex, with Ealing, Acton, Willesden and Tottenham continuing to grow, but now joined by Wood Green, Palmers Green, Southgate, Wealdstone, Finchley, Hendon, Wembley, Southall, Norwood, and Heston and Isleworth; and 132,000 to Surrey, mainly in Croydon, Barnes, Wimbledon, and Merton and Morden (the fastest-growing area in London in the Edwardian period, adding 8,700 people or 159 per cent) between 1901 and 1911.

In the Edwardian years it seemed as though London was growing faster than ever. The decades from 1901 to 1921 added 931,000 people to the outer ring, an increase of 47 per cent on the Victorian legacy. Most – 670,000 – were added in the Edwardian years. ' "London's creeping", ' warns Helen Schlegel in E. M. Forster's *Howards End*, pointing at 'a red rust' eight or nine meadows away. ' "You see that in Surrey and even Hampshire now . . . I can see it from the Purbeck Downs." '[49]

But in fact, and unexpectedly, London's growth slowed down as it entered the twentieth century. For the next twenty years, and for the first time since censuses began, the national growth in population exceeded London's. In 1921, the census authorities were to look back mistakenly to 1901 as a 'turning point' in London's development, the moment when the capital ceased to absorb an ever greater share of the nation's people.[50] An indication of the difference in pace of suburbanization between the last hectic years of the nineteenth century and the Edwardian period is glimpsed in the numbers of houses built in London in 1899, some 27,400, compared with 8,600 in 1913.[51] The First World War brought this relative trickle to a dead stop. As the echoes of the Armistice celebrations died away there was little in the past twenty years to suggest that London stood on the brink of its fastest geographical expansion in history.

In the twenty years between 1919 and 1939 London doubled in size on the ground. By the Second World War its built-up area could be encompassed only by a circle thirty-four miles across, from Cheshunt in the north to Banstead in the south, and from Uxbridge in the west to Dartford in the east. Outside this circle substantial urban islands were linked as by causeways to the mass in all directions. That mass had, by means of 'an unbridled rush of building . . . in the form of a scamper over the home counties', filled in the spaces between Edwardian London and the swelling dormitory villages and towns around it.[52] From the end of the First World War to the beginning of the Second, around 860,000 houses were built in Greater London. The boom lasted from 1924 to 1939. In the peak year of 1934, some 1,500 suburban houses were being run up every week in the capital.

This was a land-rush never seen in Britain before or since. The last remaining farms were sold and cut up for building, country house estates surrendered to the revolutionary forces of brick and concrete, fields between the ribbon developments along the roads leading into London were covered over, villages were absorbed leaving original buildings and street patterns visible only to antiquarians, old towns became new London districts with main shopping streets looking much like one another. The roads and crescents and avenues were filled with those semi-detached houses that make the inter-war suburban style so immediately recognizable: every house obsessively marked out from the one next door by tiny distinctions between gate or gable or glazing; mock-Tudor black-and-white half-timbering and clay-tile roofs; stained-glass whimsy in doors and fanlights; bay windows giving a wide-eyed and innocent, faintly undraped and sporty look in comparison to the frumpy standoffish domestic architecture that had gone before it.

London's unprecedented spatial expansion was not matched by a comparable growth in its population. Building densities in the suburbs were low and population growth in the years between 1921 and 1939 at 16.6 per cent was not much above the Edwardian low point (13.7 per cent between 1901 and 1921). But London's growth rate in the 1920s and 1930s was double that of the rest of the country, in sharp contrast to the earlier period. And London was now so huge that the numbers involved were enormous. Greater London's net population growth in eighteen years was 1,228,000, one-third the growth of the population of Great Britain as a whole. The outer ring housed 810,000 more people in 1931 than it had done in 1921; that was comparable to adding the population of Manchester in a decade. Almost 900,000 more were added in the next eight years, nearly as many as if the people of Birmingham, Britain's second city, had migrated lock and stock to the capital. In 1939 more than one out of five of the people of England and Wales was a Londoner. In that year London reached its historic maximum population of 8,615,000, a figure unlikely ever to be reached again.

Evidence of this unparalleled growth, with the paint hardly dry and the mortar barely hard, could be seen in every direction. The northern suburbs showed almost the slowest growth in these years, but even here population grew at nearly three times the national average in both the 1920s and the 1930s. The most dynamic point was just outside the Greater London boundary at Potters Bar, which showed an expansion of 129 per cent in the 1930s; but the population was still, at 13,000, very small and the largest absolute

gain of any northern suburb was Enfield's 62,000 (43.5 per cent) during the
same decade.

East London showed the slowest growth in the outer ring. In contrast to
north London, there were dramatic differences here between the two
decades. The LCC's huge estate in Becontree and Dagenham, creating from
nothing a town of 90,000 in the 1920s, distorted the pattern of growth in
the east. Without it the growth of London in Essex would have halved to
8.8 per cent; even including the huge new estate, growth in the east slumped
to 4.7 per cent in the 1930s, still just above the national average. The other
big increases in Essex were Ilford, which grew in the 1920s by 54 per cent
to 131,000, adding a further 38,000 in the 1930s; Chingford, which achieved
the exceptional feat of doubling its population in both decades, reaching
close to 40,000 by 1939; and 'the straggling suburbs of Woodford, Buckhurst
Hill, and Loughton, all of them consisting principally of good-class houses
. . . built with due regard to the choice character of this locality' bordering
Epping Forest.[53]

The north and east, then, generally followed development patterns set
from the turn of the century. Kentish London, however, had shown the
lowest growth in the outer ring in 1901–21 but between the wars was to
produce one of London's boomtowns. The 1901–21 figures had been
deceptive. The inner London boundary was anomalous in including large
areas of undeveloped land in Woolwich and Lewisham and much of this
had been filled with suburbs before the First World War. Exceptionally,
some suburban development for skilled Arsenal munitions workers had
taken place in Eltham (Woolwich) during the war itself. But Lewisham and
Woolwich were practically full by 1926 and developers had to look for sites
further out. The result was startling, especially in the 1930s. Bexley grew by
143 per cent to 80,000 people in just over eight years; at the peak, new
houses took less than three weeks to complete. 'Never before or since
has housing development gone so quickly. A rural landscape could be
transformed in a month.'[54]

Bexley, through its overspill links with Woolwich Arsenal artisans, was a
more proletarian suburb than most others on the edge of London. In the
south and south-west, by contrast, most of the fastest-growing areas were
exclusively middle-class. Their names, more than any others, have come to
epitomize suburbia and the virtues and vices attaching to it. Sutton and
Cheam, Epsom and Ewell, Esher and Surbiton, Wallington and Carshalton,
home of the tennis-playing classes and the carpeted sitting rooms of a
thousand *Brief Encounters*. Select and expensive, the southern and south-
western suburbs were still able to find sufficient prosperous immigrants to
grow consistently faster than the average for the outer ring. Nearly 400,000

people moved into the Surrey sector of Greater London during the inter-war period, almost as many as the Essex and Kent sectors put together.

But by far the most dramatic growth in terms of numbers of people took place north of the Thames in Middlesex west of the Great North Road. In west and north-west London, 800,000 people were added to the 1921 total by 1939. These years represented a decisive shift westwards in London's economic centre of gravity. Many areas shared in this expansion but the largest effects were seen in the 1920s in Wembley (a 200 per cent increase to 48,000), Kinsgbury immediately adjacent (800 per cent to around 17,000), and Hayes, Harlington and Harrow, which all showed rises of over 150 per cent. Neither did the flood abate in the 1930s, when Harrow again doubled in size to reach 190,000 (as big as Salford), when Ruislip trebled to reach nearly 50,000, and when Wembley and Kingsbury absorbed another 56,000 between them. These were the suburbs of Metro-Land, each with its station on the Metropolitan Railway line out of Baker Street, each with its estate agent's selling point – of 'residences' rather than houses, of golf clubs, 'breezy heights', 'amiable undulations' and beech woods of 'tremulous loveliness'.[55]

The middle-class settlers of Metro-Land could take the 5.30 out of 'The Smoke' and out of the suburbs proper into the dormitory villages of Buckinghamshire and Berkshire. But the motor car was opening out an ever greater variety of routes from London for those who worked in the metropolis but could choose not to live there. Between the wars bits of London were to be found all over south-east England, hedge-hopping here, tunnelling out there, stepping out with seven-league boots somewhere else. There was London deep in the country, London invading a town which had never had anything to do with it before, London at the riverside both east and west, London at the seaside.

While the largest share of the south-east region's population growth was absorbed by London, the region as a whole grew by a fifth between the wars. The main urban beneficiaries were London's unacknowledged satellite towns. These were industrial centres in their own right in the case of Slough, Luton and Watford; commuter towns for 'City men' in the case of Guildford and Woking. And at the seaside an anarchic confusion of shanty towns took root in the sandy soil. Largely lower-middle-class in origin, seasoned with bohemia and leavened by proletarian enterprise, the bungalow towns of Essex and Sussex aroused most excitement and antagonism between the wars. London deposited an urban jetsam of shacks, old trams, buses and railway carriages converted to rural arcadia or beachside chalets, most notoriously at Camber, Peacehaven and Shoreham (Sussex) and Pitsea, Laindon, Canvey Island and Jaywick Sands (Essex). 'London-by-the-Sea' grew in other ways, as at Bognor Regis, where Billy Butlin established an amusement

park in the early 1930s; and Brighton, which became endowed with all the
trappings of Soho and Fitzrovia, including gangsterdom, sexual licence,
bohemia and hard-drinking metropolitan novelists.[56]

It was between the wars that London came to subjugate the whole of the
south-east of England: 'Travelling by road to-day [1934] you must travel at
least 30 miles before you have shaken off the fact and rumour of London.'[57]
The outskirts of London began to epitomize the twentieth century and the
'New England' described by J. B. Priestley in his *English Journey*, undertaken
in 1933:

This is the England of arterial and bypass roads, of filling stations and factories that
look like exhibition buildings, of giant cinemas and dance-halls and cafés, bungalows
with tiny garages, cocktail bars, Woolworths, motor coaches, wireless, hiking,
factory girls looking like actresses, greyhound racing and dirt tracks, swimming
pools, and everything given away for cigarette coupons. If the fog had lifted I knew
that I should have seen this England all round me at that northern entrance to
London, where the smooth wide road passes between miles of semi-detached
bungalows, all with their little garages, their wireless sets, their periodicals about
film stars, their swimming costumes and tennis rackets and dancing shoes.[58]

Why did London grow in this extraordinary way?

First, the capacity to make it happen derived from the strength of London's
economy during the Depression years. Londoners could more easily find
work than people anywhere else in the country and their earnings were
higher for comparable skills. Most important, the growth of bureaucracies
and distribution and service industries produced a rapid expansion of white-
collar (or 'black-coated') work in offices, shops and the leisure industries. It
was this sector which fuelled the demand for suburban living between the
wars.

Second, the transport revolution of 1900–1914 had equipped London
with the means of making suburban expansion work. Tubes, railways,
electric trams and, above all, the motor bus could bring the new suburbanites
into London's offices and shops in the City and West End and take them
home in a reasonable time. And a reasonable time commonly meant a
journey of more than an hour each way by the 1930s. By the end of that
decade around 1.7 million people were making journeys towards the centre
of London and out again every day, around twice as many as in 1921.[59]

The 1920s and 1930s made their own significant addition to the Edwardian
transport revolution, especially by expanding motor-bus routes and tube
railways. There were hardly any new electric tramlines laid down after the
First World War except in Lewisham and Woolwich, and these were mainly

to connect LCC estates to the existing network. Similarly the overground rail system was almost entirely in place by 1904. But the improved technology of the motor bus put it into every main road in Greater London. Even so it could not meet the demand. Milling crowds jostling for places on crowded buses were a frequent rush-hour scene, especially outside railway or underground stations. In the early 1920s the demand led to dozens of independent or 'pirate' bus companies, from big firms running many buses to owner-operators with a single bus bought with wartime honoraria who set out to compete with the mighty 'General', the LGOC. The free-for-all caused considerable chaos. Street accidents soared as drivers raced one another to be the first at a crowded bus stop. Gradually, by around 1930, the anarchy was quelled as most of the independents were bought out by the monopolizing LGOC.[60]

That was a small example of a long-standing trend. The continuing growth of London and its population, the increasing complexity of its transport arrangements, the threat to profits of companies competing for passengers and the huge investments needed to maintain and extend the network produced a tendency to combination among the various private transport companies in London. The London Traffic Combine had brought together many underground railway companies in 1921. The LGOC controlled 88 per cent of London's bus services by 1925. There grew a close working relationship between the Combine and the General. Discussions between them and the LCC led to a proposal to merge all these operations, including the LCC's trams, in a private monopoly. Through the intervention of Herbert Morrison, Labour Minister of Transport, this proposal was vetoed in favour of a 'socialized' public corporation on the lines of the Central Electricity Board (1926) and the BBC (1927). In 1933, public transport in London (at least buses, trams and the underground) was in effect nationalized under the control of the London Passenger Transport Board (LPTB).[61]

The new arrangements boosted an already booming industry. In 1937–8 there were around 2.2 billion journeys in Greater London by bus and coach, more than twice the 1922 figure. Suburban trams began to be replaced by an extensive network of trolley buses from 1934. And there was continuous modernization of the underground system. The tubes inherited by the LPTB had already been extended in a number of directions since 1919. In every case the tube had followed the suburbs, chasing passengers rather than opening out new frontiers for settlement. The Northern Line drove south from Clapham Common to serve the new suburbs of Merton and Morden (1926) and north-west to Edgware (1923–4); the Piccadilly Line was extended from Finsbury Park, scene of some of the worst passenger congestion in London, to Cockfosters (1932–3); the District Line east from Barking to Upminster (1932); and the Bakerloo from Wembley Park to Stanmore (1932).

There was a self-conscious suburban modernity and lightness of touch about the architecture of the stations along the new lines. The brick and glass hat-boxes designed by Charles Holden quickly became world-famous icons of the tube and of twentieth-century London. Holden, London's most influential architect between the wars, was the designer, too, of London Transport's Olympian headquarters at 55 Broadway, St James's Park, with sculptures by Jacob Epstein, Eric Gill and Henry Moore gracing its façade and palatial interior. Under the inspired leadership of Frank Pick, the Board's first chief executive, even underground posters, signage, tickets and, above all, Harry Beck's 1933 London tube map were redesigned for the new world of the 1930s.

Above ground, the increasing demands of motorized road transport led to a road expansion programme. This was criticized at the time as too modest, but it seemed impressive enough with hindsight. The most notable additions to London's road network were the Great West Road, which 'looked very odd' to J. B. Priestley in 1933 – 'Being new, it did not look English. We might have suddenly rolled into California';[62] the North Circular Road, from Woodford to Ealing, built by the Ministry of Transport as an unemployment relief scheme in the 1920s; the Great Cambridge Road; Eastern Avenue and the Southend Road; and a number of bypasses around Kingston, Croydon, Barnet and other places. Motor traffic did nothing to relieve the congestion of central London streets in these years – by 1938 traffic speeds had dropped below those of the horse-drawn era. But for the 350,000 car owners in the County at the end of the 1930s (there were 2.28 million in Greater London in 1997), London outside the very centre seems to have been open touring country. According to Rupert Croft-Cooke, novelist and circus fan, who lived in Marylebone in 1939 and ran an Opel, 'one could speed from one point to another with scarcely a moment's hold up and park anywhere for as long as one liked'.[63] That was a pattern that changed little until the late 1950s.

So a buoyant London economy made suburban growth possible and a continually improving public transport system made living in the suburbs and working in town a practical reality for more people than ever before. But, most of all, the suburbs grew because people – millions of people – wanted to live in them.

Inter-war suburbia was, above all, a middle-class phenomenon. The suburbs spoke to middle-class values of privacy, status, pride in ownership and a fear of being left behind (literally) by the tide of fashion. The suburbs combined individualism with a restrained sociability. They established difference while eschewing eccentricity. These were precious privileges given added value by the financial sacrifice necessary to pay for them.

The suburbs offered a distinctive break with inner London ways of living. Their unique selling points were trumpeted on posters, blazoned in advertisements and brochures, praised in verse and ditty. They promised modern labour-saving homes, especially important at a time when servants had never been more difficult to find and keep. They gave better value for money, because rents were proportionately lower than in inner London and would buy more space, or because mortgages were relatively cheap compared to renting and deposits low. And they offered a better lifestyle: a more healthy life with 'good air', high ground and 'sand and gravel subsoil'; a more active life, with golf, tennis, boating and skating; and a more organic life, in touch with English history ('the tranquillity of bygone days') and the English countryside ('whin-clad common', 'golden corn', 'good tillage').[64]

It was to the suburbs that many of the hundreds of thousands who left inner London went to live. The novelist and short-story writer V. S. Pritchett was born at Ipswich in 1900, the son of a feckless shop assistant with ambitions. The family moved all over London before the First World War, from Finsbury Park to Brixton. But when father gained some prosperity from manufacturing fancy goods in 1916, they moved to Bromley, 'half country town and half suburb'. Louis Heren was born in Shadwell in 1919, becoming deputy editor of *The Times* in the 1970s. Although Shadwell was one of the poorest and roughest districts of London throughout the century, Heren's upbringing was comfortable – his father was a printer on *The Times* and his mother owned and ran a coffee shop. She aspired 'to the promised land of Bromley or Beckenham', but in 1937, when they moved, could reach only Crofton Park, Brockley. And John Osborne, the angry playwright, was born in Fulham in 1929, father an advertising copy-writer, mother an unstable barmaid. In 1936 the family moved to Stoneleigh, near Ewell, with its

small Woolworth's, the dry cleaner's, newsagents and a twopenny library, butchers, florists and empty shops which had not yet been sold, gaps in the townscape, corners which had not yet been built on, patches of fields and stubble between houses and shops. It was not Stockbroker's Tudor but Bankclerk's Tudor.[65]

As John Osborne reminds us, the new London was as class-stratified and nuanced as the old London from which it had so spectacularly grown. So, in the early 1930s, Palmers Green and Winchmore Hill are 'much superior to Wood Green'; Edmonton is upper-working-class while Enfield has a 'most select quarter'; Walthamstow is home to 'city clerks and their families', but Ilford invites 'favourable comparison with Ealing or Wimbledon'.[66] And suburban Lewisham, largely a twentieth-century product, was by 1940 made up of 'Catford, Rushey Green, Ladywell, Forest Hill, Honor Oak Park, Sydenham, Grove Park, Lee, Downham, Hither Green, Bellingham, South-end, Brockley, Blackheath or Bell Green . . . Very few people live in Lewisham. They tell you they live in one of these portions of it, often with a sly stress on the social implications of the name.'[67]

As the suburbs matured under the forced pressure of huge numbers of families with other needs than merely those of servicing a City-commuting salary-earner, they became more self-sufficient, with less of a new dormitory feel about them. Steen Eiler Rasmussen, the Danish architect and town planner who was an eloquent champion of London's squares and domestic architecture, recognized this tendency as early as 1934. He welcomed it, too, as a means of decentralizing work from central London, reducing commuting and mitigating 'the drawbacks of modern traffic':

A pronounced spreading of town-centres in London *is* taking place. In suburbs far removed from the city, there are big shops, theatres, places of amusement with artificial rinks and large cinemas so that people need not go into the town itself either for shopping or for pleasure.[68]

This was a tendency bolstered by the suburbanization of industry, as we shall see. And it was to have an important influence on the future shape of London from the 1960s on.

Rasmussen's optimistic insight into London's suburbs was, though, against the grain of most intellectual opinion. For the suburbs raised great anxieties in the minds of metropolitan literati and government policy-makers. The anti-suburban prejudice of London intellectuals was a dominant theme in writing about the city from before 1900 until 1940. C. F. G. Masterman, in an influential 1909 study, launched into 'the Middle Classes, the suburbans': 'no one respects them' or their 'tyrannical convention of manners'; they were 'unreasoning and resolute' and 'without leadership'. He blamed 'those enormous suburban peoples' for throwing over progressive government in London in 1907. Worst of all, these benighted residents of ' "Acacia Villa", or "Camperdown Lodge" ' were 'clerks' – 'adding up other men's accounts, writing other men's letters'.[69]

Twenty-five or thirty years later the view from intellectual or bohemian London had not grown more rosy. Jan and Cora Gordon thought that 'To live in an outer suburb is to enrol yourself one of a tribe' – so much less chic than a 'set':

Such people do occasionally return to town parties, and seem so like ghosts from the past that you almost expect them to converse by rapping out their messages on the top of the table. They rise up thus resurrected from Wimbledon, Streatham, Dulwich, Highgate, Golders Green, or Willesden, and talk lightly with specious nonchalance about 'catching the last'.[70]

From the Kensington Olympus, Rachel Ferguson, a witty and observant chronicler of that Royal Borough, exposed the shameless snobbery permanently attaching to the suburbs by 1939:

Which of us, on hearing that a person is 'suburban', does not instantly conjure up an over-eager half-sir who talks of 'the wife', and . . . mows a ridiculous lawn on Saturday afternoons, while his wife, saying 'pleased to meet you', sets out 'the preserves' on a d'oyley before her whist party. And the fact that in these days of high taxation and monstrous rents the suburbs are just as likely to house an eminent professor of Greek and a deposed monarch, who respectively wish to retrench and enjoy the better air, makes no difference at all, and probably never will.[71]

It certainly didn't to Rosamond Lehmann, Girton novelist, who made one of her heroines want to set fire to the latest 'outbreak of bungalows' in the middle of the night: ' "I'd – just like to blow the whole thing up." '[72]

But if the suburb dwellers were the victims of élitism, then there is little doubt that they gave as good as they got. In many ways, of course, the suburbs were the creation of a desire to better oneself and put distance between the suburban and an increasingly working-class inner London. The very product of status consciousness, it was annoying to find suburbs and suburbans patronized by smart opinion-formers in novels and the press. But it was even more so when the suburbs were not always the haven from proletarian influence that they had seemed.

The LCC rehoused over 250,000 Londoners in cottage estates in the suburbs between the wars. Around 90,000 of these were at Becontree and Dagenham, an area not in competition for development as middle-class housing. But the rest were. For working-class Londoners these estates offered about the only chance of a house (rather than a flat) with a bathroom, with electric light and power and, of great importance, a garden. An Eltham housewife 'always felt she had her own bit of country on that council estate' when she moved there in the 1930s, and tens of thousands of Londoners rehoused from inner areas to the suburbs felt the same.[73]

In many ways, though, the council estate was an intrusion in the suburbs and its tenants were certainly made to feel it at the time. 'People would say to me, "Oh, so you're from the estate?" as if you were from a leper colony,' remembered one early resident of the Mottingham Estate in Bromley in the late 1930s. That was typical. Perhaps the most extraordinary instance of class hatred was the saga of the Downham Wall. This was built by a developer around 1927 across a road which otherwise would have allowed LCC council tenants to walk through a private estate. The council tenants were forced to go the long way round to shops and buses. Built of concrete panels and posts, the wall was not finally demolished until 1946.[74]

Yet, at least for their impact on the future of London, the most important anxieties were not to come from within the suburbs, or from metropolitan literati. They were voiced by those professionals and policy-makers who, in the 1930s and 1940s, were gaining greater influence in town-planning in Britain. The 'London problem' was at the heart of their concerns.

Worries about the spread of London had been heard since the time of Elizabeth I and were resurrected during the growth of the city in the Victorian period. The garden city movement had been born out of these concerns at the end of the nineteenth century and for the next forty years it urged the decentralization of London in theory and by practical example: Letchworth was joined by Welwyn Garden City from 1920. As the inter-war suburbs speedily outpaced any previous period of growth, it became common ground that something had to be done to stop London growing.

A green 'belt' or 'girdle' around London which would hold back building had been mooted since 1901. But the first steps to curtail development at London's edge were not made until January 1935, when Herbert Morrison, Labour leader of the LCC, announced a scheme to buy up agricultural land to prevent it being sold for house-building. The LCC agreed to offer £2 million in grants to help outer London authorities effectively freeze the boundaries of London at their present position. Their policy was legitimized by the Green Belt (Home Counties) Act 1938. By 1939, 14,000 acres had been bought and 60,000 more 'provisionally approved' for purchase. But this seemed a little like Canute on the beach with house-builders riding the waves, and for many it was too little too late.

Fear of London's growth had turned into something like panic by the late 1930s. The worst years of the slump had passed, but parts of the nation, especially South Wales and England's north-east, continued to suffer apparently terminal decline. On the other hand, London was ever fattening as new factories opened daily and workers flocked to fill them. Many put two and two together and concluded that London was sucking the vitality from the nation's very bloodstream, like some gluttonous parasite.

The first influential calls for the compulsory restriction of London's growth came in 1936 from the commissioner responsible for development policy in the 'Special Areas' of England and Wales. At first the target was

London's industrial expansion, which was thought to be at the expense of investment and jobs elsewhere. Soon this broadened into questions about the regional distribution of the nation's people, who seemed more and more to be tilting Britain south-eastwards. Hostility to London's industrial growth between the wars forged a common agenda with those metropolitan aesthetes and others who attacked the suburbs on different, but no less passionate, grounds. And with those military planners who contemplated the effects of aerial warfare on a dense mass of 8 or 9 million people in a city in which the major defence industries of the country had also been unwisely clustered.[75]

So by 1937 London was a 'national menace', 'in an advanced state of hypertrophy and strangulation', a 'Daemon', 'gobbling up a vast percentage of the decelerating national increase in population'. 'Can we save . . . Britain from London and London from its tumultuous, irrepressible self?' asked the novelist and journalist Ivor Brown. He was joined in a chorus of metrophobia in the town-planning press by Aldous Huxley, Ellen Wilkinson, Sir William Beveridge, Patrick Abercrombie, Clement Attlee, David Lloyd George, Hugh Dalton, Herbert Morrison, J. B. Priestley and many others.[76]

In July 1937, Neville Chamberlain announced a Royal Commission on the Distribution of the Industrial Population, under the chairmanship of Sir Montague Barlow, a Tory barrister. Patrick Abercrombie, one of the country's leading town planners, was a commissioner. The Barlow Commission had finished its work by August 1939 but events delayed its publication until January 1940. It called for a new central authority to oversee, among other things, the 'decentralization or dispersal' of 'industries and industrial population' from 'congested urban areas'. In particular, the 'urgency of the problem of London and the Home Counties . . . demands immediate attention'.[77]

But by then it was all too late. Events, as so often, had overtaken the planners. Soon the bombs would begin to fall.

The Blitz and After

London had experienced a certain amount of bombing in 1914–18, at first from Zeppelins and then, more destructively, from Gotha bombers. There had been some tragic loss of life. In one daylight raid in June 1917 158 East Enders were killed, eighteen of them children at Upper North Street Schools, Poplar. A direct hit in early 1918 on Odhams Press, Long Acre, killed thirty-eight, mostly women and children sheltering there. In all, some 600 died from bombing in London during the First World War. Since then, though, bombing had gained fearful notoriety during the Spanish Civil War and the Abyssinian conflict. It seemed that London – the world's most unmissable target, so densely packed with people at its core – must be made a charnel house from the first bomb that fell. Official forecasts envisaged 58,000 dead Londoners from the first raid and a maddened population clamouring for peace at any price.[78]

That these prophecies were wildly defeatist was, of course, little consolation to the Londoners who experienced the Blitz in its various manifestations from the autumn of 1940 to the spring of 1945. The figures are unreliable, but officially 29,890 civilians died in London from bombs and rockets, and 50,507 were seriously injured. And London withstood more than its share of hostilities: with a fifth of the nation's population, it suffered about half the nation's casualties from air attack.

The air war against London had a number of phases. The 'phoney war' from September 1939 to the fall of France was punctured for Londoners only by an IRA bombing campaign that blew up telephone and police boxes, and damaged postal sorting offices, West End stores and the Paddington Air Raid Precautions (ARP) control centre – schoolboy pranks by later standards. While Britain's airfields and ports were bombed in the summer of 1940, on Hitler's orders London remained immune from attack in the hope that Britain and Germany might conclude some sort of non-aggression pact while Germany pursued its territorial ambitions in the east. But by error, bad luck or mischief, the East End and City were bombed on the night of 24–25 August 1940 and a retaliatory raid was made on Berlin. Overnight London became the Luftwaffe's primary target. It was code-named Loge – Wagner's god of fire.[79]

The Blitz began on 7 September 1940 – 'Black Saturday' – with daylight and night-time raids that left the East End and docks burning so fiercely that fire crews were brought in from Birmingham, Nottingham and elsewhere; at 1,800 killed or seriously injured, casualties were heavy but clearly indicated that pre-war fears would not be realized. London was then bombed virtually every night for the next three months until an unofficial truce brought a nervous peace for three nights over Christmas. This first period of the Blitz was the most sustained of the various attacks on the capital. By the end of 1940, London had suffered 40 per cent of its war casualties, with over 13,000 killed. Another 6,500 were to die before this main phase of the Blitz ended (for London) on the night of 12–13 May 1941. The onslaught was as ferocious at the end as it had been at the beginning. Indeed, the most destructive night of the war for Londoners was 10–11 May 1941, when 100,000 incendiaries fell and some sixty-one local government areas in London suffered bombing. But the 'Full Moon' as it was called at the time was nearly matched by 29–30 December 1940, 'The Second Great Fire of London', when Herbert Mason captured on camera St Paul's emerging magically from the tumult of fire and smoke around it; by 'The Wednesday' of 19–20 March 1941, when the East End and docks endured a merciless battering; and by 19–20 April, the country's heaviest raid of the war when measured by bomb tonnage.

Then, apart from nuisance raids, sleep was restored to Londoners. Their city was free from attack for more than two and a half years, until the 'Baby Blitz' of January to April 1944. This comprised fourteen night raids, some of them comparable in devastation to the first phase.

Finally, Londoners were to relive some of their earlier agonies late in the war through the V1 flying bomb (the 'doodlebug' or 'buzz bomb') and the mighty V2 rocket. Some 2,340 V1s fell on London between 13 June and 1 September 1944, with a further seventy-nine from then until the end of the war. They killed over 5,000 people, about twice as many as the 517 V2s which hit London between 8 September 1944 and 27 March 1945.

Through all this bombardment, London never came close to the terminal dislocation that the Luftwaffe hoped for and the pre-war planners feared. It was so vast, its infrastructure so capable of finding ways round the damage, that it could absorb the blows and get on with life. Even so, the destruction was enormous. 'London looked like the moon's capital', thought the Anglo-Irish novelist Elizabeth Bowen, 'shallow, cratered, extinct . . . People stayed indoors with a fervour that could be felt: the buildings strained with battened-down life, but not a beam, not a voice, not a note from a radio escaped. Now and then under streets and buildings the earth rumbled: the Underground sounded loudest at this time.'[80]

The most devastated quarter of the capital was at its very heart – the City. It lost nearly a third of its pre-war floorspace, much of it on the night of 29–30 December 1940. Virtually every building between Moorgate and Aldersgate Street was 'razed to the ground'. Older buildings fared worst. Post-1900 steel-framed construction stood up well to high explosive and fire. It did not seem much like it at the time, but the Blitz was thus a great modernizer, shifting great swathes of central London and the East End decisively into the twentieth century.

Outside the City, figures for the damage caused by bombing in London are elusive. Probably 50,000 houses in inner London were destroyed or damaged beyond repair, with a further 66,000 in outer London. Some 288,000 more houses London-wide were seriously damaged and another 2 million slightly.[81]

Despite the enormous pounding absorbed by the East End, next to the City London's most ruined district, it is clear from these figures that the bombs respected no divisions between the two Londons, old and new. Stepney, in the heart of the East End, had lost a third of its housing stock, 10,800 houses destroyed or incapable of occupation without major repair. But V1s alone damaged to some degree 54,000 houses in Croydon and 18,000 out of 22,000 in Sutton and Cheam. Twice as many V2s fell on outer London as on inner, and the frontline status of London's Essex suburbs later in the war was sufficient to win it the nickname 'Doodlebug Alley'.[82]

The war, which brought Londoners together in so many ways, made the psychic divisions between city and suburb no longer sustainable. The snobbery which had provoked John Betjeman to call down bombs on Slough in 1937 seemed criminal madness by 1945. Indeed, the suburban ideals of a reserved collectivism, a stoic desire for improvement within reasonable bounds – a better life but not too much better – seemed the quintessential values of wartime England. In contrast to the vilification heaped on the suburbs for a generation, the war transformed their image in the popular imagination. It did so mainly through the cinema, where the suburbs were glorified in films like *Mrs Miniver* and *In Which We Serve* (both 1942), *This Happy Breed* (1944) and *Brief Encounter* (1945).[83]

Despite this unifying tendency, the wartime London plans which attempted to conjure a new city from the ashes of the old remained predicated on the old divisions. Plans emerged for City, County and Greater London, making it impossible to construct one integrated proposal for a new metropolis. Confusion was compounded by the City producing two plans: one in 1944, rejected as insufficiently visionary; and another in 1947 by Charles Holden and William Holford. Even so, a clear enough picture had emerged by 1945. In the County and Greater London plans, affecting the vast majority of Londoners, one overarching idea was common to both. It derived less from the experience of war than from the state of debate about London before the bombs fell. And it was decentralization.

The main author of the London plans was Patrick Abercrombie. He was fifty-eight when he became a member of the Barlow Commission in 1937, and although he was one of the most experienced academic town planners in the country, he knew little of London, being based there only from the late 1930s. In 1941 he was asked by Lord Reith, Minister of Works, to produce a plan for the County of London with J. H. Forshaw, the LCC's chief architect; and in 1942 he was commissioned to produce a similar plan for Greater London.[84]

Abercrombie's vision had been formed in the Barlow Commission with its London-as-problem paradigm. Moving people and jobs out of London was the plans' primary concern. London was to be stopped in its tracks by hardening up the Green Belt for leisure and food production, by restricting new development to the few remaining greenfield sites in the suburban ring, and by moving out just over a million Londoners from the crowded areas of inner London and the older suburbs to the east and north. Even this would only hold London at its pre-war level, with the million emigrants merely making way for the natural growth in London's population.

If decentralization was the big idea borrowed from Barlow, the plans' second concern had a much longer history: traffic congestion. London's radial road system, like spokes in a wheel with the City as hub, dated back in outline to Roman Britain. It channelled traffic into the crowded centre before letting it flow elsewhere in London. The centre needed protection by a system of 'ring roads' to allow traffic to move round it. Each plan provided for one or more ring. The City's plans proposed one on its northern boundary with the County connecting with a new embankment on the river between Blackfriars and London Bridges. The County's proposed two: an inner ring linking the main railway stations, and an outer 'fast motor ring-road', the route of which was to blight thousands of homes for thirty years to come through the middle of boroughs like Islington, St Pancras and Hackney. Greater London's proposed three: the completion of the North and South Circular Roads; an entirely new route, the 'Express Arterial D Ring', on a twelve–fifteen-mile radius from Charing Cross; and the completion of the north and south orbital road system further out into the home counties.

A third concern was modernization. Abercrombie envisaged enormous redevelopment schemes for inner London in which everything – streets, houses, factories, schools – for mile after mile would be entirely cleared away and rebuilt. London's slate had to be wiped clean, at least in areas like the East End, where crowded worn-out districts were no longer fit for modern living. These 'Comprehensive Development Areas' would fill the spaces between the new ring roads and the old radial routes.

The wartime plans for London provoked passionate debate over what the metropolis might become. Yet, no matter how noble the aspiration of Abercrombie and his peers, it is difficult to avoid the conclusion that much of the planners' project was misconceived. Imposing one man's vision of order on the chaotic, ancient, changeling, untamable disorder of London seemed an unholy impertinence. Abercrombie paid due homage to London's huge diversity, but his lust for neatness would not let him leave anything as it was. Difference had to be hardened into 'segregation'; London's character-istic promiscuity of land uses in a single area had to be sieved out into separate 'zones'; people had to be sorted into standardized numbers per acre depending how close to the centre they lived; the height of buildings should be ordered in the same way, with the highest in the middle, like a pyramid;

London's communities could be reorganized 'as separate and definite enti-
ties', divided from one another by the new road network.

In the event, the wartime plans were to have little effect on the physical
development of London. Holden and Holford's City plan faded away in the
face of market freedoms and a new fashion in architecture. The 1943 County
of London plan was never adopted by the LCC, which made its own in
1951 under the new legal framework of the Town and Country Planning
Act 1947. The Greater London plan never had a planning authority to adopt
or implement it. By the time one came about, in 1965, all of Abercrombie's
assumptions of a generation before were dated, irrelevant or wrong. Those
elements of the plans which were made real, like the Green Belt and New
Towns for decentralized Londoners, were already policy or had long been
practical proposals before the plans were put on paper. Politics and profits
dispensed with many of the more concrete proposals, like the ring-road
schemes or retaining the 100-foot restriction on the height of buildings.[85]

The first of the political realities facing the plans was the mess to be cleared
up when hostilities ceased. It was so big that corner bomb sites, weed-strewn
behind advertising hoardings, were discernible in London for the rest of the
century. But in 1945, desolation on a Pompeian scale had obliterated much
of the City's medieval street pattern and wiped away its tightly packed
Victorian offices and warehouses. Acres of housing had been laid waste in
the East End and dockside. Great rents in London's fabric scarred nearly
every neighbourhood.

Housing was the top priority. The first major repairs programme, organized by the government-run London Repairs Executive, was begun in late
1944. By March 1945, and despite V1 and V2 attacks, 800,000 houses in
London had been repaired 'to a tolerable emergency standard' in something
like six months.[86] By 1947, the greater part of the work of making damaged
houses habitable had been completed. But building new homes began only
slowly, just 37,600 in Greater London by the end of 1948, mostly schemes
already in design before war began.

Some progress was also made out of London in the New Towns, the
decentralization plan for London adopted by Clement Attlee's post-war
government. Stevenage was the first, designated in 1946. It was followed in
1947 by Crawley, Hemel Hempstead and Harlow; in 1948 by Hatfield and
Welwyn (building on its Garden City core); and in 1949 by Basildon and
Bracknell. By 1953, over 17,500 new houses were occupied by almost 50,000
people.[87] A further 84,000 would join them by 1961. But this was small beer
when set beside Abercrombie's decentralization ambitions.

Commerce had to take a back seat in the early years of reconstruction.
Tight central control over building materials was in place for the whole of

the 1940s. This impacted particularly on the City and West End, where damage to nineteenth-century offices, warehouses and shops had been most severe. Houses in Mayfair were requisitioned for offices to make good some of the shortage. The Berkeley Square house of the notorious procurer Gino Messina was taken in this way around 1944, for instance. Land values in central London, after a war-panic slump, had begun to rise once victory seemed assured in the spring and summer of 1944. And by 1947 the post-war demand for offices, 'any offices, however difficult to reach, however badly lit, however remote from the centres of trade activity', was feverish.[88] Although controls meant that almost no new offices could lawfully be provided, building licences could be had to repair 'war-damaged' offices and other commercial premises. Profits were such that a black market in building licences operated in London, provided for a bribe or more usually fiddled by developers who carried out the 'war damage' themselves. In the City a limited amount of rebuilding had taken place by 1950, including a 'crude' Portland stone office block by Rudolph Palumbo in St Swithin's Lane (1948). But while construction was restrained, ideas lay thick on the drawing boards: by 1951 planning permissions had been granted in the City to replace 4.8 million of the 6 million square feet of office space lost in the Blitz.[89]

On the whole, by 1950 not much of a phoenix had risen from the ashes of the five-year barrage to which London had been exposed. It would be a phoenix with wings permanently clipped. By 1950, for all practical purposes, London had stopped growing. The many centuries of steady growth, capped by 100 years of hectic expansion, had been brought to a halt by war and its consequences. The Green Belt, initiated by Morrison and the LCC in 1935, had been incorporated into the Greater London plan of 1944 and was set definite boundaries for use by local planning authorities in 1950. Ironically, the LCC was the main spoiler of its own initiative by buying Green Belt land in Oxhey (Watford), Debden (Loughton), Harold Hill (Romford) and elsewhere to build estates from 1946. But even the LCC was brought to heel when Lewis Silkin, once its own planning chairman, was Town and Country Planning Minister. And from the end of the war, apart from these LCC estates, building in the Green Belt became practically impossible for the rest of the century.

Simultaneously with the closing of London's borders its population began to fall. The war had involved huge movements of people out of London and back again. The evacuation of September 1939 moved 660,000 women and children to country areas, including half of London's school population. That was the official figure. Probably a further 880,000 moved out under their own steam. Many had drifted back to London by the time bombing began in earnest, just over a year later. Between then and the end of the main Blitz, around 140,000 were officially evacuated once more, and this time there is no estimate of evacuees who made their own arrangements to stay with family, friends or acquaintances. When the V1s began to fall in the summer of 1944, the third evacuation shifted 308,000 mothers and children from London and other vulnerable areas of the south-east.[90]

The volume of movements out of London, whether through evacuation or conscription into the armed forces and other services, was enormous. Inner London's 'resident civilian population' fell to 2.3 million in 1941, a drop of 43 per cent in two years. There is no estimate for how much this huge gap was bridged by servicemen and women, swelled as they were by forces from all over the world by 1944, Americans prominent among them. But even by mid-1945 and the beginning of peace, there were only 2.6 million civilians in inner London and 6.7 million in the metropolis as a whole. Recovery to what can reasonably be considered normal times took until 1948 to effect. In 1951, Greater London at 8.2 million had come close to regaining its pre-war population, while inner London's 3.4 million was about 15 per cent down on the 1939 estimate.[91]

Half-way through the twentieth century there was little to indicate that London was within a decade of a precipitous fall in population. War had half-emptied inner London and policy had decreed that more than a million Londoners should move out. But the 1951 population of suburban London, at nearly 5 million, was bigger than ever before. It looked capable of soaking up all of inner London's loss and more.

Similarly, despite the war's demolition of the psychic divide between city and suburb, the two Londons, new and old, appeared still to live side by side. Far from bringing inner London deeper into the twentieth century, the legacy of war looked to be holding it back. 'London was a sordid and miserable place' after the war. The Blitz-created open vistas and wide horizons, once an intriguing curiosity, had worn thin. Still, eight or nine years after the war, 'many a melancholy notice board tells in the the ruins of the City where churches and where public houses once stood'. London looked broken, drab, patched, tired out and essentially Victorian still. David Lean's poetic reconstructions in film of Dickens's London – *Great Expectations* (1946) and *Oliver Twist* (1948) – spoke directly to the everyday experience of Londoners in the 1940s: this was their London too. A nineteenth-century pall seemed to have descended on inner London, shrouding over forty years of change. Even the new buildings were smoke-stained, shrapnel-scarred and essentially old-fashioned: 'to this day the City has hardly a major building which is in the style of the [20th century],' complained Nikolaus Pevsner in 1957. For Eric de Maré, an acute mid-century

London observer, 'The central London we know today is still largely the London of the 19th century.'[92]

But all this was to change, and fast. For the 1950s saw the beginning of a process that was, finally, to remake London in an inescapably twentieth-century shape. For good or ill.

2. London Remade: 1951–99

The Triumph of the New: 1951–70

On 3 May 1951, King George VI opened the Festival of Britain in a speech from the steps of St Paul's. The next day, a wet Friday, the people were allowed into the Festival site. As the crowds streamed over the temporary Bailey bridge to the South Bank, there was little to indicate that this day marked the end of the bleakest decade in London's modern history. Wartime heroism had been rewarded by six years of pinching and rationing, patching up and making do, queues, shortages, big freezes and long power-cuts. At last Londoners, and the rest of the British people with them, were allowed a collective 'pat on the back', as Herbert Morrison – or 'Lord Festival' as the press dubbed him – had put it.

It was a typically modest pat. Just twenty-seven acres of war-blasted Victorian warehousing and backstreet industry had been cleared at the side of County Hall, on the forgotten side of the river, to house it. But the Festival offered – for the first time in a dozen grim years – colour, light, innovation, flair and the excitement of the new. It offered, at last, a future. If that future was more Stockholm than New York, well, that suited the restrained mood of the times too.

Some 8.5 million people visited the Festival in the five months it was open, and almost as many the 'Pleasure Gardens' at Battersea Park, a couple of miles away by steamer. They thronged the Dome of Discovery; wondered at the Skylon, an illuminated 'vertical feature' designed by young architects Philip Powell and John Hidalgo Moya; marvelled at a 'water mobile' outside Basil Spence's Ships and Sea Pavilion; watched the Tele-kinema goggle-eyed through 3-D Polaroid spectacles; and lunched or dined at the restaurant in London's most famous post-war building to date.[1]

This was the LCC's brand-new Royal Festival Hall. And, indeed, the LCC was in many ways the star of the show. Morrison himself was the LCC personified, although his top ministerial posts had kept him away from council business for more than a decade; the Council had cleared the Festival site as part of its South Bank redevelopment plans; and it had built the Lansbury Estate in Poplar, the biggest part of the Festival's off-site 'living architecture' show. Just along the Thames from the main exhibition, the elegant white arc of Sir Giles Gilbert Scott's Waterloo Bridge, a six-year-old playing ducks and drakes with the river, was further testimony to the Council as sire to a new London, for the LCC had beaten down a chorus of conservationist opinion and overcome government parsimony to get the new bridge built.

All in all, then, no LCC, no Festival. And just as the Council and its world-famous Architect's Department were willing midwives to the Festival as symbolic herald of a new Britain, so they shaped up to be Romulus and Remus to a new London as well. Theirs was less political vision than technocratic consensus: London needed modernizing. And modernization had three key components: comprehensive redevelopment, new roads and an architecture fit for the twentieth century.

This last was more contentious than the first two, about which in these early post-war years there was little debate. The wartime plans had envisaged tight controls over the height and diversity of buildings. Appalled by the lottery of pre-war development, with its anarchic individualism and chaos of roof lines and façade design, they all wanted to retain the 100-foot maximum height in the centre of London; and to impose a continuous cornice line which developers would have to build to along main streets. This did not, however, suit the young tyros of the LCC, moved by Le Corbusier's radical vision of streets in towers stretching to the stars, by light and airy Scandinavian high-rise, and by the brash confidence of New York's astonishing skyline.

It was the LCC technocrats who had the whip hand. They represented the planning authority for London County and for the City. During the early 1950s their aspirations for London were emboldened by advances in construction technology, which could now overcome the problems of building high on pliable London clay, and deal with many of the difficulties of fighting fires above 100 feet. But controls on development, put in place during the war and not removed for almost a decade after, meant that some years had to pass before the full potential of the new could be realized in London's war-scarred centre. When the new arrived it came with a bang that changed the face of London for ever. And it came in the shape of offices.

There were many factors that contributed to the office boom of 1954–64, but it could not have happened in the way that it did without the cooperation of the LCC, even though that zealous partner of the first years had turned into guilt-ridden accessory before the fact by the end. For the office boom appeared to deliver part, at least, of the planners' agenda: comprehensive development of those seedy inner areas that seemed obsolete in the modern age; eye-catching design that marked a distinctive break with almost everything that had gone before; and, most of all, new, bigger and 'better' roads.

But neither, of course, could the boom have happened without the developers. By the mid-1960s, the office boom's property developers had become the most vilified men in London.[2] For the most part men with roots in the pre-war London property market, usually as agents seeking tenants or buyers, predominantly Jewish (which gave an anti-Semitic edge to their demonization), combining mastery of detail with entrepreneurial vision, this small cluster of individuals made huge fortunes from London's insatiable post-war demand for office space. Essentially they were deal-brokers, assembling sites, finding architects, greasing the wheels at County Hall by calculating how a development might give the planners what they wanted. Necessarily secretive in a highly competitive world, where a rumour that they were interested in a site could send the asking price through the roof, they were often reclusive and shadowy men, generally (but not all) shy of public attention. Their names resonated as the nerve-strings of the London that emerged in the 1950s and 1960s: Charles Clore, Jack Cotton, Joe Levy, Max Rayne, Harold Samuel, and Harry Hyams, 'the daddy of all developers' but well under forty by the end of the boom he had done so much to push. Hyams's chosen designer, Richard Seifert, found himself thrust into the mantle of a modern Christopher Wren as the most influential London architect for nearly three centuries. Seifert and his peers – Basil Spence, Denys Lasdun, Robert Matthew, Eric Lyons and others – were given nothing less than the task of wiping clean the biggest slate of all: London's 250-year-old skyline.

The developers' job was made easier by two factors in addition to the LCC's ready assistance. First, as we have seen, the demand for new office space was insatiable at almost any price. By November 1954, when the government's revocation of building licences fired the starting pistol for the central London land rush, hardly any new offices had been built for fifteen years. Yet the aspirations of modern office users were sky-high, for the post-war world had seen an explosion in office employment through company formations and mergers, the expansion of government bureaucracy, and the enlarged economic significance of advertising and marketing over manufacturing. Brand-new headquarters in London were an essential requirement for domestic and foreign firms, for new government departments and for newly nationalized industries. By 1962, 60 per cent of City floorspace would be devoted to offices as against 45 per cent before the war.[3]

In time, this demand would have released the land needed to meet it. In fact, land was more readily available in central London than perhaps ever before. Large tracts of inner London had been laid waste by bombing. The City Corporation had acquired compulsorily 115 acres by 1948 for rebuilding or for selling on for development. Other owners without the wherewithal to build were ready to sell at low site values. Many districts, the product of the earlier boom years of the 1840s and 1850s, were at the fag-end of ninety-nine-year building leases, full of property starved of investment and ready for the asking. The Church Commissioners, for instance, were desperate to unload 300 acres of their Paddington Estate, embarrassed by owning for years one of the densest concentrations of brothels in Europe. And the great aristocratic London estates, burdened by high death duties and low rent yields, were forced to raise capital by selling off their more troublesome property: 150 acres of the Portman Estate in Marylebone was sold from 1948, the Grosvenor Estate sold on much of Pimlico around the same time, and the Duke of Bedford let go land in Bloomsbury south of the British Museum in 1953.[4]

From the beginning, and understandably, the developers wanted to build high. That way they got most rent and profit out of the land. The architects wanted to build high, too. That way they showed their prowess on a world stage where size was everything. The LCC's planners wanted to give the developers and architects what they asked for as long as they got their planning objectives fulfilled in return. Chief among these were new roads. It is one of London's little paradoxes that roads, so earth-bound, should have freed the developers to reach for the sky.

Events moved so fast that there was no single place or time which can be identified as the moment London's skyline erupted like some slumbering volcano. But a few hot spots were especially significant. The City, inevitably, was the hottest of all. A fourteen-storey building in Queen Victoria Street, Bucklersbury House (1953–8), was the first decisive penetration of the 100-foot barrier – at the insistence of the LCC and contrary to the instincts of the City's own planners. Broken once, the ceiling was shattered for ever. But the seminal development in the City which demonstrated that the financial sector had espoused wholeheartedly the virtues of architectural modernism was the development of London Wall. Typically, this was part of a new road scheme – Route XI, the northern section of the east–west City bypass envisaged in the Holden-Holford plan. It was a road never built, and London Wall became a super-highway that ran a few hundred yards between bottlenecks. But it was straddled by six anonymous curtain-walled towers and lower slabs which proved irresistible to modern commercial tenants. They sealed the fate of development in the City from the moment the plans were published in 1955.[5]

By 1959, when construction was well under way at London Wall, high-rise office blocks were pushing through the London clay as easily as a child's fingers through Plasticine. Basil Spence's fourteen-storey Thorn House at Upper St Martin's Lane was already topped out; former LCC chief architect

Sir Robert Matthew's New Zealand House, an undistinguished building on one of central London's most distinguished corner sites, was nearly finished; so was the more successful fifteen-storey Castrol House in Marylebone Road; the much-deplored Shell Centre on the South Bank was beginning to fill some of the space left when the Festival of Britain buildings were demolished eight years before; Millbank Tower was just about to start lording it over the Thames between Lambeth and Vauxhall Bridges; and the three ghastly hulks of the Marsham Street towers, soon to be filled with civil servants, were stretching up to dominate the Westminster skyscape.

Developments of even greater significance were going on behind Londoners' backs. Two conspired more than any others to bring the office-based property boom into terminal disrepute.

Joe Levy, a bookmaker's son steeped in the London property world as an estate agent since the early 1920s, had secured for a client as early as 1952 outline planning permission for an office development at a corner site on the north side of Euston Road west of Hampstead Road. Behind it was an area of rundown residential and commercial streets, including Seaton Street market, typical of London's mixed land use and typically abhorred by Abercrombie and the LCC planners. The LCC had designs on the area: to widen Euston Road at a notorious traffic pinchpoint; and to redevelop the worn-out backlands to the north. When, in 1956, Levy revived the scheme for a new client, Charles Clore, the LCC told him he could not develop the site because it was needed for road widening. But the planners had forgotten the permission they had granted four years before. Levy coolly told them they could have his client's one-acre site to widen their road, but that it would cost them £1 million in lost development rights.

Levy held the key to a cherished road scheme. The LCC, without a spare million in its over-subscribed roads budget, was forced into a deal. Levy put together a jigsaw of secretly linked property companies and began patiently to buy houses, factories and land along the north side of Euston Road. It took him four years. At the end, he offered to give the LCC the Euston Road frontage in return for generous office planning permissions based on the site he would have had if the road had not been built. In this way Levy broke through the LCC's 'plot ratio' of floorspace to site area, a rule designed to prevent over-development of hemmed-in spaces. The result was a wider Euston Road, enabling the LCC to build an underpass beneath the Hampstead Road junction; and Joe Levy's (Stock Conversion's) huge Euston Centre – offices, shops and luxury flats, with twin towers of seventeen and thirty-four storeys. The whole deal was kept darkly secret. The story of one of the biggest developments of twentieth-century London broke in the *Evening Standard* in 1964, but only after demolition was thoroughly advanced.[6]

Even more notorious was Centre Point, half a mile to the south and contemporaneous with the Euston Centre events. This was Harry Hyams's baby. He had been put in touch with Richard Edmonds, chairman of the LCC's Planning Committee, by a mutual contact – Edmonds's solicitor, Arnold (later Lord) Goodman. Goodman portrayed Hyams as the man capable of solving the LCC's difficulties at St Giles's Circus, the frantic junction of Oxford Street and Tottenham Court Road. The LCC wanted to build a roundabout there to ease traffic flow and for this it needed land. But efforts to acquire it had been frustrated by local property owners, who knew that the more they delayed the more, in its desperation not to lose their government grant, the LCC would pay. By 1958, when Hyams dropped in the LCC's grateful lap, negotiations were at a halt.

Hyams's solution was simple. He would buy out the canny landowners at a price higher than the LCC could give, and he would buy up the adjoining land too. When the site was assembled he would give the LCC the land for its roundabout and it would give him planning permission for an office development at a density that took into account the whole site, including the roundabout. Hyams got his land and Seifert built the thirty-five-storey Centre Point for him. But the LCC never got its roundabout. By the time the deal was concluded, the Ministry of Transport had installed an experimental one-way traffic scheme for Tottenham Court Road, one of the first of its kind, which proved so successful it made a roundabout redundant.

Centre Point (1963–7), a fine building squeezed too tightly into the wrong place, its minimalist pavements endangering a generation of pedestrians, remained empty for over a decade, despite an invasion of squatters in 1975. It was more profitable that way, inflating the book value of Hyams's assets faster than any rental agreement could have done. Contributing nothing to London for so many years, Centre Point symbolized the monumental absurdities of so much of the office boom.[7]

As early as 1960 the LCC had become worried about the office pressure-cooker building up in central London, contrary to all invocations, from the Barlow Commission's report on, that employment in the capital must not grow and should, if anything, shrink. But it had effectively put itself in the developers' hands. Without their contribution the Council could never afford to assemble sites alongside London's major roads. As long as it continued to want new or improved roads, the LCC had to deal with developers who wanted offices in exchange.

That was the case with the disastrous Elephant and Castle scheme. Although not built until the 1960s, this was a road improvement plan designed in 1948, ten years or so before the motor car began to present its hideous new challenge to London's roads. The redevelopment eventually provided a shopping centre that few seemed to wish to use, an unlovely (but quickly filled) office block by Ernö Goldfinger, and a twin-roundabout traffic scheme causing so much congestion that the GLC seriously considered building a bypass around it within a year of its opening in 1965. Similar combinations of roads and offices were implemented in Knightsbridge (Harold Samuel) and Notting Hill Gate (Jack Cotton).

It could have happened, too, with Jack Cotton's Monico Restaurant redevelopment proposal at Piccadilly Circus, supported by the LCC but stopped, untypically and in response to a public outcry, by government. Experts and working parties were commissioned to recommend a scheme for the whole of the Circus. By 1965 the planners were contemplating the 'vertical separation' of cars and pedestrians, giving ground level to the traffic and lifting shoppers on to raised decks and walkways. This 'segregation', a dominant ideology in city-planning in the mid-1960s, had grown so large in the bureaucratic mind that a network of 'pedways', linking the West End and Soho with the City, was enthusiastically advocated. So things might have been worse.[8]

It was George Brown, the new Labour government's economic supremo, who brought the boom to a halt by banning new office permissions in central London in 1964. By that time office development had already passed its 1962 peak. Nor could the 'Brown Ban' stop the implementation of dozens of schemes already permitted. By 1966 there were 178 million square feet of offices in central London, compared with 78 million in 1945. The designs of the 1950s and 1960s, their concrete cladding quickly streaking a dirty grey in the London rain, went on sprouting like hair on a corpse. And office rents in London, responding to a demand which could not be banned, climbed ever higher.

The 1950s and early 1960s were generally acknowledged as the worst period of the century for London architecture. Criticized at the time for its routine functionalism or pugnacious 'Brutalism', nearly half a century's familiarity hardly softened contempt. Many of the boom buildings weathered sourly and looked tawdry beyond their years. Even when not especially high they dominated by their bulk and breadth on the streetscape and many (like Paternoster Square around St Paul's Precinct, or the South Bank's Hayward Gallery) seemed designedly ugly. At the end of the century only the Barbican, its first plans published in 1956 and built between 1959 and 1979, still impressed by the self-confidence of its vision; but its segregation from neighbouring areas and its alienating and confusing deck access made even this an equivocal success.

The office boom of 1954–64 changed for ever the London skyline. By

1969 there were over 100 office blocks in the City and West End above the 100-foot barrier, sixteen above 300 feet.[9] Even if few yet rivalled St Paul's Cathedral (365 feet to the top of the dome), the tall buildings dwarfed the City's and Westminster's spires and turrets. The Post Office Tower added its distinctive shape, 230 feet taller than St Paul's, to London's profile from 1966. And Seifert's NatWest Tower (1970–81), Britain's tallest building of the time at fifty-two storeys and 600 feet, was to dominate London's skyline in the 1980s. Yet observers looking City-wards from Parliament Hill or from Greenwich Observatory around 1970 would have been struck less by the cluster of tall buildings at the centre than by the forest of towers stretching east and west across London's panorama as far as the eye could see. For the years of the office boom saw another boom too: of tower blocks in gargantuan council housing estates.

The council estate was a twentieth-century construct but the problems it sought to solve were much older than that.[10] Broadly, the problems were twofold: old and worn-out housing that had to be cleared as slums; and the housing shortage, which left a substantial minority of Londoners having to share a house and its facilities with other families. This 'multiple occupation' was, in its scale, a peculiarly London problem; and the zone of multiple occupation expanded in the first fifty years of the century due to middle-class emigration, even though the most severe overcrowding within it had diminished.

To meet this twin problem, two sorts of council estate had developed. In the inner areas cleared as slums, the old houses were replaced with blocks of flats. Building high, traditionally up to five storeys without lifts, was the only way to put almost as many modern dwellings back on the site as the number of families displaced by clearance. Blocks of working-class flats had been an increasingly common sight in London's old central areas since the 1850s, and especially from the 1880s, mainly built by philanthropic housing societies. When the first sizeable council estate in London, the LCC's Boundary Street scheme on the site of the notorious 'Jago' in Bethnal Green, was opened by the Prince of Wales in 1900, it looked an improved version of much that had gone before: twenty-two arts-and-crafty blocks, 1069 flats for over 5,000 people, with tenants' club-rooms and a bandstand. Slum clearance accelerated from 1930. And by the end of the 1930s the LCC alone had built around 190 inner London estates. Few were as big as Boundary Street but a number rivalled it in size and one, the huge White City Estate in Hammersmith, was far bigger at 2,300 flats. In all, inner London councils had built some 67,000 flats for about 250,000 people (around 6 per cent of the population) by the outbreak of war.[11]

The second type of council estate we have already met with. This was the cottage estate of suburban semis, more utilitarian than their private neighbours, but with garden city aspirations and gardens to go with them. The first of these of any size was, again, by the LCC – 1,300 houses at Totterdown Fields, Tooting, just inside the County boundary and dating from 1903. But the real suburbanizing moment for the council estate, just as for London as a whole, was the inter-war years, the 1920s more than the 1930s. Becontree, a new town before New Towns existed, was on a scale of its own – the biggest council estate in the world at the time. Begun in 1920, it contained nearly 26,000 houses by the time it was finished in the late 1930s. By 1939 the LCC had built around 64,000 cottages, with the biggest estates (apart from Becontree) at St Helier (Merton and Morden and beyond), Downham (Lewisham and Bromley), Watling (Hendon), Bellingham (Lewisham) and Mottingham (mainly Bromley). Suburban councils in outer London had added, widely scattered, another 48,000 homes.[12]

The war, of course, exacerbated both sides of London's housing problems by reducing the number of houses available and damaging many of those left. To cope with a problem of this size councils had to build fast and – because London could no longer expand – they had to build high.

High flats had been a European-inspired dream for British architects since before the war. Some luxury private developments – like Lubetkin's famous Highpoint 1 and 2 (1936–8) at Highgate, praised by Le Corbusier as 'a vertical garden city' – had taken off in the late 1930s. Although the public sector had not yet followed suit, LCC architects had travelled to study the latest municipal architecture in 1930s Vienna, Rotterdam, Stockholm and elsewhere.[13]

One of the first post-war LCC estates, Woodberry Down, with its elegant white nine-storey blocks overlooking the New River reservoirs at Manor House, was a near copy from pre-war Stockholm. So were the high flats at Lansbury and the famous eleven-storey 'point blocks' at Alton East Estate at Roehampton (Wandsworth), opened in 1954. These were all schemes of the LCC's young Architect's Department. They were rivalled, sometimes outstripped in adventurousness, by borough-council commissions like Lubetkin's Spa Estate (Finsbury, opened 1950), Powell and Moya's bright new world of the Churchill Gardens Estate (Pimlico, first blocks opened 1950), Denys Lasdun's eccentric point blocks in Bethnal Green (Usk Street, 1952, and Keeling House, Claredale Street, 1960), the 'sudden drama' of the Hallfield Estate by Drake and Lasdun at Paddington (1951–9), and Chamberlin, Powell and Bon's Golden Lane Estate, just north of the City, brilliantly joyous and colourful and including a sixteen-storey tower (1957–9). These estates became icons of the new Britain emerging from the shades of war.

They were models for municipal architects from every corner of Britain and, indeed, the world over.[14]

A notable feature of even these early post-war council estates was their scale – generally much larger than any inner-London estate of the first half-century, apart from White City. That fitted the aspirations of the time for 'comprehensive development': the Stepney-Poplar Comprehensive Development Area, adopted by the LCC in 1946, proposed the clearance over thirty years of much of 1,300 acres housing 75,000 people. And the years 1949–55 were the busiest of all for the LCC, which built nearly 65,500 dwellings over the period. Where its efforts were most concentrated the effects were drastic. As early as 1961, Ashley Smith noted that

the writing of a book on the East End just now has an immediate urgency . . . for such as the East End is today it has never been before and will never be again . . . A pattern that has existed for generations is breaking and what the new pattern will be is unclear even to those who are making their way across the shifting sands.[15]

So by the beginning of the 1950s the virus of tall buildings had crossed sectors from the office boom and was attacking drawing boards in County Hall and in town halls across London. Its passage was fatally assisted by government subsidy changes in 1956 which gave councils more money per flat the higher it was from the ground. As usual the LCC led the way.[16] Eighteen-storey blocks were put up at the Brandon Estate, Southwark, twenty-one storeys at the Warwick Estate, Paddington, twenty-four storeys at the Pepys Estate, Deptford. The GLC, which from 1965 inherited the LCC's housing stock and its building programme, accelerated the high-rise and slab-block combination. Industrialized building methods, with factory-made components assembled on site by a number of proprietary methods, boomed from 1962 and were made an essential part of GLC housing policy from 1965. In ten years, the GLC alone built 384 tower blocks. The brand-new London Boroughs were keen to keep up. In all, some 68,500 flats in blocks of ten or more storeys were built in London before the fashion eventually ended.

There had always been some doubts about the wisdom of building high flats and those doubts were not much allayed by the experience of living in them. The 1964 Labour government, while ambitious to maintain the building programme, was more sceptical than its Conservative predecessors. It scrapped the high-flat subsidy in 1965 and made building high even more difficult by introducing the 'housing cost yardstick' in 1967. This encouraged councils to reduce the cost of individual dwellings, and high flats cost more per unit than traditional building forms. Within the architects' profession, too, a schism had grown between those who favoured high blocks set in communal grasslands and the advocates of 'high-density low-rise', squeezing flats and private gardens into as much of the site as possible while keeping building heights to just four or five storeys. This new trend had gone so far by 1968 that 'the tower blocks had vanished from the drawing boards at County Hall', although long lead-times ensured towers were still being built in London throughout the early 1970s.[17]

But the death knell rang loud and sudden for the tower block on 16 May 1968. In her flat on the eighteenth floor of Ronan Point in Canning Town (Newham), Miss Ivy Hodge, a fifty-six-year-old cake decorator, put the kettle on for an early-morning cup of tea. It was not, as gas explosions go, an especially fierce blast, but it blew out the load-bearing walls of Ivy's flat and a progressive collapse brought every living room crashing on top of the one below down to the podium. The timing was fortuitous. Most people were still in bed. Next day it was announced that just four were killed and eleven injured. But the aftershock was enormous. Within weeks, all gas installations were ordered to be removed from towers. Within months, the strengthening of the culprit Larsen-Neilsen System blocks, and other system-built towers, was ordered throughout the country. Although new towers and industrialized slab blocks continued to rise where projects had been started, Ronan Point drastically hastened the end of the most expensive folly in British housing history.[18]

Some of these giant estates were more successful than others. More than a few, like Broadwater Farm (Tottenham) or Holly Street (Hackney), became some of the most notorious urban neighbourhoods in post-war Britain. But their fate was not necessarily avoided by the late-1960s high-density low-rise alternative, epitomized in the projects of architects Darbourne and Darke. Despite returning to the traditional verities of brick and timber and slate, estates like Marquess Road (Islington) managed to create a gnomic confusion of claustrophobic walkways, ill-lit living space, and walls and roofs that sprang mysterious and obstinate leaks.[19] In all, some 201,000 council homes were built in inner London between 1945 and 1970, and a further 247,000 in outer London. This was the most productive quarter-century of all for public housing. Although many thousands of good houses were demolished to make way for the new styles, and although London's architectural balance sheet for the period shows more losses than gains, gains there certainly were, as we shall see in Chapter 6.[20]

Not all the improvement in London's housing conditions can fairly be ascribed to the efforts of public housing authorities and their often faulty towers. Between 1951 and 1971 the population of inner London had dropped by over 17 per cent. Even though the fall in households was less dramatic at

8.5 per cent, it is clear that the housing problem had eased because there were fewer people to house. Less decisively, this was a picture mirrored too in outer London, where the population had begun to fall during the 1950s for the first time in modern history. It looked, then, as though the Barlow-Abercrombie policy of decentralization from London had begun to take effect.

Decentralization from the centre of London to the suburbs within and just beyond the Greater London boundary had largely been stopped by the Green Belt, but not entirely. The Green Belt was not finally in place until 1958. By then the LCC's post-war overspill estates had eaten away some of the land intended for it. Elsewhere inside the Greater London boundary the suburbs still expanded where they could – in the backlands of suburban mansions now demolished to make way for Closes and Groves, along estate roads laid out before 1939 but not yet built on, and infilling the few spaces left between developed land and Green Belt. These 1950s suburbs were necessarily small-scale and scattered except in three or four areas. In west London, the closure of Heston Airport freed up a large site for building, and the development of what would become Heathrow, London's main airport from 1946, stimulated new building in Feltham and Stanwell, the latter just outside the Greater London boundary. In east London north and south of the river, suburban development north of Hornchurch in Harold Wood and Harold Hill in the 1940s and 1950s (including a big LCC overspill estate), and similar expansion at Orpington, kept alive the suburbanizing impetus of twenty years before.[21]

The biggest planned expansion within Greater London during the post-war period was Thamesmead. The master plan was prepared as one of the first acts of the new GLC in 1965. This huge project, post-war London's answer to Becontree, involved draining and laying out 13,000 acres of the Erith marshes south of the Thames and crossing the border of the Boroughs of Greenwich and Bexley. This was to be a new town for 60,000 people, incorporating the unlikely feature of a marina for the yachting classes of Barking Reach. Its architecture was to become a cross-section of the shifting London housing styles of the time, from the white concrete grandstands of the early 1970s to the brick-and-tile 'Pixie' format which became the hallmark of private and public developments in the 1980s. Its 1960s aspirations were scaled down step by step as constraints on public funding for house-building became ever tighter from 1976 on. And at the end of the century the yachtsmen were still awaiting their harbour.[22]

As these post-war suburban extensions put their finishing touches to London's built-up area, the inter-war suburbs themselves were coming of age. With maturity came a closer integration of the new and old Londons that had coexisted for the first half of the century.

Integration did not come from any new transport revolution. The underground's Victoria Line represented the most significant post-war extension of the London transport network between the 1930s and the 1980s. Completed in 1971, it took twenty-three years to plan and build. When completed, it connected Walthamstow to Brixton. With the Jubilee Line from Baker Street to Charing Cross (opened 1979), these extensions brought welcome relief to travellers across central London, but did little to speed the connection of suburbs to centre. The Piccadilly Line extension to Heathrow (1977) did, though, make one important contribution to the west of the suburban network.

Most of all, integration was brought about by the centre moving outwards. The office boom of 1954–64 was not just a central London phenomenon. Offices sprang up everywhere. Market forces wiped out ancient snobberies: 'Pressure of demand abruptly ended the former prejudice against a head office south of the river', with Shell, Costain, Decca and the United Africa Co. sensibly planting staff close to Waterloo and London Bridge Stations. Large numbers of offices spilled over into Paddington and Marylebone by 1960 and as far west as Fulham (including International Computers and Tabulators, a forerunner of ICL) by 1963. And offices were 'decentralized' to the suburbs, especially from 1958, helping produce high-rise cityscapes across the Greater London panorama. The sky-high price of land in central London led many firms to review cost benefits in favour of a suburban venue where land was cheap and labour plentiful. Good transport connections were critical factors in office location, and so the towers tended to cluster at important road and rail junctions. All this was welcomed by the outer London local authorities, greedy for their share of the metropolitan action, who put few obstacles in the way of high-rise development. And councils themselves became office builders when reorganization in 1965 prompted a number of new civic centres to mark a fresh start – often to the chagrin of ratepayers, who found themselves footing the bill.

Outer west London had sprouted over 100 tall office blocks by 1967 from Hammersmith to Heathrow. But the 'most sensational phenomenon' of this suburban office boom was Croydon. It became a 'mini-Manhattan' with East Croydon Station the busiest in England outside the main London termini. Largely the vision of one man – Sir James Marshall, the local council's Conservative leader – as many office blocks were built and filled in Croydon in these frantic years as in the centre of Birmingham.[23] Croydon's Whitgift Shopping Centre, begun in 1965, was also one of the first in a trend which newly valued the 'regional' role of some suburbs as a resource for large parts of London. Similar early examples were Brent Cross (Hendon) and Wood Green Shopping City. They provided alternative shopping attractions to the West End for all but the most discriminating, or wealthy, of consumers.

All these developments increased work prospects outside the centre of London and complicated commuting patterns. They also helped merge the boundaries between old and new Londons. The remaking of London had as a large component this unification into a more cohesive urban entity, taking further the process that had begun in the minds of Londoners during the war years.

To a large extent, these commercial growth-points in the suburbs were contrary to the spirit of London planning policy, where 'decentralization' meant movement out of London altogether; indeed, the Location of Offices Bureau (LOB) had been set up by government in 1963 to do just that. As for population, Abercrombie's policy had been to stop London exceeding its pre-war figure. In fact, between 1951 and 1971, London's population fell by 745,000 or 9 per cent. Three-quarters of this loss was from inner London, where the main exporting boroughs were Tower Hamlets, Islington, Southwark, Hammersmith and Fulham, Westminster and Camden. But all London Boroughs apart from Bexley, Bromley, Croydon, Havering and Hillingdon lost population in these twenty years; and outer London lost most heavily from the older Essex working-class suburbs of Newham (mainly West Ham) and Waltham Forest (mainly Leyton).

On the face of it, then, the decentralization policy for London was working. But this was more by luck than judgement. Certainly the New Towns were an undoubted success in continuing to offer what London's suburbs, now incapable of expansion and beginning to show their age, no longer could: modern homes, built for a car-owning society, with spick and span shopping centres, factories and offices. Yet they were as attractive to people moving into the south-east region – as many continued to want to do – as those moving out from still-crowded inner London. The eight New Towns for London established between 1946 and 1949 showed a net population growth of 424,000 by 1986. From 1952, a tranche of 'Expanded Towns', twelve in all, from Swindon in the west to Haverhill and Thetford in the east, gave room for another 120,000 or so. A second wave of New and Expanded Towns in the 1960s – Milton Keynes, Northampton and Peterborough – added a further 181,000 by the mid-1980s. Around two-thirds of this provision went to Londoners. But these planned movements were swamped by voluntary migration out of the capital, especially as jobs declined, so that even in the peak planned migration years of the 1960s voluntary movements exceeded planned overspill by two to one.[24]

Where did these volunteer emigrants go? Most of the evidence shows that they did not go very far. London may not have been able to grow, but the idea of London grew still. The south-eastward drift of population that Barlow had warned and agitated against continued. This no longer had London as its primary destination. Instead it produced a London-connected region of New Towns, Expanded Towns and commuter villages – an industrial suburban penumbra of apparently limitless dimensions. In the 1960s, while Greater London's population fell by 7 per cent, the Outer Metropolitan Area's increased by 817,000 people, or 19 per cent. The 'Rest of the South East', excluding London, grew by nearly 1.5 million within a decade, showing how vigorously the pre-war drift had resumed its flow. By the 1980s it was necessary for planners to talk of a 'Greater South East', encompassing Wiltshire and Dorset to the west and Cambridgeshire and Suffolk to the north-east. It was like the inter-war years writ large, with the place of inner London taken now by Greater London as a whole.

A lot of this expansion was clearly fuelled by Londoners moving out, of their own volition or through state-given opportunity. They moved for reasons similar to those of the suburbanites a generation before. However fast London was changing and modernizing, it could not move as fast as the aspirations of Londoners demanded. The south-east beyond the Green Belt offered all the benefits of suburban living while jobs were now as likely to be outside the capital as in it. The 1960s accordingly showed a marked expansion of London's 'commuter field' into a belt thirty–forty miles from Charing Cross and, in some parts of Kent and Essex, well beyond that. From there 'The Smoke' was no longer even a smudge on the horizon.

And 'The Smoke' itself was changing, although not without a memorable moment of trauma. From the evening of Thursday 4 December until the morning of Tuesday 9 December 1952, London suffered the worst smog in recorded history. A combination of dense winter coal-smoke pollution and a freak anticyclonic fog brought London to a halt for four days. It was a lethal combination, causing around 3,500 deaths from asthma-related conditions. The 'Great Smog' came, as it were, almost out of a clear sky. Despite London's huge growth in the twentieth century, the great fogs so common in Victorian London had become much less frequent from the early 1900s. Even so, the 1952 events belatedly cleared the way for far-reaching clean-air legislation, although London (and the nation) had to wait four years for a Private Member's Bill by Gerald Nabarro in 1956. The Clean Air Act introduced smoke-control areas, and the local authorities' mighty task of converting London's countless coal-burning grates and boilers to smoke-less fuel began that year. It was largely complete by 1970, and the last dense fog really to trouble the capital seems to have been in November 1974. After the demise of the horse-drawn era, this was the second great step forward to a brighter London.[25]

The emergence of a smokeless London was part of a transformation which, even by 1963 when the journalist Harry Hopkins summed up its effects, was clearly changing the capital for ever.

As in the grey old [C]ity of London[,] office 'slab' or 'tower' outbid spire or turret, the break with the past which had once seemed so continuously present appeared complete and irrevocable. The much vaunted architectural materials, the vast gleaming curtain-walls of glass and aluminium, the alloys and the plastics, bright, sterile, precision-machined, seemed to belong not merely to a different period but to a totally different universe from the mellowed brick of the Bloomsbury Squares, the Regency stucco, the Victorian pomp and idiosyncrasy, the velvety sooty Portland stone, gently shading under the rain. Each year the familiar old London now seemed more fragmented, well on the way to becoming a series of quaint museum or tourist pieces.[26]

But, even as Hopkins wrote, London's past was about to bite back.

Past and Present: 1965–80

A passion for London's past had been a private obsession for many Londoners throughout the first half of the century. It followed a long tradition that stretched back without a pause to John Stow in the 1590s and which had drawn fresh inspiration from photography in the last quarter of the nineteenth century. The demolitions of the Edwardian period were followed like mourners at a funeral by enthusiasts who lovingly recorded the old city disappearing under their gaze: artists and sifters of esoterica like Philip Norman, Hanslip Fletcher and James Ogilvy; antiquarians and historians like C. L. Kingsford, Reginald Blunt, Walter Bell and G. Laurence Gomme (who combined his passion for London's past with a full-time job with the LCC, first as its Statistician and then as its Clerk); journalists and writers like E. Beresford Chancellor and James Bone; and architects like C. R. Ashbee and W. R. Lethaby.[27] They and their predecessors formed societies to mark the passing of London: the Society for Photographing the Relics of Old London (1875), the Topographical Society of London (1880), the Committee for the Survey of the Memorials of Greater London (1894), the London Society (1912). National bodies with a wider than London remit – the Society for the Protection of Ancient Buildings (1877), the National Trust (1895), the Royal Commission on the Historical Monuments of England (1906), and later the Ancient Monuments Society (1924), the Georgian Group (1935), the Civic Trust (1957) and the Victorian Society (1958)

– were formed often by prominent Londoners and had always a sharp metropolitan focus within their work.

From the beginning, these voluntary associations combined the scholarly chronicling of 'disappearing' or 'vanishing London' with agitation to stop the demolition of treasured buildings. But in general there had been more of the former than the latter, for the modernizing tide in London swept almost everything before it, largely unprotesting, for the first sixty years or so of the century.

There had, though, been some protests and some preservationist victories. These had most often been won through an uneasy alliance between voluntary action and public authorities. The role of the LCC, in particular, paradoxically combined a rapacious zest for knocking down old London while protesting loudly over the loss of chosen buildings. In 1900, with Gomme the keeper of the Council's conscience, it paid for the first volume of the *Survey of London*, at the start of the Survey's venture to record parish by parish London's old buildings. From 1910 the Council took on joint responsibility for the Survey's future work with the Committee which had set it up in 1894; it still flourished at the end of the twentieth century, with about half the old County's parishes documented. In 1900 the LCC bought and restored the 'Tudor palace' at 17 Fleet Street. In 1901 it took over from the Royal Society of Arts the 'blue plaque' scheme for marking the former homes of London worthies. A few years later it saved the fifteenth-century merchant's house of Crosby Hall from destruction – the Council moved it from Bishopsgate, where its owners wanted to demolish it to make way for a bank, and rebuilt it on the Chelsea Embankment (1907–10).[28]

At the same time, of course, the LCC was busy obliterating all traces of Wych Street and Holywell Street and, far more often than not, progress meant demolition. A symbolic moment came when the LCC planned to replace Dodd and Rennie's Waterloo Bridge (1811–17). When first built, according to the sculptor Canova, this had been the finest bridge in Europe. In May 1924 the bridge was closed for temporary repairs because one of its arches had sunk. This marked the start of a ten-year battle to save it from destruction waged, it was said at the time, by 'antiquarians' and 'short-sighted fanatics'. Demolition began in June 1934. Herbert Morrison, the newly elected Labour LCC's leader and progress personified, was photographed triumphantly wielding hammer and chisel to knock out the first stone.[29]

The Blitz, while moving forward the renewal of London, ironically gave conservation a boost. Its destruction of Wren churches and other famous buildings gave cause for much lament, brilliantly chronicled at the time by photographers like Cecil Beaton and artists like Sydney Jones, Wanda Ostrowska, Hanslip Fletcher and Joseph Bató.[30] And a revived interest in

London's architectural history was stimulated by John Summerson's *Georgian London* (1945) and later by the formation of the Victorian Society by John Betjeman and others in 1958.

But none of this activity, valuable as it was for London's future, was as significant as the changing preoccupations of ordinary Londoners. What had been the burning obsession of a few gradually became a lifetime investment for many. This was not so much apparent in the study of London's old buildings for study's sake, although there was to be more of that than ever before. Rather it was the conscious decision by a substantial part of the London middle classes to seek the good life, not in the suburbs as their parents and grandparents had done, but in the very areas that had been abandoned in that first suburbanizing process.

As we have seen, bourgeois 'frontiersmen' had found happy hunting grounds in Chelsea and Hampstead since the 1920s. But in the 1940s and 1950s this process accelerated and spread. It was most noticeable in those areas which had always retained a middle-class core despite the various waves of emigration since 1900. Parts of Westminster (including Pimlico) and Marylebone thus joined Hampstead and Chelsea as up-and-coming areas for middle-class owner-occupiers and tenants just after the war. The first improved houses were marked out in the public consciousness by brightly painted front doors in Festival of Britain colours. Pink was favourite. Stella Gibbons called her 1959 comedy of manners, set among the new Hampstead settlers, *A Pink Front Door*:

In those days [*c*. 1952], the Muirs' cottage had been the only one so transformed and painted; now, the tenants who had lived there for many years were gradually dying off or being tempted by speculators to sell their charming inconvenient houses for large sums, and tenants of another type were eagerly buying and moving in; young prosperous artists, dress designers, advertising executives, rising Television personalities and a few bright young business men and their families . . . Oh, a madly inconvenient, unbelievably picturesque, passionately sought-after residential quarter was Bottle Court, N.W.3.[31]

A friend of the Muirs, married to 'a bright young film man' and much better off, lived in Canonbury, and if this post-war transformation had anything like a starting point it is there we should look. An area of east-central Islington in 'gentle social and structural decline' since the turn of the century, some renovation had taken place in Canonbury Square, where George Orwell had been a recent resident, by 1948. In the late 1940s and early 1950s, a property company specializing in the rehabilitation of Georgian housing – it is notable that Georgian property, rather than anything more recent, was the special object of the pioneers – bought out the Marquess of Northampton, whose predecessors had owned the estate since Tudor times. This company renovated empty properties and sold them on to 'relatively well-to-do middle-class buyers'. Tenants of parts of houses were moved round the estate to create vacant houses or were found accommodation elsewhere, a more caring process than later became the norm.[32]

Middle-class colonization, or the 'return-to-town' movement, was given a hefty push by the 1957 Rent Act. This 'decontrolled' in phases tenancies begun since 1939, so that wave after wave of tenants could eventually be moved on by notices to quit. And the 1960 Building Societies Act, which discouraged lending to property companies, freed up funds for leasehold and older-property purchases. By the mid to late 1950s the first signs of improvement had broken out in Camden Town by Regent's Park and Primrose Hill – spurred on, it was said, by the arrival of the Italian ice-cream parlour Marine Ices in Chalk Farm Road at around the same time; in Notting Hill, where 'even . . . the shady parts' were being occupied by what Monica Dickens called the 'philodendron and unmatched wallpaper brigade'; in Barnsbury, Islington, where Gibson Square proved an early attraction and where the nascent antiques market at Camden Passage (as, even more famously, at Portobello Road, Notting Hill) provided an irresistible connection between restoring an old house and collecting things to show off in it; and in Clapham, where a sudden loss of caste in the late 1930s and during the Blitz received an equally sudden reversal from 1958. House prices in London rose by around 10 per cent between 1958 and 1963, disappointingly modest by later standards but worthy of remark at the time.[33]

The early 1960s saw all this take off sufficiently to be given a name – the sociologist Ruth Glass coined 'gentrification' in 1964[34] – and to be noticeable in many parts of inner London. Gentrification did not move by contagion alone. It could break out anywhere as fortune dictated – a property company here (Sigismund Berger's in Paddington from 1963), a rich entrepreneur there (Australian stockbroker Richard Harris in Battersea about the same time), a local propagandist somewhere else (Mary Cosh, Gibson Square, around 1959). Parts of Paddington, Battersea, Lambeth, Camberwell and Kennington were thus added to the canon of newly fashionable areas by the mid-1960s. Indeed, the first 'green shoots' of gentrification were discernible in every borough in inner London and in some of the suburbanized London 'villages' beyond.

This was a process which, in a decade between the mid-1960s and the mid-1970s, was to change the fortunes of London for the rest of the century. For all its little absurdities, and not a few obscenities, it changed them immeasurably for the better. Many of the successes that London could with justice lay claim to at the end of the century began with this sea-change in fashion. Just why did it come about?

Upper-middle-class but more or less impecunious young married couples not yet burdened by school-age children, politically left of centre but generally free from party ties, balancing otherworldly bohemianism with up-to-the-minute careers in television or journalism or film or stage, the early gentrifiers were marking out their own space in self-conscious contradiction to that of their parents' generation. They chose 'real life' against the 'genteel London suburb, perfectly named Parkwood Hill' of the radio serial *Mrs Dale's Diary*.[35] They chose to widen their life experience among working-class neighbours rather than live among the sort of people they had met at school. They took a risk rather than playing it safe. Through gentrification they rejected consumerism and the mass product of suburb or luxury flat or New Town house. Their energies went into reviving, with individual flair, the beauty of neglected old buildings.

Most of these early ideals probably didn't survive the late 1960s, when gentrification turned into a popular – and so less chic – craze. This produced its own consumerism in the ubiquitous antiques shop, the architectural salvagers', the lumpen-bourgeois barrow-boys' curio stalls in Camden Passage or Camden Lock, Portobello Road or Bermondsey Square.[36] And another early victim was class diversity, the newcomers imposing their own orthodoxy by stripping pine, painting stucco white or cream, and banishing net curtains to a prudes' oblivion. No room here for the 'Cypriot, West Indian or Mauritian home-owner' meticulously picking out the bricks in red and white, with green and black detailing around the windows; or, that startling trend of the early 1970s, mock stone cladding that turned London town houses into Cotswold cottages.[37]

Even so, gentrification continued to bring with it a decameron of delights – tales of rifling junk shops for just the right door handles or fingerplates or firebacks and marble surrounds; of the antics of the old lady in the basement or the 'coloured' men across the way; of perfidious builders and tin gods in the town hall; of celebrity-spotting ('The [Jonathan] Millers' and Alan Bennett in Camden Town, Albert Finney in Camberwell, Yehudi Menuhin in Highgate, Robert Kee in Kew), proof certain that the right area had been chosen and that the old could be found so enticingly *au courant*; most of all, the comforting dinner-table tales of profits to be made, of the price-watch in estate agents' windows, the eager scanning of the Sundays' property pages, the knowing chuckle at Roy Brooks's shameless advertisements.[38] It was all more exciting than shares, almost as spectacular and glitzy as the fine-art auction rooms, profits without limit from buying and selling in the gentrification game.

House values in London reached for the stars during the 'Barber Boom' of 1971–2, when high inflation and low interest rates meant that home owners were paying literally nothing for their housing costs. But these huge rewards disguised the dark side of gentrification. From the beginning, the 'winkling' out of working-class tenants to make way for middle-class owner-occupiers had been a disturbing feature of the colonization of inner London. At worst, tenants were terrified and bullied from their homes, as Peter Rachman had done in west London from 1954 to 1960, selling off houses to owner-occupiers or renting to prostitutes and other high-payers.[39] At best, tenants were paid substantial premiums to leave, which might put a deposit on a house in outer London or beyond; or they were offered improved, but smaller, accommodation nearby or elsewhere. But always there was a cost in disruption, in cutting family and neighbourhood ties, and in the fear that this was an offer that could not be refused lest something far worse should happen.

Few gentrifiers, though, had to get their hands dirty in this way. The work was done for them by an epidemic of estate agents, whose smart offices, often in Georgian shop-fronts, occupied a substantial proportion of commercial property in the gentrifying areas. And, certainly from the late 1960s on, the newcomers could salve any troubled consciences by allying with indigenous residents to wage war against a common enemy: the council.

Revulsion against comprehensive housing redevelopment had begun to set in during the mid-1960s but it took ten years for it to gain overwhelming force sufficient to check and change public policy. It had two origins. One was dissatisfaction with the new housing estates and their system-built towers and New Brutalist slab blocks. The other was an abhorrence of the waste of Victorian houses which could be perfectly usable with money spent on them, and which would make infinitely more popular homes than anything likely to be put in their place.

One of the earliest manifestations of this critique, eventually as strongly held by tenants to be moved out as by entryists anxious to supplant them, was in the Packington Street area of Islington in 1965–6. Here a ministry inspector had turned down a compulsory purchase order for demolition after hearing 426 objections at a public inquiry. Richard Crossman, Labour Minister of Housing, visited the area and agreed with his inspector: 'It wouldn't become as good as Canonbury but could become a second-class Canonbury', he thought. But his officials and Bob Mellish, his London housing number two, were hot for clearance. Islington Council had long lagged behind in the housing programme and to reject its prize scheme would deter it beyond recovery. Crossman stood firm until he was told that current tenants would have to be evicted even if the houses were saved. 'This shook me: and since I didn't want to turn it into a completely middle-class area I finally agreed.' So he put his name to some chicanery which, after considerable embarrassment and a parliamentary debate, eventually secured redevelopment. The system-built Packington Street Estate, notorious for so many years, was the consequence.[40]

Some other campaigns were more successful at saving their areas from the bulldozers, although generally only after some redevelopment had already taken place nearby and people could gaze, horrorstruck, at what would happen if the council went on having its way. Like Gospel Oak, another area that was drawn to Crossman's attention:

a curious little village in the middle of Camden . . . where you see gigantic tower blocks going up all round you among little artisan houses built in 1820 or 1830, very poor in quality, no damp courses, no modern conveniences. Yet certain developers will pay £12,000 [in 1966] for those little houses in order to turn them into immensely profitable luxury accommodation.[41]

Part of Gospel Oak 'Village' was duly saved and so, after a long community struggle that lasted from 1967 to 1972, was most of De Beauvoir Town, Hackney. Similar part-victories were notched up all over inner London – including the Railton Road area of Brixton, ironically so in the light of later events. Even some of the architects who were designing the new estates were guilt-laden at being part of a process that required the demolition of basically sound and attractive houses. But local and central policy was based on a belief that housing had a certain useful 'life' beyond which it had to be replaced. This ideology of obsolescence ignored the increasingly obvious reality that as long as a house was loved enough it could last, apparently, for ever. London's irredeemable slums had probably all gone by the mid-1950s. Indeed, the great bulk of these eighteenth- and early-nineteenth-century cottages, built in courts and alleys, had been demolished before the war. For many years after, though, policy continued to triumph over common sense. Around 70,000 houses were demolished in London between 1967 and 1976. Some of this demolition was pursued by Labour councils deliberately to frustrate middle-class owner-occupation within their borders; although the presumption that working-class tenants would be more loyal to Labour than middle-class migrants would not in fact hold true for long.[42]

As gentrification gathered pace, so conservationism emerged from being the concern of what seemed an aristocratic and eccentric minority into something like a popular movement. The demolition by British Rail Property Board of the Euston Arch in 1962 served to warn a wider public than any other conservationist issue since the war that, without vigilance and sturdy resistance, London was in danger of losing its landmarks one by one, in the interests of either profit or a misconceived public weal. The change of popular mood found its hero in an unlikely warrior. Duncan Sandys, a former Conservative minister with distinctly right-wing views on race especially, was instrumental in providing the first defence against area redevelopment. His 1967 Civic Amenities Act, which he moved as a Private Member's Bill, enabled councils to declare Conservation Areas in addition to existing powers to protect individual buildings. The Act responded to a real need. Seventeen out of thirty-three London councils declared Conservation Areas by the end of 1968; all but Barking had one or more by 1971.[43]

These new powers coincided in the 1970s with a popular passion for resurrecting London's past that was without historical precedent. It ranged across the political spectrum, from new left to old right. It took many forms: amenity and local history societies, groups recording popular memory and publishing 'people's autobiography', 'history workshops' involving local patriots and academic outsiders, family history societies, industrial archaeology enthusiasts and more. In 1958, eighteen local amenity societies in London were registered with the new Civic Trust; twenty years on there were more than 100, and that was on the more bourgeois architectural-preservationist wing of what had become a popular front. This was a mobilization with influential and eloquent tribunes speaking out for old London against the new – Christopher Booker, Simon Jenkins, Ian Nairn and Nicholas Taylor prominent among them. And it scented blood when, in revenge for the Euston Arch, government plans to demolish the Tate Gallery in 1968 were beaten off by public clamour and by the GLC's revamped Historic Buildings Board, now with Summerson, Betjeman and Osbert Lancaster among its number. There was an impact, too, on government housing policy when General Improvement Areas were offered from 1969 as a corrective to the inevitability-of-obsolescence thesis, giving grants to preserve houses that might otherwise have been cleared.

Inchoate, fractured and localized as it undoubtedly was, this growing feeling – that the old was worth saving and the new not worth having – led to a host of skirmishes and two major battles that added up to a war against planning in London. By 1976, when the economic prospects for major public investment in redevelopment were anyway dire, it had led to a conclusive shift away from the new and all it offered in favour of conserving what was left of pre-twentieth-century London. The war was over and the planners had lost.

The two battles were simultaneous but separate, spanning the fulcrum years of 1968–73. One, the future of orbital roads in London, affected the whole city. The other affected a small part. Both had repercussions for the rest of the century and beyond. But perhaps the local struggle, over just ninety-six acres in the heart of London, was the more defining moment of the two.

Covent Garden was a seventeenth-century suburb renowned for over 200 years for its theatre and opera and its vegetable market. Of these the market was of greater importance – for London as a whole and for the economy of the Covent Garden district in particular. The market was privately owned until 1962, when it was nationalized, surprisingly by a Conservative government. There had been plans to move it since the end of the First World War, but these had been fiercely opposed by locals and by most of those who depended on it for a living. But in 1964 its new state-industry owners announced it would move to Nine Elms, Battersea; in 1966 Parliament approved the move and in 1974 it was shut.

From the mid-1960s many people had been busying themselves with what would happen when, as by then was inevitable, the market should close. Some main players on the Covent Garden stage were strangers to the drama, like the GLC, the City of Westminster and the London Borough of Camden, all newborn in 1965. Others were old hands – Bovis, the Prudential Assurance Company and Taylor Woodrow – thoroughly schooled in the London property market, especially the office boom recently ended. Both sides were interested in just one thing: comprehensive redevelopment – or as comprehensive as possible given the continued existence of some buildings (like the Royal Opera House) that could not realistically be removed.

The first plan was published jointly by the three councils in 1968. About 60 per cent of the area was to be demolished, including 82 per cent of its housing. This would be replaced by offices, hotels, housing estates (both council and private) and (of course) a new road. In a genuflection to the conservationist tide, the most valued old buildings were to be retained along a single 'line of character'. Over the next two years the plan was worked up against some opposition, mainly from the minority Labour group on the GLC, and submitted to the Conservative Secretary of State for confirmation in December 1970. By that time, the redevelopment proposals had reduced to cover some 50 per cent of the area.

As the plan went in to government opposition began to grow. The inter-authority planning team put into the area to run the process split over the devastating effects for local residents and small businesses. In April 1971 a Covent Garden Community Association (CGCA) was formed. Its first demand was a new home in Covent Garden for every resident displaced by clearance and it sought protection for those small workshops and specialist retailers who had long made their livelihoods there. Opposition to the whole thrust of the plan broadened and became more explicitly political as Labour sided increasingly with the protesters. By the time of the public local inquiry into the plan in July 1971, Camden Borough Council, which had switched control from Conservative to Labour that spring, was a formal objector to a plan it had helped work up just three years before. Redevelopment was now the objective of an increasingly isolated Tory GLC and, less important, the City of Westminster.

First blood, though, seemed to go to the GLC. The plan was entirely upheld by the inquiry inspector in his recommendation to the Secretary of State in July 1972. But as the champagne glasses chinked in County Hall, the plans so laboriously crafted for five years and more were about to turn to dust. First, Lady Dartmouth, the conservationist-minded Conservative chairman of the joint local authority committee set up to oversee develop-ment, resigned within weeks of the inspector's recommendation, 'unable to work for a project in which I no longer believe and which could do unnecessary and irreparable damage to an historic part of London . . .' Second, public outcry against the scheme gained in volume and weight of argument, the conservationist flag waved energetically by Simon Jenkins in the *Evening Standard* and others. Third, Secretary of State Geoffrey Rippon's extraordinary decision on the inspector's recommendation, announced in January 1973, ostensibly approved the plan while effectively killing it. For, in endorsing the GLC's 'general objectives', Rippon required a new plan providing for more residential accommodation; and – the death blow – he added 250 buildings in the area to the list of those already protected because of historical or architectural merit. Finally, in April 1973 Labour recaptured the GLC. Under new masters the planners had to start again. And although they held out at first for more redevelopment than locals would accept, the CGCA had most of its demands met when eight out of nine key sites marked for demolition were changed to rehabilitation in the final plan published at the end of 1976. Although there remained much shouting over the future of individual buildings, notably the Jubilee Hall, which was also eventually saved, the conservationist argument had clearly triumphed. By 1973, Covent Garden had effectively laid to rest most of the shibboleths of post-war planning: comprehensive redevelopment, zoning to separate residential from commercial uses, and notional residential densities in inner London.[44]

Similar conservationist victories were won in Bloomsbury, where long-standing plans to extend the British Museum by clearing the area between Great Russell Street and Bloomsbury Way were finally abandoned in 1975, after a campaign lasting at least a decade, thus saving London, according to Crossman, from a 'disgusting . . . skyscraper-cum-piazza' by Sir Basil Spence.

And, around Tolmers Square, a potential extension eastwards of Joe Levy's Euston Centre was beaten off by a combination of student activists and stubborn residents. A high-profile battle against developers that had begun in the late 1960s became consciously conservationist only in 1972, when residents called on Camden Council to rehabilitate the neglected houses.[45]

At the same time as these hectic events, sometimes spotlighting for the nation tiny parts of London previously unknown to all but a few hundred residents, a London-wide battle was raging against plans, inherited from Abercrombie, to build a ring road network.

Some of the 1940s road proposals had already fallen on stony ground in the twenty years since the war, mainly because of cost. Indeed, road improvements had been constricted to important but relatively small-scale schemes like the Elephant and Castle roundabouts, the Hammersmith Flyover (1961), the Hyde Park Corner Underpass (1962) and the LCC's second Blackwall Tunnel (opened by the GLC in 1967). Of the grandiose orbital road proposals, three remained on the drawing board by 1965: an inner fast route, Abercrombie's B Ring, by now known as the Motorway Box and soon to become Ringway One; his C Ring, a completed and upgraded North and South Circular Road; and the D Ring, later translated into the M25 London Orbital Motorway. With misplaced optimism, plans to build the inner London Motorway Box were confidently unveiled by the Labour GLC on 1 April 1965, the new authority's first day of power. All the rings were incorporated into the Greater London Development Plan (GLDP), published and submitted to the Secretary of State for ratification in 1969.

But 1970 would prove a bad year for roads. Two umbrella groups were formed to coordinate the assault on the GLC's proposals: the London Motorway Action Group and the London Amenity and Transport Association. In the 1970 GLC elections a Homes Before Roads Party won 100,000 votes (though not a single seat). And all this campaigning gained real point from the opening of the M40 extension, the Westway. Residents of run-down Acklam Road in North Kensington, the roaring traffic just feet from their bedroom windows, displayed huge banners crying 'Get Us Out of This Hell' and disrupted the new road's traffic with demonstrations. According to Sir Desmond Plummer, then Conservative leader of the GLC, Westway did more to turn public opinion against motorways than any other single event.[46] By the time the public inquiry into the GLDP was opened in October by Sir Frank Layfield, there were 28,392 formal objections to the GLC's plan for London. Three-quarters dealt with transport and most of those with roads.

But the shift in public opinion did not sway Layfield. When he reported on the GLDP over two years later in February 1973, he recommended that

Ringway One should be built, while proposing that the other ring roads be scaled down. Geoffrey Rippon – the saviour of Covent Garden – immediately announced that he accepted most of Layfield's recommendations, including Ringway One.

Rippon knew that he was taking a huge political gamble. The GLC elections were just two months away. The London Labour Party had by this time responded to the unpopularity of the roads issue, had reversed after fierce debate its long-held support for motorways as a key element in modernizing London and had pledged to scrap Ringway One. Rippon gambled badly. In the April 1973 elections Labour was victorious. On its first morning of power, in an ironic replay in reverse of events eight years before, the Labour GLC announced that it would abandon Ringway One and lift the 'safeguarding' of the route which had blighted thousands of homes for so many years.[47]

Abandoning the road plans gave conservation and gentrification a push that moved both on through the 1970s and beyond. By 1974 and a new Labour government, renovation of older housing had become the preferred means of dealing with so-called 'twilight areas' of multi-occupied houses, still the major component of London's housing problem. An extensive programme of Housing Action Areas helped change for good London's traditional tenure patterns. Councils bought out landlords by compulsory purchase and rehoused the tenants; or the landlords removed the tenants and sold to owner-occupiers who improved their houses with the aid of grants. In the 1970s, rehabilitation in London was nearly as disruptive to neighbourhoods as comprehensive redevelopment had been. Population turnover in inner London was immense. In Islington, the very crucible of change, it was clear by the early 1970s that a major transformation was taking place in the class make-up of its population. Skilled working-class people, the district's backbone for fifty years, were moving away to the new opportunities in New Towns or the outer metropolitan areas of Hertfordshire, Essex and elsewhere. Their place was being taken by a polarized population of middle-class gentrifiers and unskilled workers, many of them newcomers from the Caribbean, Africa and the Mediterranean. Two-thirds of Islington residents in 1961 were no longer there in 1971, having died or moved away, and it is certain that turnover increased during the 1970s. All this was to have a major impact on the shape of inner London politics.[48]

Islington was a microcosm of the extraordinary double paradox of these years. The backward-looking conservationists and gentrifiers were, in fact, the harbingers of a new prosperity which was fast becoming characteristic of large parts of inner London. On the other hand, the inheritors of the new post-war settlement, the residents of the towers and slabs, were becoming poorer and increasingly marginal to the world of work and the consumer society. This polarization was symbolized by the simultaneous creation of two new Londons in the 1970s: the 'Inner City' and 'Village London'.

The economic decline of inner London from the mid-1960s had many interacting causes. Deindustrialization and the leakage of manufacturing jobs were reflected in higher than previous post-war unemployment rates from 1966. These worsened considerably from 1974 to 1980, and then rose dramatically through the 1980s and beyond. Migration from inner London, most telling among skilled manual and white-collar workers, caused a 27 per cent fall in its population between 1961 and 1981 to 2.35 million, just over half the 1901 figure. Those workers left behind were often the poorest, and they were increasingly clustered in the council estates.

The rise and fall of the council estate was dramatic: from paradise to pit in a generation. For all practical purposes the thirty years from 1951 to 1981 saw the beginning and end of the post-war council new-build programme in London. And they saw a transformation within the estates themselves. At the beginning, prized for their astonishing looks, their modern amenities, their generous living space; by the end, feared for their violence, their vandalism, their inhuman scale and their dog-eat-dog collective life. Symbols of hope in 1951, of independence from the rentier, of the prosperity of workers participating at last in the consumption of all that society could offer; symbols of despair in 1981, of dependence on state benefits, of a morass of indebtedness to the council and the moneylender, of isolation from neighbour and kin and society at large.

The corridor is a thieves' highway . . . At the corners where blocks join are dark passages, blind alleys, gloomy staircases. It is easy to get lost in these labyrinths, and easy for robbers to lurk or to lose their pursuers. The fear of muggings is so widespread that people, if they have to venture out at night, stick to the lit areas and walk hurriedly. Burglaries occur more frequently than in the richest leafy avenues of Hampstead Garden Suburb. In a single week in 1980 there were 21 break-ins on the estate. The front doors on the fourth floor are made of glass and flimsy wood and break open at a kick.[49]

That was the Holly Street Estate, Dalston (Hackney). Things got worse during the 1980s and early 1990s, so that the flimsy doors had to be replaced with steel armour-plating. Even so, burglars would smash through the very corridor walls with sledge hammers and pickaxes to enter a flat where, anyway, there was generally little to steal. Yet five minutes' walk to the west of Holly Street lay De Beauvoir Town, also in Hackney, a gentrified area already accorded the treasured 'Village' tag by 1980; and five minutes to the east was an up-and-coming area saved from demolition a few years before and known as London Fields from the name of the nearby open space.

In the literature of the time, the Londons represented by Holly Street and De Beauvoir Town might have been separate cities, occupying different dimensions of space or time – as, to a considerable extent, they were. In fact, of course, they were not unknown to each other, as the stout iron bars and grilles over basement windows and the razor-wire on garden walls in the gentrified areas or the 'Mug a Yuppie' graffiti on council estate walls indicated. And interaction at a variety of levels (at primary school, in shops and markets) was more extensive than superficial observation might have assumed. Even so, De Beauvoir Town and the Holly Street Estate can stand as twin poles of a divided London as wide apart as ever Mayfair had been from Mile End or Belgravia from Bethnal Green. And their back-to-back proximity was becoming a defining feature of the London emerging at the end of the 1970s.

Everywhere, it seemed, these local paradoxes were replicating themselves in different corners of London like botanical hybrids forced in a greenhouse, however unlikely the aspect or unpromising the soil. By the 1970s nowhere was safe from the middle-class invaders, even areas so utterly proletarian that there had been no bourgeoisie to flee from them in the 1920s and 1930s. Like Rotherhithe, its redundant warehouses turned into 'lofts' for film-makers; Limehouse, its Georgian inns and merchants' mansions attracting a particularly hardy but wealthy breed of gentrifiers (including David Owen, Labour Foreign Secretary from 1977 to 1979) who had begun to settle in Narrow Street in the 1960s; Wapping, Ratcliff – even Cable Street, the 'London Avernus' of the 1950s with its dope dens and brothels, had an artist in residence (Dan Jones, the son of a Labour attorney-general) by the 1970s. Almost as extraordinary, given the opinions of intellectuals just forty years before, scattered among the traditional villagery (Hampstead, Chelsea, Dulwich, Clapham, Blackheath) were now a host of suburban villages where the inner-city delights of gentrification could be indulged without the attendant disadvantages of grime and crime. Some were riverside settlements, grossly swollen in the twentieth century, like Barnes, Chiswick, Kingston, Richmond or Twickenham. But many others were suburbs proper, now making surprising guest appearances in the London village guidebooks: 'Carshalton Village', Hanwell, Merton Park, 'Northolt Village', or Mill Hill, where Richard Seifert had lived from 1946. Thirty years later, as biter bit, 'he fervently trusted that Westminster City Council would not try to cover land it owned farther down the hill with [high-rise] council housing'.[50] Fears like that would become even sharper during the tumultuous 1980s.

Post-industrial London: 1980–99

Of all the decades of London's twentieth century, the 1980s proved the most socially unsettled, dangerous and paradoxical. In the 1980s London seemed to be moving fast in two opposing directions: into terminal decline, its traditional industrial base deconstructing, its public realm shabby and withering, large numbers of its people pauperized without work or hope; but at the same time there was a booming London, the City prosperous as never before, a new office explosion colonizing unexpected parts of the East End, conspicuous consumption symbolized by the 'yuppie' in his or her Porsche. It was only towards the end of the century that a resolution or synthesis of these opposing forces seemed to heal some of the breaches in this more than usually divided city.

The decline of London's industrial base continued throughout the 1980s. Even from the beginning of the decade huge tracts of the city had been effectively taken out of commission. London's historic upper port was among the earliest and biggest casualties, with dock closures from 1967 to 1981, leaving passengers and cargo to and from London to be landed at Tilbury, north of Gravesend.

Alongside the docks, the manufacturing areas of the East End were the first to suffer wholesale decline. By the early 1980s, industrial decline was also laying waste large areas of west and north-east London, the expansion zones of the second industrial revolution just fifty years before. Besides the major 'industrial cemetries' of West Ham, Park Royal and the Lea Valley, the run-down of many industries left gaping holes in London's urban landscape. Swathes of railway land, made redundant by the growth of road transport, became impromptu nature reserves at King's Cross, New Cross, Stratford and elsewhere. The decommissioning of coal gasworks wiped out industry from Beckton and the Greenwich peninsula. The closure of electricity generating stations all over inner London posed problems of what to do with massive industrial buildings filled with asbestos. London's old wholesale distribution markets were no longer convenient for the road haulage industry's needs, and so Covent Garden moved to empty railway land at Battersea in 1974, Billingsgate fish market shifted from the City to Docklands in 1982, and Spitalfields market went to Leyton in 1991. Across inner London, population losses and changes in retail patterns that favoured supermarkets and suburban shopping centres had fatally sapped the energies of the capital's town centres. This was a trend that dated back to the mid-1960s, but by the 1980s town centres in Hackney, say, or Tottenham,

Peckham and over much of inner London were run-down and silent and abandoned at night.

The 1980s saw London's population slump to its lowest point of the century – around 6.77 million in 1983 – the bottom of the trend established unevenly from 1940. Inner London was home to fewer people in the 1980s than in 1851, before the great expansion of the mid-nineteenth century. Other evidence of regression reinforced the Victorian connection. London's infrastructure, so much of it in place before the twentieth century began, appeared to be on its last legs. The disastrous King's Cross fire of November 1987, in which thirty-two people died, brought home the run-down state of the underground, daily frustration to half a million commuters. Elsewhere on the tube, the 150-year-old East London Line tunnel built by Marc and Isambard Kingdom Brunel, had to be closed for some years while it was repaired to stop the Thames flooding in. Indeed, water ingress throughout the system became an increasing problem as reduced industrial draw-off caused London's water table to rise. The Clapham rail disaster of December 1988, when three trains collided, killing thirty-six and injuring 111, raised similar questions over worn-out track and signalling on the commuter network. And despite reduced economic activity, rush-hour traffic speeds in central London were down to ten m.p.h. in 1990, 40 per cent less than in 1974.

The public sector generally in London seemed to be as much in decline as manufacturing industry. Street litter, always a problem in the capital, grew to such disgraceful proportions that the Royal Fine Arts Commission made it public enemy number one when proposing *A New Look for London* in 1988.[51] The fortunes of London government reached their nadir with the abolition of the GLC in 1986. Unemployment approached levels not seen in the capital for fifty years and, uncharacteristically, it was worse in London than in the country as a whole by the end of the decade. The number of recorded crimes in London rose 46 per cent between 1981 and 1991. It was in this decade that London was most riven by communal conflict. A few council estates tore themselves to pieces in mutual terrorism, much of it due to drug-dealing vendettas. There was ferocious rioting during the 1981 disorders in Brixton, Southall and elsewhere; again in Brixton and Tottenham in 1985; and then in the poll tax riots in central London and elsewhere in early 1990, all adding up to the most serious civil disturbances anywhere on the British mainland this century. The 1980s were to find a worthy chronicle and chronicler in the apocalyptic vision of Martin Amis's *London Fields* (1989).

Yet despite the dangers of this most traumatic decade there were many 'green shoots' which held the promise of a different direction for London and Londoners to take. At the century's end, although there remained many uncertainties over the sustainability of the London economy, it was these more creative and productive aspects of the 1980s that seemed likely to leave the more enduring legacy. And the most creative and productive of all was the replacement of London's Docklands by something entirely different.

St Katherine's Dock had been sold by the Port of London Authority to the GLC in 1969. After a design competition was won by Taylor Woodrow, endowing them with a 125-year lease, the dock and warehousing were quickly turned into a marina with housing, shops, a pub and the huge Tower Hotel (1973). But just what would replace the docks further downriver, away from the tourist-hungry Tower of London, was much less certain.

Consultants' studies of what could be salvaged from the Docklands wreck and what might replace redundant docks were commissioned by government and the GLC in 1971. A feasibility study was published two years later and in 1974 a Docklands Joint Committee of the GLC and the five riverside boroughs (Tower Hamlets, Newham, Southwark, Lewisham and Greenwich) was set up to oversee the redevelopment of the redundant docks and their hinterland. In 1976 the Joint Committee published the London Docklands Strategic Plan. The plan was out of date before it was printed. It called for new homes (mainly council-owned), open spaces and industrial jobs based on manufacturing. In the face of later developments, this was a hidebound and unimaginative approach to the biggest opportunity to change the face of London since the Blitz. But perhaps that was inevitable, given the local constituencies the Joint Committee had to please and the shallow contemporary understanding of the true state of Britain's manufacturing industry.

In any event, the plan required £1,140 million of public money and £600 million of private investment. It was silent on the sources of the latter and the former had effectively dried up in the International Monetary Fund crisis of 1976. In particular, the Treasury short-sightedly (but resolutely) opposed paying for the plan's proposal to extend the underground's Jubilee Line to Docklands as a spur to private investment. So virtually nothing happened. More dock closures followed amid the poisonous recriminations of local politics, where it served the interests of borough councils to blame everyone else for inaction but themselves.

A decade of dithering in Docklands gave the first Thatcher government every excuse, and not a bad reason, to experiment with a Development Corporation on the lines of the New Towns Corporations of the 1940s. This meant taking the area out of the control of local government and appointing a board of businessmen to carry out a plan for business. And in 1981 the London Docklands Development Corporation (LDDC) was put in control of the riverside from Tower Bridge to Beckton, to the outrage of the boroughs and to the consternation of locals, who found themselves no longer able to shout at the devil they knew.

It was the creation of most of the Isle of Dogs as an Enterprise Zone in 1982 that lit the Docklands fuse. Tax and other investment incentives, not so much seductive as wanton, sucked capital into Docklands from all over the world. 'The result has been [by 1994] a whirlwind of development producing a physical transformation that has been rapid and spectacular', where the landscape could alter out of recognition in weeks, and where the roads shifted on the ground from one month's end to the next so that even a frequent sightseer would inevitably be lost within a few minutes of entering 'The Island'. [52]

Some 70 per cent of investment in the Isle of Dogs in these years came from abroad. Foreigners were said to be less prejudiced against the East End than the British, still put off apparently by the discordant resonances of 'Whitechapel' and 'Cable Street'. And it was the decision in 1985 of a consortium of North American investors to build a speculative office development of 8 million square feet at Canary Wharf that was really to change the fortunes of Docklands – and of east London – into the twenty-first century and probably beyond.

Prior to the Canary Wharf proposal, development in Docklands had by London standards been fairly small-scale – generally schemes of less than 100,000 square feet. After Canary Wharf, developers thought big. They were helped to do so in October 1985 by a relaxation of the Bank of England rule that banking headquarters had to be located in the Square Mile; by the virtual abolition of tax breaks on development outside Enterprise Zones in April 1986; and by 'Big Bang' that October. Anticipation of this event – the deregulation and computerization of London share-trading – had already stoked demand for superior infotech-friendly office space in the City. Now this spread to Docklands. By the summer of 1986, things had gone far enough for the President of the Board of Trade, Norman Tebbit, to gush over Docklands as 'Manhattan-on-Thames' and 'Wall-Street-on-Water'. And such extravagance found some justification as Canary Wharf began to take shape from the middle of 1988.

By this time control of the scheme had passed to the Canadian property company Olympia and York, owned by the exotic Reichmann brothers. They inherited the main design from two firms of American architects, one of whom – Skidmore, Owings and Merrill – was to play a major role in the late-century development of central London. But they brought in Cesar Pelli, Argentinian-born though American-based, whose Canary Wharf Tower (1988–91) at once made a unique and defining contribution to

London's skyline: 'I wanted it to look un-American, to step outside the three main styles of classical, Gothic and art deco.' In the end his design was compromised by the need to remove five storeys for air-safety reasons while adding the missing floorspace to the remaining fifty floors. This bulked out the tower to a disproportionate stoutness. Even so, Pelli's 824-foot tower, more than twice the height of St Paul's, the tallest building in Britain at the century's end and Europe's second highest, its stainless-steel cladding glistening icily in the sun, was an extraordinary achievement. It established Docklands as 'central London's third office district'. But it also proved big enough to bring Olympia and York to bankruptcy in May 1992. At the century's end the Canary Wharf development remained unfinished and part of the tower unlet.

The pace of development on the Isle of Dogs was so fast that by 1990 the office market east of the City was saturated, supply far outstripping demand. A contributory factor had been yet another wave of redevelopment in the Square Mile. This was a final fling in the City's century-long process of continual renewal that had hardly paused for breath, and which needed no tax incentives to get started or keep going.

The causes of the City's late-1980s office boom were similar to those fuelling the expanded office sector of Docklands. Indeed, there was a reciprocal process. Docklands competition caused the City to look to its own laurels, encouraging architectural innovation within the Square Mile to compensate for the poverty of much of the building there in the 1950s and 1960s. And Docklands freed up space in the City by seducing tenants away with lower rents and high-tech accommodation. A case in point was Fleet Street where Rupert Murdoch and News International changed the face and location of newspaper printing in London. By 1988, 'The Street of Ink' had largely run dry, its passing marked by a *Farewell to Fleet Street* exhibition at the Museum of London, its old tenants thick on the ground at 'Fortress Wapping', just west of the Isle of Dogs. Here took place the last great London industrial struggle of the century in 1986–7, over the power of the printworkers in an age of computerized text production. It was a struggle decided, after much violence, in favour of the employers. Fleet Street became as hectic a site of demolition and rebuilding as it had been between the wars. But now, through buildings like Goldman Sachs's 'groundscraper' at Peterborough Court (1988–91), it was consolidated into the financial services world of a City that had lost much of the traditional diversity it had inherited from the Victorians.[53]

The 'Atrium Office Block' was the 'characteristic product of this boom' of the 1980s. The City's first dated from 1972–78, but it was somewhat later that those astonishing glass fronts exposing lifts, escalators, reception areas and what appeared to be the looted relics of tropical rain forests became a familiar feature of the City street scene. Richard Rogers's Lloyd's of London building (1978–86), the Standard Chartered Bank (Bishopsgate, 1980–85), and Ove Arup's 1 Finsbury Avenue (1982–4) stood out impressively within a successful genre.[54]

This last was part of the Broadgate development on the site of the former Broad Street Station, incorporating the renovated Liverpool Street Station. Broadgate was fairly judged in 1997 to be 'by far the most attractive and impressive piece of post-war planning in the City' and, indeed, the whole of London. It rose dramatically in just six years from 1985, when, after a decade of abortive plans, public inquiries and conservationist opposition to the loss of Liverpool Street Station, Stuart Lipton's Rosehaugh Stanhope Developments were appointed developers. Ove Arup and Skidmore, Owings and Merrill were prominent and distinctive among the designers. The result was an architectural feast – some eclectic art deco-ish and retro-chic, some (like Exchange Building) uncompromisingly modern – and a huge commercial success that pushed the boundaries of the City north-east into Shoreditch and east to touch Spitalfields. Happily, Skidmore, Owings and Merrill continued to contribute to central London's streetscape, designing more buildings around Ludgate Circus just before the collapse of the boom in 1992, notably the stunning 10 Fleet Place, Limeburner Lane. By the end of 1993 it was claimed that half the City's stock of office accommodation had been built since 1986; and although that might have been a claim too far, it gave some idea of the speed and scope of development, almost matching that in Docklands.[55]

The City boom spilled over into the parts of central London that the first post-war office-building wave had not quite reached. So, for instance, the developers got their office block on Tolmers Square (a fat ark for the Prudential Assurance Company), although the 'square', on a meaner scale than the original, was rebuilt as a Camden Council estate. And a beautiful new British Library was eventually opened on the Somers Town side of St Pancras Station in 1997, some fifty years after an urgent need for a new library had first been identified.

Most positive of all, the new world emerging in Docklands helped refocus developers' attention on London's river. A river view from office or penthouse was at a premium. A river-bank location granted designers an almost unlimited breadth of vision, and it was exploited with a flamboyant self-belief that London architects had rarely equalled at any other time in the century. The riverside buildings of the Terry Farrell Partnership – 'Farrell is the key figure . . . in the development of Post-Modern London', it was said in 1991 – were temples to an infallible god of commerce worshipped by a corporate state. They were as secure in their faith as the work of any medieval master mason: like the green and beige ziggurat of Vauxhall Cross on the unfashionable Albert Embankment (1989–92), home to MI6 at the century's end, or the cathedral bulk of Embankment Place at Charing Cross Station (1987–90), or the Conran Roche development at Butler's Wharf and nearby (1987–91).[56] The riverside remained a focus of imaginative, if controversial, exploitation through the 1990s, not least with Lord Rogers's Montevetro glass ski-slope in Battersea (1998).

This last wave of renewal, in contrast to all those preceding it, reached a considerable accommodation with conservation. No longer were old streets or buildings singled out for demolition. By the end of the 1970s any struggles over conservation (like Liverpool Street Station) were largely settled in the preservationists' favour. Rather, it was the product of the first post-war office boom that proved most vulnerable to redevelopment: 'well over a quarter', it was estimated, of post-war City buildings had been demolished by 1997, a trend destined to continue when renewal revived yet again at the very end of the century. Of those office buildings from the 1950s and 1960s that escaped demolition in the 1980s and 1990s, a few were 'refitted' with postmodernist facelifts, spicing up Brutalist façades for a more fanciful age.

As conservation flourished in these years, at least in its adaptive and compromise form where old buildings were amended for new functions, so did its new-money twin, gentrification. Its continued prosperity had two main characteristics in the 1980s and 1990s: spreading into new areas and consolidating its hold on those it had colonized for a decade or two or more.

In these years gentrification invaded areas that it had only just reached, or hardly touched at all, in the 1970s. Stoke Newington (sold first as 'Islington borders', then under its own brand name when the market had been sufficiently educated) became especially desirable around old-villagey Church Street with its diverse charms, recovering middle-class ground lost from the 1930s to the early 1950s.[57] Parts of south Shoreditch that had not seen an indigenous middle class for over a century found abandoned warehouses turned into lofts in an intriguing district where a Victorian streetscape had been imposed on a medieval street pattern. Even Hoxton, the safe-cracker's sanctuary, began an unlikely new career in the early 1990s in media production and the arts, with a few creators-in-residence. Similarly, some gentrification that had begun in the 1970s now expanded into formerly unacceptable streets at King's Cross, despite its reputation as perhaps London's lowest-caste red-light district; and at Waterloo, building on the gentrified nucleus of Roupell Street. Here the redevelopment of Coin Street produced more of a wealthy middle-class enclave than the revived working-class community that GLC purchase of the site for housing in the 1970s had ostensibly promised.

Most astonishing of all was Spitalfields. In 1981, the Spitalfields ward of Tower Hamlets was the most deprived area in London, its living conditions rivalling the worst slums anywhere in the Western world. Yet, it had already become the quarry of a dedicated band of gentrifiers who would squat empty houses, occupy property companies' offices, arrange media stunts, do almost anything to save Spitalfields' early-eighteenth-century houses from spoliation. Within a decade a few streets in the midst of London's Bangladeshi community had seen an unimaginable rise in property values, to the delight and enrichment of a few and the disgust and chagrin of others. A celebratory book, *The Saving of Spitalfields*, lavishly relayed the story and begged, but did not answer, the question, 'Saved for whom?'[58]

It was difficult to applaud without reservation a conservationist project where property values rose geometrically when a street was translated into a Conservation Area, where sweatshops were squeezed out by office conversions, where the super-rich turned out impoverished Bangladeshi settlers, where houses were 'restored' to a pristine 'Georgian' state they had never known in reality, and where newcomers fought the retention of Spitalfields' messy fruit and veg market despite the jobs it provided. Raphael Samuel, historian and unfashionable Spitalfields resident, summed up the self-deceptions of gentrification around 1987: 'Office development . . . now threatens to engulf Spitalfields in a sea of neo-Georgian fakes.'[59] The same could have been said for Covent Garden, where the residents and businesses for which the CGCA had so passionately fought had largely moved on by the 1980s.

All over inner London a similar story was writing itself out in whitened stucco, jet-washed bricks and remodelled railings. Yet the office trend in Spitalfields was against the grain of tendencies elsewhere. It was in the 1980s, and especially in the 1990s, that London saw a reversal of its age-old transformation of residential accommodation to commercial. Deindustrializ-ation meant that commerce – at first factories and warehousing, by the mid-1990s offices – had abandoned many areas. Sturdy nineteenth-century buildings, often empty of commercial tenants for a decade, were at last finding a market through conversion into flats and penthouses. By the 1990s this was a tendency encountered throughout inner London. It converted the art-deco Gilby's gin offices and distillery at Camden Town to luxury flats. It snatched up warehousing at Bankside, where the construction of the Globe Theatre brought in a middle-class population for the first time almost since records began: 'five years ago, hardly anyone lived between Waterloo and Tower Bridge except council tenants', *The Times* disarmingly claimed in 1998.[60] It magicked Mediterranean riverside apartments from gas board offices in Fulham. And it reclaimed for occupation by the super-rich early-eighteenth-century houses in Queen Anne's Gate, Westminster, that had been offices for sixty years or more.

Besides extending its boundaries, gentrification also consolidated its hold on areas colonized in the 1950s and 1960s. Thirty years on these had lost their bohemian and faintly risqué air. Now they were prey to a pervasive complacency founded on ready money. The diversity that had been so much valued at the beginning – and was so quickly under threat – had in many areas been largely ironed out, at least within the gentrified streets of Barnsbury, say, or 'Islington Village'. Or Notting Hill, which had shifted from Edwardian upper class, to 1930s bedsit land, to a low point of peeling stucco and 'problem families' and the 'ghetto' of the Caribbean influx in the late 1940s and 1950s, and then once more to an object of middle-class desire from the late 1950s. By the mid-1990s, it 'has metamorphosed from a colourful but somewhat frayed corner of London to the happening haunt of the young film/media/music set, and those who aspire to join its ranks,' with housing space only within the grasp of the very rich indeed.[61]

There was change, too, and most welcome, for the council estates. This transformation also had a 'back to the future' feel about it. Just as the City redevelopments of the 1980s and 1990s had targeted as sacrificial victims the buildings of a generation before, so councils attempted to remedy the mistakes of their own very recent past. They did so by rebuilding estates, replacing concrete towers and wasteland with streets and houses akin to what had been knocked down in the 1950s and 1960s. The first London tower blocks were demolished as early as 1981 – in Newham, home of Ronan Point. By 1984, Hillingdon had resolved to demolish all its system-built flats erected between 1967 and 1971 because of structural failure and damp from condensation.[62] Demolitions across London gathered pace during the 1980s and 1990s, especially in Hackney, where many borough and GLC towers had been built. By the end of the century London was living through the break-up of the council estate. Holly Street was an early example. From late 1994 its dreadful 'snake blocks' of linked low-rise maisonettes, and three of its four towers, were demolished to make way for houses built on a traditional street pattern. The most expensive were to be sold on the open market for owner-occupation, some were retained for council tenants and most were rented by housing associations.

These progressive trends of the 1980s had an effect on the capital's demography. From 1984, London's population decline went slowly into reverse. Inner London, which had been losing people since the turn of the century, recovered from 2.31 million in 1983 to 2.41 million in 1991. Outer

London's population picked up more slowly. The 1991 figure for Greater London of 6.89 million was projected to grow to 7.17 million by 2001, a rise of 4 per cent in the 1990s and 6 per cent on the 1983 low point. That was hardly spectacular growth in eighteen years. It was based almost entirely on the natural increase of population, from the excess of births over deaths, alongside a continuing (but slight) net migration away from inner London. And it indicated that the 7 million mark was likely to be London's 'natural' population for the opening decades of the twenty-first century. That was nearly one in five fewer people than in 1939. Even so, the long decline from 1940 to 1983 seemed to be over.[63]

Despite these substantial gains from the new London emerging in its post-industrial phase, the 1980s legacy of partial disintegration remained all too tangible and potent throughout the 1990s. It not unreasonably inspired doomladen commentaries, notably Patrick Wright's *A Journey Through Ruins: The Last Days of London* (1991); Andy Thornley's *The Crisis of London* (1992) – 'London is in a mess . . . London is failing'; and Iain Sinclair's *Lights Out for the Territory: 9 Excursions in the Secret History of London* (1997).[64]

Many factors seemed to justify pessimism. Traffic, perhaps the most enduring of the problems that London had inherited at the start of the century, had worsened at the end. The road plans of the 1960s, once abandoned, had been replaced by no plans at all. Yet the number of cars licensed in London had risen from over 1.5 million in 1967 to over 2.7 million in 1996.[65] Traffic movements slowly increased, especially in outer London, and traffic speeds fell by about four m.p.h. from the mid-1970s. In the meantime, the road infrastructure aged, requiring disruptive bridge and road closures. In December 1996 an eight-hour traffic gridlock affected most of east London north and south of the river when a lorry was stuck in the Blackwall Tunnel at the moment other road works had shut down alternative routes: 'This is the jam that people have been dreading,' lamented the Automobile Association, and it was considered only a matter of time before it happened again somewhere in London.[66] By the end of the century London's chronic transportation problems were increasingly cited as a reason for business relocating from the capital.

Many signs that business had, indeed, packed its bags and left could still be seen all over London. The Docklands experience and the Broadgate development had soaked up some empty land but enormous tracts were left. The Royal Docks in Newham had been excluded from the Enterprise Zone and were largely unaffected by the efforts of the LDDC; despite a number of ideas, they remained merely an unrealized 'opportunity' at the century's end. So did the King's Cross railway lands, where a comprehensive redevelopment scheme had foundered by the early 1990s, undermined (it was said) by Civil Servant gentrifiers who had moved into nearby streets in the 1980s and who fought a secret struggle in Whitehall to keep the developers out. And similarly no miraculous solution to the empty sites strung out along the Lea Valley or clustered in Park Royal had materialized by the end of the century, although the Millennium Dome brought a reprieve for Bugsby Marshes, the old site of the massive South Metropolitan gasworks at the Greenwich peninsula. Whether that proved a sustainable development much beyond 2001 remained to be seen.

Even so, it was clear by the end of the century that London had escaped the worst of what the 1980s had seemed to promise for its future. Some sort of synthesis had been reached.

A balance had been struck between old and new London, for instance, that seemed to provide scope for dramatic new buildings while valuing as never before in the century the capital's heritage. On the one hand, over £360 million Lottery money was quickly allocated to twelve prestige projects in London, all ready for reoccupation, or nearly so, by the turn of the twenty-first century, including the Tate Modern at the redundant Bankside power station, and a revamped Royal Opera House reopening (with snags) in December 1999. On the other, London's riverside was providing inspiration unique in the capital's history to the best of the world's architects. Maybe, given the excellence of modern design and construction from the mid-1980s, the balance had tipped too far in favour of the old, although few signs of a shift away from the conservationist consensus were detectable by 1999.

A new balance, too, had been struck between the classes in London. The capital's middle classes had grown, as they had in the nation as a whole, across a gentrifying century. But the middle-class evacuation of large parts of inner London that had been such a feature of the first fifty years was more than made up for by the last fifty. The middle-class recolonization of the second half of the century had still not run out of steam by its close. What Angela Carter, in her 1991 novel *Wise Children*, set in Brixton, called 'the diaspora of the affluent' was to some extent a homogenizing influence on London life. It went some way to cover over the age-old breaches in London's class geography between north and south, east and west.[67] And the reuse of empty commercial buildings and land, and the break-up of the council estate, seemed likely to allow room for yet further expansion of middle-class London.

This class change in the capital added up to a momentous transformation in the meaning of London's districts, wilder in its fashion swings than even the turbulent period from 1900 to 1939. Some gentrified areas had lost the class mix they had thirty years before. But as long as the council estate stayed cheek to cheek with the gentrified streets (as, indeed, was the case in

Barnsbury), then some considerable diversity at the level of shopping and street life and primary school seemed assured long-term. And the solidly proletarian areas that had been such a feature of inner London up to the 1960s – Shoreditch, say, or Bethnal Green, or Walworth – by the end of the century had more of a class mix than at any time since the 1880s, if not before.

One other traditional element in London's diversity had risen triumphant from the planners' ashes: the intimate mixture of land uses that had been for so long a characteristic of inner London. Segregation into zones was always an unfeasible anti-London project. With the disappearance of most noxious or bad-neighbour factory uses with deindustrialization, there seemed to be positive advantages from mixing uses to bring life back twenty-four hours a day to central London and London's 170 or so town centres.[68] Perhaps the Oxo Building, a Victorian factory at Waterloo rehabilitated as part of the Coin Street redevelopment, could stand as the epitome of mix at the end of the century, incorporating as it did within a single shell retail outlets, an ultra-smart restaurant, craft workshops and sought-after flats.

Another, and also distinctively *fin-de-siècle*, balance had been struck between London's centre and its periphery. The suburban ring might remain the junior partner to central London, but even the junior had taken on grey hairs sixty years after its precocious early years. And considerable energy, of the traditional parish-pump kind of local patriotism, went into reversing the decline of town centres, into celebrating a suburban 'village' feel and heritage, and into seizing outer London's share of the capital's employment prospects. So the suburbs were slowly urbanizing; and inner London, with its population decline and its replacement of tower blocks and slabs by two- and three-storey houses, seemed in part increasingly suburban.

Some elements of the century's-end synthesis appeared to have more long-term effects than others. London's boundaries were largely fixed inside a south-east that continued to grow in economic significance within the nation. The valorization of London's past had a firm place in the cash nexus of tourism, rapidly becoming the world's greatest industry. The brighter, cleaner London that emerged from the horse-powered and coal-fired ages seemed relatively immune from regression; despite the end-century dangers of smog from vehicle emissions, a repeat of the 1952 disaster seemed hardly likely.

Other elements of the 1990s synthesis were more mobile. The future of London's economy, and how that might affect its mixture of classes, was a big unknown despite the tendency to gentrification showing no signs of expiring by 1999. The performance of London's experimental governance arrangements, just in place at the turn of the twenty-first century, was likely to have an unforeseen impact on investment, especially on transportation. It hardly looked possible that road-building would get back on the political agenda within a generation. But in its absence it seemed that some drastic alternative solution to London's snarl-up would have to be found and implemented.

As hundreds of thousands strolled bemused or delighted through the Millennium Dome on Bugsby Marshes in 2000, there remained the greatest uncertainty of all. How might 7 million Londoners and 60 million Britons, many of whom were past or potential citizens of London, alter their view of the capital and exercise what choice they had to stay in it, to come to it or to leave it? For if a century of ceaseless change had immeasurably transformed the scale and fabric of London since 1900, then that was nothing compared to the changes wrought by that same century on the Londoner. And whereas many of the twentieth century's physical changes to the capital were likely to prove relatively short-lived – with the commercial capital settling into a cycle of urban renewal every thirty years or so – the changes to the Londoner within the last fifty years of that century would last, as far as anyone could see, well into the twenty-first century and beyond.

PART TWO

People

3. Londoners: 1900–1947

Londoners and the Nation

There grows in the North Country a certain kind of youth of whom it may be said that he is born to be a Londoner. The metropolis, and everything that appertains to it, that comes down from it, that goes up into it, has for him an imperious fascination. Long before schooldays are over he learns to take a doleful pleasure in watching the exit of the London train from the railway station. He stands by the hot engine and envies the very stoker. Gazing curiously into the carriages, he wonders that men and women who in a few hours will be treading streets called Piccadilly and the Strand can contemplate the immediate future with so much apparent calmness; some of them even with the audacity to look bored. He finds it difficult to keep from throwing himself in the guard's van as it glides past him; and not until the last coach is a speck upon the distance does he turn away and, nodding absently to the ticket-clerk, who knows him well, go home to nurse a vague ambition and dream of Town.[1]

This yearning for London from afar, its fascination as Dream-City (the term is Ethel Mannin's),[2] its promise held out, its gauntlet thrown down, its terrible vengeance wreaked on failure were all well known to Arnold Bennett when he wrote *A Man from the North* (1898).

He was not alone, for Londoners made up something more than a fifth of the population of England and Wales for much of the first half of the twentieth century. And Londoners came from everywhere. At any one time around a third of people living in the County had been born outside it, mainly in the provinces of England and the nations of Britain. In outer London this rose to more than half. Londoners were 'an alloy of the people of Britain', it was said in 1941.[3] They would become an ever more complex amalgam of elements before the century was much older.

The place of the Londoner in the nation was far more important than even the sheer bulk of numbers at any one time would suggest. There was a limitless flow of people in and out of London whose lives the capital might touch for many years or just briefly, grist for a time to its perpetual mill. Ever since the railway age at least, migration to London seemed to affect every hearth in the country:

The subject is one of universal interest. There is hardly a household in the land that is not more or less concerned with it. There is no parish, however remote or obscure, from the Hebrides to Cornwall, from which young men do not find their way to London. There is, perhaps, none who has not a relative or friend who has made his journey to the great city and fought his battle there . . . [4]

Not only young men. In fact, from before the start of the twentieth century young women had outnumbered them as new Londoners. Their predominance grew in the 1920s and 1930s. And throughout the century, despite independence for most of it, Ireland remained as much a part of 'the nation' as ever it had been, at least in her desire to send her daughters and sons to London.

The idea of London was an irresistible force in the national consciousness. Its allure was planted in the imagination of every child brought up as British – wherever in the world that might be. Born in Dublin in 1899, the novelist Elizabeth Bowen's first 'picture' of London 'came out of books' and 'gained on me something of the obsessive hold of a daydream': 'All through my childhood, London had a fictitious existence for me', wrought from the pages of Dickens, Conan Doyle, Compton Mackenzie and others. Sam Myers, a young teacher from Lancashire, arrived at Euston in 1912, with 'my bowler hat and my dreams': 'London called me with a thousand voices of which those of Chaucer, Chatterton, Blake and Keats were the sweetest.' 'It was in Llandudno, when I was very young, that I first heard about London,' remembered Glyn Roberts, a talented journalist whose life in the capital was cut tragically short in 1939: 'Then I saw the name on covers of magazines – *London Opinion, The London Magazine* – and the idea of a London where everyone was tall, efficient, terrifying and rich took shape in my head.' '[F]or years we have had in our heads a London of our own,' according to Bradford's J. B. Priestley, 'pieced together from scraps of reading and talk, a queer jumble in which the Strand and the Monument and Shaftesbury Avenue and Limehouse and the Houses of Parliament and Kensington Gardens are thrown together in a most fantastic fashion'. And David Low, the Australian who became the best political cartoonist of his generation, reached London from Melbourne in the gloomy strike-hit November of 1919. Leaving his sister to unpack their bags at a hotel near Euston, he 'set out for my first London walk . . . What delight! What joyful promise of treading the fabulous streets, entering the enchanted places until then only known at second-hand in books and photographs! I was for evermore a Londoner. But then I had always been a Londoner.'[5]

It was a job offer on the *Star*, the most radical of London's nine or so evening newspapers of the time, that had brought Low 13,000 steamship miles across the world. And the 'paved-with-gold' image of London as a city where the rewards of talent and enterprise were beyond limit shone brightly across the century. It was a provocative challenge to what Priestley called 'pugnacious provincialism', the feeling that London was a treasure-house to be stormed and taken by main force by those with the wit and energy to do it. ' "Up in London, George, things happen",' urged Wells's Teddy Ponderevo, a reckless but lovable speculator desperate to escape the 'Cold Mutton Fat' of small-town life in Sussex. And that very same feeling inspired tens of thousands every year to try their luck in the biggest lottery that the Empire – perhaps the world – could offer.[6]

This was more than a matter of coming to London for work – even though for much of the century London had generally more work to offer than anywhere else in the country. Coming to London meant a job *and* the opportunity to transform your life-chances. It was always a new turning.

So it proved for Stephen Hobhouse, a Somerset Quaker, who put an idle existence behind him in 1904: 'I was drawn to a life of service in the London slums . . .'; he was to become a conscientious objector in the First World War, imprisoned in Wormwood Scrubs and cruelly treated. Service of a different kind was on the mind of Harry Pollitt, a boilermaker from Droylsden in Lancashire, where an old street singer's favourite song had begun:

> The greatest city in all the world is London.
> At least, that's what the wealthy people say.

Pollitt came to London in 1918, when he was twenty-eight, finding work at a ship repairer's in Blackwall (Poplar). Within a year he was a London-region trade union official, launched on his way to becoming general secretary of the Communist Party of Great Britain. John Murphy, another communist engineer, born in Manchester, journeyed to London in 1922 – not to work on the bench but to try his hand at journalism and lecturing. By 1928 he was the English correspondent of *Pravda* and had moved up in the world from Fulham to Highbury.[7]

Or London might be an escape route, say from long-term unemployment between the wars. As for Bill Rounce from Jarrow, a former shipwright who found work in the building industry, assisted by a network of Jarrow 'lads' who had already found their way into the capital. Or George Mason, an unemployed miner from South Yorkshire, who came to London for work in 1929. From inauspicious beginnings in a Salvation Army lodging house in the East End, he soon found work as a canvasser for the *Daily Herald*, settling eventually in Hammersmith. And London offered an escape, too, from 'rural idiocy' for Dolly Davey from North Yorkshire. In 1930 she answered an advertisement in her local evening paper from a Streatham dentist's wife seeking a live-in domestic servant. Just seventeen and from a narrowly religious home, she wrote and got the post. She overcame her parents' objections partly through making contact with the nearest south London branch of the YWCA:

I had to do it that way, otherwise I'd never have got away. I'd have ended up an old maid, with no future in front of me . . . It was really and truly a sense of adventure. I wanted to do something that nobody else in the town had done. I was about the first one to leave and come to London.[8]

Those, like Dolly, who stayed and made their home in London did so for many reasons. They relished the anonymity of the giant city, immune from the petty scrutiny of provincial life; found soul-mates among others at work or play who had come to London with similar objects to their own; were fascinated by the inexhaustible variety of the London streets; were intrigued by the endless possibilities of chance encounters; were enlivened by the capacity for enjoyment in dance halls or nightclubs, music halls and concert halls, cinemas and galleries; were expanded by its intellectual opportunities in college, night class and adult education group; and were fulfilled by its very life-force and energy.

But London did not suit everyone. Some, eager to explore its glittering window display, found it to be meretricious once the dazzling surface had been penetrated. They felt empty and lonely and pined for the life they had left behind. Even when they stayed in London for the sake of a career difficult to pursue elsewhere, they knew they were in a more or less intolerable exile. 'For a year or more I was also a part-time assistant in a London bookshop,' recalled George Orwell, 'a job which was interesting in itself but had the disadvantage of compelling me to live in London, which I detest.' Tom Hopkinson, a journalist brought up in the Lake District, found that even 'After six years in London [1927–33] I was quite unreconciled to living entirely among brick walls and found myself constantly thinking of the countryside, at times imagining there were mountains visible from the Fulham Road.' And Storm Jameson, the Whitby-born novelist, came to London in 1919 to work for an advertising agency:

I was dying of discontent with myself. And with London. This – these endless cold streets smelling of mud, sweat, petrol, these cafés and restaurants I could not afford to enter, these people with their flattened voices and faces, seeming to be nothing and nowhere, like shadows in water – was the London I had been praying to return to . . . Fool![9]

Newcomers to London ranged widely across the capital, but they did not settle evenly. Some parts of London were more London than others – at least in the proportions of the London-born living there. The highest densities of London-born were to be found near the centre, especially Shoreditch, Bethnal Green and Bermondsey (in both 1921 and 1931 all with over 87 per cent of their populations born in London), closely followed by Finsbury, Southwark and Poplar. In 1931 Deptford and Camberwell also had four-fifths or more born in London.[10] These districts, on any indicator based on poverty or job title, were also the most working-class boroughs of London, and it is clear that those many thousands of working men and women who flocked to London to escape industrial decline in Wales and northern England in the 1920s and 1930s tended to settle in the newer industrial areas of outer London in the west, north-east and south.

Conversely, London's most middle-class districts showed the lowest proportions of London-born and the greatest numbers of newcomers. Westminster, Hampstead and Kensington in 1931 had half their population or fewer born in London, with Paddington, Holborn and St Marylebone managing a bare majority. Despite inner London's proportion of London-born rising between 1901 and 1921 (from 66.5 per cent to 70.7 per cent), the gap between the most middle-class and the most working-class boroughs widened in this regard up to the Second World War, so that the proportion of London-born in Westminster fell from 47.2 per cent in 1911 to 42.9 per cent in 1931, while Bermondsey's rose from 84.7 per cent to 88.7 per cent.

The explanation for this wide variation lies largely in London's huge demand for female domestic servants, which remained insatiable even after the First World War. This was a demand that, because of middle-class migration out of the County, became increasingly concentrated in fewer areas, especially during the 1930s. Domestic service had long been unpopular among London girls, and London girls had long been unpopular – as too worldly and independent – among the servant-keeping classes. So young women from the country were imported in droves to burnish the silver and stoke the grates in Mayfair mansions and Bloomsbury boarding houses.

This migration of young women domestics to London helped distort its gender balance. London had traditionally shown a greater ratio of women to men than the country as a whole: 1,140 women to 1,000 men in Greater London in 1931, for example, compared to 1,088 in England and Wales. In the County of London the figure reached 1,151 and in Hampstead an extraordinary 1,547.[11]

Women or men, incessant migration constantly renewed London's lifeblood. Londoners shifted out of the County to make room for newcomers. And Greater London beyond the County filled from a tank that included

Londoners spilling out from the centre and migrants moving in from the provinces and nations of Britain and beyond.

Of the non-English nations historically part of Britain, the main reservoir of new Londoners in the first half of the twentieth century remained Ireland, as it had in the nineteenth century too. But that single continuity disguised many fluctuations over time. Residents of the County of London born in Ireland, Scotland and Wales totalled over 150,000 in 1901 but fell to 130,000 in 1911 and 1921. Immigration revived in the 1920s, depressed years especially in the mining districts of South Wales and in strife-torn Ireland, so that the figure for 1931 climbed sharply to 179,000. In Greater London as a whole the figure of Irish, Scots and Welsh approached a third of a million. The nationwide Depression of the 1930s brought in more migrants. And a wartime and post-war influx of Irish people pushed the 1951 total from the three nations in inner London alone to 234,000. There were 203,000 Irish in the metropolis in 1951. That was more by far than at any previous time in history and nearly twice as many as in the post-famine peak of the 1840s. The numbers of Irish continued to grow in the 1950s and 1960s, showing that the Irish diaspora was, for London at least, more of a twentieth-century phenomenon than it had ever been in the nineteenth century. Irish migrants were dominated by women: 62,000 against 50,000 Irishmen in inner London as late as 1951. Neither partition nor independence seem to have made a difference to the London-Irish connection: that same year around 84 per cent had migrated from the Republic rather than the North.[12]

London's Scottish-born population stayed fairly steady around the 50,000 mark in the County for the first half-century. There were probably twice as many in Greater London, at least after the First World War. The Scots showed the nearest balance of all the feeder nations of Britain between men and women migrants, although women remained slightly in the majority in all census years except 1901. But the Welsh-born population of the County fluctuated greatly, more than doubling in size between 1921 and 1931 (from 28,000 to 60,000). In 1931 in Greater London there were 115,000 Welsh-born, the largest of all the national migrations to the capital at that time, temporarily displacing the Irish as main providers of new Londoners. And there were 1,600 women for every 1,000 Welshmen resident in London.[13]

London's main provincial reservoirs are somewhat more difficult to fathom. Northerners made up a greater share of London's provincial-born population during the Depression and after: loosely defined, they represented about an eighth of English newcomers in 1901 but nearly a quarter (of a smaller number) by 1951.[14] In contrast to Wales and Ireland, men migrated from the north in almost equal numbers with women. That was untypical, too, of migration from England as a whole, where women migrants out-numbered men by 1,249 to 1,000 in 1901 and still 1,223 to 1,000 fifty years later, when live-in domestic service was virtually coming to an end.

The greatest English reservoir of new Londoners throughout the first half-century remained the south-east, including East Anglia. It accounted for about two-thirds of English migrants to the County of London. Women were predominant among them, so that, for example, 44,000 Essex-born men were resident in inner London in 1901 compared to 58,000 women. That dominance, as for migration from East Anglia itself, had declined by 1951 but was still marked.

As we shall see shortly, there were strong tendencies for foreigners to cluster in London districts that they made very much their own. But the patterns of settlement among the Irish, Scots, Welsh and English were much less segregated. Irish people were distributed across the city, although borough-wide statistics tend to disguise local concentrations in areas like Camden Town, North Kensington, Paddington, Kilburn, Wapping, the Borough, Camberwell and Peckham. But the high densities of Irish-born women in Kensington (4,716 to 1,982 Irish men in 1931), Hampstead, Westminster and St Marylebone were almost entirely accounted for by the demand for domestic servants in these areas, despite some anti-Irish prejudice among employers.[15]

There were similar concentrations of Welsh women after the 1920s and 1930s influx, although the drapers and dairymen who made up such a high proportion of the male migrants from Wales in the early years of the century were distributed pretty evenly across London. The post-First World War dislocation of the mining industry, however, seems to have brought large populations to the areas of industrial expansion in west London in particular, at least for a time: Harrow was said to be 'largely Cymric' around 1932, for example.[16]

These proved generally temporary adjustments in the early period of migrations. Diffusion throughout the metropolis was the general experience of the British coming to London. There were fewer reasons – institutional, economic or social – to keep newcomers in one place after an initial period to settle in. Diffusion revealed itself in every street outside those inner areas where the London-born squeezed out almost everyone else. And diffusion was most complete in the new suburbs of London, especially in the west and south-west, so that, in 1931, only 21 per cent of people in Hendon were Middlesex-born, just 29 per cent in Mitcham had been born in Surrey and 31 per cent of Dagenham residents originated from Essex (mainly West Ham and other parts of London-in-Essex). Of around 700,000 who moved into outer London in the 1920s, it was estimated that 300,000 were Londoners moving out from the County and 400,000 provincials and others moving in.[17]

Often these newcomers brought with them not only their accents and attitudes to add spice and variety to London life, but their institutions too. Indeed, they created new ones to help maintain their national or regional identities in the great melting pot of London, and to construct a safe bridgehead from which they might attempt their first assault on the capital. In general, these tended to be built by and for middle-class men, despite the dominance of women among the migrants. Domestic service probably played a significant part in isolating women who might have shared a common background but had no opportunity to take advantage of the connection once in London. It is also likely that these regional and national institutions were more robust in the early years of the century than later, probably due to the dislocation of the First World War and the post-war flight of the middle classes from inner London.

Before 1914 the Scots, widely represented in London's professions, in Fleet Street and in the Metropolitan Police, had a flourishing and old-established network of institutions in London, with 'many county associations . . . the Highland Society, the Caledonian Society, the Gaelic Society, and various other organizations'. There was said to have been a London-Scottish public dinner on St Andrew's Night since 1665. There was an orphanage for London Scots in the Caledonian Road, established in 1815, a Caledonian Club in St James's, a Scottish Golf Club at Wimbledon, a London Scottish rugby club and 'Burns' nichts' at the Royal Albert Hall. A number of these institutions survived intact throughout a century where the Scottish contribution to London's legal, medical, literary and political life remained no less vigorous at the end than at the beginning.[18]

The Irish, too, were prominent in the law, police force, journalism and civil service, as well as providing a large element of the artisan and casual trades in building, road transport and the docks. They brought with them the added excitement of a culture divided by religion and politics. Irish nationalism continued throughout the century to view London as its very own battleground. Waging the struggle by peaceful means before the First World War, the Gaelic League ran fifteen Irish schools in London and an annual music festival at Queen's Hall. There was an Irish Literary Society, an Irish Peasantry Association to promote education among poor Irish children in London, an Irish Club in Holborn and an annual Irish concert on St Patrick's Night in St James's Hall. The Gaelic Athletic Association federated eight or nine clubs, offering hurling, football and athletics on the Hackney Marshes and at Alexandra Palace. And the Roman Catholic Church impacted on all classes of Irish people in London in a way that no

Scottish church attempted: 'The religious service in honour of St Patrick at the Roman Catholic Church, Dockhead [Bermondsey], is unique, the hymns, sermons, and responses being respectively in Irish and Latin. It attracts a crowded congregation.'[19] Catholic church processions, sustained especially by Irish congregations, were frequent London spectacles up to the Second World War and probably beyond. And another feature of the London Irish, the Irish-run and patronized pub, was prevalent in many parts of London throughout the century, unmatched by any other immigrant group from home or abroad.

The main institutions of the London Welsh were choirs, rugby clubs, churches and chapels. Religion secured some commonality of interest across classes among migrants from the principality. The Edwardian 'Revival' of evangelical Methodism built a 'remarkable' number of Welsh chapels and churches in London – thirty-four in the County in 1913 and possibly as many again in the suburbs – all using the Welsh language and most relying on itinerant 'hellfire' preachers from home to supplement local ministers. The 'Calvinistic Methodists' were said to 'act in close co-operation in tracing and visiting Welsh people settling in London'. The strong 'clannishness' of the London Welsh, remarked upon in the 1930s, suggested that these connections had not broken down despite heavy migration and a more secular environment.[20]

English provincial migrants brought with them much less in the way of cultural institutions than those from the nations of the 'Celtic fringe'. What few efforts there were to maintain provincial identities in a city that 'blunts, by its vastness, their peculiarities',[21] seem to have been made by middle-class men and were based almost entirely on junketing. 'Of late years,' it was said in 1900, 'nearly every county has its London dinner, whereat all the provincials settled in town enjoy a banquet and eloquence of a more or less excellent order. We have the festival of the Devonians in London, and the East Anglians in London, and many others.' A generation and more later, in the mid-1930s, similar efforts were noted among Cornishmen and men from Wiltshire, Nottinghamshire, Cumberland and more: 'There is something very English at those 30 dinners where the folk of 30 counties forget the toils and the immense anonymity of London, and are once more back home among their own people.' And at home in London a regional heritage was kept alive in the kitchen at least: 'I have eaten the apple pasty of Yorkshire in a London home, and the Lancashire hot-pot, and cream sent from Devonshire, and the true, the perfect pork pie . . . of Nottingham. I have eaten the asparagus of Worcester, and heard it called grass. And in the homes of Scotsmen I have heard porridge talked about in the plural.'[22] All this, of course, was partaken – metaphorically rather than literally – alongside the more spicy cockney fare of jellied eels, pie and mash and green liquor, cockles and whelks and whitebait, with salad called green-meat and water-cress talked about in the plural as creases. For Londoners – even if not in that pure form that could lay claim to the title of cockney – were still mainly people who had been born in the capital. Seven out of ten of the County population were County-born in 1921. Such were the dynamics of London's shifting population, though, that the London-born were likely to have at least one parent who had migrated to the metropolis from somewhere else in Britain. Even in the 1930s it was apparently almost impossible to find London schoolchildren whose parents and all grandparents had been born there.[23]

The great population movements constantly operating on the metropolis, both in and out, led to a distorted pattern of family make-up when compared to the nation as a whole. It showed a marked 'surplus' of people between twenty and thirty-nine, especially single women, when compared to the countrywide figures. And the average household was smaller in London – 3.46 persons in the County against 3.72 in England and Wales in 1931, including servants living in. This was due mainly to a large surplus of one-person, and a smaller surplus of two-person, households in London: only 6.7 per cent of households in England and Wales in 1931 were made up of persons living alone; but in Greater London the figure was 9.8 per cent and in the County 13 per cent. By 1951, one in five households in inner London was a single person, compared to one in ten in England and Wales.

There were other differences in this family make-up between the two Londons, old and new. Inner London had a deficit of children under fifteen compared to outer London, because young families tended to move out to the suburbs and beyond if they could afford more house-room and a greener environment. But this generally worked only for the middle classes and those artisans rehoused by the LCC: the deficit of children, most marked in Hampstead and Westminster, turned to a surplus in Shoreditch or Southwark when compared to the nation as a whole.[24]

But whether in inner London or the suburbs, among newcomers or London-born, everyone had to construct what the novelist William Plomer called 'a London of one's own'.[25] Everyone had to come to terms with what it meant for them to be 'a Londoner'. H. G. Wells struggled to put into words the ineffable vastness and mystery and wonder of it all:

I could fill a book, I think, with a more or less imaginary account of how I came to apprehend London, how first in one aspect and then another it grew in my mind. Each day my accumulating impressions were added to and qualified and brought into relationship with new ones, they fused inseparably with others that were purely personal and accidental. I find myself with a certain comprehensive perception of

London, complex indeed, incurably indistinct in places and yet in some way a whole that began with my first visit and is still being mellowed and enriched.

London![26]

Landmarks with a world-sounding resonance struck chords for everyone. Just to move to London was to claim a place in the limelight and quicken the heartbeat. 'Do you go to the night clubs?' the girls of Thornaby-on-Tees asked Dolly Davey, a mere Streatham slavey in the early 1930s. They might have had 'the wrong conception of it', but it was a conception that had seduced Dolly herself to London Town.[27]

This stardust, though, shone less brightly for the London-born. 'Up West' held its inimitable glamour throughout the century. But the tourist wonders and rich trappings of London, including even the West End, were a closed book for many home-grown Londoners, at least until the 1950s. Clarence Rook, from South Kensington, met a girl from Tooting 'on a Russian steamer' around 1907: 'She had been to Samara, but she had never been to the Earl's Court Exhibition . . . And then I had to admit that I had never examined the exhibition of Madame Tussaud, never ascended the Monument . . . We stood far apart as Londoners who knew not London.' 'I took,' remembered Harry Pollitt of his early London years around 1920, 'every possible opportunity to find my way around London and explore all the places I had read about and longed to see as a kid. Talking with my mates in the shipyard made me realize how little Londoners know about their city.' H. V. Morton noted, in 1940, 'The ignorance of, and indifference to, London, which are characteristic traits of the Londoner . . .' Even in the 1950s East End, after the immense dislocations of war, the sociologists Michael Young and Peter Willmott found that 'for a few people places beyond Bethnal Green are another world'.[28] And maybe a pair of 'Home Birds' reported in George Lansbury's *Daily Herald* (17 September 1923) might stand for the archetypal parochial Londoner: 'Mr and Mrs Hickey of Bow, East London, have just completed 60 years of married life. Neither has ever spent a night out of the East End. Mr Hickey is 82. Mrs Hickey, who is 81, has never seen Westminster Abbey, Hyde Park, or the Tower of London.'

Localism was a virus that also infected newcomers to London. In becoming Londoners they might never lose the thrill of watching St Paul's emerge from Ludgate Hill, or viewing the river from Waterloo Bridge, or experiencing that very personal tingle that came from walking down a street that seemed peculiarly to represent their 'London': Islington High Street, say, or the King's Road, Chelsea, or Borough High Street near the George Inn. Or, most evocative perhaps of all, 'their' London station: Euston for the

Brummies, Waterloo for the Hampshire Hogs, King's Cross for the Yorkies. All that, after only a few months, became situated in a context of neighbourhood that did indeed define a London of one's own. It was only at particular moments that citizens of Rotherhithe or Clerkenwell or Hornsey or Crystal Palace might see themselves as Londoners: on great state occasions in the imperial city, like the 1902 Coronation and the 1935 Silver Jubilee; on meeting provincial newcomers and tourists; on seeing archetypal cockneys portrayed on the cinema screen or music-hall stage; on travelling out of London and returning to it, especially by train; in the aftermath of a disaster like the Thames flood of 1928, which inundated only a small part of London, mainly Bermondsey and Pimlico, but which seemed to strike the whole city with a hammer-blow, personally felt.

There was no greater hammer-blow in the twentieth century, of course, than the Blitz. It involved, uniquely, all London's localities in a single shared experience. And it recast 'the Londoner' in the national imagination. Despite those most dedicated lovers of London who celebrated it in print in the first forty years of the century – E. V. Lucas, Thomas Burke, William Margrie, William Kent – all being 'sons of London', the label of 'Londoner' was more brickbat than boast. Glyn Roberts and Douglas Goldring had noted how, in the early 1930s, 'The Londoner . . . is the only Englishman who is not proud of his birthplace. To be labelled a Londoner is regarded, particularly by Londoners, as rather a slur.' This feeling gave an added push to the desire of many to leave the city's taint for the suburbs if they could. Cockney was called 'a pariah' among dialects in 1938. Londoners were labelled 'physical undesirables in a civilized country' in 1937: 'their teeth are a family of Borgias, their gums smell like lazar-houses . . . Strip the clothes from a trainload of Londoners and no huckster of bodies would bid for more than ten per cent of them.'[29]

But from 7 September 1940, literally overnight, the image of the Londoner was remade in the eyes of the English-speaking world. Just as the war healed many of the divisions between old London and the suburbs, so it bridged the gulf between London and the nation that had grown so wide in the 1920s and 1930s. Pluck and a ready wit, balancing elements in the negative image of the Londoner since Sam Weller if not before, became building blocks on which a new character could be readily erected. The staunch and steadfast citizens of London, undaunted in the face of a bombardment never before endured by a civilian population, revalorized 'the Londoner' into a title of honour. 'London can take it', 'London's spirit is unbroken', 'London will stand fast', 'Every district in London, every street, contains its heroes' and 'when London beat him, Hitler was doomed' were all plaudits written within the first two weeks of the Blitz beginning.[30] 'Londoner' became a badge of courage which people wished to wear, 'like the eminent Chinese who drank a pledge to "Us Londoners", or the American correspondent . . . who said to me, with mock wistfulness, after he had been dug out of a wrecked shelter: "Can I call myself a 'Londoner' now; I've been initiated?" '[31] This 'London pride' cast an afterglow on the post-war years: 'Who, indeed, could not feel proud of London and Londoners who lived and worked in the Metropolis through the years 1939 to 1945?' wrote Harold Bellman in his autobiography *Cornish Cockney*.[32]

There was one other change wrought on the Londoner during these tempestuous wartime years. The war brought more foreigners than ever before to London. In ways totally unrecognized at the time, it was to herald an era when the cosmopolitan character of the Londoner would become a dominant factor in the life and fortunes of the metropolis.

Londoners and the World

Throughout its history London had always been one of the world's most cosmopolitan cities. From the first century to the fifteenth this reflected its position as one of the premier ports of northern Europe. Its mix of peoples was immeasurably enhanced from the sixteenth to the nineteenth centuries as the great capital of the furthest-flung empire that civilization had ever seen. The world's circulatory system had London as its heart. And the seamen and adventurers of every trading nation on the globe knew London as their main port of call, with civilization's richest and most populous metropolitan hinterland adjoining it.

The number of foreigners in inner London, and their share of its population, grew significantly from the 1880s, mainly as a result of Jewish immigration from Eastern Europe. This trend continued in the first decade of the twentieth century so that, by 1911, there were 176,000 foreign-born Londoners, nearly 4 per cent of the County's population.[33] London was then probably more cosmopolitan than at any time since the aftermath of the Norman invasion.

Or than it was to be in the 1920s and 1930s. Three factors in particular combined to make London more British between the wars than before 1914. From 1905, the first restrictions on immigration had been put in place, largely as a result of anti-alien (mostly anti-Semitic) agitation. The new law's emphasis on excluding a small number of undesirable or pauper foreigners deterred a far greater number, who could migrate from Europe to America without restriction. Then, from 1914, the First World War slashed London's big German population, which never recovered its pre-war vitality despite an influx of refugees from Nazi rule from 1933 on. It also tightened restrictions on immigration so that, by the mid-1920s, 'London has half closed her door to the foreigner', even French chefs and 'girl' shop assistants, and German and Swiss waiters, all characteristic elements in cosmopolitan London before the war. Finally, the very strong tendencies to assimilation among a Jewish minority demonstrably 'foreign' before 1914 but increasingly (if still decipherably) integrated from the 1920s diluted London's cultural mix. By 1931 the foreign-born population of the County had fallen by more than a quarter to 127,000, less than 3 per cent of the total. Even so, the diversity of Londoners was extraordinary. And it was to be complicated beyond all past compare by the Second World War and the world that emerged from it.[34]

Not all London, by any means, was cosmopolitan. South London, it was said in 1931, 'is almost exclusively English ... more genuinely and thoroughly English than any other part of London'.[35] Even north of the river London was not uniformly cosmopolitan and we have already noted those districts where the density of the London-born allowed little room for newcomers, especially foreigners. In the history of the Londoner from abroad in the first half of the century two areas in particular stand out: Soho and the East End.

Soho was London's 'cosmopolis'. The few acres between Leicester Square and Oxford Street had attracted foreign residents almost as soon as the fields were built on in the seventeenth century. Soho's Greek refugees from the extension of Ottoman rule around 1670 were quickly followed by French Protestant Huguenots fleeing religious persecution in the 1680s. The Huguenots took over the Greeks' chapel, sold to mitigate bankruptcy in 1682, and a French community clustered nearby for over 250 years thereafter. Each succeeding century had brought its own crisis and washed up a skeleton army of French refugees in its wake: the Revolutionary Terror of the 1790s – Dickens had taken Dr Manette to Soho on his release from the Bastille some years earlier – and the bloody revenge on the Communards in 1871 were prominent among them. Many Belgians followed this well-worn path after the German invasion in 1914.

Although Soho was still London's 'French quarter' in 1900, the French were not the only component in its kaleidoscopic character. Germans and Italians had lived there in some numbers since the 1850s, and the 1890s brought Polish and Russian Jews from the East End. In the early 1900s it was the extraordinary diversity of Soho that captured the imagination of London, and the globe. 'No part of the world presents in such a small area so many singular and interesting pictures of cosmopolitan life as Soho,' wrote Count Armfelt in 1903: he listed among its residents Greeks, Jews,

Frenchmen, Levantines (Arabs), Swiss, Italians, 'Kabiles' (Berbers), Africans, Turks, Syrians, Persians, Montenegrins, Russians, Poles and Germans; and he might reasonably have added Dutch, Belgians, Algerians, Austrians and Americans to their number. To Alec Waugh in the 1920s, 'Soho is the city's foreign quarter, and there is a quality peculiarly un-English in the life that seethes and shudders about this dozen acres or so of streets.' And Thomas Burke summed up the meaning of Soho at the beginning of the First World War: 'Soho – magic syllables! For when the respectable Londoner wants to feel devilish he goes to Soho, where every street is a song. He walks through Old Compton Street, and, instinctively, he swaggers; he is abroad; he is a dog.'[36]

In the 1920s and 1930s Soho became more Italian than French. But the French community centred on Soho remained of considerable importance to London up to the 1940s. There were some 16,000 French people in London County in 1911, 54 per cent of them women, and probably 25,000 in the whole of Greater London. Although the largest concentration was to be found in Westminster, there were substantial numbers in the middle-class areas of Kensington, St Marylebone, St Pancras and Lambeth. Further out there was a small colony of City Frenchmen in Croydon. Wherever they lodged, the French formed a London community that generally defied assimilation. Even though born in London, the children of French couples generally 'returned' to France and all male children had to be registered in Paris for military service. French culture was preserved in London newspapers like *La Gazette*, in Soho and West End café society, in Soho's French restaurants that had provided such temptation to English gourmets since the 1870s, and in a variety of charitable and religious institutions dating from the nineteenth century or before: like the French Hospital and Dispensary in Shaftesbury Avenue (1867), the French schools in Lisle Street (1865) and four churches, the largest being the Catholic l'Eglise de Notre-Dame de France, just off Leicester Square (1868). Old Compton Street, even in the 1930s, was said to be 'as French as the rue St Honoré', and French butchers, grocers, bakers and greengrocers abounded, including a shop that sold just snails and frogs: 'In the window [around 1905] is a two-storied doll's house constructed entirely of snails' shells; live snails cling to the window-panes . . .' The York Minster, in Dean Street, was famously known for years as 'the French Pub' and was eventually renamed the French House. And Soames Forsyte met his second wife, Annette, in her mother's '*Restaurant Bretagne*' in 'Malta Street', Soho, with its 'little round green tables with little pots of fresh flowers on them and Brittany-work plates' so alluring (like Annette) to the City man's wandering eye. The number of French waiters and waitresses, chefs, shop assistants and prostitutes declined in

London after the First World War. Even so, in 1931 there were still 10,500 London French in the County and 16,000 in Greater London.[37]

A much more dramatic decline was experienced by the London Germans. Up to the 1890s they had made up the largest foreign community in the capital. Then they were rapidly outnumbered by the Jewish influx from Eastern Europe. Nevertheless, the German community continued to grow and there were over 31,000 in the County in 1911, with perhaps another 10,000 in outer London.

Despite the Germans' extensive cultural networks, theirs was a more integrationist migration than the French. In particular, there was considerable intermarriage between German men and English women, hardly surprising when nearly two-thirds of the migrants were men. Their main areas of settlement were north of Soho, in west London and in the Leman Street area of Whitechapel, in the east.

The area north of Soho, called Fitzrovia from the 1940s after Fitzroy Square and Street, had long been a German colony. Charlotte Street, its main commercial artery, was nicknamed 'Charlottenstrasse' and retained the ghost of a German connection through Schmidt's restaurant until the 1970s. The high point of German London was in the period just before the war that would destroy it. Then, besides its inner London colonies in east and west, there were German settlements in bourgeois Forest Hill and Sydenham for stockbrokers and other City men; a community of skilled glassblowers in Silvertown (West Ham); and other clusters in Kentish Town, Camberwell, Highbury and Brompton. There were a dozen German churches in London, all but one Protestant, and there were enough German workers in the streets north of Oxford Street and around Regent's Park for the Salvation Army German Corps to hold 'open-air services in the German tongue'. There were a dozen or so *Vereins*, clubs based on a common trade or interest – the German Gymnastic Society, the German Industrial and Theatre Club, a *Verein* of German cyclists and so on – each with their own premises and administration. There was a forward-looking German Hospital at Dalston that survived the First World War but not the Second, at least as a hospital run by and for Germans. There were hostels, each with library and reading room, employment agencies, benefit societies, *Lieder-Tafels* ('social gatherings for song'), restaurants, Hans Ratschüler's German-language bookshop, two newspapers (the *Londoner Zeitung*, and *Die Finanz-chronicle* for City men) and a German Military Union which met in Wardour Street, Soho. To the east, in Leman Street and the turnings off it before the First World War, there were 'numberless German names over the doors of the shops and the brass plates of the German business houses. There are bakers and confectioners, boot makers, butchers, drapers, fruiterers, grocers, hosiers, publicans, tailors, tobacco manufacturers and cigar makers, and wine, beer, and spirit merchants' and restaurants and Christmas card makers and more.[38]

The First World War devastated this community, one of the most extensive and deeply rooted in London's history. From August 1914, all Germans were registered as 'alien enemies'. Some German shops were attacked, looted and wrecked within a week of the declaration of war. There were serious anti-German riots after the sinking of the *Lusitania* (May 1915) and after the bombing raids of 1917. The *Vereins* and newspapers were closed down and some German-owned businesses trading with Germany confiscated. The ubiquitous – but notoriously unmusical – German bands disappeared overnight from the London streets, where they had for sixty years been a popular entertainment. Thousands of London Germans were interned from October 1914 as potential spies or possible recruits for the German army – at first in Olympia, later in the great hall of Alexandra Palace, in Stratford Camp on the Hackney Marshes, and in hulks off Southend. Some were deported to internment in Holland. The treatment meted out by a few brutal commandants provoked deep resentment.[39]

By 1921 the German community in London had shrunk by over two-thirds to 9,000 in the County. Of these, just 4,700 were of 'alien nationality', the rest British by birth or naturalized. In Stepney and Westminster, where 4,500 Germans had lived before the war, fewer than a thousand were left by 1921. Some post-war recovery was noted among German financiers in the City during the 1920s; and German restaurants and *delikatessens* were back in Fitzroy Square and Charlotte Street by 1926. Then, with the rise of the Nazis, a trickle of left-wing Germans and Jews migrated to London, turning into a rush after 1938, when immigration restrictions were eased for a few precious months. Among them were Ernö Goldfinger and Berthold Lubetkin, whose impact on London we have already encountered. But the German colonies of inter-war London, in Belsize Park and Swiss Cottage, could never re-create the cultural vibrance of the Edwardian community.[40]

In contrast to the London Germans, the Italians were Britain's allies in the First World War and London's Italian communities survived it unscathed. Again, census numbers peaked in 1911, at 12,000 in the County, but these fell by only a couple of hundred by 1921. London's 'Little Italy' was the Warner Street and Eyre Street Hill area of Clerkenwell in Finsbury and (mainly) Holborn. Around 2,500 Italians lived there in distinctive style before the First World War and for some years after, cultivating their own industries (organ-building, player-piano roll-making, laying mosaics, making ice cream, monopolizing the London trade in goldfish) and catering for their own needs with cafés, delicatessens, restaurants, clubs, a theatre and dance hall. The brilliantly colourful procession every July from the Italian church of St Peter's, Saffron Hill, was 'one of the sights of London's summer' between the wars. The community sustained two newspapers (*Londra-Roma* and *Gazetta Italiana di Londra*) and founded in 1884 a hospital in Queen Square, Holborn, which served London for the next 105 years.

This main Italian area had been settled since at least the 1850s but had moved northwards as residential accommodation close to the City was demolished to make way for commerce. Saffron Hill, the old centre, had been turned over almost entirely to warehousing by 1900 and we have already glimpsed the same process beginning around Warner Street a few years later. The upshot was a drift westwards – some to Notting Dale (North Kensington), but most to Soho, where Italians increased in numbers before the First World War but more noticeably after it. In doing so they brought a new culinary experience to the Londoner. The Italian restaurant 'is such a peculiarly British institution', remarked Joseph Conrad in 1907, and it was Soho he had in mind for its location. Radclyffe Hall set her fine novel *Adam's Breed* (1924) among the Soho Italians before and during the First World War. By 1934 Soho was 'essentially the Italian quarter of London'. 'The Italians learnt their profession of chefs and waiters from the French and the Swiss,' wrote one rueful French writer on London in the early 1930s; 'now they are the masters of Soho.' He could not resist pointing out, 'Their very active Fascism has its headquarters in Greek Street', and it is true that from the early 1920s most of the cultural life of the London Italians was permeated by the trappings – if not the ideology – of fascism. There was to be some anti-Italian rioting in Soho when Italy entered the war in the summer of 1940.[41]

In the early 1930s trouble also broke out between Soho's Italian street sellers and Cypriots, who had just begun to move into the area in their first wave of migration to London from that beautiful but troubled island. And immediately before the Second World War the Soho cosmopolis seems to have been just as densely populated by newcomers as it had in Armfelt's day, despite London having become less cosmopolitan in the same period. French and Italian 'café bars' found themselves next to Cypriot cafés; there was an Armenian café in Great Windmill Street, a café for black Londoners in Great White Lion Street, the proprietor of which unsuccessfully sued *John Bull* for a libel on his clientèle in 1927; and in 1937 Thomas Burke listed, among the numerous French and Italian establishments, Spanish, Chinese, Indian, Hungarian, Greek and Jewish restaurants in Soho.[42]

A Jewish quarter had rooted itself in Soho by 1900, aptly enough around Poland Street, where there was a Poor Jews' Temporary Shelter for a time. Chaim Lewis, born nearby in 1911, was one of a family of seven among the 2,000 or so foreign Jews of Soho before the First World War. His father, a grocer, had settled there with his wife in 1902. They had come from two different Russias – 'She was big town to my father's village hovel' – and his father 'remained [a] backwoodsman for all the years he spent in the world's greatest metropolis'. His shop survived until 1959 with no accounts, with communication in Yiddish or badly broken English, with credit contentiously noted in 'the grubbiest ledger I have ever set my eyes on'; and in defiance of the laws of hygiene or marketing, its shop window sported a 'fly-paper cemetery . . . as bait for prospective customers'.

Father was *froom*, strictly orthodox and fiercely disputatious in matters of observance. He rose at six each morning, drank a glass of Russian tea and trudged with Chaim to whichever of the five or so rival local synagogues or *shuls* he 'was still on praying terms' with. The preparations for *Shabbas*, the Friday night to Saturday night Sabbath, absorbed the household in frantic cooking and cleaning and bemused those *goy* neighbours who would be obliquely enlisted into stoking the fire or turning off the lights before bedtime on Friday. His *Shabbas* suit, 'dandy in the wild days of his village youth' in the 1880s, was paraded in Regent Street on fine Saturdays forty years later, to the squirming embarrassment of his London-born children.

Mother was less resistant – culturally and spiritually – to anglicization. She was 'ambitious for her children' and the door to success was more school than *shul*. She shared in her children's experience not through education but through the cinema, where she was taken weekly by her daughters without the knowledge of her husband; she 'gave herself over to the screen completely'. At home, 'Nothing pleased her more than to feed us as though the act of feeding answered every maternal instinct in her.' Chaim recalled the '*lokschen* swimming in the fat of our chicken soup' and home-made *gefüllte fisch*. And he lamented that, by the 1950s, a taste for these dishes had become the 'sole test and witness' to a 'tenuous Jewish allegiance . . . otherwise indifferent to all religious observance'.

Yet Chaim was himself an unwitting agent in the dissolution of the East European Jewish inheritance within two or three generations of its arrival on London clay. A bright boy, he immersed himself in competing educational systems – the public elementary school and the unofficial *cheder* or Hebrew school of his father's choosing. He did well at both. But matriculation and university was the path he had selected by the late 1920s. Or perhaps it was selected for him by a London which seemed ideally adapted to mould the Jewish immigrant to its own image. 'I can phase my intellectual growth in terms of Soho's topography' and nearby – the second-hand bookshops of Charing Cross Road, the South Audley Street public library, the prostitutes, street fights and ceaseless stimulation all around him: 'Only the multilateral life of a city's centre can rise to the occasion of an adolescence.'[43]

Four miles to the east, in a similar world writ large, thousands of adolescents were working their way into English society and making themselves
Londoners in the process. The 100,000 or more 'alien Jews' of the East End
'ghetto' made up the biggest immigrant community since the Irish influx of
the 1840s. For most of the pre-1914 period their strangeness to the Londoners
around them was largely undiluted by assimilation. A foreign-born element
was still entering London, although much deterred by the Aliens Act 1905,
up to the First World War. But by the early 1930s, when there were
estimated to be 234,000 Jews in Greater London, the foreign complexion of
East End Jewry was greatly diminished and the 'ghetto' itself was in an
advanced state of dissolution. Despite a gender balance which seemed able
to sustain the community without the need for marriage outside it, and
despite a uniquely strong cultural, spiritual and economic inheritance that
had survived centuries of oppression and change, London Jewry had become
noticeably more London than Jewish within just twenty years of the First
World War.[44]

There can be no doubting the strength of the inheritance that the East
European Jews brought with them to London. The *shuls* and *chederim* of
Soho were multiplied a hundredfold in Whitechapel and Stepney, frequently
based on gatherings of *landsleit*, men originally from the same town or
country district. The *shuls* ranged in size from the Great Synagogue in Brick
Lane (the Machzikei HaDath) to back-room *stiebels* in every street in the
Jewish East End. Shops of every kind and services like ritual steam baths,
wig makers, Hebrew booksellers, religious artefact makers, savings banks,
friendly societies, ritual slaughterhouses and a Yiddish theatre and library
catered for every need. Yiddish newspapers and journals, short-lived and
long, dozens of them over the years, reflected every shade of religious and
political opinion in a community where controversy was life. Clubs for
the like-minded provided for dialogue beyond the newspaper columns.
Discussion overflowed into coffee houses, Jewish-run pubs and back kitchens of tenement flats and mean slum houses. Jewish trade unions represented
clothing, bakery, boot and shoe, cigar and cigarette workers, often in
competition with one another, folding and re-emerging under a new banner.
There has never been an immigrant community in London to match the
extraordinary institutional inventiveness of the East European Jews.[45]

The self-contained society which the foreign Jews made for themselves
in the East End was no homogeneous 'community'. It was a microcosm of
London itself, with all its divisions of class and background and topography
and world-view reconstructed on unique lines. The *landsleit* brought with
them cultural differences and prejudices that separated to some degree
Pollacks (Poles) from *Litvaks* (Lithuanians), Galicians from '*Mummaligge* Mer-

chants' (Romanians), and the *Choots* (non-observant Dutch Jews already settled in the East End before the East European migrations) from almost everyone else. Religion divided as well as united, fundamentalists despising the compromisers of heterodoxy, and atheists despising believers: in 1904 a 'full-scale riot' broke out around the Machzikei HaDath at Yom Kippur when socialist and anarchist Jews taunted the fasting worshippers with *troife*, non-kosher food including bacon. And the economic turmoil of the East End's sweated industries and backyard enterprises, constantly making masters one day and breaking them the next, fractured class solidarity by seeming to offer so many ways out of poverty and dependence on an employer.

The Jewish East End's internal divisions were energetically widened by an aristocratic Anglo-Jewry that had painfully made its own way into English society since the eighteenth century. It saw the influx of poor Jews from Eastern Europe as an unwelcome and destabilizing burden, fearing, not without reason, an anti-Semitic reaction that would not stop at Aldgate Pump, where the East End joined the City. But whatever the motive, this was a burden that rich Jews shouldered none the less. In doing so, their explicit objective was to anglicize the foreign Jews, remaking them as Londoners in their own image. To assist in the process they extended existing institutions – like the Jews' Free School (1817) and the Jewish Board of Guardians (1859) – and created others, like the Jewish Working Men's Club, the Jewish Lads' Brigade, clubs and settlements on the lines of Christian Toynbee Hall, and a Four Per Cent Industrial Dwellings Company to build tenement flats for Jewish workers.

From the beginning, dispersal had been perhaps the main objective. Making the foreign Jews less conspicuous by sifting them out across the great city seemed one antidote to the growth of anti-Semitism. Dispersal, though alien to many, struck a chord within the fissiparous community of the Jewish East End, where worldly success was equated with leaving the 'ghetto' and all it seemed to stand for. This was a process that did not affect the mass of East End Jews until the suburbanizing moment of the late 1920s and 1930s offered more chances to move out (and so up) than ever before. Even so, dispersal was a distinctive feature from the turn of the century. In 1902 Charles Booth noted how 'Dalston and Canonbury are said to be among the first steps upwards of the Whitechapel Jew, and Highbury New Park is called the New Jerusalem'.[46] A number of staging points on the road to Hampstead, where 'a large colony' of rich Jewish families was established by 1910, were already visible: Dalston, Stoke Newington, Stamford Hill, with a poorer community at High Cross, Tottenham. These were joined after 1919 by Golders Green, Brondesbury, Wembley, Finchley and Harrow – or the 'north-west passage', as it was wryly known. And there was a distinctive suburban movement eastwards from around the same time or slightly later to Chingford, Harold Hill, Hainault and Ilford.

Foreign Jewish immigration to London revived in the wake of Nazism. Most settled in or near the newer north-western areas, away from 'the ghetto'. Although the Jewish East End retained its distinctive flavour until the early 1950s, by the 1930s the main focus of London Jewry had shifted more to the west. Jewish Londoners became prominent less in the pre-1914 domain of tailoring and boot-making than in the professions (notably medicine and the law), in academic life, in the arts and in the entertainments industry, especially popular and classical music and the cinema. Wardour Street, Soho, the centre of Britain's inter-war film industry, was called a 'glossy Ghetto' by 1933.[47] As the influence of talented individuals expanded and held its own in the wider society, the 'small planet' of 'Jewish' trade unions or politics was abandoned for the bigger stage, giving another turn to the screw of assimilation. There may have been a sneer behind the 'glossy Ghetto' tag, but it recognized the unmistakably energizing influence of the Jewish immigrant community and its descendants on London life – then and, indeed, throughout the century. No other immigrant group could claim such a share in London's cultural development until migration from the Caribbean began to establish itself, fifty years or so after the main Jewish influx had ceased.

The East End, in which the great bulk of the foreign Jews had settled by 1914, had long been a reception area for migrants to London from around the world. Mostly they were transient groups of seamen lodging briefly in the great port in the leeway between one berth and another. Over generations, institutions had become established to cater for such passing trade – lodging houses, coffee shops and eating houses at first; then a church or mission, and maybe a library, usually funded by charitable subvention in the home nation. So, for the first thirty or so years of the century, there was a Scandinavian flavour to Shadwell, east of the London Docks, and to Rotherhithe, across the river near the Surreys, with Norwegian and Swedish churches, general shops, lodging houses and curio dealers; and there was a Danish church in Poplar and a Finnish in Ratcliff.

Lodging houses, cafés and Christian missions also marked the East End's age-old connection with seamen from the Indian subcontinent and from Africa. The Strangers' Home in Stepney routinely assisted destitute sailors from India, Ceylon, Japan, Mauritius, 'Africa' and elsewhere before the First World War. A small colony of black seamen, mainly West Indian, had settled in Canning Town (West Ham) around 1900. Cable Street, Stepney, had many cafés run by 'lascars' (Indian seamen) or West Africans who had settled ashore to rent out board and lodgings to fellow countrymen on their odyssey through the world's metropolis. A few seamen from Sylhet (Assam, then in north-east India) set up lodging houses in Spitalfields in the 1920s and Whitechapel in the 1930s.[48]

Once having decided to stay in London, however, there were no barriers to settlement spilling out of the East End and numbers of black and Asian Londoners were to be found in Fitzrovia and Tottenham Court Road, Camden Town, Bloomsbury (where many colonial students boarded and some settled), Brixton and elsewhere. The few hundred black and Asian settlers in London before the Second World War were a heady mix of former seamen, adventurers with no fixed backgrounds or horizons, intellectuals from emerging nations battling against imperial domination, and others who had done well from imperialism. Bayswater was sufficiently connected to a high-living community of 'rich and cultured Orientals' to be called 'Asia Minor' by some in the early 1900s.[49] A few Indian restaurants were open in Soho and off Piccadilly by 1914. The *African Times and Orient Review* was published in London for black intellectuals from 1912 to 1920. And Indian, African and West Indian doctors, Sikh pedlars, black street entertainers and Prince Monolulu, the famous tipster who claimed to hail from Abyssinia and whose raucous 'I gotta horse!' became a nationally recognized catchphrase between the wars, were all prominent features of an enduring black presence in London before it began to be greatly enlarged at the end of the 1940s.[50]

The East End was home to others besides East European Jews and black and Asian settlers from the sea. Non-Jewish Russians and Poles settled in Whitechapel, Stepney and West Ham in considerable numbers before the First World War. There were many anarchists and revolutionaries among them. They included, in 1902, both Lenin and Trotsky, flitting between the Russian political émigré communities of London, Paris, Zurich and elsewhere. There were enough Russians in London for Trotsky to get by in the small world of East End Russian cafés, clubs, restaurants and newspapers without adding to the skimpy English he had picked up in an Odessa gaol.[51] A similar, but more sustained, closed world was constructed by the London Polish socialists, whose journal *Robotnik* ran from 1894 to the early 1960s.[52] But the numbers of Russians and Russian Poles, both Jew and Gentile, diminished somewhat from 1917, when repatriation into the Russian army began, followed by a voluntary movement of exiles back to Russia after the revolutions later that year.

There was one other East End community that had an impact on the imagination of Londoners out of all proportion to its size – and to its clear desire to keep itself to itself. 'Chinatown', in east Limehouse (Poplar), had become a definable community based on a street called Pennyfields some time in the 1890s. By the First World War there were around 300 to 400 Chinese men there, a few with English wives or consorts. The Chinese population of the area probably never reached more than 500 at any time until it began to fade away from Limehouse by the late 1930s.[53]

Despite these small numbers, the area's reputation had distinctly lurid overtones. The taint of John Jasper's opium addiction in *The Mystery of Edwin Drood* seemed always to hang over the London Chinese, although Dickens had set his 'den' in Shadwell, a mile or so to the west. Restrictions on opium selling began to be put in place from 1908 and were tightened considerably in the First World War, when any tendency to 'demoralization' was firmly stamped on. The sensational details of 'disgusting orgies', opium parties and cocaine habits revealed at the inquest of the young West End actress Billie Carleton late in 1918 fuelled the Chinatown myth. Carleton died of a cocaine overdose and Ada Lo Ping You – a Scot married to a Chinaman living at 24 Limehouse Causeway – received five months' hard labour for cooking opium in Mayfair and Limehouse. Partly because of the hypertension caused by the Carleton affair, prosecutions for opium smoking in Chinatown, and for allowing premises to be used for the purpose, were fairly common in the early 1920s. One raid in 1920 netted forty-nine opium smokers, all Chinese, and a trickle of prosecutions reached the courts in the 1930s.[54] Police raids on illegal gambling houses also brought the area to public notice. A series of novels, stories and poems by Thomas Burke from 1916 to the early 1930s focused on the exotic side of Chinese Limehouse and its imagined dangers, though Burke later confessed that he had known little of the district at the time he wrote his popular tales. As the local rector commented in 1930, 'This may be literature, but it is not Limehouse.'[55] Yet Chinatown itself, with its cafés and gambling houses, shops and restaurants, its clubs, masonic hall for Tong members and Chinese school, was truly one of the most fascinating but secretive of London's foreign communities in the twentieth century.

Pennyfields and the other Chinese streets nearby were already run-down, some of the houses derelict, when the Blitz demolished substantial parts of Chinatown. This seems to have pushed its nucleus westwards to Soho, where a few Chinese restaurants had established themselves by the end of the First World War. Although a Chinese presence could still be detected in Limehouse at the century's end, a new and much more vigorous Chinatown emerged after 1945 around Gerrard Street, Soho.

The Limehouse Chinese were not the only foreign community to be affected by war. War brought newcomers to the capital in unprecedented numbers. In the First World War thousands of Belgian refugees began to arrive in London from August 1914. They were billeted across the capital in empty houses and temporary hostels, like the old Soho parish workhouse. By 1917, the numbers of strangers in London made it seem as though it was 'in the hands of the conquerors':

The Strand . . . is blocked for pedestrian traffic by Australians and New Zealanders; Piccadilly Circus belongs to the Belgians and the French; and the Americans possess Belgravia. Canadian cafeterias are doing good business round Westminster; French coffee-bars are thriving in the Shaftesbury Avenue district; Belgian restaurants occupy the waste corners around Kingsway; and two more Chinese restaurants lately opened in the West End.[56]

Black and Asian sailors were also settling in greater numbers than usual in the East End.

In the Second World War this trend was repeated but on a far greater scale. Inner London, half-deserted by its pre-war population, became a vortex of strangers. Poles more than filled the place of the Belgians. Poland's government-in-exile was established in London at the same time as the French, in June 1940. The Polish army regrouped in Britain and its head-quarters and civilian personnel were largely London-based. Numbers continued to rise throughout the war and after, reaching a peak of around 157,000 Poles in Britain in 1949. Some 38,000 to 40,000 lived in London. With shades of the Jewish influx fifty years before, a host of political, religious (largely Roman Catholic), charitable and educational institutions were established in 'Polski Londyn', including a daily newspaper (*Dziennik Polski*) and many weeklies and monthlies. The London Poles in the 1940s were, if only fleetingly, the largest foreign-born community in the metropolis, with local concentrations around Earls Court Road ('the Polish Corridor'), Ealing, Battersea, Clapham, Croydon and elsewhere. In contrast to the previous patterns of foreign settlement in London, there seem to have been as many Poles south of the river as north.[57]

Other communities on a smaller scale accompanied the Polish invasion. The Maltese made their presence felt in London for the first time during the war, settling mainly in Stepney and moving out to other, less bomb-damaged, parts of east and north London from there. A few settled in the West End, with notorious consequences.[58]

Then, especially from 1943, United States servicemen came to London in their thousands. There had been an 'American invasion' of London in the early years of the century, and Americans had always been among the most admiring of London's visitors and settlers (though only around 5,500 lived in the County before the First World War). But the American love affair with London took on a wholly new passion during the war years, especially after the Blitz, in which the radio journalist Ed Murrow played a major role in sanctifying the reputation of the Londoner. The Rainbow Club, at Piccadilly Circus, became the 'centre of American life in the capital'. And that life had never been more lively.

Most wartime newcomers joined communities that had already put down some roots, however tender, in the decades before the war or earlier. Sylheti settlers – and London's Indian restaurants – increased in number during the war as colonial labour was encouraged into the merchant marine and as sailors made their home ashore in London. The first East London mosque was opened in Commercial Road in August 1941 and reflected the strength of numbers of the new settlers even that early in the war. Similarly, engineers and seamen from the West Indies were recruited into active service or the munitions industry, some of them settling in London. By 1944 it was estimated that 400 West Indians, West Africans and Indians were living around Cable Street, Stepney, in what was fast becoming London's 'coloured quarter'.[59]

It was to be some of these ex-servicemen, former munitions workers and merchant seamen who were to return from the West Indies on the *Almanzora* and the *Empire Windrush* to try their luck as Londoners in 1947 and 1948. Already many of them would have learned the knack, and the pitfalls, of making their way in the metropolis and finding how best to live with their neighbours. And many would know how difficult that could be.

Getting On Together

But in London there are no neighbours, nobody knows, nobody cares . . . Neighbours in London! The Ramboats did not know the names of the people on either side of them.[60]

So wrote H. G. Wells of lower-middle-class Ealing at the turn of the century. Thirty years later, from a background in upper-middle-class Canonbury, Molly Hughes brooked no contradiction: 'Londoners have no neighbours.' Ian Niall's family, his father an engineering foreman from Glasgow, moved to suburban Southall in the 1920s: 'There was one thing about life in this place. People did what they decided to do quite unselfconsciously and without asking the opinion of neighbours, or caring what they thought. Everyone was an island, every family lived in a keep, and no one came to cross the drawbridge.' And in the lowlife Soho of novelist Gerald Kersh in the late 1930s things seemed much the same: 'I said, he lived in a room next to mine. But in London you may live and die in a room, and the man next door may never know.'[61]

Just because lots of people say the same thing and say it over a long period of time – the eighteenth-century novelist and London magistrate Henry Fielding wrote of 'London . . . a place where next-door neighbours do not know one another'[62] – does not make it true. Yet although anonymity among neighbours was not the whole story of neighbouring in London, it contained a large element of truth. For many it seemed a defining characteristic of the metropolis when compared to other places. It was especially noted – and often welcomed – by newcomers to the city. Clearly, though, the absence of neighbours did not adequately describe life everywhere in London. It was impossible to generalize about neighbourhood and community in the capital. In any street or tenement block or estate of flats there was an infinite mingling of mutuality, hostility and indifference. And if the greatest of these was indifference it did not dominate every place or for all time.

Certainly not in the Tabard Street area of Southwark, cleared as an 'unutterably bad' slum by the LCC mainly from 1919 to 1921. Part of the medieval pilgrims' road from London to Canterbury, it had long been notorious as a nest of mean courts and alleys, the homes of costers, rag dealers and thieves. Condemned in 1910, demolition had been delayed by the war.

'I believe', says the headmaster of a local school, 'that no immigration and little emigration has taken place in this little back-water since the Fire of London. Occasionally we may still observe in the speech of the children archaic colloquialisms long forgotten by other Londoners. The people inter-married for generations, almost everybody was related to everybody else, and many of the children to-day are descendants of an old Alsatia, and their dwarfed stature and short stumpy fingers, to my mind, bear witness to generations of in-breeding.'[63]

A similar sort of rooted kinship seems to have been a feature of Bow Creek, Poplar, perhaps the last of these isolated London 'villages' to fall under the housebreaker's hammer. Here a community had built itself up from the 1820s in almost complete separation from the rest of London: 'Even the people who live within a mile of it . . . have never heard of it.' In the early 1900s, Booth called it 'the "Orchard House"' after an old mansion that had once stood there and which had given its name to Orchard Place, the main street. He condemned it as an 'Alsatia for dock thieves'. Even then, 'Many of the families have been here four or five generations . . . and the place is as full of gossip and scandal as a village.' Home to about 200 people in the mid-1930s,

Most of the children are brothers and sisters or cousins. The men of the village seldom bring their brides from beyond the long road . . . There are whole tribes of Scanlans and Jeffrieses – but the biggest tribe of all are the Lammins . . . And so there is no formality among the people of Orchard Place and Boat Street and Salters Buildings. The woman next door is not 'Mrs Smith' but Aunty Kate, and Mr Smith is only Uncle Fred. They know each other's pedigrees and failings; they know how long Uncle Bill stays at the Steam Packet of an evening, and what Uncle Frank does for a living.

But they did not go on doing so for long: the area was cleared by the LCC shortly before the Second World War.[64]

Bow Creek and Tabard Street were exceptional. But in the more home-grown London-born areas of the city kinship continued to play a large part in neighbouring throughout the century. In Bethnal Green, Violet Lee, later Kray, mother of the formidable twins, had so many relatives nearby that 'They called our bit of Vallance Road "Lee Street".' Shoreditch (especially Hoxton), Finsbury, parts of Stepney (like Wapping), Poplar, Southwark, Bermondsey, north Lambeth and more had within them clusters of streets with a similar, if less overwhelming, village feel. Yet extensive kinship did not substitute for neighbouring. Kinship actively promoted relations between non-kin, rather than excluding them: 'The Bethnal Greener is . . . surrounded not only by his own relatives and their acquaintances, but also by his own acquaintances and their relatives.'[65]

Kinship played a part, too, in those areas known as dysfunctional, unsettled communities notorious for their 'rough' behaviour and their truculent attitude to the London around them. Here, though, the pattern was very different. In Campbell Road, Finsbury Park (north Islington), 'the worst street in North London', a few settled families coexisted with a whirlwind of people moving in and out of the street's cheap and very poor accommodation – renting a furnished room by the week or even for a night at a time.[66] What we know of Essex Street, Hoxton – sometimes called 'the worst street in London' in the 1920s – or Hales Street, Deptford, or Rope Yard Rails, Woolwich, or a couple of dozen more London streets with similar reputations, indicates that this would have been true of them too.

So it was in Notting Dale, among the most notorious of all London's neighbourhoods for the first half-century and more. This south-west corner of North Kensington, the Royal Borough's Norland ward, had been infamous since the 1830s. It was then that pig keepers became established near the 'Potteries', where manufacturers had been digging out the local clay for many years. By the 1840s, deep pits and ditches were filled with pig blood and manure and human sewage. By the 1860s it was known as the 'second great [Metropolitan] Gypsyry', and gypsy families were prominent in the local population for almost the next 100 years. Although the last pig left in 1878, the people of Notting Dale were in bad odour ever after.

The streets of three- and four-storey houses built there in the mid-nineteenth century were known as the 'London Avernus', a hell on earth, from before 1900. Bangor, Crescent, Kenley and Wilsham Streets and part of Sirdar Road received particular attention from the sanitary authorities as the 'Notting Dale Special Area'. In 1907, of its 208 houses, 107 were let out as furnished rooms, many by the night. These included all thirty-four houses in Bangor Street, the worst of all. A very high turnover of people moved through the furnished rooms and common lodging houses, where people rented beds in shared dormitories at a few pence a night – one for women in Crescent Street was ironically known as 'The Golden Gates'. Things had much improved by the 1920s, but insufficient ever to recover from its reputation as an irredeemable slum, and Bangor Street and most of the others were cleared in the early 1950s. Yet there were many residents whose families had settled permanently in the area. 'The happiest place we lived in was Bangor Street. They used to be all friends, just like friends and neighbours,' remembered one old resident in the 1980s. And if her hindsight was rose-tinted, it was at least a corrective to the 'no neighbours' view of London life even in an area where there was a constant change-over of personnel.[67]

Notting Dale was almost matched for notoriety by the Southam Street and Golborne Gardens area of Kensal New Town, North Kensington, and by the Clarendon Street area of Westbourne Green, Paddington, just north of the Harrow Road. Two well-known sociological studies of the 1940s and early 1950s – *Branch Street* and *The Deprived and the Privileged* – took their evidence from the Clarendon Street area.[68] But perhaps nowhere was quite so wild in the first half of the twentieth century as a suburban shanty-town in Kenton, Harrow. Known as 'the shacks', hutments had been built along Clay Lane, later Preston Hill, after the First World War. By the early 1930s the area was more like a North American hobo camp than the greenfield fringes of suburban London. It gained some unwelcome public attention in 1931 when a new arrival in the shacks known as 'The Pig-Sticker' was beaten to death with an axe by two established hut-dwellers called 'Moosh' and 'Tiggy'. They tried to burn the body at a rubbish dump at Scratchwood Sidings, Mill Hill, a suburban Avernus where a fire had burnt continuously for at least twenty-three years.[69]

The shacks were soon swept away for 'bankers' Tudor' in the 1930s. And that should remind us that London was constantly creating new communities and destroying old ones through expansion and redevelopment, just as it had in the nineteenth century. In the new areas the kinship networks which aided neighbouring in even the least settled of the older districts were absent and special effort was needed to foster mutuality and community. On the LCC's Becontree estate, for instance, thousands of workers arrived in a short space of time from all over east London and beyond. More than a decade after estate development began,

> Neighbours sometimes look after the children or look after the gardens in cases of illness, send round subscription lists in cases where there is a death in the family, etc. But neighbours do not know each other so well as they do in the areas from which Estate people have come and the general impression is that such help is far less frequent than it is in the older established working-class districts.

Even more alienating were the first few years of the Honor Oak Estate in Deptford and Lewisham, five-storey blocks of flats rather than a cottage estate like Becontree: at the end of the Second World War, 'after nearly 10 years, it is obvious that the people have no roots here'.[70]

Yet it is difficult to generalize about neighbouring even in these new implants in the metropolitan fabric. The LCC's Watling estate in Hendon, not far from 'the shacks', proved more successful at organizing neighbouring than Becontree. Local snobbish hostility to the estate-dwellers provoked a proud reaction. A community centre was built and sustained by the amalgamation in 1930 of the 'Association of Residents' and a separate 'Association of Neighbours'. By 1939 the centre was organizing some thirty activities for Watling residents, from an orchestra to a weight-lifting club and rose society, from a psychology class to a guild of players and table-tennis club, from the 'Young Watlers' for children to a 'Cripples' Parlour' for disabled ex-soldiers and others.[71]

We know more about neighbouring in working-class areas than in middle-class ones, where domestic servants made each household more or less self-sufficient, where commuting put distance between home and men's work, where women's networks were based on schoolfriends and the wives of husbands' business contacts, and where private schooling often disconnected the crucial link between child and neighbourhood. London's working-class areas usually provided for a mutuality of some richness. But it rarely lived up to the reputation, nurtured in nostalgia to the status of an urban myth, that 'every door was open'.

Crisis brought out the public side of neighbouring most visibly. When Doris Bailey's four-year-old sister Rosie died of meningitis in 1920s Bethnal Green,

There was the usual collection among the neighbours and they all gave liberally. Then they gave a huge wreath, the 'Gates of Heaven' . . . 'From the Neighbours' it said, in big purple letters. The wreaths were lined up in the street outside the front door for all the neighbours to see and they all came along and stood in silence. Then they began to gather, crowding either side of our door, as we always did ourselves at other funerals . . .

In another East End street, in the 1930s, a woman (Mrs Shepherd) was taken seriously ill in the night and an ambulance arrived:

When we came out into the street, I was amazed to find that there were about 200 people standing round the ambulance. There had been nobody about when Shepherd's boy had run for the doctor, but now nearly everybody seemed to be up and there were lights in almost every house . . . When the [ambulance] men closed the doors, there was a great sigh from the crowd, as if the doors had shut on something infinitely precious to them.[72]

Looking after children and the home while mothers were in hospital would be the normal expectation of a neighbour's duty. Sometimes this might lead to informal fostering over a long period of time, and the informal or legal adoption of a neighbour's orphaned child. Help with child-care, like collecting children from school, was also to be expected – within limits. So was helping out those in desperate straits – at least for a time. Cooking and delivering a Sunday dinner for elderly neighbours too poor or shaky to look after themselves was common enough. Ted Willis, the playwright and creator of *Dixon of Dock Green*, recalled one Sunday at home in Stanley Road, south Tottenham, in the 1920s:

we were waiting for our dinner – a savoury lamb stew which was bubbling on the stove – when my mother came bustling in, whipped up the saucepan, and hurried off with it to a house down the street, where she dished out the stew to a family of six children. I am ashamed to admit that I was not impressed by this gesture, but when I complained . . . [s]he delivered a fierce and stinging blow to the side of my head, and said in a voice sharp with anger and disgust: 'Oh shut up! Stop whining! You're hungry. They're starving!'[73]

Assistance was most readily forthcoming in those very close areas where settlement over the years meant that neighbours were well known to each other. Here some lending between neighbours was expected, even small cash advances to tide a family over for a day or so until wages or benefit was received. And when time came to marry, then husbands and wives were often chosen from what the street, even the next-door house, had to offer. As in 'The Island', an isolated group of streets near Hackney Downs, where communal life centred on the pub, the few general shops that everyone used, and on weekend parties with dancing to a hired piano: 'The Island was marvellous. Life will never be the same again. We all used to help one another. We were all like a family concern.' This attachment to neighbourhood was revealed in the thousands of wooden plaques erected in 1919 to commemorate the First World War dead, name by name and street by street, across working-class London – just as was being done in nearly every other village throughout the land. And it was revealed at that supreme moment of crisis in the Blitz. Cheltenham-born Barbara Nixon, a Newnham-educated ARP warden in Finsbury, 'knew that the Cockney was seldom happy for long, away from London, but one had not realized how extraordinarily devoted he is . . . to his actual street'. This was especially so among elderly Londoners.[74]

Yet, for all except the elderly, attachment to street and neighbourhood did not imply attachment to a particular home. Moving house was very common and the main (unsurprising) reason for doing so was to find better accommodation. Londoners were highly mobile within narrow boundaries. A study of schoolchildren in 1930s Shoreditch – one of the most 'rooted' of London boroughs with its high proportion of London-born – showed that 30 per cent of the families in the study had moved home within the past five years. A. S. Jasper began life 'in a hovel on the ground floor' of 3 Clinger Street, Hoxton, in 1905. By 1919 he had lived in Canal Road, Salisbury Street, Ebenezer Buildings (Rotherfield Street), Loanda Street, Scawfell Street, Shepherdess Walk, Bridport Place and New North Road – all within a half-mile radius. Coming and going was not just a working-class experience: John Osborne's fly-by-night mother moved around the south-west London suburbs and beyond 'thirty or forty times during the first seventeen years of my life'.[75] Even when such high mobility was restricted to a small area of London that families knew well, 'neighbours' could not have meant the same as they did to a family rooted for some fifty years in, say, 'The Island's' handful of small streets.

It is possible to indicate some patterns of mobility from a study of a group of a dozen streets in Lower Clapton, Hackney, housing about 8,000 people between the wars. The streets were a mix of poverty and comfort, and of casual, unskilled and skilled workers, and there was nothing especially distinctive about them. As far as anything can stand as representative of London's kaleidoscopic reality, then this area was typical of those thousands of streets of two- to three-storey houses, occupied mainly by two families, which covered large tracts of London from Fulham to Poplar and Battersea to Deptford.

In the 1920s and 1930s, from an analysis of the electoral registers, the streets of skilled workers were more mobile than the unskilled, which in turn were more mobile than the poorest streets. Yet in every street there was a substantial nucleus of deeply rooted families who continued at the same address for at least sixteen years: 32 per cent of 1923 households in the skilled streets were at the same address in 1939, 37 per cent in the unskilled streets and 43 per cent in the poor. Newcomers in all groups were apparently more prone to move on again than settle. It is clear, too, that there was much more mobility in the 1930s than in the 1920s. In the skilled streets in 1939 over half the households had occupied a different address six years before, and in the poorer streets over a third. And there seems to have been a loss of housing function in the poorest and unskilled streets, with a significant decline in household numbers between 1923 and 1939; whereas the streets of skilled workers held up well, actually gaining in numbers over the same period. All this reflects the greater opportunities to find improved accommodation after the middle-class drive for the suburbs from the late 1920s, and after the local authorities' efforts to clear slums from 1930. Although slum dwellers were rarely rehoused in the new flats, better housing could more easily be found for rent than at any previous time in the century.[76]

Even in the out-County LCC estates, mobility was high. The ideal of finding a home that would cater for a family's needs for a generation was not realized very often. Inability to afford the new cost of living on an out-County estate, with high rents and travel-to-work expenses, or failure to adapt to a community where all were strangers, sent many families back where they had come from. Others, perhaps growing in prosperity as children left school for work, moved further out to the suburbs proper, taking on the risk of a mortgage in the process. Emigration from Watling and the other estates had been 'enormous' in the early years but had settled down to under 10 per cent annually by 1939.[77]

This constant movement of people into and within and out of London made the capital and its citizens so difficult to pin down and pigeonhole. To some London was the anonymous city; to others a metropolis of villagers; to yet others a 'cosmopolis' of immigrants from the nation and the world. All of these were true, but none was the whole truth. To Maurice Gorham, in his 1951 study of Londoners, London was 'a city of emigrants, for you will meet Londoners all over the world'.[78] And that was true too.

In all the typologies of the Londoner the contradictions and paradoxes of London life tended to be ironed out. So, for example, kinship shored up community. But it also led to dissension and schism. Vendettas within working-class streets, over old grudges or new slights from the trivial to the grievous, centred round 'families' and their tenuous network of kin. As in 'The Battle of Toulon Street', Camberwell, in the summer of 1930, when a row between the Tuck and King families apparently involved bayonets, razors, bottles through windows and tiles thrown from roofs. Four of the Tucks needed hospital treatment. The *New Survey of London Life and Labour* noted in the 1930s that 'Terrorism is still rampant' in the poorer tenement blocks, as it had been at the turn of the century: 'the fear felt by the decent tenant of the bad is pathetic'. That was certainly true of life in the poorest streets as well.[79]

Similarly, class shored up community. But it, too, led to divisions, because the London working class was split between rough and respectable, skilled and unskilled, the aspiring and the barely surviving. The writer John Holloway was brought up in Waverley Road, South Norwood (Croydon), in the 1920s, his father a stoker, his mother a former nurse:

Coventry Road we should have thought an impossible place to live in: it was a working-class slum. But we didn't live in Apsley Road, or even Harrington Road, either. Even as a small boy I was conscious of the slightest distinctions between the streets – whitened steps, bow-windows, frosted glass in the front doors, fences, iron railings, front gardens, hedges, golden not green privet, a myrtle bush, and a great deal else.

And it was just the same – give or take the privet – in proletarian Stepney, where writer Willy Goldman's street 'was a "divided" community . . . The people on our side tended to be more neighbourly with each other than with the people across the way – and distance was not the reason. The fact is our homes were more substantial. We had a basement as well as the two floors above.'[80] So in nearly all of London's '20,000 streets', side by side lived settlement and mobility, anonymity and community, mutual aid and hostility, neighbourliness and privacy.

Privacy was treasured because it was so hard to come by. The average working family's expectation of a home was two rooms and a kitchen in a shared house. That held good for the first fifty years and more of the century in London. In one of Dolly Davey's early moves around Southwark with her newlywed husband, 'You have no privacy, especially with a big family like his mother had, you see. For about seven weeks, he had to stay in the same room with his brother, and I had to be with his sister.' Once a home was obtained it might be jealously guarded against outsiders. When the journalist Horace Thorogood lodged in a Poplar room in the early 1930s he saw nothing of his fellow lodgers:

A family consisting of a stevedore, his wife, and their two young children lodged upstairs. They kept strictly to themselves. It is astonishing what privacy can be maintained in the small houses of the poor. I never saw any of them, partly because the stevedore put his home-made radio set on as soon as he came home, and that glued them for the rest of the evening.[81]

Maud Pember Reeves, in her classic study of north Lambeth house-wives before the First World War, characterized them as 'quiet, decent, "keep-themselves-to-themselves" kind of women'. And this desire for privacy – for secrecy within limits – could be a deterrent to neighbour-ing and a foil to best intentions. Decent motives might be misinterpreted through suspicion; or maybe the motives weren't so decent after all. 'Shepherd', whose wife was taken to hospital at night in that neighbourly East End street, steadfastly refused the frequently proffered help of women neighbours to look after his home and children while she was in hospital: ' "They only want ter poke their noses in 'ere ter see 'ow I'm situated," said Shepherd.'[82]

The reporter here is Hugh Massingham, a journalist responsible for one of the best-observed but least-known studies of London life in the 1930s. He lived in an East End street to relate what went on around him and to sell a book for his trouble. But what trouble he had. For Massingham clearly did not blend in easily. And he was to find that the desire for privacy was one end of a spectrum that could climax in a paranoid and hostile suspicion of strangers. In the end, Massingham's neighbours concluded that he was some sort of spy, though for whom was never made clear. There was a nationwide survey of overcrowding at the time and some linked him vaguely to that. 'It was the knowledge that I was being perpetually watched and criticized that unnerved me. I was in a strange land, inhabited by strange people . . . Being lost in a foreign country seemed to me a pleasant experience by comparison.' When, through a misunderstanding, he was held responsible for bailiffs distraining Shepherd's goods and, in a moment of frustration, punched him on the chin, the street organized against him. Things were stolen from his rooms, his milk was taken from the doorstep and once replaced with watered carbolic acid, children hustled him off the pavement and rubbish was tipped on his floor. Massingham withstood it all. 'But in the end they were too much for me. One Saturday night I returned home to find that my visitor had . . . smashed the rest of my crockery and had then done his business in the frying-pan and left it in the middle of the table.' He went on the Monday.[83]

Some of these contradictions were ironed out in the Blitz. Then all were faced with one common enemy and many were dying in the struggle.

Elizabeth Bowen memorably recalled the influence of London's anonymous dead on the living during those awesome moments of the first Blitz:

These unknown dead reproached those left living not by their death, which might any night be shared, but by their unknownness, which could not be mended now. Who had the right to mourn them, not having cared that they had lived? So, among the crowds still eating, drinking, working, travelling, halting, there began to be an instinctive movement to break down indifference while there was still time. The wall between the living and the living became less solid as the wall between the living and the dead thinned. In that September transparency people became transparent, only to be located by the just darker flicker of their hearts. Strangers saying 'Good night, good luck', to each other at street corners, as the sky first blanched then faded with evening, each hoped not to die that night, still more not to die unknown.[84]

But even the Blitz couldn't heal all divisions. 'He's a stranger, heave a brick at him', had summed up the attitude of people in Hoxton, according to Robert Hyde, a church missionary there before the First World War. Suspicion and hostility were greatly magnified when the stranger was a 'foreigner'. The American sociologist E. W. Bakke noted fierce antagonism to 'foreigners' who came to Greenwich looking for work in the Depression. The term would have included anyone from outside the district, but hostility was directed especially at the Welsh and Irish. George Orwell listed 'suspicion of foreigners' as one of the 'salient characteristics of the English common people' in 1944, a time when there were more foreigners in London than ever before.[85] And there were two main manifestations of this suspicion and hostility which disfigured London life throughout the first fifty years of the century: anti-Semitism and the 'colour bar'.

Anti-Semitism hurt more people if only because there were more Jews in London at the time than black or Asian people. Like the colour bar, anti-Semitism was a vice of intellectuals as well as the urban poor, and it ran the gamut from mild antipathy to single-minded loathing. But it had most resonance in those working-class areas near where the immigrants clustered.

Anti-Semitism was a political force from the beginning of the century. Major William Evans-Gordon, the Conservative MP for Stepney, helped raise the British Brothers League to become a significant influence on government immigration policy from its foundation in 1901. Its power base was the East End. Waging an anti-'alien' agitation on the supposed ill-effects of the Jews on rents, overcrowding and jobs, the League called for an immediate halt to immigration. Its large and noisy public meetings were conducted to cries of 'Wipe them out'. Attacks on Jews in the street, window-breaking and violent resistance to immigrants attempting to move into some streets in Shadwell and Wapping were common enough in the first years of the century, yet 'failed to ignite the East End'.[86]

After the 1905 Aliens Act, anti-Semitic agitation receded. But the hostility to Jews in a few places on the borders of the main areas of Jewish settlement never abated. It was kept alive by competition for house-room and work, especially in the furniture and clothing trades. Wapping (where Irish Catholics predominated), Bethnal Green and parts of Shoreditch in particular became the most fertile soil for Sir Oswald Mosley's British Union of Fascists (BUF) when it shifted to an anti-Jewish line from September 1934. From then until 1940, east London fascism held out the prospect of organized violence against Jews who had been settled there for thirty to fifty years. Fears of a pogrom were never realized, but the fears were real enough. Assaults on Jews and synagogues, window-breaking and arson, the daubing and chalking of anti-Semitic slogans and swastikas, marches with chanted slogans on the margins of the Jewish area, rabble-rousing street-corner meetings, all accompanied by tough black-shirted men whose appearance was designed to intimidate, stoked a climate of fear in the Jewish East End.

The 'Battle of Cable Street' of 4 October 1936, when Mosley and his blackshirts were prevented by a huge demonstration from marching through the Jewish East End, was a signal victory for a broad anti-fascist alliance. But a guerrilla warfare against the Jews of east London persisted throughout the 1940s. The first nights and days of the Blitz provoked a wave of anti-Semitism that made sensible commentators fearful of a pogrom in the East End. Rich Jews were said to be fleeing London to rural safety and poor Jews to be squeezing 'Britons' out of the shelters. Although this antagonism subsided, it was revived in March 1943 by the Bethnal Green tube station tragedy. No fewer than 173 people, sixty-two of them children, were crushed to death when an air-raid warning caused a rush for the underground. An evening paper blamed the disaster on a 'Jewish Panic', a theme seized on by William Joyce ('Lord Haw-Haw') in his broadcasts from Germany. In the East End, anti-Jewish feeling was such that Home Secretary, Herbert Morrison, set up an official inquiry into the causes of the tragedy. The report publicly quashed the 'Jewish Panic' theory but the myth survived. And fascism resurfaced in the East End as soon as war was over. A Bethnal Green psychological survey of 1947–9 found over 26 per cent of the sample to be 'extreme anti-Semites', believing Jews to be 'traitors', 'warmongers' and worse. When Mosley formed the Union Movement in London in March 1948, he brought together a number of extreme anti-Semitic (and by now anti-black) organizations, almost all with a presence in the capital. Despite the unspeakable sufferings of the Holocaust, beatings of Jews, violent attacks on Jewish meetings and the vandalism and fire-bombing of synagogues throughout London scarred the immediate post-war period just as they had the last years of peace.[87]

Hostility to blacks in London never approached this sustained virulence prior to the late 1950s. Even so there were violent moments. And an informal – sometimes official – colour bar operated as a daily obstacle to normal life for blacks and Asians in the capital right across the first half of the century.

In the troubled summer of 1919 attacks on black seamen took place in a number of British ports, triggered by sudden unemployment and the use of cheap foreign seamen. The most serious episodes, where a rioter and victim were shot dead, were in Cardiff, but considerable anti-black rioting also took place in Liverpool, Newport and in the East End. There were attacks on lodging houses occupied by blacks in Stepney, Poplar, Limehouse and Canning Town from May to August 1919. Furniture was dragged from houses and burnt in the streets, blacks in fear for their lives fired revolvers over the heads of the crowd and the weapons used against them included razors lashed to sticks. Yet things quickly calmed down. For the next thirty years London was virtually free from violent anti-black hostility, although there were some isolated street attacks on black men by the BUF in the 1930s, and Louis Gillain recalled 'gangs of toughs who wrecked a café which served only coloured men' in the East End around 1933.

But overt hostility was sublimated into a more covert colour bar. Refusal to serve blacks and Asians in London hotels, dance halls and restaurants was not uncommon throughout the first half of the century; blacks were frequently rejected as lodgers or tenants by landlords; there was discrimination against blacks in employment; 'coloured boxers' were banned from fighting in the Royal Albert Hall, although a few exceptions were allowed in the 1930s. During the war, large numbers of black US servicemen were reputedly better treated by Londoners than by their white comrades and compatriots, but there was little room for self-congratulation. Indeed, the war exposed the most notorious instance of the London colour bar in operation. The Imperial Hotel, Russell Square, banned Learie Constantine from staying there in 1943. Constantine, known across the world as a West Indian test cricketer, was at that time working for the government, settling migrant workers to help with the war effort. He thought the hotel was reacting to 'American pressure': 'someone . . . had said: "The Imperial is coming to something if you are going to take niggers in!"' Constantine successfully sued the hotel for breach of contract and went on to write a book called *Colour Bar*. Yet despite the Imperial's humiliation in court, the colour bar remained an undercurrent of London life through the 1940s. In 1948, for instance, Tom Boatin, a West African lecturer at London

University, was refused service at Rule's Restaurant in Covent Garden. The Ministry of Food forced Rule's to apologize.[88]

A survey published in 1947 of landlords' attitudes to renting rooms to black students revealed that London landlords 'show an "aversion" [to black students] of 44.2 per cent', compared to 37.3 per cent of landlords in the rest of the country.[89] These results did not bode well for post-war London. Migration from the Caribbean would begin, hesitantly enough at first, almost from the moment the survey was published. Within a decade, that first migration would be followed by an unparalleled influx of newcomers from every corner of the New Commonwealth. For London was on the brink of one of the greatest of all changes experienced in its long history: the making of multiracial Londoners and of a truly multicultural metropolis.

4. The Remaking of the Londoner: 1948–99

Multiracial London

On a bright afternoon in May 1955, the sociologist Sheila Patterson made her first acquaintance with the Coldharbour Lane area of Brixton.

As I turned off the main shopping street, I was immediately overcome with a sense of strangeness, almost of shock. The street was a fairly typical South London side-street, grubby and narrow, lined with cheap cafés, shabby pubs, and flashy clothing-shops. All this was normal enough. But what struck one so forcefully was that, apart from some shopping housewives and a posse of teddy boys in tight jeans outside the billiards hall, almost everybody in sight had a coloured skin. Waiting near the employment exchange were about two dozen black men, most in the flimsy suits of exaggerated cut that, as I was later to learn, denoted their recent arrival. At least half of the exuberant infants playing outside the pre-fab day nursery were *café noir* or *café au lait* in colouring. And there were coloured men and women wherever I looked, shopping, strolling, or gossiping on the sunny street-corners with an animation that most Londoners lost long ago . . . [I] experienced a profound reaction of something unexpected and alien. In fact, I received what I was later to hear Professor Ira de A. Reid describe as a 'colour shock'.[1]

The strength of Sheila Patterson's reaction is a measure of the extraordinary rapidity with which the Londoner was remade in the second half of the twentieth century: an 'alloy of the people of Britain' in the 1940s, an alloy of the people of the world just forty years later.

In 1951 only one in twenty Londoners had been born outside the United Kingdom. Even that was the highest proportion of the century thus far in a city then still home to refugees and former soldiers from all over Europe. But only a tiny fraction of these newcomers would have been black or of Asian origin – maybe 4,000 West Indians and far fewer Indians and Pakistanis in a population of over 8 million. Of the foreigners, most were Poles (nearly 50,000) and Germans and Russians (60,000 between them, mainly Jewish, and most in London for forty years or more).[2]

By 1991, 1.35 million black and Asian-origin Londoners accounted for just over one in five of the Greater London population. Some 535,000 described themselves as black and 690,000 as Asian (including Chinese).

Many, of course, were Londoners born and bred. Even so, the foreign population of London was very large and growing still. In 1991 18.5 per cent were born outside the UK and Eire, up from 15.2 per cent in 1981. Thirty-three foreign countries each had over 10,000 nationals resident in London (compared to fourteen in 1951). The capital's children shared 307 home languages, making London probably the most linguistically diverse city in the world. By 2001, one in three Londoners were expected to be of ethnic minority backgrounds or of foreign birth.[3]

From a pre-war London where 'cosmopolis' was confined to Soho and the East End, by the mid-1980s virtually any main street in the capital could cater for the needs and desires of every major culture round the globe. Neither was this a reflection of changes in the nation with which London had merely kept pace. In 1991 just 3 per cent of the people of Great Britain had described themselves as non-white. London, with 12 per cent of Britain's population, contained 45 per cent of its black and ethnic minority people. Of the twenty-nine local authority areas with 15 per cent or more of ethnic minorities in their populations, twenty-two were in Greater London.

Of all the changes to London and Londoners in the twentieth century this was the greatest. It was entirely unanticipated, coming after a generation from 1914 to 1940 when London had become less foreign and more British. It changed the face of the Londoner more significantly than any event since the Norman Conquest, almost a millennium before. Its consequences would mould the fortunes of the city and its people well into the third millennium of London's history. And, astonishingly, this was a change irrevocably established in just a decade and a half, between the mid-1950s and the late 1960s.

The West Indian diaspora of the late 1940s and 1950s was the key event in the remaking of the Londoner. Young West Indians were the first to claim their inheritance from a fast-dissolving Empire. The emerging post-colonial world dislocated markets and industries, creating unemployment and provoking independence struggles, civil wars and the wholesale ejection of minorities. London, the imperial capital, would feel the full blast of these upheavals. The winds of change rattled windows in Notting Hill Gate and raised the dust on Brixton Hill. For the imperial citizens of Highgate and Middlesex (Jamaica), of Waterloo (Trinidad) and of Woodford (Grenada) were coming home to roost. And coming to colonize London.

Much has been made of the docking of the SS *Empire Windrush* at Tilbury on 22 June 1948, with almost 500 mainly Jamaican migrants on board, as the start of it all. But London – and history itself – knows no such clear-cut openings. For migration from the West Indies had begun before the *Windrush* tied up, and did not become a significant mass movement until some six years after its passengers had found their way into London.

The Second World War provides as good a beginning as any. West Indian men had come to Britain as servicemen and as recruits to war industries. They received training, good wages, assistance with board and lodging and appeared, generally, to be welcomed. Some stayed on. Most had returned to the Caribbean by 1947, even though many returners hankered after England as their new home. There were several factors pushing them away from the post-war West Indies. Unemployment was high and migration to find work and a better life had long been an escape route from poverty in the islands – to Panama before the First World War, to the USA and Cuba after it. But it was the post-1945 labour shortage in Britain that determined thousands of West Indians to capitalize on that wartime experience and migrate. When US borders were closed by the McCarran Act in 1952, Britain became virtually the sole destination of the migrants.

' "[E]very man want a better break," ' says a character in George Lamming's 1954 novel *The Emigrants*. Lamming, from Barbados, voyaged to London in 1950 on a boat filled with men – and a few women – seeking opportunities for fulfilment through a better education, a better job, a better standard of living, a better status in the world. 'They were taking flight from something they no longer wanted. It was their last chance to recover what had been wasted.'[4]

England, uniquely, seemed to offer this better break – indeed, had promised it in a contract between colony and mother country. And London, of course, was the epitome of England, taken in with mother's milk. The calypso singer 'Lord Kitchener' composed a famous number while sailing on the *Empire Windrush* itself: 'London is the place for me, London that lovely city.' 'I had decided long before I was ten that I would come to London,' recalled Donald Hinds, who migrated from Kingston in 1955. 'I cannot be certain at what age the thought first occurred to me.' 'How excited I'd been at the prospect of seeing the great old city, the centre of the world we had learned about at school,' remembered Jamaican Eric Ferron, who stayed on in England after RAF service but didn't get to London until 1947.[5] And the Trinidadian novelist Sam Selvon found his way there in 1950, soon to write triumphantly of the delight he found in conquering this city that he'd dreamed of from afar, and conquering it for good.

Oh what it is and where it is and why it is, no one knows, but to have said: 'I walked on Waterloo Bridge,' 'I rendezvoused at Charing Cross,' 'Piccadilly Circus is my playground,' to say these things, to have lived these things, to have lived in the great city of London, centre of the world. To one day lean against the wind walking up the Bayswater Road (destination unknown), to see the leaves swirl and dance and spin on the pavement (sight unseeing), to write a casual letter home beginning: 'Last night, in Trafalgar Square . . .'

What it is that a city have, that any place in the world have, that you get so much to like it you wouldn't leave it for anywhere else? What it is that would keep men although by and large, in truth and in fact, they catching their royal to make a living, staying in a cramp-up room where you have to do everything – sleep, eat, dress, wash, cook, live. Why it is, that although they grumble about it all the time, curse the people, curse the government, say all kind of thing about this and that, why it is, that in the end, everyone cagey about saying outright that if the chance come they will go back to them green islands in the sun?

In the grimness of the winter, with your hand plying space like a blind man's stick in the yellow fog, with ice on the ground and a coldness defying all effort to keep warm, the boys coming and going, working, sleeping, going about the vast metropolis like veteran Londoners.[6]

The numbers of West Indian migrants kept in close step with job vacancies in the English labour market. Even so, numbers in the early years were tiny – never more than 1,000 a year before 1951, around 2,000 in 1952 and 1953, and then a substantial jump to 10,000 in 1954 and 27,500 in 1955. Virtually all migration was voluntary, with hardly any direct recruitment – probably fewer than 6,000 came to England under schemes organized by London Transport from 1956 and the National Health Service in the 1960s. Three-quarters of these migrants came to London and by 1961 there were over 100,000 West Indians in the capital. In fact, the census of that year counted fewer than it should have done: widespread evasion of the enumerators was due to impending immigration controls which some feared might lead to repatriation. Eventually, restrictions in the Commonwealth Immigration Act 1962 limited new migration to voucher holders for work or study, and to the dependants of those already in Britain. By 1968, new migration from the Caribbean had ceased for all practical purposes. In 1971 the West Indian-born population of London reached its highest recorded figure at almost 170,000.[7]

At the beginning of this migration men had predominated – there had been just two women migrants on the *Empire Windrush*. But the numbers of women noticeably increased from around 1953 and by the end of the 1950s women formed the majority of newcomers. In 1961 the proportion of West Indian men to women in London was 1,196 to 1,000, but by 1971 this had fallen to 961 to 1,000. That was a distinctively higher share of women than among migrants from other Commonwealth countries, whether old

or new. Nearly three-quarters of West Indian women were single, migrating
for the same economic opportunities as men. Virtually all of child-bearing
age, they helped create a specially fertile group that would ensure the
numbers of black Londoners would rise faster than the natural increase of
the population at large.[8]

As with other migrations, there were many divisions among the newcomers themselves. The distinctions between people from different islands
were manifold and sharply drawn. ' "I don't want no kiss-me-arse Jamaican
living with me," Bat say', in Selvon's *The Housing Lark* (1965): ' "You can't
get a Trinidadian instead?" ' ' "Who the hell you calling Bajans[?]" ' someone
on Lamming's migrant ship asks a Grenadian: ' "The people from Barbados
are called Barbadians." ' Trinidadians were said to be 'gay', Jamaicans 'touchy
and flamboyant', Barbadians 'dull and hard working'. 'Big islanders' were
considered more worldly-wise, and so less trustworthy, than 'small islanders',
who 'wrote off Jamaicans as bullies'. As late as the mid-1970s, a sociologist
noted the 'lingering distrust' among Montserratians 'of other islanders,
a feeling that they are somehow different'. Some 'small islanders', like
working-class migrants from St Lucia and Dominica, spoke a French 'creole'
patois as their first language. All of these differences were overlain with
others – between West Indians with Asian origins, 'incompletely assimilated'
into a majority black culture; or with differences of skin colour, within a
'pigmentocracy' or 'colour-class' hierarchy that valued light over dark; or
between evangelical Christians, Rastafarians and those of no religion at all.
These were the traditional divisions that had fatally undermined the cause
of West Indian nationalism, a nationalism which some militants hoped to
build on English soil.[9]

Some of these divisions would melt away in a city where the newcomers
were all 'coloureds' or 'blacks' or 'spades' or worse. But in the early years
they were influential in determining the unusual patterns of Caribbean
settlement in London.

Most attention at the time, fuelled by fears of black ghettos on the
American model, focused on concentrations or clusters of migrants. There
had been one significant cluster from the beginning. The Cable Street area
of Stepney was the earliest so-called 'coloured quarter' in the second half of
the century. But it did not grow with the new influx. Its black population
peaked in 1949 and in 1951 was only around 450. Probably the area's
unsavoury reputation, and the consequent hostility of surrounding whites,
deterred many from making a long-term home anywhere near it.

By 1953, Stepney still figured in a list of just four principal West Indian
communities in London. The others were Camden Town, Paddington and
Brixton. Five years later, two much larger concentrations had evolved. One

was in west London (Bayswater, Paddington, Shepherd's Bush and North Kensington), the other south of the river (Brixton, Stockwell and Camberwell). A popular explanation for this clustering relied on London's radial transport network to explain the choice of where newcomers settled. The Plymouth boat train terminated at Paddington, Liverpool's at Euston and Southampton's at Waterloo. Migrants burdened by cases and confined to shanks's pony were constrained to find a home minutes away from the station.[10]

But Brixton is quite a step from Waterloo and in explaining its attraction for West Indians the *Empire Windrush* has again figured large. Some 242 Jamaicans from the ship were billeted temporarily at a huge underground air-raid shelter on Clapham Common in the autumn and winter of 1948–9. In a famous story recounted by Joyce Egginton in 1957, forty Jamaicans were treated to tea by the Mayor of Lambeth and the local MP at the Astoria Cinema, Brixton. 'In the unknown and perplexing vastness of England, the Jamaicans now felt they could be sure of one place. Brixton was friendly. In Brixton they would make their homes.'[11]

Maybe. But the Jamaican presence in Brixton seems not to have become especially noticeable until 1952–3, four or five years later, and probably this extension of the *Windrush* arrival myth is also misleadingly simple. For there were numbers of black people in Brixton for at least twenty years before the ship docked. A West African, remembered locally as 'Massa Johnson', ran nine lodging houses for black students in Brixton before the war and these remained 'in coloured ownership or occupation' through the 1940s and 1950s. Their tenants were added to by '[m]any coloured [American] troops' in Brixton in 1944. A lively street market gave a flavour of home. Serendipity probably explains the rest, and chance was nowhere more crucial than in the changing fortunes of the local housing market. In the early years, the main migrant presence in Brixton was confined to just two streets – Geneva and Somerleyton Roads, running south out of Coldharbour Lane. Owned by an absentee family estate, the houses had long been farmed out and neglected, and leases were at their fag-end and cheap. This ready availability of two entire streets of low-cost housing made settling in Brixton easier than almost anywhere else. They became known for a time as 'London Harlem'.[12]

The housing question was central to which areas were settled when. High costs usually put renting more than a single room beyond the migrant's reach. So choice of accommodation was largely confined to the belt of mid- to late-Victorian multi-occupied property at the outer edge of inner London, and in places just beyond.

Yet this was a very large area indeed. Although it later served some militants to write of 'the ghetto', as Michael X did about Notting Hill,[13] the most remarkable factor in the pattern of Caribbean settlement was its huge geographical spread. As early as 1958, a survey of 4,700 West Indians found them living in all but two of the twenty-eight Metropolitan Boroughs of inner London. The exceptions were St Marylebone (probably a sampling quirk) and Bermondsey, one of the most 'London' of all the capital's districts, its small houses not well suited to subdivision. The 1961 census showed West Indians living everywhere in the County and in every borough in Middlesex. They were even more dispersed than the Irish, despite the latter's well-trodden tracks into every neighbourhood in London. This pattern was something new in the migrant settlement of the capital, where clustering in 'the Jewish East End', 'Little Italy', 'the French quarter' or 'Chinatown' had been the traditional pattern. Nor was it a model that others found so comfortable to follow: by the end of the century, West Indian-born migrants were far more dispersed across London than Indians, Pakistanis, Cypriots and others who arrived at the same time or slightly later.[14]

Even so, clusters there were. Brixton and Stockwell accounted for almost one in five West Indians surveyed in 1958, and this Lambeth settlement grew in importance from the late 1950s as the other main cluster declined. That was North Kensington, where 'the return to town movement' – not yet known as gentrification – was tending to push migrants out almost as soon as they arrived. In 1958, though, North Kensington still contained one in eight of London's West Indians.[15]

This distribution reflected the geographical legacy of the subcontinent the migrants had left behind. Geneva and Somerleyton Roads were called 'Little Jamaica' by the people who lived there. Notting Hill had a Trinidadian character that determined carnival should start from there rather than the larger area of Caribbean settlement in south London. Montserratians were mainly found in Finsbury Park and Stoke Newington, the Dominicans and St Lucians in Paddington. There seemed some desire not to be confused with migrants from other islands and it pushed settlements apart in London's sea of faces. Later there would come a sensitivity to reputation which made some migrants wish to move away from Notting Hill after the 1958 riots and from Brixton by the early 1960s.[16]

This dispersed colonization of London by the West Indians gave a substantially different character to the appearance of the Londoner almost overnight. Dispersal meant that white Londoners did not have to visit particular districts to notice it. The change was everywhere. 'A coloured population – and this means a growing half-caste population – is now a stable element in British social life,' noted the London-born but Australian-reared novelist Colin MacInnes as early as 1956; his *City of Spades* (1957) would be the first account by a sympathetic outsider to get under the skin of this newly emerging phenomenon. The journalist and broadcaster Clive James migrated to London from Sydney in January 1962. His first trip by underground from Earls Court to Piccadilly was a shock: 'Half the people in the crowded carriage seemed to be black or dark brown . . . I had entered my first multiracial society, and all for the price of a tube ticket.' By 1966, *The New London Spy* could claim, with some exaggeration, that 'London is now one of the most cosmopolitan cities in the world. It is possible for an Irishman, an African or a Pakistani to live, eat, sleep, work and die in London without ever catching sight of a native Englishman. Just think of County Kilburn, British West Hampstead or Belsize Pakistan.'[17]

As this suggests, by the mid-1960s the West Indian migration had already been joined by many others. The Maltese had been first off the mark. They were London's most prominent new migrant group of the early 1940s, mainly young men escaping poor prospects and repressive morality on their dusty island. Some 1,600 Maltese had settled in London, or were passing through, in 1951. Just over a third lodged in the East End, where Eastman Street (Bethnal Green) and Christian Street (Aldgate) were particular pockets in the late 1950s. Numbers peaked in those years at probably not many more than 4,000.[18]

The slightly later post-war migration from Cyprus, though, was on a far bigger scale. There had been some 8,000 Cypriots in London in 1939 but this grew rapidly in the 1950s to reach around 75,000 by 1966. There was considerable clustering early on in Camden Town which then spread east through north Islington and Stoke Newington into Hackney; later it would move decisively north into Harringay, Wood Green and beyond. By 1970, shopping streets like Seven Sisters Road (Holloway) and Green Lanes (Harringay) seemed entirely given over to Cypriot clubs, grocers, banks and travel agents. It was a migration particularly of married couples, and the gender and age balance ensured that this, like the West Indian migration, was especially fertile compared to the population of London as a whole.[19]

Steady migration from Hong Kong brought the Chinese in unprecedented numbers to London while retaining their reputation as the 'least assimilated' minority in the capital. Their main areas of settlement were scattered in the East End, Camden Town and notably Soho, the new Chinatown of post-war London. Gerrard and Lisle Streets acquired many Chinese restaurants from the late 1950s. By the middle of the 1960s Gerrard Street was known in Cantonese as *Tong Yahn* or 'Chinese People's Street'.[20] And Chinese migration, three-quarters of it from Hong Kong, doubled in the 1970s to reach 20,000 in 1981.

Around 1961–2, the balance of newcomers to London shifted away from the West Indies. In these two critical years, tens of thousands of Asian migrants rushed to beat the restrictions that the whole world knew were about to be imposed by the Commonwealth Immigration Act. From migration totals of 8–12,000 a year from India and Pakistan to Britain between 1956 and 1960, a 'remarkable surge' pushed numbers to 50,000 in 1961 and 90,000 a year later.[21]

All this built on two significant migrations from the Indian subcontinent that predated the great influx of 1961–2. One was the steady build-up of Sylhettis from East Pakistan (later Bangladesh) who had already put down roots in pre-war Spitalfields. By 1956 the connection between East End and East Pakistan was sufficiently strong for a Dhaka travel agent to open an outlet in Sandys Row off Middlesex Street (Petticoat Lane). Only 800 Pakistanis were enumerated in Stepney in 1961 but 'Pakistan Exports' in leather and clothing were already prominently announced on shop-fronts and factory signboards. A network of villages which had sent migrants to Spitalfields and prospered through cash remitted home were known as *Londoni* to explain their good fortune. By 1991 there were more than 38,000 Bangladeshis in Spitalfields and nearby.[22]

Even more significant was the remarkable growth of an Indian community in Southall. This was the first prominent example of a suburban migrant cluster, an important harbinger of a tendency that would become well established by the century's end. There is an arrival myth here to rival the *Empire Windrush*. In the mid-1950s, it goes, the personnel officer of Woolf's Rubber Company in Southall found himself with a shortage of workers willing to labour in the factory's tropical atmosphere. Having met, or officered, men of a Sikh regiment in the Middle East during the war, he had a high opinion of their potential as a workforce. So he set out to recruit them direct from the Punjab. The company bought houses near the factory to billet the newcomers until they could find their own way into the Southall housing market. Other factories – there were several similar in the Rubastic Road area – followed suit, and other Indians followed the rubber workers. Great organizers, as early as 1957 there was a Southall branch of the militant Indian Workers' Association and an Indo-Pakistan Cultural Society. A Sikh temple opened there in 1959. This first settlement, south of the railway line that divides Southall in two, became known as *purana* Southall to distinguish it from the newer (*nava*) Southall settled later to the north. By the late 1970s,

nowhere else in Britain does an Asian community now have what Southall provides – its own cinemas (two show only Indian films), travel agents, marriage bureaux, banks, grocers, insurance agents, cafes and clothing and jewellery stores. Three Pakistani newspapers are produced in the town and Southall has developed a whole generation of craftsmen. Asians from all over Britain, and even from Europe, look to Southall for their household, social and cultural needs.[23]

From 1965 Southall was incorporated into the London Borough of Ealing, and by 1991 over 44,000 Ealing residents described themselves as 'Indian'.

Other areas had been settled during the 1950s and 1960s. The run-down Drummond Street area beside Euston Station was known as 'Little India' for a time, and a large Sikh community settled in Woolwich in the 1960s. But the most important extension of London's migrant communities during the later 1960s and early 1970s arose from the Africanization policies of the newly independent nations of East Africa.

Black Africa had already sent perhaps 30,000 of its sons and daughters to London by 1971, mainly Nigerians and Ghanaians. This important migration of West Africans set in from the Second World War. Seamen and students were prominent among the early arrivals. It was largely an inner London migration, most moving to areas like Lambeth, Hackney, Islington and Paddington, already settled by West Indians, with whom they established an uneasy rapport.[24]

But West African migration was to be overwhelmed by the movement out of East Africa of Asians who had gone there as indentured labour on railway construction just as the century opened. In sixty years those indentured labourers had worked their way up in the world. Forming an important stratum of shopkeepers, merchants, professionals, clerks and craftsmen, Asians were displaced from jobs and country as an objective of state policy. Beginning from about 1960, caught up in the surge of 1961–2, sustained in considerable numbers through the next few years as the direction of change in Africa became unavoidably clear, East African Asians were eventually subject to forced expulsions from their homeland. First Kenya from 1967 and then, notoriously, Uganda in 1972 forced the Asians abroad. Some 10,000 Ugandan Asians expelled in August and September 1972 were absorbed into London, just under half the UK total. By 1981 there were nearly 92,000 East Africans in London, nearly all of them Asian, compared with 37,000 ten years before.[25]

East African Asians extended the migrant settlement of suburban London that Southall had begun in the 1950s. The Gujarati Patidars, two-thirds of them from East Africa, were prominent from the 1970s in the north-east suburbs of the North Circular Road (Wembley, Neasden, Golders Green) and in suburban south London (Norwood and Croydon). East African Sikhs from Kenya, sufficiently strict in their religious observance to be tagged 'Victorian Sikhs', settled around Southall rather than in it. True to the suburban ideal, virtually all households became owner-occupiers within just a few years of arrival. And the suburbanizing potential of this particular migration was epitomized by families who quickly made their mark on the league table of wealthy Londoners: the Viranis and the Chatwanis from Uganda and the Bhutessas from Kenya all owned substantial slices of London real estate by the early 1980s.[26]

This suburbanizing tendency of the migrants soon established itself as a dominant trend, despite the popular identification of immigration with the inner city. In 1971 an estimated 58 per cent of black and Asian migrants lived in inner London. But by 1991 the pattern had reversed, with 56 per cent of a minority population now twice as large living in outer London. Reflecting the Southall tradition, most of the outer London minorities were of Asian origin.[27]

The Ugandan Asian crisis of 1972 was the first of several world shocks whose waves were powerful enough to wash migrants and refugees on to the streets of London. There was nothing new in that, of course – remember the Huguenots. But now they chased each other almost without pause.

The 1973 oil crisis seemed to create a new Arab homeland in west London, centred on Bayswater ('Beirut-on-Thames') and Marylebone, but stretching west to Shepherd's Bush and north to Regent's Park, where the great mosque was built in 1978. Shepherd's Bush market was said to be like a Middle Eastern *souk* in the 1970s and so was Queensway in the 1980s. Even the super-rich end of the London property market represented easy pickings for oil millionaires or merchants from Kuwait, Saudi Arabia, the Lebanon and elsewhere, like the Al-Fayed brothers, from Egypt, who bought Harrods in 1985. Arab tourism accounted for 200,000 visitors to London each year by the mid-1970s, rising to an estimated (and almost incredible) million in the 1990s. By 1996, London could be described as the 'intellectual and political capital of the Arab world', with some 150 Arabic papers and magazines based there. The Middle East Broadcasting Centre had its main studios in Battersea, and London was 'the centre for Arab banking, investment, and . . . arms dealing'.[28]

Just a year after the oil crisis, the Turkish invasion of Cyprus in 1974 brought fresh migrations of Greek and Turkish Cypriots without, from the outside at least, allowing much inter-communal dissension to spill on to the streets of Stoke Newington, Harringay and Wood Green. It was in the 1970s, too, that the suburbanizing tendency among the Greek Cypriots got firmly into its stride, moving north through Wood Green and Bounds Green to Southgate, Finchley and Enfield. In 1975 the end of the war in Vietnam brought the first South Vietnamese settlers to London, with more following between 1979 and 1981 especially. By the end of the century, nearly 12,000 Vietnamese Londoners were largely scattered around the inner boroughs of

Hackney, Tower Hamlets, Southwark and Lambeth. In the early 1980s, Kurdish migrants escaping brutal regimes in Turkey and Iraq moved in large numbers to Hackney, Stoke Newington and south Tottenham in particular. Largely a migration of men, especially at first, the Kurds brought with them militant politics grounded in armed struggle. In London this was waged in print from smoke-filled community centres and through loud-hailers at street-corner rallies. Nor was all of their tradition of direct action left behind: there was some fire-bombing of Turkish and Kurdish clubs in Stoke Newington in the late 1980s and early 1990s. Indeed, refugees from civil strife anywhere on the globe ended up in London throughout the second half-century, from Hungary in the 1950s to Somalia, Sri Lanka, and the former Yugoslavia and Romania in the 1990s.

Not all minorities, of course, arrived in London shaken by trauma. World trade sent its emissaries in their thousands to one of the globe's great centres of finance, culture and communications. The 1991 census counted nearly 33,000 Americans (almost three times as many as 1951 in a population one-sixth smaller), 23,000 Australians, 12,000 Canadians and over 17,000 Japanese Londoners – all unprecedented numbers. Britain's entry into the EEC brought London closer to Europe than ever before: 32,000 Germans, more than at any time since 1914; and 30,000 Italians, 21,000 French, 19,000 Spaniards and 13,000 Portuguese – mostly figures never seen before in history and all without a calamity to precipitate them. Even London Jewry had expanded through the migration of *hassidim*, forming in Stamford Hill the largest ultra-orthodox community in the world outside Israel and New York. And, to prove that migration for domestic service did not die with the Second World War, 13,000 Filipinos, nearly three-quarters of them women, had moved to London by 1991 to polish the silver and mind the silver-spooned infants of South Kensington, Mayfair and Barnsbury.

In this astonishingly variegated profile there had to be less room for the British. And London was, indeed, greatly more foreign in the 1990s than ever before. Yet its British character – as a true melting pot of the nations of the UK and Ireland – was peculiarly intact. The Scots, at 113,000 in 1991, held on with extraordinary pertinacity to roughly the same numbers they had contributed across the century. There were fewer Welsh in 1991 (70,000) than at any time for seventy years, but their numbers had always varied greatly, depending on prosperity in the Principality. But the passion for London among the Irish still seemed to know no bounds. They provided the largest group of non-English-born Londoners in 1991, despite huge competition from a host of exporting nations. There were 256,000 Irish-born, 214,000 of them from the Republic, just 27,000 down from the historic peak of 1971. And as always, most were women.

So London was not so much 'less British' by the century's end as less English. Indeed, it was less English than at any time in probably a millennium. A growing separation between London and England, and Londoners and the English, was sharply perceived by newcomers from abroad. Like Kathy Acker, the New York-born novelist, who settled in London from 1967: 'I love London, and I do understand the differences between London and the rest of the country. I could never become English. A Londoner is something else.' Or Shari Peacock, of Iranian parentage but born in Bulgaria and a Londoner since 1975: 'I'd say I was part of London, but not part of England.' Or Paloma Zozaya from Mexico City, in London since 1980: 'I would never live out of London, or far away anyway. Because I go to the local shop in some little village and at first people are incredibly friendly . . . but from the moment you talk with an accent, the attitude changes.' 'They all come to London, not England,' noted Maureen Duffy in *Londoners* (1983).[29] This was a fine irony at the end of a century when the possibility of the break-up of Britain threatened to leave London as merely the capital of England rather than the capital of a United Kingdom.

Despite these changes, London still worked its old magic for the English. The special lure of London for the nation was pinned down by Colin MacInnes, that perennial outsider. He wrote in 1962, but his message would have rung as resonantly for the English at the beginning of the century as at the end, and, indeed, for some centuries before:

there can be found in London, among every class and each locality, more of those true *princes* of our country than in any other English city that I know of. More members of the maquis of the brave, the spirited, the talented, the irreverent, the witty and the physically attractive and unjudging. And more, I must say – in justice to the weaknesses as well as the virtues of my fellow-countrymen – of those gamblers with their lives who are the only true ones. To be a Londoner is always to take a chance: an instinct that manifests itself . . . by their perpetual willingness to take the most improbable human risks. And I believe the spirit of the ugly old indifferent capital encourages the presence of such people; and by its very incoherent informality, enables them to discover one another more freely and happily than elsewhere in our land.[30]

Princes and *princesses* it should have said. For as MacInnes wrote, a storm was just about to break over the heads of two English migrants who might stand for many, and who qualified under most of his criteria: Christine Keeler, from Wraysbury, near Staines, who started table-waiting at Murray's Cabaret Club, Beak Street (Soho) in 1958, when she was sixteen, and Mandy Rice-Davies, from Birmingham, also sixteen when she came to

London for the first time as Miss Austin at the 1960 Motor Show, and stayed.

But there is no doubt that London was touching the lives of fewer English people, and a smaller proportion of the English, by the 1960s and 1970s than it had earlier in the century. In 1951 there were 7.4 million English-born Londoners, who made up 89 per cent of the city's total population. In 1991 this had dropped to 5 million, forming 75 per cent, and looked likely to fall still further. In the same years, the population of London as a proportion of that of England and Wales fell from 18.7 per cent in 1951 to 13.5 per cent in 1991, the smallest of the century so far; that fall, too, looked likely to continue.

The most English parts of London at the century's end were no longer to be found squeezed into the old inner areas round the City and riverside, like Shoreditch, Bethnal Green and Bermondsey. Now they were found out on the furthest edges in eastern Greater London north and south of the Thames: Havering, Barking and Dagenham, Bexley and Bromley. The rest of London was truly cosmopolitan. There were now three great areas influenced by the Caribbean migration, with south London (Southwark, Lambeth, Lewisham, Wandsworth and Croydon) and north-west London (Brent, North Kensington, north Westminster) joined since 1960 by north-east London (Hackney, Haringey and Waltham Forest). Indians and Pakistanis had settled densely in east London (Tower Hamlets, Newham and Waltham Forest) and less so in south-west London (Wandsworth, Merton and north Croydon); but the biggest numbers of all occupied a great arc of north-west London from Hillingdon to Haringey, with the highest densities in Heston (Hounslow), Southall (Ealing) and Wembley (Brent). Brent and Newham, largely due to their populations of Asian origin, housed the greatest proportions of non-whites in London (45 per cent and 43 per cent respectively); both were confidently forecast to have non-white majorities by 2001. The most cosmopolitan areas of all in terms of the variety of backgrounds to be found among their people were the boroughs of north-west London – Camden, Barnet, Brent, Westminster, Kensington and Chelsea, Hammersmith and Fulham, and Ealing. But huge diversity could be found in other parts of inner London, too: Hackney in the 1990s had over 100 home languages spoken by its school population, for instance. Indeed, *most* of London by the 1990s was as diverse as only the world-renowned Soho had been before the war.

So, in something less than forty years, the population of London had transformed itself. London could genuinely lay claim, at the century's end, to be one of the world's greatest cosmopolitan cities. The whole world, of course, had been affected by the same forces that had reshaped the Londoner, and urban areas around the globe had become more ethnically mixed than ever before in history. But it was the sheer diversity of its peoples and their numbers that set London apart. And so, for many, did something else. London was seen as a *successful* cosmopolis, relatively free from the inter-communal strife that had bedevilled the great urban areas of North America, for instance, and free from those 'guest-worker' tensions of continental Europe, where citizenship was denied to migrant populations.

At the end of the century there was, no doubt, some cause for celebration, if only because things could have been much worse. And this, for many years, they promised to be.

Hard Feelings

London was spectacularly ill-prepared for the mass migrations of the 1950s and 1960s. The culture and traditions of the pre-war Londoner were unpropitious for a generous welcome to outsiders, especially to outsiders with black skins. Xenophobia, anti-Semitism, colour prejudice – vices of all classes – overlay a wary antipathy to any newcomer within London's more settled working-class communities: 'He's a stranger, heave a brick at him.' Hostility was bred in ignorance, abysmal ignorance in the case of people of other nations whether near or far, black or white. But especially if they were black.

It was this ignorance that most struck the earliest West Indian migrants. Not that ignorance was all one way. The migrants' cardboard suitcases carried as many stereotypes and illusions as hopes and anxieties. 'What did I know of London?' mused V. S. Naipaul, whose first experience of England was an Earls Court boarding house in 1950: 'The London I knew or imaginatively possessed was the London I had got from Dickens. It was Dickens – and his illustrators – who gave me the illusion of knowing the city.' But the reality, for everyone including Naipaul, was a shock: 'I had come to London as a place I knew very well. I found a city that was strange and unknown.' The Jamaican novelist Andrew Salkey, a migrant of the 1950s, recorded the expectations of many: 'Yet the man had said, and I had believed implicitly, that London's that big cinema of a city where trees are banks and money plus freedom is as easy to come by as leaves on an autumn pavement.' Disappointment set in from the very first moment, as on the rail journey into Waterloo or Paddington or Euston: 'I never think London she look so old and dirty and poor and so different from the way I picture.'[31]

But this ignorance of London was nothing compared to the benighted condition of the natives. Mervyn Morris, a London University student from Kingston, Jamaica, was asked how many wives he had by Londoners who were surprised he spoke English. Eric Ferron was asked if the black washed off and if his blood was red or black. A Jamaican bus conductor told Donald Hinds that passengers would touch his hands to feel if they were warm and that he feared baldness from the number of times his hair had been touched for luck. The 'overpowering, warm, animal smell' of West Indians is a minor obsession of Lynne Reid Banks's 1960 novel *The L-Shaped Room*. Nell Dunn, in *Up the Junction* (1963) records the new urban myth of the 'spades' living off Kit-E-Kat. The East Pakistani settlement in Spitalfields was known, through some geographical stab in the dark, as 'Little Singapore'. No wonder that a migrant recalled his sense of ' "shock to discover people knew nothing about us . . . My loyalty at age 15 was to England. I felt that Jamaica was part of England. The shock was to find I was a stranger." '[32]

And usually an unwelcome one. Of course there were myriad instances of kindness to strangers. But the atmosphere that met the new arrivals was generally mean-minded. It is hardly surprising that indifference, that characteristic component of London life and one of the building blocks of tolerance, should be interpreted by the newcomers as unfriendliness. It made London seem less approachable than other parts of Britain. S. Weeraperuma, a Ceylonese student who spent his first English years in Leeds and elsewhere, considered his introduction to England 'smooth sailing. It was not until I started looking out for accommodation and a job in London [around 1960] that the ugly monster of colour prejudice raised its challenging head.' Eric Ferron found Doncaster, Manchester, Blackburn and Glasgow all friendlier than late-1940s London, where 'People seemed indifferent. You had to have a lot of nerve to approach them because you felt they might rebuff you . . .'[33]

A rebuff could be just around the corner. Black men were attacked at a hostel in Deptford Broadway in the summer of 1949 – two were seriously injured and police had to cordon off the hostel from a crowd of 800–1,000 whites. Lambeth Borough Council called for immigration restrictions as early as 1951, three years after the Brixton welcome for the *Windrush* contingent. There were two nights of trouble in Baynes Street and Prowse Place, Camden Town, in August 1954, when whites tried to turn blacks out of their homes: two houses were briefly set on fire. In the specially fevered climate of Cable Street, where luridly blatant prostitution must have been an oppression for most residents, and where vigilante patrols and petitions against immigration were frequently in the news, white hostility was persistently violent against ' "the blacks and their women . . . It's the blacks. Send the cunts back from where they come from." '[34]

As the numbers of migrants rose in 1954–5 so did hostility to them.[35] And increasingly it focused on an objective difficulty which the migrants were seen to be aggravating: the London housing shortage.

We have already glimpsed various components of the post-Blitz housing problem: 116,000 houses were destroyed and 288,000 seriously damaged. Much of what was left entirely lacked the basic amenities needed for modern living. And the demand for housing was fuelled by the near-recovery of the pre-war population of inner London by 1948, while the number of separate households seeking accommodation actually grew. The London housing shortage revealed itself in rising rents and property values and in hopelessly long council waiting lists: 160,000 families (maybe 750,000 people) on the LCC's list in May 1955, 50,000 in the top-urgent queue alone, with several boroughs (like Paddington) having closed their lists altogether. Households with young children and low incomes found it virtually impossible to find decent accommodation – indeed, any accommodation at all. Objectively there was no crisis: overcrowding and multi-occupation had reduced from 1931 due mainly to middle-class emigration. But it *was* a crisis of expectation, stoked by wartime sacrifice, full employment and the right to reap the rewards of triumphant democracy. But these were expectations that London just could not satisfy.[36]

There could hardly have been a worse time for thousands of West Indians to attempt to settle in London. And thousands there were by the mid-1950s. Their problems were made greatly worse by almost universal discrimination against them in the London housing market. A survey of landladies in 1952–3 showed that nearly 85 per cent would not let rooms to students who were 'very dark Africans or West Indians', and ordinary workers fared even worse. 'No Coloureds', 'Whites Only', 'Europeans Only' were common proscriptions on newspaper adverts for rented accommodation, and on cards in the windows of rooms to let or on newsagents' noticeboards. Even when prejudice was not brazenly advertised, it was met with on the doorstep more often than not. Similarly, the threatened sale of a house to a black or Asian owner-occupier could provoke protests and petitions: property values in Southall were said to have fallen 50 per cent in 1963, and a white Residents' Association formed to halt immigration. And council housing was virtually unobtainable by migrants because of the five-year residence rule that the LCC and most boroughs applied before they would consider rehousing anyone from their lists.[37]

Yet accommodation was to be had, at a price. Prejudice was not strong enough to resist the lure of lucre. It meant, though, that black people were blatantly charged more for a room than whites, often two men each paying the normal rent for one room while sharing it. Cases were reported in 1955 of six men each paying 25s for their share of a single room; £2 for a room was not uncommon where rents for whites would be £1. Similar 'colour premiums' were charged when migrants tried to buy a house – £50 or £100 on the purchase price, a substantial mark-up in the 1950s. Even so, the newcomers were generally willing and able to pay. Almost all were in work at wages they had never enjoyed before and they could secure at least some sort of roof over their heads. A 1955 survey of London West Indians showed that 69 per cent reported 'no trouble finding housing when they arrived' and 47 per cent thought they were not paying too much. By this time, too, a growing number of West Indians and Asians had bought their own homes, the West Indians aided by their tontine or 'pardner' schemes, where a group of people contributed so much a week while one could draw out the whole kitty in turns. The growth in this way of migrant landlords no doubt made finding a room easier, but exploitation of tenants in terms of overcrowding, overcharging, disrepair and insecurity of tenure was just as bad, if not worse.[38]

There were other areas of discrimination. Motor insurance had its 'colour premium', some vicars excluded black worshippers from their churches, only the least pleasant and worst-paid jobs were readily available, and there was discrimination in the workplace. All of these, though, were pinpricks compared to the overwhelming difficulties of the London housing question. Nowhere was more difficult than North Kensington. The worst slums of Notting Dale – Bangor and Crescent Streets – had been demolished by the early 1950s to make way for Henry Dickens Court before many West Indians had moved nearby. Indeed, few migrants lived in the long-notorious Notting Dale. Memories were conveniently short, however, and the area's reputation was quickly forgotten in the charge that it was 'the coloured people' who had 'lowered the neighbourhood'. Parts of North Kensington had long been incapable of being lowered at all.[39]

There were four main clusters of West Indians in North Kensington in the late 1950s. One was north-east Notting Hill, mainly east of Ladbroke Grove in the Powis-Colville area. It was here that Peter Rachman owned a few dozen houses from 1955 to 1960. Rachman made it his business to let to migrants; indeed, he was apparently better known for this tolerant side of his nature than for the aggressive and unscrupulous landlordism to which he later gave his name.[40] To the north of the main railway line to Paddington, the Golborne ward of north-east Kensington had the second main cluster, between Wornington Road and Ladbroke Grove, with the northern portion of Portobello Road running through the middle. Third, to the west of this, around Bramley Road, there was a much smaller cluster inside the northern edge of Notting Dale. And then the fourth area was Kensal New Town in the north-east corner of the Royal Borough, virtually separated from the rest of North Kensington by a railway line and including the notorious Southam Street. Further north and east, outside Kensington altogether, there were large numbers of West Indians in the Kilburn Park, Maida Vale and Westbourne Green areas of Paddington.[41]

It was in North Kensington that London's worst race riots of the century took place for five days and nights in August and September 1958. It was not, perhaps, surprising that resentment against blacks should boil over into violence here rather than elsewhere. Poverty, rootlessness, violence and crime were already part of life in North Kensington. Its poor whites were slipping far behind the rest of working-class London by the 1950s: 'Certain near-slum standards which have vanished from a dockside area like Bermondsey still persist here. Today there cannot be many youngish housewives in London who pad round the house in mid-morning with bare feet; nor homes that an official notes as being in "utter chaos and filthy" . . . Another anachronism is the number of street fights, including those between women.'[42] West Indians found themselves competing for housing in this tense and desperate area. It was a competition made more ruthless by the 1957 Rent Act. This new law precipitated evictions of long-standing unfurnished tenants to make way for furnished lettings, a process that often meant that whites were forced to make way for blacks. The newcomers brought another competitive component, too: sex. The explosive mixture of black men and white women readily provoked sexual jealousy among white men with low self-esteem. In some places the association was particularly brazen, as in the Rachman houses, where prostitutes lodged openly with West Indians, and where basement clubs, loud music, drink and drugs were a clearly visible feature of the Notting Hill scene.[43] Then the rise of the Teddy Boy from the early 1950s, a potent symbol of aggressive white working-class masculinity, seemed to provide muscle to meet the challenge of the newcomers.[44]

There was one further element. Notting Hill had provided a base – there were others – for fascism in post-war London. Jeffrey Hamm ran the British League of Ex-Servicemen and Women from Arundel Gardens from the late 1940s, and Victor Burgess's Union for British Freedom operated from Westbourne Grove.[45] Fascist street meetings, leaflets and wall slogans – 'KBW' ('Keep Britain White'), 'People of Kensington Act Now', 'Niggers Go Home', 'Nigger Leave Our Girls Alone' – all added tinder to smouldering litter.

There were isolated assaults on black men in the streets of west London through the summer of 1958. Gangs of Teddy Boys smashed up cafés used by West Indians and attacked a house in Shepherd's Bush. In the early morning of 24 August, a Sunday, nine white youths went 'nigger-hunting' in a car. Aged seventeen to twenty, mainly from Notting Dale and the White City Estate, they were armed with a knife, chair legs, a car starting handle and 'iron bars torn from street railings', the traditional weapon of the London tough. They assaulted five black men in separate incidents in Shepherd's Bush and Notting Hill; three West Indians were seriously hurt. That same night, there was prolonged rioting involving whites against West Indians in Nottingham. A week later, North Kensington went the same way.

The 'Notting Hill Riots' began around midnight on Saturday 30 August. Crowds estimated at 400 strong attacked houses occupied by West Indians in Bramley Road, Blechynden Street, Lancaster Road and Silchester Road in the north of Notting Dale, where, of all the clusters of West Indians in North Kensington, fewest lived. Majbritt Morrison, the young Swedish bride of a Jamaican – she would later earn a good living as a prostitute – thought it all began from sexual jealousy: 'The Teds were after a coloured man named Sporty who had two young girl friends.' Windows were broken and at least one house was set on fire by a petrol bomb. Weapons included milk bottles, favoured for throwing, choppers, iron bars and knives. On Monday and Tuesday, 1–2 September, petrol bombs and milk bottles were thrown in an attack on a house in Blenheim Crescent, Notting Hill, and windows were smashed in Oxford Gardens. Thousands of people were said by police to be roaming the streets of North Kensington and there was trouble in the Harrow Road, Paddington. Violence continued in the north of Notting Dale, where one of the most famous and dramatic incidents of the riots took place. A black student, Seymour Manning, was attacked by three men in Bramley Road. He ran towards nearby Latimer Road underground station but, nearly overtaken, he turned into a greengrocer's shop and slammed the door behind him. 'A moment later the shopkeeper's wife . . . appeared in the doorway, locked the door behind her, and turned to face the trio of toughs.' With a housewife friend and 'a boy in his teens', she kept what was by now a crowd of angry locals at bay – to shouts of 'Lynch him!' – until the police arrived.[46] Similar scenes took place in North Kensington (on the borders of the Powis-Colville district, Portobello Road and elsewhere) and to a lesser extent in parts of Shepherd's Bush, Paddington and Marylebone until 5 September, when the riots petered out. The streets were tense and conspicuously policed for some time after.

In all some 140 people were arrested. Some of the whites involved lived in Notting Dale, but others came from further afield – White City, Tottenham, Acton, Barnes, Hayes, Greenford, so from the suburbs as well as the inner areas. Despite whites clearly being to blame for the rioting, many blacks were arrested too – for possession of 'offensive' weapons carried for defence, and for responding to verbal taunts. Some whites who defended blacks were also charged. It was in North Kensington in 1958 that black mistrust of the Metropolitan Police first found popular expression.[47]

Exemplary sentences of four years' imprisonment were passed on the nine 'nigger-hunting' youths ten days or so after North Kensington grew quiet. But although the rioting stopped, hostility to blacks did not. Isolated assaults continued as they had before the riots grabbed the headlines. And there was a chilling coda. Kelso Cochrane, a thirty-two-year-old carpenter from Antigua, was stabbed to death in Southam Street (Kensal New Town) in May 1959, apparently by a gang of white youths. In what was to become a familiar pattern, the police discounted any racial motive and his killers were never caught.[48]

The riots and Kelso Cochrane's murder inevitably shed lurid light on race relations in London and in Britain as a whole. Smelling blood, Oswald Mosley returned from self-imposed exile in France to contest North Kensington in the 1959 general election. He lost his deposit, a measure that, however disgruntled some local whites were with West Indian immigration, their traditional political allegiance remained unshaken. For although the riots had brought hundreds of angry whites on to the streets, most locals stayed away, many loathed the violence and some came out to stand up for the blacks. Keep Britain Tolerant groups, inter-racial Harmonist Clubs and International Friendship Committees, established in many parts of London, were one consequence of the riots.

This was the mixed pattern of responses that established itself through the 1960s, the main decade when migration was consolidated from Asia as well as the Caribbean and elsewhere. From the mid-1960s it became clear that, like it or not, the population of London had changed for ever. There was no going back, no possibility of sending 'home' the growing numbers of black children who knew no other home than London. West Indians and Asians were claiming a stake in the capital through these children, through investment in houses, corner shops and other businesses, and through extensive daily contact with whites at work and home: seven out of ten Jamaican men surveyed in London in 1963–4 had social contact with 'English' people and 61 per cent had been in an English home.[49] It was also becoming clearer, especially after the Race Relations Acts of 1965 and 1968 outlawed the most blatant forms of discrimination and incitement to race hatred, that London would not follow the ghettoization model of North American cities, or South African apartheid, despite frequently voiced fears that it would. But it should be said that it needed discrimination to be made a criminal offence for many Londoners to start treating the newcomers like human beings: in 1966–7, forty out of sixty personal applications for housing by a West Indian in London resulted in him being told the rooms were let when they had not been; and in one London lettings agency three-quarters of files were marked 'Whites Only'.[50]

There was worse. Some Londoners could never entirely shake off their fear, mistrust, even hatred of the newcomers. Extremist politics could always find sympathetic resonance, if only at the fringe. And a decade after the North Kensington events a new object for their loathing had materialized: Asians.

Asians more than replaced the declining numbers of Caribbean migrants after 1962. They seemed much more foreign than the West Indians, one reason for the special ferocity of the backlash against them. Another was economic envy, especially of the East African Asians, who began coming in larger numbers as the 1960s wore on. Expulsions from Kenya in 1967 coincided with a regrouping of the far right in a new unity movement, the National Front. Enoch Powell's 'river of blood' speech of April 1968 – 'we must be mad, literally mad' to allow 50,000 dependants in each year, the country 'heaping up its own funeral pyre' – seemed to give legitimacy to the expression of racism. The speech was well received in the East End of London, where most migrants from East Pakistan had settled. Dockers and Smithfield porters struck for the day and marched on Westminster in Powell's support. The speech and its aftermath coincided with civil unrest between blacks and whites in America on an unparalleled scale, and the importation of Black Power ideology to Britain. It seemed that 1968 could be a moment when race relations in London and elsewhere went catastrophically wrong.

Designedly or otherwise, Powell's intervention was literally murderous. Attacks on Asians in the Drummond Street area of Euston prompted the Pakistani Workers' Union to call for vigilante patrols. Blacks across London saw how, post-Powell, racist sympathies could be openly, even proudly, proclaimed. Prafulla Mohanti noted the change straight away in his Wapping GLC flat, where he'd lived peacefully enough for four years. After Powell's speech children started calling him 'Paki' and he and a neighbour's family had stones thrown at them. Mohanti was then badly beaten up in the street: 'After two days I was discharged from hospital. I had developed a fear of the East End and was frightened of living alone in my flat. When I went to see my doctor I could not stop crying.'[51]

By 1968, crop-haired youngsters styling themselves skinheads had aligned themselves as stormtroopers for the militant right, in a far more conscious and dedicated way than the Teddy Boys had ever done in the 1950s. Especially active in Hoxton and Bethnal Green, meeting at pubs like the Bladebone and the Salmon and Ball, fascist haunts for a generation, skinheads and their more discreet cronies carried out attacks both opportunistic and organized on East London's Asians. 'Paki-bashing' was the even more savage updating of the 'nigger hunts' of more than a decade before. Increasingly it focused on the East Pakistani (Bangladeshi from 1971) community of Spitalfields and the scattered Asians who, like Mohanti, had gravitated nearby. Things came to a head in April 1970 with a riot in Brick Lane. Marauding skinheads smashed shop windows and any Asians they could lay their hands on. Through that month there were dozens of assaults, provoking reprisals on whites in Pakistan and diplomatic protests. It culminated in the murder of Tosir Ali, his throat cut by two white youths on his way home from work as a kitchen porter at a Wimpy Bar.[52]

There were further outbreaks of skinhead violence in the East End and Southall from 1970 on. The Ugandan and Malawi Asian expulsions of 1972 and 1976 provoked a contagious fury against London Asians. And more murders accompanied Powell's 'repatriation' speech of 1978. Indeed, Tosir Ali was just the first of many Asian victims in London and elsewhere in these troubled years. They included Gurdip Singh Chaggar (Southall, 1976), Altab Ali (Whitechapel, 1978), Kennith Singh (Newham, 1978), Ishaque Ali (Hackney, 1978) and Akhtar Ali Baigh (Newham, 1980). There were 110 attacks on East End Asians in the autumn of 1977 alone, 'an almost continuous and unrelenting battery of Asian people and their property'.[53] It is necessary to focus on these terrible events if only to remember, first, the victims and, second, that the final outcome for some sort of tolerant multi-racial London hung for many years in the balance.

For every violent racist there were dozens of whites who escorted harassed Asian mothers and their children to school; who helped protect threatened families on council estates in Bow or Poplar; who joined the Anti-Nazi League from 1977 and various militant left groupings; who marched with the Labour Party, trade unionists and others in the East End chanting, 'Black and White Unite and Fight'; who fought the National Front at Red Lion Square (1974, where Kevin Gately was killed), at Lewisham (1977), at Southall (where Blair Peach died, 1979), and elsewhere; who thronged 80,000 strong to the Rock Against Racism Carnival at Victoria Park in April 1978. Throughout London, communities worked desperately hard to involve newcomers of all colours and backgrounds in the festivals that began to be held annually in streets, parks and estates, especially after the Silver Jubilee celebrations of 1977. And the failure of the National Front in the 1979 general election – securing less than 5 per cent of the East End vote – once more showed that politicized racism did not mobilize working-class whites, even in that most disturbed part of London.

The 1980s wrought major changes in the balance of tolerance and intoler-ance in London. They came partly through violence, but violence of a very different kind to the subterranean terrorism of what had gone before. Out of the Black People's Day of Action in March 1981, which followed a disastrous fire that had killed thirteen black youngsters in Deptford two months before, and out of the Brixton 'Uprising' of April 1981 and the summer riots of youth (white as well as black) against police and property, a new self-confidence emerged among London's black communities and a new self-consciousness. 'Come what may, we're here to stay', Linton Kwesi Johnson's response to the Deptford tragedy, expressed the irrevocable nature of multiracial London. There was no going back. And staying demanded equal treatment. When, at Southall in July 1981, local Sikhs set about skinheads and police, they felt 'they had earned their right to be in England permanently [and] elders and young alike became proud of the prowess displayed by their own during the riots'.[54]

No one could argue that the new settlement after 1981 ended all of the difficulties that London's migrant communities had experienced up till then. We shall see more of this (in Chapter 7) in the furious antagonism between some black Londoners and the Metropolitan Police that persisted through the 1980s and into the early 1990s. Nor did murderous assault, provoked solely by the colour of the victim's skin, entirely abate, as we shall also see. There can be no doubting the intransigent intolerance and tension that accompanied the remaking of the Londoner from 1948. But that was not the whole story. And it was no mean achievement that by the end of the 1990s the harmonious racial and cultural diversity of the city – though far from perfect – was cited as one of its most valuable features by citizens and visitors alike. No mean achievement indeed.

Live and Let Live

The migration of black and Asian settlers to London put all its fragile superstructure of neighbouring and community life under immense strain. In the first half of the century, relationships between Londoners, even when they lived next door to each other, had varied greatly according to length of residence, housing type, local tradition, tenure, class, whether inner city or suburb, and happenstance. They spanned the spectrum from mutual aid to internecine terrorism, with a large expanse of arm's-length contact and indifference somewhere in the middle. Now the spectrum had broadened with an influx of strangers never seen before. And such a sudden influx at that. Elspeth Huxley caught the astonishing rapidity of it all in her *Back Street New Worlds* (1964). At the end of 1963 she visited an Islington infants' school, open for ten years. 'For the first three years it had three non-English pupils. By 1960, this had risen to ten. Now there are 163, which represents fifty-five per cent of the roll.' Most were Cypriots but there were fourteen other nationalities, including Irish, West Indian, Indian, Nigerian, Latvian, Czech, Polish, Spanish, Mauritian, Italian and Burmese. The most recent intake had just nine British children out of thirty-five.[55]

Change on that scale and at that pace would have been enough to deconstruct any stable community. Indeed, perhaps it was the very instability of so many of London's inner areas, their constant coming and going around a core who stayed on, that helped London adapt. But immigration was only one of many seismic shocks to the London system. And they all bore mercilessly on the capital in the twenty years between 1950 and 1970.

We have glimpsed three already: redevelopment, gentrification and decentralization. Redevelopment caused huge communal disruption in some parts of London. It followed close on the already extensive dislocation caused by bombing. By 1972, 54 per cent of dwellings in Tower Hamlets had been built since the war, 36 per cent in Southwark and Hackney, and 28 per cent in Newham.[56] In Lambeth, where one dwelling in five was post-war, a survey of Stockwell in 1973 showed that a half of all households were 'relative newcomers', in their present homes for less than five years, compared to about a third in Greater London. Redevelopment was the main cause of this 'major upheaval': 'Some of those displaced have been rehoused near their former homes, but it seems clear that most have not. In estates in Stockwell . . . we meet people rehoused under clearance schemes from Peckham, Kennington and South Clapham.' Such high mobility was destructive of 'neighbourliness, local social contacts, mutual aid and a sense of community'; 'most Stockwell residents . . . have not apparently found it easy to strike up friendships with the strangers around them or to feel at their ease among them'.[57]

Gentrification ensured that population movements would be just as high in those Victorian terraces that escaped the bulldozers in the slash-and-burn 1950s and 1960s. Jonathan Raban lived in an Islington square declared a conservation area in 1969 or 1970, where 'Nigel and Pamela, Jeremy and Nicola' from 'Kensington, or the northern outer suburbs, or the Home Counties' displaced 'the shawled Greek widows, the clowning blacks on the pavement outside the pub, the wise and melancholy Irish and the Cockney wits'. These were pushed or bought out to 'Finsbury Park, the darker reaches of Holloway Road, and brazen GLC estates on the Essex border'. All that remained of them were their cats, 'the real permanent residents of the square, these animals for whom the rest of London, and the wheels of changing social fortune, were not even rumours'.[58]

Both redevelopment and gentrification gave a push to the decentralization of people from London. But other factors were involved. Moving out of London was for many an object of desire. The 'return to town movement' by no means displaced the suburban ideals of private space privately owned, of green fields, clean air and Home Counties English spoken at school. These dreams had pervasively infected the middle classes in the first half of the century and remained powerful enough, among working-class Londoners too, in the last two-thirds. And working-class emigration from London had become a matter of state policy through the New and Expanded Towns initiatives. In the five years from 1966 to 1971 an estimated half a million people moved out of the working-class areas of inner London, 47 per cent to outer London and 34 per cent to the Home Counties. As the main route was buying a house, non-manual and skilled workers were prominent among the movers.[59]

Those who were left behind often wanted to join those who had gone. 'More than half the people living in London would like to move out because they do not like the neighbourhood,' declared a Thames TV survey in 1977. And journalist Paul Harrison, exploring a new Dark Continent at the beginning of the 1980s, discovered that, 'For a large proportion of Hackney's residents, the principal ambition is to get out of Hackney. Away to Romford or to Milton Keynes, to Enfield, Basingstoke – anywhere.'[60]

This sense of being left behind in the older neighbourhoods was sharpened by a feeling that only those who could not leave remained. The elderly were noticed first. Redevelopment had already forced married daughters in 1950s Bethnal Green to move away from their parents. Yet the 'main concern' of the old folk 'was to live near members of their families'. Despite this, allocations policies in the suburban council estates removed any chance of parents moving nearby. 'In Stepney', it was noted a few years later, 'one person in every eight is an old age pensioner and sometimes their presence gives an air of mournful eccentricity to the place.' David Downes, an enumerator at the 1961 census, had a Spitalfields tenement block as his patch, among the grimmest housing that soon-to-be-Swinging London had to offer. He noted 'very poor, old women live alone . . . recluse-like and unapproached except by welfare workers from the nearby Toynbee Hall . . . Age-structure is loaded with the old. The needs of several of these old people approach the desperate . . .'[61]

The younger poor moved into the inner London vacuum created by those moving out, as in fast-gentrifying Kentish Town in the early 1970s: 'semi-criminals, drug addicts, alcoholics, runaway teenagers, the human flotsam which *has* always floated to the slums . . .' Among them were black people and Asians and other newcomers from abroad. For it was the whites with jobs, or skills to get jobs elsewhere, who were moving out fastest: 22 per cent of whites living in Greater London in 1971 were living outside it ten years later, a rate of emigration three times greater than for ethnic minorities. If the figures had been run for inner London alone they would have been much higher.[62]

All these pressures – immigration, redevelopment, gentrification and decentralization – were peculiarly London issues. But there was one last cluster of influences which impacted momentously on the collective life of almost everyone in Britain: privatization. The rise of the domestic – the fetishization of the home, its possessions and its decoration, embodied in television and do-it-yourself and reflected outside the home in the motor car – drove families in on themselves. They were not unwilling victims. The desire for privacy had been an unrequited passion in pre-war London. Now, in the bright new council flats and in the suburban semis, everything was possible. 'We keep ourselves to ourselves' became more than ever a statement of policy and a badge of respectability.

Ashley Smith saw the first fruits of it in the East End in 1961 and quickly recognized what a transformation the new consumerism meant for the unfulfilled ambitions of a whole class. 'Elizabeth' lived in a brand-new Stepney tower block:

There was going to be G-plan furniture in the bedroom – a fitted wardrobe beside the built-in one: a bedside light; in the living room there would be white Venetian blinds and lime green curtains, a velvet occasional chair in pale green, a long John table, a small cocktail bar and a Kang couch which I knew nothing about but which Elizabeth described to me as a special affair in which you could sit both ways and which cost £140. There would be another cabinet in the kitchen and a dining room suite in white and gold. Oh – and the Kang couch is in pale Turquoise and charcoal grey. Elizabeth will not feel abashed when her furniture is unloaded in the sight of 2,000 windows and drawn up through seventeen flights of stairs.

Elizabeth got more out of this than her husband. He hated the flats: ' "He had to give up his pigeons, you know, when he came here." ' And others thought the new way of life had most effect on women: ' "The men don't change much but the women do." '[63] One further change was that women frequently worked outside the home to pay for what went into it. The rise of the 'symmetrical family', with male and female breadwinners, removed many mothers from their old collective role as the backbone of neighbouring and community life.

Under these earth-moving influences everything changed. But the change cannot be construed as some golden age of London community life slipping relentlessly into declining communal values and alienation. There had been no golden age. There may have been nothing, by the 1960s, to compare with Bow Creek or Tabard Street forty years before, but they had always been exceptional. Some 'village' forms persisted into the second half of the century. Indeed, new forms of neighbouring emerged from the changes themselves. Even in the least promising areas – the great council estates – it was not all bad news. And in the middle-class suburbs there may well have been more mutual contact than ever before.

The traditional ideal of a working-class community in inner London was described by sociologists Peter Willmott and Michael Young in the mid-1950s. In Bethnal Green 'we discovered a village in the middle of London'.[64] Here, 53 per cent were Bethnal Green born and bred; mothers could always find housing nearby for their married daughters, if necessary by offering the rent collector a bribe; 'two out of every three people, whatever their sex, have their parents living within two or three miles'; over half a sample of married women with mothers still alive had seen them in the previous twenty-four hours. And there was a distinctive pattern of lengthy local residence, as yet undisturbed by the bulldozer: ' "They're new here – they've only been here 18 years," ' remarked one sixty-two-year-old of her neighbours; and one man couldn't remember a new family moving into his street of seventy houses in the past forty years.[65]

But Bethnal Green was exceptional. And it is difficult to know whether it or Guinness Buildings, just south of the river, was more typical. Here, in 1947–9, Raymond Firth found 'communal unity in crisis', with little visiting between kin, rows over cleaning common parts, 'very little relationship with others in the Buildings, even their neighbours', a fearful isolationism (' "we keep ourselves to ourselves, and then we can't get into trouble" ') and a combative privateness: ' "On the stairs, if the door is ajar and you happen to look in, they ask you what the b— h— you are looking at!" '[66]

Somewhere in between came Hannah Gavron's 1960–61 sample of young wives in St Pancras. Her findings may well have been more typical of the older multi-occupied areas of London before many of the forces of change had fully worked themselves through. She found that over a third had been born in St Pancras, four out of ten had parents living within a mile, and over six out of ten had sisters living nearby. But a quarter said neither they nor their husbands had friends, not one of the wives who claimed to have 'one or two friends' ever had them to visit in the evening, and over seven out of ten claimed to have no contact at all with their neighbours. 'Without a doubt, neighbours played a relatively unimportant part in the lives of these couples . . . [A] picture emerges of a rather isolated, extremely family centred existence, with the focus not on the extended family but on the nuclear family.'[67]

It is clear from this that the new post-war pressures did not have to oppose some immovable object. There was often no traditional way of life which could put up values and mechanisms effectively to resist change. Communal life in most of inner London was essentially malleable, impermanent, contingent. It was a highly workable soil. There were many elements within it ready to embrace the new world emerging, a better standard of home comforts and a passion for privacy prominent among them.

This was certainly the case in the suburbs of outer London, where the majority of Londoners lived throughout the second half of the century. By 1960 most of inter-war London was between twenty-five and forty years old, enough for a second generation to have come to adulthood there. Suburban culture was intrinsically receptive to the new consumerism and the glorification of the domestic. Yet, paradoxically, it was here that patterns of neighbouring and mutual aid were closer to pre-change Bethnal Green than were other more working-class parts of inner London. This was true irrespective of the class make-up of the suburb.

For instance, Dagenham had taken time to settle down as a neighbourhood in the 1920s and 1930s. But by 1960 nearly seven out of ten Dagenham residents had been born there or had lived there twenty years or more, and four out of ten had parents on the estate. By now it was a neighbourly place, and when surveyed in 1958–9 60 per cent of households had been visited by a friend or neighbour during the past week. Mutual aid included borrowing, donating excess provisions, dealing with the rent man or workmen in a neighbour's absence, letting neighbours use domestic appliances and helping with gardening or DIY. On an even more public scale, the estate had produced the nationally famous Dagenham Girl Pipers, a television favourite of the 1950s and early 1960s, and the lesser-known Dagenham Choral Society. By 1994, 51 per cent of people in Barking and Dagenham had local kin, compared to 44 per cent at the end of the 1950s; and an astonishingly high 72 per cent of a sample of local schoolchildren 'had a relative visit their home within the last week'. And it seemed that the post-war LCC estates in the Green Belt – like South Oxhey, Hertfordshire – were fast adapting to this new climate. They grew more quickly into settled places, with far lower removal rates than had been common in suburban council estates before the war.[68]

There were similar patterns in post-war middle-class suburbia. Willmott and Young found Woodford a far more friendly place in the late 1950s than their prejudices had led them to expect. In Woodford, as in Bethnal Green, kinship networks were extensive. A 'remarkably high proportion of all people had friends or neighbours into their homes' – 74 per cent within the previous week – and most visitors were locals living in Woodford. There was far greater readiness here to let neighbours into the home, probably because there was less reason to fear betraying traces of poverty and of scrimping on limited means. In Woodford, people could be more relaxed about their circumstances: 'The common pattern, it seems, is to belong to a small, intimate network of "friends", mostly coming from the surrounding 20 or 30 houses.' This brought with it more mutual obligations than in areas where there was little contact with neighbours, including help with dropping and picking up schoolchildren, or with shopping, and child-care during family illness. In sum, 'People in the suburb are on the whole friendly, neighbourly and helpful to each other.' This friendliness, especially a receptiveness to newcomers, was also found in 'Greenbanks' (outer north London) in the early 1960s, and in the very different London suburbs of 'Rivermead' and 'Purlbridge' around 1975.[69]

When Woodford was revisited in a follow-up study by the sociologist Anthea Holme in the early 1980s, friendliness continued a feature of life there. In general, 'immediate neighbours were known "very well"'. Yet this was by now an area much affected by decentralization (just 16 per cent of Holme's sample were considered to be 'local'), by thirty years of intense consumerism and privatization, and to some extent by Asian migration.

Holme also revisited Bethnal Green, an area in the very front line of all London's post-war changes. Perhaps here the surprise was the continuity with 1950s Bethnal Green. Only eight out of fifty families sampled had no birth or long-term local connection and 'the single feature most often commented on was its friendliness'. There were, though, worries about Bethnal Green becoming less friendly and Holme also considered the bond of matriarchal kinship to be 'loosening'. '"Coloureds"' were blamed by some for bringing the area down, and friendliness did not extend to the Bangladeshis in the west of the borough: '"They're filth,"' remarked one woman of '"the Indians"'. But the biggest problems seemed to be associated with redevelopment and the growth of the council estate rather than the results of immigration. Redevelopment had affected forty-six out of fifty in the sample. On the council estates, mothers were deprived of their old devices for manipulating or fiddling their daughters into a home nearby. It was these 'flat-dwellers' who were most alienated from neighbours and other Bethnal Greeners:

As many as 14 (not including the recently arrived families from Bangladesh) did not know either one or the other [neighbour] at all. And among the majority who did, it was mostly 'just to say hello to' or 'quite well'. Only a handful knew them very well; a minority regarded them as friends. As for other people in the block or on the estate, the majority knew fewer than ten people.

In thirty years of utterly momentous change, there was much in 1980s Bethnal Green that had been familiar among St Pancras housewives twenty-five years before; it may not have been the Bethnal Green of old, but it was still recognizably a London pattern of getting on together.[70]

New patterns were also emerging. The early years of migrant settlement forced newcomers to put aside differences of background and culture, and the prejudices they involved, when faced with white Londoners to whom they were all black strangers. West Africans and West Indians, despite some mutual avoidance, were frequently found sharing houses where one of them was the landlord: like a West Hampstead house owned by a Ghanaian and home in the 1960s to himself and his brother, six West Indian women, a Greek-Cypriot couple, an Irish single mother and her two children, and a West Indian man. These could be fragile marriages of convenience, as the Lagos-born novelist Buchi Emecheta found while living in Wellesley Road, Kentish Town. Her landlord was a Yoruba, she was an Ibo, and he harassed her out of her home during the Nigerian civil war.[71]

Kinship networks were just as important as an aid to communal life among the migrants as among long-settled white Londoners. This happened surprisingly early. At a Yoruba christening in Hackney in the 1960s, the guests included the father's half-sister and her husband, his brother and his wife and two children, his sister's husband's brother and his wife, a male relative of his mother's mother, and an uncle, all resident in London. In the Louvaine Road area of Battersea in 1978, 52 per cent of ethnic minority locals had kin in Battersea or elsewhere in south London. Migrant institutions creatively filled some of the gaps in mutual aid that longer settlement might otherwise have provided: voluntary organizations, funded especially by local councils from the late 1970s, provided specialist advice about benefits or housing or jobs, or gave subsidized meals and entertainments, or formed clubs and housing associations specifically for migrant groups. Hackney, for instance, in the 1980s was home to dozens of organizations run by and for West Africans, West Indians, Pakistanis, Indians, Vietnamese, Turkish Cypriots, Kurds and others. And length of residence among migrants in some areas of London was quickly replicating the old patterns found among white Londoners in 1950s Bethnal Green or even 1920s Bow: as with 'Mrs Greenaway', from Jamaica but in Brixton for twenty-seven years – 'London beyond Brixton was almost totally unfamiliar to her.'[72]

If immigration brought its own patterns of neighbouring to London, so did gentrification. The combination in the same street of owner-occupation and private renting, mixed with some council-owned 'street properties', proved a more dynamic, adaptive and tolerant environment than the council estate. The mixture of classes seemed to make it easier to cope with a mixture of races, too. Prafulla Mohanti escaped from his Wapping council flat to gentrifying Pimlico around 1970: 'The moment I moved in I liked its cosmopolitan character, with Italian and Indian shops, fish stalls, and open-air markets', and the Irish newspapers for sale outside the Catholic church on Sundays. Maybe competition between blacks and whites for jobs and services was just not so intense in areas like this; in Stockwell, in the mid-1970s, those who were most positive about the area were white professionals and black people.[73]

There was in general an anything-goes non-judgemental inclusiveness about these changing areas, where so many were newcomers. It aided the integration of strangers while never demanding assimilation to any cultural norm. How could there be conformity to one code in an area like Notting Hill: ' "Fairies, tarts, coffee-bar wierdies, unwashed geniuses, juvenile delin-quents, old ladies living and dying under sheets of newspapers on the benches by the playgrounds. Drunks and thugs and Maltese pimps, all living cheek by jowl with people like you who are madly normal, and people who are madly chic . . ." '[74] The gentrifying areas celebrated difference, at least until the very rich merged hegemony with homogeneity. But that did not happen everywhere or at once, and for most of the years of migrant consolidation – right through the 1950s, 1960s, 1970s and early 1980s – they were markedly fluid. Some, like David Thomson's boozy Camden Town in 1980, seemed destined never to be set in aspic or capable of simple categorization, where novelist Beryl Bainbridge might join Thomson for a chat in the pub on the same day that he is involved in an attempt to persuade Tipsy Davy, a Scottish alcoholic and rough sleeper, to take himself to hospital before his leg got too bad to be saved from amputation.[75]

The inclusiveness of the gentrifying areas was aided by a number of factors. The 'town hall' had paradoxical effects here. The threat of demolition could unite a neighbourhood, forming a community almost overnight irrespective of class or race or background: Gillian Tindall counted '[s]ome eighteen residents' and tenants' associations' in one square mile of Kentish Town around 1970, many of them set up to fight the council bulldozers.[76] But local councils could also play more positive roles, especially in giving migrants a stake in their new neighbourhoods.

Education, for instance, was a partial but unsung success story of the first generation of multiracial London. Not that education authorities got it all right: the dissatisfaction of black and white parents with the quality of their children's education was a powerful inner London theme from the 1970s on. But from the beginning of mass migration the authorities fought hard to be inclusive, to treat the children of migrants with respect, to value their culture and to make them feel essentially welcome. Parents were similarly valued, aiding integration between mothers from all backgrounds at the school gate and in the life of the school. Only in Southall (later Ealing), from the early 1960s to the late 1970s, were misguided attempts made to bus Asian children away from their local schools once a notional 'quota' had been exceeded. Elsewhere in London things were different, and Buchi Emecheta has left a heartfelt testimonial to her children's primary school in Camden Town in the early 1970s: 'before I knew my way about the universities and polytechnics, my friends were the Head and teachers of St Mary Magdalene. The school became an extension of our home . . .'[77] Had the education authorities made the same mistakes as the Metropolitan Police, then the prospects for race relations in London would have been bleak indeed.

Education assisted integration on the council estates, of course, as well as the gentrified areas. But the second positive achievement of local authorities impacted especially on the older housing areas and the suburbs. For councils were generally far more ready to make house purchase loans to migrants than most building societies in the early years. The LCC (from 1963) and GLC (from 1965) were especially far-sighted here, filling the gap left by other lenders who, largely through prejudice, were unwilling to give mortgages to 'risky' investors making risky investments. Some boroughs followed the GLC's lead. By 1966, it was estimated that half the black owner-occupiers in London had a mortgage either with the GLC or Lambeth Borough Council. House purchase was immensely popular among migrants, who did not wish to be dependent on unreliable landlords, or could not get help from the council. Some 40 per cent of a 1973 sample of Jamaicans in London were home-owners, and among Asian migrants owner-occupation became almost a matter of religious observance: 82 per cent of London Mauritians were home-owners by the mid-1980s and apparently 100 per cent of East African Sikhs. Owner-occupation was inevitably higher in the smaller suburban properties of outer London, the larger multi-occupied houses in the centre generally deterring all except absentee landlords, local councils and well-off gentrifiers.[78]

But it was all much more difficult on the council estates. West Indian and Asian migrants were not much met with as council tenants until the very end of the 1960s. As well as the lengthy residence qualifications on waiting lists which discriminated against newcomers, there was the common practice in redevelopment areas of excluding furnished tenants from rehousing once their houses were knocked down. This enabled councils to demolish run-down multi-occupied housing without rehousing the new migrants who had crowded into them, for unfurnished tenants were almost invariably white Londoners of settled residence. When black people *were* rehoused, it could lead to white protests, as at the Loughborough Estate, Brixton, in the mid-1960s for example. Just how reluctant councils were to be seen rehousing the newcomers was shown at the time of the Ugandan Asian crisis in 1972. Faced with 10,000 Asians needing housing in London, councils offered up just seventy-five dwellings.[79]

Even by then, though, things were beginning to change. The Land Compensation Act 1973 required councils for the first time to rehouse virtually all those affected by redevelopment or rehabilitation, irrespective of tenure; thousands of black tenants in houses bought by councils were immediately protected from eviction. In addition, most migrants had by now been in one place long enough to overcome the residence bar on waiting lists. And they were having less competition from the very stratum whom council housing was established to help – the skilled (and generally white) working class, clerks and shop assistants who were now solving their own housing problem by buying houses in the suburbs or the New Towns. All these tendencies were given a mighty push in 1977, when councils were made responsible for rehousing most families made homeless or likely to become so. The later 1970s produced a massive increase in the numbers of black people housed on council estates in London.

For reasons of policy – or because of the institutional racism of procedures that linked the poorest accommodation to migrant tenants – black households began to end up on estates where no one else wanted to live. Often these were the worst of the inter-war estates, neglected and outmoded after forty years' heavy use: White City (Hammersmith), Kingsmead and Haggerston (Hackney), Boundary Street and Bow Bridge (mainly Tower Hamlets), Kennington Park (Lambeth) and Kingslake (Southwark). They were joined by the new 1960s system-built estates that so quickly lost caste. As on the Holly Street Estate, Hackney, where 63 per cent of allocations between 1970 and 1975 were to whites but where between 1977 and 1980 77 per cent went to black households. And on Broadwater Farm, Haringey, where about half the households were black and where, in 1980, 70 per cent of lettings were to homeless families.[80]

Council estates produced the most hostile environments of all for black and Asian newcomers. In Tower Hamlets, the Canada, Montmorres and Hollybush Gardens Estates were 'known as "no-go areas" among the Asian community' in the late 1970s. Others petitioned against the rehousing of Asians and when their pleas were ignored kept them out by organized abuse, intimidation and thuggery. Conditions were so bad that they led in 1978 to debate about the need for segregated estates for Bangladeshis in the East End, a proposal fortunately taken nowhere. In 1982, on the Holly Street Estate, 'frightening and indiscriminate racial warfare' broke out between black and white tenants over who should control the Saturday night disco at the community centre. And incidents of racial harassment remained a sordid feature of life on many London estates right through the 1980s and 1990s.[81]

Yet even on the estates the picture was not uniformly hopeless, despite the dislocating effects of redevelopment, privatization and immigration. On Broadwater Farm, just after the disastrous riot of 1985, 21 per cent of tenants said they knew no neighbours; but 28 per cent said they knew most and 51 per cent a few. And Broadwater Farm was an estate with a quite remarkable record of pulling itself up by its bootstraps, led by a powerful black tenants' leader, Dolly Kiffin, and facilitated by Haringey Borough Council. From 1981, when things had been at their worst, the residents had formed a Youth Association, day nursery, mothers' project (with a library, keep fit and advice sessions, a Turkish women's group and English classes), a play centre, pensioners' lunch club, summer festival, community launderette, food cooperative and workshops for sewing and photography. No sign here that the collective enterprise of the 1930s Watling Estate had disappeared from London's working-class culture. Kinship and neighbouring on the 'Parkview Estate' in Hammersmith similarly revealed no terminal malfunction: 77 per cent of tenants had at least one relative living 'locally' and 62 per cent felt able to call on neighbours in an emergency.[82]

Of course, even within the same estate there were those who felt good and those who felt miserable. Tony Parker's 1983 study of a south London council estate, *The People of Providence*, was a powerful corrective to Paul Harrison's one-eyed cataclysmic view from Hackney of the same year. Parker's sensitive ear caught the diversity of responses that 'Providence' evoked among its tenants: 'Oh yes, it is a sad place now'; 'the community sense has all gone, there's no question about that at all'; 'from my neighbours I have never received anything but courtesy and friendliness'; 'I think that's the thing that's struck me most of all about living on this estate . . . all the people being so nice and friendly'.[83]

This was the complex reality that underpinned a general tendency to recovery that became apparent from the early 1990s. But things got worse before they got better. The proportion of lone-parent families on the worst estates rose dramatically. Squatting – often by a motley of confused youth loosely grouped under the banner of 'Class War' – increased in the 1980s and peaked in the early 1990s, bringing anarchy to some estates. And in others, whole neighbourhoods could be terrorized by a single family involved in drug dealing, receiving stolen property or organized burglary: in Hackney's Kingsmead Estate, a flat could be stripped of its contents while the tenant was restrained at knife-point. In circumstances like these, those who could get out did. Better-off tenants continued to leave the public sector by migrating to suburban homes they owned themselves or exercising their 'right to buy' from the council. Being a council tenant had become, by the 1980s, the most visible proxy for 'being poor'.[84]

In the worst cases, improvement only came about with the break-up of the council estate. This usually involved extensive redevelopment, with much of the land then sold off for rebuilding by housing associations (for renting) and private house-builders (for sale). In Holly Street, before demolition began to recast it, 44 per cent of tenants surveyed claimed to have witnessed a violent incident on the estate in the past year; that fell to 2 per cent among residents of the first new houses occupied during 1995–6. Those experiencing 'fear of the area' reduced from 60 per cent to 16 per cent. By 1997, 48 per cent of tenants in the new homes said they had friendly neighbours and 71 per cent had visited, or been visited by, them since moving in. On Hackney's Clapton Park Estate, which had also undergone substantial redevelopment, including the demolition of tower blocks, a survey noted 'a strong sense of the estate as a community', especially among young people. Even so, despite many local achievements like these across the capital, the most unpopular places in the country in which to live at the end of the century were the inner London housing estates of Tower Hamlets, Islington, Hackney and Southwark.[85]

The majority of people experiencing improvements on estates like Holly Street and Clapton Park were non-white. And by the 1990s, in virtually the whole of inner London and much of its suburbs, the experience of living among black and white neighbours was now thirty years old and more. Adults had been children at school together and their children were now sharing the same experience, often at the same schools. Inter-marriage and mixed-race relationships – such a bane of the 1950s and early 1960s, raising spectres of 'mongrelization' for race-purists – were now more an accepted fact of life than almost anywhere else in the world. That was an extraordinary measure in itself of how attitudes had changed, not least in working-class London. The politically organized and violent hatred of the 1970s had virtually disappeared. Whether this was for good or just for a time was too soon to tell, and the bombing campaign in Brixton, Spitalfields and Soho of early 1999 showed what destructive power one lone extremist could wield. But sheer weight of numbers had left little scope for collective intimidation by the 1990s. The building blocks of community – length of residence, kinship, a balance between privacy and mutual obligations, the capacity to throw up community leaders, that London indifference which at its best meant 'live and let live' – had never entirely disappeared from most neighbourhoods. Borough councils had devised strategies to uncover and punish racial harassment and to restrain the worst 'anti-social' tenants, whether white or black. Some action was being taken at last to invest in those places that had gone so utterly to the dogs in such a short time.

At the century's end this was still a fragile settlement. The future of collective relations in London remained uncertain. But the disasters that had seemed to stare London – or parts of London – in the face in the late 1950s and in the 1970s and first part of the 1980s had so far been avoided. A settlement had been reached, even if it was not always a comfortable one – as in post-'Uprising' Brixton, fast gentrifying at the century's end: 'For now [1987, but true enough at the end of the 1990s], the new residents, wine drinkers in Habitat-furnished houses adorned with glossy Athena prints, must coexist with the old Brixton of obstreperous, proud, middle-aged Jamaican women, menacing-looking black youths, and the pounding bass-filled sounds of reggae music on Saturday nights and Sunday mornings. It is not always a harmonious marriage.'[86]

A marriage, though, it did not have to be. Indeed, London's multiracial character at the century's end looked less like a marriage or melting pot and more like separate cultures negotiating to share the same space. It was remarkable, forty-odd years after the main Greek Cypriot migration for instance, how very distinct London Greek Cypriot culture remained: the language, the grocers' shops, the travel agents, the jovial weddings of London Cypriot girl to London Cypriot boy, even 'shawled Greek widows' on Green Lanes, Harringay, or in Palmers Green. Or the London Italians, revived by a constant flow of new blood from Italy, in close touch with the village communities of 'home' (even though the head of the London branch of the family might have left it in the time of the *fascisti*), and much more noticeably 'Italian' than sister communities elsewhere in England or Scotland.[87] Or the West Indians, with their own Pentecostal churches and rhapsodic evangelism, their own hairdressers, pay parties and spectacular weddings. Or Sikhs and Muslims, with their London temples and mosques, cinemas and sari shops, community centres and yet more weddings of youngsters marrying 'into' the community. And so on.

The private spheres of London's diverse communities were marked more by this separate development than by 'assimilation' to an English – or even London – way of life. In London, remarked Hanif Kureishi in *The Black Album* (1995), 'the races were divided. The black kids stuck with each other, the Pakistanis went to one another's houses, the Bengalis knew each other from way back, and the whites too . . . The divisions were taken for granted, each to his own.'

This did not necessarily imply mutual antagonism or dislike or mistrust. No doubt there were some or all of these on occasions and in certain places:

'where did such divisions lead to, if not to different kinds of civil war?'[88] Yet perhaps this semi-detached development provided the private space where difference could find expression while providing for cultures to come together in a safely negotiated and circumscribed public space. For separate development was never complete segregation. There were always points of conjuncture and combination – routinely, of course, at school and at work, in shops and nightclubs, in council chamber and meeting rooms, and on buses and tubes; but also at moments when coming together could mean much more.

Festivals, conscious celebrations of the diversity of Londoners, were prominent among these more meaningful moments. Most spectacular by far was the Notting Hill Carnival. Its origins, so recent, were yet lost in myth. Some gave the start date as 1959, others 1961 or 1962, others 1966; some said it was started by whites, others by Trinidadians; others still said it sprang from an older Notting Hill 'Pageant' tradition resurrected for the new times.[89] Whatever, by the 1990s the three days of carnival were attracting a million celebrants, and 'carnival arts' had become a backstreet industry all the year round from Dalston to Brixton. The Chinese New Year celebrations in Gerrard Street, Soho, also attracted huge crowds. But in many ways the most impressive events were local – the annual Kurdish Festival in Clissold Park, Stoke Newington, for instance, or the many street festivals and borough shows which brought together a fertile mix of local cultures.

Other elements, too, were genuinely assimilationist in character. Popular music was probably the most fruitful, where the fact that Louis Armstrong was black saved at least one West Indian from Teddy Boy trouble on the tube; and where even skinheads could not remain immune from black musical influences.[90] And professional football, where black players and white sympathizers valiantly fought off racist abuse from the terraces. And eating out, where the traditional (or subtly adapted) foods of scores of migrant cultures could be found on every Londoner's doorstep. Just how far London had travelled in this single direction is evidenced by Jane, who lived in the *L-Shaped Room*. Pregnant, she had a sudden craving for curry; but 'where am I to find curry, in God's name, in this benighted neighbourhood?' The place, reader, was Fulham, and the year, 1960.[91]

Forty years on, the most dramatic changes in the history of the Londoner had worked themselves through with patterns of collective give and take that remained recognizable from the earlier years of the century. In the process, they had created a culture hugely enriched by a world of diversity. And, as if all this were not enough, there was one other change that had also been negotiated in these same years without catastrophic dislocation: nothing less than the biggest transformation in the London economy since the industrial revolution.

PART THREE

Economy

5. Capital and Labour

Mart and Workshop of the World: 1900–1914

London is a city of trade. Commerce, the buying and selling, wholesale and retail, of goods of all kinds from machine-guns to money, is the circulatory system of the London economy. Yet there was always more to London than that. Until the mid-1960s the capital was also the nation's main manufacturing district. 'Made in London' was a mark of reliability and sophistication. This dual strength in making and selling gave London an economy as diverse, robust and productive as that of many European nations. From the middle 1960s, though, London's manufacturing industry virtually bled away, along with the port that had fed it with raw materials and shipped its commodities all over the world. But despite that impoverishment, changes in the way the world circulates capital had once more put London at the heart of the 'global economy' by the end of the 1990s.

Looking back across the century, two trends were most apparent. One was the increasing specialization of the London economy, its declining diversity and its narrowing focus on particular elements of world commerce. The other, going hand in hand with the internationalization of its population, was the offshore separation of London's economy from the nation's, so that, in its guise as 'world city', London at the end of the century seemed to belong more to the world than to Britain.

London had, of course, been a world city in 1900. Indeed, it had been 'the world's metropolis' for a generation or two before that. It constituted without challenge the world's greatest port, its greatest bank and its greatest workshop. But in 1900 the port came first.

It is impossible to exaggerate the place of the Thames in the economic life of London for almost two millennia. The produce of the world was brought upriver for consumption by Londoners or for onward transfer. The nation's goods sailed downriver to the sea on their way to clothe and furnish an empire and to indulge luxury everywhere. Wherever Thames water found its level, commerce and industry fetched up on its shore. Wharves and factories were deposited along the banks of its navigable tributaries (the Wandle, Deptford Creek and the Ravensbourne, Bow Creek and the Lea, Barking Creek and the Roding) and along the canals that opened into it, manmade to bring the river into the heart of the city and to link London by water with other great towns.

The map of London's principal factories and businesses drawn for the Royal Commission on London Traffic in 1904 shows commerce and industry in a continuous belt along Thameside from Barking in the east to Brentford in the west, narrowly clinging to the river banks at the extremities but bellying out as the river approached the centre. There, factories and warehouses clustered in a great knot at the City and Southwark and in the West and East Ends, with straggling industrial suburbs stretching north through Finsbury and Islington and south into Camberwell. It was only on either side of this central point that industry pulled clear of the river's tidal sway. That domination of the Thames was a pattern set for centuries. It had been exaggerated rather than dislodged by the frantic growth of Victorian London.

Yet at the beginning of the century the river and port faced a crisis. In 1900 much of the port's infrastructure was almost a century old, the product of a revolutionary modernization in the middle of the Napoleonic Wars. Then the old quays and wharves from Billingsgate to Deptford had been greatly extended by a system of docks, cut behind the shoreline to expand the areas for loading and unloading, to improve security and to aid onward movement into the great city. The West India Docks on the Isle of Dogs; the London Docks in the Pool of London east of the Tower; and the East India Docks on Blackwall, downriver of the Isle of Dogs, were all excavated and built between 1800 and 1815, hedged in by a bustling hinterland of wharves and giant warehouses. Each dock group was built and run by a separate company and so were the hundreds of wharves on the riverside. Burgeoning trade led to further competition and expansion. New companies built St Katherine's Dock by the Tower of London in the late 1820s; the London Docks were extended about the same time and again in the 1850s; Victoria Dock opened at Canning Town (West Ham) in 1855; the Surrey Commercial Docks on the south side of the Pool at Rotherhithe (where some docks were quaintly called 'ponds') were greatly extended in the 1860s and 1870s; Millwall Dock (on the Isle of Dogs) was opened in 1868 and the Royal Albert Dock (mainly East Ham) in 1880. By then the upper port was largely complete. Only the King George V Dock, just south of the Royal Albert, was added in the twentieth century, planned from 1910 but not opened until 1921. The lower port at Tilbury, some twenty-six miles downriver of London Bridge and on the north side of the Thames opposite Gravesend, was also Victorian, opened mainly for passenger traffic in 1886.

Despite company mergers and rising trade throughout the nineteenth century, the port was in severe difficulties by the start of the twentieth.

Huge investment and company cooperation were needed to dredge silt from the river to accommodate modern ships of deep draught. Neither money nor mutuality was forthcoming, for the port was at war with itself. Dock company revenues were choked off by ultra-competitive price cutting and by the freedom of wharfingers and shipping companies to have their barges unload and load from the docks without charge, the so-called 'free water clause'. By 1899 the 'financial collapse' of the dock companies 'was almost imminent'.

The dock companies' proposal to charge the wharf- and ship-owners dock fees per barge, which they introduced as a bill in Parliament, caused uproar. Yet something had to be done. So in 1900 the Conservative government set up a Royal Commission to inquire into the port's problems. It showed itself not to be afraid of radical solutions. The Commission reported in 1902 and urged nationalization of the dock companies, their assets to be vested in a public authority on behalf of London and the nation. It was seven years before the various interests could be pacified with sufficient gold and political safeguards for the Port of London Authority (PLA) to be established, in 1909. The PLA proved a great success. It dredged the Thames, regulated dock labour, extended the docks and improved gateways to the river. After a generation of bickering, it heralded a new era of prosperity that survived two world wars and retained London as the world's greatest port for the next fifty years.[1]

The port was London's biggest employer. Something like 20,000 men – labourers, porters, stevedores (skilled men who loaded ships), blacksmiths, crane-drivers, coopers, tally clerks, lightermen (the river's single-handed bargemen) and others – worked at the docks on an average day before the First World War. But another 10,000 on average were turned away at the dock gates, men who, knowing the vagaries of the shipping trade and the fluctuating demand for 'hands' it produced, clamoured each day for work. This huge crowd of casual and more regular workers provided a pool of labour from which employers could take their pick. At the various 'calls' at the dock gates, foremen shouted out the names of men they wanted, or pointed to those they did not know but wished to select, or – for mischief – threw brass tallies into the crowd of hungry men to allow the fittest to win a day's work in the ensuing bloody scramble. It reminded some observers of a Roman slave market and was one of the sights of Edwardian London. As late as 1937 a man was reportedly crushed to death in the daily press for jobs.[2]

Within the million-ton storage capacity of the enormous port, the handling of coal bulked largest. London ran on coal until well into the second half of the twentieth century, consuming 16 million tons in 1900 and 21.5

million in 1938. Coal for industry, gas and electricity production mainly
arrived by collier to the port; coal for domestic hearths, about half the
capital's demand, came by rail, mainly into Euston and St Pancras and
then into 400 or so railhead sidings, wharves and coal depots across the
metropolis.[3]

Coal was moved from the stacks by horse-drawn waggons, and so until
around 1919 was virtually every other commodity in London. In that year
horse-drawn trade vehicles outnumbered motor lorries by three to one on
London's streets, and motors were not comfortably in the majority until
around 1930. As late as 1939, Watney's kept 100 horses at their Pimlico
brewery, about a fourth of their team in 1900. So the horse remained an
integral part of London's transport economy for another generation after it
was displaced from pulling passengers. It needed a service industry of its
own, an army of drivers, stableboys, grooms, farriers and vets still 64,000
strong in Greater London in 1921. The traditional London stables – around
a courtyard where horses were driven to the first floor up slippery ramps –
were a feature of the backlands behind main streets, ripe for conversion to
industry once the horses left.[4]

Coal and the other commodities brought into London by ship and rail
had their own markets for wholesale exchange, and each market had its own
specialist labour force for buying and selling and transit. Cattle shipped live
to the port from Ireland and Canada were moved for sale and slaughter at
the Metropolitan Cattle Market at Caledonian Road, Islington – about
280,000 animals were killed there each year after the slaughterhouses opened
in 1907; carcasses not sold there would be taken to Smithfield, the London
butchers' great wholesale market, along with chilled and frozen meat
imported from Argentina, Australia, New Zealand and elsewhere. Fish,
mainly brought in by train from the east-coast ports but some landed by
boat, was sold wholesale at Billingsgate, game and poultry at Leadenhall,
fruit and vegetables and English and foreign flowers at Covent Garden and
Spitalfields, hides and skins at Bermondsey leather market, dogs at Club
Row (Bethnal Green), horses at the Elephant and Castle, costers' donkeys
at Caledonian Road Market every Friday, diamonds and other jewels in the
shops and on the pavements of Hatton Garden, old jewellery on costers'
barrows at Duke's Place ('a receiver's paradise'), Christmas stocking fillers
from pavement sellers on Ludgate Hill and furs at the Hudson Bay Company's warehouse at Lime Street. Wool, rubber, metals (copper, tin, lead
and zinc or spelter), coal, hops, corn and shells were all sold at their own
London exchanges. Grain, timber, oilseed, soya beans, flour and tallow were
sold at the Baltic Exchange, the 'most cosmopolitan' market in London, which
moved to new premises at Jeffrey's Square, St Mary Axe, in 1903. Some 97

- **A Traffic Lock at the Mansion House,** *c.* 1900
  Road congestion was London's most enduring problem. Scenes like this led to a Royal Commission on London Traffic in 1905, but by the end of the century gridlock threatened not just the centre but the whole metropolis.

- **Little Italy, Holborn,** 1907
  Looking down Eyre Street Hill to Warner Street, the heart of the Italian community in Holborn. Little Italy was one of London's several migrant areas that maintained a distinctively foreign flavour in the early part of the century.

- **Providence Place, Stepney,** *c.* 1909
  A typical London court, built in the early nineteenth century. Its like was to be found all over inner London before the First World War. Almost all had been cleared as slums or for commercial redevelopment by 1939.

- **The Siege of Sidney Street, 3 January 1911**
  Winston Churchill, guarded by armed police, looks on as troops besiege the East End hideout of Russian anarchists who had shot dead three City policemen a month before. Two anarchists and a fireman died in the blaze that ended the siege.

- **Monkey Parade, Rye Lane, Peckham, 1913**
  The joyful gathering of young men and women in the streets on fine weekend evenings was a feature of London's towns and villages until the 1920s. Here the Monkey Parade overwhelms a respectable suburban high street by 10 p.m.

- **Troops Leaving Victoria Station for France in the First World War**
  The First World War was a defining moment for London. Around 60,000 of its men died in the trenches, some of these no doubt among them. And the war had revolutionary effects on London's economy, its night life and on women's lives.

- **Poplarism, 1921**
  With high unemployment in the East End, Poplar Council refused to collect rates for the LCC and the Metropolitan Police. Thirty Poplar councillors, here seen marching to the High Court to state their case, were imprisoned for contempt.

- **Dock Work, 1930s**
  The port was the largest employer of manual labour in London. Here skilled shipwrights and engineers repair a ship's propellor at the brand-new King George V dry dock, East Ham.

- **Labour Gets Things Done!**
  Herbert Morrison, new Labour leader of the LCC, helps demolish Waterloo
  Bridge, a Regency masterpiece, in June 1934. Its replacement, a twentieth-
  century masterpiece, adorned the river in time for the nearby Festival of
  Britain in May 1951.

- **Going to the Dogs, 1938**
  London's relative immunity to the slump showed in the huge crowds with
  money to burn at greyhound racing, a London craze from 1928. Ten years
  on and a meeting is captured by Bill Brandt, one of the capital's great visual
  chroniclers.

- Boys of Webb Street School, Bermondsey, 1890s and 1930s
  Eloquent representation of social change in working-class London either side of the First
  World War. Webb Street ran out of Tower Bridge Road, just south of London's main
  leather-making district.

- Coronation Celebrations at Bangor Street, Notting Dale, May 1937
  This was probably the most notorious street in London's twentieth century until its
  demolition in the early 1950s. Its poverty, its links with costermongers and gypsies, and i
  antique dress styles are all on display at the Coronation tea-party.

- **The Glass Man, Petticoat Lane**
  The street market was one of the enduring features of London life.
  The sheer theatre of the Sunday-morning market at Petticoat Lane,
  Spitalfields, is captured here, *c.* 1936, by the wonderful Hungarian
  photographer L. Moholy-Nagy.

- **Caledonian Market**
  The Friday-morning Pedlars' Market at Caledonian Road was one of
  the great sights of London. World-beating bargains – and the world's
  biggest distribution centre for stolen goods – made this an unmissable
  lure for dealers and collectors.

QUEEN VICTORIA STREET, No.23 is seen collapsing in flames, Sunday 11th May 1941.

- **The Blitz, City, 10 May 1941**
  'The Full Moon' of 10–11 May 1941 was the most destructive raid of
  London's Blitz. One dramatic moment among many, the collapse of 23
  Queen Victoria Street, provides a memorable image of London's most
  dangerous time.

- **Bank Station Disaster, 5 February 1941**
  The 'largest crater in London' opened when a bomb
  exploded in Bank Station, killing fifty and
  completely destroying the point where seven City
  main roads met. But in three weeks the crater was
  cleared and shored and this steel bridge thrown
  across it. Things were back to normal by May.

- **Rescue at Bexleyheath, 1940**
  Although the East End, the port and the City suffered most in the Blitz, no part of London
  escaped the terror of bombing. In all 30,000 Londoners were killed. Here a factory worker
  is rescued after a raid on a south-east London suburb.

per cent of the nation's tea was shipped to London, 350 million pounds of it each year; it was sold, along with sugar, coffee and cocoa, in the London Commercial Sale Rooms, Mincing Lane. Here, around 1900, Robert Hyde, founder of the Industrial Society, bought and sold at the weekly dried fruit auctions – 'Valencia and Muscatel raisins from Spain, sultanas from Smyrna, dates, figs, plums and currants' – jostling with brokers from Armenia, Turkey, Spain, Greece and Italy. The youngest salesman at the auctions, just seventeen at the time, he proudly wore the Rooms' customary silk top hat.[5]

At the celebrated Number 6 Warehouse, London Dock, its ivory, cinnamon, spice and bark floors laid out the world's treasures to the view of merchants before the weekly auctions. It took twenty-one African elephants to die for a ton of ivory and over 284 tons were imported in 1913 for carving into billiard balls, piano keys, cutlery handles and trinkets. This would have included narwhal tusks, hippopotamus teeth ('sea-horse tusks'), rhino horn and mammoth or 'fossil' ivory from Siberia: 'I have seen as many as 50 mammoth tusks on the Floor at once,' recalled A. G. Linney in the 1920s. Spices came in their distinctive containers: nutmegs in mahogany 'Singapore boxes', cinnamon in bales like cheeses, boxes of cloves wrapped in sacking. Tobacco arrived in huge American hogsheads, its quality assessed by PLA samplers, whose 'judgment is never questioned'. And in the 'Crude Drug Department', around 1902,

There is the dried juice of aloes in gourds, and even in monkeys' skins; and there is sarsaparilla from Jamaica. We see cinchona, camphor, and strophanthus, a deadly poison from Africa. There are drugs in horns, and in barrels; bottles of musk, sold by the ounce; a parcel of musk-skins [the scrotum of the musk deer]; bales of ipecacuanha; gums, myrrhs, eucalyptus, sandal-wood, and turmeric.

In London there was a market for everything: 'the centre of the world's market for human hair is in Soho', with the convents of France, Spain and Italy the main suppliers of dark hair, 'while fair hair is obtained from the women of Germany, Austria, Hungary, and Alsace-Lorraine'.[6]

Money made all this go round. And the City of London was the hub on which the money of the world spun. There was never a time, before or since, when the world's finances were more in thrall to the City of London than in the twenty years or so before 1914.

London exchange markets set the world prices of staple commodities like metals, wool and rubber, and the principal foodstuffs. London was 'the world's chief lender'. Its accepting houses (merchant banks) guaranteed the credit arrangements necessary for world trade through the 'bill on London'. Its joint stock banks converted these same bills into gold should merchants need it for new speculations. By adjusting the bank rate, the Bank of England ensured that London attracted sufficient funds to fuel investments across the globe. The exchange rates of the world's currencies were adjusted to the price of gold, and that price was fixed in sterling and fixed in London. When the world's governments wished to raise capital for new railways or canals or cities or wars, it was to London they came, and to a handful of merchant bankers whose international creditworthiness was greater than that of most governments. The houses of Rothschild or Baring or Kleinwort, London's 'financial institutions specializing in foreign credits', were 'at the height of their power'. The financial fortunes of nations ebbed and flowed to the gravitational pull of the London bank rate and the London bankers' view of their prospects. The City's invisible earnings from banking, insurance and shipping cancelled out the pre-1914 trade deficit on commodities; and the nation's trade surplus was created by dividends and interest on Britain's enormous foreign investments, mainly in the Empire and South America, and all negotiated through the City.

The Edwardian City, with the Bank of England, held the world's purse strings in its hands. But it was also expanding its influence on the pockets of the nation. In the years before 1914 the joint stock clearing banks, headquartered in and around Threadneedle Street, were centralizing and transforming the financial affairs of Britain's citizens. The absorption of private banks by the clearing banks, and then the amalgamation of the clearing banks to form institutions of apparently inexhaustible resources, had begun in the mid-nineteenth century but did not conclude until the twentieth. It was in the early years of the century that the banking habit took hold in Britain, with the appearance of high-street branches and the universal acceptance of cheques. Deposits and transactions per head of population rose by about 25 per cent between 1906 and 1914. Amalgamations of banks and mergers of insurance companies – who became major institutional investors in domestic industry before 1914 – fuelled the redevelopment of the City with headquarters that trumpeted their new majestic status, as we saw in Chapter 1.[7]

The City had a vital role within the London economy, as well as the world's and the nation's. At first sight, the commission on raising a loan in the markets for Mexican railroads would seem to have little impact on the lives of ordinary Londoners. Yet some 364,000 people worked in the City in 1911, an increase of a fifth since 1891. And the City's global manoeuvres required an army of services to grease the wheels – and palms – of international finance: accountants, actuaries, adjustors, advertisement agents, appraisers, arbitrators, auctioneers and auditors; barristers, solicitors, clerks, conveyancers and law-hand copyists or scriveners; hairdressers and wig-makers, tailors and tobacconists. As the City's was business made of paper, most important of all were the printers and stationers. In 1904 there were some twenty-two printing firms in the City each employing 100–200 people, eighteen with 200–500, and three with over 500 workers. The biggest firms served the 'Street of Ink' or Fleet Street, the newspaper capital of the whole nation; but many printed the shares and securities and bonds and bills and cheques and even the banknotes that the City and the world depended on. They printed and bound its account books and diaries and calendars, and made envelopes, tracing paper, carbon paper, and notepaper embossed to impress.

The City's printers and bookbinders remind us that the heart of London's commerce was also to a considerable extent its manufacturing heart. Printing and other machines, gold plate, cigarettes, clothing, china, glass, cork and beer were all made in City factories employing 100–500 workers in 1904. In the smaller workshops, in backyard outhouses and the basements and garrets of old houses long turned over to industry, hundreds of enterprises made almost anything capable of manufacture: from bows and arrows and scabbards to weighing machines, from asphalt to whips, balloons to black lead, cattle food to dog biscuits; and of course the tools of the City's trade – pens (quill, steel, gold), pencils (aluminium, lead), ink (marking, writing, copying), rubber bands, gum, paper fasteners, rulers, sealing wax and writing slates.[8]

The City revealed in microcosm the extraordinary diversity of London manufacturing and its importance in the local economy. In the County as a whole in 1901, the occupied population divided roughly into two-fifths employed in manufacturing and three-fifths in services, including retail, transport and building. Just as the City formed a huge market for the nearby printing and stationery trades, so Londoners formed the largest and wealthiest domestic market in the country. And a large proportion of those engaged in manufacture were making things for Londoners alone. London 'brews and drinks her own beer', according to Charles Booth – indeed, 'more than her fair share' – and this self-sufficiency was true of many other necessaries of London life. Like clothing (but not boots and shoes, increasingly imported from Northampton and Leicester); cigarettes and cigars and everything for the smoker; bread and most canned or bottled foods for immediate consumption; furniture (but not chairs, bought in mainly from High Wycombe); everything for the horse in the way of saddlery and harness; every vehicle for private and public conveyance, including omnibuses and the new motor cars (but not so many bicycles, mainly made in Birmingham and the West Midlands); most building materials, most manufacturing machinery; and all its own gas, water and electricity. Many of these industries also exported to the rest of the country, the Empire and the world. London was the national and imperial centre of production for items like scientific instruments (surveying and optical in particular, by 1900 under increasing competition from Germany), electrical instruments, light bulbs, musical instruments (with Germany also strongly competitive in piano-making) and armaments of all kinds.

This enormous range of industries tended to cluster in districts. So some parts of London were defined as much by their industrial character as others were by their connection to fashion or the shifting nuances of class.

Heavy industry, which depended on huge consumption of coal and raw materials, or industry that made a particular stink, tended to cluster on the river downwind of the main residential areas. A walk along the industrial rim of the Isle of Dogs around 1900 revealed:

Works succeed one another all along the shore. Here is a list: Vulcanizing wood yard; Bermuda's yard; oil-storage wharf; Cubitt Town Dry Dock; Rice-mills Wharf; boiler-makers' works; the Poplar Dry Dock; Alpha Wharf; saw-mills; decorative earthenware works; copper-depositing works; lead-smelting works; iron, lead and glass warehouse; oil-wharf; iron and bridge works; oil, colour, paint, and varnish works; disinfectant fluid works; iron and brass foundry; antimony and gold complex ore works; metal and machinery works; the Platinum Metal Company; shipbuilding-yard; the Patent Cask Company; van and cart works; oil-mills; tank and cistern works; ships' stores; chemical works; steel-plate factory; gas-tubing works; boiler maker's works; Electrical Power Storage Company; barge-building works; a timber-yard; a Stave and Cask Syndicate; a Coal and Coke Company; bottle-makers; mast, block and oar makers; lubricating oil works; a Preserving Company; Chain and Anchor Wharf; hard-wood merchant's yard; sack, bag and canvas factory; sail-maker's works; steering-gear works; wire-rope maker's works; foundry-furnisher's works.[9]

Immediately downriver of the Isle of Dogs, West Ham was another district of large factories. Outside the County boundary, it was immune from LCC by-laws restricting 'offensive trades'. Its County Borough Council offered the cheapest electrical power in London at a time when most electricity was produced at varying tariffs by local councils; and its nineteen miles of canals, docks and river banks gave easy access to coal and raw materials brought in by barge. Along the Thames and up the Lea to Stratford, the great sugar refineries of Tate and Lyle clustered near to Keiller's jam factory; guano works found suitable neighbours in manure processors and in Knight's soap factory, varnish, oil and colour works, and in indiarubber and telegraph works making telegraphic and electric cable, one giant firm employing 3,000 men. Some 600,000 footballs a year and millions of golf balls were made in one Silvertown rubber works. Further east still, the giant Beckton gasworks in East Ham were the largest in the world, covering 350 acres and employing several thousand men. Opposite Beckton at Woolwich the South Metropolitan gasworks, giant chemical works, the Royal Arsenal and Dockyards, and Siemens's telegraphic cable works, employing 1,500 men, lined the southern bank of the river.[10] The picture of London as a pre-industrial economy of small workshops and sweated homeworkers, primitive when compared to the north and Midlands, has been much overdrawn.

Further west, London's industrial neighbourhoods made a rich functional patchwork. In most instances they shared space with residential occupiers, usually the same street and often the same house or backyard. So the Royal Army Clothing Factory, employing over 1,000 women in 1904, was a close neighbour to St George's Square in residential Pimlico; and not far away around the same time, an investigator found 'a frock-coat of beautiful cloth' being finished 'in one of the poorest rooms I have ever entered, where a Polish Jewess, neurotic and ill, was making perfect button-holes' at 1¼d each.[11] In rooms like that there was no dividing line between home and workplace, life and work.

Clothing was, indeed, one of London's great industries. It employed nearly 250,000 workers living in inner London alone in 1901, two-thirds of them women. Large clothing factories employing over 200 workers were found all over east, south-east and central London. But the main clothing districts were Soho and Whitechapel. In both, Jewish immigrant workers were prominent, but clothing was far from exclusively an immigrant industry.

Soho was the workshop district pre-eminently for bespoke gents' tailoring. Some of that sort of work was also carried on in the small workshops and homes of Whitechapel and west Stepney. They – together with the large clothing factories of Westminster, Finsbury, the City and elsewhere – were the home of ladies' tailoring and the gents' wholesale trade, clothes made for retailers to sell off the peg; and of 'wholesale bespoke', making up customer orders taken by cheaper retailers in imitation of the West End's Savile Row. Whitechapel, too, was the centre of the very poorest end of London clothing. This was the so-called 'Kaffir trade', garments 'of a cheapness and shoddiness almost unknown to the consumer in this country', for export to the black nations of South Africa; seams were sometimes stuck together with soap and parted in the first shower of rain.[12]

Clothing illustrates the diverse range of markets for which London produced – from Park Lane diamond-mine speculators like Barney Barnato to

Kimberley diamond miners themselves – and its extraordinary range of production units. There were large factories 'where every mechanical appliance is employed, and where subdivision of labour is carried to the extremest point'; workshops 'of all dimensions, which may be on the premises of a retailing firm, or in those of a small master [living] in the same room or rooms'; and homework in the poorest slum or in comfortable quarters. It was also an industry of 'extraordinary efficiency in the art of small-scale production', quick to adapt to changes in fashion and to switch from class-specific home demand to export shoddy. Despite the growth of great clothing factories in Leeds and elsewhere, and despite these antique appearances in a world of 'modern' factories, London had the most productive clothing industry in the country.[13]

Differently organized from clothing, London's furniture industry turned a single district into something approaching one giant factory. That was Shoreditch and west Bethnal Green. Its centre was south of Old Street in Curtain Road ('The Road'), where Shakespeare's plays had first been performed at the end of the sixteenth century. It spilled out into Finsbury, where there were several large factories, and then followed the Lea to Tottenham as the tendency to seek a competitive edge by centralizing mass production demanded more floorspace. Furniture production was extensively subdivided, but each part of the production process was usually carried on by separate businesses or independent craftsmen on their own premises. So that a cabinet-maker with an order for dining-room suites (one couch, two armchairs, six small chairs) would buy the timber in planks from a local merchant, then mark it out and take it to a sawmill; if fine fretwork was needed, that would be done by another sawyer working on his own account at the same mill; carving would be done by a carver on his own premises, and so would veneering, marquetry, inlay or engraving, each by its own specialist; the 'maker then planes, shapes, dowels, glues, cleans and glass-papers' the frames and would then take them to the Curtain Road wholesaler who had given out the order; the wholesaler himself would arrange French-polishing and upholstery. All these functions were carried out at the most competitive prices within a five-minute walk of the wholesaler's or maker's premises. One of the distinctive sights of east London until the 1950s was a muddle of frames 'in the white' being wheeled on a barrow from one craftsman to the next. Everything (glue, screws, castors, buttons, filling, fabrics, tools) the 1,000 or so furniture-makers' workshops needed in Edwardian Shoreditch and Bethnal Green could be had nearby, either direct from the manufacturer or from specialist dealers. This was a wholly self-sufficient industrial district, merging seamlessly with a residential population of some 240,000 people, many of them working in the furniture industry. As in the clothing trades, Jewish migrants were prominent among cabinet-makers too.[14]

There were many similar but smaller patterns of local concentration in London's other industrial districts. Like Bermondsey's leather industry, its tan-yards and markets distinctively flavouring the air of Tanner Street, Market Street and the area south of Tower Bridge, where 'Men in the streets tramp about in heavy clogs; some have high boots, while others have their legs tightly bound in matting to protect them from the damp and dirt in which they work.'[15] Clerkenwell's watch- and clock-making, and its scientific instrument and electrical equipment industries, still gave the area great character in the Edwardian years: a watch might go in and out of twenty different workshops here in the course of its manufacture, and a 'watchmaker' might spend a lifetime knowing just how to cut a fusee or coil a hair-spring and have no clue about how a watch got put together.[16] The Lambeth potteries, including Doulton's, behind the Albert Embankment and St Thomas's Hospital, made everything in stoneware: sinks and lavatories, chimneypots and drainpipes, and bottles for beer, gingerbeer, blacking and ink. Camden Town was the centre of the piano-making trade; Little Italy the place for organ-building; Hoxton made cardboard boxes; bicycle-makers found strength in numbers at Holborn Viaduct; Enfield was the home of the rifle called after it; Vauxhall gave its name to a famous motor car; and there were so many French jewellers working near Fitzroy Square that 'the trade name for this district [is] "La Petite France"'.[17]

London's service industries also clustered in districts they made peculiarly their own: laundries in Kensal New Town and the Bollo Bridge Road area of South Acton, both known as Soap Suds Island to locals; medical men in Harley Street and Wimpole Street – Pill Island, some called it; lawyers in Holborn, Fleet Street, Temple and the Inns of Court; banking around Threadneedle Street and insurance around Holborn Circus; music publishers around Denmark Street, travel agents in Cockspur Street, car showrooms and garages in Great Portland Street, estate agents in Maddox Street, film-makers in Wardour Street and broadcasting in Marylebone – some of these only coming into their own in the 1920s and after.

Traditional ties and local connections did not indicate a conservative habit of mind. Above all, London had an inventive economy. That did not necessarily eliminate industrial backwardness: watch-making, shipbuilding and silk-weaving were on their last legs before 1914 yet still clung on to outmoded working methods in the face of foreign or provincial competition. And many jobs, from banking to bricklaying, were inherited by sons from fathers, perhaps especially on the Thames: 'The name of the river postman has been Evans since 1809 [it was reported in 1934], and the men have all come from the same family.'[18] But there were always rising industries ready to take the place of the hidebound – especially, in the years before the First World War, chemicals, processed foods, vehicle manufacture and electrical engineering.

The last two were the most inventive of all. At the John A. Prestwich (JAP) motorcycle works at Tottenham, around 1911, R. M. Fox and his workmates marvelled at the new machinery that seemed constantly to revolutionize production:

Scarcely a week went by but some new glistening mechanical contrivance entered the workshop . . . Pride of place was given to one intricate monster which occupied the centre of the shop. This was an automatic machine which ate up hexagonal rods of steel and turned them into sparking plugs . . . When this machine first entered the workshop groups of men stood round watching it perform its miracles.[19]

Much car manufacture in the early years in London depended on French engineering know-how, with some French firms setting up London factories. And there was a notable west (and south-west) London bias to the industry. Legros and Knowles had their factory in Hammersmith, AC Cars made 'Amazing Cars' at Thames Ditton from 1900, the Century Motor Engineering Co. made the 'Tri-Car' with a French engine at Willesden from about 1902, Napiers established a large factory at Acton Vale in the same year, Clement-Talbot were at Ladbroke Grove, Vauxhall were at Wandsworth until 1905, when they moved to Luton, and Wilkinson Sword made motor cycles in Acton from 1909. The owner of the Albany Motor Co., Scrubbs Lane, was an enterprising inventor, and the engineer W. F. Watson worked for him around 1905:

He was one of the first to experiment with a rotary engine, not unlike the aeroplane engines of to-day [1935], and of course there were many others trying out improvements on internal-combustion engines, carburettors, stearing-gears, gear-box designs, crank-cases, clutches, brakes – every conceivable thing. These people brought their inventions to places like the Albany where they could personally supervise the construction of the child of their genius.[20]

This inventiveness encouraged the development of the aeroplane as a peculiarly London product. The first aeroplane factory in Britain was opened by Handley Page at Barking from 1909; Airco at Merton and De Havilland at Fulham merged in 1914 and moved to Hendon in time for war; speedometers and altimeters and pressure gauges were perfected in Clerkenwell.

Clerkenwell's extensive scientific instrument trade also gave London a sound launch-pad for the fine work involved in the new electrical industries. These had developed in nearby Hatton Garden from the 1880s, where Sebastian de Ferranti had perfected his electrical switches and transformers, and Robert Paul the 'kinetoscope'; and the cathode ray tube was developed in Clerkenwell from 1902.[21] But electrical engineering had developed a suburban presence through Edison, who brought electric lamp making to Ponders End, Enfield, in the 1880s; GEC made Osram lamps in north Hammersmith and Siemens their own light bulbs in Dalston from 1908. In 1911 two-thirds of the nation's electric lamp makers lived in the counties of London and Middlesex alone.[22] Other products were also developed in London: the Gramophone Co. Ltd made its first HMV machines from 1899 and Hubert Booth his first vacuum cleaner a few years later.

As production expanded to meet consumer demand, this suburbanization of industry expanded too. Growing firms moved to greenfield sites where land and rates were cheaper, and where a reservoir of skilled labour had already moved from the 1880s on. This was a strong trend in the early years of the century and not one confined to the 'new' industries: printing and furniture-making, where gains were to be had from centralizing production in one big factory, had already begun to move out from central London by 1900. Most of these migrating businesses moved to north London, especially along the Lea Valley (Enfield, Edmonton, Tottenham, Walthamstow, Hackney, Stratford), but also Willesden, Acton and Ealing in the west, so that the residential clerk and artisan suburbs of late-Victorian London had also become established industrial suburbs by 1914.

All this world of work outside the home was largely a man's world. No part seemed more so than the City:

The streets of the City are thronged at morning, evening and noonday; in the morning, by countless tribes of men of all sorts and conditions, but all in black, all in tall hats, and all hurrying to their respective offices or places of business; in the evening, by the same men returning; and at noonday, by the same men swarming, like ants, out to lunch, at their particular club, restaurant, or humble 'aërated'.[23]

No other district of London was quite so segregated. But industries certainly were. All transport – the railways, docks, road haulage and passenger transport – was almost exclusively a male domain; so were the building industry, vehicle manufacture, and gas, water and electricity supply. Yet women played a more or less important part in all other sectors of manufacturing, including printing and bookbinding, metals, furniture (mainly upholstery) and tanning. And in some manufactures, notably clothing but also tobacco (mainly cigarettes) and food (except bread), women were in the majority by 1901.

In the London professions, women had only just begun to make their mark at the turn of the century: ninety-two medical doctors; no barristers or solicitors but 184 'law clerks' (so might the formidable Sally Brass of *The Old Curiosity Shop* have found herself enumerated); no clergyman but 1,508 'missionaries, scripture readers and itinerant preachers', and almost as many nuns and sisters of charity; while women teachers and lecturers outnumbered men by almost three to one. There were 19,000 women 'commercial or business clerks'; 5,000 Civil Servants and local government officers; and a further 500 or so in banking and insurance. Some of those, at least, must have been beginning to brighten up the City's black. One important industry, of course, was almost exclusively female – domestic service. Nearly a quarter of a million women domestic servants lived in the County of London in 1901, over 90 per cent of them unmarried. In all, the County's workforce was 34 per cent female in 1901.[24]

Ten years later the figure was 35.4 per cent, as an additional 50,000 women living in inner London had entered the labour market, compared to just 4,000 extra men. The main growth areas for women's employment were food manufacture, shopwork and business clerks, telecommunications and the public service, professional occupations, metals manufacture and paper and printing. Domestic service had declined by 23,000, almost a tenth of the 1901 figure, reflecting the suburbanizing tendencies of the servant-keeping classes. The biggest rises in women's employment were in the more middle-class outer areas of the County: Fulham, Hammersmith, Lewisham, Wandsworth, even Woolwich. Here, the home of patriarchal artisanship where a working wife was a shameful thing and even daughters were not expected to work outside the home, the number of working women rose by 22 per cent between 1901 and 1911, as daughters moved into respectable positions as shopgirls and clerks. A similar trend was detectable in outer London, where the female commuter first emerged as a new-century phenomenon: there were over 10,000 women clerks and shopgirls living in the main outer London suburbs in 1911, compared to fewer than 4,000 a decade before.[25]

All this growth in employment for women, none of it at the expense of men, was a sign that the London economy was continuing to expand. Indeed, working London at the beginning of the century looked utterly invulnerable. And the key element in its invulnerability was its diversity, as Charles Booth eloquently recognized:

Ship-building may leave the Thames; silk-weaving decline in Spitalfields; chair-making desert Bethnal Green; books be printed in Edinburgh or Aberdeen; and sugar-refining be killed by foreign fiscal policy; but the industrial activity of London shows no sign of abatement. Individuals and individual trades may suffer, but her vitality and productive energy, stimulated by a variety of resources probably unequalled in their number and extent by those of any other city either ancient or modern, remain unimpaired. London is supreme not only in variety, but in total magnitude.[26]

And its unassailable position was to be strengthened even further by four years of total war.

Brave New World: 1914–40

The First World War, which did so much to halt London's outward growth, which turned off the streetlights and closed the pubs, at the same time gave a great push forward to the capital's economic development. It had repercussions for the next fifty years.

There were several reasons why the war should have affected London's economy in particular. As the hub of the nation's road, rail and port networks, London was where men, munitions and supplies converged before embarkation for the short journey to France. Just as important, London was the Empire's arms and armaments capital. London and war shared a long history. Woolwich was the site of Henry VIII's arsenal and since then had matured as the home of the Royal Ordnance Factories – the Royal Gun Factory, the Carriage Factory, and the Royal Laboratory for experimental explosives and ammunition manufacture. The Royal Small Arms Factory (RSAF) at Enfield had first made muskets in the Napoleonic Wars. Clerkenwell had also long been a cradle of destructive invention: Hiram Maxim had perfected his machine-gun at 57 Hatton Garden in 1894, for example. London's fertile motor industry was crucial even in a static war where supplies and men had to be brought quickly to the front. London was an important base in chemicals production, helpful for making explosives and poison gas; and it was home to the nation's electronic communications and scientific instrument manufacture, especially vital when German imports ceased overnight.

The enormous capacity of London manufacturing was turned over to war production and everywhere it fattened on the proceeds. In north-east London the RSAF was greatly extended, employing over 10,000 people and turning out 2 million Enfield rifles in the four years of war. Nearby,

National Projectile Factories were built along the Lea Valley from Ponders End to Hackney Marshes. In the north-west, aircraft and munitions factories were run up at Colindale and Park Royal; the local motor industry changed from car production to army lorries, and the engines for the first tank were made in Wembley. In the east, a disused soda factory in Silvertown (West Ham) was taken over by the Brunner Mond Corporation for the manufacture of TNT: it exploded in January 1917, killing at least sixty-nine people and flattening property within a half-mile radius. In central London, Cossor's at Clerkenwell switched production from fluorescent tubes to wireless transreceivers and valves, needing to move to larger premises at Highbury in 1918. In the south-east, the Woolwich Arsenal, employing just 8,500 men in June 1914, grew to be the largest factory on a single site in Europe, with 75,000 working there in May 1917. Backstreet engineering firms turned into gold mines as if by alchemy: as, for instance, in Tottenham, where Thomas Glover's gas meter and stove works made radiators, and aeroplane and gun parts, employing 2,000 against at most 200 before the war; and where JAP worked on government contracts for dispatch riders' motor cycles and aeroplane parts. All over London, war work penetrated to unlikely industries – to the garment trade, where work on 'the khaki' brought unheard of riches to East End sweatshops; to furniture, where cabinet-makers turned out bunks, tables, benches, boxes and even army huts; to the manufacturers of electrical wiring, and rubber goods, and watches and paint and canvas and an endless list of requisites to satisfy the greedy maw of modern warfare.[27]

The most important of these wartime industrial developments was in Park Royal, an area which straddles the borders of Willesden, Ealing and Acton. In 1915, this wedge of wasteland just west of Willesden Junction, had been an 'unsuccessful showground' with a few factories on its fringe. It was then appointed the inspection and storage point for bullets made in Enfield and the Midlands before being entrained for France. Government shell-filling factories were soon put there, and then others found vacant sites elsewhere in west London: Hammersmith, Willesden, Acton, Hendon, Hayes, Greenford and Southall. All this marked a westward shift in London's industrial capacity which had significant effects on patterns of suburbanization after the war.

London's swollen manufacturing base and the mobilization of hundreds of thousands of its men for the front produced a demand for labour never before seen in British industry. It created a labour supply where none was thought to exist. Within the first full year of war the supply of working men had more or less dried up. Engineers and other craftsmen migrated to London to work in the new government munitions factories. They could virtually name their price. Skilled men in west London moved from one firm to another and back again, demanding a pay rise with each move, until Munitions Act prosecutions stopped the practice. For probably the first time in London's history, the casual labour fringe of under-employed men in building, road transport and the docks entirely disappeared. The average percentage of unemployment among London building workers, 9.6 per cent in 1914, fell to 1.9 per cent in 1916 and kept below that until the Armistice, despite the catastrophic fall in building work. The docks were so short of men that as early as January 1915 dockers had to be drafted in from South-ampton and east-coast ports; and soldiers of the Transport Battalions were directed to dock work under military discipline from 1916.[28]

When the casual labour supply was exhausted, then demand ate into the so-called 'residuum' of 'unemployables'. Gone from Victoria Station were 'those strange figures from the underworld, who begged, touted and stole there night by night. The war has charmed them all away.' Gone were 'All the itinerant musicians', according to a London diarist, 'disappeared' by August 1916. 'Old men have come out of the workhouse, and sick men have come out of the infirmary', and bad men came out of the prisons. The London workhouse population fell by a third between 1914 and 1918, and the casual wards, which had taken in over 29,000 homeless or destitute people in the first year of war, needed to open their doors to only 6,000 in the last. In 1914 the LCC's winter survey of the homeless sleeping in the street and under arches found 434; in 1918, just nine. Even the London lunatic asylums, in a sharp reversal of an otherwise rising trend from 1890, lost over a fifth of their inmates between 1915 and 1919.[29]

When the supply of men, any men, was exhausted, there was a return to child labour on a scale not seen since the 1860s. Nationally, some 600,000 schoolchildren had been lawfully released 'prematurely' for work by 1917. Then there were the children unlawfully put to work. In London, sum-monses for non-attendance at school increased sharply from around 7,500 in 1914 to 12,500 in 1918. High wages and endless job opportunities were irresistible seductions. 'Boys used to be boys in England,' complained one Fleet Street employer in 1916. 'They are tyrants now . . . [If] you are not careful they fold their tents like our proverbial Arabian friends and silently steal away to any one of the dozen or more better jobs that stretch out their hands for them.'[30]

Most startling of all, the war drew 1.4 million women nationally into manufacturing, commercial and service industries. London led this trend, especially in commerce and office work, where women permanently dis-placed men from routine positions. But the very significant wartime rise of the 'business girl' was overshadowed at the time by women in engineering and transport. During the war some 400,000 girls and young women across the country left domestic service for better-paid and more liberating employment – at the factory bench, on trams and buses ('conductorettes'), on the railways, driving lorries, delivering milk, and dozens of other jobs which men had always kept to themselves. The new tube station at Maida Vale had an all-women staff in 1915; only women worked at the LCC ambulance station at Bloomsbury; 'Thousands of girls are earning their living in City offices'; and more than 28,000 women and girls were filling shells and bullets at Woolwich Arsenal by 1917 (they were known as 'canary girls' because the TNT turned their skins yellow).[31]

Some of these wartime effects were largely transitory. The employment of women in transport went quickly into reverse when men were demobilized. The post-war slump of 1921–2, which hit London engineering especially hard, re-created the labour surpluses that had been absorbed by war so that only the most skilled men were secure in a job. But some changes were to have a lasting effect, and none more so than the expansion of London's industrial capacity, especially in west London.

London was not immune from the great slump that overshadowed the 1930s in much of the rest of Britain, and Londoners were not insulated from unemployment or the fear of it. But compared to the industrial areas of South Wales, Scotland and north-east England London was a boom town. And it was a boom town that grew to over a fifth of the nation's population as more and more Britons flocked to claim their share of it.

Work was the key. Of Britain's net increase of 644 factories employing twenty-five or more persons in the years 1932 to 1937, 532 or 83 per cent were located in Greater London. Around three-quarters of these were entirely new enterprises and most of the rest were firms expanding and migrating from inner London. Workers from all over the country left home to take up the opportunities these new jobs offered. Between 1928 and 1934 'the new industries in and around London have attracted more than half a million persons', many of them from the depressed areas. A Hammersmith policeman recalled, 'At the height of the depression literally every park seat, shelter, cart, van and lorry held its sleeping figure' from some Welsh or northern 'derelict town or village'. When the recovery of the middle to late 1930s got under way, the tide of workers to London slackened as they found more jobs at home. But it is true to say that between the wars the age-old lure of London as a city where the streets were paved with gold was burnished more brightly than for generations before.[32]

All this new industrial development was at its most dense in north-west London, but it had important extensions in the north-east (Edmonton and the rest of the Lea Valley); the east (Dagenham, where Ford's, Briggs' Motor

Bodies and Kelsey Hayes Rim and Wheel Co. settled from 1931); the south-east (Woolwich, Erith and Crayford); and the south-west (the Wandle Valley and Kingston Bypass).

Besides the accidental fortunes of war, west London had two key advantages: it had a ready supply of young female labour not yet in factories, due to the predominance of domestic service on that side of town, and it was where the nation's new road network connected to London. Access to roads and the potential of motor lorries for long-distance haulage overtook proximity to waterways and railheads as a key locational factor for industry, especially in the 1930s. Just as Britain's railways converged on London, so the nation's new trunk roads reinforced the 2,000-year dominance of the capital.

The most important west London centres of development were Park Royal, which grew from eighteen factories in 1918 to some 250 by 1939; Willesden Green and Harlesden; the Great West Road (Brentford, Osterley and Feltham), where fifty-three factories in a two-mile stretch were employing 11,000 by the late 1930s; and Alperton, Perivale and Greenford. In 1931, the nadir of Britain's Great Depression, 'many new factories' were opened along the Great West Road, and in North Acton alone '15 new factories were built during the year'; that was when, for a three-month period, just one of Scotland's eighty-three blast furnaces was firing. In the five years before 1928, employment in west London between Acton and Slough rose from 60,000 to 150,000 jobs. By 1934–5, so many jobs had been created that labour shortages were inhibiting new factories from opening. And giant firms became a feature of this suburban industry in a way they had never managed before the First World War: by 1930, 60 per cent of the output of electrical goods came from factories employing over 1,000 workers, and four out of ten of these workers lived in London.[33]

This was the *Brave New World* of Aldous Huxley's Electrical Equipment Corporation and its Gamma-Plus dwarfs. And of Wallis Gilbert's great Hoover Building on Western Avenue and his giant Firestone and Pyrene factories, jostling for place with the Coty factory and Trico Windscreens, all on the Great West Road; and the Gramophone (EMI) Company's sprawling complex at Hayes, employing up to 15,000 mainly women workers. That and Plessey's of Ilford, Siemens of Woolwich, Standard Telephones of Hendon and GEC of Erith and Wembley helped corner the market for London in electrical equipment. They rubbed suburban shoulders with firms that had moved from inner London: the Rego Clothing Company, with about 1,000 workers, who moved from Shoreditch to Edmonton in 1928, straight into a famous strike; Heinz moved from cramped Southwark to twenty acres at Park Royal in 1925; Stork Margarine flew to Purfleet in

1918, and other household names were shouted from factories along the roads out of London – Lyons Bakeries, McVitie and Price, Guinness (Park Royal), Dunlop-Macintosh (who moved from Manchester to Edmonton in 1933), Glaxo Pharmaceuticals, Ilford Photographics and scores more. These were the years, too, when multinational firms, especially American motors and motor-parts, took a substantial stake in industrial London; three-quarters of foreign firms locating in England between 1931 and 1935 settled in the London region.[34] This was a sign of things to come.

Not all of London's industries grew. Thames shipbuilding and repairing – not yet a vestigial industry at the time of the First World War, with Thornycroft making torpedo boats at Chiswick, for example – lost 4,000 out of 14,000 jobs between 1923 and 1938. But it had not been a major London industry since the 1870s and the world downturn in shipbuilding had little effect in London compared to the devastation wreaked on the Clyde and the Tyne. But the collapse of the London piano-making trade had greater effects, especially around Camden Town, Kentish Town and Holloway. Musical instrument makers fell in number from over 23,000 in 1929 to under 8,000 in 1938 as the gramophone and the talkies displaced the piano from home entertainment and from the cinema. A similar shift in taste led to the demise of London cooperage, reflecting a decline in beer-drinking generally and a move to bottled beer. And industrial expansion could cause some dislocation of the link between certain industries and the areas in which they had traditionally clustered. So the heavy tanning yards had mostly 'vanished' from Bermondsey by 1933, and a year later there was just one clock-maker's workshop left in the whole of Clerkenwell.[35]

But in general, as the economist M. P. Fogarty wrote in 1945, 'London was outstandingly prosperous before the war. London's industries and services were not merely not declining; they were advancing rapidly . . .'[36] Prosperity was not confined to the western suburbs or the other areas dominated by the 'new' industries based on electrical engineering or the motor car. For most of London's traditional industries expanded in the glow of rampant consumer demand from Britain's biggest and best-heeled market. Thus, in Islington, to take one primarily residential borough for example's sake, the number of registered workshops increased from 1,316 in 1913 to 1,860 in 1937. And the Camberwell *Borough Guide* for 1936 pointed out that in this residential district, too,

industries are not obtrusive, but they are nevertheless numerous and varied. Chief among them is . . . the South Metropolitan Gas Company's works in the Old Kent Road . . . Other industries include the building of buses, motor-car bodies and caravans, engineering, and the manufacture of printing, book-binding and allied machines, electric potato-peeling machines, preserved foods, patent medicines, flour, butter, pickles, sauces, corks, scales, stationery products, gummed paper, rugs, architectural metal, varnishes, and a vast number and range of other commodities.[37]

In inner London alone in 1938 there were nearly 37,000 factories employing 744,000 people. Surprisingly, perhaps, the most 'industrial' borough measured by number of factories was Westminster, with 4,414; but if measured by workers it was Finsbury, with nearly 67,000.[38]

The port of London 'more than held its own' across the slump, its share of the nation's combined imports and exports rising from 29.3 per cent to 37.3 per cent between 1913 and 1937, even though this meant little more real trade than in 1913 because of the world downturn.[39] In this shrinking trade world the role of the Empire waxed large. The Empire attained its maximum extent as late as 1937. And the British Empire Exhibition of 1924 bequeathed a memorial to London and the nation for the rest of the century in the shape of Wembley Stadium, as well as attracting millions to see, among other things, the newly discovered treasures from Tutankhamun's tomb.[40] This vast Empire, which needed bureaucrats at home and abroad, was one element in the growing tide of office workers in London, which had twice the national proportion in 1931.

There were, though, costs to all this growth. Mechanization spelled the demise of the London craftsman. Machines invaded every industry from pen-pushing to road-building. 'The old type of craftsman, who was a very special figure in the industry of the metropolis a generation ago, has virtually been wiped out,' according to the communist Allen Hutt in 1933. Certainly, in glass-making, 'bevellers and cutters are being displaced by the entry of the "robot"', costing 70 per cent of skilled workers their jobs in the industry in London in the seven years after 1921. Most cabinet-makers were becoming assemblers of machine-cut parts, carvers were made redundant by machines that 'press-carved' designs into wood, and there was little call for 'the old-fashioned french polisher with his trade secrets'. There was a 'disappearance of the skilled workman' in most food and drink production, and although 'all employees [in factory bakeries] call themselves bakers they are for the most part skilled machine minders'. Bookbinding by hand was in 'decay'; the saddler's, harness-maker's and piano-action maker's skills were no longer required; and 'the skilled clock-maker, who still makes high-grade domestic clocks, may soon be as much of an anachronism as the hand-loom weaver'. Even the clerk 'is just a machine minder. The typist has replaced the penman.'[41]

On the other hand, machines were also taking the strain and danger out of heavy handling; the 'unskilled' factory operative gained from minding machines; driving motors was considered more skilled work than handling horses; and some new specialists emerged from the demands of reinforced concrete and steel erection in the construction industry, for instance. So there tended to be a bunching of skills below the level of handicraft but above the level of lifting and toting.

But undoubtedly the losses hurt more at the time. There was a widespread feeling that work was getting harder and was taking more out of a man, even though the length of the working day was cut for many by the end of the First World War. The switch from horses to motors, affecting thousands of London's working men in the 1920s and 1930s, meant a harder day: 'Motors have quickened the pace of the driver's work . . . The carman [horse-driver] still leads a more leisurely life, with time to feed his horses and clean the harness . . .' And the pace of work, and its effects on the health of the London bus crews, was a major element in the Coronation bus strike of 1937. For mechanization had taught road transport employers an important lesson: men could be worked harder than horses.[42]

These were pre-eminently the years of the mechanical clocking-on system, of night shifts encroaching into engineering and other industries, of endless rows over night baking, spreadover and time schedules. Max Cohen, an East End cabinet-maker who had 'never been pampered in the workshop' and 'was not exactly a loiterer at the bench', worked at one London factory in the 1930s where

The speed at which my mates worked astonished me . . . And yet I had to emulate them if I wanted to keep my job . . . I forgot everything, I forgot even myself, in the tense effort of keeping up with my mates. I kept my eyes glued on the output, and, by straining myself to the utmost, managed somehow to keep mine somewhere near theirs.

And a London car-maker testified, 'We often work with sweat pouring out of us. It's necessary to move like lightning.'[43] This pace and pressure of work was reflected in the number and severity of accidents on the job. An acute London example was the Earls Court Exhibition Centre building job of 1936–7, where, according to the unions, speed and cut corners led to 2,000 accidents, the local hospital treating 600 men from the site, and nineteen deaths.[44]

Worst of all for men was the sense that they were expendable and that jobs chopped into their component parts could now be done equally well – perhaps better – by women. 'On almost every kind of work, men are being replaced by girls and boys, who are, of course, cheaper for the boss,' wrote an aggrieved worker at Berger's paint factory, Hackney, in 1932. Doris

Bailey, daughter of a Bethnal Green French polisher on short time, left school that same year: ' "Plenty of work around, if you look for it," ' he told her. ' "Take a penny bus ride and walk through Shoreditch. Lots of vacancies for girls. It's only men that are not wanted." '[45]

He had a point. Industry in London between the wars revolutionized women's employment prospects. The economic effects were felt more in the quality of opportunities than in their number, though numbers were important, too. In the County of London in 1931, the workforce was 36.8 per cent female, compared to 35.4 per cent in 1911 – no huge shift there, even though it meant a rise of over 80,000 in the number of working women. No doubt the proportion rose again during the 1930s. Perhaps more important, there were significant shifts in the jobs women were taking up. Domestic service was far less popular after the First World War than before, but the drop in the numbers of indoor servants was less dramatic than the fall in its share of women's employment. There had been 201,000 domestic servants in inner London in 1911 and there were still 185,000 in 1931; but now their proportion of employed women in the County had fallen from 26.1 per cent in 1911 to 21.7 per cent.[46]

Jobs in many sectors of manufacturing grew faster for women than they did for men, especially electrical engineering and equipment, food, leather, clothing, printing and stationery. In London manufacturing as a whole, insured employment for women increased by 113,000 jobs (39 per cent) between 1923 and 1938, compared to 170,000 (36 per cent) for men. And a consistently greater share of women in the County of London were economically active than in Great Britain as a whole: 44.4 per cent compared to 34.2 per cent in 1931.[47]

The attractions of factory work, especially in the newer suburban industries, lured London girls away from domestic service. The 'factory girls looked down on us as inferior, calling us "drain 'ole cleaners",' recalled Edith Hall from Southall, who followed her mother into general service in 1923. Probably three out of four London servants were provincial born around 1929–30 and the proportion was higher among young servants aged between seventeen and twenty-five.[48]

The shortfall had to be made up by provincial migration. Voluntary migration was supplemented by the Juvenile Transference schemes, operating for boys from 1928 and girls a year later. The latter took 37,000 girls from Britain's depressed areas and resettled them in London and other prospering districts, many in domestic service. Prominent among them were girls from Wales, and the plight of the Welsh servant girl in London provoked vociferous concern from around the time of the miners' strike of 1926. That summer a 'protection movement' had been mooted to save young female

Presbyterians from the perils of the 'white slave trade'. The tragic case of Annie Hatton, an eighteen-year-old from Glamorgan, who was murdered by a rejected suitor while general servant to a Hackney kosher butcher, seemed to crystallize the risks of coming to London. Her widowed mother was too poor to travel to London for the inquest. When Annie was buried in her home village, 'thousands of people lined the route' and floral tributes included one in the shape of a harp 'From a Welsh unemployed miner in London'. The Salvation Army Girls' Home in Clapton had succoured 'hundreds of girls between the ages of 15 and 18, who have come from South Wales to take up domestic service and then run away owing to the conditions of their work'. Many, of course, ran away to factories, where work was more friendly and less all-consuming of time.[49]

But not, though, less dangerous. In June 1928, an inquest was held into the death of Ethel Violet May Waite, seventeen, who worked packing Boli-Varu scouring powder at a factory close to her home in Battersea. Death followed headache, nose bleeds, weight loss and shortness of breath and was due to 'industrial silicosis': 'Her lungs were like rubber, with green knobs the size of peas.' 'Skin diseases' were said to be common among women wiredrawers in electric cable factories; screwing up wireless cabinets all day produced painful lumps under the arms; and in one of the worst industrial accidents in London between the wars, four young women aged between fifteen and twenty-seven were burnt to death in an explosion at a St Pancras film store in September 1927. A ball of flame flashed across the room where they were winding celluloid film.[50]

Nor were the jobs less exhausting. Women in factories were perhaps even more susceptible than men to the frantic search for a competitive edge in the new world of machines and 'speed-up' between the wars. The torments of time were made most exquisite under Charles E. Bedaux's work-study system, where work was divided into standard tasks known as Bs and where workers had to achieve 60Bs an hour. Devised in America before the First World War, the system did not infect British industry until the late 1920s. But London, with its great new factory investment, fell under the spell of the Bedaux stopwatch faster and more completely than any other manufacturing area. And girls and women were in the Bedaux frontline:

resentment against the Bedaux system is very keen in the factory. One girl fainted during the timing operations of the Bedaux experts . . . They are making one girl do two or three girls' work for less pay, and if the poor girl even stops to blow her nose she's put all behind. Why, when we even want to wash our hands, etc., we have to ask, and we're watched and timed. The Bedaux men stand over you, not giving you breathing room, with a clock and a board, watching every movement and giving the girls all the sarcasm they think . . . Oh! please help us make it well known the conditions at the wonderful Nestlé's Chocolates, the conditions that the girls work in.[51]

The disadvantages attaching to factory work were less evident in the new world of service industries opening out to women in these years. The *New Survey of London Life and Labour* in 1933 noted the growth of new types of shop, like 'the wireless shops – usually combined with music shops – the camping and scout shops . . . and shops dealing in motor accessories . . . Specialty shops which sell nothing but stockings, or lingerie, or inexpensive frocks – the shops which are termed by the trade "Madam shops" – are increasing in numbers in response to the prevailing fashions.' Even more important, the cheap imitation of the middle-class superstore – the threepenny and sixpenny bazaars – flourished from the 1920s. They also provided valued employment, even though Woolworth's wages were notoriously low, in the 1920s at least.[52]

Opportunities increased, too, for usherettes in the super-cinemas and waitresses in the catering industry. These were the knickerbocker-glory years of the Lyons Corner House and the department store teashop and restaurant. Uniformed waitresses like the Lyons Nippy and her cheaper imitations captured the public imagination. They starred in documentary films of London life like Edgar Anstey's *Dinner Hour* (1935), and in novels like J. B. Priestley's *They Walk in the City* (1936), where Rose Salter, a Yorkshire girl with drive, gets her first London job at one of the 'Copper Kettle Cafés', close to the Strand. No masculine symbol of work could compete with these young women in standing for the new Britain emerging from Depression. And even more than the Odeon usherette or the Woolworth's shop assistant, and even more than Priestley's 'factory girls looking like actresses', the Lyons Nippy was the defining symbol of the modern world of work that London represented in the 1930s: 'She was . . . a jolly laughing girl,' wrote Winifred Holtby of a favoured character, 'brisk as a terrier, and capable as a head waitress at Lyons Corner House'.[53]

Those would be qualities useful to London when the bombs began to fall.

Office World: 1940–65

The industrial effects on London of the Second World War were a reverse image of the First. The four years from 1914 concentrated manufacturing and distribution in London to an unprecedented degree; but the five years from 1939 pushed commerce and industry out of the capital more than at any time since the Great Fire.

Air warfare made the difference. Between 1914 and 1918 just one bomb damaged the port of London, despite it being a primary target. But from September 1940 the port became 'the most consistently and heavily bombed civilian target in the British Isles', the victim of nearly 1,000 high-explosive bombs and thousands of incendiaries. A third of its warehouses and transit sheds and half its storage accommodation were destroyed and the river was 'threatening to silt up for lack of six years' dredging'. The destruction was so great that some of it was never made good in the thirty years or so that the upper port remained open for business.[54]

The fear of bombing had already been a factor in the reaction against London's industrial growth: to concentrate so much of the nation's productive capacity in one place, apparently so vulnerable to destruction from the air, seemed strategic madness. When rearmament got under way from 1935 new munitions factories were urgently needed. The three Royal Ordnance Factories – Woolwich, Enfield and the Royal Gunpowder Factory at Waltham Abbey – expanded to fourteen between 1935 and 1939, but the other eleven were put far from London in Wales, north-west England and Nottingham. Similarly with aircraft production: where London had dominated for the first thirty-five years of the century, it lost its lead when the new factories also moved west.[55]

When war was declared there was little voluntary evacuation of manufacturing industry from London but 'business' proved more nervous. Firms moved their office staff from the City to south London especially, 'where so much of their clerical labour lives, taking over large houses there'. The Civil Service sent many departments out of London, the railway companies moved their head offices to railway towns and manufacturing companies relocated theirs to factories they owned elsewhere.

But when bombing began, 'wholesale' and 'hasty' evacuation took place, this time involving industrial production too. Engineering and clothing moved from central London, where the East End, Shoreditch, Finsbury and the City were particularly badly hit. They moved to suburban north-west London, the Home Counties and further north, some clothing factories relocating near Leeds, the home of ready-made gents' outer-wear. Of those who stayed, many switched production lines to war materials, just as they had done in the First World War: a canning factory in Mitcham made shells, Bryant and May switched part of their production from matches to fuses for demolition work, the Chrysler motor body assembly works at Chiswick went 'over to bombers', and so on.[56]

Some firms and industries could not move out. Retail, for instance, had to stay or close. And to the destruction by bombing was added the steady withdrawal of anything to sell as supplies for consumer industries were diverted more and more to the war effort. Yet despite these extraordinary setbacks, it was the sheer indestructibility of London's economy under fire that stood out most at the time.

Sidney Chave walked down Oxford Street the day after it had been heavily attacked. Bourne & Hollingsworth was devastated, 'not a window remained and the interior was a shambles'. Waring & Gillow was closed by an unexploded bomb. John Lewis was a gutted ruin. Selfridge's and Peter Robinson had both been hit. It seemed that shopping in Oxford Street must be a thing of the past. Yet within four days nearly all were open again; Bourne & Hollingsworth had draped the ruins in Union Jacks and sales girls were serving a few yards from the great hole ripped through the centre of the shop. Only John Lewis defied repair . . . [57]

It was not only the 'business girls' of the West End who could proudly put up those famous notices on the outside of blasted shop-fronts: 'More Open Than Usual'. Maybe one incident, in the heart of the City, can stand for many. On the night of Saturday 11–12 January 1941, a high-explosive bomb penetrated the roadway in front of the Mansion House and burst in the booking hall of Bank Station. It collapsed, and so did escalator shafts and tunnels, killing more than fifty and injuring many more. The 'largest crater in London' had opened up in the middle of one of the busiest junctions in the capital, where seven of the City's main thoroughfares meet. But by 3 February the crater had been cleared and shored up and a temporary steel bridge slung over it to link Queen Victoria Street and Poultry with Cornhill; by 17 March the station was re-roofed and working again; and by May the roadway was rebuilt and the bridge removed.[58] All this in a city where, on that same night, forty-three had died at Liverpool Street Station, where fires and explosions had damaged an area from Stepney to Kensington and Finsbury to Lambeth, and in the middle of a Blitz that raged almost nightly from September to May. It was the remarkable inventiveness, confidence and diverse capacity of workaday London that helped it mend its wounds so quickly and so well.

But the war did damage London's economy. In some respects the harm was permanent. Some firms chose not to return after 1945, having increased their workforce and markets away from London. In the heavily bombed East End there was no possibility of as many jobs locating there as before the war, not only because of the amount of destruction but because comprehensive redevelopment plans would no longer allow industry to mix in with 'residential zones'. And some industries learned they could survive away from the capital: it was in the war years that it first became apparent that routine clerical functions could take place more cheaply elsewhere even if 'key business employees must remain in Central London, in close contact with the financial and business market'.[59] Even so, the growth of employment in outer London more than made up for the decline at the centre. By 1951, employment in Greater London at 4.23 million workers had recovered its 1931 position (4.12 million).[60] Employment in London peaked at 4.43 million in 1966, although it is unlikely that it ever exceeded the share of national jobs it attained in the late 1930s.

The centre of London never recovered its historic role as a manufacturing district. Despite property in run-down residential areas continuing to turn over to industry as population declined, inner London lost over one in five of its manufacturing jobs between 1938 and 1947, some 170,000 in all, and nearly a quarter of its factories and workshops. Most Metropolitan Boroughs shared in the loss, with Finsbury shedding nearly half its jobs. Manufacturing continued to decline in these areas during the 1950s, so that the East End furniture trade lost 55 per cent of its workshops between 1939 and 1958. There were losses outside the County, too, at least in West and East Ham.[61]

The decentralization of expanding firms from inner London, a trend apparent since before 1900, was given a huge push by the war. Despite the continuing decline of factory jobs in the centre, manufacturing actually increased in London as a whole as industrial expansion continued to take place in the suburbs. But manufacturing in London grew more slowly than in post-war Britain. So that where, between 1951 and 1962, manufacturing employment in the capital grew by 66,000 jobs or 4.4 per cent, that was less than half the nation's growth of 9.6 per cent. London lagged behind, especially in chemicals and vehicle production, both strong metropolitan sectors before the war. But outside the Greater London boundary, the 'London Region' continued to expand its capacity, at a rate of 17 per cent over the same period.[62]

If industry struggled, though, commerce bounced back, and fast. The tonnage of goods handled through the port of London had surpassed the pre-war peak by 1952, the difficulties still experienced from war damage partly overcome through mechanical handling by mobile cranes and fork-lift trucks.[63] And one new post-war development in particular aided London's economic recovery.

This was the opening of Heathrow Airport. It originated in a government decision in 1943 to build a military transport base in west London capable of adapting to civil use once there was peace. The site chosen had been used by the Fairey Aviation Co. as a test runway from around 1929. It was further out – and so less cramped by suburban development – than the airports at

Heston and Croydon, the latter London's main airport between the wars. Heathrow opened as 'London Airport' in February 1946. Its growth in traffic was phenomenal: 282,000 passengers in 1947, 523,000 in 1950, 1.2 million 1953, 2.7 million 1955, 5.3 million 1960. Freight rose from 5,351 short tons (2000 lb) to 88,000 over the same period, and aircraft movements from 30,000 to 147,000 a year.

Heathrow's success attracted to it huge numbers of jobs on the airport itself – 26,000 by 1958 – and a busy hinterland of warehousing, hotels and transport depots. London's air business was so hectic that the need for a second airport was identified by the late 1940s. Gatwick opened in that role in May 1958, greatly expanding the previously modest air traffic it had carried from the end of the war. By 1964 a *de facto* third airport was operating at Stansted after the closure of five smaller suburban airports, including Croydon, between 1956 and 1964.[64]

The resurrection of London commerce after the war reshaped the London economy in an entirely new image for the second half of the century. For the 1950s and 1960s saw the rise of the office as London's quintessential and symbolic workspace.

It took the City, London's premier office district, years to recover from the devastation caused by bombing. In one respect it never recovered. Employment in the City had climbed throughout the nineteenth century and the first forty years of the twentieth, reaching an estimated half-million in 1939. It would never reach that again. Bombing destroyed one-third of its floorspace (office, warehousing, industry and retail predominantly). By 1949 there had been almost no recovery and even in 1962 floorspace was still at just 86 per cent of the 1939 figure. But the 1939 *office* floorspace had been recovered by 1957 and in 1962 there was 6.1 million square feet in excess of the 1939 figure; offices now accounted for over 60 per cent of City use compared to 45 per cent pre-war. The shift to offices after the Blitz largely eliminated City warehousing as 'the trading of physical goods was replaced by the trading of rights to goods'.[65]

The office boom added about 56,000 jobs to central London in the 1950s, some compensation for the loss of manufacturing. But it was the shift in emphasis rather than the rise in numbers that was of historic significance. Up to 1961 the typical London worker had been a factory or workshop operative (34.4 per cent of the workforce, 1.51 million workers). From 1966 it was the office worker – 34.7 per cent, 1.54 million – with the operative slipping back to just less than a third.[66]

This brought a shift, too, in the gender of the typical London worker. Women were providing an ever larger share of the workforce. In 1931 for every 1,000 men at work in London there had been 520 women; in 1966 there were 615. But in office employment, now London's main sector, 62 per cent of clerical workers were women. The rise of office work and the woman worker kept in step with each other. By 1985, 'Nearly half London's working population can be described as office workers', and by the end of the century women made up half the London workforce.[67]

The gender shift brought another shift, too, and one a long time coming. Before the First World War 'the "superiority" of the clerical worker over the manual worker was still not in question'. From 1919 the universal application of the typewriter and comptometer opened up clerical employment to the sons and daughters of skilled and semi-skilled manual workers in particular. This process had gone far by the 1930s. Consciousness of the declassed office was nicely captured by Michael Bonavia, who started as a clerk at N. M. Rothschild's, New Court, in 1931. He was told by the manager to arrive after 10 a.m.: '"We are not one of those beastly nine o'clock places."' And around the same time J. B. Priestley noted the rise of a class of office 'girls' 'who may not make any more money than their sisters and cousins who work in factories and cheap shops – they may easily make considerably less money – but nevertheless are able to cut superior and ladylike figures in their respective family circles because they have succeeded in becoming typists'.[68]

Office work never really lost its 'superiority'. In 1939 it was noted that 'office work of any kind is preferred to factory work, and this is having a marked effect in London – particularly in the Great West Road area. The resulting tendency is to push new light industries farther out to places where there is less office competition.'[69] That competition redoubled in the 1950s, when the opportunities to exchange a factory job for clerical work, with its continuing cachet and status, had never been greater. And there was no lack of compensating opportunities for middle-class Londoners who felt themselves too good for run-of-the-mill office tasks:

With the advance of technology, with the increase in the division of labour and of consumer expenditure, new occupations have developed, especially middle-class occupations. (Look at the advertisements in the "quality" newspapers. Wanted: project engineer, production executive, system analyst, computer shift leader, sales promotion specialist, attitude tester, beauty operator, public relations manager, window-dresser, and many more of different kinds.) Some of the old menial occupations are becoming extinct, or are likely to disappear.[70]

Ruth Glass gave no examples of the latter in her 1964 comment on social change in London but she might have had in mind the most 'menial' of all. Domestic service fell away as a London employment, from 185,000 women indoor servants living in the County in 1931 to some 85,000 in 1951, and from more than one in five of all occupied women to fewer than one in eight.[71]

Apart from office work, other service industries also grew to mop up the declining role of manufacturing in the London economy. The capital's sales force grew steadily until the mid-1960s, and the nature of retailing changed. 'The day of the small independent shopkeeper was almost over in 1939', according to the town planner C. B. Purdom in 1945: 'The growth of large-scale organization was bringing London shops into the hands of quasi-monopoly concerns . . . The necessaries of life in food, clothing, and furniture were being more and more subject to mass distribution.'[72] That trend accelerated during the war and after. But side by side with this shift to mass retailing there coexisted a remarkable tradition of continuity among the great names of London shopkeepers who had dominated the West End for so long: Fortnum and Mason (founded 1710), Dollond and Aitchison (1752), Debenham's (1791), WH Smith (1792), Savory and Moore (1806), Maple's (1848), Harrod's (1849), John Lewis (1864), Austin Reed (1900), Foyle's (1905), Selfridge's (1909). Some of these, of course, were to become the 'quasi-monopolists' of the second half of the century.

Retailing was boosted, too, by the availability of new products. Crucial in the 1950s and early 1960s were television and the motor car, the latter beginning to transform beyond compare the use, sound, smell and appearance of the streets of London and the habits of Londoners from the late 1950s on. Mass ownership of motors conjured up its own service industries, from advertising agencies to thousands of mechanics' backstreet workshops, busily displacing manufacturing from London's railway arches and mews stables.

Among all this activity it was easy enough for migrant workers to carve out a living. That, of course, was why they had come to London in the first place. Labour shortages in industry, transport and the health service – jobs deserted by white Londoners because of low pay, lower status and blossoming opportunities elsewhere – made work readily available, at least after training. Discrimination at the point of recruitment to the labour market was not as pernicious as when trying to enter the housing market, although there were many slights and oppressions. Selfridge's, for instance, employed black kitchen staff in the early 1960s but only white waitresses and counter-hands; and migration involved 'to an almost staggering extent' a downgrading of employment, so that men who were clerks in the West Indies would find themselves sweeping streets in London.[73]

But the migrants also added to the capacity and diversity of London's economy in the 1950s and 1960s. The boom period for Chinese restaurants opening in London was the five years or so from 1955, and Indian restaurants from 1962. Indian and Pakistani entrepreneurs penetrated the East End clothing industry in the 1950s, so that by 1960 'there were between 25 and 30 workshop establishments run by Indians in the East End'. The immigrant communities quickly became self-sufficient, creating service industries to satisfy their particular needs, from wedding-car hire to hairdressing, and with their own groceries and butchers with supply chains to Asia, the Caribbean, the Middle East and beyond. For the largest communities these local (but international) economies were all in place by 1960.[74] They became one of the city's selling points in the 'Swinging Sixties' era that took off shortly after.

By the early 1960s, then, London had experienced a generation of job surpluses and economic expansion. The Barlow Commission Report of 1940 had bemoaned London's economic superiority within the nation as a pernicious phenomenon to be stopped at all costs. The London plans had called for controls to prevent industries returning to peacetime London and to stop new enterprise choosing it as a location. But despite London taking a smaller share of post-war manufacturing expansion, employment in the capital just kept on growing. The office boom from 1954 offered a new target for those who worried about London's economic hypertrophy. And fears were hardly eased by delays in publishing the 1961 Census results, which might have corrected misapprehensions over the numbers of central London office jobs created in the 1950s, in reality about a third of those most popularly quoted.[75] So London still seemed in the mid-1960s an unstoppable juggernaut.

With hindsight, though, there were signs that the London economy – so robust in the face of a turbulent sixty years and more – was beginning to enter an entirely different phase. Road transport created one watershed. The motor lorry came of age around 1930. The arterial road network was also a product of the 1920s and 1930s. Fast lorries on fast roads revolutionized the relationship between producers and markets. Road transport proved far more flexible at door-to-door delivery than rail could ever be. Proximity to the London market was now less important than many other business factors like space to expand, the cost of premises and the availability of affordable labour. By 1964, under the influence of the expanding motorway network, firms were moving from Park Royal to take advantage of better road connections further west.[76]

Inner London manufacturing was fatally undermined by this historic shift. Backyard enterprise in narrow streets, now clogged by private cars and lorries, found deliveries and collections awkward or impossible to organize. And there were other reasons for moving from inner London. Successful firms wanting to grow found expansion impossible because neighbouring interests were too complex and expensive to acquire or because the LCC put obstacles in the way. It was often an attractive proposition to sell out interests to an LCC ambitious to clear industry from the residential zones and replan for a new post-war world. The office boom gave another spur to decentralization. It pushed central London land values so high that any industrial user with a site to sell would generally have been foolish not to take the money and run – to outer London or away altogether. Then there was state help to move industry to the New Towns, although this assisted only a small fraction of those moving voluntarily; and there were state-imposed penalties on staying put, like converting coal-burning furnaces and boilers to smokeless fuel, for instance. Finally, but crucially, the suburban migration of skilled workers pulled jobs after it. As so often, work chased the workers just as much as the other way round.[77]

The emerging superiority of road transport also strongly affected the post-war port. Tilbury had been built with no road connection at all – it was linked to London solely by rail and the river. For more than fifty years that hardly mattered and road connections were put in place only by 1939. Yet the growing significance of the motor lorry meant that as early as 1946 'road traffic exceeded rail traffic in and out of Tilbury'. Road connections to the upper port, however, were notoriously congested, inconvenient and time-wasting. The move to roll-on roll-off (ro-ro) ferries, with their promise of 'immediate delivery' from ship to customer – a development learned from beach-head landings during the war – and containerization, with its bulk carriage of packaged items ready for loading into freight lorries, defined the future for the world's ports by the early 1960s. In that future the upper port was damned by its geography to take no part. And by its history. For the traditions of trade union struggle and job control had produced inflexible working methods and a bloody-minded reluctance to change and adapt. Mechanical handling was introduced to the port 'only' from 1946. And unpredictable work stoppages – thirty-seven strikes between 1945 and 1955, for instance – led shipowners to take their custom to continental Europe, to Felixstowe, Harwich, Folkestone, Dover, Southampton or elsewhere.[78]

With hindsight, all these factors are readily apparent. But it really did not look that way at the time. The growth of office jobs at the centre seemed to be 'submerging' London when Peter Hall wrote *London 2000* (1963), a sustained call to move jobs out of the capital into the wider London region. The sociologist John Greve noted 'the self-generating momentum of London's growing domination of the economy', and forecast – in 1964 – a rise in London's population, even that of inner London, which had been falling for sixty years. The years 1962–4 saw record shipping in the port of London and record tonnages of goods handled. James Bird, a meticulous observer of the post-war port, could rhapsodize in 1964, 'The growth of the port – its physical extension and the increase of its trade – from the past into the future forms a continuum. London still makes demands on the Thames, and there is still plenty of room for their further fulfilment. Such great opportunities: such great expectations . . . The story continues.'[79] But not for much longer. No one could tell it at the time, but it was to be all downhill from there. For a generation, at least.

Great Slump, Green Shoots: 1966–99

Even at the end of the 1960s there were few signs of just what the London economy faced. But the first cracks had appeared. They opened fastest and widest in the port. Despite growing trade, the Rochdale Committee's report on Britain's port industry recognized that the future of the port of London lay in deep water and close to the shipping lanes at Tilbury. The Committee called on new investment to be targeted there rather than the upper port, and urged that the future of the docks furthest upstream – the St Katherine's and London group – 'be considered'. At that time the PLA seemed largely oblivious of the long-term implications for the upper port of ro-ro ferries, already well established in the industry, and containerization, still in its early days. So investment in the upstream docks continued undeterred, a brand-new 'Dock House' office and warehouse complex opening at St Katherine's as late as 1964.

Trade fell off in the difficult years of the mid-1960s. Partly that was due to Britain's economic problems as a whole, partly to competition from European ports exploiting containerization, and partly to the port's own intrinsic shortcomings. From 1966, the PLA began to plan Britain's first 'fully integrated ocean container ship terminal' at Tilbury, to be opened in 1968–9. In order to cut costs at the upper port, where 'immediate delivery' was already making the large Brunel warehouses of the early nineteenth century redundant, St Katherine's, London and East India Docks were to be closed as the new facilities at Tilbury opened.

The port now entered the worst period in its recorded history. Looking back, the years from 1966 to 1981 had a surreal quality about them. Whether anything in the way of a working port could realistically have been salvaged upriver of Tilbury remained questionable. But the attitude of the dock labour force rendered the point academic and wiped away any chance of the upper port surviving world change in the industry. It was as though an ageing workforce – the average over forty-five in 1977 – had determined that no jobs should be left when they were too old to work. Dancing all the way to the scaffold, the dock workers – 'unofficially' or with the connivance of a myopic trade union leadership also rooted in an obsolete past – brought the upper port crashing down on their own heads. Shipping companies and distributors gave up on London as, year after year, dispute after dispute closed the quays. A weekend overtime ban caused massive delays and congestion in 1964; the port closed from May to July 1966 through the seamen's strike; a nine-week unofficial strike brought the Royals to a halt in 1967, 'a disastrous blow' according to the PLA; 'terribly disappointing' delays over negotiating the decasualization of dock labour led to the new container facilities at Tilbury being 'blacked' in 1969 – 'The damage is incalculable' – and the switch of vessels to Antwerp meant that 'most of the general cargo trade to and from Australia has been lost to London'; the port closed for six weeks in the summer of 1970 because of a national dock strike, making it as difficult a year 'as any ever experienced by the Authority'; there was another national dock strike in the summer of 1972, triggered by the imprisonment of five London dockers who had picketed the 'stuffing and stripping' of containers at the Midland Cold Store (Stratford) by non-dock labour; the port closed for around six weeks in 1975 through a jobs dispute between dock workers and lorry drivers using the port; there was an unofficial strike over payments for abnormally stowed cargoes in 1977; 100 ships were lost to other ports because of more strikes in 1978; a lorry drivers' strike caused severe congestion at the port in 1979, there was a two-week strike over dock pay in 1980, and a seamen's strike and a six-week strike by cornporters in 1981. These were just the star turns in a music-hall farce that played a crazy accompaniment to the steady downstream drift of the historic port.[80]

After the closure of the East India, St Katherine's and London Docks in 1967–9, the last timber ship left the Surreys in December 1970 and the docks closed a month later; by then, transport developments meant that a single package timber berth at Tilbury could handle the whole of the Surreys' tonnage capacity. There was then a pause in the closure programme. In 1976 the PLA expressed hope of retaining the docks on the Isle of Dogs and in West and East Ham. Indeed there was much continuing investment in the upper port throughout the 1970s, all wasted money as things turned out. For by this time the port of London's share of UK imports and exports had fallen from a third in 1964 to about 12 per cent in 1975, comfortably overtaken by airports (mainly Heathrow and Gatwick) at 15 per cent. From 1977 the confidence of just a year before seemed badly misplaced and the future of the docks on the Isle of Dogs seemed more and more bleak. The

West India and Millwall Docks closed as an emergency financial measure after the pay strike of February 1980. Then, in a final blow, all business was moved from the Royals to Tilbury. The last vessel left the upper port in October 1981. The registered dock labour force had fallen from 29,250 in 1960 to 2,315 in 1982 and was shrinking still.[81]

The fall of the port and the rise of the airport again shifted London's economic balance of power westward. That trend continued through the collapse of London's manufacturing base from the late 1960s on. Closures happened first and worst in east London, in the older industrial areas that had grown up around the river. West London was last to be affected, but it was inexorably ravaged in its turn.

London's manufacturing workforce was 1.29 million strong in 1966, already a drop from 1.43 million just five years before. By 1974 it had fallen to 940,000, by 1989 435,000, and by 1997 274,000. In the thirty years from 1966, manufacturing in London lost nearly 80 per cent of its jobs. By the early 1980s every part of London was affected. Areas like Park Royal, west Middlesex, and the Lea Valley, which had developed as industrial areas mainly in the 1920s and 1930s, and which were still gaining jobs in the 1950s, saw the practical end of their industrial existence by 1985.

Every sector of manufacturing was affected, too. London sweet-making lost Clarnico (Hackney), Barrett's (Wood Green), Callard and Bowser (Hayes); the north London furniture industry employed 16,390 in 1960 but 1,320 in 1984, with '[m]any of the big names of British furniture such as Lebus, Great Eastern Cabinet Company, Beautility and Cabinet Industry' closed; employment at Ford's, Dagenham, peaked in the early 1970s at 28,000 but was down to 15,000 by 1984; the west London vehicle-parts industry virtually evaporated with the closure from 1979 of Smith's Industries, Firestone Tyres, Champion Spark Plugs, Zenith Carburettors, Lucas, Glacier, British Leyland and others; Hoover and United Biscuits left west London around the same time; AEI and four other major engineering firms including Norton Villiers closed at Woolwich in 1968–9; the Beckton gasworks closed at East Ham in the 1970s and Battersea Power Station in 1980; the RSAF closed at Enfield in 1987; six out of ten of Newham's largest firms closed between 1975 and 1981 and others shed jobs (3,000 at Tate and Lyle, for instance); and so on – for the litany of closures was endless.

The gaps that firms left in the 1960s – just like the bomb sites of twenty years before – stayed empty or ruined because there was just nothing to take their place. In Tower Hamlets, the amount of 'dead and disturbed space' rose from fifty-seven hectares in 1964 to 277 in 1977, three times the land area still occupied by factories. 'Some of these sites still [in 1985] stand empty and broken windowed . . . Others have been demolished. There are whole roads of corrugated iron and guard dogs.'[82] At the end of the century great tracts of evacuated industrial space were still marketed as 'opportunities' in east and south-east London, the Lea Valley, Park Royal, the Wandle Valley and elsewhere.

Much of all this reflected trends in the British economy as a whole. But London lost more manufacturing jobs faster than anywhere else. Between 1959 and 1974, London lost 38 per cent compared to 24 per cent in Manchester and 3 per cent in Liverpool; and Tyneside manufacturing grew by 4 per cent. During the 1970s manufacturing jobs fell in Great Britain by 25 per cent, in Greater London by 36 per cent and in inner London by 41 per cent. By 1996, fewer than 10 per cent of the London workforce was employed in manufacturing compared to 18.3 per cent in the UK. And London contained about 7 per cent of the nation's manufacturing jobs, compared to a fifth in the 1950s. So the peculiar disadvantages of London that had begun to harden in the 1950s and 1960s effectively destroyed London's historic role as the 'premier manufacturing district of the country' by the 1980s.[83]

Because of the inevitable delay in assimilating the figures, London's demise took time to dawn on the policy-makers. The decentralization policies of the post-Barlow London plans dominated official thinking through the 1950s and 1960s. Some cautionary voices were raised around 1969 on the need to reduce the flow of job losses, though not stem them altogether. These anxieties reached a wider public only when David Donnison and David Eversley published their review of London urban policy in 1973, warning that a reduction in economic activity could 'seriously weaken the economic and social fabric'.[84] Yet government and GLC decentralization policies did not alter until 1976, when, overnight, the Council's emphasis switched to attracting jobs back to London, and to inner London in particular.

By then service industries in London were also affected by decline. Policy impacted here, too. In 1964, doing something to stop the growth of offices in London was a top political priority. The 'Brown Ban' of November, one of the first acts of the new Labour government, required the grant of office development permits before new offices could be built in London; and permits proved hard to get. The Location of Offices Bureau had been set up that April to move office jobs out of London. It was still going strong, despite the fears for London, in 1977: '"Move out, before London costs strangle your business" the posters in the underground leer invitingly.'[85] By 1978 the LOB had helped move over 150,000 office jobs from central London, although about a third had gone only as far as places like Croydon, Hounslow and Romford in outer London. Among the moves out was a significant part of the insurance industry, which decamped to Bristol. It cited cheaper premises and labour costs and the difficulty of recruiting suitable labour in inner London as primary reasons for moving. Bristol proved popular among office workers. The emergence of the 'M4 Corridor' from Heathrow to the west pulled jobs away from London, with long-term effects. In December 1995, the relocation of around 3,000 Civil Servants to the Ministry of Defence Procurement Agency at Bristol showed that the tide was still strong.[86]

In all, London lost 1.36 million jobs between 1962 and 1994, 30 per cent in just over thirty years. The worst year of the century for London employment was 1994. The mid- to late 1990s showed some recovery, and London employment was forecast to reach 3.4 million in 2001, some 200,000 above the 1994 figure. It was possible that could prove an under-estimate.[87]

London's population fell in 1983 to its lowest point of the century, and it was theoretically conceivable that the fall in jobs was merely catching up with population movements, producing little unemployment as a consequence. But that was not the case. A measure of London's relative decline when compared to the economic fortunes of the nation was the capital's deteriorating unemployment position. For as long as reliable records had existed, the London unemployment rate was lower, frequently substantially lower, than the nation's, although some industries fared worse in London from time to time (building before the First World War, engineering immediately after, for instance). Even after twenty years of manufacturing job losses from the mid-1960s, unemployment in London in June 1984 was 9.7 per cent, compared to the UK's 13.1 per cent. And no doubt the relative prosperity of the rest of the south-east helped Londoners commute against the flow to find work beyond the Green Belt.

But from 1990, job losses overall in London accelerated faster, and then recovered more slowly, than elsewhere. For the whole of the 1990s London's unemployment rate was about two percentage points higher than that of the country as a whole. In 1995 the seven worst unemployment districts in the country were all inner London boroughs; and worklessness was distributed unequally, affecting black youth worst of all. Never before in history had the capital city's economy lagged for so long behind the country's.

Yet side by side with London's great depression, overshadowing its economy for the last third of the century, there were London industries that showed nothing less than boom conditions. Just as London had been the boomtown antidote to slump in 1930s Britain, now the City seemed to keep the capital afloat during its own long recession. Or less the City itself, perhaps, and more the buoyancy of its primary industry, for which 'the City' served as shorthand: 'banking, insurance and financial services', especially the first and last.

The inter-war period had seen the City's place in the world retrench. The German banks, just like the bands, never returned to the London they deserted in 1914. Instead of being banker to the world, the City settled into the more limited function of banker to the Empire and the sterling bloc, and the dollar took on an ever more vital role in the rest of the globe. Conservative American banks stayed at home rather than locate in London – in 1939 there were just eight American branches in the City. Yet if its world role diminished, domestic business continued to extend as banks amalgamated and as more and more British multinational firms were quoted on the Stock Exchange to attract investment worldwide.[88]

A resurrection of the City's position in the world followed the relaxation of British foreign exchange controls in 1958. Unlimited sterling could now be exchanged for foreign currencies. At the same time, artificially low US interest rates sent dollars abroad in the search for the better return that could now be had in London. These 'eurodollars', dollars traded outside the US and mainly from London, became the basic currency for international trade. They were exploited most of all by multinational companies, who needed one flexible currency worldwide, and by syndicates of banks who jointly funded the world's biggest loans, where the involvement of more than one bank was essential to spread the risks of lending. The eurodollar was made more attractive still by protectionist US capital controls which deterred foreign borrowers – including the foreign subsidiaries of US multinationals – from raising loans in New York or any other American financial centre. Those controls were later scrapped, but the damage to New York and the benefit to London were done. They were in place long enough to give London an overwhelming competitive advantage in eurodollar dealings that had not been lost by the century's end.

The eurodollar 'brought to the City a new era of international prestige' in the early 1960s.[89] Homage was paid by the movement of American banks to London, eager to circumvent interest rate ceilings imposed on their domestic customers and to facilitate borrowings by American subsidiaries abroad. London was chosen over potential European competitors because of its world expertise in shipping, commodities and insurance; a liberal regulatory and tax regime; the use of English as the world business language and English law as the framework for international trade; its excellent communications and its position as a time zone. These were all powerful advantages that served London well for the rest of the century. Then the enormous 'petrodollar' market which followed the OPEC oil price rises of 1973 swelled beyond anticipation the funds available for world investment.

Most of those funds were disbursed through London as well. So other
foreign banks now followed the American lead in the move to London. In
1959 there were seventy-six foreign banks in the City; at the end of the
1990s there were around 580. London had more American banks than New
York and more Japanese banks than Tokyo, the highest number of foreign
banks of any city in the world by far.[90]

The growth of international banking in the 1960s was followed in the
1970s by the rise of the financial investment institutions and the creation
and marketing of an enormous range of financial commodities for the
personal and the institutional investor. Once more, the City led the world,
turning all its expertise, including that newly acquired in the eurobond and
eurocurrency markets, to account.

All of this hyperactivity led to employment growth as other – larger –
elements of the London economy began to slip into near-terminal decline.
Despite the movement out of some large insurance firms and 'back office'
number-crunching and paper-shifting functions to cheaper locations outside
central London, employment in banking, insurance and financial services
increased from 275,000 in 1966 to 575,000 in 1982.[91] That was at the
beginning of a decade which was the most hectic of all for the City in the
twentieth century. And the most rewarding, for those lucky enough to have
been in the right place at the right time.

The run-up to 'Big Bang', the deregulation of the London Stock
Exchange in October 1986, was an episode of feverish greed unparalleled
since the days of the gold and diamond rushes a century or more before.
The removal of foreign exchange controls in 1979, one of the first acts of
the first Thatcher government, began to expose expensive flaws in the way
the Stock Exchange handled share dealing. New York, deregulated in 1981,
began to lead London in the volume of international trading in shares,
including the privatization of British utilities. Then the 1982 Third World
debt crisis reined in international lending, one of the big props of City
finance. These two factors amounted to an impending crisis that threatened
to knock the City off the pinnacle of the financial world that it had stoutly
reoccupied since the late 1950s.

The City's response was quite extraordinary. Under pressure from a canny
government, it swept away the traditional (and lucrative) closed shops that
separated stock jobbers and stockbrokers, merchant and lending banks, and
foreign and British banks. It seemed to be essential in the new world for
financial institutions to become multi-functional – all-singing, all-dancing
in the jargon of the time – offering an entire range of services to clients
across every financial specialism. So banks bought up the London brokers
and jobbers to create a winning team in the world's most competitive league.

At huge transfer fees. It was a 'Gadarene rush', with unconscionable fortunes made overnight, and top brokers demanding 'golden hellos' as high as a king's ransom. It was also a technological revolution, with 'screen-based dealing' through instantaneous communications with Tokyo and New York; an architectural revolution, with the need for enormous open-plan dealing rooms creating the 'groundscrapers' that began to replace the 1960s City; a style revolution with its essential trappings of Porsches, wine bars and nightclubs. Yet it worked. At least in the medium term. Despite unforeseen local difficulties – the Stock Exchange crash of October 1987, the Robert Maxwell and BCCI scandals of 1991, the IRA bombing campaigns of 1992–3, the Barings crash of 1995 – at the end of the century the City was still on top of the world.[92]

The job implications of all this excitement for London were volatile but generally in the right direction. The first long rise in employment in London's financial services peaked in 1989 at around 650,000, then fell to 617,000 in 1991. By 1998 it had risen again, this time to 790,000, nearly a quarter of the London workforce. The productivity of the sector meant that it created around 38 per cent of London's GDP at the century's end. But, and this was a worry for many, 30 per cent of these 'City' jobs were held by people who were commuting in from outside the Greater London boundary.[93]

By the end of the century, as we saw in Chapter 2, 'the City' had expanded east in the 1980s even more dramatically than it had expanded west in the 1950s. Indeed, employment in the City itself had halved from its 1939 peak to under 250,000 in 1991. With ups and downs it stayed at around that level through the 1990s. But some of that loss was now made good in the office district of Docklands. And by 1999 that was recovering from the drastic over-supply of offices in London that had in part caused the collapse of the Canary Wharf project. The Isle of Dogs was providing about 50,000 'City' jobs outside the City. Even half-complete, Canary Wharf was 'the largest ever single office development in the UK'.[94]

In the 1990s, the City and its financial services industry had put London in the very top drawer of 'world cities'. It was not uniquely powerful, as it had been before 1914, because it now had to share world power with two other great cities, New York and Tokyo. But by 1990, according to some observers at least, these three cities were no longer in competition. They had, like an imperial triumvirate or robber-baron junta, carved up the financial world between them and seemed in a stable, if tense, state.[95]

The special place of London in the world was reinforced by another industry that hypertrophied from the 1970s on. Tourism had been an important London industry from the late nineteenth century, although it had notoriously lagged behind Paris in the quality of service it offered foreign visitors. But by 1900, 'In nothing has London altered more of late years than its hotel accommodation, which is now on a par with that of any great capital.' In 1902 it was estimated that London received 120,000 visitors each day and provided overnight accommodation for 50–60,000 in hotels, boarding houses and private apartments.[96] The 1920s and early 1930s saw the development of large modern hotels, especially around Park Lane and Marble Arch, and in 1924 the British Empire Exhibition attracted 17 million visitors, three or four times those visiting the Millennium Dome. It was also twice those attending the 1951 Festival of Britain, and there is no doubt that war damage, the housing shortage and rationing curtailed tourism to London by any but the most spartan in the 1940s and early 1950s.

But the growth of international air travel and improved economic circumstances in the 1950s brought around 1.5 million foreign visitors to London in 1960. And it was the London style and fashion revolution of the early 1960s that brought sightseers and consumers from mainland Europe, America and Australasia. The London Tourist Board (LTB) was established in 1963 to help swell and manage the flow. Some 3 million visitors a year arrived by the mid-1960s, and the industry received a boost from the devaluation of sterling in 1967, when the pound in everyone else's pocket became suddenly worth so much more. Overnight, 'Swinging London' was magicked into a bargain boutique for the world's spenders, big and little. As if the cheap pound was not enough, the first Wilson government, desperate for dollar earnings to offset the trade deficit, made frantic efforts to attract Americans to London. Between March 1968 and April 1971, government grants of £1,000 per bedroom were paid for new London hotels completed by April 1973. In 1966 there had been some 44,000 hotel bedrooms in central London; by 1977 there were 150,000, accommodating 8.1 million foreign and 11 million domestic visitors that year. Among them were an estimated 200,000 Arab tourists, making their petrodollars go further in cash-strapped Britain.[97]

By the 1980s tourism was recognized as an industry of major importance to London in the context of falling manufacturing and office jobs. Employment at Heathrow Airport peaked at over 57,000 in 1979–80 and fell by a quarter in the next four years.[98] But the rising productivity of those who remained facilitated the passage of more and more foreign visitors to London: 9.1 million in 1985, 10.3 million in 1990, 13.5 million in 1997. Americans easily topped the poll each year, providing about one in five of all foreign tourists to the capital, followed by French and Germans (another fifth between them). Overseas visitors to London spent some £478 per head in 1997, seven times more than the roughly equivalent number of domestic visitors in the same year.

These were huge numbers – in all, four visitors for every Londoner – and needed a huge industry to resource them. Even attractions like the British Museum (6.3 million visitors in 1996), the National Gallery (5 million), Madame Tussaud's, the Tower of London and Westminster Abbey (all 2.5 million or over) could satisfy only a fraction of tourism's needs. In order to attract tourists back a second time or more, new attractions outside central London had to be discovered (or reinvented) and popularized. In the 1990s, even what appeared to be the most unlikely parts of the capital set out their stall to lure visitors from the City and West End. Islington had its own tourist office for a time. And Hackney, where the National Trust opened the sixteenth-century Sutton House to visitors from 1994; Tower Hamlets, where the Ragged School Museum and other attractions were opened at about the same time; and Stratford (West Ham), which made a visitor centre of its industrial heritage at Three Mills on the River Lea, were among the more surprising of the tourism developments that flaunted London's hidden treasures from the early 1990s on. Indeed, conservation turned into miraculous resurrection with the Globe, Sam Wanamaker's vision of a rebuilt Shakespearean theatre on Bankside: this improbable venture quickly became one of London's premier tourist attractions from its partial opening in 1995, and especially from its first full season in 1997. In all, hotels, restaurants and distribution accounted for 15.2 per cent of London GDP in 1996, and tourism contributed much to transport, storage and communications (a further 10.1 per cent). And quite a lot, too, to the 'other industries' section, especially cultural industries.[99]

London's cultural industries had as troubled a history as any other employment sector after the onset of economic decline in the 1960s. But in the late 1990s there was no doubting the value they brought to London in foreign earnings, or to its status in the world. The London theatre had its periodic and much lamented crises – and its periodic and much vaunted 'renaissances' – but it never lost its leading position in the theatrical world, and around 60 per cent of ticket sales were usually taken by non-Londoners.[100] The London orchestras, or all but the exceptionally brilliant London Symphony Orchestra, lived under almost continual financial strain because of parsimonious state subsidies and suffered from a dearth of good recording, practice and performing venues. But they attracted world-class conductors and recording contracts and, with the Proms a unique summer music festival celebrated in almost every year throughout the century, London could justifiably claim to be the world's music capital, from the 1960s if not before. It was less fortunate in opera. The antics of workforce and management at the Royal Opera House, Covent Garden, in the last thirty years of the century showed it was not just the London dockers who could slit their own throats in the cause of greed and reckless extravagance, this time wrapped up as the pursuit of artistic excellence. The fate of the renovated opera house still looked uncertain in Millennium Year, its place in the arts and hearts of London and the nation far from secure. On the other hand, there was something of a genuine renaissance, if still with potential unfulfilled, in the London film industry, so drastically run-down from the 1950s and early 1960s. London led the world in television production films by 1990. It was also a world leader in the visual arts.[101]

In all, London's cultural industries were said to employ 215,000 people in 1991, 6 per cent of the capital's workforce. They had grown by 20 per cent in the 1980s alone.[102] And cultural production in film, video, animation and 'multi-media' was transforming the old workshop and warehouse districts around the City, incongruously bringing wine bars to Hoxton and studio lofts to south Shoreditch, and cutting rooms, editing suites and recording studios to the City fringe from Soho to Spitalfields.[103] These new industries, high-tech and rising higher by the day, took the same comfort from agglomeration – face-to-face contact between innovators, labour market and commissioning networks – that had kept the furniture and scientific instrument industries flourishing in the same spaces sixty years before.

One new element in post-war London offered a special bonus to its cultural industries: its role as a centre of world culture. Black popular music had revolutionized the listening and performing fashions of the world from the late 1950s. Musical production by West Indian migrants, and then by indigenous black Londoners, was an important branch of the city's cultural industries by the end of the century. More generally, London's migrant communities had generated considerable economic diversity, providing both culturally specific services (including such green-shoot sectors as banking and tourism) and those catering – literally – to wider markets. London's international restaurant trade was as varied as any in the world by the 1990s and was viewed as an integral component of 'Boom Town London'.[104] A survey in 1997–8 concluded that about a fifth of London employers were from ethnic minorities, roughly in line with their overall proportion in the London population. But within this group there was a very large bias to people who described themselves as 'Indians', many from East Africa. They owned over a third of non-white businesses.[105]

Taking stock at the end of the century, many observers saw dangers in the enormous changes to the London economy since 1945. Others, relying perhaps on the city's infinite resourcefulness, were unconcerned. The slump in the financial services sector from 1989 set the context for some of the anxieties of the early 1990s. Globally, questions were raised over the world's capacity to sustain three financial mega-cities. The world's economy seemed far more susceptible to seismic shock at the end of the century than it had at the beginning. And each one rocked, to greater or lesser effect, the towers and groundscrapers of London. Nationally, London seemed to be losing out to Birmingham and other cities that were sharing in the country's urban renaissance. Without its own government from 1986, with its cultural industries deprived of the municipal subsidy that was building new concert halls and theatres elsewhere, with its major industrial sector focused on the world rather than the nation, and with national events long associated with London (Cruft's, the Ideal Home Exhibition, the Motor Show) shared or moved elsewhere to a better home, the notion of 'the capital city' seemed more contingent than it had ever been. And then London seemed to be divided within itself, 'the City' divorced from the city's deindustrializing heartlands and suburbs. More and more it seemed to have just one arrow in its quiver, ending up 'with a highly volatile and unbalanced economy' where a 'collapse in the financial services sector would see London's economy in a very bad way'.[106]

By the late 1990s, with the British economy generally sturdy and unemployment lower, prospects for London seemed brighter and intelligent commentators more upbeat.[107] There were many reasons to be cheerful. London's economy remained diverse. Manufacturing had not entirely disappeared, and in clothing, computer software and cultural production it had a base that could be built on. The service industries clustered round tourism and leisure were diversifying and growing still. By 1999 yet another City building boom was under way, this time again reaching for the sky in back-to-the-1960s fashion, and showing that London's lead industry was still in vibrant mood.

Even so, no possible formulation at the end of the century could match Charles Booth's 'Ship-building may leave the Thames' etc. at the beginning. Just compare the Isle of Dogs with its docks and industries in 1900 to its offices and offices in 1999. If the moneychangers were to leave the City, then few would dare to venture that London could still be 'supreme'. And if they were unlikely to leave tomorrow, then London's financial services industry did seem vulnerable to chaos caused by an unexpected ripple in some far-off place: a bank crash in Tokyo, a revolution in the Far East, an investment bubble bursting over the Internet. Jitters had never seemed more infectious. They were not eased by the thought that many of the City's most powerful institutions were merely camping out there while the going was good. UK banks were responsible for just 14 per cent of the City's international lending in 1990. After Big Bang the American, European and Asian ownership of great City names was hugely extended, just as foreign multinationals had absorbed British manufacturing from the 1960s. World ownership of 'the City' did not end with financial services. It spread across central London, so that significant, even characteristic, real estate had gone the same way as the financial institutions that had made it all possible, selling themselves first and London after. Battersea Power Station and County Hall, owned by Hong Kong and Japanese investors respectively, were outstanding examples. Maybe none of that would matter when the jitters came to call. But it was all a far cry from the traditional ties of family to business and business to locality that had knit together a fair proportion of the London economy till the 1960s at least.

Another apparently unavoidable by-product of the global city and the rise of the money industries was – a favourite word of the time – polarization. Everything was polarized. Indeed, within the financial services industry itself, an overnight bonus could reward one individual with wealth that a back-office keyboard operator might struggle to earn in a working lifetime. And on the streets of London, the young Porsche-owner and the young beggar – side by side but a world apart – became a symbol of the new London, its woes and its allures, that had emerged from the 1980s.

But then London, of course, had always been one of the most divided – polarized – cities on earth. And there was some evidence across the century that while certain breaches had widened, others had healed.

6. Richer and Poorer

Always with Us

East London in the 1980s. A lone parent with four children aged sixteen and under. Her two school-age children 'do not have raincoats. She and her eldest daughter go without breakfast . . . She herself does not possess a raincoat and she has only two pairs of stockings . . . None of the children could be allowed to go on any outing in 1985.' Terry, twenty-eight, a single mother with three children:

'We're getting low now. We've got food for today, but there's none for tomorrow . . . I make sure the kids eat all right, they get fish fingers and beefburgers, and if we're lucky once a week we'll have mincemeat [*sic*]. I just have one meal a day, sometimes I don't eat at all, sometimes I have soup or boil up potatoes and put cheese with them. I've had to get the little one out of nappies – I couldn't afford them any more.'

'The Calane family . . . run one bath, which costs 50p in the meter, then get in one after the other, using the same water: father first, wife and baby next, 10-year old boy last.' A better-off family of four, husband a foreman packer, and wife, a school cleaner, were ' "usually without electricity every Wednesday, that's when the money runs out, because I get paid Thursdays. If I don't have more than 50p left, I use it to cook their dinner. Then we go without electric for an hour or two, sometimes all evening. Sometimes I'll read a book by torchlight, sometimes we go to bed early." ' [1]
West London in the 1930s.

The Hodgsons occupied two rooms on the ground floor. The back room where we were had an old-fashioned grate piled high with coal. The atmosphere was, as usual, torrid. On a deal table, spread with a newspaper, was a loaf, the inevitable lump of 'marge', and a few odd plates and cups. The floor was bare, but there was an old curtain at the window, a springless armchair, and a large bed. This was the living-room in which husband and wife and five children had their being. The front and smaller room held the overflow – a cupboard, a tottery washstand, an odd table, and two truckle beds.

Mr Hodgson was unemployed, Mrs Hodgson 'the frailest creature, with a perfectly flat figure, a thin face with starved eyes, and a sudden smile of revealing sweetness': ' "Groceries, coal, a bit of meat, and bread and potatoes take most of the money after the rent, and we use a lot of soap and soda . . . I make all their clothes . . . and, when a jumper wears out, I undo it and knit up the wool again." ' 'Did she, I wondered, ever go out? "There isn't time", she said. "Pictures? We couldn't afford the money. It's difficult enough to manage a bit of baccy for dad" ', as she called her husband.[2]

A family of five, with one on the way, also in two rooms, the husband unemployed; bread and margarine, sometimes with jam, made two meals a day at breakfast and tea. The bread was bought stale for cheapness and they got through two loaves a day. A target of mutton, purchased late on a Saturday night for a shilling, made dinner for three days. Another three days were meatless. 'All children's clothes made out of old clothes. Mother repairs children's shoes. Can buy an old motor tyre for 2d or 3d at the rag fair. Strips the tyre and uses rubber for soles and heels.'[3]

South London, around 1910. Mrs X, 'a deserted wife, with three children under eight'. She worked as an office cleaner in the City and lived in two rooms, but 'Owing to her lack of beds and bedding she and her three children were forced to sleep all in one bed . . .' She could afford only sausages or 'pieces' (offcuts of meat), with potatoes and 'pot herbs' or greens for Sunday. So her midday meals from Monday ran: 'Remains of sausages and potatoes . . . [Tuesday:] ¼ lb bacon, half a loaf of bread . . . [Wednesday:] halfpennyworth of fish for Lulu [who was ailing], and halfpennyworth of potatoes. Landlord downstairs gave Mrs X some meat pie and potatoes . . . [Thursday:] Bread, margarine, and tea . . . [Friday:] Bread and three bloaters.' Breakfast and tea, seven days a week, were '[h]alf a loaf, margarine and tea', so on Friday that served for all three meals. 'The eldest boy of seven has dinners at school five days in the week in term-time . . . All the children are extremely delicate.'

Then,

A woman with a sick child – one of six – living in one room, was allowed milk [by the poor law authorities] for the use of the child, who was extremely ill. The only place where she could keep the milk was a basin with an old piece of wet rag thrown over it. The visitor found seven flies in the milk, and many others crawling on the inner side of the rag. The weather was stifling. The room, though untidy, was tolerably clean. But over the senseless child on the one bed in the room hovered a great cloud of flies. The mother stood hour after hour brushing them away. On the advice of the visitor the sick child was carried off there and then to the infirmary, where it ultimately recovered. Once the child was removed, the flies ceased to swarm into the room.[4]

The destiny of that mother and child in Kennington before the First World War was fixed in the clear lens of Maud Pember Reeves's *Round About a Pound a Week* (1913). Families with just that to live on were emphatically 'not the poorest . . . Far from it! . . . The poorest people – the river-side casual, the workhouse in-and-out, the bar-room loafer – are anxiously ignored by these respectable persons whose work is permanent, as permanency goes in Lambeth, and whose wages range from 18s to 30s a week.'[5] But Reeves's classic study, and those that followed it over the next eighty years or so, reveal something of the continuities of poverty in London across a century: the plight of women, on whom poverty always fell hardest; the blighted life-chances of children growing up poor; the anxiety of an empty purse, gnawing at the guts as sharply as any hunger; and the inability to take advantage of a general rise in living standards so that the full participation of the poor in society was tantalizingly, almost mockingly, withheld.

There was perennial debate over just what proportion of Londoners at any one time could be considered poor. Charles Booth, the wealthy son of a Liverpool shipping magnate, set out in 1887 to debunk the socialists' contention that 25 per cent of working-class Londoners were in poverty, living on wages that could not sustain them in proper health. But when he published the first results of his investigation two years later, he concluded that over 350,000 Londoners were 'very poor' and 'at all times more or less "in want". They are ill-nourished and poorly clad.' A further 938,000 were 'poor': 'Their lives are an unending struggle, and lack comfort . . .' Adding these together made 30.7 per cent of the County of London population in 1889 – the whole population, not just the working class. So Booth gave a far worse picture of London than even the Marxist Social Democratic Federation had ever dared to paint.[6]

Charles Booth drew his poverty line at 'a fairly regular though bare income, such as 18s or 21s per week for a moderate family'. The very poor earned less than this, and some of those getting more could still be poor if they had four or more children. His massively documented findings and dramatic conclusion were much argued about at the time, but they were never replaced by any more convincing alternative. When the last of his great series of seventeen volumes on *Life and Labour of the People in London* was published in 1902, he felt no need to revise his estimates, despite some few years of unexampled prosperity and regular employment at the end of the 1890s. But it is interesting to note the enormous gap between Booth's estimate of almost a third of Londoners in poverty and the numbers of those relieved by the poor law as destitute or incapable of supporting themselves. Even including 'lunatics', orphans and the 'insane', less than 3 per cent of the County of London population received poor relief in 1913, the year *Round About a Pound a Week* was published, and pretty typical for poor relief in pre-1914 London. Three-quarters of these had to go into the workhouse before aid was granted. In that same year around 55 per cent of Londoners over seventy were receiving the new old age pensions and some unemployed men in insured trades were receiving benefit; but even taking all these into account, probably fewer than 5 per cent of Londoners at any time were receiving state assistance between 1900 and 1919.[7]

Nor had those figures changed greatly forty years after Booth first published his poverty findings. In 1929 around 4.4 per cent of the County's population were in receipt of poor relief, although nearly three out of four of these were relieved in their own homes rather than the 'House'; and it is true that old age pensions and unemployment benefit helped many more in the 1920s and 1930s than before the First World War. It was in 1929 that a team based in the London School of Economics revisited the Booth findings in a *New Survey of London Life and Labour*. The project, directed by Sir Hubert Llewellyn Smith, a former Civil Servant sympathetic to the cause of labour, and published in nine volumes between 1930 and 1935, found great difficulty in choosing an appropriate poverty line for the fundamentally changed circumstances of the late 1920s. Professor A. L. Bowley, the leading statistician of the age and main author of the *New Survey*'s poverty chapters, confessed to its 'twenty-six or more estimates, varying from 3.3 to 13.4%, of the proportions in poverty, any one of which might be quoted legitimately'.[8]

Adjusting Booth's 18–21s to 1929 prices produced 38–40s a week, or 39s for a couple with two children aged ten and under. This was such a stringent standard that – as in Booth's day – 'There is no surplus for beer, tobacco, amusement, trade-union subscription or voluntary expenditure of any sort. Emergency can only be met by some windfall or by stinting food or clothes', or rent.[9]

This updated Booth standard came under considerable criticism during the 1930s. It left too little scope for taking advantage of new commodities which society now considered essentials, even if in Booth's day they were luxuries or not yet thought of; neither did it accord with what modern scientific opinion considered a satisfactory dietary for health, hotly contested though that question was, too. The most influential critique of the *New Survey*'s poverty line, taking account of a new minimum dietary published by the British Medical Association, was that of R. F. George in 1937. He concluded that the *New Survey*'s poverty line was 18 per cent too low (excluding rents). At 1929 prices that would have pushed the 39s figure to 47s 4d. Similarly, Seebohm Rowntree, whose first great study of poverty in York was published in 1901, calculated a 'Human Needs Standard' in 1937 that at last provided a modest allowance for 'inessentials'; and that would have cost 59s at 1929 prices for a family of five.[10]

Applying the Booth standard in 1929, the *New Survey* concluded that just 6.6 per cent of the London population were in poverty in the week they were surveyed. That was a dramatic reduction, even over forty years, and truly reflected Bowley's view 'that poverty, as a former generation knew it, has fortunately become very rare, when a regular wage is received . . .' But poverty is experienced in relation to its own time, not that of a former generation. And if the R. F. George reworking for a healthier dietary was used, then the proportion in poverty rose to 9.3 per cent; and some 23 per cent of Londoners in the *New Survey* area in 1929 fell below Rowntree's more modern needs standard. That was still a smaller fraction than in 1900, but it represented a very substantial minority, some 1.3 million Londoners in all.[11]

The long summer of full employment after the Second World War coincided with the first years of a nationalized welfare system. The 1940s and 1950s maintained the low levels of state support to the poor that had characterized the first forty years of the century. Even in 1966, at the start of London's economic problems, just 5.4 per cent of the Greater London population over fifteen years old received supplementary benefit and three-quarters of these were old age pensioners. London in the late 1960s was the 'least poor' region in the country.[12]

But by 1983 the picture had begun to alter drastically. The re-emergence of mass unemployment pushed the numbers on supplementary benefit in London to 10.4 per cent, and by now the proportion of pensioners among them had dropped to four out of ten. Over 580,000 individuals were on benefit in London. Dependence on state aid in some parts of the capital was such that a strike of Civil Servants in the summer of 1981 threatened rioting by panic-stricken families with no resources to fall back on; town halls stepped in with food parcels and cash advances until officials returned to work. By 1994, the numbers in receipt of income support had risen to 936,000, one in every six Londoners aged fifteen and over, including the poorest pensioners. And London's position was notably worse than the nation's as a whole: it had 25 per cent of households with at least one member on benefit compared to Great Britain's 21 per cent; 26 per cent of households on housing benefit compared to 20 per cent; and high rents meant that London claimed a fifth of the country's housing benefit while having just an eighth of its people.[13]

Nor did this extraordinary rise in the numbers of Londoners on state aid exhaust the ranks of 'the poor'. Supplementary benefit was not claimed by everyone who qualified for it. In any event, benefit scales were considered inadequate to sustain a reasonable standard of life, so those on benefit were still poor. And those with incomes less than 40 per cent above the benefit scales were on the margins of poverty, likely to become poor with any adverse change in financial circumstances. A London poverty survey carried out by Peter Townsend and others concluded that in 1983 around 300,000 were living below benefit level but not claiming it; 600,000 were claiming it but were still poor; and 900,000 had household incomes of no more than 140 per cent of benefit scales, and were therefore on the margins of poverty. In 1996 the comparable figures were 200,000, around a million and 900,000 – in all some 2.1 million or 30 per cent of the London population. So back to Booth.[14]

And in more ways than one. For if there were many similarities in the relative experience of poverty across the century, and in the proportion of Londoners considered to be poor, then the causes of poverty – as indicated by those groups most at risk of being poor – seemed to be enduring facts of London life too.

Unemployment – which in Booth's day was as much under-employment through casual labour – was a dominant cause of poverty across the century, fluctuating with the economic fortunes of London and the nation but at its worst for Londoners from the late 1970s through to the late 1990s. So were low wages a constant factor, especially in the service sector: 18 per cent of London employees, many of them part-time, were considered low-paid in the summer of 1995, for instance. Although these economic factors were significant across the century, in the last quarter they were impacting differently on Londoners according to race: 16 per cent of white employees in London were considered to be low-paid in 1995, but 33 per cent of non-whites, and black and ethnic minority people were more likely to be unemployed than whites.[15] That of course was a new element overlaying the distribution of poverty since the days of Booth or the *New Survey*.

Old age was another factor commonly associated with poverty across the century, and so was the proportion of households headed by women. But during the century the relative position of these two groups changed. The elderly gradually became generally more prosperous as those who retired on employment pensions or with savings were able to protect themselves from penury; although those who had to rely on the basic state pension, never on its own a sufficient safeguard against poverty, remained poor. On the other hand, the proportion of poorer households headed by women grew very considerably. Women who were breadwinners suffered labour-market discrimination in the low-wage jobs that were generally open to them; and their hours of work were restricted by the demands of child-care. The families of widows had always been notoriously prominent among examples of 'the deserving poor' before the First World War. But the rise, through more frequent marriage- or relationship-breakdown, of the 'single-parent family' in the 1960s greatly extended this particular source of poverty. This was peculiarly an inner London phenomenon. In 1991 8.1 per cent of families in Great Britain comprised lone parents with dependent children; in Greater London it was 10.9 per cent. But in inner London the proportion of lone-parent families was more than twice the national average at 16.8 per cent, with Lambeth, at 21.5 per cent, the highest in the country.[16]

One final factor was more strongly related to poverty in Booth's day than in subsequent generations. Trying to raise a large family on even a reasonable working-class income almost invariably involved penny-pinching and frequently real want. Large families alone accounted for about 8.5 per cent of poverty discovered by Booth. But by 1930 this was down to 6 per cent. That reflected a decline in the proportion of large families within the London working class. The birth-rate in London halved from around thirty births per 1,000 population each year in the 1890s to fifteen in 1931, and it kept remarkably close to that figure for the rest of the century. The loss of 60,000 London men in the trenches caused an especially sharp dip in the birth-rate during and after the First World War. It never recovered to its pre-1914 level. To some degree, that was a result of birth control becoming better known about and more readily available in the 1920s. But that in itself was a function of women and men choosing to avoid the harsh economic consequences of having too many mouths to feed, a lesson apparently permanently absorbed.[17]

The seemingly indelible stain of poverty – which continued to make London a vale of tears for a substantial minority of its people across the century – must not be allowed to mask the rise of comfort, even for the poor, since the days of Charles Booth and Maud Pember Reeves. The steady rise in the standard of life, in which Londoners partook and in many ways led, affected all classes – and, for once, the poor more equally than others.

The First World War was a crucial turning point for the London poor. For perhaps the first time in history the war economy provided full-time employment for all who needed it. It gave opportunities for improved living standards beyond the dreams of the boom years followed by bust that had characterized the Victorian and Edwardian economies. Despite rampant price inflation and some shortages of materials, despite the ill-effects of the London housing shortage, which pinched even tighter in the war years, the standard of life and comfort rose dramatically for virtually every section of the London working class. Looking back to Booth's time from 1929, the most fruitful comparison is not so much between now and 40 years ago as between post-war and pre-war conditions – so much greater and more striking have sometimes been the sudden changes wrought in the conditions of London Life and Labour by the great catastrophe, than by the slighter and more gradual movements of the whole of the preceding generation.[18]

   War increased family incomes through a ready availability of jobs for men, women and adolescents, at uniquely high wages and with endless overtime for those who could work it. The free choice of jobs tended to benefit the poor and unskilled most of all. So did flat-rate wage increases, often called a 'cost of living bonus', designed to protect everyone equally from wartime inflation; so did the rise of trade unionism, said to have grown by 80 per cent in the East End, and the collective bargaining power that went with it; and so, too, did the freeze on most unfurnished rents from the end of 1915, and the food rationing that came later in the war. Inequality within the working class reduced in these years, tending to shorten the economic and social distance between the ultra-respectable bowler-hatted craftsman and the ragged-arsed general labourer who had represented the extremes of pre-war working-class life in London. Before the war, a London hod-carrier had earned under 70 per cent of the wage of the bricklayer he had laboured for; after the war he earned 81 per cent. Before the war, a labourer in a London engineering works had earned 52 per cent of a pattern-maker's wages; after, he earned 75 per cent. Before the war, a London dock labourer, the most ragged of them all, had earned 5s 10d a day; at the end he earned 11s 9d, a rise of 101 per cent, with more days' work into the bargain. Women's wages, too, tended to come closer to men's and in a few cases employers made gestures towards equal pay for equal work, responding to a steep rise in trade union membership among women.[19]
   The change was such that economic distress seemed to be just a bad memory. It was plain to see in the East End during the bitter winter of early 1917:

During the last great frost in 1895, for instance, there was distress and suffering . . . Yet in the greatest of all wars . . . there is very little unemployment and no distress funds are needed, in spite of the fact that the winter has been the severest for 22 years and that prices are higher than they have been for a couple of generations.[20]

'You cannot buy a cheap piano for immediate delivery,' complained a middle-class Londoner in 1916. 'They have all gone into the cottages of the workmen, who have never made so much money.' And the urge to put cash into the home was a universal working-class response to improved conditions, even if there wasn't much of a home to speak of. Florrie Roberts's Walworth family, members of the poor labouring class before 1914, could put four adults to work during the war, including mother, who made gas masks: 'I used to spend my money as soon as I got it. I was all for making the house look nice. I bought something each week: curtains, a new blind, an aspidistra to put in the window, carpets on the floor – little things to make the place look nice.' And in Dolly Scannell's Poplar home, mother

visited Killwick's at Stepney and bought a green plush sofa and matching armchairs. They had mahogany curved arms and legs and beautiful cream roses on the seats of green plush. A carved mahogany occasional table, a rug by the marble fireplace and a mahogany overmantel with many mirrors on it completed the furnishing of this luxury room. Father [a plumber pre-war] was very cross when he arrived home from the war; he thought mother was turning into an extravagant woman . . . [21]

Indeed, working-class women led this drive to conspicuous consumption, aggravating the sensibilities of the middle classes in the process. A couple of months after the Armistice a

queue of over a thousand women and girls was to be seen outside Tottenham Employment Exchange on Friday morning. They were waiting to receive their 25s out-of-work bonus. It was a well-dressed queue; the musquash and seal coat, eloquent of the former munition worker, was not absent, while most of the queue-ists appeared to be under 21 . . . On the same day the [*Tottenham and Edmonton Weekly*] *Herald* advertisement columns contained 187 advertisements for domestic servants, and about a hundred more for female assistants for businesses and laundries.[22]

These high times did not last for ever; or even for very long. The engineering slump of 1921–2 saw many a wartime treasure pop into the pawnbroker's, never to be redeemed. Life for the long-term unemployed, for widows' families, for the elderly on a state pension, was miserable enough, and by no means assuaged by the feeling that there were fewer really poor people about than there had been. Yet the fear of the workhouse diminished as authorities increasingly withdrew it as a pre-condition for relief. Unemployment benefit staved off starvation without the need to grovel to the Poor Law Guardians. Improved literacy, more libraries, and the radio – literally more common in London by the end of the 1930s than the kitchen sink – offered previously unavailable solace. In general, London workers never looked back after 1914. They never experienced again the grinding, scraping, grubbing hand-to-mouth existence that had scarred the lives of one in three Londoners before 'the great catastrophe'. Small wonder that sharp-eyed London watchers like Tommy Burke considered 'the end of the Great War' to be the beginning of the twentieth century: 'Not until 1920 did London enter upon its new era of structural or spiritual change. Thus, in writing of London before the war one has a feeling of writing of the London of the last century. And really one is.'[23]

The 1920s and 1930s consolidated the rise in the standard of life of the London working class that the First World War had so unexpectedly fan-fared. Luxury commodities for the home – sideboards, three-piece suites, linoleum, gramophones – were available on the 'never-never' for those in regular employment. The working week was cut by seven hours, giving 'the average London worker . . . an extra day to himself', since Booth's day. 'Inessentials' like holidays at the seaside or entertainments (unknown by Booth) like cinema, greyhound racing and speedway accounted for some 24 per cent of working-class expenditure at the end of the 1930s. Con-venience foods in bottles and cans and packets were changing eating habits for the better. There was some sharing of middle-class indulgence by labour aristocrats, like compositors on *The Times*, who 'drove up to Printing House Square in Rileys or Rovers when the average reporter was lucky to run an Austin 7 or Morris 8'. Several observers noted that the 'most remarkable outward change of the Twenties was in the looks of women in the towns. The prematurely aged wife was coming to be the exception rather than the rule.'[24]

It was perhaps in the lives of poor children that the post-war rise in living standards was most noticeable. Selecting London school photographs from the 1890s and then contrasting them with the same school in the 1930s was a favoured way of showing social progress, the bright-eyed well-groomed sleek youngsters in blazers, shiny shoes and open-neck shirts a breathtaking improvement on their ragged, crop-haired scowling forebears, bare toes sticking through the gaping uppers and soles of their unspeakable boots, and some with no boots at all.[25] By 1925, the LCC's chief child psychologist considered that free school dinners for the poor had 'almost entirely abolished gross instances of under-feeding'. Horace Thorogood, writing of east London in 1935, remarked how 'bare-footed, ragged, and mal-nourished children are very seldom seen today'. He recalled pre-war Shadwell on a 'hot day [when] the narrow, crowded streets smelt foully. Sluttish women lurked in doorways . . . There was a steady traffic to and from the public-houses, where babies crawled about the dirty steps . . . All that has been abolished.' Louis Heren conceded that even Shadwell, one of the poorest and most crowded London districts of Booth's day, 'was not a bad place' by the time he moved away in 1937: 'There was more work in the docks, and therefore more money to spend.'[26] Even so, all this improvement would still not diminish the shock experienced by middle-class provincial England confronted by evacuated schoolchildren from inner London and elsewhere in 1939; in part, it appears, because of the prevalence of head lice in urban areas.[27]

Heightened working-class expectations between the wars resulted in a palpable narrowing of the capital's class divide. 'To an increasing extent the rich and the poor read the same books, and they also see the same films and listen to the same radio programmes,' George Orwell wrote in 1941, admittedly with a patriotic point to make. The *New Survey* also remarked that 'the visible signs of class distinction are disappearing':

The dress of the younger generation of working men and women, so far from having any distinctive note of its own [compared to the choker, Derby coats and ostrich feathers of pre-war days], tends merely to copy, sometimes to exaggerate, any particular fashion current in the West End. In the same way paint and powder, once regarded in this class as the marks of the prostitute, are freely used by respectable working girls. [1,500 lipsticks were said to be sold in London shops in 1931 for every one just ten years before.] With men the pipe has given way to the cigarette, and where it persists it is no longer a clay but a briar. The Cockney dialect and rhyming slang are slowly disappearing while the Cockney twang is spreading to other classes.[28]

The rise of what later would be known as 'estuary English' was accompanied by other evidence of a narrowing class gulf with the growth of the suburbs and the decline of the servant-keeping habit. This cross-class experience was powerfully extended by the forced egalitarianism of war and rationing in the 1940s; by the rise of mass spectator sports; by the television and motor car-led consumer boom of the 1950s and early 1960s; and through and beyond Swinging London with its common culture based on fashion and pop, and the new sexual and social freedoms which happily hopped over all known class boundaries. Even the widening inequalities that re-emerged in the late 1970s and 1980s failed to disturb that truly popular culture which emerged between the wars to take an unshakeable grip on the experience of the great mass of Londoners.

In all this transformation the lives of the rich changed far less than the lives of the poor. The rich are always with us – especially in London, where, on any index at any time, both average earnings and top earnings were higher than anywhere else in the country. The consumption of the rich in London may well have become less conspicuous after the First World War than before, as Tommy Burke thought it had, because 'the rich and privileged

... have learned something of good taste and renounced ostentation', if only, perhaps, to give a more democratic age less to complain about.[29] But at the end of the century they sent their children to the same schools that they had at the beginning, where manners, curriculum and teaching styles largely bypassed the huge changes in education experienced by the mass of Londoners over the same period. The weekend habit, country motoring, and foreign holidays had all been features of London 'society' before the First World War, when 'town' had emptied after the London 'season' of May to July. The survival over many generations of smart provision shops (Fortnum and Mason, Simpson's), jewellers (Asprey's, Tessier's), tailors (Gieves, Poole), private banks (Hoare & Co., Coutts & Co.) and one-stop stores (Harrods, Barkers, Harvey Nichols), in streets where the wealthy had only ever shopped (Bond Street, Savile Row, Knightsbridge, Piccadilly), utterly defied trends to multiples, supermarkets, shopping centres and big high-street names. A similar immortality attached to famous restaurants (Rules, Wheeler's, Prunier's), bookshops (Hatchards, Quaritch, Sotheran), art galleries and gentlemen's (from the 1970s often ladies', too) clubs in St James's. The debutantes' ball may have stopped rolling by around 1960 and music hall for the louche man-about-town may have given way to the more genteel West End musical show, but Buckingham Palace garden parties, smart nightclubs, private functions at galleries or City guilds, dinners at the Inns of Court or Guildhall or Mansion House, the crush bar at Covent Garden or the Long Room at Lord's were few of many golden threads connecting the wealthy or patrician Londoners of 1900 with their successors of 1999. A Piccadilly buck transplanted from Mafeking Night to Millennium celebrations would, with a few adjustments of costume and vocabulary, have been readily at home in a London where he could still find everything he wanted, and more or less where he had known it always to be. Neither would he have been put to shame by any false modesty. Conspicuous consumption in *fin-de-siècle* London was once more raucously in vogue. The rise, especially around the time of Big Bang and after, of the yuppie, the 'buppie' (black urban professionals), the 'swell' (single women earning lots in London), the 'dinkie' (double income no kids), the 'dockney' (living in Docklands and working in the City) and the reinvented 'Champagne Charlies', all re-created a 'loadsamoney' provocative extravagance that would have been entirely familiar to the swells and toffs of the Edwardian West End.[30]

One important change, though, in the configuration of the London rich cannot be allowed to pass without notice. In Booth's day the rich were curiously ghettoized. There they are, fittingly marked in gold on Booth's street maps of poverty and wealth, clustered round the West End's great green spaces like crows round a cornfield. John Galsworthy peopled the ghetto with a single family who represented the intricate geography of a class and the subtle symbols of a whole way of life.

The position of their houses was of vital importance to the Forsytes, nor was this remarkable, since the whole spirit of their success was embodied therein . . . Their residences, placed at stated intervals round the park, watched like sentinels, lest the fair heart of this London, where their desires were fixed, should slip from their clutches, and leave them lower in their own estimations. There was old Jolyon in Stanhope Place; the Jameses in Park Lane; Swithin in the lonely glory of orange and blue chambers in Hyde Park Mansions – he had never married, not he! – the Soameses in their nest off Knightsbridge; the Rogers in Prince's Gardens . . . The Haymans again – Mrs Hayman was the one married Forsyte sister – in a house high up on Campden Hill . . . the Nicholases in Ladbroke Grove, a spacious abode and a great bargain; and last, but not least, Timothy's on the Bayswater Road, where Ann, and Judy, and Hester, lived under his protection.[31]

Ninety-odd years on and there were many more rich Londoners than the park's perimeter could accommodate. They still held on to the territory the Forsytes had staked out. But whereas in Booth's day the poor had penetrated the rich man's ghetto in scattered mews and back alleys and in the crowded streets behind Westminster Abbey, now the rich had overwhelmed the purlieus of the poor. In 1999 inner London was proclaimed 'the richest area in the European Union', with average wealth per head more than twice the European average.[32] The richest area in inner London, judged by household income, was not in Mayfair, Belgravia or South Kensington but the City Corporation's Barbican Estate, a run-down commercial and industrial area in Booth's day. Reassuringly, five of the ten wealthiest postcodes were indeed in Forsyte territory (plus Dulwich, Highgate, Wimbledon and Hampstead – all prosperous commuter villages for City men at the turn of the century). But the spread of wealth in 1990s London was better revealed by the poorest ten postcodes. Virtually all would have looked grotesquely out of place in such a list in Booth's day. His most deprived areas were Waterloo and St Saviour's; Old Street and south Shoreditch; St George's-in-the-East and Shadwell; Bethnal Green; Whitechapel and Spitalfields. But in the late 1990s not one of these figured in the list of London's poorest districts. All housed sufficient wealthy residents to balance out some of the poverty they without doubt still contained. The lowest average household incomes in London were now to be found in central Woolwich; the less well-off part of Putney (including 'the notorious Roehampton Estate', astonishing epitaph for the LCC's Corbusian dream);

south Bermondsey and north Peckham; Plashet (East Ham); and East Camberwell and adjoining parts of Peckham. And suburban poverty – not exactly a new phenomenon, as a few cases of starvation or suicide through destitution on LCC estates in the 1920s and 1930s testified – was rediscovered as a larger and more sinister problem in the 1990s, this time among home-owners rather than tenants.[33]

All this added up to a far more heterogeneous class geography in London at the end of the twentieth century than probably ever before. Inevitably, this reflected a more even distribution of Londoners between the classes, as in the country as a whole. London in Booth's day was very largely working-class, even if there were many shades and distinctions within the class itself. Around 82 per cent of Londoners in the County were manual wage earners at the turn of the century. That picture had shifted considerably by 1930 (72 per cent) in a survey area that included significant parts of outer London. By 1991, the rise of the office worker had pushed the proportion of Greater London households headed by manual workers down to 61 per cent and inner and outer London showed no great variation from each other.[34]

Despite this class cohabitation, there was much evidence at the end of the century that the better-off in these mixed areas were getting richer and the worse-off getting poorer. It was another classic London paradox: living closer together but moving further apart. Analyses of London incomes showed the poorest 10 per cent of households falling further behind average earnings during the 1980s and 1990s, and the top 10 per cent pulling further ahead. And, largely because top earnings in London were higher than in the nation as a whole, this widening income gap was more pronounced in London than anywhere else. In 1994–5 11.5 per cent of Greater London incomes were less than £80 per week, compared with 10.4 per cent in England; and 20.5 per cent were above £650, compared with 14.2 per cent. The 'richest area in the European Union' contained within it nine of the twenty most deprived local authority districts in England in 1998. London was not a more polarized city than in Booth's day, but it was hardly less so. And it did seem more polarized than during at least the four middle decades of the century, from 1930 to 1970.[35]

There were, though, two significant areas where – if inequality had not disappeared – basic standards had risen so far from Charles Booth's time that the experience of living in London at one end of the century and the other seemed worlds apart. Those were the health and life expectancy of Londoners and their housing conditions.

Public Health, Private Space

The death-rate, a traditional indicator of the health of a society, fell in London by just over half between 1901 and 1997. The inner London figure, the only available index for such a long run of years, showed a drop from 17.1 deaths per 1,000 living in 1901 to 8.3 in 1997. Compared with the population of England and Wales as a whole, inner London's population was less healthy than the nation's until the end of the First World War; then slightly better or about the same from around 1920 to 1970; it then became less healthy than the nation's again, especially during the late 1980s and early 1990s, when inner London failed to benefit as much as the rest of the country from a marked improvement nationwide; and then, catching up some lost ground, it was about the same as the nation's once more by 1997. That pattern seemed a pretty accurate indicator of inner London's relative prosperity over the same period. Outer London's population, though, always had a lower death-rate than the nation's, often by a wide margin. That meant that Greater London as a whole seemed generally healthier than England and Wales right across the century.[36]

That swarm of flies where the Lambeth family lived eight to a room (and eight to a bed) in 1913 was one measure of how far the health prospects of Londoners had come by the end of the century. And there were others from about the same time. Official medical examinations of men of military age conducted in 1917–18 classed 31.5 per cent nationally as having 'marked physical disabilities' or disabling 'evidence of past disease' and 10 per cent as 'totally and permanently unfit'; the figures for the 'London Region' were significantly worse – 37.4 per cent and 11.1 per cent respectively. Of all London men examined, 7.8 per cent were considered to have 'valvular disease' of the heart and over one in twenty to have 'Deformities, Congenital and acquired (including Flat Foot, Hammer Toe, etc.)'.[37]

It was during the 1920s, after wartime benefits had worked their way through, that the life expectancy of Londoners, as measured by the death-rate, took a sharp and apparently permanent turn for the better. The County of London death-rate of around 12.5 per 1,000 living in 1921 was not greatly different from that of sixty years later (11.9 in 1981). The improvement was especially marked in the reduction of avoidable deaths among London infants. In 1901 over one in seven children born alive in the County of London died before they were a year old (14.8 per cent). Infant mortality had already begun to fall in the 1890s and that trend strengthened even before the First World War. By 1910, just over 10 per cent of County children died in their first year, and the figure was 9.5 per cent in Greater

London. In this regard, London was healthier by far than many other great cities – the rate in Manchester and Liverpool was 15.1 per cent, for instance. There was then a dramatic fall in the London infant mortality rate at the end of the First World War to around 6 per cent in 1923, dipping again at the end of the 1930s. By 1938, infant mortality in inner London was almost a third of the 1901 figure, and there was another sharp fall through the war years and just after. For all their dour utilitarianism, the 1940s saw much attention paid to the care of infants, with practical help for virtually all who needed it. In 1948 just 3.1 per cent of London babies were dying in their first year and in 1964 the figure was 2.1 per cent. There was then a further dramatic fall in the 1970s to just over 1 per cent in 1983 and 0.7 per cent in 1996.

This heartening trend did, though, hide many disparities. Infant mortality was always seen as a significant indicator of deprivation, at least until the last thirty years of the century, when the figures dropped too low to be a meaningful signpost any longer. Between the wars, babies in working-class Shoreditch were almost twice as likely to die in their first year as babies in middle-class Hampstead or Lewisham. Inequality within boroughs could be even more extreme: Brompton ward in South Kensington averaged an infant mortality rate of 3.2 per cent between 1932 and 1934 (some fifteen years ahead of its time), while Norland (Notting Dale) in North Kensington averaged 11 per cent (fifteen years behind the inner London average).[38] Poverty, malnutrition, overcrowding, lack of washing and sanitary facilities combined in the worst streets of Hoxton and Notting Dale, and much of the rest of working-class London, to make child-rearing a hazardous business, despite the efforts of mothers and despite improving council health services.

One factor in the decline of infant mortality between 1900 and 1940 was the diminished virulence of some epidemic killers. Roughly a quarter of infant deaths before the First World War were due to diarrhoea, mostly 'summer diarrhoea' spread partly (it was thought) by flies. It was still a big problem in the late 1930s, causing between one in five and one in six infant deaths. But tuberculosis (TB) in babies had ceased to be a significant killer by 1930; the last major smallpox epidemic in London was in 1902 (7,000 cases and over 1,300 deaths); and the great childhood killers of the Edwardian years were far less ferocious, though vile enough, by the 1930s. So measles, for instance, killed nearly 2,000 in 1910, but 584 in 1936; the figures for whooping cough were 1,363 and 278; diphtheria – 'a London disease; it is endemic here and has been so for generations past' – 434 and 226; and scarlet fever 214 and forty-two.[39]

Even so, no childhood was immune from the life-threatening nature of these annual or biennial epidemics, at least until after the Second World War. It is hardly surprising that illness features to an extraordinary extent in working-class memoirs of London childhoods in the 1920s and 1930s. John Holloway, from upper-working-class Norwood in the 1920s, recalled a severe bout of whooping cough when he was seven which his mother treated by wheeling him in a pushchair to the Shirley Hills daily for fresh air; other mothers took similar sufferers to local gasworks – fumes brought on cathartic vomiting, which brought some relief from the terrible cough. The feared diphtheria was warded off by the London child's charm of 'touch collar, never swaller'. All five children in Grace Foakes's Poplar family went down with scarlet fever and were distributed around the London fever hospitals either side of Tower Bridge. Long stays in hospital were common-place. George Cook from Hackney wrote about a childhood taken over by his struggle against pulmonary TB, rather rare in children, and his years in hospital and sanatorium. Rose Gamble and her brother were both laid up at the same time in Chelsea's Tite Street Hospital, she with meningitis, he with peritonitis. And in 1920s Walthamstow, poor Robert Barltrop, future historian of the Socialist Party of Great Britain, copped the lot:

I was an ailing small child. According to my parents I had bronchitis fearfully when I was two. I remember having whooping cough at three, and being given ipecacuanha root to make me vomit. Measles, mumps and scarlet fever (in the isolation hospital at Chingford for that, with my skin peeling and my parents not allowed beyond the doorway). When I was five, in my first year at school, I had nasal diphtheria; and while I was recovering from it, having made no contact with any other child for weeks, I got chicken pox.[40]

These diseases had largely (but not entirely) evaporated as a threat to life by the end of the 1940s, with polio, which reached epidemic proportions in London in the mid-1950s, providing for a time a new nightmare of childhood.

Similarly TB, the 'White Death' or 'White Scourge' of the Edwardian years, which in all its ghastly guises killed almost 10,000 Londoners in the County in 1906, had become less pernicious by 1936, though still accounting for over 3,000 deaths. But by 1956, with the rise of antibiotics, it was killing fewer than 500 a year, and that was down to 160 in 1971. TB was a disease associated with poverty and crowding, with morbidity rates highest in Bermondsey and Southwark and lowest in Hampstead; and it was notoriously prevalent among workers in the East End tailoring sweatshops, especially the pressers, who worked in damp air all day long.

Infectious diseases were killed off mainly by better living conditions, and partly by improved vaccination rates between the wars, and antibiotic intervention and better vaccines from the 1940s. But the nineteenth century could still, as it were, bite back. Water from a contaminated well at Croydon caused an epidemic of typhoid fever which affected over 300 and killed forty-three in the autumn of 1937, the last severe outbreak of the disease during the century.[41] But as the Victorian diseases diminished then new killers emerged. TB had killed twice as many Londoners as cancer in 1906 but that picture had completely reversed thirty years later. And heart disease was causing over one in every three deaths among men and women aged forty-five or over in 1936, compared to fewer than one in seven in 1912.

Cancers seemed to bear a confusing relationship to poverty. A comparative study in Hampstead and Shoreditch for 1913–20 showed highest rates of lung and stomach cancers in Shoreditch men; but for all other types Hampstead's rates were distinctly higher, especially of breast and uterine cancers. But heart disease showed a far stronger allegiance to social class, with the five highest rates in London in 1934–6 presenting in Poplar, Stepney, Bethnal Green, Battersea and Southwark. That class connection was still strong in the 1990s, by then overlain by the presence in working-class areas of minority communities whose vulnerability to 'coronary heart disease (among Asians) and stroke (among African/Caribbeans)' was notably high. And the death-rate overall among adult men in inner London was adversely affected by the concentration there of men dying from AIDS-related illness.[42]

Despite huge advances in life expectancy across the century, health inequality remained stubbornly a fact of life and death within London at the millennium. It was not, though, as wide as it had been. Variations of infant mortality and the all-age death-rate were nothing like as wide in the 1990s as in the 1900s. The range of crude death-rates across London Boroughs in 1997 was 7.3 to 11.7 per 1,000, where that of Greater London authorities in 1906 was 8.8 to 20.7, and the infant mortality disparities were far more marked than that. Even so, the geography of poor health outcomes and high mortality in the 1990s would have been recognizable to any Medical Officer of Health in Edwardian London, with its concentrations of illness and premature death in the East End and south London close to the river. Hackney, Tower Hamlets, Newham, Islington and Southwark had the highest proportions of households where at least one individual had a limiting long-term illness in 1991. In Hackney's case the proportion was 35 per cent above the national average and nearly 40 per cent above Greater London's. And it was of real concern to many commentators that, beginning in the 1970s and accelerating through the 1980s into the mid-1990s at least, life chances in inner London seemed to be relatively worse, when compared to the national average, than they had been during the 1950s and 1960s. That was similar – and entirely connected – to the widening gap in household incomes between rich and poor over the same period, despite inner London's status as richest area within the European Union. The poorest got relatively poorer compared to the average Londoner; and they died relatively younger, too.[43]

In general, though, the poorest did not suffer the extremes of inadequate housing conditions that had for so many generations been the lot of the Londoner. Housing was *the* London problem for at least the first eighty years of the century. And it was the biggest worry for Londoners too until crime, unemployment and race relations knocked housing off the top of the anxiety agenda in the 1980s. By that time huge strides had been made in the basic provision of housing in London, so that – dwelling for dwelling – London had probably the best-housed population of any world metropolis by the end of the century. That did not mean there were no problems of shortage or quality remaining; none the less, the improvement since 1900, for all classes but especially the poorest, was quite staggering.

'I do not blame the working man because he stinks,' wrote Somerset Maugham in 1922, 'but stink he does. It makes social intercourse difficult to persons of sensitive nostril. The matutinal tub divides the classes more effectively than birth, wealth or education.'[44] But the tub, matutinal or otherwise, did not become generally available to the working man or woman in inner London until – extraordinary though it seems – the 1970s, fifty years after Maugham wrote. Over half a million Greater London households in 1971 had access only to a shared bathroom or none at all. That was one in five of the households in Greater London. But for those renting from private landlords, still in 1971 the majority tenure for working-class Londoners in inner London at least, around 50 per cent were denied exclusive use of a fixed bath or shower. The author recalls entire streets in Islington in the early 1970s where the houses had not one bathroom between them. At that time Islington had the lowest proportion in London of households with exclusive use of a bath or shower (just 56.4 per cent), but matters were not greatly better in the multi-occupied or older parts of Brent, Camden, Hackney, Hammersmith, Haringey, Kensington and Chelsea, Lambeth, Newham, Southwark, Tower Hamlets, Wandsworth and Westminster, all with borough-wide figures under 75 per cent.[45]

By 1971, of course, things had never been better. Until the late 1930s there were still parts of London where water was not piped to every house and where shared standpipes in a yard, and shared water closets in tumbledown brick shacks nearby, stood in for sanitary arrangements. Even where water was laid on in the house there would often be just one tap in a back-addition scullery, shared by all the tenancies in the house; or maybe an additional tap for the upper floors over a tiny triangular stone sink on the half-landing; those arrangements, too, were common enough in inner London in the 1970s. In these circumstances a bath even in a tin tub was frequently impracticable to arrange: there were often no facilities to heat more than one pail or pan of water at a time. It was the 'bodily dirtiness' of evacuated children that contributed to the collective sense of shame with which they were received in the reception areas. Other domestic tasks were often practically impossible, too. Laundry facilities were totally inadequate in tenement houses; before the Second World War 800,000 visits a year were still being made to council washhouses, and the 'rather pathetic processions of baby chairs and ancient perambulators' piled with laundry was one of the sights of working-class London. In Southam Street, North Kensington, in 1934 hardly any of the 1,500 or so families living above basement level had any facility 'for washing-up or for preparing food . . . for some years one of the great handicaps from which people have suffered in this particular area'. Conditions like that were not just confined to notoriously poor districts like Kensal New Town. They were utterly commonplace. A survey of 1,066 dwellings off Theobald's Road, Holborn, in 1930–31 found just 14 per cent with satisfactory cooking facilities and half the houses had only an outside WC shared by the four or five households in each property. And in 1951 in London County nearly one in three households had to share a water supply, over one-third shared a WC, 16 per cent had no sink for their exclusive use and 44 per cent had no access to a fixed bath, shared or otherwise. Before 1951 such matters were not even thought worthy of inquiry by the Census.[46]

Nor were figures collected of the numbers of London dwellings considered to be verminous, but it is clear enough that large proportions were infested with bedbugs and with mice or rats. In the absence until the 1940s of an insecticide with staying power, bedbugs were the king of the London worker's castle. 'No woman, however clean, can cope' with them, concluded Maud Pember Reeves; 'bugs have dropped on to the pillow of the sick woman [lying-in after childbirth] before the visitor's eyes. One woman complained that they dropped into her ears at night.' 'I have lain in a filthy bed in a Hackney lodging house,' recalled Chris Massie in 1932, 'and bugs have dropped on my face from the ceiling, and when I struck a match the wall was one maze of moving insects, and the atmosphere reeked with them.' Rats, too, were common enough. In a survey of Kentish Town carried out by the indefatigable housing reformers Irene Barclay and Evelyn Perry in 1932–3, 'rat trouble' was a constant complaint.

The tenants say the rats come through holes at the back of the kitchen grate and they feel nervous about leaving the baby alone in the room . . . The wife [in another house] said that rats were a nuisance and that last summer they caught sixteen in one week. The tenant on the top floor had seen a rat on the top flight of stairs in the afternoon three days previously (January, 1933).[47]

Some of the worst of all London living conditions were found in basements, sometimes subterranean cellars, of tall houses built in the nineteenth century for single-family occupation. Basements designed as kitchens, sculleries and pantries were turned over to a family, sometimes two. Rarely built with a damp course, the walls could be wringing wet. Shoreditch had some 2,000 substandard basements around 1931, all occupied, and in the County as a whole in 1934 it was estimated that '100,000 people are existing in underground insanitary homes'. 'In one front basement' in the Clarendon Street area of Paddington in 1930,

live a man and wife, a boy of seven, and girls of 11, 10, nine, six, four and three. This basement room is one of the worst in the street. The front room on the ground floor was at one time a shop, and the area has been partially covered in, so that light only reaches the room below through the bars of an iron grating. The room is consequently very dark. The walls are distempered in a dingy blue colour, and need repair. Plaster is falling in places. There are no cupboard doors [probably burnt at some time for firewood] and coals are heaped in a corner with an old curtain across them. The tenant states she is *obliged to use an oil lamp* for lighting, as the gas company will only let her have the use of gas on a quarterly meter which she cannot afford . . . The family at one time rented the back addition room, measuring about 7ft square, for 2s 6d weekly, but gave it up as it was too damp and dilapidated to use.[48]

Rooms like this could flood when heavy storms forced filth back up the sewers and drains of London's overstretched sewerage system. But the most disastrous flooding of the century in London occurred in the early hours of Saturday 7 January 1928, when a uniquely high tide and gales caused the Thames to burst its banks from Woolwich to Richmond. The greatest damage was in Rotherhithe, Bermondsey, where 'more than 600 homes have been ruined', but both sides of the river were partly inundated for sixteen miles in the coldest January for over thirty years. The force of the water tore the walls from some houses. The greatest loss of life – ten of the fourteen deaths – occurred in the Horseferry Road/Grosvenor Road area of Pimlico, including the four Harding sisters aged eight to eighteen drowned in their basement bedroom. In all, 2,000 houses were damaged and thousands made homeless, losing much of their few belongings in the process. In

Ponsonby Place, Pimlico, a couple of days after the flood, 'sad-eyed men and women – some of them with very little clothing on – groped about among the wreckage, trying to find anything worth taking'.[49]

Poor living conditions were made much worse by almost universal overcrowding in inner London until well into the 1950s. 'Two rooms and a kitchen' was the best a working-class family – of almost any size – could reasonably hope for and they often had to make do with much less. In 1901 there were 150,000 one-room dwellings in the County of London. By 1931 the number of one-room dwellings had only fallen slightly to 145,000, housing over a quarter of a million people. The national overcrowding survey of 1936 revealed that the worst crowding in England and Wales was in inner east and central London, and on the north-east coast of England. The County of London contained 70,731 families living below the legal overcrowding standard in 1936, compared with just 7,815 in the whole of Middlesex.[50]

All these households would have been living in rooms in multi-occupied houses (often called 'tenement' houses until the 1960s). This was the characteristic London housing problem. Even a two-storey family house was usually occupied by two families, one up and one down. In 1961 30 per cent of inner London households shared houses in non-self-contained dwellings. With less than a fifth of the nation's housing stock, Greater London contained 'well over half of all multi-occupied dwellings in the country'. Multiple occupation was then most dense in Islington and south Hornsey, with Hackney, Willesden and Paddington close behind. But the most densely crowded district of London at that time was the Golborne ward of North Kensington (including Southam Street), where 40 per cent of the population lived at a density greater than 1.5 persons per room. Even so, by 1961 things had never been better.[51]

It was London's councils that transformed the living conditions of working-class Londoners. They did so largely in the 1960s and 1970s, mainly the latter. In 1961 the proportion of local authority dwellings in inner London was 21 per cent;[52] in 1971 34 per cent; and in 1981 46 per cent, with a further 7 per cent owned by housing associations. In those boroughs noted for their poor living conditions the proportion could be much higher: Islington 60 per cent, Southwark 67 per cent, Hackney 72 per cent, Tower Hamlets 82 per cent. No doubt council housing programmes were eased considerably by the post-war haemorrhage of working people from inner London to the suburbs or even further afield, but even so these figures were a considerable achievement. There were two major effects of all this activity apparent by the mid-1980s. One was that some parts of London which would undoubtedly have become comprehensively rich and gentrified were perforce shared by working-class council or housing association tenants: North Kensington, for instance, or Barnsbury and 'Islington Village'. And the other was a dramatic improvement in Londoners' living conditions.

By 1991, 97 per cent of households in inner London had the exclusive use of a bath or shower and WC; just one in twenty had to live at a density greater than one person per room (it had been over one in six in 1961); in five London Boroughs, including Tower Hamlets and Southwark, the proportion of households with central heating exceeded the proportion in Greater London and the inner Home Counties (82 per cent), by far and away the most prosperous population in Britain; and just 0.7 per cent of dwellings in Greater London were shared by more than one household.[53]

This remarkable progress was dented considerably by the defective design and construction of much council housing built in the 1960s and early 1970s which caused almost a third of council dwellings to be considered 'unfit' in 1991, mainly because of disrepair and damp.[54] So bad living conditions were not eliminated and were deplorable enough for those forced to endure them. Even so, the condition of London housing at the end of the century was unrecognizably better than just thirty years before and worlds away from anything commonly experienced before 1950. It was, though, one more London irony that the overstretched incomes of the poorest inhabitants meant that they were unable to take full advantage of improved housing. Central heating, a bath with hot water supply, even electric lighting were all there to be had, but many tenants could not afford to use them.

There was also a substantial minority of households in London who were left out of this general improvement altogether, at least for a time. These were the Londoners with no permanent home at all. This was a dimension of the housing question that, taking everything together, was worse at the end of the century than at the beginning.

Homelessness in London had always taken two forms. One, the 'rough sleepers', mainly (but not exclusively) men worn down and out by mental illness and drink, was a permanent but small-scale London phenomenon, symbolized throughout the century by the Embankment tramp and his park-bench and shop-doorway fellows. The other, family homelessness, had tended to come in waves, with crises from time to time.

The wandering Briton spawned a rich literature. It consisted of memoirs of those who took to tramping by choice or force of circumstance, and those who donned the garb for a time to see what it was like and to write a book about it after. Apparently all came to London, if only for a time. 'London is a sort of whirlpool which draws derelict people towards it,'[55] wrote George Orwell, responsible for perhaps the greatest achievement of the vagabond genre, *Down and Out in Paris and London* (1933). Once in the metropolis, there were special laws to move vagrants on – or move them directly to gaol – and a special charity superstructure made great efforts to cater for their wants within that narrow span that stretched from bed to Bible and soup to salvation.

The numbers of the single homeless in London have always been difficult to compute. It is reasonably certain, though, that they were highest at the beginning of the century. Before the First World War the 'tramping man', often a skilled artisan in search of work, was still to be found in some numbers in those largely pre-Labour Exchange days. But then homelessness did not usually mean sleeping rough. There were around 27,000 common lodging-house beds in London in 1914 rented at 4d to 1s a night and catering for two main types of clientele: one settled, who may have had their bed in a shared dormitory or a matchboard cubicle for years, and the other 'the flotsam and jetsam of the road'. At the top end of the London common lodging houses were the Rowton Houses (first opened 1892), accommodating about 5,000, and in the middle the Salvation Army and Victoria Home hostels (another 1,000). The rest, extremely shabby, were privately owned and run, making for the proprietors some large fortunes from the pennies of the poorest. In addition to the common lodging houses, there were the workhouse casual wards, known as 'spikes' for their unyielding discomfort. They provided beds free but at the cost of a work penance – usually stone-breaking, sometimes wood-chopping, or at worst oakum-picking, scratching out the knotted ends of tarred rope; and inmates had to move on after two nights. About 1,100 a night were accommodated in this way in London County casual wards until about 1912, around 90 per cent of them men; but a closure programme cut the number of casual ward beds considerably by the outbreak of war in 1914. Finally there were those who slept in the streets – 2,747 were counted in central London in 1910, 535 in 1914 and just seventy-eight in 1931 – though the accuracy of these censuses was always disputed and they were conducted in deepest midwinter when only the most desperate or case-hardened would be outside.[56] Some of those who were could be in a very bad way, like this woman, 'incredibly old', spotted in the City around 1929: 'Her skin was wrinkled and pitted with disease, her face pinched, her eyes bleared. And she crawled rather than walked, dragging her ragged skirt, which was all she wore, along the pavement. But her body from the waist upwards was covered with horrible sores and ulcers, that, smeared with dirt, gave her an appearance past description.'[57]

Her like could have been found in central London at any time in any year of the century and photographs of London vagrants in the 1990s were shockingly similar to photographs of their predecessors in, say, the 1870s.[58] For even in the most prosperous years this culture of London vagrancy was never entirely extinguished. Thomas Callaghan, a Geordie on the tramp in London, recalled the 'nightly over-occupied embankment benches, the bomb-site camp fires and the cider groups squatting in the condemned houses in the East End' in 1950, 'despite the fact that there were plenty of jobs available'. And in the 1960s a fresh supply of young homeless people was provided by the hippies who chose, or readily adjusted to, a life without ties in communal squats and who clustered scruffily around Eros in Piccadilly Circus, to the discomfort of the authorities. By 1971 it was said, with no hard figures to back it up, however, that the 'number of plain down and outs, apart from the hippies, is also on the increase: it is thought that there are now as many people sleeping out in Central London as there were in the 1920s'.[59]

The phenomenon of disaffected youth living rough in London seemed a new creation of the later 1960s, at least as far as twentieth-century London was concerned. Adopting different guises, it was to be a continuing London presence until the end of the century, growing in numbers and self-confidence in the 'new age', Class War, 'grunge' and 'crusty' styles of the 1980s and 1990s. These young people shared their London hunting grounds with the methylated-spirits drinkers, the deluded, the depressed, the run-aways, the addicts – 'I have never seen so many destitute people sitting for warmth in [Camden Town] tube station as this year,' noted David Thomson in January 1981, 'not the usual drunks and winos.' The newcomers were swollen from 1988 by unprecedented numbers of sixteen- and seventeen-year olds deprived of social security benefit and unable or unwilling to hold down a job in London or anywhere else. They and their traditional companions filled the Arches off Villiers Street until they were taken out of commission for the Charing Cross redevelopments of the late 1980s; and they created 'cardboard city' at the Waterloo Bull Ring underpass until that, too, was cleared out and closed off in 1994. The 1991 Census recorded 700 rough sleepers in central London, back to pre-1914 figures; by 1996 it had fallen again to below 300.[60]

The number of homeless families in London, as distinct from the single homeless, peaked in the 1990s. This was no nagging ache of London life but a problem that erupted in sharp and painful crises. Family homelessness did not rank as a social problem until the end of the First World War. Before then the London housing market had provided accommodation to match the poorest or most insecure pocket and the direst emergency: furnished rooms could be rented for pennies by the night, as we have seen in Notting Dale, and in dire necessity there was the workhouse. The moonlight flit to avoid the importunate rent collector was a popular device just because there was always somewhere to flit to if your standards were not exacting.

But at the end of the First World War rising expectations were bolstered by full employment and relatively high wages; and many demobilized soldiers 'were now animated with the sole desire to found a home of their own, and to settle down'. Yet virtually no new accommodation had been built for five years. And, to make matters worse, many landlords were evicting tenants in order to sell houses to owner-occupiers cashing in their war gratuities, or to developers who wanted to demolish them to make way for businesses or flats. Once tenants were out, houses would be kept empty or part empty until a purchaser could be found. Working-class accommodation virtually dried up in London in 1919. That December, a hoaxer who advertised a house to let in Lewisham caused crowds, including many soldiers and sailors in uniform, to converge on the address all day long until 10 p.m. Rent strikes to fend off landlords taking advantage of the shortage by raising rents, and the organized squatting of empty houses, occurred throughout 1920–22. Squatting seems to have been most aggressive in south London – in Camberwell, Peckham and Herne Hill in particular. As late as 10 September 1923 a 'House to Let' sign in the inner London suburbs was sufficiently remarkable to warrant a photograph in the *Daily Herald*.[61]

Suburban development and the middle-class exodus from inner London solved this first crisis, but the next erupted after the Second World War. Blitzed housing and acute demand from returning servicemen and servicewomen re-created in an exaggerated form the circumstances of 1919–22. This time squatting broke out nationwide, with some 45,000 people moving into 'empty military camps the length and breadth of Britain'. The most celebrated instance occurred in September 1946, when the London District of the Communist Party organized a mass squat of an empty block of luxury service flats in Kensington called Duchess of Bedford House. Around 400 families moved in there and into a further eight buildings in Kensington, Marylebone, Pimlico and St John's Wood. A few days later the empty Ivanhoe Hotel in Bloomsbury went the same way. For the twelve days it lasted, the mass squat became a world event, provoking similar action in France, Canada and America. The Attlee government, to whom a Communist Party success was only marginally less palatable than Red Army tanks in Trafalgar Square, flung the full weight of police, security services and the criminal and civil law against the squatters' leaders. Ted Bramley, a Communist housing campaigner and LCC councillor, and four other activists were prosecuted for the most serious offence that could be devised in the circumstances – conspiracy to incite trespass. They were convicted but a sympathetic judge merely bound them over for two years. One effect of the furore was a more vigorous requisitioning policy in central London, with councils taking over empty property and equipping them as temporary homes for the homeless.[62]

Family homelessness in London reached a first post-war peak in 1951, when nearly 3,500 women and children were taken into LCC hostels. Then a second crisis broke after the Rent Act 1957 brought tens of thousands of London dwellings out of rent control. Catering for the 1,000 or so families made homeless a year in inner London around this time was the responsibility of the LCC's dreadful 'rest centres', where husbands were denied a bed and so separated from wives and children in case things got too comfortable. But that was unlikely. A scandal erupted in September 1961, when the journalist Jeremy Sandford discovered thirteen beds in one room at Newington Lodge (Southwark); new arrivals were subjected to anal swabbing to test whether they might be carrying dysentery. It was as if putting homeless people through these degrading rites of passage would somehow deter them from becoming homeless in the first place.[63]

This time, the numbers of homeless families kept rising year on year. Like lone-parent families, this was a peculiarly inner London phenomenon. In 1968 the twelve inner London boroughs contained just 6 per cent of the population of England and Wales but 37.5 per cent of 'registered homeless persons'. The main reason seems to have been the sharp decline of private rented accommodation, taken over by councils or sold for gentrification. This sudden change – private renting represented 42 per cent of Greater London dwellings in 1961 but 14.5 per cent in 1981 – deprived the London housing market of virtually all flexibility, especially for the poor. Only councils wanted to rent to working-class families in inner London; but the pressure on council housing became such that, unless you were in a redevelopment area awaiting clearance, or already a council tenant wanting a transfer, there was virtually no hope of rehousing. From 1969 organized squatting in empty council-owned properties awaiting demolition or rehabilitation, mainly by single people but also by families, had become one way round the shortage for those who could not qualify legitimately for council housing. By 1976 there were estimated to be 50,000 squatters in London. Some were given licences to occupy premises as one way of reconciling an inadequate supply and an apparently bottomless demand. In that same year, councils were given the statutory duty of rehousing virtually all families with children who claimed to be homeless or threatened with homelessness. Soon, meeting their duty to homeless families exhausted the available stock of dwellings. At first, those families who could not be housed permanently were put into bed and breakfast accommodation, some of it in as scandalous a condition as the old LCC rest centres; then privately owned flats and houses were leased by councils to accommodate the homeless. The number of homeless London families in temporary accommodation peaked at 43,166 in September 1992. That fell to 28,000 in 1997 but was rising again at the century's end.[64]

So this was a complex picture. There had been much progress. For even the poorest, living conditions at the end of the century were vastly improved on pre-1914, even pre-1950, London. The lives of most Londoners had moved closer together as the century grew older. But for those who were most deprived, housing remained in short supply and health outcomes were bleak. And the poorest were relatively worse off, compared to the average, at the end of the century than they had been in the middle.

Yet survival, if not easy for those on a low income or dependent on benefits, had some economic and cultural assistance in London, especially inner London. For if inner London was peculiar in some of its problems, it was peculiar in some of its solutions, too.

The London Factor

'I like this life,' says Del Boy, the senior partner in Trotters' Independent Trading Company, introducing himself in his very first outing in front of the public. 'Ducking and diving, wheeling and dealing – it's exciting!' The lovable London wide-boy already had a long history, but it was in the television age that he became a cultural hero. Sid James in Alan Simpson and Ray Galton's *Citizen James* (1960–62); the same writers' unforgettable *Steptoe and Son* with Wilfrid Brambell and Harry H. Corbett (1962–74); James Beck as Private Walker in *Dad's Army* (1968–77); George Cole's exquisite used-car dealer Arthur Daley in *Minder* (1979–85); and finally John Sullivan's wonderful *Only Fools and Horses* (1981–91). Old sitcoms never die, and as the millennium dawned David Jason, Nicholas Lyndhurst, Lennard Pearce, Buster Merryfield and the rest seemed never to have left the small screen; as, indeed, they hadn't. It was more than this, though, that gave in the late 1990s an antique feel to the Trotters of Peckham. There was something archetypal about Del Boy which overrode the up-to-the-minute mobile phone or Filofax gags, or radioactive mineral water and hang-gliders. For he was a character who might have stepped off the London streets (or music-hall stage or radio studio or film set) at any time this century. Del was a spiv. And we all knew one when we saw one.

The spiv as icon emerged in London in the late 1940s. That, at least, was the moment of demonization. The word had been around at least fifty years before that and John Worby's *The Other Half: The Autobiography of a Spiv* and *Spiv's Progress* were published in 1937 and 1939. But when Worby used the word, apparently 'Nobody knew what it meant', and it did not gain real currency until about 1947. Spiv seemed perfectly to encapsulate yet another type who had been 'always with us'. He (the image of the spiv was exclusively male) lived on his wits, usually on the right side of the law but sometimes on the wrong if the risks weren't too great. He remained content with small rewards but was always 'wide' to the deal that might make his fortune. He was politically conservative, valuing independence and individual flair against the burdens of wage labour and commitments of collectivism; so he was from the London working class but not of it. He was a cheat and a rogue but likeable none the less, because his victims didn't usually suffer too much and because those who did were unsympathetic bureaucratic elements who deserved what they got. It was this last point that helped make the spiv represent in the 1940s something of a universal attitude of mind: 'he was the caricature of us all. He tricked authority with a grin. He talked fast and laughed himself out of tight corners. He got away with it.' These were virtues indeed in that grey decade, when anything colourful made a welcome splash and when Jack the Lad would always be preferred to Citizen Food Inspector. But the spiv did not just rise and fall in the 1940s. He lasted throughout the century – and maybe all London centuries – as the popularity of Ally Sloper, Max Miller, Charlie Chester, Sid James and Del Boy ('no income tax, no VAT') showed.[65]

The spiv was merely the sharply dressed tip of an iceberg of London spivvery. It encompassed the whole spectrum, from petit-bourgeois individualism that could, with luck and talent, end in successful business enterprise and wealth, to the shifts and devices that could make living on wage labour or on state benefits just that bit more comfortable and, occasionally, more exciting. It had many manifestations and was called many things: it was the economy called hidden, or irregular, or black, or alternative, or cash, or underground, or tertiary, or informal. And it included all those activities called, variously and vaguely, fiddling or moonlighting or having a trade or doing a deal or having a dabble or doing the business or doing (not having) a bit on the side.

It was impossible to measure how far all this was truly of a different order in London compared to the rest of the country, but it certainly seemed so. Michael Hebbert, a sophisticated observer of London at the end of the twentieth century, speculated that it might be this 'informal' economy that prevented Newham from looking like ' "the poorest urban area in Northern Europe" ', as the statistics said it was:

But any visitor from, say, Liverpool or Glasgow who sees the thronged pavements of East Ham High Street, the vitality of local shops . . . and the continual self-improvement of thousands of terrace houses . . . must feel that the statistics are missing something . . . London has real poverty and need, but it does not have the waxen-faced, down-at-heel misery of the other industrial cities . . .

The sociologist Dick Hobbs was struck by his own early experiences as a general labourer when he moved from east London to a northern town in 1970. His new workmates were no longer 'opportunistic and alert to the main chance' or 'constantly moving from legal to illegal enterprises and back again', as they had done in London: '[I]n the East End everyone was "at it" and some were "at it" more than most.'[66]

By all accounts London was uniquely fertile in its opportunities to turn a penny. Classically, pennies were turned – just as they were once tossed with the pieman – in the streets. That was how they continued to be earned by Steptoe, Del Boy and the rest. Among some communities and families this street enterprise was bred in the bone. At least up to the motor-car age of the 1950s, the culture of working-class children was rich in ways to earn a copper or two in the streets. In north London between the wars, for example, children acted as lookouts ('dogging out') for street gambling schools; chopped up old packing cases or wooden paving blocks ('tarblocks') and hawked them as firewood from a soapbox on wheels; scavenged bottles (sometimes snatched them from the back of brewers' drays) for the return deposit and collected rags for sale to dealers; took out a guy near 5 November; collected horse dung and sold it by the bucket to rose growers and window-box fanciers; opened taxi doors for tips at railway stations and outside gentlemen's clubs (porters and commissionaires permitting); helped coster-mongers stack and pull their barrows; watched spectators' cars at the Arsenal football ground to prevent harm coming to them (a sort of protection racket in a small way); went 'fatting' at Smithfield Market, picking up discarded pieces of meat and selling them to rag and bone men; ran errands for neigh-bours; helped stall-holders claim a pitch at the Caledonian Road Market; dived into canals at traditional points to grub in the mud for pennies thrown by passers-by; cleaned doorsteps; worked a paper round or milk round; delivered provisions for grocers' shops; made toffee apples and sold them from a home-made barrow; washed cars; helped pull barrel organs; scrounged programmes from the first house leaving a music hall and sold them cheap to the second house queuing to go in; entertained cinema or music-hall queues with patter or songs or tumbles; made a fairy grotto and charged other children to look into it; and doubtless much more. All of these, or most, taught at an early age how best to pitch a sale and catch a customer, how to test a market and seize the moment. And they developed a lifelong taste for the unanticipated windfall and the unpredictable excitement of the chase.[67]

Most of these were boys' tasks but some were shared by girls, who made doorstep cleaning largely their own. And in adult life women played a big part in street selling, that archetypal spiv trade. Indeed in the very early years of the century women comprised nearly half the street traders in London. There were few women 'barrow boys' pushing or pulling a 'walking barrow' but plenty ran their own market stall, some had highly profitable newspaper pitches (passed on in the family and capable of sale like real estate – one at Victoria was said to have changed hands for £5,000 in 1966, more than a suburban house might have fetched at the time), and many more sold from a basket (the flower girls of Piccadilly Circus were one of the sights of London before the First World War – they sometimes dipped their flowers in dye to improve their appeal). Women also sang in the street for coppers – 'Of all the multifarious ways of earning a living that lie open to the "down-and-outer" I am certain that street-singing is the hardest' – and they were prominent among the London beggars.[68]

Street selling was an important part of the London economy and a unique feature of London life. 'The itinerant vendor plays a part in the life of London which has no parallel in any other city with which I am acquainted,' wrote Harold Hardy for Charles Booth's survey, and in fact street selling grew in importance in the London economy over the first forty years of the century, despite no new licences being issued in the City after 1911. There were over 12,000 'costermongers, hawkers, and street sellers' in the County of London in 1901 but more than 19,000 in 1931. It was probably only the full-time sellers (and not the many who moved between street selling and casual labouring jobs) who revealed themselves to the Census in this way, and the *New Survey* estimated there were probably 30,000 street traders in London 'all told'. Neither was there any certain count of London's street markets. The *New Survey* listed eighty-two with licensed pitches, all but six of them in the County; Mary Benedetta in *The Street Markets of London* (1936), illustrated by the fabulous photographs of Moholy-Nagy, listed eighty-six in the County alone; and a government count in 1930 found 106 'in the Metropolitan area'.[69]

Many ex-servicemen used their war gratuities to set up a market stall after the Armistice and a number of new markets, none of them very large, were established with or without borough council consent. But the growth of motor traffic caused the police and councils to suppress some from 1921. Sometimes considerable force was necessary to persuade the costers to move to new sites. In 1927 street markets became regulated by a system of licensing by local authorities. Despite the costers' fears, markets flourished as a consequence. The morning scramble for pitches was no longer necessary and nor was the systematic petty bribery of the police who controlled it.

The new system also provided a means to put down markets deemed unsuitable: so no stalls got a licence at Notting Dale's Sunday morning 'Rag Fair' in Bangor Street, for instance (although it seems to have survived up to the outbreak of the Second World War).[70]

There were two main consequences of the licensing system. One was a decline in the numbers of perambulating barrows on the streets, more likely than ever to be 'moved on' by the coster's perennial foe, the 'cozzer'. And the other was increasing patronage of street markets by the respectable working class and even middle-class housewives in search of a bargain and a colourful shopping experience. Although some markets had a long history and strong connection with the poorest, it was between the wars that the street market became one of the great institutions of London life.

But the Second World War upset the street market economy of London. Blitz and rationing drove many stall-holders (indeed, some streets) out of business. In 1948 Harry Williams toured 'the once glamorous and lively street markets' of south London and was most depressed by East Street, Walworth, known to locals as East Lane, 'a drab, dead thing, infinitely remote from the Cockney spirit and tradition'. He noted the 'white, drawn faces of the women shoppers, picking over the rubbish on sale with dispirited fingers' and 'the threadbare poverty of these once-groaning stalls, the lack of commodities, the endless restrictions and a widespread loss of good manners and cheerfulness – the hallmark of London street markets before the war . . .'[71]

But despite the appearance of terminal decline, the London street market quickly recovered. The main revival accompanied the gentrifying urge of the 1960s and 1970s. Camden Passage, off Islington High Street (antiques and second-hand books, from 1960), Camden Lock, off Chalk Farm Road (crafts, opened 1973), and Swiss Cottage (crafts), Nag's Head, off Seven Sisters Road (clothes), Putney Flea Market, Hampstead Community Market, Greenwich Antiques Market and Jubilee Market Covent Garden, all opened around 1974–5, were among the new street enterprises noted in Alec Forshaw's well-informed survey of nearly ninety markets published in 1983. By then the revival of East Lane was so thoroughgoing that it could be called south London's 'answer to Petticoat Lane', with an eight-year waiting list for a pitch. And the Mercedes- or Jaguar-driving barrow boy, living in Chingford and holidaying in the Bahamas, had become the stuff of London myth.[72]

If the state of street selling in London's markets was probably never more healthy than at the end of the century it is likely that many other types of street enterprise barely survived the Blitz. Indeed, many in the 1920s felt there had been a sad falling off since the First World War; and others old enough to remember said that London's street enterprises had never been the same since the 1850s and 1860s.[73] Even so, London's streets in the first forty years of the century nurtured a bustling and lively culture of economic enterprise outside the licensed street markets. The 'little tradesmen of the streets are not dwindling,' James Jones claimed in 1934. 'Rather their ranks are swelling every year.' He and others listed up to the Second World War: lavender sellers, muffin men, flower sellers, hawkers of wood, cats' meat men, milk sellers, men selling vinegar by the pint and table salt by the block, trolleymen hawking coal, ice cream and roast chestnut or baked potato salesmen (mainly Italians, alternating between winter and summer trades); chimney sweeps, chair menders, knife grinders, mat menders, window glaziers, knockers-up for early risers, and a man who could translate 'old-fashioned umbrellas into "stumpies"'; hawkers of razor-blades, buttons, bootlaces, oriental rugs, *Old Moore's Almanacs*, flypapers, carbolic from drums slung on a yoke, fancy stationery, 'funkum' (fake perfume), bath salts, tooth powders, mechanical toys, eggs, onions, draught excluders called 'window-sandbags'; gypsies selling clothes pegs and charms, tinkers or whitesmiths mending pots and pans; street dentists, street photographers, street tattooists, street chiropodists; and the rat catcher with tame white rats crawling all over him (gone with the First World War, according to Compton Mackenzie).[74] All this besides the man on 'the fruit game', selling whatever was in glut at Covent Garden or Spitalfields from a walking barrow, and the fraternity who cashed in on crowds attending big events in the capital. These brought out the casual street sellers in droves. At Wembley Cup Finals in the mid-1930s John Goodwin noted the hawkers of 'celluloid dolls naked save for a ribbon of blue, or of white, tied like a sash round their mid-sections. Other traders stridently urge one to buy Mickey Mouse, or Dismal Desmond, or Felix the Cat, or Pip, or Squeak, or Wilfred.' And on Boat Race Day the same people hawked 'Dark Blue or Light Blue rosettes, and paper caps of the same colours', or (shades of Mafeking Night, when their forebears must have had similar stock immediately available in cellars and sheds and stables) 'Union Jacks, paper ticklers, cardboard squeakers, and large wooden rattles'.[75]

Big events were good days, too, for the pavement artists – like George Orwell's memorable acquaintance Bozo the Screever, whom he met on the Embankment around 1930[76] – and for the buskers. A visit to a West End cinema or theatre, or a music hall anywhere, meant an evening's entertainment just while waiting in the queue. Every street market rang to the accompaniment of buskers in all their manifold guises. 'Singers, conjurers, musicians, men who make patterns out of old newspapers, men who clash spoons together like castanets, men who recite passages from

Shakespeare in throaty melodramatic voices', bones players, quack doctors 'on the crocus lay' (one with a monkey on his shoulder), escape artistes, muscle men, the reciter of Virgil in Latin, organ grinders (there were said to be 1,000 Italian organ grinders in London at the turn of the century), acrobats, men cutting capers in women's clothes, racing tipsters, fortune-tellers, Punch and Judy men, men pulling peepshows displaying scenes of old murders, the horse-drawn carousel which played music while children rode round and round, clowns, one-string-fiddle and singing-saw players, street pianists (the piano pulled on a barrow), street or park orators, men with a wind-up gramophone or radio with loudspeaker on a barrow or cart, a legless clog dancer, a felt-hat manipulator, the champion bottle carrier, fire or broken glass or razor-blade eaters, sword or pebble swallowers, the man with the little theatre on wheels showing 'Jack Payne and His Boys' made from cocoa tins, 'real kilted Scots with bagpipes (from Aldgate)', blind bands, Welsh choirs (the post-1914 replacement for the German bands, though fewer of them), men with weighing machines on a barrow crying 'guess your weight' (you didn't pay if you guessed right) and the man who could flick a cigarette out of a girl's mouth with a whip, all apparently versed in the London busker's lingo, where a penny was a *soldi*, a pound a *pfunt* and a policeman a *scarpa-omi*. This was a culture that survived the Blitz, and though its variety was much curtailed by the 1950s, Julian Franklyn could claim that 'it is doubtful whether any city in the world has as great a proportion of street performers as London has'.[77]

If the Second World War knocked much of the stuffing out of unregulated street enterprise, it gave a mighty push to another London industry long associated with spivvery, and which traditionally straddled the boundary of legitimate and illegitimate business. One part of London made a living on the stuff thrown away by the other part, or stuff sold cheap as used or second-hand, or stuff stolen but then merged unidentifiably with the rest. This recirculation of used commodities – waste, scrap, junk, second-hand, antiques – had a long, though under-regarded, place in London history: Noddy Boffin, 'the Golden Dustman' of *Our Mutual Friend* (1864–5), was Albert Steptoe's most illustrious predecessor.

Second-hand clothing, a strong trade at the turn of the century in street markets like Petticoat Lane, where working-class Londoners would bargain for the swells' and toffs' West End cast-offs, took a knock from the rise of ready-made and the '50 bob tailors' of inter-war fame; and the bottom had fallen out of women's second-hand clothing by the mid-1930s as cast-offs were firmly rejected, especially by younger women. But the London trade in second-hand books never faltered. There were apparently more second-hand bookshops than new in London at the turn of the century and the trade had its own peculiar shopping street at Charing Cross Road and its own street market at Farringdon Road, with stalls at Lisson Grove, Whitechapel High Street and doubtless elsewhere. And rag and bone men did extraordinarily well out of the war, when salvage drives for scrap metals and waste-paper, and the loot to be retrieved from blitzed buildings, fuelled a huge growth in scrap dealers in the 1940s and 1950s. Gilbert Kelland, a police constable at Walworth from 1946 to 1948, recalled 'a proliferation of scrap-metal dealing businesses': 'Sometimes the reclaiming amounted to stealing and . . . the disappearance of complete lorry-loads of valuable metal was not unusual.' Not far away, and just a few years later, the young Charlie Richardson 'developed a real fascination for scrap and metals generally. I loved keeping up with the changing prices for the various types of scrap. Lead was always very good and so easy to nick; you could tear it off a roof like soft thin toffee.'[78]

Real money could be made from scrap and so, too, from junk, bric-à-brac, curios and antiques, an industry that grew phenomenally between the wars and then again, beyond all precedent, from the 1950s and 1960s. It all began at Caledonian Road Market – the 'Cally' or 'The Stones'. Even before the First World War the huge open forum of the cattle market was turned over to traders in second-hand goods on Fridays and in 1914 there were on average 725 stalls there. But it was apparently during the First World War that browsing among the stalls became fashionable and 'Mayfair began to visit Caledonian Market in its Rolls-Royces'. During the 1920s and 1930s the 'Pedlars' Market' grew enormously. Tuesdays as well as Fridays were given over to the trade and by 1932 3,400 stalls were setting up there over the two days. It was one of the sights of London:

From five minutes to to five minutes past 10 . . . a most extraordinary scene can be witnessed there. At first there is an immensely wide and complete[ly] deserted space surrounded by high iron railings with a tall clock tower in the centre and low long sheds on two sides. Outside the railings from each of the wide gates still firmly closed the most phantastic caravans imaginable stand waiting in long queues. Private cars, old perambulators, vans, lorries, barrows, coffee-stall vans and every imaginable other vehicle with the men, women, boys, girls and children belonging to them, as well as others carrying their goods without the help of wheeled vehicles, in weird procession. Before each gate there is a throng of people not burdened with any goods pressing expectantly against the iron bars. All eyes are fixed on the great clock on the tower. Then it commences to strike and at the tenth strike the uniformed attendants throw open the gates – a wild rush! From all sides boys, youths, men and women of all ages run as fast as they can into the wide open space in a free scramble for the positions most coveted. As soon as they have reached an unoccupied place which suits them they throw down a cap, hat, coat or other garment and return to their goods or companions behind the gates. For a few seconds the square, again almost deserted, is littered with articles of clothing, while the procession of vehicles and their owners is slowly pouring through the gates. In a remarkably short time the whole square is filled with spreaded goods, their vendors and purchasers, and business commences immediately. The goods marketed vary from fur coats and jewels to old shoes and second-hand tyres, with every conceivable intermediary from bulky furniture to artificial flowers.[79]

'Probably more valuable antiques have been "picked up for a song" there than anywhere else,' mused Mary Benedetta in 1936. 'There is all the excitement of never knowing what you are going to see next. And for the real bargain-hunters it has a glamorous spell that draws them back to it again and again.' Bertolt Brecht immortalized it in verse, its images were taken by the world's greatest photographers, its vendors ranged from 'the silver kings' to desperately poor old women with a pair of battered shoes for sale, and its patrons from the depths of London toffery to the peaks of London slumdom. The story from 1932, apparently genuine, of a woman paying what she considered a pricy 7s 6d for a bead necklace which turned out to be a string of black pearls worth £20,000 fixed 'The Stones' for ever in the popular imagination.[80] Curios and antiques were also to be had in Petticoat Lane, Berwick Street market, Bethnal Green Road and in junk stalls at a dozen places from Kingsland Waste to Portobello Road, but the Cally was the second-hand market of England, if not the world.[81]

The pedlars never returned to 'The Stones' after the market was badly damaged during the war. Despite that the London antiques and second-hand trade never looked back. A 'New Caledonian Market' opened in Bermond-sey Square in May 1949. Wolf Mankowitz gives an endearing insider's account of the antiques trade – and its connections with scrap dealers, demolition contractors, thieves and fences, in his *Make Me An Offer* of 1952, a time when the break-up of country-house estates overexcited the market in London and across the Atlantic. Retail outlets expanded or emerged anew – and with them the bourgeois barrow boy – in Portobello Road by 1950, Camden Passage from 1960 and Greenwich Market in the 1970s, all feeding the inexhaustible demand for collectables; and all providing untrammelled scope for a dabble and a deal behind the back of the taxman, or cover for the thief and receiver of stolen property. At least two of the Great Train Robbers described themselves in the dock as 'antiques dealers'.

Many another London enterprise offered scope for independence and advancement by exploiting wit, charm, shrewdness, a quick tongue and courage – qualities readily available as birthright in the London working class and largely untouched, one way or the other, by schooling. Some industries especially prominent in London largely depended on this independence of mind and spirit. 'Amongst cabmen there are no employees in the ordinary sense,' remarked Booth, and this too was an industry that flourished as the century grew older. It was swollen hugely from the 1960s by the growth of the unregulated minicab trade, a favourite among migrant workers in London and with similar entrepreneurial aspirations to the black-cab tradition. In 1996 there were estimated to be 100,000 minicab drivers in London, many of them part-time, casual or moonlighters, and 25,000 black-cab drivers; in 1937 there had been fewer than 12,000 licensed cab drivers and 8,000 cabs, with a marginal hire-car industry around it.[82] And, in a related line, the used-car trade was already decidedly spivvish before the Second World War: second-hand car dealers feature largely in Robert Westerby's 1937 Soho novel *Wide Boys Never Work*. They had their own street market at Warren Street, and 'the used-car trade' was said to be prominent among old-established gypsy families in Notting Dale in the 1950s. But it had, of course, grown out of all recognition in the Arthur Daley years – while remaining recognizably spivvish.

Used-car dealers were notoriously fond of cash transactions and there is no evidence that the cash economy, as a means of avoiding the book-keeper and the taxman, diminished over time.[83] Neither did the fiddles for cash or favours that probably all classes of London society indulged in whenever the opportunity raised its tempting little head. 'Only a very foolish fellow couldn't make a pound a week extra in London merely by fiddling,' a lorry driver told the sociologist Ferdynand Zweig around 1946. Zweig estimated that London tradesmen like plumbers, gas-fitters, electricians and so on earned even more on the side, 'as much as 50% or more of their wages'. Some fiddled with sufficient vigour to cross over to genuine entrepreneurship. Steve made leather belts in a Hackney workshop when he left school in 1974: 'I used to fiddle the governor wicked, I'd buy my own materials and go in after hours for another two or three hours, and I could make 2,500 belts extra a week: stitch them one night, buckle them the next, pack them another. Sometimes I'd make only a few pence on each belt, but it came to a nice amount.' There were uncountable Steves across London and across the years.[84]

No doubt Steve stepped over the line dividing legitimate from illegitimate, and one man's fiddle was another man's villainy. There was, for instance, only a fine line between the griddler (street singer) of no talent and the beggar. The same could be said for the 'timber merchant' (match seller) or the bootlace vendor, and street begging was rife in most decades and present in all throughout the century. Around 5,500 people a year were prosecuted for begging before the First World War; that fell to around 1,500 during it, and below that (around 1,100) for the whole of the inter-war period.[85] But that gives little indication of the numbers of beggars on the streets of London. By all accounts there was a surge of disabled war veterans begging in the streets after 1918, but a liberal prosecution policy seems to have been pursued towards them. And, just like the barrow boys of a later generation, myths grew between the wars of the fabulous profits to be made from begging: 'the man known as "No Legs" . . . owns property [and] can afford to go to Paris every year for his holidays' (1930). Certainly, some begging wheezes displayed entrepreneurial flair: like the man, around the same time, who went door to door in south London collecting, with some success, for money to reopen a station recently closed by Southern Railway. And it was still possible in the poorest streets to hire children for begging purposes as late as 1930.[86]

London experienced a begging revival in the 1980s, especially among the young homeless and squatters, to an extent probably only paralleled in some of the bleakest years of the nineteenth century. In the absence of children, dogs had always been a useful prop for beggars to squeeze that extra penny from a sentimental public. In the 1980s and 1990s the small dog on a length of string was a required fashion accessory for the young beggars of Stoke Newington Church Street or Islington's Upper Street or Camden High Street and probably every other high road of inner London. And at the turn of the twenty-first century beggars from Eastern Europe, gypsy families apparently prominent among them, provided a minor moral panic in the press and among the authorities.

If it was a fine line between busking and begging, and scrap dealing and receiving stolen property – Caledonian Road Market was the most important distribution point of stolen property in England between the wars – there was also little distinction between cheap-jack buying and selling and the confidence trick. John Worby and a pal devised an amusing and sophisticated enterprise along these lines in the late 1930s. They 'took a small office in the West End, and put the following advertisement in the papers: *What Every Young Couple about to be Married should have. Illustrated, 2/6 . . .* It wasn't long before we were making £15 a week. For the two and sixpence we sent the gullible public a small illustrated Bible, which cost us about fourpence.'[87] Like so much of spivvery, his enterprise cocked a snook at civil society, and he laughed up his sleeve at the 'mugs' who were locked, like drones, into the humdrum world of wage labour. But spivs had standards. Louis Gillain, a street seller and busker for much of the 1930s, was offered a job selling vacuum cleaners but gave it up after a week: 'If I had to cheat for my living, I would cheat on my own behalf and no one else's.'[88]

The wrong side of the law was certainly crossed when it came to fiddling relief out of the poor law authorities, or benefit from the Unemployment Assistance Board (UAB), the National Assistance Board or their various successors. The very size and anonymity of London, its eternal indifference, helped Londoners fiddle the system with less risk than elsewhere. 'I have seen cases of evasion of the Means Test,' George Orwell remarked in 1937, 'but I should say that in the industrial towns, where there is still a certain amount of communal life and everyone has neighbours who know him, it is much harder than it would be in London.' Even so, the Greenwich Labour Exchange received two anonymous letters a day betraying alleged fraudsters around 1933, and the fear of disclosure seems to have inhibited many from fiddling dole or relief.[89]

But it didn't deter everyone.

Deptford [just next door to Greenwich] offers special opportunities for fraud in connection with Unemployment Insurance or Assistance, as it is one of the parts of London where hawking thrives most. The young men hire barrows and take them up to the West End of London for the evening stocked with fruit . . . Some of them make substantial profits from these ventures, and add to them by . . . drawing Unemployment Assistance.

'In one London office an intensive investigation into . . . 118 young men (18–30) on the UAB register led to 80 of them finding work, on their own, in order to avoid the trouble which the investigation was causing them . . .' George Tiley, an Islington unemployed labourer on poor law relief in the early 1920s, pulled a barrow for a woman costermonger for 9d a turn until someone told the Guardians, but the 'first floor tenant of our house in Bemerton Street was a good fiddler . . . He earned a couple of bob helping either coster-mongers or coalmen.'[90]

This connection between drawing dole and street trading was a strong one, but there were reported instances among dockers, packers, door-to-door salesmen, coalmen and shop assistants in the trickle of prosecutions between the wars. There were other fiddles, too. A 'supremely scientific socialist' in the Socialist Party of Great Britain, where aspirant members had to pass an examination in Marxism before being accepted into the party, discovered he could draw dole from two benefit offices on the same day. And Cecil Chapman, a west London magistrate until 1925, heard a case where a piano-tuner had exchanged insurance cards with a docker: 'The piano-tuner remained at the docks a little longer than the dock labourer at the piano shop, but both were informed in a short time that they were not sufficiently experienced. They returned with the refusals to the Exchange and were at once put "on the dole".'[91]

With the huge rise in benefit dependency in London from the late 1970s on, the scope for fiddles – and their volume – rose hugely too. By 1983, social security fraud in Hackney took 'virtually every form that human ingenuity is capable of devising: claiming and working; cohabiting and claiming separately; claiming under two separate names; altering giro cheques to higher amounts; fraudulently claiming that books or giros have been stolen and cashing them oneself; or selling a benefit book at a discount and then claiming it was lost'.[92]

Almost any state benefit could be turned into profit by the enterprising: student grants, housing benefit, illegal subletting of a council or housing association flat while living on benefit at another address, even the orange badges given to disabled drivers. In 1995–6 two-thirds of the country's housing benefit fraud was detected in London, while one-fifth of benefit was claimed there.[93] And on the council estates, where the poor were clustered and where benefit dependency (and the marginal fiddles that made existence on benefit tolerable) was an almost universal way of life, there seemed for many no dividing line between legal or illegal, right or wrong. Survival meant having few scruples or none at all. In Brixton in the mid-1990s Nick Danziger's laptop computer was stolen in a break-in. Pursuing it with an ally from the neighbouring council estate into which it had vanished, he came across the moral accommodation that victims and thieves had perforce made with one another:

There is a certain logic to buying stolen gear even if you don't approve of stealing. Few people on the estate can afford to insulate themselves against risk and contingency – against the lawlessness – because of the exorbitant insurance rates. So when you get burgled you can't afford to go out and replace things at market prices: your only option is stolen goods.[94]

Danziger's laptop never turned up. It had disappeared into the City of Dreadful Night.

PART FOUR

Popular Culture

7. City of Dreadful Night

Mobs, Whizzers, Hoisters and the Bobbed-hair Bandit:
Crime, 1900–1940

One Sunday evening in August 1911, Darky the Coon was drinking in the Blue Coat Boy in Bishopsgate, on the edge of Spitalfields. A tough man, leader of a 'mob' who extorted money from local shopkeepers and publicans, 'the Coon' – real name Ikey Bogard, variously remembered as both Jewish and 'a man of colour' – was also a pimp. One element in his considerable attraction for women was said to have been his stetson cowboy hat, open-neck shirt and leather leggings, startling enough in a city not then known for colourful dressing. Darky had fallen out with Arthur Harding, a.k.a. Tresidern, the most notorious of the East End protection racketeers of his day. The row appears to have been over who had the right to extort money from stall-holders in Walthamstow market. A stall had passed to Georgie King, Darky's protégé, when Harding had wanted it to go to someone else. That Sunday, Harding and seven or eight others walked into the bar of the Blue Coat Boy. Darky, in an effort to make peace, said, 'What you having, Arthur?' but when Harding got his beer he threw it at Darky, smashed the glass and thrust it in his face. Another man slashed Darky's throat with a knife, though not fatally, and others went for him with razors. 'The Coon had a face like the map of England' for the rest of his life.

A week or so later Darky and King were set upon again by Harding's mob and had to be arrested by police 'for their own safety'. They were charged with disorderly conduct. Bound over at Old Street Police Court, they asked the magistrate, Chartres Biron, for protection from Harding and his men, who by this time had surrounded the court. Harding was armed with an Irish Constabulary revolver, big enough to 'have knocked holes in a brick', and six or seven others also had guns. With Old Street Magistrates' Court under siege by armed men, Darky and King were kept inside for several hours and Biron telephoned Scotland Yard for armed police. Eventually the pair walked out of the court, Harding and his men made a rush at them, shots were fired and the police arrested eight, including Harding, some at the scene and some later. At the Old Bailey the eight received between one and five years' penal servitude and the *Illustrated Police News* announced, 'East End Vendetta. Gang of Ruffians Broken Up at Last.'[1]

Bloodthirsty civil wars were a feature of the London underworld right across the century. Unlike teams of burglars or robbers who came together for a specific enterprise, protection rackets were run by groups of men, a dozen or two strong, who gravitated to a single leader or, more frequently, a family, often two or more brothers. They depended on reckless courage and ruthless cruelty for the supremacy they waged over their smallholdings of London turf. These 'manors' might be small but they offered rich pickings none the less. Shops, market stalls and pubs were always susceptible to blackmail – pay up or get smashed up[2] – but most vulnerable of all were those who occupied that twilight no man's land dividing lawful business from the unlawful: bookmakers, nightclub proprietors, scrap dealers, prostitutes, shady landlords, spare-time buyers of stolen property. Some mobs were strong enough to levy Danegeld on the underworld itself. Things were so bad in the days of the Sabinis, complained Billy Hill, that an honest thief couldn't have a night out 'up West' without treating one or more of the Italian mob to an expensive night out too. Others also fished in this small but well-stocked pool. The protection racketeers had to compete not only against each other but with the depredations of the Metropolitan Police, as we shall see in a moment.

Every district of London had its protection racket, waxing and waning as personalities flourished or were flushed out like worms in the gut. Sometimes the mobs battened on an industry rather than a locale – gaming in the 1960s, racecourse betting in the 1920s – and these provided the excuse for the most sanguinary contests of all.

London saw nothing again quite like the racecourse gangs of the early 1920s and their battles for the right to 'protect' bookies from thieves and thugs and welchers. More attention may subsequently have been paid to the Krays' paranoid efforts to maintain 'respect' in the 1960s, or the fatal squabbles over who should control drug dealing in south London and elsewhere in the 1990s, but nothing beat for arrogant effrontery the way in which the Sabinis and their opponents conducted their disputes. For a time the police appeared powerless to stop almost nightly shoot-outs in the cafés, pubs and back streets of Holborn, Clerkenwell and the Gray's Inn Road. Shootings, stabbings and razor-slashings happened in public places in front of crowds of witnesses who would testify to nothing; unarmed detectives were shot at in the street; charabancs from Saffron Hill and Stepney, packed with armed men like chariots of war, would converge on racecourses at Epsom Downs or Brighton or Bath, or the trotting races at Greenford Park, to meet opposing mobs from Birmingham and Leeds, all after the rich pockets of terrified bookmakers who knew they would lose more than their punters if they refused to pay up and to pay well. The Sabini brothers joined in friendly rivalry with 'the East End mob' against the men from the north and the Midlands. But the Brummagem mob had many London connections south of the river (Elephant and Castle and Bermondsey especially) and also in north London (Hoxton and Islington). And the Sabinis had Sicilian rivals in Little Italy, the Cortesi brothers, who shot Harry Sabini at the Fratalanza Club, Great Bath Street, in late 1922. So around the great pitched battles – Alexandra Palace races 1921, Derby Day at Epsom in 1921 and again in 1922, when sixty police made over a hundred arrests – racecourse-related fracas erupted in London at clubs and on street corners from Euston Road to Waterloo, between 1920 and 1925 at least. The Sabinis remained active on the racecourses of southern England – some of them retired to Brighton – and in the nightclubs of Soho for years to come. Their influence did not finally wane until they were interned in 1940. But by the 1930s things were so much quieter that Walter Hambrook, lately Detective Superintendent at Scotland Yard, could 'predict with confidence that the terrorist days of the gangster as we have known them are gone, never to return . . .'[3]

The London underworld was, in reality, many little underworlds which overlapped in Soho. Indeed, largely separate underworlds could coexist in the same part of London. In the East End in the early 1900s the immigrant Jews bred their own protection racket, no doubt side by side with whoever were Darky's or Harding's predecessors at the time. In fact there was more than one Jewish protection racket, for once some enterprising men showed the way to easy money then others rose up to steal the bread from their mouths. So the 'Bessarabians' were opposed by the 'Odessians', each with their own clubs and neither afraid to kill for the spoils: Max Moses, a.k.a. Kid McCoy, a promising professional boxer, stabbed an Odessian to death and got ten years' for manslaughter around 1902.[4] Throughout the century London's migrant communities would bring their own terrorists with them or grow them *in situ*, taxing the income of legitimate and unlawful business alike, but especially the latter: from the Sabinis and the Cortesis creaming off the profits of Little Italy's drinking clubs in the 1920s, to the 'Triads' taking their share of Chinatown's gambling clubs, or the 'Yardies' their share of Brixton's drug trade and black music industry, all in the 1980s and 1990s.

These apparently 'alien' implants would be a favourite target of police propaganda and press demonization across the century. Foreign desperadoes cast deep shadows on the popular imagination. Among much self-seeking exaggeration, though, it is true that London's place as a world city made it a magnet for the world's most enterprising criminals. 'Gangs' of German burglars and sneak thieves, the best (or worst) of them organized by a Shadwell woman called Bertha Weiner, were prominent before the First

World War; and the 'Great Pearl Robbery of 1913' ended in the extradition of two Hatton Garden jewellers, both Austrian.[5] Indeed, these years before 1914 provided a genuine import of considerable menace. It was not matched for ferocity until international terrorism cast London as a world theatre of operations for bombings and shootings in the 1970s.

The Tottenham Outrage of January 1909 saw two Latvian political refugees try a wages snatch at Schnurmann's rubber factory, Chesnut Road. They bungled the job and were chased by police and passers-by six miles across Tottenham Marshes to the edge of Epping Forest at Chingford, commandeering a tram and a horse-drawn milk float on the way. They fired 400 rounds from automatic pistols, killing PC Tyler and a schoolboy and wounding twenty-seven others, seven of them policemen, before shooting themselves to avoid capture.

Nearly two years later, just before Christmas 1910, more of these armed revolutionary expropriators attempted to rob a Houndsditch jeweller's by breaking through a party wall from a house at Exchange Buildings in the City. Despite a gale blowing outside, they made so much noise that the neighbourhood was aroused and police were called. Nine City policemen surrounded Exchange Buildings and demanded entry to the house. The four Russian men inside, with a woman companion, were armed with Mauser and Dreyse automatics and decided to shoot their way out. Police Sergeants Bentley and Tucker and PC Choat were shot dead. Choat, six foot four, was shot eight times and kicked in the face before he loosened his grip on Gardstein, one of the burglars, who was accidentally shot in the back. Two other policemen had gunshot wounds but survived. Never again in the twentieth century would London policemen suffer so grievously at the hands of an armed gang, although one incident nearly fifty-six years later came close.

Gardstein was dragged dying to his home at Grove Road, Stepney, where police found him the next day. There was then a lull as police issued descriptions of his accomplices, using a photograph of the dead Gardstein with eyes fixed open to aid identification, and the City police announced a reward of £500 for information leading to a conviction. Some seventeen days after the murders suspicions hardened that two of the wanted men had taken a room at 100 Sidney Street, Stepney, and at 7.30 a.m. on 3 January 1911 the famous siege began. It lasted six hours and ended with the house gutted by fire. Its legacy was two dead anarchists, a fireman killed by falling masonry, Detective Sergeant Leeson wounded by a bullet that caused his retirement from the force, and one of the most memorable photographs of London's twentieth century: Home Secretary Winston Churchill in silk hat, watching the drama from a stable gateway, armed policemen and Scots

Guardsmen around him and a young boy perched cheekily on the stable roof above his head.[6]

These moments of extraordinary drama, etched into the city's mythology, must not be allowed to obscure the fact that the overwhelming bulk of crime in London was always home-grown. 'The cleverest thieves are . . . undoubtedly born Cockneys,' remarked Frederick 'Weasel' Wensley in 1931; he should have known, after forty years' thief-taking, mainly in the East End. And most crime was routine and humdrum, except for those on the receiving end. Fashions in London crime changed over the years, although the popularity of housebreaking, shopbreaking, burglary and 'van-dragging' or 'the jump-up' – stealing 'off the back of a lorry', sometimes hijacking the lorry itself – were perennial favourites. Within these traditional modes there was always room for technical development and variation. Gussie Delaney, said to have been London's first cat burglar, made his mark on Park Lane's tall mansions and luxury blocks of flats in 1924, for instance; and 'The 'Loid Boys' were the first to use flexible plastic to slip the catches of Yale locks in the mid-1930s. Similarly, a type of crime might be more popular in one place or time than another: 'Widespread housebreaking plagued Londoners [in Hampstead and Golders Green] in the late twenties and early thirties, even more so than it does today [the late 1950s].'[7]

For the first fifty years of the century, especially before 1930, the archetypal London male thief was the pickpocket ('dip' or 'whizzer'). And the archetypal whizzer lived in Hoxton, 'the leading criminal quarter of London, and indeed of all England', as Charles Booth characterized it in 1902. Dips ranged in proficiency from the skilled artisan working alone or maybe with one companion to whom he passed the loot (like Robert Allerton's grandfather, the best-dressed man in his Hoxton street, who picked pockets despite having one arm withered and useless) to 'mobs' (like Hoxton's 'Titanic Mob') gathered together to jostle crowds and cause confusion in which it was easier to pluck spoil from the unwary. So anywhere that crowds gathered was a hunting ground for the pickpocket. London provided countless opportunities: railway stations, shopping streets, tram and bus interchanges (where the absence of any queuing habit at bus and tram stops in London until the Second World War made things easy), fairs, race meetings (when the 'Nile Mob', 'an ugly bunch' of pickpockets from the notorious Nile Street area of Hoxton, turned up in a charabanc at Goodwood around 1930, detectives 'identified about ten of their number, all gazing eagerly from their seats as if on a Sunday School outing'), crushes around music halls and cinemas, and tourist attractions. Baedeker's London guide of 1911 noted, 'We need hardly caution newcomers against the artifices of pickpockets and the wiles of impostors [confidence tricksters], two

fraternities which are very numerous in London.' It warned, 'Poor neighbourhoods should be avoided after nightfall.' For whizzing could turn to
robbery with violence if dips went mob-handed and a victim protested.[8]

Not that well-heeled strangers were the only target. On the contrary, it
was the working man's wage packet and the working woman's shopping
money that provided the dip's bread and butter. So they were at their most
active on Friday evenings and Saturday nights. One late Friday afternoon
around 1927, nine pickpockets assembling near the bus stops outside Shoreditch Church were spotted by the Flying Squad. They were overheard
saying they were off to ' "Poplar and Canning Town to work the tubs
(buses)" ' in search of dock labourers' wages, among the lowest in London.
Police diverted to Bethnal Green police station the bus on which they were
travelling and they were all arrested. It was one of the myriad myths that
accreted to London crime that poor victims were a late-century phenomenon, symbolic of an era of moral decline from around, say, 1970. Nothing
could be further from the truth. One of the most prized possessions in
London's poorest streets in the first half of the century was a padlock to keep
other tenants out of the room when it was empty during the day. It was
unsafe to hang washing out in these poverty-stricken places. Gas meter
break-ins were another common way of the poor stealing pennies from one
another.[9]

A few whizzers were women: three from Hoxton were sentenced in 1926
for trying to pick a detective's pocket at Cambridge Circus, for instance.
But the archetypal London female thief was the 'hoister' ('oyster' as it is
sometimes phonetically transcribed) or shoplifter. These, too, worked mostly
in 'mobs'. Hoxton was also well known for supplying hoisters, but the most
famous examples came from the Elephant and Castle, passed from mother
to daughter between the 1920s and the 1950s. These were the 'Forty Thieves'
or 'Forty Elephants', less a topographical allusion than a reference to the
hoister's technique of stuffing stolen garments into specially made skirt
pockets or bloomers, so that she went into a shop thin and came out fat,
even pregnant. Good money could be made at this game, for goods were
readily marketable and quickly disposed of in the street markets of east and
south London. Successful teams could afford to travel in style, in the 1930s
hiring cars to take them to the West End or even provincial town centres.
Six hoisters who left Hoxton 'in a very flash touring car with a liveried
chauffeur' and who drank bottled beer all the way, getting 'pretty merry',
were eventually arrested at Westcliff-on-Sea after robbing a department
store of large quantities of 'silk goods, underwear, and stockings'.[10]

This use of the motor car represented one of the great changes wrought
on patterns of crime during the century. The car aided escape from capture

– especially until the late 1920s, when the Metropolitan Police tardily introduced their own fast cars. It brought rich pickings in the suburbs and even the countryside within easy reach. And it created new forms of crime. 'Smash-and-grab' by 'motor bandits' became the stuff of legend between the wars. Jewellers' shop windows were the favourite target. Windows were broken by a brick if the glass wasn't toughened, or a cut-down (sawn-off?) sledgehammer, or even rammed by the car itself; later, when the trade had adapted by installing grilles, these could be removed by ropes and grappling hooks attached to the car. Smash-and-grab was perfected by the slippery Ruby Sparks from Tiger Yard, Camberwell, in the early 1920s and it remained the most popular and lucrative form of armed robbery in London until around 1950. Ruby Sparks's female companion was the celebrated Bobbed-hair Bandit, an immensely skilled driver who captured the nation's headlines from the late 1920s to the early 1930s. She, though, was never captured.[11]

Then the motor car itself was the object of crime from its very debut on the streets. At first the motive for stealing a car was curiosity, joy-riding, a quick way home, or use as a getaway after crime. But soon after the First World War car 'ringing' – 'ringing the changes' with new number plates and stolen registration details, sometimes apparently obtained from a crooked LCC clerk at County Hall – became a substantial new criminal enterprise. As early as 1924, 'The "industry" is syndicated, with branches in various cities.' Stolen cars were 'transported in large pantechnicon vans . . . to another part of the country, where they are re-registered as new'. And a 'Great Car-Stealing Conspiracy', involving a Brixton gang with garages at the Oval and Camberwell, was broken up by police in 1935.[12]

Under these new influences, figures for crime in London fluctuated across the first forty years of the century. There was no doubt huge under-reporting of crime by the poor, and huge under-recording by the police, at least until they changed their practice in 1932 better to record 'suspected' larcenies. When they did, indictable crime known to the police in London shot up by a factor of three, from 26,000 in 1931 to 83,000 in 1932. It was not just common theft that was underestimated. Frederick Wensley made the point that in the early years of the century even murder, and certainly manslaughter, could easily go undetected:

It was not in those days a very extraordinary thing for a dead body to be found in the street during the night or in the early morning hours, and it was significant that this usually occurred not far from houses to which all sorts of bad characters were known to resort. Few of these cases were classed officially as murder . . . but that there had been foul play was often likely.'[13]

With the available statistics so comprehensively unreliable, it is possible to represent trends only with a broad brush. Even so, it is reasonably clear that crimes of violence against the person fell steadily between the early 1890s and 1910, although they increased again slightly just before the First World War. Assaults then tailed off considerably when drastic wartime controls were imposed on the hours of sale, and strength, of liquor. These controls were largely retained after the Armistice and by 1928, according to the *New Survey of London Life and Labour*, 'The social status of drunkenness has steadily fallen in the eyes of the working-class population.' It never recovered its Victorian and Edwardian acceptability. There were 70,000 arrests for drunkenness in London in 1913 and some 9,500 persons were tried for assault; in 1939 the figures were 18,000 and 4,500 respectively. By 1930, 'The old-time, ignorant brutal criminal has practically ceased to exist. He was the product of a rougher and sterner age . . .' And all observers who knew their London commented on the comparative physical safety of the streets compared to pre-1914 days.[14]

Crimes against property showed a different trend. There was a sustained and marked reduction in housebreakings, burglaries and minor larcenies between 1890 and 1930, although the under-reporting of the last has always to be borne in mind. Between 1903 and 1928 burglary and housebreaking in London fell from 553 per million of population to 473; and indictable larcenies almost halved from 2,194 to 1,135. But from around 1930 there was a steady rise in property crime, especially house- and shopbreaking. So that indictable crimes known to the Metropolitan Police were 83,700 in 1933 but 94,900 in 1939, a rise of 13.4 per cent.[15]

By later standards these figures would appear innocent enough, but it did not seem that way at the time. 'Smash-and-grab raiders', 'motor bandits', suburban housebreakings, a notable increase in the proportion of juveniles in the offending population, these were all sufficiently distinctive for some observers to feel swamped by 'a rising army of lawlessness whose members do not hesitate to use the weapons which they carry'. This was the 'great struggle of the century . . . between the modern criminal and modern society'. Much of the explanation for this rise in property crime at the time relied on the Great Depression of 1931–2 and its unsettling effects, through unemployment and wage cuts, on working-class living standards. But in London the slump had less effect than anywhere else in the country, and crime still rose when economic security returned. In fact, the 1930s saw the beginning of a world phenomenon that would soon reach unprecedented proportions: the link not between crime and poverty but rather between crime and prosperity – the superabundance of commodities to steal, illimitable opportunity to steal them, irresistible temptations to match the living

standards of neighbours and an ever-expanding choice of things on which
to spend the proceeds.

Bombs, 'The Black', Chivs and Shooters: Crime, 1940–55

On the afternoon of Tuesday 29 April 1947, Jay's jeweller's in Charlotte
Street, Tottenham Court Road, was held up by three men wearing scarves
round their faces and carrying handguns. The shopmen, both elderly, refused
to do as they were told, pressed a burglar alarm and threw a stool at the men.
Shots were fired, passers-by became inquisitive, the robbers panicked and
ran. They found their stolen getaway car blocked in by a lorry and all three
took to their heels. That was how Alec de Antiquis, a garage mechanic
riding home on his motor cycle, came upon them. He apparently attempted
to slide his machine into the robbers' path and was shot in the head at close
range.

Through a combination of good fortune, skilled detective work and the
settling of an underworld grudge, the three men involved were tracked
down, arrested, charged with murder and convicted at the Old Bailey. Their
leader, twenty-three-year-old Harry Jenkins from Bermondsey, had just
come out of borstal. His brother was serving eight years for manslaughter
for his part in the killing of another 'have-a-go hero', Captain Binney, run
down by a getaway car in 1945. Jenkins's two younger accomplices, Chris
Geraghty, twenty-one, and Terry Rolt, seventeen, both had criminal records
too, Geraghty having escaped twice from borstal. They had broken into a
gunsmith's for their pistols and ammunition. Jenkins and Geraghty, who
had fired the bullet that killed Antiquis, were hanged at Pentonville that
September; Rolt, too young, was detained at His Majesty's pleasure. Detective Superintendent Robert Fabian, in charge of the police investigation,
thought the hangings had done much good. Two of the three handguns
used in the shooting had been found in the Thames at Wapping low-tide;
and 'For weeks after the hanging of Jenkins and Geraghty we began to find
guns . . . abandoned in parks under bushes, in dustbins, dropped through
the floors of bombed houses, fished up by Thames River patrolmen in nets
from the low-tide mud. The men of the underworld had decided to think
twice about using guns in London.'[16]

A passing pressman had photographed the dying Antiquis crumpled in
the gutter, his head cushioned on a shopman's jacket, in a picture wired
round the world. But it was not just this potent image which made the
Antiquis murder so significant. For the new anxieties of post-war London

seemed to converge and crystallize in those few moments of drama and agony in Charlotte Street.

Key among them was the crisis of London youth. This was, of course, no new problem. The first official investigation into juvenile delinquency in London was published in 1816; the turn-of-the-century 'hooligans' of Lambeth Walk had found a chronicler in Clarence Rook; and between the wars many writers had rediscovered the difficulties of *London's Bad Boys* and *Boys in Trouble*. The percentage of first offenders in London aged under thirty rose from 57 per cent to 70 per cent between 1927 and 1932 and the Home Secretary decided to inquire into the problems of juvenile crime in London in 1938. So there was little doubt that the rise of lawless youth predated the dislocations of wartime.[17]

But those dislocations were enormous. The evacuation and trickle back of nearly 50 per cent of London schoolchildren, the closure of schools through evacuation and bombing and teacher shortages,[18] the insecurities of home life in the Blitz with fathers absent in the services and mothers in the factories, the excitements of the blacked-out streets and abandoned houses where collectable or saleable treasures might be had, all combined to unsettle and distract youth from the pre-war tramlines of education and apprenticeship, job and career. Deference and discipline seemed to have deserted the generation born in the late 1920s and 1930s, whose formative years, in inner London at least, were so comprehensively disarranged. Yet after the war they were confronted in positions of power by people only a few years older who had known nothing other than to expect unquestioning obedience to the word of command. It was all a sure-fire recipe for peacetime strife.

The numbers of 'juveniles' (those under twenty-one) arrested for indictable offences in London rose by nearly 25 per cent between 1938 (9,150) and 1945 (11,360) and stayed around that high level for the next eight years. The largest increase was detectable in arrests for shopbreakings and simple larcenies, but also in crimes of violence against the person. By 1949, 'The newspapers were full of the terror imposed by juvenile gangs' like the 'Elephant Boys' (which *was* a topographical reference), and the 'Cosh Boy' had become the plain-clothes predecessor of 'the Ted'. Within a couple of years the weaponry of London youth had expanded from the cosh to include flick knives, fish hooks sewn into jacket cuffs and aluminium armour to protect forearms from a knife or razor slash. A savage knife fight involving a dozen or so Teddy Boys on Clapham Common in July 1953 famously led to one boy having his throat cut and another condemned to hang, though Michael Davies's sentence was eventually commuted. In fact, 1953 had been a year of relative improvement in the post-war youth 'crime wave';

ironically, 1948 was the worst, so no deterrent effect from the Jenkins and
Geraghty hangings detectable there.[19]

Similarly, Robert Fabian's optimism over the disconnection between
guns and London criminals, at least young London criminals, proved false.
In February 1948 PC Edgar was shot dead by a twenty-three-year-old
burglar in suburban Southgate. The weapon was a Luger, one of the many
war mementoes now in the hands of the underworld. And in November
1952, in perhaps the best-remembered post-war youth crime of all, PC
Miles was shot dead by Christopher Craig, just sixteen at the time, on the
roof of a Croydon sweet factory. Derek Bentley, Craig's nineteen-year-old
accomplice, was hanged by a vindictive state despite having been arrested
by another officer at the time PC Miles was shot and despite having learning
difficulties. The murder of an unarmed policeman was especially heinous.
But it was difficult to avoid the conclusion that Bentley was killed to
discourage 'one of the most urgent problems which the domestic dislocation
caused by the Second World War has emphasized in Britain . . . that of the
young criminal'.[20]

Antiquis and all these later cases seemed to symbolize the cheapening of
life that war had brought to London. The post-war years felt incapable of
shaking free from this legacy of violent death. The war itself had seen some
of the most vicious crimes against women that London's twentieth century
ever produced, stirring folk memories of the Jack the Ripper murders more
than fifty years before. Jack the Ripper, of course, had murdered prostitutes
and they were especially liable to meet violence at the hands of men who
hated women. It was remarkable, too, how these murderers – like Jack the
Ripper – escaped capture, protected by the veil of secrecy and subterfuge
under which prostitution necessarily operated. There had been a number of
London prostitutes murdered in the 1930s – at least five in Soho and one in
Clapham. All were strangled and no perpetrator was found in the case of
four Soho women killed in a series between November 1935 and May 1936.
Later, too, well beyond the post-war period, there were other serial killers
of west London prostitutes. The deaths of six women, between January
1964 and January 1965, some found naked on the Thames foreshore,
prompted a ghoulish press to identify their unknown assailant as 'Jack the
Stripper'; and other murders took place in the early 1970s in north London.[21]

But none matched the savagery of those carried out by Gordon Frederick
Cummins. No one knows exactly how many women Cummins killed, but
he was hanged for the murder of four in one week in February 1942. Three
were prostitutes, killed in their rooms in Soho, Fitzrovia and Paddington,
the fourth was a Hornchurch woman found dead in a Marylebone air-raid
shelter. All had been 'brutally assaulted', strangled and grotesquely mutilated

after death; it was this last feature that vividly resurrected the Ripper memory.

Cummins, from Northampton and in London while training to fly in bombers, had attempted to kill other women around the same period but had been frightened or fought off. Police thought he had killed at least two others. He was hanged in June 1942 at Wandsworth.[22] In his essay on the 'Decline of the English Murder' of February 1946, George Orwell celebrated 1850 to 1925 as 'our Elizabethan period, so to speak' of 'the English murder'. He included in his canon the classic London cases of Jack the Ripper (Whitechapel, 1888, 'in a class of its own'), Cream (Lambeth, 1891–2), Crippen (Holloway, 1910), George Joseph Smith (Highgate, 1914) and Bywaters and Thompson (Ilford, 1922). 'It is difficult to believe that any recent English crime will be remembered so long and so intimately, and not only because the violence of external events has made murder seem unimportant, but because the prevalent type of crime seems to be changing.' Orwell saw a new, casual approach to murder, victim meeting murderer merely by chance – like Antiquis and Geraghty – so that 'There is no depth of feeling in it.'[23] But Orwell seems to have forgotten Cummins. And in fact he wrote during a decade when the classic London murder was about to have its twentieth-century heyday.

Four months after Orwell's essay was published, Neville Heath murdered Margery Gardner, 'a woman of 32 of somewhat bohemian ways', in a frenzy of sexual sadism at the Pembridge Court Hotel, Notting Hill. Heath had stayed at the hotel before and had booked in his real name the room in which Mrs Gardner's body was found. Sought by police, he had time to kill again, Doreen Marshall at Bournemouth, before being arrested and brought back to London for trial at the Old Bailey that September. Despite an evidently valid plea of insanity, Heath was hanged.[24]

Two and a half years later, in February 1949, another west London hotel figured in the case of John George Haigh, 'the acid bath murderer'. Haigh had almost certainly murdered at least five others previously between June 1944 and February 1948. He killed calculatedly and for gain, and it was the murder of a fellow paying guest at the Onslow Court Hotel, South Kensington, with which he was charged. Inveigling the elderly Mrs Durand-Deacon to a factory in Crawley – she was considering investing in an enterprise he had told her about – Haigh killed her and virtually destroyed her body in a bath of acid at the works. Haigh presented a palpably fabricated plea of insanity at his trial – he claimed eight victims in all and said he had drunk their blood – but was found guilty and hanged at Wandsworth in August 1949.[25]

Finally, the climax of an apparently endless escalator of horrors, came the revelations surrounding perhaps *the* classic London murder case of the century, the crimes of John Reginald Halliday Christie. He arrived at 10 Rillington Place, Notting Dale, in December 1938. During the war and despite a criminal record, Christie was a special constable at Harrow Road police station. He started killing during those four years of power in the blackout – Ruth Fuerst was the earliest of his identified victims, killed in August 1943 and disposed of in the garden of 10 Rillington Place; he used one of her thigh bones to prop up the garden fence for some years. His police career helped him avoid arrest for the murders of Mrs Evans, one of his ill-fated lodgers, and her baby daughter. Timothy Evans, the baby's father, was hanged for his daughter's murder in a tragic miscarriage of justice. Christie gave perjured (but conclusive) evidence against him. In all, Christie killed at least seven women between August 1943 and March 1953, including his own wife. Three of his victims were prostitutes, all killed in early 1953 after he had disposed of his wife the Christmas before. His motive was sexual – he was a necrophiliac. The bodies of all seven and baby Geraldine were secreted under the floors, behind the walls or in the garden of Christie's ground-floor flat. The neglected 10 Rillington Place was among the first properties in North Kensington to be bought by a Jamaican landlord, who let empty rooms to fellow migrants from 1950. It was one of these new tenants, allowed the shared use of Christie's scullery, who came across an alcove there covered up with wallpaper. When he tore the paper aside he found the naked body of Christie's last victim, and behind it two others. Christie was hanged at Pentonville in July 1953. Only the fifteen – possibly more – murders in Cricklewood and Muswell Hill by the Civil Servant Dennis Nilsen, coincidentally another ex-policeman, came close to the Christie atrocities, in London at least. But even Nilsen could not match Christie's sordid mania, nor the soulless cunning with which he dispatched an innocent man to the gallows to save his own neck.[26]

Murders like these were the unpredictable highlights of the criminal statistics, revealing more (indeed, a great deal) about prevailing codes of social behaviour than about patterns of crime. Antiquis fitted firmly within Orwell's 'violence of external events', reflecting the era's proneness to casual but tragic conjuncture of circumstances. But unlike the bomb or rocket 'with your number on it', Antiquis had died as an accidental consequence of the London 'crime wave' that began in 1944 and was to last some eight years. And it was this prevailing lawlessness that his death came to symbolize most potently of all.

The Second World War seemed to bring a new attitude to crime in London, perhaps in Britain as a whole. It did not emerge all at once. Indictable crime fell slightly between the outbreak of war until the Blitz;

then rose with the looting of bombed shops and houses but fell again, so that 1943 recorded fewer crimes known to the Metropolitan Police than in 1938. Perhaps a fall was not surprising, even after a rising trend. Inner London had lost around half its normally resident population, although some of that gap was filled with servicemen (including George Frederick Cummins). There was then a sudden rise in criminal activity from 1944. By the end of the war, indictable offences known to police in London numbered 131,000, compared to 96,000 in 1938, a rise of 36 per cent. 'Breaking-in offences' rose by 72.5 per cent.[27]

Despite all the hesitations that must attach to the use of criminal statistics, this movement was considered real enough at the time. Why did crime rise so steeply in London during the war and immediately after?

Any answer seems to contain four main components. First was opportunity. The blackout, then air raids and bomb damage, gave thieves an unprecedented easy passage. The blackout covered the shopbreaker's tracks and swallowed up the street robber; an epidemic of handbag snatching in 'the Charing Cross Road area and all around Theatreland' was noted by police early in the war. 'Air-raids . . . were the best ally London's crooks ever had,' remembered Wally Thompson, an Islington thief who had led a smash-and-grab team in the 1930s. Noise, confusion and distracted emergency services meant that any villain with more than a modicum of nerve could take what he wanted when he wanted.[28]

Second came demand. Drastic shortages of most materials and foodstuffs required rationing to ensure that the poorest got a reasonable share of what was going. Inevitably rationing was incapable of satisfying demand for domestic goods, especially as – with full employment – there was more cash to buy things than before the war. Rationing was a system to which all paid lip service but which all wished to get round and most had the ready money to do so. A huge black market organized itself nationwide to fill the gap, and was nowhere more active than in London, where the middle classes had always been more demanding than anywhere else. Getting cigarettes or eggs or nylons or steak or sugar or petrol 'on the black' created a new moral economy which some bemoaned but all exploited. No one minded how goods got into the black market in the first place and many were stolen. 'It was a thieves' paradise,' according to Frankie Fraser from Lambeth. 'I was a thief. Everyone was a thief.' Those who stole had no problem in finding those who would buy: '[T]he war created a vast legion of [receivers],' recalled Peter Beveridge, in operational charge of London's CID at the time, 'not previously criminal receivers but now prepared to buy almost anything in short supply and at inflated prices.' Salvaged or stolen metals, needed to stoke the fires of war, made scrap yards into gold mines: metals remained in short supply, and so irresistibly tempting to the thief, until a year or two after the Korean War. On the margins of the black market the rationing system created its own crime: forging petrol coupons and ration books was as profitable as, and easier than, forging banknotes, and stolen ration books or identity papers were better than cash.[29]

Third, and perhaps surprisingly given the greedy manpower needs of the armed services and industrial or agricultural production, war provided new personnel for crime. Barbara Nixon noted how the civil defence services provided refuge for London's economic misfits: 'Owing to the fact that race tracks, boxing rings, and similarly chancy means of livelihood closed down at the outbreak of war, there was a large percentage of bookie's touts, and even more parasitic professions . . . together with a mixed collection of workers in light industry, "intellectuals", opera singers, street traders, dog fanciers, etc.' Accustomed to seize the main chance, they were well placed to take advantage of the opportunities their work offered them. Like Wally Thompson, inappropriately assigned to ARP duties among City warehouses, where he organized a gang to liberate merchandise the Luftwaffe spared.[30]

Then the armed services themselves created an army of men living on their wits. These were men who had never registered for call-up in the first place and the deserters. Going absent without leave might last a weekend or the duration. By 1944, men going AWOL included not just Britishers but Poles, Free French, Canadians, Anzacs and Americans, both black and white. They were estimated to total 20,000 by the end of the war and most of them were on the run in London. None legitimately had a ration book. Identification papers forged, stolen or purchased got some into work by which they could live. The rest scrounged – a keyword of the time – or took without asking. The cafés and cellar bars of Soho had long been the information nexus for men living on their wits, and never more so than now, despite frequent raids by civil and military police. Among them were men like Alfie Hinds, a household name twenty years later as the persecutor of prison and police authorities: 'It all began when my home was bombed in 1941 and I deserted from the Army. From then on until the end of the war, I was either on the run or in civil or military prisons.' A north London magistrate who had repeatedly fined one costermonger for selling from his barrow in main roads before the war found the same man in front of him a few years later as an army deserter: '"I can't get on with this Army stuff" was the explanation of this sturdy individualist.' Some deserters were more dangerous than others, having 'been trained, some of them in Combined Operations, or with the Commandos . . . They often brought a gun with them.'[31]

And equipment was the fourth component in the wartime rise in crime. Revolvers and bayonets had been noted on the streets of London at the end of the First World War and just after. But guns were in glut by 1945 and remained so for some years to come. 'You can easily buy a gun in London's underworld,' Robert Fabian reported in the early 1950s. '£5 will buy you a big revolver, £10 will get a slender automatic pistol to fit the pocket. They are war souvenirs, or smuggled in from France, Belgium, Eire.' Around 1952 2,400 firearms were confiscated in London, including 1,613 handguns.[32]

It is small wonder that a number of those intimately involved with crime across the period from, say, 1930 to 1970 saw the war as a watershed, 'particularly that "black market" permissiveness which has done so much to corrode everyday standards of honest, decent life . . .' '[N]ew kinds of villain were bred during the war . . . We moved into the era of the spiv and the smart alec, the get-rich-quick types who have unhappily never really left us.'[33] It is certainly true that high crime rates persisted beyond peace in 1945, with indictable crimes recorded by police in London staying at around 130,000 each year until 1948. But they then fell to 103,000 in 1950, rising again to around 112,000 in 1951–2, and then falling to pre-war levels (95,000 or so) in 1954. And it is impossible to pin the dramatic, and dramatically long-lasting, rise in crime that occurred from 1955 on a specifically wartime culture that seemed largely to have exhausted itself with the end of most rationing in the early 1950s.

There were, though, two features from this time that prefigured patterns of London professional crime in the 1960s and 1970s and even beyond. Both received a boost from war. One was the protection racket, finding in the black market a huge unlawful industry from which the blood could be sucked and involving nearly every corner shopkeeper in London. The other was armed robbery, meticulously planned, of cash and valuables on the move.

When Fred Narborough took charge of the CID at City Road police station in 1945, his number-one target was the 'Corner Mob' or 'the Angel Mob', who preyed on corner shopkeepers connected to the black market. This particular gang of 'ruthless thugs' was 'a wartime innovation, and a dangerous one', and Islington was not the only district to sustain one. By the end of the war Billy Hill's Camden Town mob (some knew him as the boss of Kentish Town) brushed padded shoulders with the Whites' King's Cross mob; south of the river the 'Elephant Mob' spread their influence as wide as 'Brixton, Camberwell and New Cross. Over at Notting Hill and Shepherd's Bush another mob was in command. Down in the East End [Jack "Spot" Comer] had become king.' The West End or Soho was, of course, the most contested London territory of all. Here during the war and until 1947, the five White brothers, led by Harry, a bookmaker, had substantially filled the Sabinis' shoes, by all accounts with some brutality. They extorted a high ransom from clubs and gambling dens, more popular than ever through the floods of black-market cash that swamped the underworld. But in 1947 the Whites' reign was broken by an uneasy alliance of Hill and Comer, uniting two powerful mobs against one. Eventually Comer was forced out – but only after his face had twice been badly cut about – and Hill was left in a relatively unchallenged position by 1954.[34]

Hill unusually combined the bloodthirsty capacity for terror so valuable to the protection racketeer – 'I still am one of the best chiv [knife] merchants in the business,' he boasted in 1955 and he would readily use torture to extract information or secure compliance a generation before the Richardsons[35] – with a schoolman's skill at organization and planning. He turned these more fastidious qualities to account by organizing around forty robberies of suburban sub-post offices in 1945–6. Then he broke the mould.

The underworld latched late on to the idea that cash and valuables are most vulnerable not when locked in safes and vaults or displayed behind plate glass or grilles but when they are in transit between one safe place and another. There had been wages snatches early in the century like the Tottenham Outrage (1909) or the Treacle Plaster Robbery (1912), where a cashier was picturesquely disabled by a mask of brown paper and treacle clamped to his face, but highway robbery with violence had not been much of a feature of crime before the Second World War.[36]

Things began to change with an attempted bullion raid at London Airport in 1949, when a police tip-off led to the Flying Squad ambushing the robbers, slugging it out and arresting nine. Hill was more secretive with his planning and 'the opening of the new era' in 'the growth of the crime industry' came on 21 May 1952 in Eastcastle Street, Marylebone. A post office van laden with 'high-value packages', mainly used banknotes, was ambushed by six men in two cars, the crew were ejected and the van hijacked. Hill's team got away with £287,000 in cash, a huge sum and the biggest haul in history at the time. 'The police had little doubt who was behind the raid' but couldn't, or wouldn't, pin it on Hill, who slipped away to warm his heels around the shores of the Mediterranean. 'No robbery had ever taken place like it. No robbery has ever been carried out with such perfection, from split-second timing down to the concealment of evidence,' gloated Hill (while admitting nothing) three years later. Even more important, no one squealed.[37]

In September 1954 Hill struck again. A lorry carrying bullion worth £45,500 and just about to be unloaded at KLM Airlines' office at Jockey's Fields, Holborn, was whisked away 'in 20 seconds'. No one was caught for that robbery either and, according to Frankie Fraser, Hill's minder a year or two later, Hill 'never needed to work again'.[38] Others, though, were willing and able to carry on where Billy Hill left off.

Blaggers, Muggers and Businessmen: Crime, 1955–99

Robberies – blags or blaggings in London cant – increased in the capital by 68 per cent between 1955 and 1957. Although at under 400 they were a tiny proportion of London crime, 'their seriousness has caused considerable uneasiness, and they are still on the increase'. Robbery covered a multitude of sins, from the Eastcastle Street military-style operation to an aggravated handbag snatching on Clapham Common, but all increased during the 1950s, and so did the proportion where weapons were used. By the early 1960s, with robberies still rising overall, bank hold-ups emerged as a 'fashion-able technique' and in 'the spring of 1962 wage-snatches had become so frequent in one part of London' that police had to swamp the area with personnel to deter the robbers. 'Month by month,' recalled Richard Jackson, the Assistant Commissioner (Crime), 'I saw the total number of robberies increasing, and the arrogance and self-confidence of professional thieves growing too.' Robbery was an especially metropolitan crime: '35 per cent of all such offences are committed in London'; and when major robberies took place outside the capital it was usually London robbers who were responsible.[39]

So it proved on 8 August 1963. The raid on the Glasgow to London night mail early that morning remained nearly forty years on Britain's 'crime of the century'. The Great Train Robbery became a mythic event, accreting legends and counter-legends, not least because of the huge haul – £2.6 million in used banknotes – very little of which was ever recovered. This was a south London enterprise, involving a large team put together by a few strong personalities: Buster Edwards, born 1931, brought up near the Elephant and Castle, window cleaner, florist, by 1950 an associate of thieves and fences who used a pub called the King's Head at Vauxhall; Gordon Goody, strange but brilliant, who lived with his Irish mother in Putney; Charlie Wilson, from Battersea, who went to the same school as the talented and versatile Bruce Reynolds; Reynolds, who had been in Wormwood Scrubs in 1949 with Ronnie Biggs, born 1929 in Lambeth, a self-confessedly incompetent thief who some thought would bring bad luck to the job; the two drivers, one a Formula One racing driver called Roy James, came from Fulham; and others from various parts of London and Brighton, fifteen in all. They came together not through some masterplan but 'through a kind of personal recommendation' and 'the word' going round, and quite a number had worked together in various combinations on armed robberies before. According to Biggs, Reynolds was the 'leader'. But the whole job was probably put together by two or three of the team who were the only ones to have an overview, recruiting others as necessary for isolated tasks. Unusually, no underworld gossip leaked to the police before the event; and afterwards it needed painstaking detective work to make the first arrests and so break through the carapace of silence. Some were never publicly identified or charged; and a number of those imprisoned later famously escaped, Ronnie Biggs thrust from Stockwell to international stardom in the process.[40]

The south London connection that created the Great Train Robbery of 1963 revealed that London crime was as strongly attached to neighbourhood after the war as before. So it remained. At the century's end each London district still spawned its own villains. No serious threat to this strictly local division of spoils was ever mounted or could be. London was just too vast and complex and fiercely parochial ever to allow one 'gang' or 'mob' or 'boss' to reign supreme in south London as well as north, east as well as west. But it did not stop people trying, at least until the 1960s. This was the decade that saw the end of London's most notorious gangs of racketeers in circumstances which seemed to curb the West End ambitions of potential imitators for the rest of the century.

First came the break-up of Charlie and Eddie Richardson's 'gang' from Camberwell. In many ways the brothers, especially Charlie, were talented businessmen who ran a range of legitimate enterprises with underworld connections (like scrapyards and fruit-machine rentals), and who also engaged in long-firm frauds and provided some 'protection'. A brutal affray in which one man was shot dead outside a club called Mr Smith and the Witchdoctor at Rushey Green, Catford, in March 1966 was over who had the right to supply the club with one-armed bandits and protection; the owners had called in the Richardsons in preference to another south London group in current control. The Richardsons could also be relied upon to punish the transgressions of other south London villains who had cheated or offended their allies or those who claimed their protection. Punishment extended to torture. Charlie Richardson, apparently unable to feel pain himself, was curious to see its effects on others. He was jailed for twenty-five years at the Old Bailey in 1967. Whether his crimes merited such a savage sentence or whether they had been exaggerated by police and his other enemies was a matter of some debate at the time and later.[41]

No such doubt attached to the gaoling of the Krays. Born in 1934 in Bethnal Green, the Kray twins, Ronnie and Reggie, were about the same age as the Richardsons. Both were of that generation robbed by the war of an education and settled prospects. Their turf was the East End, where they were tough enough to work the protection racket on the local underworld even more than local businesses. They remained essentially East End villains until the Betting and Gaming Act 1960. The legalization of gaming capitalized on the uncontrollable 'gambling fever' which had seized London from the mid-1950s. Overnight, hole-and-corner 'spielers' in Soho back rooms were transformed into a multi-million-pound industry. Even so, gambling still remained under close police scrutiny. And trouble was to be avoided at all costs lest the police find a reason to withdraw the licence to operate lawfully. Clubs were glad to pay protection to keep trouble away, even when it was the protection mobs themselves who would cause the trouble. Liquid cash, that powerful adrenalin, was shot into the arm of a criminal racket that legalization had been designed, in part, to destroy. The Krays saw their chance and seized it.

With the assistance of the semi-retired Billy Hill, the Krays opened a combined gaming and nightclub called Esmeralda's Barn in Knightsbridge in late 1960. They combined it with a muscular expansion of the protection racket on gambling clubs in the West End. By the mid-1960s, Mr Justice Sparrow estimated, 90 per cent of London gaming clubs were paying protection, and a fair proportion of it would have gone to the Krays. This West End connection turned their heads. Delusions of grandeur made them the courtiers of the glitterati, taking every opportunity to be photographed with film stars like Judy Garland and George Raft (the latter had American Mafia connections the twins were also keen to court), and their small-town domestic equivalents like Barbara Windsor and James Booth. Ronnie Kray's homosexuality lubricated the twins' connections with the lower echelons of London's political smart set, like Lord Boothby. They featured in David Bailey's *Box of Pin-ups* (1965) among the most 'glamorous' progeny of Swinging London. These were all substantial distractions which turned attention away from their old power base east of Aldgate. In all this high life, any lack of respect shown them back in the East End must have seemed an intolerable affront. But lip service was more readily paid in Knightsbridge than in Stepney and settling East End scores was to prove their downfall.

The transatlantic flirtations with the Mafia, who presumably found the twins could deliver so much less of the West End than they promised, the black-tie charity fund-raising events and showbiz parties where even royalty might be expected, all folded like a house of cards with the assassination of George Cornell (who had reportedly called Ronnie 'a fat poof') in the Blind Beggar pub, Whitechapel Road (Ronnie, March 1966) and the squalid hacking to death of Jack 'The Hat' McVitie in Blonde Carol's flat, Stoke

Newington (Reggie and others, October 1967). More than half mad, the twins were imprisoned for life in March 1969, and the squeeze on the East End underworld relaxed overnight with audible relief.[42]

But the rising tide of crime abated not one jot. From 1955 reported crime rose to unprecedented levels. In 1968, which saw the Krays' last months of freedom, indictable crimes known to the Metropolitan Police totalled 299,000. That was twice the post-war peak of 1945. The disappearance of one 'gang', no matter how significant, made no visible mark on the upward trend. By 1971, indictable crimes reached 340,000 (up 14 per cent in three years), in 1974 414,000 (up another 22 per cent) and by 1978 567,000 (a further 37 per cent). Although some of this rise may have been artificially inflated by differences in recording methods, and maybe a greater propensity to go to the police about certain offences (like rape and other sexual assaults) previously under-reported, a real rise in the volume of crime could not be ignored or wished away.[43]

That rise was a national, indeed international, phenomenon. High-value crime, however, was still essentially concentrated in the metropolis. So were armed robberies, the highest-value crimes of all. These began to rise exponentially from 1963. Local teams of robbers organized all over London. In August 1966, a madly reckless team of west London robbers from Paddington and Notting Hill shot dead three policemen (DS Christopher Head, Temporary DC David Wombwell, PC Roger Fox) in a 'Q' car at Braybrook Street, Shepherd's Bush. Roy Garner, from Holloway, brought together a group of north London robbers in the daring Piccadilly underpass hijacking of yet another KLM security lorry in December 1970. By the summer of 1972 there was an armed bank robbery in London every five or six days. Police reckoned there were some 3,000 men in the capital who were ' "available" for bank robbery' and London was 'estimated to contain 80 per cent of Britain's major criminals'.

Bertie Smalls became London's (and the nation's) first 'supergrass' in 1973. He had led a west London team whom police knew as 'the Ealing mob', although their raids (like Billy Hill's) ranged all over London. Maurice O'Mahoney, another supergrass, was especially active among the armed robbers of Hounslow and outer west London, round Heathrow Airport. But the rise of the supergrass could not prevent the nation's biggest robbery of the century. This was the November 1983 Brinks Mat robbery at Heathrow, which netted £26 million in gold bullion. The rise of a prosperous criminal élite reversed the pattern that had dominated London crime in the 1930s. Instead of the Shoreditch burglar taking a car out to the suburbs for a 'job', the armed robbers of Stanmore and Pinner were commuting to central London to blag an armoured van or open a safe-deposit vault. And second homes in Marbella and the 'Costa del Crime' had institutionalized Billy Hill's Mediterranean connection of the 1950s.[44]

The 1970s was the decade when London seemed to become – was in reality – a more violent place. Indictable offences against the person more than doubled between 1968 (8,024) and 1978 (17,152), mainly woundings and serious assault, and grew as a proportion of all crime. 'Violence and how to deal with it was one of the main preoccupations of the Seventies.'[45] It undermined the gentrification movement, now thickly colonizing inner London, where violent crime was most prevalent. Among the terrifying instances of attacks on women in public places, or the apparently insoluble problem of football hooliganism, two types of violent crime stood out. Both were largely specific to London: international terrorism and 'mugging'.

Of the terrorists, the IRA – an old enemy of London – struck first. The end of the Fenian dynamite outrages of 1883–5, when the tube and railway stations were bombed and attempts were made to blow up Nelson's Column, London Bridge and the House of Commons, were followed by an Irish ceasefire bringing peace to the capital for nearly forty years. Then 'The Troubles' were accompanied by the assassination of Field Marshal Sir Henry Wilson, shot dead on the doorstep of his Belgravia home in June 1922. There were attempts to blow up the Vacuum Oil Company at Wandsworth in January 1923, and various arson attacks on railway property and hayricks, still a feature of soon-to-be-suburban London. Then, in January 1939, a new IRA campaign began, with London once more its prime mainland target. Time-bombs damaged electricity generating and post office plant, as well as shopping streets – six small bombs exploded or were discovered in the Piccadilly area on one June night, for instance. And there was more trouble in 1954–5, when service depots in the Home Counties were raided for guns and gelignite – a cache of Bren guns and other weapons was discovered in a cellar at Caledonian Road, Islington.[46]

All of this, though, was a pale harbinger of the IRA mainland campaigns of 1973–6 and 1978–82. These took a very considerable toll: 252 bombs or explosive packages in London alone and nineteen shootings. Fifty-six Londoners died. The siege of six IRA gunmen and their hostages at Balcombe Street, Marylebone, in December 1976 produced one of the most memorable moments (and photographs) in a turbulent decade. Apart from prominent individuals, the main bombing targets were service personnel (including the Woolwich pub bombing, Chelsea Barracks, the Household Cavalry at Hyde Park, a regimental band at Regent's Park), railway stations, shopping streets and stores, tourist attractions (including the Tower of London and the Hilton Hotel), and symbols of privilege or authority (like Harrods, Pall Mall, Old Bailey, Westminster Hall). The main victims, though, and intentionally so, were ordinary Londoners going about their business – over 800 were injured in the two campaigns, many maimed for life. These were difficult years for the London Irish, who suffered considerable abuse and some police harassment in a backlash against the fundamentalists.[47]

The IRA continued to target London through the 1980s and into the 1990s, helping make it probably the most continuously bombed city in European history. The destruction of the Baltic Exchange, St Mary Axe, in April 1992, and the tremendous Bishopsgate bomb of March 1993 caused the City Corporation to put a 'ring of steel' round the City, where – extraordinary to see in central London – policemen and women armed with sub-machine-guns manned checkpoints on main streets. The bomb at Canary Wharf in February 1996 reminded Londoners, grown complacent after another ceasefire, of the destructive power that a small band of fanatics could muster at the end of the century.

Middle Eastern terrorism followed hard on the heels of the first IRA campaign. It was unsurprising that London should have been such a battleground, given its prominent Jewish community and its place in the Arab diaspora of the 1970s. Among recent Arab migrants were many political exiles and refugees, some of whose governments sent assassins to London to hunt them down. In December 1977 two Syrians were killed by a car bomb. A month later the London representative of the PLO was assassinated. In July 1978 there was a grenade attack on the Iraqi ambassador outside his embassy and a former prime minister of Iraq was shot dead at the Intercontinental Hotel. There then followed attacks on Israelis: a gun and grenade assault on El Al airline staff outside the Europa Hotel, and the assassination attempt on Shlomo Argov, the ambassador, as he was leaving the Dorchester Hotel; Sir David McNee, Metropolitan Police Commissioner, was at the same function. Scary though all this was, it was at least plain that the people of London were not intended to be caught in the crossfire of what was designed, at least, as a semi-private squabble. Things changed somewhat in the most dramatic event of all, the Iranian Embassy siege of 30 April to 5 May 1980. Embassy staff and a diplomatic protection officer, PC Lock, were held hostage. Four terrorists, who had already killed one of the hostages and were planning to kill more, died and one was captured in the sudden end to the siege, shown live on television all over the world. Nearly four years later, in March 1984, PC Yvonne Fletcher was shot dead by an official from the Libyan People's Bureau in St James's Square. But the Iranian Embassy siege effectively marked the end of London's three years as a world theatre of operations for the resolution of Middle Eastern troubles.

The other problem that rose to prominence in the violent 1970s refused to go away. This was street robbery. In 1972, peak year for bank robberies, a term was reintroduced into everyday English to describe this more common, less rewarding, spontaneous and amateur crime: mugging. Reintroduced, because although adopted by the press as an Americanism for 'a frightening new strain of crime', the term was English and the crime very old indeed.

John Camden Hotten's *The Slang Dictionary* of 1865 defined one use of the verb 'to mug' as 'to rob by the garrote' – seizing someone round the neck from behind.[48] The 1860s had also been a time of high anxiety over street robberies and it was fitting that another panic 110 years later unwittingly revived an old word to describe it. From the 1970s on, a mugging was a robbery involving sudden attack in the open air; the amount of violence varied from brutal and superfluous assault to the minimum force needed to snatch a handbag; the assailant could be alone or working with others but was almost always young, if only because he had necessarily to be fleet of foot; and the term came malevolently to be associated in both the public and constabulary minds with race, so that 'black' was the spoken or silent adjective that 'mugger' conjured up.[49]

Robberies known to the Metropolitan Police jumped from 2,012 in 1967 to 6,826 in 1977, though this also included categories like armed robberies by professional thieves and may have been inflated by redescribing some 'thefts from the person' (like pickpocketing) where minimal violence had been used. A careful study of street robberies in London published in 1980 threw much light on the reality of 'muggings'. The favourite time for a street robbery was a Friday night between 10 p.m. and midnight; victims were overwhelmingly adult men, attackers almost always youths aged between fourteen and sixteen, most often working alone or in pairs; generally the victim was uninjured and less than £20 in cash or value stolen. Whereas 88 per cent of victims were 'white-skinned European type', 58 per cent of assailants were described as having black skins. That figure rose to 61 per cent in Lambeth, where street robbery had a quite extraordinary prevalence and where it remained disproportionately so for the rest of the century. In 1997–8 there were 26,731 robberies known to the police in London (four times the level of twenty years before) and Lambeth was the capital's capital of street robbery – 2,618 offences compared to Westminster's (and thus largely the West End's) 2,435. Despite this growth in street robberies, the offence had to be kept in proportion. For in 1997–8, all categories of robbery constituted 3.5 per cent of notifiable crime in London and in the 1970s, at the height of the mugging panic, less than 1 per cent.[50]

But the significance of muggings was much greater than their proportion of London crime would indicate. London felt – and was – a less safe place at the end of the century than at the beginning, despite civilizing improvements in the inner areas and despite Londoners having become hugely more middle-class in the interval. The difference in real terms was impossible to measure accurately. Certainly it was not fully reflected in the figure of nearly 27,000 robberies in 1997–8 compared to the eighty-eight known to police in 1906. Clearly definitions and police recording methods had changed greatly over the years. And although there always remained very considerable under-reporting of crime, it was likely that street robberies at the century's end – high-profile crimes committed by strangers – were more likely to be reported than in the first forty years of the century, when assailant and victim in London's working-class districts would more often have been known to each other, if only by reputation.[51] Even so, an enormous rise in actual occurrences was hardly to be denied.

The fear of crime seemed to have outpaced the real thing. It could be even more potent than actual experience of crime in determining how Londoners felt about their city and how they lived their lives. London crime surveys in the 1980s showed that nearly half of Londoners worried about going out after dark, and the proportion was even higher among women, especially those living in inner London. In 1985 71 per cent of Islington residents were worried about crime and '[n]early half of all women in Islington worry about being raped, sexually molested or assaulted'. At the end of the century Londoners worried more about 'walking alone at night', burglary, 'mugging' and most other types of crime than was the norm in England and Wales, despite vandalism, burglary and other (non-vehicle) household thefts being less common in London than in the rest of the country.[52]

If the fear of crime outran actual crime, then the latter was not far behind. The Thatcher years, with their challenging combination of record post-war unemployment and brazenly conspicuous consumption, were characteristically years of rising crime. In 1978 notifiable offences known to the police in London stood at 567,000. In 1990 they had jumped to 834,000, a rise in recorded, if not actual, crime of 47 per cent. Yet London did not suffer uniquely, or even disproportionately. In 1980 there were 5,500 serious offences recorded per 100,000 population in England and Wales, but 8,100 in London (the highest of all the country's police districts); in 1990 the national figure was 9,000, London's 11,600, but now a number of urban and even rural areas had easily overtaken the capital (Northumbria was highest with 14,200, though here again readiness to report crime could distort comparisons). Recorded crime in London peaked during 1991–3, when, for both years, notifiable offences were around 945,000. By 1997–8, they had fallen by 18 per cent to 778,000 – although a change in recording methods during 1999–2000 was set to push the figure up in the new century, while making previous comparisons unsafe.

Crimes of violence against the person and sexual offences, though, were rising against the falling trend of the 1990s overall. So that at 58,000 they comprised 7.4 per cent of all offences in 1997–8 against 44,000 and 4.6 per cent in 1991–2. One factor in that rise appeared to be the growth of London's drug culture. It was as pervasive in some parts of the capital, especially its poorest parts, as drink had been in the years before 1914. It was even more productive of violence and some types of property crime, where robbery and housebreaking were the fastest ways to raise cash to fuel an expensive habit.

By the early 1980s drugs had far outstripped gambling as the main object of London's protection racket as gangsters squeezed their share of the dealers' profits. And drug smuggling and distribution were the main sources of income for organized crime. More than any other element in the history of crime in London, the international networks on which the world's illegal drugs industry depended – growers in Colombia or Kurdistan or Afghanistan, money launderers in London, New York or Moscow, smugglers from the Caribbean and Eastern Europe – brought the world's top criminals to London as never before. Gang wars again erupted on London's streets. Once more they were confined to London's localities – Brixton and so-called 'Yardie' shoot-outs were connected from the late 1980s until the end of the century. No one was in a position to capture London's drugs economy as a whole, if only because outsiders still had to coexist with London's home-grown family enterprises. These perhaps were the toughest of the lot, kingpins in their own pieces of London turf, like the Adams family (Islington) and the Arif brothers (Stockwell). And guns, despite Britain's ever-tighter controls, seemed as readily available to the underworld as they had been in 1911 or 1947; a sub-machine-gun could be had in London for as little as £200 in the summer of 1999.[53]

All this made things hugely difficult for the Metropolitan Police, at the nation's cutting edge in the war against drugs and drug-related crime. Those difficulties were made even worse because the Met had not just to fend off rapacious criminals from all over the world, it had also to deal with the enemy within.

The Blue Lamp: Police and Public, 1900–1958

Poor George Gamble. It would have been far better for him had he never ventured out in the early hours of Tuesday 21 August 1906. Gamble, a painter's labourer for Trollope and Colls, the big London building firm, lived in a lodging house in Commercial Street, Spitalfields, and that night went out to buy sex. In Brick Lane he approached Ethel Griffiths, a married woman from South Wales, who lived in the notorious prostitutes' lodging house at 2 Flower and Dean Street, and with whom he had been several times before. He asked her for a 'short time'. As he was talking to her, PC Ashford approached the pair and told Gamble to 'move on'. This he did. Ashford then asked Ethel 'if she would go to a certain place with him, and she refused. She knew what he meant.' Probably because Gamble would pay for what Ashford would not, Ethel went after George. So did PC Ashford. 'The constable followed him up and kept dancing in front of him . . . and trod on his heels [a common provocation of the time], and shoved him, and finally the police constable knocked him down, and started kicking him between the legs.' A newsvendor round the corner in Flower and Dean Street 'heard "a man's screams"'. He rushed up to Brick Lane, and saw a man lying on the ground and a constable standing over him . . . Every time he went to get up the constable hit him and kicked him. He heard a sergeant say, "Let him alone; he has had enough."' When Gamble did get up and stumble away, the furiously jealous Ashford pursued him and kicked him again. Ethel and the young newsvendor eventually helped Gamble to the London Hospital. He stayed there three months with a ruptured urethra, his injuries 'extremely serious . . . In the doctor's opinion [he] is permanently damaged.'[54]

'Gamble's Case' came to the attention of the 1906 Royal Commission on the Metropolitan Police, set up to consider complaints about the way the London streets were policed. The Commissioners upheld Gamble's complaint. They concluded that Ashford and PS Sheedy, who had admonished but not reported him, were guilty of misconduct. But in most of the nineteen complaints they considered in detail, they concluded that the police had acted appropriately, and in most of those cases they were no doubt right. Yet the Commissioners' report was not the wholehearted exoneration of police conduct that opinion at the time and subsequently chose to construe it. The pattern of complaints that the Royal Commission considered was to be repeated for the next fifty years and more: oppressive abuse of power, violence against arrested persons especially at police stations, blackmailing street bookmakers (and prostitutes) for money (and sex), bearing false witness and manufacturing incriminating evidence against innocent people. Indeed, many complaints like these, adjusted for changed circumstances, were common enough at the century's end. Despite *The Times*'s ringing endorsement, 'beyond all cavil or doubt that our police force is a credit to the men who are responsible for it', the Commission's report revealed a state of open warfare between police and a considerable portion of the non-*Times*-reading London public that would have familiar overtones for 100 years to come.[55]

In fact, the relationship between police and public in London was fraught throughout the twentieth century. To a certain extent that was inevitable. Always and everywhere there is tension between those who enforce the law and those who break it. And the ranks of the latter rise and fall with tides of fashion in human behaviour, especially when laws criminalize activities which many consider legitimate. In London, however, it was hard to avoid the conclusion that problems between police and public were particularly deeply rooted. There seemed to be systemic morbidities in the management and organization of the Metropolitan Police that would let generations of Londoners down. And that undermined the bravery, commitment and good intentions of tens of thousands of men and women who served selflessly in its ranks.

Fault, though, was by no means all on one side. There can be no doubting the violent hostility to the police of large sections of the London working class, especially fierce during the first twenty or thirty years of the century. In 1906 the local magistrate for Notting Dale spoke of 'the terrible assaults' on police 'and how they were kicked and battered about, and many and many a time a man has gone home wounded and injured, and has had to leave the Force, because of injuries received in that district . . .' More than twenty years later it was still, according to a local policeman, 'the roughest, toughest spot in all London . . . Every time we made an arrest, a crowd would collect, booing and jeering and threatening us. Sometimes a great mob would gather outside the police station, screaming and shouting and daring us to come out. It got so bad at times that we had to barricade the doors and windows.' In one 'running battle' around 1929 that ended up with a crowd outside the police station 'challenging us to come out and finish the fight', an elderly PC, 'in his last few months of service, was kicked in the crutch and crippled by a double rupture'.[56]

Notting Dale was exceptional, but every single district of London had its tough places where it was made clear to any young policeman from his first day on the beat that he was the enemy. Like John Capstick, posted to Bow Street, Covent Garden, around 1926. His beat included a place famous at the end of the century as the home of ultra-chic wholefood faddery:

As I patrolled down Monmouth Street, painstakingly inspecting each shop door, a scruffy young fellow dashed up to me, shouting: 'Quick, mate! There's a fight in Neal's Yard.' He ducked into the shadowy alley that led to the yard, and like a mug I followed him. Too late I saw that the one flickering gas-lamp had been put out. Before I could draw my truncheon I was on the ground, with four or five ruffians working me over with fist and boot. I staggered back to Bow Street minus helmet, whistle and truncheon. My face and body were covered with bruises, and I knew I was lucky to have escaped so lightly. But there was no sympathy in my sergeant's eyes as he asked, 'And what's happened to *you*?' 'I've been attacked by a gang of roughs,' I said. 'Where? Round Neal's Yard? . . . I thought so,' he said. 'That's where they break all you young coppers in.'[57]

The phenomenon of the 'hostile crowd' threatening, sometimes interfering with, a policeman making arrests was fairly common in London until 1930 – more common before the First World War than after, and drink again played a large part in that change. Making an arrest could be difficult on any Saturday night in any main street in inner London. A high point of the hostile crowd arose in the summer of 1919 in the various riots – race, soldiers awaiting demobilization and youth – that troubled London and many other places. Things were not helped in London by a police strike that August, the second in a year – the earlier strike had brought down the Commissioner. Exuberant horseplay on the streets provoked police intervention; and that in turn led to local battles to free prisoners and batter the police. A crowd of 2,000 attacked Enfield police station to free a man arrested for discharging a firework on Peace Night, that July, and six PCs were injured in a Greenwich riot around the same time; five PCs were hurt in the 'Battle of Wood Green' in August – 'I have never in all my life seen such a hostile crowd,' remarked one veteran of eighteen years' service, most of them 'in a notorious part of London'; another 2,000-strong crowd attacked Brixton police station that same month; a 'huge crowd', some armed with bayonets, rescued two men from the police in Tottenham High Road in September; and a hostile crowd in Kilburn High Road attacking two PCs arresting a drunk included a soldier armed with a revolver. A north London magistrate complained 'that the vulgar crowd always went against the police when the latter were in difficulties', and Gervais Rentoul, a west London magistrate, noted in 1940 'the curious fact that a crowd, particularly in working-class districts, is almost invariably hostile to the police'.[58]

But how curious was it? To portray the police as an army of occupation billeted on a militant working class to subdue them for toil and deference would be a woeful travesty; although it is interesting to note the anti-cockney recruitment prejudices of the force – 83 per cent were born outside London

at the turn of the century.[59] Even so, there is no doubt that the police had
to enforce many laws which, more so before 1960 than after, were at odds
with working-class culture. The class bias of the betting laws was notoriously
brazen, with all off-course betting forbidden, so only those with time and
resources to attend the race meeting could have a lawful flutter; it was a
criminal offence for bookies to take bets in the street and penalties were
worse if a house was used as a betting shop. Street gaming with dice and
coins was outlawed; a drunken singsong after closing time could provoke
arrests; so could playing football in the streets, selling from a barrow, shouting
wares, or having sex in an alley when there was nowhere private and
affordable to go. These were all sins so much more likely to be tempting
around the Walworth Road than High Street Kensington. Even restrained,
tolerant and good-humoured policing in these circumstances would still
cause offence. But policing was not always all these things – how could it
be in those districts where feeling against the police was traditionally so
truculent? – and oppression did not have to be on the PC Ashford scale to
be bitterly resented.

Oppressions, though, there were. Drunks could be beaten in the street
and anyone could be given a whack for no justifiable reason. The old laws
of 'suspected persons' – the so-called 'sus' laws – sent men to prison on the
uncorroborated and perjured evidence of one or two policemen. Beatings
in police stations for turbulent youth or seasoned villains were commonplace,
and some stations had notably bad reputations for it. There were frequent
complaints of planted evidence: stolen property, a jemmy, a cosh. Then,
certainly until the 1930s, there was much ill-treatment of working-class
women by the police: making 'obscene remarks' to 'comely' women in the
street, or blackmailing prostitutes and other women into having sex. There
was a prominent case involving two PCs and a young Islington woman,
Helen Adele, in 1928: she refused to favour them with sex and they brought
a false charge against her. When two West End detectives swore that same
year they had observed a woman as a common prostitute for five weeks,
while a doctor at her trial declared her *virgo intacta*, it seemed to typify a
reckless and arbitrary abuse of power by police over working-class women.[60]

However many oppressions there were in reality, they were multiplied
beyond number in the popular mind. Fear of the police had similar magnify-
ing effects to fear of crime. 'If you know a good copper, kill him before he
goes bad,' Louis Heren, his mother a shopkeeper and his father a printworker,
was taught in 1920s Shadwell. 'Not for one moment would I suggest that the
police frame up charges on a grand scale,' mused Desmond Morse-Boycott, a
Somers Town high Anglican priest in the 1920s and 1930s. 'Yet one cannot
disregard the universal judgment of the poor . . . Seldom does one hear a

good word about them.' 'One of my earliest realizations,' wrote outspoken Victor Meek of his early police service in Wandsworth, 'was that few people other than dear old ladies and foreigners really liked the London policeman. The vast majority longed to score off him. Many feared and hated him as much as he feared and hated them. Things may have changed since, just as the pay has, but that's how it was in 1927.'[61]

There were other sources of popular discontent. It was readily accepted in London's working-class communities that the police were venal. Before 1933, when Lord Trenchard, the new Commissioner, moved to stamp it out, 'tipping' could provide a significant proportion of a London PC's pay, itself shamefully low and with conditions of service to match. Tipping took many forms, some of them more frowned upon officially than others. Some PCs competed with the loafer for the chance to open a car door for a wealthy passenger. Free beer donated by publicans was the commonest tip and tipple of the constable on the beat, for publicans needed his ready cooperation in the event of trouble; their fear, justified or not, was that without liquid inducement the policeman might not readily be at hand. ' "Do you drink, mate?" ' PC Bishop was asked on first taking up his duties at Limehouse around 1903. ' "Then you're in luck . . . There are sixteen pubs on this beat of yours and there is a pint bottle hidden outside each one of them. Then at one o'clock you take over half my beat, and there's another half-dozen pints on that . . . Don't worry, you needn't drink the lot. The bloke on the next beat and I and the acting-sergeant will . . . soon put it away for you." ' Harry Daley, the gay (not laughing) policeman lover of E. M. Forster, joined the Met in 1925 and was posted to Hammersmith. 'It was mildly and cosily corrupt, with a good sprinkling of street bookmakers willing to give the copper on the beat half-a-crown a day to keep out of the way.' Similarly, prostitutes, cab drivers, and costermongers were all said regularly to bribe the police to let them go about their business. The most lucrative beat in Daley's division was Olympia, where policemen took tips for seeing drivers in and out of tight parking spaces, giving a percentage to the sergeant and the station clerk each week; he could collect 30s a day at this, compared with pay after two years' service of £3 6s a week.[62]

Daley thought that tipping stopped with Trenchard: 'When our superior officers were known to be honest, the majority of us followed suit.' But the corrupt relationship with street bookmakers, at some stations at least, remained lucrative until the law changed in 1960. When Gilbert Kelland was posted as sergeant to Carter Street police station, Walworth Road, in 1951, he found all ranks up to inspector in the pay of bookies; the Chief Inspector, an honest man, was deemed a fool because he could have earned £50 a month from them when his pay was just £850 a year.[63]

There was tipping in the CID too. Around 1921, recalled Edward Greeno, an especially vigorous and combative thief-taker, 'we got a pound or ten shilling note from the Commercial Gas Company through official channels for every meter thief we jailed and my £3 5s a week [wages] became quite theoretic [*sic*]'. Just how many false charges, or false confessions, such a system provoked is daunting to contemplate.[64]

But with the CID there was worse, and this was never stamped out. Just as the uniform branch corruptly 'licensed' street bookmakers – who had, in truth, to be permitted if the police themselves were not to be even more unpopular – so the CID licensed other popular but unlawful activities: one-armed bandits in pubs in the 1930s, for instance; or gaming houses from Chinatown to Mayfair. Then they famously licensed premises which were not licensed premises: drinking clubs and shebeens all over London were closed or permitted to remain open at a senior detective's costly whim; and smart West End nightclubs would pay small fortunes to be allowed to flout the capital's nonsensical liquor laws, which made it an offence to serve alcohol after 10 p.m. By 1928, the enterprising Station Sergeant Goddard at Vine Street police station had salted away quite a nest egg from these licensing activities. In his main hoard at the Pall Mall Safe Deposit police found £12,000 in cash, some in high-value notes that could be traced to the bank accounts of Luigi Ribuffi and Kate Meyrick, both prominent Soho nightclub owners. They were prosecuted with Goddard for bribery and conspiracy offences. Goddard was also charged with taking money from a Mrs Gadda, who ran a brothel at 56 Greek Street but who was by this time 'abroad'. In the force since 1900, forty-nine by the time of his trial, Goddard ran a Chrysler car, owned a freehold house worth £1,600 and had over £17,000 in cash, all on a salary of around £400 a year. He said he had been thrifty; that his wife had money; that he had speculated wisely in business ventures (buying the copyright of popular songs, making sticky rock for sale at the Wembley Exhibition Centre); and he was a wizard punter on the horses. Despite putting up witnesses in his defence, Goddard was convicted at a sensational Old Bailey trial in January 1929. He received eighteen months' hard labour and a £2,000 fine, the others fifteen months'. On his release he used his entrepreneurial talents, and the residue of his hard-grafted cash, to found Chessington Zoo.[65]

For some time after, policemen in London had 'Goddard!' shouted after them in the street, and there is no doubt that the case dealt a heavy blow to the force's self-esteem and to its reputation in middle-class London. Maybe it was this experience that encouraged the Met to keep the lid on corruption scandals, preferring to ignore, cajole or discipline rather than expose and punish in public. But corruption in the CID remained endemic. By no means all officers were tainted but many were. Trenchard was 'scandalized' by the amount of corruption he came across in the early 1930s, with officers up to detective superintendent level taking bribes from some criminals and blackmailing others. He believed the Met was worse in this regard than other forces, if only because, as in the Goddard case, temptations were bigger. He did little – perhaps in just four years as Commissioner he could do little – to deal with it. And so corruption remained endemic in the 1940s and 1950s. Few policemen in their memoirs dealt with this aspect of their work; it became more acceptable to do so in the 1970s and 1980s, after Sir Robert Mark. Perhaps two examples from the 1940s will suffice. When Fred Narborough took charge of the CID at City Road police station (Shoreditch and south Islington) in 1945, he had been warned by the Assistant Commissioner of its unsavoury reputation. He addressed the fifty detectives under his command: 'I looked round at the faces; old faces, young faces, hard faces, some as tough-looking as the gangsters in the Hanover Arms [Oval, where Narborough had warned local thieves of his arrival in Lambeth in 1943]. Some glanced away.' But he quickly moved on to other duties and City Road retained its bad name for another twenty years at least. And when Gilbert Kelland was at Walworth in the early 1950s he came across a sickening case of a shopkeeper blackmailed by Flying Squad officers. They arranged for a thief to leave a case of stolen tea on his premises, threatened to charge him with receiving it, then told him it could all be straightened out for £100. The shopkeeper, entirely innocent but fearful of the effects of a trivial criminal record from many years before, had no choice but to pay up. Kelland later thought he identified one of the officers responsible, 'an inspector whose nickname I discovered was "One Ton [£100] Johnny"'.[66]

All this affected mostly working people and poorer shopkeepers and merely reinforced prejudices against the London police taken in with mother's milk. Not that the police were always the enemy. Nearly everyone, at some time, needed them for protection, for assistance and for advice. Harry Daley noted that when Citizens' Advice Bureaux were set up in 1939 they were a great 'boon to busy station officers at police stations' in the poorer parts of London, 'who had always given the help and advice which the new organizations were now prepared to give'. And PC Rawlings, around 1920 in Somers Town (where, remember, no good word was apparently to be heard about police), would 'always try to help with war-pension papers and separation allowance forms and do what I could in a general way to make people feel the police were their friends'.[67]

The attitude of middle-class Londoners was much more positive to the police, though this was undoubtedly dented by the scandals of corruption or oppression that erupted from time to time. Thus had pressure for a

Royal Commission built up in 1906 and more complaints led to a Royal
Commission on Police Powers and Procedure in 1928–9. Prominent among
these was a farcical case of alleged indecent behaviour in Hyde Park. The
Park was a happy hunting ground for energetic trainee detectives, and for
some it no doubt provided much scope for blackmail. Here, Sir Leo Chiozza
Money, a well-known Liberal economist, and a young woman, Irene
Savidge, were arrested for public indecency by two plain-clothes men, but
the magistrate dismissed the charges. There had been similar cases before,
including astonishingly one in 1925 involving Sir Basil Thomson, formerly
Assistant Commissioner in charge of the CID, who claimed that the charges
against him were '"not a mistake on the part of the police; it is a
conspiracy . . ."' But the main change in relationships between police and
middle classes in London seems to have come about through the Road
Traffic Act 1930 and the myriad offences it created. Well-off people were
now brought into that sphere of irksome prying, nit-picking correction and
waste of time which working people daily encountered and it was resented.
It was an argument over a road traffic violation involving the Whitehall-farce
actor Brian Rix on Putney Heath that bizarrely led to the third Royal
Commission of the century on the police (this time not just the Met),
established in 1960.[68]

When *Dixon of Dock Green* began to delight television audiences in 1955,
its portrayal of kindly and avuncular policemen integrated into the East End
community they served was pure wish-fulfilment.[69] Even though to later
generations *Dixon* seemed to embody a departed reality, it was a case of
fiction displacing more troubling memory. In fact, throughout the first fifty
years or so of the century, the Metropolitan Police had been in quite a mess.
Why?

Essentially, this was a problem of management. Managing a police force
always presented peculiarly difficult problems. Perhaps the policeman, his
job to order people about, was inherently resistant to being ordered about
himself. Certainly the constable's unfettered discretion to act as he felt
circumstances dictated required almost total delegation and individual autonomy on the streets. Conduct was not difficult to prescribe but was impossible
to control. With the personal authority of the crown mystically invested in
him, his word had generally to be believed against another's, at least in the
magistrates' courts. That all amounted to an enormous personal power,
abuse of which was difficult to detect. And the temptation to abuse was
strong: for financial gain, for career advantage, or (perhaps strongest of all)
for the constable's view of what justice demanded.

This was a difficulty common to all police forces. London's problems
were greater still. First, its size was enormous. In 1907 the Met's strength

(police officers in post) was 16,000 – over a third of all the policemen in England and Wales; in 1957, despite the great rise in crime, there were 17,000, still about a quarter of the nation's police. It was easy to see how intrinsic problems might be magnified in a force of such a size. Second, the police authority in London outside the City was uniquely divorced from the influence of the people policed. It resided in the Home Secretary rather than local people, elected or appointed to oversee their own police service. He delegated practical responsibility to the Home Office, which took an arm's-length view of its responsibilities that generally spanned the narrow spectrum from ignorance to obstruction while neatly avoiding accountability for adverse consequences: it was extraordinary how the inquiry into the death of Stephen Lawrence at the very end of the century stuck no mud to either the Home Office or the Home Secretary in their supervisory or inspectoral roles, despite clearly long-standing problems of racism in the Met.

It was the Home Secretary who chose the Commissioner, a decision of huge consequence to Londoners. This arrangement succeeded for the first fifty years of the century in securing men of considerable brilliance who were largely – sometimes disastrously – unfitted for the task. Some of them realized it, too, at first refusing to take the job and only eventually agreeing to do so after the most excruciating arm-twisting, in at least two cases by the prime minister of the day personally. The series of superannuated army and air force officers, long past their full vigour, utterly out of touch with the lives of Londoners or London policemen, resulted in shambolic leadership at the top as one man's reforms were swept away in short order by the next Commissioner's bright ideas. The age and background of the Commissioners contributed to the Met's inbuilt resistance to technological change, at least until the mid-1930s. The telephone did not reach Scotland Yard until 1903, when the police office in Reigate, for instance, had had it twenty years before – indeed, Lord 'Bungo' Byng, Commissioner from 1928 to 1931, refused to have a telephone in his office or ever speak into one. Superintendents still inspected their police stations on horseback or with a pony and trap until 1919. Police telephone boxes were developed by provincial forces and the use of fast cars came later to London than elsewhere. Small wonder that the gap in understanding between the Commissioner and, say, Sergeant Goddard's Clubs Office at Vine Street in the 1920s was so immense. Or that development of a Women's Police Force, introduced in London in the First World War, should take so long to flourish, even though it might well have had a humanizing effect on police–public relations: in 1958 there were only 486 women officers in the Met, under 3 per cent.[70]

The leadership vacuum at the top led to management anarchy in the middle. The Met was an organization marked by harsh but uneven discipline – just such a case drove Inspector Syme from the force in 1910 to become an eccentric public figure for the next two decades, making death threats against prime ministers and ending his days in an asylum, even though substantially exonerated in his original grievance. The force developed a culture of secrecy, where top detectives, terrified of having their work subverted by corrupt or self-seeking colleagues, would keep the details of complex investigations entirely to themselves. Unconstrained cultivation of underworld informants led to a corrupt system where some criminals who 'helped' individual policemen were permitted to go on helping themselves. It developed a culture of obstruction in the face of complaints from the public so that police accused of wrongdoing were often not investigated at all, or the 'investigation' was a sham: ex-Detective Chief Superintendent Peter Beveridge approvingly recalled the Scotland Yard detective in the 1920s who 'wore a police athletic club tie' so that officers he was investigating would instantly recognize him. The force was alive with backbiting and favouritism and scheming and lobbying for promotion. 'Nipper' Read, recalling the Great Train Robbery investigation, testified to the organiz-ational confusion this could cause, so that 'Every senior officer was out to make a name with *his* arrests and have *his* photograph in the papers. All gave short crisp quotes suggesting that they were really overlording the operations, and then shortly afterwards they were driven back to London.'[71] All this in an organization where two forces were allowed to grow alongside one another – uniform and plain-clothes – rife with envy and largely separate in terms of manpower and operational command.

The Met was also less effective than any other police force in the country, despite its large share of the nation's police resources, at clearing up crime. In 1958 the Met's clear-up rate was 27.5 per cent, compared to 45.6 per cent in England and Wales as a whole (i.e. including the Met). Here the difficulties of fighting crime in an immense city, known for its anonymity, with complex and innovative criminal traditions, and attracting to it the nation's, even the world's, most talented lawbreakers, could properly be cited in mitigation. And it had to be recognized that corruption could be a false charge impossible to rebut, made by criminals who had every reason to sully the name of an efficient detective. Even so, and despite brilliant men and women who were some of the greatest detectives of their day anywhere in the world, when all was said and done the Met was a police force unequal to the task that London and Londoners set it.

But in 1958 the greatest failures were still to come.

The Bill: Police and Public, 1958–99

At 10.30 p.m. on the night of Thursday 22 April 1993 Stephen Lawrence was stabbed to death on the corner of Well Hall Road and Dickson Road, Eltham. Stephen was an eighteen-year-old A-level student and he was killed because he was black. His killers, a group of five or six white youths, were never caught and after a failed private prosecution seemed never likely to be. Dissatisfaction with the police investigation of his murder led to four years of public criticism and, in July 1997, a judicial inquiry. The most senior officers of the Metropolitan Police gave evidence at the inquiry's various public sittings. The Macpherson report, published in February 1999, pre-sented the most comprehensive and trenchant criticism ever made of the competence and impartiality of a British police force.

It was not necessary to accept every one of the inquiry report's criticisms of individual officers for the findings as a whole still to be shocking enough. Perhaps the revelations of incompetence were most surprising, if only because they were encountered at every turn: the inadequate first-aid knowl-edge of officers who attended the dying Stephen; the 'abysmal' confusion on the night over just who was in charge of the crime scene and who should be doing what; the inadequate searches and investigations during the first few crucial hours; the error of judgement in not arresting and questioning key suspects early enough; the missed opportunity to gather forensic evi-dence that quick arrests might have presented; the delay in effecting surveil-lance of suspects because equipment was prioritized to a 'mugging' investigation; the 'elimination of credible suspects on spurious grounds'; the failure to communicate effectively with Stephen's bereaved parents; the inability of the force to accept that mistakes had been made when the investigation was reviewed by an 'independent' senior officer. These all tarnished the Met's carefully nurtured image of professional competence. Less surprising were the revelations of racial prejudice. This the inquiry termed 'institutional racism': the racial stereotyping that underpinned the Met's values, beliefs, recruitment and management structures, so that the police treated black Londoners differently from, and worse than, white Londoners.[72]

This was less surprising because racism in the Met had been the subject of complaint by black Londoners since the 1950s, exposed by startling investigations in the 1970s and 1980s, and was a generally understood fact of London life for the last three decades of the century. It had helped provoke some of the greatest social unrest that modern London had ever known.

Police and public relations in London had been dominated by questions of race almost since the Notting Hill riots of 1958. There had been incidents of racial abuse and victimization of blacks by police before the Second World War, enough for one observer in the 1930s to think the London police 'prejudiced against foreigners, especially coloured men'.[73] But it was the post-war Commonwealth migrations from the late 1940s that put the issue of race and the Met in sharp focus. The Notting Hill riots exposed some policemen as sharing the prejudices of anti-black rioters: some black men went to prison for appearing merely to be defending themselves, blacks complained that offensive weapons had been planted on them, and at times journalists noted blacks and whites uniting to turn on the police. 'We still maintain that we had a rotten deal from the police!' remarked Mrs Frances Ezzrecco, who helped found the Coloured People's Progressive Association just after the riots.[74] Then the murder of Kelso Cochrane in May 1959, the refusal of the police to accept it as racially motivated in case there were reprisals and their failure to find the assailant (not necessarily blameworthy in the case of a random murder by a stranger in the street) fuelled mistrust of a force which, in the experience of many black Londoners, was by now largely hostile to them.

The main elements in the black Londoner's case against the Met were all in place by the early 1960s. They were articulated by Joe Hunte, from Brixton, in a 1966 pamphlet which he titled, after hearing local police discussing their night's work, 'Nigger Hunting in England?'. He catalogued racial abuse, physical assault, failure to protect blacks against whites, police suspecting all blacks of being criminals (then pimping or drugs, later street robbery) and harassment of black social life by raiding drinking clubs. Other details soon emerged, such as beatings in police stations and complaints of abuse of the laws of 'suspected persons'. Some of these factors were, as we have seen, evident in police–public relations before black people ever came to London in large numbers; and they still continued to plague the lives of some white working-class Londoners as they always had done. But racial abuse and the stereotyping which meant that black people were objects of suspicion just going about their daily business – walking a street, driving a car, carrying a suitcase – gave a personal edge to relations between police and black Londoners. It would become a spiteful vendetta in which the police had been the first aggressors but where aggression was reciprocated and then, in a vicious spiral, escalated.[75]

By the late 1960s, in the year or two following Powell's 'river of blood' speech (1968) and the East African Asian crises, tensions between black people and police in London were running very high. Police raids on the Mangrove Restaurant, All Saints Road, in 1969 – to check contraventions of the licensing laws and search for drugs – and the case of Roland Ifill, a fourteen-year-old steward at Queen's Park Rangers football club, assaulted by whites but then arrested and charged, raised the temperature in Notting Hill; and the Clement Gomwalk case, or 'Battle of Atlantic Road', involving the unlawful arrest, racial abuse and beating of the First Secretary of the Nigerian High Commission, unwise enough to shop at Brixton Market in a new Mercedes, kept things bubbling in south London at the end of the 1960s.[76]

In 1970 Caledonian Road police station was under siege for a time by angry blacks protesting at arrests in Islington. But most significant of all, further raids on the Mangrove provoked a Black Power protest march around the local police stations that August, led by a woman holding aloft a pig's head, and ending in a ferocious clash close to Harrow Road police station. Charges of riot and affray against the 'Mangrove Nine' collapsed ignominiously after a ten-week trial: just two were convicted and given suspended sentences. A raid on the Metro youth club in Notting Hill caused further trouble in 1971. In 1972 the 'black muggers' moral panic broke. In 1973 a report on complaints of police racism was published by an independent charitable trust, and there was trouble between police and black youths at Brockwell Park fair – school students charged with assaulting police became the 'Brockwell Three'.[77]

A House of Commons Select Committee on race relations had been told in 1972 by the West Indian Standing Conference of 'blood on the streets of this country' unless police relations with the black community were improved. That this was no scaremongering was shown sensationally by the Notting Hill Carnival in August 1976. Some 400 police and 200 civilians were hurt in the worst London rioting of the century so far. This was a ferocious anti-police riot pure and simple, with some opportunistic looting and street crime in the confusion. It would set a pattern for collective recrimination in London for the next fifteen years.

The Notting Hill Carnival riot taught the police nothing about race relations, just how better to hit back. They were thus prepared – and gave as good or more than they got – when trouble again erupted at the carnival in 1977. By then a campaign against the 'sus' laws, sections of the Vagrancy Act 1824 designed to deal with persons suspected of being about to commit a crime, focused on the way in which they impacted unequally on black youth. The law was most used (and abused) in London. The Met brought 55 per cent of the nation's suspected person charges in 1976, when London had just 15 per cent of the nation's population; and 42 per cent of 'sus' arrests were made on black people, compared to 12 per cent of all arrests. The campaign was successful and the old law was repealed in 1981.

That was a year to be remembered. For 1981 was London's – and Britain's – year of riot and once more these were essentially riots against the police, with looting and other property crime as a fringe activity. This time Brixton provided the spark. Police relations with black people there had long been tense. A 'deteriorating state of relations between the police and the black community' had been noted around the time of the 1976 Notting Hill Carnival riot. The Met's Special Patrol Group (SPG – a mobile trouble-shooting force which some described as 'paramilitary') began operations in Lambeth from 1978, targeting street crime. The wholesale 'stop and search' of black youths could only make matters worse. An attempt to build a police–community liaison committee foundered in February 1979 after four months and amid much bitterness and mutual blaming. A Lambeth Borough Council inquiry into local policing received 275 representations from organ-izations and individuals – except the Met, who refused to take part. Its report, published in January 1981, was predictably 'highly critical' of the police and unhelpfully used inflammatory language to say so; but it cata-logued a long list of alleged abuses, not all of which could have been fabricated or fantasized. That same month saw the dreadful 'Deptford Fire' at a party in the Ruddock family's home at New Cross in which thirteen black youngsters died. The cause was almost certainly arson. The motive was unlikely to have been racism, but many black people believed it was and the perpetrators once more were never caught. The insouciant response of press, government and – many thought – police resulted in a mounting sense of outrage. It culminated in a march on the 'Black People's Day of Action' in March 1981. When it passed through Fleet Street, the marchers were taunted by white journalists and fighting broke out briefly. Anger, though, was not assuaged. And next month, when the SPG conducted yet another street-crime foray in Lambeth – the notorious Swamp 81 – Brixton ignited.

The 'Brixton Disorders' of Friday 10 to Sunday 12 April 1981 were the most sustained and serious riots of the century in London. The very begin-ning of these terrible events showed how tinder-dry were police and public relations in Brixton. Just after 6 p.m. on that warm Friday evening, a PC noticed a black man chased by 'two or three other black youths'. The PC attempted to stop him and both fell to the ground. 'When PC Margiotta and the youth stood up, the officer noticed that his own arm and shirt and the back of the youth's shirt were covered in blood.' The man had been stabbed and badly wounded, but he still ran away from the officer. Other PCs eventually found him and tried to render first aid. But an angry crowd gathered who assumed the police had set about him. They pushed the policemen aside, 'rescued' the youth and took him to hospital. Rumours of the police 'assault' spread and brought others on to the street. Within twenty-five minutes of PC Margiotta spotting the youth, a riot had begun and police came under fierce attack. Things were quiet by 10.30, but blood had been tasted.

Next day, Saturday, SPG forces returned to Brixton to continue Swamp 81 at 2 p.m. Three hours later the most serious rioting on the British mainland in the twentieth century had begun.

At this point Chief Superintendent Robinson was himself hit and partially stunned by a missile thrown from the crowd. Recovering himself he made his way back to the northern cordon which, again under heavy attack, succeeded in advancing a further twenty yards or so north up Railton Road. A few reinforcements arrived in response to the Chief Superintendent's increasingly urgent calls for assistance, and about six fire appliances. The fire officers fought with great determination the fires around them, in spite of the danger from collapsing buildings and the missiles of the crowd, and under the difficulty that their hoses were being cut by the glass and other sharp objects which were strewn around the ground. Many police officers were injured, some seriously: ambulances were ferrying them from a house in Effra Parade, the occupants of which had offered to help and who rapidly found themselves in charge of a casualty clearing station. As the number of police officers injured rose steadily, Chief Superintendent Robinson's calls for assistance became increasingly insistent.[78]

On that Saturday, 11 April 1981, 279 police and forty-five members of the public were injured, sixty-one private and fifty-six police vehicles damaged or destroyed, and 145 buildings damaged, twenty-eight by fire. One in three of those arrested was white and all commentators noted the large part played by white youths as well as black in the attacks on police. That summer there were further anti-police riots outside London as well as in Lambeth, Southall, Wood Green, Dalston and over twenty other sites in the capital, including a police riot in Railton Road, Brixton, when 176 officers smashed up the interiors of eleven houses, ostensibly in a search for petrol bombs.[79]

More trouble broke out in Brixton in September 1985, after Mrs Cherry Groce was shot in an armed raid by police using a Smith and Wesson .38: 'No other European countries issue their police with such large hand guns,' it was noted at the time.[80] The local police station was attacked with petrol bombs and in eight hours' rioting £3 million damage was done; a man died three weeks later from injuries he received that night. Then, just a week later, came the terrible riot at Broadwater Farm Estate, Tottenham, after Mrs Cynthia Jarrett, involved in a police search nearby, died of a heart attack.

PC Blakelock, well liked and respected as a local community policeman, was part of a unit guarding firemen attending one of the many fires started all over the estate. Police and firefighters all came under attack and were ordered to retreat down the stairs of Tangmere block, the last officers having to 'retreat backwards and protect themselves from attack with their long shields. When they reached the bottom of the stairs, all were ordered to make a run for it.' PC Blakelock ran but tripped and fell 'and was immediately surrounded and attacked'. Mr Holloway, a fireman giving evidence at the subsequent trial, said:

'I looked over my shoulder. Someone fell and the crowd descended on him. I saw things like machetes, carving knives, a pole with a blade set at right angles to it. There appeared to be a frenzied attack going on . . . with a considerable amount of noise. The people around were striking up and down with their weapons. I saw eight or ten machetes being used, or being held in the air.'

Almost immediately two of the fleeing officers, Sergeant Pengelly and PC Pandya, turned back and attacked the group of attackers. Sergeant Pengelly hit out with his truncheon, and the group began to split up. Others came to assist him, and were able to pull PC Blakelock away, although some of the group continued to attack the police. The attack on PC Blakelock was over 'in seconds' according to the judge. But it had caused 40 wounds, caused by weapons such as knives and machetes, to PC Blakelock's head, neck, face, back, hands and forearms.[81]

Between the deaths of PC Blakelock in October 1985 and the inquiry report into the death of Stephen Lawrence in 1999 there may have been some accommodation, but it was hard to say that much had improved in the disastrous relationship between police and black Londoners – at least black youth. There was yet more rioting in Brixton in 1990, and though that thankfully was the last significant anti-police riot of the century few ventured that such episodes would be permanently confined to the dark days of 1976–90.

How much of this dreadful failure was the responsibility of the Metropolitan Police? Not all, clearly. Some black youths had indeed turned street robbery into a cottage industry in Lambeth and passed it on from one emerging generation to another. But the primary responsibility lay with the Met, especially the way in which stupid and mischievous stereotypes of black people were perpetuated and acted upon where they mattered most – in the minds of individual policemen on London's streets.

This was a continuing failure of leadership at the top and anarchy in the middle, apparently unshakeable legacies of the Met's earlier history. Resistant to learning lessons, it was an organization that did not react well to outside criticism. Defensiveness, matched only by an unwillingness to accept changed circumstances, characterized even the response of Sir Robert Mark, in many ways the most outstanding and organizationally progressive of the century's Commissioners. He belaboured the makers of the 1968 BBC *Cause for Concern* programme which first gave mass publicity to the issue of racism in the Met; rubbished the 1973 report into police–public relations in Ealing; refused to accept that a huge police presence at the start of the 1976 Notting Hill Carnival had in any way been provocative. He alighted triumphantly on any error of detail in a critic's case to create a smokescreen behind which he could avoid confronting, even acknowledging, blatant racism in the force he commanded.[82]

The prevailing ideology in the Met in Mark's time and for some years later was that the police were merely innocent victims when policing 'the ghettoes of London, created by the idealist and the inept', as Mark himself put it. 'It is not the relationship between the police and minority groups which is the central issue,' said Peter Marshall, City Commissioner and formerly a Met superintendent at Brixton, in 1979, 'but the social factors underlying the position. We have no power to solve the problems – poor housing, unemployment, discrimination – but we have to bear the brunt in containing trouble.' In this world-view the police were neutral, powerless, having to pick up the consequences of society's ills, not themselves causing difficulties. 'Discrimination' was something that went on around them, indulged in by others, and in which they played no part.[83]

When the police were criticized in Lord Scarman's report on the Brixton Disorders, similar tendencies were at work. Commissioner Sir David McNee protested at the time that, because it was an inquiry under the Police Act 1964, Scarman's terms of reference 'would concentrate upon policing and not extend in depth to the wider social, political and economic context', including (a fair point) the role of the Home Office. In the event, Scarman was relatively muted on the issue of racism in the force. He thought some constables (but not senior ranks) no doubt reflected prejudice common enough in society and there had been some harassment of black youths. But he went on to criticize 'inflexible' policing and a failure to consult the local community about SPG and other special operations; and, unkindest cut of all in the Met's view, Swamp 81 had been a 'serious mistake'. That laid at least some responsibility at the Met's door for the chain of circumstances leading directly to the riots. McNee, no less defensive than his predecessor, believed that the Scarman report had an adverse effect on police morale and left the force feeling 'got at'. Inevitably, the Met got back at those who got at them. In March 1982 Gilbert Kelland, Assistant Commissioner (Crime), released highly selective figures on black youths involved in street robbery, retrospective justification of course for operations like Swamp 81. This caused, Kelland noted wryly after the event, 'quite a furore'.[84]

McNee rightly saw Brixton as a 'watershed' and he established 'community relations training' in the Met. But on the ground police seemed to have accepted and learned nothing. The self-destruct button was pressed hard down. Just before Brixton, McNee had bravely opened up the Met to a searching examination by a team of sociologists led by David Smith. Their four volumes of findings, published in 1983, contained dynamite. Here, laid out in a lurid light of which Scarman could have had no inkling, was the Met's 'canteen culture' – irredeemably racist and sexist, and cheerfully condoned by every senior officer who came into contact with it: 'there can be few other groups,' the report concluded, 'in which it is normal, automatic, habitual to refer to black people as "coons", "niggers" ["monkeys", "spooks", "spades"] and so on'. ' "How many of these niggers actually fried in this barbecue at Deptford, then?" ' a PC asked one of the researchers.[85]

These attitudes, as Smith and his colleagues rightly stressed, did not always – even often – betray themselves on the streets: people do not necessarily act as they speak. But they did so frequently enough. And every unjust act of petty oppression was told and retold in the black community, making far more enemies than victims, and fanning flames the police had long set smouldering. Perhaps the case of Mark Bravo might stand as one small example of how miserably unjust policing could be to black Londoners. This was no drama of a suspicious death in police custody or middle-aged blacks beaten up in their own homes during a police search – neither that rare – just one black boy in north London whose mother gave him a motor bike for his sixteenth birthday in 1982.

During the first week he was stopped by the police on seven occasions and this began a pattern which continued for several months. His mother kept a record of his encounters during a two-week period in April 1982: *2 April*: stopped four times; *4 April*: stopped once; *5 April*: stopped twice; *7 April*: stopped seven times; *8 April*: stopped twice; *9 April*: stopped twice; *14 April*: stopped five times. Mr Bravo eventually received 18 summonses as a result of countless stops between January and the summer; he was acquitted of ten and those for which he was found guilty included a 'defective registration plate' which contained a crack (£2 fine), careless driving (endorsements), and 'dangerous part' (£10 fine and endorsement).[86]

The inquiry into the death of Stephen Lawrence found that 'not a single officer questioned before us in 1998 [there were more than sixty] had received any training of significance in racism awareness and race relations throughout the course of his or her career'.[87] Another instance of institutional resistance to change was shown in the vital question of ethnic minority recruitment to the force. From the beginning the Met had been more reluctant than many forces to recruit black and Asian officers. Senior officers who spoke about this to Sheila Patterson in the early 1960s said they thought Londoners wouldn't stand for black policemen, although they said the Met operated no 'colour bar'. The first black officer, PC Gumms, was recruited in 1967. By 1970 there were just eight and in 1976 – the end of Mark's tenure – seventy-one, a big improvement but a tiny number none the less. In 1999 there were 890. That marked real progress. But the force had now grown to 26,600 and ethnic minority officers represented just 3.4 per cent of the strength; only twenty-three of these were of the rank of inspector or above; and all this in a city with a population over 20 per cent non-white in 1991 and that a growing proportion. The scandalous treatment that some black officers received at the hands of their white colleagues made the national press in 1996, and an uneasy relationship subsisted between the Commissioner and the Met's Black Police Association, increasingly critical of senior officers' lack of understanding of race issues in the police and in society at large.[88] As the century ended there was evidence, too, of a recidivist response to outside criticism, with leaked figures and off-the-record briefings on stop-and-search, condemned for its racial distortion by the Macpherson report. The fight-back against Macpherson was as rapid and hard-hitting as that against Scarman eighteen years before.

Race was the great issue for police and public relations in the second half of the twentieth century, but within the Met itself another, older, issue received greater attention, at least until 1981, and that was corruption. There was not much success here either.

The Challenor case of 1963 did not involve bribery but it concerned the wholesale abuse of power by yet another police sergeant in the West End who was entirely out of control. Challenor was routinely racist – he loathed Italians (he had served in special operations there in the war) and racially abused, falsely imprisoned, assaulted and maliciously prosecuted Harold Padmore, a West Indies test cricketer, in 1963. But his downfall came when he was found out planting bricks on political demonstrators and then charging them with possessing offensive weapons. He was quickly retired from the police and conveniently found unfit to plead at his trial; but he remained something of a hero in the force for 'cleaning up' Soho and was fit enough to pen an unrepentant autobiography some years later.[89]

Londoners did not have long to wait to discover just how clean was Soho. And how clean the Met. In November 1969 *The Times* accused three officers, a detective inspector and two detective sergeants, of blackmailing a Peckham thief. The newspaper had decided to publish rather than give the evidence it had to the Met, not trusting it to investigate the matter properly. One of the three men was DS John Symonds, whose name floated to prominence again thirty years later when his subsequent history as a KGB agent came to light. He was famously recorded as saying to the thief, '"We've got more villains in our game than you've got in yours, you know." And – even more memorably: "I know people everywhere. Because I'm in a little firm in a firm." '[90] The Home Secretary established an inquiry under Frank Williamson, HM Inspector of Constabulary. But the Met attached to it as senior investigating officer Detective Chief Superintendent Bill Moody, himself in the expensive pay of Soho pornographers, and Williamson received little but obstruction and vile treatment ('virulent, poisonous') from the Met's top brass, Commissioner Waldron down.[91] Symonds fled the country but was eventually imprisoned, and so were the two other officers named in *The Times*. But the investigation had been neatly circumscribed and little was done under Waldron, as under his post-war predecessors, to address the problem in any root-and-branch way.

Soon there were revelations about the Drug Squad under Victor Kellaher – like Challenor retired on health grounds, too ill (it was said) to answer charges brought against him – where it was clear that drugs seized in raids and marked for destruction were reappearing on the streets with the Met as main supplier.

It was Sir Robert Mark who took on the CID when he became Commissioner in April 1972, after five unhappy years as Assistant and Deputy Commissioners in a force where he was largely hated, at least at the top. Mark knew exactly what he was up against: 'I had served in two provincial police forces [Manchester and Leicester] for 30 years and though I had known wrongdoing, I had never experienced institutionalized wrongdoing, blindness, arrogance and prejudice on anything like the scale accepted as routine in the Met.' Shortly after being appointed Commissioner he made a highly significant organizational change to bring the uniform and plain-clothes branches closer together, and to give precedence to the first. The CID serving in divisions – 2,300 out of 3,200 – were to report to uniformed divisional commanders rather than the four area detective commanders at Scotland Yard. He then called a meeting of CID representatives.

I told them simply that they represented what had long been the most routinely corrupt organization in London, that nothing and no one would prevent me from putting an end to it and that if necessary I would put the whole of the CID back into uniform and make a fresh start . . . The message got over loud and clear. The century-old autonomy of the CID had ended.

Police connections with Soho pornographer James Humphreys were exposed following his arrest in 1973, leading to the trial and conviction in 1977 of eighteen officers from constable to commander, including a former head of the Flying Squad, although some convictions were overturned on appeal. 'This ended the "firm within a firm" of which *The Times* had complained . . .' and by the end of Mark's tenure some 400 officers had 'left the force either voluntarily or under compulsion'. In fact, he thought that by '1974 police corruption in Soho had virtually ended'.[92]

If only. It all proved much more difficult than that. Such a change needed sustained management action and restless vigilance over many years in pursuit of the reforms that Mark had begun. It needed the courage to admit there could be no quick fix and even more courage to expose the Met to further opprobrium by admitting that problems continued. Somehow, too, the honesty and commitment of many talented CID officers – a factor that Mark confessed he had not stressed enough in his public statements or even in the force – had to be valued and built upon without covering up iniquity. These requirements put immense pressures on an organization already dealing with the most demanding policing context that the Met, and London, had ever faced: responding to a multicultural city, the great rise in crime, international terrorism, the spread of the drug culture.

It was, really, small wonder that, after a period when heads kept low, corruption flourished again. Here the absence of effective middle management told once more. Senior officers seemed reluctant to put in place any checks and balances that might restrain the autonomy of the detective. To respond in any positive way to external criticism was portrayed as weak-kneed pandering to the Met's enemies, or the oppressive investigation of hard-working officers who were always going to be slandered by villains. Some senior men were probably unable to act because they were vulnerable to subordinates who knew too much about them. And things were made more difficult still because a detective might be corrupt but he might also be effective at putting villains away. 'Bent or Brilliant?' asked one national newspaper about a controversial detective superintendent in 1989. The answer, of course, could well have been 'both'. The officer in question was suspected of sharing the reward money from robberies by putting his informant's name forward as providing the vital clue to an arrest and conviction, even though the informant had provided nothing, and of stealing part of the proceeds of robberies he 'cleared up'; but he also, with the help of his top-villain informant, put many robbers in gaol. Others were thought to be in on the planning of robberies, providing crucial intelligence and, in some cases, police uniforms to confuse robbery victims over who was the policeman and who was the thief.

Indeed, in London it was not always easy to tell. One detective chief inspector in the Robbery Squad was remembered by Freddie Foreman, a top south London thief, as 'a rebel cop . . . as much a crook as any of us'. But he would 'nick you as quick as look at you if it was safe to do so' and, though corrupt, he was still waging his private war against the underworld, bending judge's rules at will and getting what he could on the side. He was a key member of the team that secured many convictions with Bertie Smalls's supergrass evidence in the mid-1970s.[93]

So, after Mark, the Met's litany of disgrace continued still. The farcical demise of Operation Countryman, an investigation into allegations about both Met and City police officers, occurred in 1982. It cost £3 million; four years' work resulted in the prosecution of eight Met officers, none of whom was convicted. Allegations of drug dealing by police at Stoke Newington police station dogged the force from the late 1980s to the mid-1990s and a number of officers were suspended and one or two convicted. 'Every law enforcement officer we met,' relayed some investigative journalists in 1990, 'had a story of the good guys at the Yard . . . who had shared information [about drug trafficking] with Customs and Excise and eschewed glory in the fight against organized crime. But there was always the same refrain; corruption and incompetence are alive and well at the Yard. Worse still, when caught out, the reaction is, too often, one of cover-up and deceit.'[94]

The Police and Criminal Evidence Act (PACE) 1984, and the Prosecution of Offences Act 1985 (which set up the Crown Prosecution Service) both helped quell the worst abuses of police station intimidation to exact confessions and malicious prosecutions. But only sound values and good management could defeat corruption, and this proved harder to crack. In the late 1990s Sir Paul Condon declared there were 250 corrupt officers in the CID, some 6 per cent of its strength, though who could tell whether that was the iceberg or the tip? By late 1998, fifty were suspended and two Flying Squad officers had confessed to stealing cannabis worth £1 million from an east London flat. *The Times* commented in May 1998:

Some of the Yard's leading detectives are alleged to have pocketed up to £100,000 a time to recycle drugs or lose evidence against major underworld figures. Officers are accused of investigating an armed robbery using an informant and then taking up to £400,000 from the robbers. Others stole drugs ranging from cannabis to heroin from dealers and then sold those drugs to other dealers.

Police were hoping that some of those charged would turn supergrass and give evidence against corrupt colleagues. Just how successfully remained to be seen.[95]

By the end of the century it was clear that in some ways the Met had responded positively to changing circumstances. Women officers had increased to over 4,000 (15 per cent) and were represented at all ranks. It was a more open and accountable organization than in the past, a good sign when responsibility was at last about to move away from the Home Secretary to a more representative police authority for London. The clear-up rate of 22 per cent was still low, but it had recovered somewhat from figures of 17 per cent in the early 1980s, and some 44 per cent of crimes of violence against the person were now solved. Intelligence seemed better able to deal with terrorism than ever before. And maybe the Stephen Lawrence inquiry report and more black police officers would at last show benefits where change had been so difficult to effect – on the streets of London.

Maybe, too, one other lesson might be learned from a problem-strewn past. So much police effort over the century had been put to stopping Londoners enjoying themselves to no one else's detriment. Where pleasures had been desired but proscribed, then individual policemen had ended up 'licensing' them on their own account. There was quite a list: street betting; liquor licensing; gaming; pornography; drugs. Liberalization – even legalization – did not always prevent criminals cashing in, as with gaming in the 1960s. But liberalization, even legalization, seemed inevitable. Demand, in the end, would not be stifled or wither away. It had to be satisfied – by hook or by crook. For the Londoner in pursuit of pleasure and thrills would not be deterred by the letter of the law.

8. The Swinging City

Roaring Crowds: Street Life, 1900–1999

On Sunday evening punctually at seven I arrived, and there was Bert, in a big check cap, sitting on the railings, smoking a Woodbine. 'Hallo, thought you were never coming!' he said, jumping off. We walked down the pathway, passing the wooden seats scattered at intervals along the Green. Bert had his hat cocked at an acute angle and walked with a swagger. For a hundred yards by West Green Corner the wide pavements were thronged with groups of lads and girls. Some had gathered round the seats in the Green, and from these groups came whisperings and giggles. Others strolled with lofty disdain but turned at the end of the lights and repassed the same spot. Eyes flashed invitation as they passed . . . Scuffles, nudges and shrieks of laughter came from every group . . . 'You should see it later on,' he gurgled. 'This ain't nothing. You'll see 'em all over the bloomin' road, pavement an' all, an' so thick you have to fight your way through!' . . . Two other girls came along arm-in-arm . . . I was amazed when Bert suddenly leaned forward and gave one of them a loud smack on the shoulder. And I was quite unprepared for the squeal of delighted laughter which followed . . . Flowing towards the corner, by the lighted windows of West Green Road, came one human stream. It was joined by another which flowed along the quieter and more shadowy pathway by the Green . . . At the corner both streams met, eddied and swirled.[1]

Swinging Tottenham, around 1910, during the Sunday evening Monkey Parade. Saturdays were just the same. And so was every high street in London, from East Ham to Ealing and Barnet to Balham. Photographs of the Monkey Parade at Rye Lane, Peckham, on a summer night about the same time show the road filling from seven and packed wall to wall by ten, buses easing a passage through the crowds, all other traffic squeezed into the side roads, young men in boaters, young women in summer hats and long dresses, a thousand faces caught white in the glare of the photographer's roof-top flash, a thousand more lost in the gloom beyond the camera's gaze. For Edwardian London was still very much an outdoor city, with as much of the eighteenth century about it as the twentieth. Even the modern suburbs retained patterns of street life familiar to Londoners from time out of mind, where tradition (the Monkey Parade, the street market, the political meeting place) overlapped with spontaneity (Mafeking, the 'hostile crowd', the street accident, the riotous assembly). The London streets provided entertainment, commerce, communication, information, politics, sex. All human intercourse was here.

This was to change across the century as a home-loving people gained the space, comfort and stimulation indoors that they had previously encountered only by going out. The London crowd and its use of the streets changed most noticeably from the early 1950s, when the appeals of domesticity and the rise of the motor car began to impact comprehensively on working-class life. It was not necessarily that crowds were smaller – the Millennium Eve crowd of 3 million may well have been the biggest in history. But for most of the time streets were emptier, and crowds were marshalled and regimented into big events, in fewer spaces, for shorter periods of time. Beyond these exceptional moments of crowd as spectator, outdoor London had shrunk in on itself so that, by the 1980s especially, crowded streets had become a feature largely of the West End and London's regional shopping areas; and the fear of crime was playing its part in keeping streets empty, especially after dark. At the end of the century, though, the revival of London's town centres had begun to re-create some of the crowd patterns that were so much more a feature of the first half of the century than the second.

It was an unrepeatable mix of spontaneity and big set-piece events that distinguished London street life in the era of imperial splendour before 1914. The excesses of Mafeking Night may have been the century's biggest tumult of unorganized popular rejoicing but it had almost been matched by celebrations for the relief of Ladysmith a couple of months earlier on 1 March 1900. The biggest crowd of all turned out for the return of the City Imperial Volunteers (the 'Lord Mayor's Own') from South Africa in October that same year; two people died and thirteen were badly injured 'in the crush'. These were the great years of imperial display in London, of crown princes, maharajahs and potentates. The 'ordinary Londoner of 1910 was used to pageants', recalled the journalist J. B. Booth, pointing up the differences a generation later, and certainly there were many more grand occasions of state packed into the fifteen years before the First World War than in any subsequent comparable period: the funeral of Queen Victoria in February 1901, the packed but silent streets between Victoria and Paddington Stations decked in imperial purple; the delayed coronation of Edward VII, August 1902; his lying-in-state and funeral eight short years later, when 'a vast multitude', an 'endless human stream', filed for three days past his catafalque at Westminster Hall; then the triumphal coronation of George V in June 1911, when 50,000 troops fronted crowds of 'hundreds of thousands'; and there were dozens of royal weddings and state occasions in between.[2] The next ninety years would yield only that same crop of two monarch's

funerals and two coronations (in 1936–7 and 1952–3). Though royal weddings were common enough, and the state funeral of Winston Churchill
(1965) was a momentous event, only the funeral of Diana Princess of Wales
in September 1997 could match for tragic solemnity those moments of 1901
and 1910, but by then in an age when television competed with the street
as vantage point, and when people could experience its multi-layered
emotions in their own homes.

There were other instances of how the 1990s had come closer to the
1900s than probably any other decade. Perhaps the London Eye of the
millennium year and the Great Wheel of 1900 showed London coming full
circle. The Great Wheel at Earls Court, 300 feet high and revolving from
1894 to 1907, was one of London's premier turn-of-the-century outdoor
attractions. Its forty 'roomy saloon-carriages' could each carry thirty people
– the wheel once stuck overnight and passengers received £5 a head
for their ordeal. Earls Court and the nearby 'pleasure resort' of Olympia
represented a late-Victorian revival of the eighteenth-century pleasure
garden. These west London suburban ventures – 'theme parks' a later
generation might have dubbed them – were joined in 1908 by the White
City, 'the largest and most magnificent exhibition ground ever seen in
London down to that time'. Here the Franco-British Exhibition and the
Olympic Games were held that same year of opening, an administrative feat
the organizers apparently took in their stride. The White City's main purpose
was as a multi-functional pleasure garden, with funfairs, bandstands, its
Flip-Flap rivalling the Great Wheel, social club, lake, illuminated cascade
and ornamental gardens – all out-glistering the charms of Earls Court, by
that time twenty years old and more. Alexandra and Crystal Palaces provided
older and staider sister-attractions north and south of the Thames. And then,
each year, the peripatetic pleasure gardens of London brought rural traditions
into suburban London, providing days out for 'Arries and 'Arriets from
Bethnal Green or Walworth, 'the girls with their gaudy shawls and heads of
ostrich feathers like clouds in a wind, and the men in their caps, silk
neckerchiefs and bright yellow pointed boots'. The most prominent of these
were the Bank Holiday fairs at Hampstead Heath, Epping Forest and
Wanstead Flats; and the more extensive Southall Fair, Mitcham Fair and
Barnet Fair, where gypsy horse-dealers rubbed shoulders with Hoxton
wide-boys until the Second World War.[3]

Inevitably, the British weather constrained the scope of outdoor London.
But, befitting the greatest city the world had ever seen, the seasons were
overborne by something called 'The London Season'. Beginning on the
Friday nearest 1 May with the private view of the Royal Academy Summer
Exhibition and ending after the Goodwood Races at the end of July, the

Season was a living reality for London's aristocracy and upper middle classes into the 1950s. In fact it affected all Londoners to some degree, and the main events of the Season's calendar – the Derby, Ascot, the Royal Tournament, the Chelsea Flower Show, Wimbledon, Henley – would outlive the more exclusive toffery of Queen Charlotte's Ball and the Horse Show into the twenty-first century.

Opera, ballet and the theatre adjusted their programmes to the Season and so, although never quiet at any time of year, the West End was especially hectic from May to July. This, according to some, was a relatively new phenomenon in 1900. 'As late as the '80s and '90s,' recalled Ralph Nevill (an old-Etonian diplomat who knew his West End), 'the West End was a sort of separate part of London into which the inhabitants of other districts seldom strayed. In Mayfair, most of the residents knew one another well, and the majority of the passers-by one saw in Piccadilly were not workers but people of independent means out for a stroll.' But by 1900 the West End streets were Londoners' premier playground for every class, from artisan and clerk to rentier. Any man with gold in his pocket could satisfy every need in the square mile from Park Lane to Charing Cross Road and Oxford Street to Pall Mall. In the years before the First World War 'a veritable carnival of extravagance raged in the West End', and luxury 'reached an almost excessive point'. This was the most brilliant spot in the Empire – literally so, for Leicester Square was 'lit by 10,000 electric lamps' in 1902 and the lights of Piccadilly were 'one of the most extraordinary things in the world'.[4]

The West End's hub was Piccadilly Circus. Here it is, captured on a July night in 1902 by Robert Machray. Here too is West End night-life's defining feature in the Edwardian years:

As the theatres and music-halls of London empty into the streets, the Circus is full of the flashing and twinkling of the multitudinous lights of hurrying hansoms, of many carriages speeding homeward to supper, of streams of people, men and women, mostly in evening dress, walking along, smiling and jesting, and talking of what they have seen . . . It is now midnight . . . You are back again in Piccadilly, and its northern pavement is filled with men and women, mostly women, tramping up and down . . . You move with the crowd; you may be in it, not of it, but the mere fact that you are there subjects you to incessant solicitations; you are addressed as 'darling', 'sweetheart' – what not? Your ears are deaf, and you take a look into 'Jimmy's' [the St James's Restaurant, demolished around 1905 to make way for the Piccadilly Hotel], the chiefest temple of the demi-monde . . . Once upon a time . . . the ghastly pilgrimage of the Women of the Town was from St James's to Drury Lane; now it is from 'Jimmy's' to Waterloo Road . . . About 20 minutes past 12 you notice a singular movement in the streets; it sets in towards 'Jimmy's' and stops there. You go with it, and find yourself once again in front of the place. And the very first thing you see is that a couple of policemen (one of them a sergeant or a superintendent) are on guard a few feet from the door. Slowly people emerge in pairs from the restaurant . . . And about half-past 12 a crowd of demi-mondaines and men pours forth, but by this time there are four policemen outside the door standing there to preserve order. Four policemen! (Is there such another sight to be seen night after night in any other spot on the globe?)[5]

Indeed, the Edwardian West End at night was the world's largest flesh market, of that or perhaps of any other time. Its streets after dark were almost entirely given over to sexual commerce. Prostitution was so pervasive that it was inconceivable to contemporary Londoners that a woman unaccompanied by a man could be in the West End at night for any other purpose: 'scarcer than virgins in Piccadilly' was a quip of the day. In 1906 a woman who said she was waiting for her husband 'invited reasonable suspicion in the mind of anyone conversant with the neighbourhood and its condition at that time of night': the neighbourhood was Regent Street and the time was 10.30 p.m. – and yes, despite vehement protestation to the contrary sufficient to secure her discharge by the magistrate, she was indeed a prostitute. Certainly the West End gave 'scandalous licence to the solicitations of vice', though in 1906 some felt it had improved from a few years before and prostitution in London as a whole was thought to have 'diminished very much during the last 40 years'. Prostitution was not confined to the West End alone. Streets around the main railway termini and docks, and the main parks and open spaces were notorious for it. One Christian rescue organization claimed to have closed 'upwards of 700 brothels' in the Waterloo Road area of the Borough and north Lambeth alone between 1894 and 1906. But it is likely that with the rise of the West End as the city's main pleasure ground by 1900, prostitution clustered most visibly there rather than in the rougher areas of London. Tommy Burke noted how, by 1914, 'The two fiercest streets of the Metropolis – Dorset Street [Spitalfields] and Hoxton Street – are as safe for the wayfarer as Oxford Street; for women, safer.'[6]

This was the other side of the coin. The prostitutes' invasion of the West End made it unsafe for other women to go there from dusk, and sometimes earlier, not just because of the risk of wrongful arrest but because of the persistent attentions of predatory men hunting for sex. Swan and Edgar, the Piccadilly Circus haberdashers, complained in 1906 of the 'pests' who loitered near their windows to accost women shoppers, 'some of whom have been absolutely terrified by the persistence of these blackguards'. At the turn of the century, George Gissing memorably sketched the 'typical woman-hunter' of Piccadilly in 'cautious pursuit of a female figure, just in advance': a 'light and springy and half-stalking step; head jutting a little forward; the cane mechanically swung'. Perhaps the most terrifying picture of all was given by H. G. Wells a few years later. Ann Veronica Stanley, a biology student of twenty-one who runs away from an oppressive father in the Home Counties, reaches London, books into a hotel and walks to the West End in search of a job and somewhere more permanent to live. She adores London at first sight, its grandeur and its freedom, until she is brought down to earth by a 'gentleman' of her father's age in Piccadilly: ' "Whither away?" he said very distinctly in a curiously wheedling voice.' Ignored, he drops behind. But in Oxford Street she discovers she is being followed by another man, this time more persistent: 'She went from street to street, and all the glory of London had departed. Against the sinister, the threatening, monstrous inhumanity of the limitless city, there was nothing now but this supreme, ugly fact of a pursuit . . . [That] night she found he followed her into her dreams. He stalked her, he stared at her, he craved her . . .'[7]

This false position of women in the West End streets – hunter or hunted – would soon change. And so would one other feature of London street life that was not confined to the central entertainment district. This was street fighting. For the tramp-poet W. H. Davies, who came to London in the first years of the century, 'what struck me most in those early days was the number of street fights, seen almost hour by hour . . . it was this savage fighting spirit, which was almost as strong in women as it was in men, that surprised me more than anything else I saw in London'. The Shakespeare scholar and London antiquarian William Margrie recalled his working-class childhood in the Borough at around the same time: 'When I was a boy I could take a walk along the Old Kent Road on a Saturday night and see half a dozen public-house fights in half an hour. Now [1934] you never see one.' And Eileen Baillie, a vicar's daughter brought up in Poplar before the First World War, watched fascinated the fights 'in that convenient open space before the vicarage gates', where onlookers would form a 'rigorously kept' ring. 'Fortunately it was rare, though not unknown, to see two women fighting', where one or other might resort to 'use their long hat-pins on each other's eyes', but there were many between husbands and wives. She saw so many over the years that she 'developed a kind of instinct, an embryo ability to tell when a fight was going to peter out or flare up into a scrap worth watching'.[8]

Sex and violence on London's streets both had the stuffing knocked out of them by the First World War, a fulcrum of change in so many ways for the capital and its people. 'Strong ale' had been responsible for street-fighting

London, W. H. Davies thought, and the war both watered beer and made it harder to get. The position with prostitution was more complex. 'War, she thought, was sex', the novelist Henry Green wrote of a character caught up in the London Blitz, and that rang equally true for the first great conflict. In both, spontaneous promiscuity combined with widespread prostitution, finding a huge market in London as the premier transit station and pleasure-dome for troops from all over the English-speaking world. In place of the full-time pre-war streetwalker, young girls from all over the country flocked to London 'with only a few shillings in their pockets' in search of men in uniform. It was this profusion of 'amateurs' that made some commentators speak of a doubling in the number of women 'practising their trade in the capital city' during the war. Even so, prosecutions for prostitution-related offences in London fell by 37 per cent between 1914 and 1918, and 'the work of the London police courts' in general 'almost disappeared'. It appears that blacked-out streets, early closing hours, the use of White City and Earls Court for war purposes, and the new Women Police all rendered street-prostitution less flamboyant than before the war. In the West End prostitutes tended to move off the main promenades and cluster notably in the back streets of Soho: Wardour Street was 'alive with them' between the wars. Whereas south of the Strand, around the long-notorious Villiers Street, only 'a sprinkling' of prostitutes were left by the early 1920s, 'not so gaudily attired' and 'unquestionably . . . better behaved' than before the war. It was in these years that the peculiar closed-in world of ponce and prostitute became one of the defining features of twentieth-century Soho.[9]

Yet an even more significant and noticeable wartime change took place in the independence of women in London. It was this that probably did most to push prostitution off the main streets and claimed them for entirely new relations in public between men and women. Born of the revolutionary expansion of work opportunities, especially for young women, and nurtured in a tumultuous intellectual climate where received opinions had no or little value, a new woman emerged in wartime London. She it was who reaped the benefits of the militant suffragette years of 1906–14 which had brought such chaos to parliamentary precincts. Inside a year of war unaccompanied women fearlessly trod streets that formerly would have been entirely out of bounds. And that was despite the fearful darkness of the streets: lights were extinguished to confuse Zeppelins and London was pitched into a gloom that elderly residents hadn't seen since the 1870s, where even the street markets' naphtha flares were put out, so that cabbages and joints had to be examined in the pale gleam of bicycle lamps. Wearing a uniform was a useful midwife here, aiding confidence and announcing a right to be anywhere any time: 'There were the khaki women of the W.A.A.C, the blue women of the W.R.N.S. and the women of the Red Cross . . . There were the short-skirted women bus-conductors and women taxi-drivers, the women guards and porters of the underground, and the brown-frocked girl-messengers of the Government offices', as well as the first women police in London.[10]

The journalist C. Sheridan Jones, writing of the changes wrought on London by the war, singled out – distinctly from a man's point of view – the significance of the new independence of women on the streets at night:

the old wayfarer in Cockaigne . . . will observe a strange and quite distinct type of woman in the streets. He will find women, many in uniform and with high boots, who walk through the streets of the Metropolis at midnight, unprotected, unmolested, safe in the new-found confidence that war work has given to their sex! . . . Nobody speaks to them; no one seeks to attract their attention. Before Armageddon this would have been impossible. Five years ago, three years ago, every other man would have considered them fair game and every man in three would have spoken to them . . . Well, the war has changed all that. This much, at least, it has done for us – it has taught us to realize that not every woman out after 10 o'clock at night is abroad for our pleasure.[11]

The feminist novelist Ethel Mannin, born near Lavender Hill, Battersea, in 1900, held a similar view from a different perspective. The 'assertion of woman' was 'the most startling change' of 'war-time London':

She had begun to make herself heard before the war, but it had been a faint voice . . . But this war-time woman, who smoked cigarettes in public and drove motor-cars and lorries and worked on the land and strode about in breeches and went to France – one had to recognize her as a force. The war had smashed down those doors upon which she had been knocking for admission and she had swept in – a great new force flooding into the most amazing places.[12]

The celebrations of Armistice Day and Night recalled something of Mafeking jubilation in the numbers taking to the streets and in their sexual abandonment – 'orgy of rejoicing', 'complete surrender of self-control'. A disapproving Malcolm Muggeridge 'observed with wonder and some alarm crowds surging through the streets and into the parks to couple under the trees'. And the official celebrations of Peace Day, 19 July 1919, were said to have seen the birth of the children's street party in London, an occasional feature of street life in the capital revived in the last quarter of the century during the 1977 Silver Jubilee celebrations.

London was changed considerably by the experience of war. The crowds became less raucous and more staid, and the streets were safer from violence because of the reduction in drunkenness. The pleasure gardens never regained their pre-war popularity, and were largely used for indoor events and organized sport. Londoners would have to wait another seventeen years after the Armistice for a royal event to approach anything like pre-war splendour and joy with George V's Silver Jubilee celebrations of 1935. The Monkey Parade in suburban high streets fell out of fashion as new indoor entertainments (radio, the cinema) gained unprecedented mass appeal and as police took a tougher line with traffic obstruction, horseplay and assertive youth: 'I am told,' relayed the American sociologist E. Wight Bakke, who studied Greenwich in the early 1930s, 'that the "Monkey Parade" . . . used to be a far more popular institution before the police became active and decided to keep the couples moving.' The rich texture of London children's games – Norman Douglas had named nearly 1,000 in his classic study published in 1916 – was also stretched thin by traffic and the vigilant policeman; by 1931, in a second edition, Douglas was wondering how many were now still played. The uproarious celebration of Boat Race Night, when Edwardian London would be invaded by drunken undergraduates and when the Women of the Town had a high old time, was much muted from 1920, although it continued to light up some West End nightclubs until the Second World War. Similarly Derby Night, when horse-drawn buses and brakes had paraded home through the Elephant and Castle, and 'the world came out, old and young, to line the main road from Newington to Tooting, and cheer the homeward procession', 'an impromptu pageant' of '[c]lowns, niggers, dudes, costers, harlequins, pierrots, dustmen, and red-robed devils', 'cab-horses wearing women's hats, donkeys' fore-legs in trousers', popular choruses played on 'cornet, concertina, tin-whistle, coach-horn, clarinet, accordion, fiddle, "bones", guitar, ocarina, mouth-organ and jew's-harp', and 'the audience, and the squirts and the ticklers, and the blow-outs and the rattlers and the squeakers and the monkey-nuts and the confetti and the coloured ribbons and the air balloons – the fluttering hair – the bold eyes – the audacious hats and flying frocks, and the Things Said'. It was all just a memory by 1924, when the motor buses sped everyone home through streets, if not deserted, then a poor shade of their former vivacity.[13]

The same was true of that other great feature of the pre-war streets, prostitution, which was thought by the *New Survey of London Life and Labour* in 1935 to have undergone 'a great reduction' since the early 1900s. It never recovered from the wartime changes in women's use of the streets at night; and diminished poverty, expanded and more congenial work opportunities, and a greater openness about sex and contraception among young women affected both supply and demand.

Despite this decline in raucous spontaneity in the London streets, many traditional patterns of crowd behaviour continued through the 1920s and some into the late 1940s and beyond. Exhibitionism ('flashing') 'may be considered [in 1932] as one of the commonest of London vices'. Street gaming with dice and cards (craps, sevens-fours-and-elevens, crown and anchor) or coins (pitch and toss) was common in the poorer and rougher streets, especially quiet courts and alleys or open spaces (like the Hackney Marshes) where approaching police could be easily spotted. The celebration of 'the Fifth of November' in independent do-as-you-please places remained a key date in the cockney calendar until the Second World War at least: 'Guy Fawkes night in slumland is [in 1931] a sight for the gods . . . Backyards give up their old bedding and their broken chairs, and bonfires are built feet high every few yards along the public highway. I have counted as many as thirty . . . the length of one short street, surrounded by kiddies . . . dancing and yelling excitedly and waving flaming brands around their heads.' Elections, too, provoked feverish excitement through the night as results were announced from town-hall balconies. Funerals continued to bring large crowds to watch a special passing – a murder or tragic accident victim, or prominent locals from villains to saints. When Will Crooks, long-standing Labour MP for Woolwich, was buried at Bow Cemetery in June 1921, 'Thousands were debarred admission to the cemetery prior to the last rites, and this caused a demonstration uncanny in that no sound was uttered by a huge crowd that attempted to force the gates.'[14]

Rumours of haunted houses would set hundreds on to the street in question to watch for ghosts – there were two such cases in early 1928 alone, one in Elland Road, Battersea, and another in Penge. News of injustice could also lead to a crowd forming bent on retribution or at least a show of public displeasure, in part the motive of those hostile crowds who attacked police making arrests in the street. When a man who tried to cut his wife's throat at a house in Bedford Row, Holborn, in September 1922 was taken out of his house a 'dense crowd' made a rush for him and had to be fought off by police. In January 1924 a crowd of 3,000, mostly women, attacked the home of a slaughterman at St James's Road, Holloway, because neighbours felt he had driven his wife to suicide. When that 'Clerical Micawber', the Reverend Desmond Morse-Boycott, 'smote' a Somers Town boy who had given him 'sauce most rich and rare', the boy went home 'and "fainted" on his doorstep'; soon after, outside the vicarage door, 'I found Sally [the boy's big sister], and several hundred people, waiting to devour me. Dogs yapped, children booed, and more restrained adults hurled invective, occasionally stressed by a good hard stone. A policeman [but just one!] shifted them off at last . . .' And then troublesome youth continued to make a nuisance of itself by gathering in numbers on prominent street corners and open spaces, pushing, jostling and abusing respectable elders beyond endurance just as it had always done – as at Highbury Corner, Islington, between 1926 and 1928, for instance.[15]

It is likely, though, that all these traditional spontaneous forms of behaviour in London's streets diminished between the wars. Quantification is difficult, if not impossible, but certainly the press reports of events like these are more common in the 1920s than the 1930s, and more common still in the early 1920s than the late. But, in contrast, from the mid-1920s the London crowd began to assume forms which, if not entirely new, took on a distinctive virility not previously encountered.

The catalyst here was professional sport. Although the Football Association was formed in London in 1863, and the early FA Cup Finals were held at Kensington Oval and then at Crystal Palace (where a crowd of over 120,000 gathered in 1913), professional football came late to the capital. The Football League was founded in 1888–9 but no London club joined until 1893–4. That was Woolwich Arsenal and it remained the only metropolitan side in the League until 1905–6, when it was joined by Chelsea and Clapton (later Leyton) Orient. In 1910–11 there were just five professional clubs in London, out of forty in England, the average weekly attendances in London totalling some 84,000.

The capital did not take its full place in the game until 1921–2, when the eleven clubs who represented professional football in London for the next fifty-five years became League members. In that season the average total weekly attendance rose to 217,000, nearly 20,000 a club, with the big three (Arsenal, who moved from Woolwich to Highbury during the First World War, Chelsea and Tottenham Hotspur) achieving around 35,000 or more each week. The new stadium at Wembley, home to the FA Cup Final from 1923, set the seal less on London's place in the game than on the place of the game in the nation's culture. Even so, football got ever-larger crowds on to London's streets for almost the next thirty years, excluding 1939–45: nearly 250,000 each week in 1938–9, and 335,000 in the nation's favourite football season of 1948–9. That was an average weekly gate of 30,500 for the eleven London clubs, 51,500 for top-flight Arsenal. There was then a decline, but even in the late 1960s weekly total gates ran at 236,000. Then a steep, almost catastrophic, fall halved this by 1985–6 (twelve clubs, 134,600). That was the worst year of the post-1919 game. From then on things looked up, so that the thirteen London professional clubs in 1997–8 just overtook the gates of eleven clubs some seventy-five years earlier.[16]

London's football crowds matched the nation's in the rise, fall and rise again of the professional game's fortunes. They were affected by the same passions and fears as the rest of the country (post-war national pride and a thirst for any entertainment in the 1940s, 'football hooliganism' in the 1970s and 1980s). Even so, eleven League clubs out of eighty-eight was a poor showing for one in five of the national population, up to the 1950s at least. But then, in the peak sporting decades of the twentieth century – the 1920s, 1930s and 1940s – London had other attractions, some even bigger crowd-drawers than football.

The biggest were greyhound racing and speedway. These were new attractions and in the late 1920s and early 1930s they took the country by storm, especially London. Greyhound racing for betting purposes was reintroduced into England from America in 1926, reaching London from Manchester a year later. By the end of 1927 fifty courses were open or planned and 100,000 people were turning up in a single night at the reborn White City that summer. The main London tracks were at Catford, Clapton, Harringay, Stamford Bridge, Wembley and West Ham. Within a year the dogs had another competitor for mass audiences when dirt-track or speedway was introduced from America and Australia in late 1927. It reached London early in 1928 and became a peculiarly metropolitan attraction. Eight of the country's sixteen stadiums were located in the London area, with week-night gates of 90,000 at the bigger tracks like White City and Stamford Bridge, and with star riders as much heroes for boys and girls alike as any footballer. Even without the incentive of a flutter, speedway provoked great excitement. 'Crowd of 50,000 Storm London Speedway' at the opening night of West Ham's 1932 season; at Crystal Palace in 1933 an 'angry crowd stormed the speedway track' because they disapproved of the way a race had been started; and there were minor riots at Harringay in 1938 and 1939 – once when a crowd turned away from the stadium because of rain sought spectacle at an indoor roller-skating competition nearby.[17]

Sporting traditions went deep into London's working-class culture but at no time did sport draw bigger crowds than in the thirty years from 1920 to 1950, whether for new fads like all-in wrestling, ice-skating, ice hockey, the dogs and speedway or old favourites like boxing, athletics, cycling, horseracing, football and cricket. The presence of women in large numbers at all these events signified for many their new independence, forged in wartime London and sustained since. The active participation of young people in amateur sport responded to the contemporary cult of the body and physical fitness that youth movements in Britain and abroad heartily espoused. And improved public transport was able to nurture the young Londoner's new passion for hiking and sunbathing.

The reinvention of the London park in the 1920s and 1930s owed much to this absorption with sport. Parks increased in number and area in London as suburban local authorities preserved open space (especially around country mansions) from the depredations of house-builders; and as the LCC and the inner boroughs cleared slums and replaced some of them with small parks and gardens. Greater London's parks and open spaces increased in area from 30,000 acres in 1927 to 40,500 in 1937, a rise of 35 per cent. They also became better used. The number of cricket matches for which payment was made to the LCC rose from 15,000 in 1926 to 18,500 in 1933, and football matches from 13,000 to 18,300. And the use of municipal swimming baths in the County of London rose by 40 per cent to 6.7 million swims a year between 1920–21 and 1932–3.[18]

This sporting pressure, and a new interest in the outdoor life, became a hot political issue in 1929. George Lansbury, one of the century's great Londoners, was appointed First Commissioner of Works in Ramsay Mac-Donald's ill-fated second government of 1929–31. London's royal parks were part of his responsibilities. Although seventy years old, radical George seized the banner of youth. He created a 'British Lido' for men and women swimmers and sunbathers at the Serpentine, Hyde Park, in June 1930. The very idea of mixed bathing in central London provoked intense opposition at the time, whipped up by *The Times* in full bluster. So did his plans for a children's boating lake at Regent's Park, creating 'a furore among the middle class families occupying the flats and houses' near Hanover and York Gates. When Lansbury ordered the railings to be pulled down from around the flower beds and freed the lakes for swimming and play, he opened the royal parks to Londoners as never before in history. In doing so he encouraged, consciously or otherwise, movement away from the streets as a legitimate space for self-expression.[19]

One small example of this move from street to park – a corralling, a penning-in of Londoners' energy and joy – is dancing. Dance was a vital element in London's popular culture throughout the century. Before the First World War it was more an outdoor activity than indoor. Wherever the barrel organ stopped and turned, wherever the music of the automatic gramophone or piano or concertina spilled from a pub doorway, children, women and men danced on the pavements or in the middle of the street. A London crowd could not celebrate together without dancing. Eva Hubback, charity worker and feminist, was appalled by the crowds at the 1911 coronation: 'A really damned thing was to see some drunken women carrying tiny babies (one of them feeding hers) and dancing.' Often no music was needed: 'If you go to Whitechapel, Lambeth Marsh, or any low-class districts,' reported the brilliant Japanese water-colourist Yoshio Markino in 1907, 'you will see many young girls, mingled with boys, doing a cake-walk in the streets, and shouting loudly some meaningless and tuneless songs.'

Even amid the horrors of Gallipoli in 1915 an officer was struck by this readiness for a dance among 'the cockney lads': 'Suddenly one of them would shout – Come on let's have a "Riley", and a dozen would form in two rows facing each other, and off they would go, to the tune of "Knees up Mother Brown" – advance and retire, and turn around with much shouting and Oi!'[20]

Dancing in the streets was as frowned upon after 1919 as many another activity, and a rise in the number and luxuriousness of dance halls from the 1920s doubtless made it seem an old-fashioned pastime. But the LCC recognized the Londoners' passion for dancing out of doors and they introduced dance bands to the parks in August 1938, high summer of the 'Lambeth Walk' craze. At Highbury Fields, Islington, 20,000 dancers turned up and 'the official arrangements broke down under the strain'.[21]

'Dancing Through' was how Mass-Observation described Londoners' attitude in the months of war before the Blitz, and traditional elements in the culture of the London crowd no doubt assisted the city's resourcefulness under strain. Certainly Londoners were used to getting on together in large numbers and adapting to each other's company. With sporting events postponed for the duration, street crowds were now entirely functional – walking to work in the absence of buses and trains, and sharing in the ubiquitous queues, long, deep and for just about everything. Then, in the worst of the bombing, crowds gathered underground. On 27 September 1940 an estimated 177,000 Londoners sheltered in the tube tunnels. And as underground living established itself home-grown entertainments were supplemented by weekly ENSA concert parties and adult education classes: 'for the enjoyment born of good fellowship there has been nothing to compare with . . . the air-raid shelters during the Second World War', it was said in 1950.[22]

There were other changes in London street life, too. The prostitute came into her own once more during the blackout. Girls carried torches to uplight their faces for the punters, 'giving the effect of candles illuminating a holy picture in the shadows of a church', as the novelist Anthony Powell recalled. Later in the war they were supplemented 'by an outbreak of terrible, satanic and ghastly young girls, who invaded the West End and Piccadilly to prey upon the American troops . . .' 'Just in their teens', they invaded London 'in swarms' and 'were hated by the professional prostitutes, for whom one really felt sympathy'. For the first time since the First World War, prostitution – holy or satanic, depending on one's point of view – swept showily out of Soho to become a prominent feature of West End street life in the 1940s and 1950s.[23]

Not that prostitution spread to entirely new areas of London. Euston and

Paddington, considered the 'worst plague spots in London' in 1942, had long been associated with sex for sale, probably ever since the railways brought male travellers in large numbers to these cheap rooming districts. But the large numbers of girls and pimps, the ready availability of abandoned or cut-price bomb-scarred houses, the support industry of shops selling 'indecent literature, abortifacient drugs and contraceptives', the sheer brazenness of it all, represented a return to conditions not seen since the early 1900s. 'Pimps, panders and bullies infest the street corners. It is impossible for a man or woman to walk any distance along most of the streets of this area [Paddington] after 1.30 p.m. without being accosted by these women and the men who live on their earnings.' Prostitution in the West End and inner west London seemed both to flourish in old haunts in the 'square mile of vice', Soho, and to push the boundaries outwards, so that by the end of the war notorious areas for prostitution included Shepherd's Market, Curzon Street, Maddox Street and Bond Street (all in Mayfair), Bayswater, Maida Vale, Notting Hill and, of course, Soho, where prostitutes 'were so thick on the streets that as a kid coming home from school I had to say "Excuse me" to get to my own front door'.[24]

This highly visible prostitution survived the Second World War in a way that had not happened after the first. But whether there were more prostitutes than before or their behaviour was just more immoderate was hard to tell. Estimates of the numbers of prostitutes in London varied wildly – from 8,000 to 80,000 in the early 1900s and 1,800 to 80,000 again in the late 1950s – and were generally inflated. In fact, only tiny numbers ever seemed to come before the police and the courts. A careful study of prostitute arrests in a single year (1949) showed 457 women arrested in Soho, 259 in Hyde Park, 221 Paddington, 198 Mayfair, ninety-six in Victoria and Pimlico, forty to fifty around Euston and King's Cross, twenty-five on Clapham Common, twenty-two each near Waterloo Station and Finsbury Park, sixteen in Stepney and thirteen outside Woolwich barracks; and these figures could stand as a proxy for the respective significance of the main prostitute areas of London from 1919 through the rest of the century. An apparently well-informed view put the number of full-time streetwalkers in London in 1958 at 3,000, with 1,000 of them in the West End, and that is the best estimate we are likely to obtain.[25]

Whatever the truth about numbers, post-war prostitution in London became a national scandal. The Wolfenden Committee on prostitution of 1957 noted the view of many that 'some of the streets of London are without parallel in the capital cities of other civilized countries'. Certainly, flagrant soliciting, with its side effects like 'gutter-crawling' by motorists, was an intolerable nuisance for most Londoners and in some districts utterly out of hand. But public hysteria on this issue was stoked by xenophobic press campaigns against foreign pimps, most notoriously the five Messina brothers. They were Maltese sons of a Sicilian father, true cosmopolitans who had learned the brothel-keeping trade in Alexandria. They were active in the West End from the mid-1930s to the late 1950s, despite sensational press exposés and Old Bailey trials keeping one or the other out of circulation from time to time. This demonization of the exotic foreign ponce found a new outlet from the late 1940s with West Indian migration. The connection between white prostitute and black pimp was especially strong in Notting Hill and the Cable Street area of Stepney, though blown out of all proportion as a 'social problem' at the time. So was the influence of foreign prostitutes, famously French women, in reality a tiny fraction of the London street workforce.[26]

The visibility of prostitution in London changed completely on Sunday 16 August 1959. That was when the Street Offences Act 1959 introduced prison sentences for a second soliciting offence – previously punishable by a small fine, easily recouped almost at the door of the court. The streets emptied literally overnight. Instead, girls went 'on the phone', contacted by cards in newsagents' windows – quite an earner for the lucky shopkeepers – or pinned to Soho doorposts ('Erection and demolition by an expert' was one that raised a smile), and later by graphic advertisements in West End telephone kiosks. All that was supplemented by discreet soliciting, which had returned to some streets by the early 1960s, becoming flagrant again in some areas but never reviving the bad old days post-war, at least in the West End.

The 1940s and early 1950s also saw the last flowering of traditional London street life. The great popular demonstrations of joy at the end of the war – VE Day, 13 May 1945, and VJ Day, 14 August 1945 – brought back memories of 1918 and even 1900. Starved for so many years of colour and interest, people came out in droves to participate in anything that smacked of pomp and ceremony. To see the new fountains at Trafalgar Square floodlit at night, 'an enormous crowd stood silently in the dark, feasting their eyes on the first sign of public entertainment that they had seen since 1939' – 'one of the most pathetic chapters in the history of London and Londoners', Maurice Gorham called this morbid interest in cold water in 1951. The crowds for sporting events were never bigger, before or since, than they were in the late 1940s, although mid-week sporting events were curtailed by the fuel crisis from 1946. Wembley Stadium was filled for 'the austerity' Olympic Games in 1948, when Germany, Japan and Russia didn't compete. The wedding of Princess Elizabeth (November 1947), funeral of George VI (February 1952) and the coronation (June 1953) filled the streets for the first royal occasions since the coronation of May 1937. And, most important, the Festival of Britain brought crowds from all over the nation to war-scarred London, some 8 million through May to September 1951.

As television, comfortable council flats and the motor car seduced and prised Londoners off the streets, one portion of the population remained more immune than others to the lure of indoors, the domestic interior at least: youth. Young Londoners, of course, had always played a large – perhaps the largest – part in London's street life. The Monkey Parade was entirely their creation and part of its charm was no doubt its hostility to adults – there were plenty of complaints of young people linking arms to force old-timers off the pavements and into the roadway. So the conscious celebration of young people's strength was no new phenomenon. But a new self-confidence emerged from the 1940s, after almost a generation of Hollywood's irresistible influence. Before the movies, not much of style had penetrated London's youth culture. Clarence Rook described 'Alf', a turn-of-the-century 'hooligan' from Lambeth Walk, as wearing 'a dark-brown suit, mellowed by wear', 'a cloth cap' and 'a neatly-knotted necker-chief, dark-blue, with white spots, which does duty for collar as well as tie'.[27] A wide leather belt with a heavy buckle, which doubled as both ornament and weapon, was something of a 'hooligan' trademark. For the next forty years and more dress expressed little of a self-conscious group identity, cocking a snook at adult life, despite some aping of the movie gangster before the Second World War, as we shall see in a moment.

It was in the late 1940s that youth style in London became more formalized, marking off from adult life a section of young people by their appearance alone. There were strong Hollywood influences here. The '"Dago" or "Spiv" types' in London around 1948 were 'dressed in their own, or rather the American, singular style – i.e. cut back collar with large knotted tie; "Boston Slash Back" hair cut; and a "house coat" style of jacket usually in a light fawn with brown flannels to match.' The capacity of these and other youths to hang around, 'going nowhere in particular, just walking along the street and going into cafés and amusement arcades, or else standing for hours on end at street corners or in shop doorways', perplexed the spiv-watchers of Mass-Observation.[28]

Some of these elements influenced the Teddy Boys, blending into the 'Edwardian' look that gave them their name. The Teddy Boy was London-grown. From 1950 on, most youth fashions in Britain would originate in the capital and mould the rest of the nation in their image, although there was always scope for adventurous provincials to alter the metropolitan pattern. Just like Rook's 'Alf', the first Teds were claimed as a south London working-class invention, but myth and legend have obscured their origins beyond convincing resurrection. Despite some of the evidently American influences – not least, of course, in their favoured rock'n'roll music – the Teds' style was said to have emerged from a 1940s Edwardian revival in Savile Row that failed to catch on with Mayfair but magically reappeared, transmogrified, at the Elephant and Castle a few years later. However conceived, there is no doubt that the Teddy Boy electrified youth culture, first in London and then nationwide. 'Aggressive', 'anti-social', 'a pretty rough lot', the Teddy Boy, in dress code and lifestyle, gave a confidence-building framework to young unskilled workers who, in an era of full employment, had money to spend and more to spend it on (records and record-players, cars and motor bikes, innumerable fashion accessories from jewellery to flick knives) than ever before in history. It was in these same 1950s that the 'teenager' with sufficient purchasing power to create a world market for his or her own indulgence was discovered – or invented – as one of the most important social phenomena of the century.

The Teddy Boys' first distinctive and intimidating look in the early 1950s – long, draped, usually black jacket, waistcoat, white shirt, 'Slim Jim' bootlace tie, tight 'strides', heavy shoes with toe-caps or crêpe-soled 'creepers' – went through several changes but remained a feature of London streets until around 1960. The style attracted only a small minority of London youth but a larger share of those who habitually spent much of their time on the streets. And, as we have already seen, the Teddy Boy was often there when trouble flared: the Clapham Common murder of John Beckley in 1953; the *Rock Around the Clock* riots of 1955, when jubilant audiences smashed up cinemas showing Bill Haley's film, beginning at the Trocadero, Elephant and Castle; the Notting Hill race riots of 1958; and the stabbing to death of PC Summers in Seven Sisters Road, Holloway, in December 1958 – Ronald Marwood was hanged for the crime despite riots outside Pentonville in protest at the sentence. The Teds' uniform, their cult of toughness and their attachment to a particular strand of musical culture combined to make them the first real youth movement of the century. For good and ill, the history of youth on London's streets over the next fifty years could in part be viewed as the chain reaction triggered by this metropolitan innovation.[29]

Although, as we shall see in a moment, there were other significant places where youth could strut its stuff, the London streets provided the premier catwalk for youth fashion. In this, some streets became more equal than others. Carnaby Street, Soho, and King's Road, Chelsea, were indelibly associated with the Mods ('moderns' or 'modernists'), who emerged at the end of the 1950s in a reaction against the vicious Teds (and scruffy Beatniks) – even a musical reaction, at first championing modern jazz. This was a movement said to have been born in east London but no more topographical certainty can attach to the Mods than to the Teds – except to say that, once more, this was a phenomenon made in London. It was a cult of smartness and 'cool' sophistication. 'They wore suits and desert boots, ankle swingers they were called, and Ben Sherman button-downs or giraffe-necked gingham shirts and black leather jackets. Buttons, flaps and vents were all very important,' recalled Twiggy, 'The Face of '66' and a Neasden Mod from 1962. For girls, 'Our Mod uniform was a long plastic . . . Pakamac' over 'whatever was the thing to wear at the time'.[30] The boys rode Vespa motor scooters or more fashionable Lambrettas, in contrast to the powerful motor bikes of the leather-jacketed Rockers, inheritors of the Teds' macho legacy. Running battles between London Mods and Rockers at the capital's traditional seaside playgrounds of Clacton, Margate, Brighton and Hastings provoked much fear and fury on the Bank Holiday weekends of 1964.

From then, fashions seemed to change with lightning speed. The Mods' short hair was one of the inspirations of the skinheads, who went through a number of metamorphoses from their birth (in east London, some said) in the mid-1960s, fading away into various youth styles in the early 1970s, reviving once more as an ally of the militantly racist far right around 1980. The skinheads developed the Teds' cult of violence, specializing in racial attacks and 'football hooliganism' from the late 1960s on. From around 1975 an alternative London-generated youth movement emerged in the punks, evolving their own music greatly influenced by an Islington-based band, the Sex Pistols. By 1978, youth style in London had become fluid and transient. Shifting rivalries led to alliances around music or politics and sometimes both. And rock music events continued to pull huge crowds of young people to the parks, like Hyde Park where the Rolling Stones had played to 250,000 in July 1969, or to Wembley Stadium, until the end of the century.

From the mid-1960s but especially from the 1980s, youth was joined by others who gave a new complexion to the London crowd: foreign tourists. Many of these, too, of course, were young, sampling the charms of 'Swinging London' and 'The Coolest City in the World'. They added greatly to the interest, colour and vivacity of the West End and to celebratory events of world fame, like the Notting Hill Carnival. By the late 1990s, youth, foreign tourism, some revival of London's town-centre night-life beyond the West End, the local festivals that had become a feature of many London districts, great outdoor events like the Notting Hill Carnival and the London Marathon, extended licensing hours promoting a '24-hour city', all combined to put back something of the old zestful patterns of street life into London. Its local high streets, if not as well trodden as in the days of the Monkey Parade, had at least recovered something from the fearful and lonely places they had become between the late 1960s and the early 1990s. The city's great attractions had never been busier. And the millennium celebrations – 3 million people lining the banks of the Thames on Millennium Eve, thousands every day visiting the much-maligned Dome on Greenwich peninsula, the queues for the new and even greater wheel – recaptured London for the crowd, if only for a time. It was less spontaneous, perhaps, than 100 or even fifty years before, but where there were crowds there was life.

In Town Tonight: Night Life, 1900–1959

Virtually all the elements of London night life at the end of the century were in place before the First World War. Restaurants, cafés, pubs, theatres, cinemas, dance halls, social clubs, nightclubs, massage parlours – all present in 1909 and still there in 1999, in different numbers, sometimes under new names, generally (not always) looking very different, but essentially the same and sometimes still where they had always been. By 1999 the music hall had disappeared, but not without trace. Brothels were reportedly far less numerous. The circus had almost departed – long gone the days (1900–1909) when the vast underground 'runs' of the Hippodrome, Charing Cross Road, had housed for public display 'Seeth's 40 forest-bred lions; Woodward's seals and sea lions; Bjornsen's 12 huge white polar bears; Saunder's 20 Bengal tigers; Jamrach's rattlesnakes and anacondas; the Chinese Cormorants; Consul, the Chimpanzee; the Bucking Donkey . . . [and] Louis de Rougemont's famous turtle'. And vanished entirely were displays of physical deformity – the one-legged high-diver or the Armless Wonder who played the violin with his toes.[31] On the other hand, entertainment for the voyeur (strip clubs, 'live performance shows', pornographic movie theatres) and places dedicated to sexual minorities were much more openly and readily available. Whatever the changes, throughout the century London was one of the world's great pleasuredomes – 'the gayest city in the world' (1935), 'The Swinging City' (1966), 'The Coolest City in the World' (1996).

When the century dawned it had not been so for long. 'The great feature of modern London – its excellent and palatial restaurants – is an entirely modern development,' wrote Ralph Nevill in 1912, dating the change from the early 1880s. Even at the turn of the century, London was still contrasted unfavourably with the liveliness of Paris. But a decade on, the sophistication of London night-life under a king who knew something of pleasure had expanded and grown in confidence. 'When I returned from the Near East some years ago,' recalled the journalist Sydney Moseley in 1920, 'I discovered

a new London ... London no longer needed to blush for Paris.' And
'"London's a much wickeder city than Paris,"' opines a character in Compton Mackenzie's *Carnival* (1912).[32]

In pre-1914 London the great centre of night life and enjoyment was, of
course, the West End. By the First World War the Strand had lost much,
though not all, of its celebrated Victorian reputation as a showcase for
luxury, fashion and sexual licence. Romano's Restaurant's famous proprietor
died in 1910, taking much of its bohemian gloss with him; but Simpson's,
the Savoy, Gatti's, the theatre district round Drury Lane and the new hotels
round the Aldwych (including the Waldorf) kept through the century
something of a toehold in London's night-life for the Strand, Holborn and
Charing Cross. The West End itself was divided into two. The smartest
places were to be found round Piccadilly and Regent Street – the great
Criterion, Monico and Trocadero restaurants and the Café Royal. But
wherever you went in the West End before 1914, sex was on the menu. As
at the 'Café d'Orange', Leicester Square:

In a corner left by the sweep of the stairs a quartette of unkempt musicians in seamy
tunics of beer-stained scarlet frogged with debilitated braid were grinding out
ragtime. The noisy tune in combination with the talking and laughter, the chink of
glasses and the shouted acknowledgments of the waiters made such a din that
Michael stood for a moment in confusion, debating the possibility of one more
person threading his way through the serried tables to a seat ... At one table four
offensive youths were showing off with exaggerated laughter for the benefit of
nobody's attention. Behind them in the crepuscule of two broken lamps a leaden-
lidded girl, ivory white and cloying the air with her heavy perfume, was arguing in
passionate tones with a cold-eyed listener who with a straw was tracing niggling
hieroglyphics upon a moist surface of cigarette-ash. In the deepest corner a girl with
a high complexion and bright eyes was making ardent love to a partially drunk and
bearded man, winking the while over her shoulder at those who watched her
comedy. The other places were filled by impersonal women who sipped from their
glasses without relish and stared disdainfully at each other down their powdered
noses. At Michael's own table was a blotchy man who alternately sucked his teeth
and looked at his watch; and immediately opposite sat a girl with a merry, audacious
and somewhat pale face of the Gallic type under a very large and round black hat
trimmed with daisies. She was twinkling at Michael, but he would not catch her
eye ...

'You're very silent, kiddie,' she said. 'I'll give you a penny for them.'[33]

The most bohemian, stimulating, intimate part, firmly established as such
by 1900, was Soho. Soho remained one of the most significant districts of

London throughout the century – for the history of London's pleasures perhaps the most significant of all. Here the foreign restaurant, the coffee house, the nightclub and the pub had long clustered, venerably linked with prostitution and the other specialities of London's sex industry. Soho's most famous restaurants pre-1914 were Kettner's (Church Street, later Romilly Street), a 'French house'; Maxim's and other French places, in Wardour Street, Coventry Street and Old Compton Street; and there were Italian restaurants in Rupert Street, Gerrard Street, Old Compton Street and elsewhere. Greek Street was famous for its brothels, and some of the restaurants and 'hotels' across Soho were *cabinets particulier* where sex and a meal could be combined in a private booth or room: 'If you pay 10 shillings extra, you are not bothered there.' Innocent Ann Veronica was taken to one by the predatory Ramage in 1909 but did not succumb.

Then pubs were ubiquitous in Soho. At the turn of the century the temperance reformer Arthur Sherwell counted seventy-six in eighteen Soho streets, 'most of which are exceedingly short', some having as many as eight. Indeed, in 1894 the Metropolitan Police C Division, covering Soho and nearby, contained 357 pubs and beer houses and 192 other premises with on- or off-licences, 545 for an area of seven-tenths of a square mile. These numbers had fallen drastically by 1908 as licensing laws were tightened in response to puritan reformers' zeal, so that just fifty pubs remained in Soho – a number roughly retained for the rest of the century. They included the famous York Minster in Dean Street, run by German licensees until 1914, when control passed to Victor Berlemont; 'the French pub' remained in the hands of Victor and then his son Gaston for the next seventy-five years, becoming a bohemian icon, perhaps the most famous pub in London across the century. And then there was 'an enormous number of social clubs and private drinking saloons', 'accounted for partly by the large foreign element in the population' who preferred places above all where their countrymen gathered. There were 214 licensed clubs in west and west-central London in 1897 and in one small part of Soho Sherwell counted eighteen. From about 1911, newly fashionable Soho nightclubs set out their stall to the upper middle classes and intelligentsia. They included, around 1913, the Cave of the Golden Calf run by Madame Strindberg, wife of the gloomy Swedish playwright: its decorations were by Wyndham Lewis and Jacob Epstein, and it boasted a Galician gypsy floorshow. Another, the Crabtree in Greek Street, was established by Augustus John, the Chelsea painter. And the well-known Murray's in Beak Street reputedly introduced the tango to London around the same time.[34]

None of these attractions belonged to Soho alone. The public house, in particular, was a London-wide phenomenon, one of the working man's main sources of recreation and relaxation – and increasingly the working woman's. Indeed, the pub-going habit had been growing more popular among London women since before 1900, including respectable young women: 'Young people do their courting in public-houses, since both sides are rather ashamed of their homes, and like to make themselves out a class above what they are', one of Charles Booth's informants reported. Late on a Saturday night, after the weekend shop, was a favourite time for women – in a Fitzroy Square pub women callers outnumbered men by 219 to 150 between 10 p.m. and midnight, and there is no reason to think that untypical.[35]

The London pub was a versatile cultural resource for men and women alike, capable of adapting quickly to changing times. It had given birth to the music hall in the mid-nineteenth century. It could specialize to accommodate thieves and fences, prostitutes, the smart set, bohemians, gays, poets, actors, policemen. From the late 1950s it hosted striptease and jazz, in the 1960s it revived variety and the music-hall tradition, in the 1970s it discovered rock and punk bands and in the 1980s family entertaining and poetry readings. It adapted to every wave of migration, so that before 1914 there were German and Jewish pubs, and West Indian pubs after 1950. It was constantly reinventing the way it looked – neo-Tudor-Shakespearian in the 1920s, post-utility Formica in the 1950s, neo-Victorian in the 1980s. And the pub provided London novelists with the ideal stage for bringing characters together in London, from Arthur Morrison's *The Hole in the Wall* (1902) to Graham Swift's *Last Orders* (1996); the popular TV soap opera *EastEnders*, running twice-weekly from February 1985, could easily have been called *The Queen Vic*.

Despite this enduring fame there were fewer and fewer pubs in London – from around 7,800 in the County in 1900, to 6,700 in 1908, 5,900 in 1915, 4,900 in 1938 and 3,400 in 1992. There were no doubt many reasons for the fall: the population of the County had dropped in about the same proportion, although tourism and the growth of the leisure industry might reasonably have tended the other way; a shift to drinking at home and the rise of domestic comforts made the pub a less attractive alternative to poor housing conditions than it had been even up to the 1970s; redevelopment of older areas had destroyed pubs that were not replaced in the new estates.

One other reason was the assault on 'liquor' by London reformers that made licences harder to get and restricted the time during which drinking could be enjoyed. Between 1872 and 1914 London pubs opened on week-days from 5 or 6 a.m. and stayed open till 12.30 a.m. Hours were much reduced on Sundays, closing from midnight on Saturday, reopening from 12.30 to 2.30 p.m. and 6 to 11 p.m. Restaurants usually stayed open an hour longer till 1.30 a.m., and 11.30 p.m. was a common late supping hour. In general, Londoners kept later hours before the First World War than any time up to the 1990s, if then. One instance: Bill Hubback, a Civil Servant at the Board of Education, relayed a night out in 1912 consisting of supper at Maxim's until 12.30 a.m. and then 'we went to a club . . . called the New Palais Club – a sort of night club where people dance – rather subduedly respectable', and was there till after 3 a.m.

Hubback's late night, like so many of the time, had begun at a music hall. There were then fifty-one music halls and 'theatres of varieties' in the County of London and numerous suburban places outside the County boundary. Just half of them were licensed to sell 'intoxicants', for the LCC had adopted from its inception in 1889 a puritan policy to disconnect variety from drink. That the LCC failed to clean up the halls in other ways, though, was singularly apparent. Indeed, many men did not go to the music hall to look at the stage at all. Compton Mackenzie wrote of the 'promenade' – the foyer and downstairs bars – of 'the Orient', Piccadilly (in fact the Alhambra, Leicester Square) that, 'For many who visited the Orient, the stream of prostitutes ebbing and flowing upon the Promenade was enough.'[36]

That was also around 1912, and by then music hall was on its way out. Its greatest stars were dead or past their prime, and its musical glories largely behind it, apart from a late flowering of popular song in the First World War. One element in its demise was the cinema, which the halls had brought in, like a Trojan horse, to attract matinée audiences. The Empire, Leicester Square, had a season for Lumière's Kinetoscope as early as March 1896, and the Alhambra retaliated with Robert Paul's Animatograph that same month. Before the end of the year the American Biograph was showing at the Palace, and Léon Gaumont brought his improved cinematograph system to London in 1898. The world flocked to exploit London for the new invention within months of its first development. By 1900 hardly a music hall was without its cinema show. Soon cinemas were set up in former halls and the 'collapse of the [roller] skating rink fever . . . left numerous sites and building shells free'. In 1912 there were no fewer than 347 premises licensed for film shows in the County of London, 271 of them devoted solely to cinema. They far outstripped the 269 places licensed for music and dancing, which usually also doubled as cinemas, music halls, mission halls or pubs.[37]

London's vibrant indoor night-life suffered as much as outdoor entertainment from the outbreak of war in 1914. From September, the month the blackout came into force, pubs and licensed clubs closed from 9 p.m. Then, from November 1915, the notorious Defence of the Realm Act (DORA for short) and its Liquor Control Regulations began to bite. Opening hours were cut from 12 noon to 2.30 p.m. and 6 to 9 p.m. Off-licences closed at

8. Spirits had to be diluted to not less than 30° under proof, beer was watered, and 'the long pull' or generous measure was prohibited. Worse, the conviviality of pub-going was attacked to make the whole experience less pleasurable: 'treating' – buying a drink at the bar for someone other than yourself, even husband for wife – became a criminal offence, and so was a 'slate' or any credit arrangement which deferred payment for drink. Some of these regulations were probably honoured more in the breach – Tommy Burke recalled one notice in a London pub which read 'No Treating Aloud' – but there is no doubting the stifling effect of DORA on the city's night life.[38]

Even so, for those who knew where to go, 'Things happened quickly then in London town . . . Mad, hectic, crazy war-days! . . . Everybody was having a good time.' For DORA had some unintended consequences. Nightclubs for dancing and dining could remain open till 12.30 a.m. as long as no drink was detected being served after 9. 'During the war the night clubs of London prospered amazingly. Newly-made young officers . . . fairly swamped the better-class places.' A nightclub sideline was gambling – illegal of course but, despite higher wartime penalties, 'never have there been in London a larger number of gambling establishments run for men of all classes' than in 1917. Another consequence was the rise of the illicit drinking clubs or shebeens, 'which have sprung up like mushrooms throughout those districts in London where workmen do congregate . . . in the neighbour- hood of Waterloo Bridge Road [*sic*] they are as thick as blackberries in August'. Mushrooms or blackberries, good fellowship in London was pushed – quite literally in many cases – underground. 'London, in fact, has become a city of clubs, of secret rendezvous, of meeting-places that are known only to a comparatively few *habitués* . . .'[39]

Once driven underground by the liquor laws, the clubs attracted other illicit pleasures besides the gaming table. Pushed from the blacked-out streets, it was to the Soho clubs that prostitutes increasingly resorted, despite DORA raising the penalties for this as well. And the wartime 'cocaine epidemic' – an unsurprising passion for the drug developed among young infantry officers and was passed on to their girlfriends – also centred on Soho, even though DORA prohibited its sale and possession from mid-1916. By 1919 illicit drugs were easier to obtain in the clubs and cafés of Soho than anywhere else in London, or Britain as a whole.[40]

DORA's dead hand survived the Armistice. Continuing restrictions on licensing hours after the war lost London its Edwardian reputation for gaiety rivalling or exceeding that of Paris. 'London probably is the only capital in the world where out of war time the authorities would dare to make early going to bed compulsory . . . Who but a madman indeed would in these days come to London for a pleasure trip?' complained Ralph Nevill in 1922. And that was after a liberalization in 1921 of the wartime restrictions which established the London licensing laws as they would be for much of the rest of the century: 11 a.m. to 2.30 p.m., and 5.30 to 11 p.m. That was nine hours each weekday compared to some nineteen and a half pre-1914. All this represented a severe loss, felt by all old enough to remember pre-war London: 'it is not a little shocking to the lover of individual liberty to compare London life to-day [1929] with what it was in the beginning of the century', and some wondered 'if, after all, we really did win the war'.[41]

The extension of DORA perpetuated the wartime West End's underground culture well into the 1920s. Those nightclub proprietors who were tempted to breach the preposterous and oppressive liquor laws reasonably felt they might as well be hanged for a sheep as a lamb. So clubs, drugs, sex and Soho became the dominant theme of West End night life in the immediate post-war years.

The diversity and creative energy of the Soho nightclub from 1919 were astonishing. Live music, soon extended to cabaret, was the premium asset. Musicians and performers from all over the world were attracted to London, black Americans prominent among them. A 'versatile four of coloured men' entertained Murray's clientele in 1919, stoking 'the craze for jazz-ragging and dinner-dancing'. Two black song and dance men made the Café de Paris's name in the early 1920s. 'All the famous coloured stars' were seen at the Nest in Kingly Street – its cabaret included a one-legged tap dancer. Black musicians were in sufficient numbers in London in 1919 to form the sixty-strong 'Synco-Synco orchestra', incorporating just one white musician who made up with burnt cork. And American jazz bands like the world-famous Paul Whiteman's, Paul Specht's and Hal Kemp's all played at Kate Meyrick's 43 Club, Gerrard Street, and elsewhere in the early 1920s.[42]

After good music, then eccentric decor, a glitzy guest list and beautiful hostesses were the main attractions. The Prince of Wales (the ill-starred Edward VIII) frequented many clubs – three times a week, apparently, at the Café de Paris (Coventry Street). Maple from his Alberta ranch had been used for the dance floor of the Lambs Club over Leicester Square tube station – Robert Fabian raided it for liquor infringements in January 1924. Then the eccentrics. The Morgue, Ham Yard, run by Dalton Murray after his Beak Street club closed, had a receptionist dressed as a nun (though 'far from virtuous'), doormen and waiters as devils with made-up eyes that 'glittered like twin balls of fire', coffins as tables and 'skeleton' lamps hanging from the ceiling. The Blue Peter, Great Windmill Street, was decked out like a battleship. At the Bullfrogs Club, electric lights shone through oiled silk and the waiters dressed as Mexican bandits. The Gargoyle, in an alley off Dean Street had a roof-top dance floor with Christmas trees in pots, neighbouring chimneys painted red, tables with frosted-glass tops and light-ing under them, a large Matisse on the stairs and a guest list that included Noël Coward, Arnold Bennett and Hermione Baddeley. Kate Meyrick's Silver Slipper in Regent Street had a glass dance floor, copied from Paris, lit 'from underneath by hundreds of different-coloured lights, and there was an ingenious mechanism to make the lights ripple, giving an imitation of sea waves'. And the Hell Club, Gerrard Street, had 'hidden lighting that changed colour slowly, at a time when this was quite a novelty, and sank from pink to deep red and into ghastly purple and with various effects to make flickering shadows'. A few clubs catered especially for black men – the Big Apple in Gerrard Street, for instance, and a notorious place known as 'Black Man's Buddy' near Tottenham Court Road. And so did a few for homosexual men: Jack 'Ironfoot' Neave ran one called the Caravan Club in the early 1930s.[43] In general, though, the Soho nightclub was an expensive pleasure for those rich men who bankrolled the 'bright young things'. A box of choco-lates costing 3s 6d would be sold at the 43 Club for 2 guineas. The entrance fee at the Embassy Club, 'a sort of super-dance club' in Old Bond Street, was £21 in 1926, nine months' rent for a London worker's family. Other places were cheaper, but evening dress was compulsory almost everywhere.[44]

The combination of beautiful young hostesses and cocaine became a thing of scandal in Soho's nightclubs in the early 1920s. Freda Kempton, a dancer and hostess at the 43 Club, died of an overdose of cocaine in September 1923. Police thought her supplier was Brilliant Chang, Billy to his many friends, who ran a Chinese restaurant, at first in Regent Street and then opposite the 43 Club. Chang employed a number of dealers, including some Chinamen. And Eddie Manning, a Jamaican dubbed by a sensational press the 'most wicked man in London', was another notorious cocaine supplier of the time. Other dealers included hostesses, waiters and nightclub habitués. Chang was deported in early 1926 after serving a fourteen-month sentence for supplying cocaine to an actress called Violet Payne, who got three months' hard labour for possession – deterrent sentences to discourage the Soho dope trade. Indeed, cocaine was more freely available in early 1920s London than it would be again for almost the next sixty years. It was smuggled in by merchant ships from Hamburg and other German ports, where it could be bought for £5 a pound; profits from dealing were fantastic, for cut into useable doses of two grains at £1 a time its street value was £1,400–1,500 a pound. But international action to stamp out the traffic began to have an effect from the mid-1920s, and maybe the sentences passed on Chang and Payne helped, for by 1932 '"snow" is very infrequently obtainable in London'.[45]

- **Alec de Antiquis Shot Dead, Charlotte Street, 29 April 1947**
  The murderous violence of London's troubled post-war period was epitomized in the shooting of Alec de Antiquis, who tried to stop the getaway of three young armed robbers. Two of them were hanged for the crime.

- **West Indians, Southam Street, 1956**
  Roger Mayne's famous photographic record of Southam Street, Kensal New Town, captured the first years of Caribbean migration to this notorious multi-occupied district. Kelso Cochrane was to be one of the first of London's racial murder victims here in May 1959.

- **Notting Hill Carnival,** *c.* 1970
  Not so many years on and a multiracial London celebrates the city's tempestuous character transformation at the annual Notting Hill Carnival, already one of the largest events of its kind in the world.

- Last Flowering of the Port of London, 1958
  Despite a terrible pounding during the Blitz, the port recovered its trading position by the mid-1950s. But its time was running out, undermined by containerization, the demands of road transport and suicidal labour relations. Closures began in 1967 and the whole of the upper port had gone by 1981.

- Swinging London: Carnaby Street, 1968
  Fashion, music and sex – the magic ingredients of swinging London – centred on Soho. Carnaby Street, made famous by John Stephen's Mod clothes empire, was the fashion end of Soho's allure.

- **Before Gentrification: North London, _c._ 1960**
  Don McCullin brilliantly captures that other reality of 1960s London – mean
  streets, poverty, racial tension and economic decline. This is pre-gentrification
  Islington, at the King's Cross end of the Caledonian Road.

- **After Gentrification: Chelsea, _c._ 1975**
  The restoration of inner London Victorian housing in the 1960s and 1970s
  became a middle-class fetish. It was perhaps at its most exclusive and aristocrati
  in Chelsea, where workers had been displaced in favour of the rich from the
  1920s on.

- **The Rise of the Council Estate, Poplar, 1953**
  William Whiffin recorded the new world emerging from the Blitz in this East End
  panorama where council high-rise housing bulks large, and would soon bulk even larger
  and higher. In many respects, though not all, this would turn out to be a false dawn.

- **The Fall of the Council Estate, Hackney, 1998**
  Demolition of tower blocks on the Nightingale Estate, a spectacular experience for
  sightseers on Hackney Downs, signals the break-up of the inner London council estate.
  London towers had begun to be dynamited in the 1980s, some just twenty years old.

- **North London Suburbia, 1982**
  For all the satire of John Taylor's shot, suburbia outlived the snobbish superiority which had beset its origins in the 1920s and 1930s. Of all London's twentieth-century housing, this proved the most enduring and successful.

- **The Brixton Disorders, 10–12 April 1981**
  The worst rioting on mainland Britain in the twentieth century occurred at Brixton in April 1981. Essentially this was a youth riot against the police. Most anger was vented by young blacks against a racist police force.

IRA Bombing of the Baltic Exchange, May 1992

The IRA were London's most persistent enemy in the twentieth century, with terror campaigns in six decades out of ten. They killed fifty-six Londoners between 1973 and 1982 and maimed many more. This huge bomb in St Mary Axe devastated a substantial part of the City, for a time at least.

Full Circle at the Dome

In 1951 Herbert Morrison had presided over the Festival of Britain, with its Dome of Discovery on the South Bank. Forty-nine years on and Peter Mandelson, Good Old 'Erb's grandson, puts the final touches to a new but more derided dome some five miles downriver.

- Loadsamoney, *c.* 1996
  The yuppie, personified by the City winebar loafer, was an object of
  envy and spite, especially after Big Bang, the Stock Exchange reforms
  of October 1996. Yet London's economy had never depended so much
  on the world-beating City trader as it did at the end of the twentieth
  century.

- **No Money at All: Ian,** 1996
  If the City trader represents one end of London's economic and social
  spectrum, then Nick Danziger's photograph of Ian captures the other.
  The gulf had been no wider in Victorian London than it was in the
  London of Tony Blair. Even so, a much smaller proportion of
  Londoners were now in dire need than at any time before.

Around and between the sensational nightclubs in Soho there were innumerable quiet drinking clubs, just as transient (through bad debts rather than police raids) as their glamorous neighbours. Like 'Foppa's club', which Anthony Powell's fictional narrator Nick Jenkins frequents around 1931–3 – 'a small, smoky apartment', a table for 'Russian billiards', 'vermouth bottles above the little bar', 'a party of three or four playing cards gravely at one of the little tables in the corner'. And similar places, stretching the licensing laws to the limit and beyond, closing when raided and opening up under a new name nearby, could be found anywhere in London. Wally Thompson, the Islington thief, opened one off Gray's Inn Road, the Iris Club, around 1928–32. It made him a small fortune and the nightclub remained a potentially thriving venture open to all business-minded London villains for the rest of the century.[46]

Soho abounded in another institution with lively underworld connections which also began to come into its own between the wars: the café. The traditional London coffee house had already given birth to the modern café by 1900, small round tables and bentwood chairs gradually easing out the old benches, settles and heavy oblong tables of Victorian days. Some, like the Café de l'Europe around 1906, had 100 tables and a band, and served wine and beer just like any continental original. Most, though, were modest and it was these smaller versions that began to take on a large place in London culture, especially from the 1920s. Cafés catered to a loyal clientele who could make the place their own as much as any members-only club: local youth in the cafés of Holloway, say, or Brixton; thieves, fences, prostitutes, dope dealers and impecunious intellectuals in Soho; market porters in Smithfield, Billingsgate, Covent Garden and the rest; printers in Fleet Street, dockers in Canning Town, communists in Clerkenwell. But it was youth who provided the main stimulus to the rise in London's café society between the wars. And cafés laid more and more bait to bring them in. Penny-in-the-slot automatic gramophones had been popular since the early years of the century – the prostitutes of Euston Road would sing and dance to them at the Rising Sun pub in 1907, for instance – and in the 1930s more sophisticated versions of these were augmented by pintables (bagatelle), slot machines (though most for gaming were illegal) and occasionally billiards and pool. There tended to be fashions in cafés, perhaps more than in pubs. So that the 'café bar', usually run by Italians, later by Cypriots, arrived in Soho in the early 1920s, featuring 'a mahogany-coloured horseshoe or lemon-shaped bar' behind which coffee, tea and sandwiches were dispensed. George Scott Moncrieff wrote a good novel about one in 1932, *Café Bar*: 'the *Nine* was the principal café in Soho, with a regular clientèle of about a hundred, the centre of all gossip and news, the meeting place for crooks of many grades, for prostitutes and their ponces, for a few communists and philosophers, inferior artists, buskers; it was the heart of "the West End", Soho'. Then the milk bar, an American import of the late 1930s, became a popular innovation for a time, though milk shakes did not endure so well as coffee, as the 1990s reinvention of the coffee house in London would show.[47]

Cafés often closed late, around 2 a.m., unfettered by the imbecile liquor laws or (until the late 1960s) other controls and many of their customers, especially the young, went there after the cinemas closed. For the cinema was the great mass entertainer of the period from 1920 to 1955, with attendances – like professional sport – peaking after the war, in the case of cinema around 1946. It easily outweighed any other popular leisure activity, whether sport or dancing, despite the increasing luxuriousness and modish-ness of facilities for the latter: the Hammersmith Palais de Dance was a seductively glitzy spectacle from the 1920s on. But the rise of the supercinema put all else in the shade for exuberant extravagance, especially when the American 'atmospherics' came to London, from 1929. The Brixton Astoria was an Italian garden, the Finsbury Park Astoria a Moorish walled city, there was an Egyptian temple in Islington, Venice at Tooting, Gothic Spain at Woolwich, a hacienda at Ealing, a Chinese pagoda at Southall and a 5,000-seater wonderland at the Trocadero, Elephant and Castle. These were magnificent people's palaces in which to live a dreamworld, for a couple of hours a night at least. What a lure they must have been for a youngster whose home was a crowded two-rooms-and-a-kitchen in a tenement house – warmth, a comfortable armchair, visions of luxury on the screen. Many young Londoners would go to the cinema four times or more a week. When a 1947 survey asked young Londoners what they had done the previous evening, 21 per cent had been to the cinema – just 8 per cent said 'indoors' and 7 per cent said 'dancing'; and 41 per cent of London youth surveyed in 1949 went to the cinema every weekend.[48]

Cinema played a huge part in London youth culture through the 1920s to the 1950s – fearfully so, for many adults. A journalist visiting 'Islington's most notorious café' in April 1934 found four youths playing dice for pennies, rolling them into 'a round, greasy cardboard box'. When the nearby cinema emptied the place filled with young people 'of the same kidney', including girls badly and heavily made up:

They acted all the time. Movie mad. The youths are just as bad. Clothing, 'the latest worn', ridiculous styles and with a horrible 'cut price' appearance about it . . . The conversation [was] mostly in American accents. Nearly every girl there was acting a 'hard boiled Kate' role. Nearly every youth, with a very long overcoat and a round black hat on the rear of his head, was to himself a 'Chicago nut'.[49]

A few years later and those same Kates and nuts would be propelled – as heroines and heroes – into the whirlwind of total war.

London's second blackout from 1939 to 1945 did not have the disastrous ill-effects on its night life that 1914–18 and produced. There were, of course, famous casualties. Eighty-four died when a direct hit destroyed the Café de Paris on the night of 8 March 1941, among them the dance-band leader Snake-Hips Johnson. By this time the Café de Paris had become a popular broadcasting venue, so its name was well known to hundreds of thousands who had never set foot in it. Yorke de Souza, the Jamaican pianist of Johnson's band, had £60 on him when the bomb hit but when he got home to Rupert Street it had gone, probably 'taken from me by the looters. There were many of them.' Someone took the cufflinks from the manager's corpse. This tragedy, one of the most ghastly of London's war, figured largely – as the Café de Madrid – in Anthony Powell's re-creation of wartime London, *The Soldier's Art* (1966).[50]

London's night-life in the second blackout may have lost part of its pre-war glamour, for some at least of the super-rich avoided London, even England, altogether. Yet not all brilliance departed. In place of glitter came the thrill attaching to uniforms in war and sexual appetites kindled among strangers living for the moment. Clubs flourished. There, in Henry Green's words, with 'long-haired sheaved heads too heavy for their bodies collapsed on pilots' blue shoulders', women danced 'gorged with love, sleep lovewalk-ing'. Americans in the flesh, Hollywood really come to town, endowed London with a unique excitement that even the revolutionary changes in manners wrought by the First World War had not quite matched. Americans alone would have kept London's night life alive and more than kicking. London had to be invaded before Normandy and this was an occupying army that killed first with kindness. When the American forces left for France, the Horse and Groom pub off Regent Street was christened 'The Whore's Lament' 'after the tears shed by the ladies of the bar' for the good times that had left with them.[51]

Besides these exotic newcomers, wartime London nurtured a largely new state-supported intellectual class – writers, artists, film-makers, actors, entertainers, spies, boffins, bureaucrats. Everyone had a job to do. All were swept up. Even writers could be useful. So Henry Green (Eton and Magdalen) was drafted into the London Auxiliary Fire Service; Graham Greene (Berkhamsted and Balliol) became a spycatcher based in Queen Anne's Gate; Nigel Balchin (Dauntsey and Peterhouse) worked in Civil Service personnel; William Sansom (Uppingham and public house) was another fireman; Patrick Hamilton, at risk of being made a clerk, pulled strings and got himself into ENSA, writing links between songs for radio broadcasts. Stoked by a regular income, the appetite for pubs, clubs and cafés grew rather than declined. It was during these years that Fitzrovia briefly flowered as a bohemia. 'North Soho', as some called the district west of Tottenham Court Road, south of Euston Road and north of Oxford Street, was the great watering hole of the broadcasting classes employed round Langham Place, which, with Regent Street and Portland Place, bounded Fitzrovia on the east. The Fitzroy Tavern, already known for its eccentricities pre-war, became a renowned haunt for homosexuals, joining Soho's holy canon – the French pub, the Swiss, the Highlander and more – as a place to meet significant others for all sorts of connections.

North or south, Soho flourished as never before and continued to do so even into the bleak 1940s. 'Despite all the difficulties,' a commentator wrote around 1946, 'the Soho restaurants are enjoying the biggest boom in their history', and he counted 'dozens of little clubs which are properly run and handy for talking business'. Among these, from 1948 or 1949, was Muriel Belcher's famous Colony Room in Dean Street – its 700 members included the painters Francis Bacon, Lucian Freud and Nina Hamnett (until her gin-induced incontinence began to ruin the bar stools). And around the pubs and clubs other elements of London night-life recovered from the war faster than anyone expected. In the face of austerity, the debs' ball and the smart restaurant were resurrected, even if all faculties were not yet fully restored: the chaperone apparently failed to survive the war, for instance. *The Girls of Slender Means*, at their club-cum-boarding house in South Kensington, had to share a single Schiaparelli dress so they could take their turn at 'the Milroy' and 'Quags' (Quaglino's restaurant, Bury Street, St James's): 'it's getting known all over London'. By 1951 Francis Marshall was able to celebrate the full-blooded revival of the London Season – 'In the middle of World War Two it seemed incredible that all this would ever come back again . . .'[52]

To this strong recovery of London's night-life after 1945, three elements soon introduced fresh blood. Although each built on a traditional base, two were sufficiently different from anything that had gone before to rank as entirely new influences on London's popular culture. These were black immigration, most particularly from the West Indies but also from Africa; and the teenage musical revolution that first expressed itself in London's café society. The third, with links to both those, was the return of a phenomenon from an older post-war generation: recreational drug use.

The West Indian migration from 1947 rapidly began to work its magic on London's night life. The migrants' musical traditions rooted quickly – calypso was especially suited to informal small-scale performance venues like cafés, clubs and pubs. Their capacity for enjoyment created its own leisure industry of drinking and gaming clubs, with appropriate annexes for casual sex, and a passion for noisy parties that did not always go down well with the neighbours. They popularized the use of marijuana among the young and young at heart. Known in London only to a few insiders in the 1930s, marijuana became a Soho favourite as early as 1948. Frank Norman, playwright and ex-villain, was an enthusiastic acolyte and set out to cultivate the plant surreptitiously (but unsuccessfully) in the hot-houses of Kew with the help of 'Snowball', a Soho West Indian. Snowball and his fellow travellers went on virtually to create a new pleasure district which would be of great significance to London for the rest of the century.

This was Notting Hill. It had always been a queer place, with the 'London Avernus' of Notting Dale on the very doorstep of grand neighbours in Lansdowne Crescent and Ladbroke Grove. This was a district which, ever since it was developed in the middle of the nineteenth century, had been competing for caste. But by the 1940s the rich had lost out comprehensively to the poor. These were the years of Heath and Christie, when the great terraces of W11 had never been in a sorrier state. These were the years, too, when Notting Hill was chosen as one of the first major areas of West Indian settlement in London. The dominant Trinidadian character of the migration to Notting Hill brought with it a passion for entertaining, food, music, drink and carnival. This combined well with do-as-you-please local traditions among a shifting population that had never cared much for authority or property. The result endowed London with a new jewel rivalling Chelsea, Fitzrovia and Soho for bohemianism, and Soho for its underworld and sex-commerce connections. Taking over from the old prostitution district west of Paddington Station, now being redeveloped, the area within a half-mile radius of the junction of Talbot and Ledbury Roads was known as 'the biggest brothel in Europe' by 1960, and dubbed 'Jungle West 11' in the cheap press. It was liberally sprinkled with shebeens – Christie's old rooms, disguised under their new name of 10 Ruston Street, were turned into the Celebrity Club for a time around 1960. Yet Notting Hill was also one of the earliest sites of post-war gentrification. Adventurous middle-class settlers were lured there by the potential beauty of much of the Victorian housing, by its proximity to the West End and by the Portobello Road market, becoming almost as famous for its antiques and bargains in the 1950s as Caledonian Market had been twenty years before. When, in the late 1950s, the young British disciples of Kerouac and Ginsberg trekked to London in search of dope and enlightenment, it was to Notting Hill they headed rather than any other district. And when Colin Wilson, their early chronicler, wrote *Adrift in Soho* (1961, but set in 1955), most of the novel's action took place in a Notting Hill multi-occupied house filled with painters, poets, dope-heads and friendly women.[53]

Music was the common ground that connected, if not united, black migration with the teenage revolution of the late 1940s and 1950s. The café was the crucible. The 1950s were the heyday of the London café, Soho the premier location of the 'coffee-house craze'. In 1958 there were 'at least 50 of them'. 'They bring a different character to Soho, they are the teenagers and skiffle merchants . . .' The most famous café in London – in Britain, maybe the world – was the 2i's Coffee Bar in Old Compton Street. This was one of the first to exploit its deep cellar for music and dancing, and one of the first to give talented young working-class Londoners a stage that stretched from Soho right around the world. Brilliant exponents of skiffle and rock'n'roll were 'discovered' and launched to a mass audience in the cellar of the 2i's and nearby Soho cafés: most famously Tommy Steele (Bermondsey) and Cliff Richard (mainly Enfield), but also Billy Fury, Terry Dene, Lonnie Donnegan and the significantly named Laurie London (just fourteen when he had an international hit) all started in this way. Besides the cafés and their basement clubs – the real stars of films like *Expresso Bongo* and *Sapphire* (both 1959) – pubs (like the Swiss, Old Compton Street) and clubs (the Flamingo, Wardour Street, and the Blue Gardenia, St Anne's Court) were important venues for aspiring young artistes in jazz and rock: the Beatles' first London performance, in December 1961, was at the Blue Gardenia. This was also a culture in which the use of recreational drugs was increasingly common. Pill-popping in cafés and clubs became an easy way of keeping going at these late-night dance venues: the contents of benzedrine inhalers, which were chewed, and then 'benz' tablets were apparently the earliest available.[54]

Colin MacInnes was the London writer most in touch with this rising generation, even though his own background was staid, upper-class and Edwardian. He did not miss the mark when he spotted in February 1958 the first thunderclouds of the gathering storm about to hit London in the shape of teenage culture:

In general they're gayer than English people seem to have been for 50 years at least. Contemporary England is peculiar for being the most organized country, in the social sense, for ensuring the moral and material welfare of everybody – pullulating with decent laws, with high-minded committees, with societies for preventing or encouraging this or that – and yet it has produced, in consequence, the *dullest* society in western Europe: a society blighted by blankets of negative respectability, and of dogmatic domesticity. The teenagers don't seem to care for this, and have organized their underground of joy.[55]

And the underground was just about to break through the crust.

From Swinging London to Coolest City in the World:
1960–99

In April 1966 *Time* magazine proclaimed London as the world city of the decade – 'London: The Swinging City'. It blazoned the notion of 'Swinging London' (the neologism was used several times in the editorial and cover story) to the world. That was not the first time that London had received recognition for its sudden blooming in the 1960s. There had been earlier rave notices in *L'Express* (September 1964), the *Weekend Telegraph* ('London – The Most Exciting City', April 1965) and *Epoca* ('the happiest and the most electric city in Europe, and the most nonconformist', November 1965). But it was *Time* that fixed London in the world's imagination for years to come.[56]

It was fashionable then and later to decry the myth of Swinging London and, of course, it was a grossly misleading tag: this was the decade, after all, when the plug was pulled on the London economy, when the bulldozer and the Brutalist architect had full reign, and when crime and racial antagonism took a turn for the worse. These were all realities that the rhetoric of 'The Swinging City' ignored: 'The "swinging sixties" did not swing in Lambeth', at least for a rueful John Major. Even for youth, joy and adventure and freedom would always be the lot of the few rather than the many, so that when 'Petronius' compared London favourably (if ungrammatically) to New York in 1969 as 'one of the easiest cities in the world for a man to get laid in', he did not speak for all his peers.[57]

None the less extraordinary things had happened to London by 1966. Despite her breathless prose, Piri Halasz in *Time* was on to something real enough. She was right to stress the attraction of a city where youth and the new combined so intriguingly with tradition, and where upper-class elements of the London Season seemed to blend effortlessly with working-class talent. 'Ancient elegance and new opulence are all tangled up in a dazzling blur of op and pop', and she juxtaposed the Rolling Stones with the Changing of the Guard, Princess Margaret with Michael Caine, the 'incredibly exclusive' Clermont Club (Berkeley Square) with Dirty Dick's pub (Bishopsgate), and the West End theatre with Carnaby Street's Mod clothes shops. 'London has shed much of its smugness, much of the arrogance that often went with the stamp of privilege, much of its false pride – the kind that long kept it shabby and shopworn in physical fact and spirit.' Now it had a 'large measure of . . . civility . . . tolerance . . . simple humanity . . .

gentleness . . . ease, a coziness and a mixture of its different social circles that totally eludes New York . . . "In London, everyone parties with everyone else." '58

It was this demotic element of class mix that marked the Swinging Sixties out from the Roaring Twenties in London and, indeed, from any previous decade. It is not unreasonable to consider the 1960s a genuine period of 'social revolution' for the way in which working-class talent was plucked from obscurity and pitched into worldwide stardom and riches overnight – not a new phenomenon but new in its apparently inexhaustible cast list. Photographers, hairdressers, actors and actresses, models, above all rock musicians and singers loomed large among the new stars. At the end of the decade the journalist Christopher Booker charted the careers of the 200 or so who made the 1960s what they were. Working-class London was not the only seedbed – Liverpool had its own musical revolution from the late 1950s – but it produced a host of golden orchids from 1960: David Bailey (East Ham), Terence Donovan (Stepney), Terence Stamp ('East End'), Michael Caine (south London), the Dave Clark Five (Tottenham), the Rolling Stones (Dartford, on the London fringe), the Kinks (Muswell Hill), Twiggy (Neasden), the Pretty Things (Dartford again), Sandie Shaw (Dagenham), The Who (west London), Helen Shapiro (East End), the Small Faces (East Ham), Adam Faith (Acton) – indeed, the list was almost endless.

The musicians among them were greatly assisted by the connection between club life, café society and musical performance which had expanded so much in the 1950s. Even those not bred in London had to come there to record; and usually, for sensible business reasons of accessibility to studios and session musicians, agents and tour promoters, photographers and journalists, ended up living there, if only for a time. The long connection of London with recorded music put it in an invincible position to take advantage of a 'social revolution' founded largely on popular song. Its own Gramophone Company (later EMI) provided 'The most important recording studio in Rock and Pop history' at Abbey Road, St John's Wood. A telling moment symbolizing London's irresistible superiority in the field was recounted by George Melly, himself an ex-Liverpudlian adopted Londoner. When the première of *A Hard Day's Night* took place in Liverpool in 1964, 'It looked as though nothing had changed that night. The Beatles appeared after the film on the balcony of the Town Hall. They were cheered by 50,000 people, but they didn't wait for the reception. They flew straight back to London.'59

London, of course, had other assets, too, and post-war developments directly paved the way for Swinging London. London's strongly rooted and flexible garment industry was well placed to respond to quick-change fashion and style from the late 1940s on, and it built on home-grown talent emerging from the capital's art and fashion colleges. Mary Quant came straight from Goldsmiths' College of Art to set up Bazaar on the King's Road, Chelsea, giving London its first 'boutique' in 1955. An unparalleled leader of style, Quant was one of the formative figures – and a bottomless resource – of Swinging London. By 1960 she was designing for wholesale and selling her styles to America. By then, too, John Stephen, from Glasgow and still in his early twenties, opened the first of his men's clothes shops in Carnaby Street – when *Time* reported, he had nine there. Stephen promoted clothes in the Italian-cool Mod style which, with his help, had fully emerged in London by 1962. And, of huge significance for working-class London girls desperate to be 'with it' but unable to afford Quant's Chelsea prices, Biba was opened by Barbara Hulanicki at Abingdon Road, off High Street Kensington, around 1963. The adventurousness of the London fashion world at this time might be gauged by the response in Milan, where, in 1967, a department store re-created 'Carnaby a Milano' – 'You enter and have the real impression of finding yourself in London, Carnaby Street.'[60]

And then there was sex. London was able to build on a sex industry as old as the Romans and kept very much alive in the twentieth century. The Street Offences Act might have driven the prostitutes off the streets but it largely created the Soho strip club. Striptease did not come new to London at the end of the 1950s. By 1935 there were nude tableaux, the girls having to sit or stand quite still, at the London Casino, Old Compton Street. The first true striptease seems to have arrived about the same time at a 'very smart club' called the Venetian and a little later at the Gaucho Club.[61] After the war the tradition of nude tableaux was kept alive by Collins' Music Hall, Islington Green, and striptease was a feature of some London pubs and the odd Soho club before 1959.

Nor were the more extreme versions of pornography and live-sex exhibitions entire strangers to the capital. When Ted Greeno raided a brothel for 'top-notch people' at Dover Street, Mayfair, in 1938, he found a small theatre where four women and two men were on stage with 'not so much cover as a handkerchief between the lot of them', presided over by 'the mistress of ceremonies, a glistening six-foot Negress in thigh boots and nothing else. This was Carmen.' Something called 'the "French Circus"' provided exhibitions at a flat in Marylebone High Street, probably around the same time. In the war Nigel Balchin wrote knowingly of something similar which he called 'Liberty Hall' and placed in a cellar in Albemarle Street, Piccadilly:

It was a big room with a dance floor in the middle. All round the sides were cubicles, going back quite a long way like a theatre box, and looking out on the floor. Each cubicle had horseshoe-shaped sofas and a table. To get into a cubicle you opened a half-door in front, like going into an old-fashioned pew. There were curtains in front so that you could shut yourself in completely if you liked. There were a few people there. We sat down in a cubicle and rang the bell. A waitress came. She was the usual sort of cabaret beauty, blonde with a rather tired skin. She was wearing a little scarlet jacket and the world's tightest pair of white silk trousers . . .

'Do you wear masks later on or just trust to the curtains?'

Edwardes said, 'You've seen this sort of thing before?' He seemed a bit surprised.

'Not in London,' I said. 'But there's a place in the Rue Druot in Paris very like this.'

'It's run by a Frenchman,' said Edwardes.

'Do you bring your own women or are they provided by the management?'

'Liberty Hall,' said Edwardes. 'You please yourself.'

'And the floor?'

'Used for dancing,' said Edwardes with a grin.

'And for l'exhibition, l'attraction et la demonstration, I suppose?'[62]

There was also a venerable connection between Soho and the dirty-book trade, established when the booksellers moved from Holywell Street ('Bookseller's Row') to Charing Cross Road in the early 1900s. Pornography remained, though, a small-minority taste. In 1932 it was said that 'Pornography, considered as a vice in London, is not a grave one, less frequent here, I think, than in almost any big city and less frequent now than at almost any time . . . Obscene cinema shows are practically unknown in London.'[63]

But with the girls off the streets from August 1959, voyeurism quickly became big business. It centred on Soho and lasted in its most brazen form for the next twenty years at least. The Soho striptease club mushroomed from 1959, just as its nightclub forebear had from 1919. Indeed, it often displaced the nightclub and coffee bar from their former haunts as this new craze took over the old. 'Within a few months [of August 1959] there were at least a dozen of these Strip Clubs around the manor', with girls imported from Paris by impresarios like Paul Raymond (from Liverpool originally) in a reverse of the 'White Slave Trade' that had so fascinated reformers in the early years of the century. Strip clubs were joined by 'clip joints', clubs selling 'near-beer' to avoid the licensing laws, where punters were lured into paying fantastic prices by beautiful 'hostesses' who might, or might not, go to bed with them. The glamour, exoticism and excitement of this new Soho triggered a sympathetic resonance in both the fashion and music industries.[64]

Soho figured overwhelmingly in all these elements of music, fashion and sex. It was rivalled in fashion by Chelsea, where the King's Road provided an *al fresco* catwalk of unique appeal. And it was rivalled in bohemianism – drugs, sex and music – by Notting Hill, spiced as it was with rich lacings of Caribbean culture, and the new trendiness of antiques and the trappings of gentrification. Maybe this was Swinging London's fundamental asset, its possession of districts where all the diverse elements of the entertainment industry – photography, models, printing, art and music publishing, agents, performers, venues, sexual gratification – could cluster, network and add value, helping each other adapt to and lead the era's chameleon changes of taste and fashion. Certainly it was difficult to imagine Swinging London without Soho and all it had to offer.

When *Time* printed its encomium in 1966 the phenomenon it celebrated was almost nearing its end, or at least the end of its first phase. The high summer of Swinging London probably dates from 1963 to 1967. Its temples were the boutique and the discothèque (as their names suggest, hardly London originals); its high priests the pop star, the fashion designer, the model and the photographer; its emblems the miniskirt and the haircut. It was an era of sexual freedom made easier by homosexual law reform and the oral contraceptive. It was a time of political optimism – the election of the first Wilson government in October 1964 frankly encouraged experimentation and a passion for the new.[65] And London was able to attract to it creative individuals from all over the world who played a large part in the next, and in many ways more significant, phase, among them a clutch of brilliant Australians (including Richard Neville, Germaine Greer and Martin Sharpe).

Swinging London's Indian summer was 1967 to 1972. This was the era of hippiedom and flower power. It took fewer Londoners with it than the more populist Swinging London phase and it had to battle against more opposition and repression. This was the London of real high priests and temples, of floor-length skirts and no haircut at all, of 'alternative' (a keyword of the period) reality constructed through hallucinogenic drugs and mystical subjection, of an underground press more stimulating and exasperating than anything known in the capital since the 1820s. And where the contradictions of a sexual 'freedom' that both liberated and objectified women began to emerge in an icon-shattering feminist revival, which was mirrored in struggles to assert the rights of minorities, especially gays and blacks.[66]

Much of this extraordinary harvest from 1963 to 1972 was ephemeral. Some of it was made by Londoners following in the footsteps of radical citizens elsewhere (like New Yorkers, who took the lead on gay rights, for instance). Not everything changed and not everyone was affected. Even so,

London and Londoners would never be the same again. This was a cultural revolution with long-term effects.

What did the 1960s give to London? There were several legacies, some more positive than others. The London women's fashion industry never lost the place that Quant won for it in the world's premier league. It had begun to catch up with Paris – at least in seeking the favours of fashionable Englishwomen – from 1920; and Norah Crampton and Norman Hartnell were great names from the 1930s to the 1950s. But in the 1960s London led the world, and the cachet of young London-bred designers was hardly diminished, if diminished at all, at the end of the century. That in itself may not have been an achievement that affected much in the lives of ordinary Londoners. Yet a world-beating London fashion industry helped both stimulate and satisfy the changing inflections of style among young Londoners that would be an enduring feature of the post-1960s metropolis.[67]

Indeed, the 1960s passed on to the youth of later decades a gilded baton that included more institutions than ever before. For the boutique survived the decade and so, most importantly for London night-life, did the discothèque. The discothèque arrived from Paris on the wave of the twist dance craze of the very early 1960s (although the name was apparently first taken up by a Soho coffee bar which called itself La Discothèque from 1954). By 1962 the Saddle Room, Hamilton Place, Mayfair, was, according to George Melly's eagle eye, 'certainly the most fashionable discothèque in London'. 'The dècor [sic] is harness and hunting pictures and horse-box panelling. It's so English it couldn't look more French', and it was indeed run by a Frenchwoman. This was the place where the 'Chelsea Set' came to be seen – 'people connected with the rag trade, and, most noticeably, a great many fashion models'. The Saddle Room was a members-only club and the discothèque as originally constructed was a nightclub where people went, above all, to dance. The London nightclub as it emerged after the First World War had dancing to live music as a distinctive element, but dining and drinking were equal partners in a night's entertainment. The 1960s discothèque offered food and drink, too, but subordinated both to dancing – the tables for eating and drinking had their legs cut down to give the experience a transient picnic feel. Music was usually recorded rather than live, which must have helped with the overheads. And the premises were necessarily larger than the average London nightclub, miniature versions of the Hammersmith Palais with exclusivity guaranteed through members- and guests-only entry.[68]

This new 1960s form of the London nightclub was a distinctive creation that lasted through the changing fashions of style – Mod, hippie, Sloane Ranger, punk, disco, yuppie – that followed in some great pop dialectic over the next forty years. It never lost its appeal, partly because from the beginning each discothèque targeted a special audience from whom it claimed loyalty within an increasingly diversifying and eclectic London pop scene. And it retained its 'classless' feel, at least in so far as birth mattered less than wealth. So that Annabel's, Berkeley Square, was open (from 1963) to anyone who could fit into 'the world of the Glossies, the quality ads, the private yacht and the house in the Bahamas' – no matter how new their money. Indeed, if they were pop or movie stars, the newer the better. The Ad-Lib, Leicester Square, was less exclusive, 'dedicated to the triumph of style' – 'the clothes reflect [1965] Carnaby Street at its most extreme'. And there were many many more, including the Scotch of St James's, Mason's Yard, Duke Street, where tables on a dais were roped off for the exclusive use of any passing Beatle or Rolling Stone; the UFO (Underground Freak-Out), Tottenham Court Road, a hippie mecca from 1967; and the Flamingo and the All Nighters in Wardour Street, especially favoured by West Indians and blues fans.[69]

In the 1970s, especially, the discothèque nightclub was supplemented by a host of live and recorded rock music venues. Most of these were pay-as-you-enter downmarket versions of the nightclub disco and ranged from purpose-adapted halls or club rooms and church halls hired for the night, to upstairs rooms in Victorian pubs (like the Hope and Anchor, Islington, the George Robey, Finsbury Park, and the Mean Fiddler, Harlesden). This suited the more oppositional music of the punk era and its various spawnings from the mid-1970s on. The tendency also expanded the geographical spread of musical performance venues in London. Camden Town, for instance, rivalled almost anywhere by the late 1970s, with 'the Roundhouse, Dingwalls, the Electric Ballroom and the Music Machine, all within a few minutes walking distance of each other, plus the Dublin Castle and various other pubs where bands could play live'. By 1986, the journalist and London-watcher Michael Elliott could count in one week 'over 550 rock, folk and jazz gigs' in London, with over 100 to choose from on any Friday, Saturday or Sunday night. And the survival of the nightclub in this lively scene was demonstrated by seventy listed each week in the listings magazine *Time Out*, itself one of the great survivals of 1960s London.[70]

Clubbing (a favourite late-century verb) and disco remained a generally available cross-class and (to an increasing extent) cross-race feature of London night-life, waxing and waning with the fortunes of the London economy and youth unemployment but generally a sturdy survivor. It was a particular favourite of suburban youth, in general the most consistently prosperous among London's young people. London clubs continued to offer, as was said of Peter Stringfellow's Hippodrome (Charing Cross Road) in the mid-1980s, 'the young workers from Bromley and Croydon' the equivalent 'in cold old London' of their brief summers of 'sun and sex in Spain'. Indeed, from around 1988 through the rest of the century the London disco-club dance scene continued to expand and diversify. 'Acid-house' or 'house' music went through a stage of illegal 'warehouse raves', where empty industrial buildings would be squatted for a tempestuous weekend, and 'jungle', created by young black Londoners in the early 1990s but proving irresistible to youth of whatever race, class or gender, were just two of the innovations with most appeal. As in the 1960s, clubs catered specifically for those who pledged allegiance to one of these shifting strands or another. Whatever you wanted to hear, from 'Mod' to 'psychobilly', 'trance' to 'techno', 'trip hop' to 'rare groove', there was a London scene. Frequently these strands could be had in different rooms in a single multiplex club, with quiet ('chill') rooms, coffee and cake shops and retail outlets creating a self-contained world of dance and its accessories.[71]

Some other boundaries breached by Swinging London stayed down for the rest of the century. Fringe or experimental theatre boomed – *Time Out* could list fifty venues in 1972, all sparked off by Jim Haynes's exciting Arts Lab in Drury Lane (from 1967). So did the popularity of London as a venue and subject for the American film industry: *Time* noted how, in the spring of 1966, 'film makers from all over the world have been attracted to London by its swinging film industry', including Chaplin (born in Walworth in 1889), Truffaut, Polanski, Aldrich, Lumet and Antonioni (*Blow-Up*). This fad hardly abated and spilled over into the tourism industry; Michael Moorcock, in a felicitous phrase, described the fashion for making over pubs in pastiche Victorian – one in the East End was renamed the Jack the Ripper – as 'Hollywood Cockney'.[72] It was a trend still apparently with much mileage in it at the end of the century, as the success of *Notting Hill* in 1999 showed.

The 'permissiveness' of Swinging London also had much life in its legacy at the end of the century, at least in its expression through sex and drugs. The London sex industry blossomed seedily in Soho right through the 1960s and 1970s. By 1970 there were at least forty Soho shops dealing, more or less openly, in the dirty-book trade. By 1977 Soho had 185 sex-industry establishments of one sort or another, from strip clubs to blue film shows. It was, without any serious rival, 'the porn capital of England' and reaped a tourist whirlwind as a consequence, though at the expense of much of the energy and diversity that had made it such a truly fascinating part of the capital for generations. This nadir, though, was relatively short-lived. By 1989 a clean-up in Scotland Yard (whose senior officers had corruptly sanctioned the takeover of Soho by the porn merchants), tougher licensing laws for sex establishments and rising office rents elsewhere in London which helped push small creative industries into Soho left it with just thirty-five sex-industry premises intact. Continuing red-light entertainment seemed to coexist reasonably amicably with a partially restored social and economic diversity. The pornography trade reduced and scattered to the Tottenham Court Road area (Fitzrovia getting Soho's leftovers again) and the main central London prostitution districts.[73]

The drugs legacy of the 1960s was, though, more complex, more enduring and more worrying. Marijuana remained a popular recreational drug, in particular among the young, among 1960s veterans and among black Londoners. Its use was legitimized by default as police and prosecution authorities, with other more sinister drug targets in their sights, turned a blind eye to possession, if not dealing. The whiff of spliff became a universal street smell in the metropolis by the late 1990s, as Millennium Eve revellers along the banks of the Thames could readily testify. For many, if not for the law-makers and moralists, marijuana had ceased to be any more of a problem to London than alcohol, and conceivably less.

But the slow rise of heroin, from its absorption into the hippie counter-culture of 1967–72 to gaining a terrible popularity among working-class youth from the late 1970s, proved a far more urgent difficulty. It produced a craving very hard to break and hugely expensive to feed, so that drug-related property crime, sometimes accompanied with violence, was the great scourge of the last two decades of London's century. It combined, from around the same time, with the rediscovery of cocaine as a fashionable leisure drug among City yuppies and Soho clubbers. In the mid-1990s a 'new cocaine epidemic' was said to be reaching more plebeian consumers of the schoolteacher and librarian class through the nightclub network. And the underground marketing of 'designer drugs', most prominently ecstasy, was another emerging complication of the London club scene. In 1996 the British Crime Survey estimated that 29 per cent of Londoners aged sixteen to twenty-nine had taken some kind of illegal drug in the previous twelve months, compared to 24 per cent in England and Wales as a whole. That was higher than any other region of the nation, although the north was thought to be catching up.[74]

There was, finally, one legacy of the 1960s that had lasting beneficial effects. That was in its life-giving consequences for significant London districts. Swinging London was built fundamentally on Soho and, to a lesser extent, Chelsea. But the nightclub discothèque reinvigorated Mayfair – long the smartest part of London – which had lost cachet through the intrusion of offices after the Second World War. More important, it consolidated Notting Hill as a new bohemia for white and black intellectuals where there 'were lots of communal houses where you could always drop in and get a joint or a cup of tea, or companionship, conversation and music'. As we have seen, it was the Black Power movement's chosen battleground, its rallying point the Mangrove Restaurant, its intellectuals including Horace Ove, Darcus Howe, Courtney Tulloch and the unreliable Michael Malik; Jimi Hendrix took his fatal overdose at a basement in Lansdowne Crescent in September 1970; and blacks and whites came together to establish the All Saints Church Hall as a rock venue and community resource, planning the early Notting Hill Carnivals there. Swinging London also helped save Covent Garden from destruction and turn it into another pleasureground for London. It was said that the 'Arts Lab was the first thing that made Covent Garden vaguely trendy', although Denmark Street's already established music-publishing industry must have helped bring rock musicians into an ever-interesting location. Once saved, Covent Garden became perhaps the most self-conscious inheritor of the Swinging London mantle, complete with boutiques, discos, 'alternative' stalls and shops, clubs and street theatre.[75]

Much of the optimism of Swinging London turned to dust in the authoritarian reaction, the economic difficulties and racial tensions of the 1970s; and in the social disturbances and unemployment crises of the early 1980s. But the institutions that the 1960s created never entirely withered away. And it fell to the 1990s to revive something of that decade's peculiar excitement. The 1990s were less naïve, more prosperous, more culturally diverse, financially astute and technologically adept than the 1960s, and what they lost in innocence, idealism and revolutionary discovery, they gained in inclusivity; they could offer most young Londoners greater accessibility to their benefits. Just how much was on offer was celebrated almost exactly thirty years on from *Time* by yet another American journal.

In October 1996 *Newsweek* rediscovered London as 'The Coolest City in the World'. 'Outrageous fashion, a pulsating club scene and lots of new money have turned Britain's capital into the coolest city on the planet.' 'London is a hip compromise between the nonstop newness of Los Angeles and the aspic-preserved beauty of Paris – sharpened to New York's edge.' Much of this excitement was due to its unBritishness. Its mix of European and world cultures could be seen in 'an amazing variety of international food. Chefs are mixing Asian and European styles in a way I ['a Malaysian-Briton' chef] haven't seen anywhere else.' 'London clubs are said to pull in about 500,000 people every Saturday. If a slick superclub like the Ministry [of Sound, Elephant and Castle, opened 1991] doesn't appeal, the sheer variety in London promises that something will – whether Goa trance nights, acid-jazz evenings or bongo-beating, incense-smoking Caribbean funk at a tiny hole in Soho.' 'Over the last three years London has . . .

become fashion's "Boom City"', with the leading Paris houses both choosing London designers educated at St Martin's College of Art. 'Not everything
cool about London is new' – Changing of the Guard, Houses of Parliament,
the Tower of London, St Paul's – 'In fact, one of the things that makes
London so entertaining is its mix of the old and the new.' Featuring pop
stars, fashion models and designers, and artists, the parallels with *Time*
were virtually exact. One difference, though, was in the various maps
accompanying the piece. There was a separate one charting the virtues of
Notting Hill, mainly for eating out: '192 Restaurant. The place to see/be
seen'. The map of central London featured Clerkenwell, Southwark, the
City and Covent Garden, as well as Soho – and it could reasonably have
been extended to Camden Town and Hoxton. Chelsea, though, was off the
map.[76]

Newsweek ended with a note of caution: 'London's boom may last, oh,
another few months. Better get there soon.' In fact, as the century ended,
there was no sign of the violent swing 'between booms and busts' that was
the 'secret to understanding London'. No sign at Millennium Dawn anyway.
Newsweek was surely right in its proposition that 1990s London was booming
because young people had money in their pockets and purses; and if that
spending power faltered then much would come crashing down with it.
But Armageddon seemed safely deferred by a number of factors. The election
of the Blair government in May 1997 seemed to give 'the coolest city'
another flip, just as Harold Wilson's had done in 1964. The celebrations for
the new millennium were set to generate tourism and investment in the
Greenwich peninsula, on Bankside and probably in London as a whole, for
at least a year or two into the new century. The benefits of a multicultural
city seemed unshakeable and ever more widely spread, so that for eating out
Stoke Newington Church Street, say, or Upper Street, Islington, had
become as exciting as Notting Hill or Soho, and more exciting than almost
any provincial town or city centre in the nation. And Hollywood Cockney
seemed to be going from strength to strength, bringing dollars and tourists
in its train.

There was one further – but unknown – quantity that also seemed to
promise benefit to London, even if it could not decisively safeguard the
capital's economy or its place in the nation's. This was the prospect of new
government arrangements for London from May 2000. For it had long been
a wonder indeed that the coolest city in the world could also have been, for
much of the century, just about the worst-governed in Britain.

PART FIVE

Politics

9. Governing the Ungovernable

Progressives, Moderates and 'Good Old George':
London Government, 1900–1933

'Who governs London? The answer to that question is a simple one. The people of London govern the city in which they live. In no other way could a great body of Englishmen be ruled.'[1] Brave words, but not the whole truth even when Hugh Arnold-Forster penned them (for 'young readers') in 1900. They were more true then, though, than they would have been in 1999, when London – at least the big idea of London as a unified city – was not 'ruled' by Londoners at all. For in the twentieth century London self-government virtually withered away.

The insoluble puzzle of how best to govern London had been inherited from the Victorians, and even in their day the question was an old one. If only the City Corporation had responded to the great expansion of Elizabethan London by letting the City's boundaries move out as the town spread, then things might well have been different and better. But the 'City fathers' hadn't and wouldn't, clinging like rigor mortis to their ancient boundaries, adjusted a few yards here or there, with a grip that even the twenty-first century seemed unlikely to shake. When the reformers of the 1830s began to grapple with the democratic consequences of the growth of towns, London was just too big and complex for the solution they applied to Birmingham, Manchester, Bristol and elsewhere. There the ancient borough or city boundaries were pushed out to take in the new built-up area. In London no single authority could hope to carry out all functions in a gargantuan town where the connections between, say, Bethnal Green and Fulham were non-existent and which the Thames broke almost unbridgeably in two. This great contradiction between the local interests of London's diverse parts, once towns and villages in their own right, and those less tangible interests which united London and Londoners, would be resolved temporarily in the local interest in 1986, but only at the preposterous cost of no London-wide government at all.

That, of course, necessitated direct rule from Whitehall. And this was the second great contradiction of London government. The overpowering importance of London to the nation state – its enormous wealth based on international trade, the seat of parliamentary government and the monarchy, its huge concentration of the nation's most energetic and enterprising people, its symbolic and actual place in the nation's history – meant that governing Britain could not be divorced from the idea of governing London. To the world, London and Great Britain were one and the same. What happened in Birmingham or Bristol might generally be ignored with equanimity by the nation's legislators. What happened in Threadneedle Street, in the side streets of Westminster or on Kennington Common could not be left to London alone to determine, for the whim of Londoners could upset the governance of the nation. So, as we have seen, the police of London were directly accountable to the Home Secretary from 1829 to 2000. So, as we shall see, the rivalry of Whitehall and London government would be a running sore that showed no sign of healing at the century's end, despite a new beginning for London government in the year 2000.

The year 1900 was a new beginning too. In 1855 a London-wide government had been put in place covering more or less the city's then built-up area and provided by the Metropolitan Board of Works (MBW). The Board was not directly elected by Londoners. Instead, London was divided into thirty-nine localities, each the responsibility of a vestry or 'district board' (unions of smaller vestries). Vestries were elected by ratepayers, on the narrow franchise of the time, and had some important public health and safety functions. The vestrymen then went on to elect some of their number on to the MBW, and it was the Board that had the great task of providing London's mains sewerage and street improvements, and clearing its worst slums. It was the MBW and its brilliant engineer Sir Joseph Bazalgette who cleaned up the Thames, solved London's sewage disposal problems and built the Embankment. But its business was conducted behind closed doors and it ended its days in the stink of scandal, hustled ignominiously out of office by a directly elected London County Council (LCC) in March 1889.[2]

From 1855 to 1900 London-wide government was conducted at the expense of local self-government within London. The vestries and district boards gained a bad name for small-mindedness, parsimony and turpitude. Although standards of public life in London were higher at the end of the vestries' existence than at the beginning, reform was without doubt overdue at the end of the 1890s. But it was less the demands of administrative and democratic advancement that led to the strengthening of the local tier than the desire to reap party political advantage. And it is this – after the tensions between London as a whole and its localities, and those between London and Whitehall – that provides the third defining fact of life for the history of government in the capital: the peculiar pervasiveness and ferocity of its party politics.

This, too, was a Victorian inheritance. The LCC had been 'Liberal' from its beginnings – a unique metropolitan form of liberalism that brought together radicals and Fabian socialists in a 'Progressive' alliance. With so much of the nation at stake in the battle for London, a Conservative government was determined to clip the Council's wings. It did so by strengthening local self-government within London as a counterbalance to the London-wide body. So rivalry and conflict and controversy were bred in the bones of London governance from the very start of the century.

The London Government Act 1899 created twenty-eight new Metropolitan Borough Councils (MBCs), which took office from November 1900. They lasted sixty-four years. They had greater power to influence the lives of Londoners than the old vestries and district boards they replaced. Not only were they the sanitary, paving and streetlighting authorities but they took on responsibility for baths, washhouses, burial grounds and public libraries. A few insignificant powers also passed down from the LCC and a few others were shared with it; of more importance was the power of the boroughs to buy land and build their own council houses. Perhaps most significant of all was the symbolism of borough status and its improved position in the world of local self-government, each council with its own mayor, aldermen and all the trimmings.[3]

Although the new boroughs were conceived as a counterweight to the LCC, the County Council's power was barely dented. In fact, the opposite was true. By 1900, even though London proper had long outgrown the County boundary by some miles in almost every direction, the LCC was undisputed champion of the capital. The administrative credit of the LCC ran high enough for it to be endowed with more and more functions, even by a government of a different political complexion. The first and greatest of these was education. From 1870, London's schools had been built and run by a directly elected special-purpose authority, the School Board for London. It was a popular institution and had done its job well, but in 1902 school boards outside the capital were abolished. State education was widened to include responsibility for church schools and all schools were given to County Councils to run. By the Education (London) Act of 1903 the reform came a year later to the capital. The LCC already had some education experience, distinguishing itself by establishing and maintaining technical institutes and art schools, the first mono- and polytechnics in London. Now, from May 1904 it took on the task of schooling nearly three-quarters of a million children in 940 schools with 17,000 teachers. Its responsibilities and financial burdens doubled overnight.[4]

The School Board for London had been just one ad-hoc body among many. The most important of the rest were local boards of guardians, thirty-one of them in the County, who administered the poor laws through workhouses and out-door relief. The 814 elected guardians then went on to nominate their own central body – the Metropolitan Asylums Board (MAB), responsible for poor law hospitals (the infirmaries), some mental hospitals and all fever hospitals. The MAB had a few government appointees, but in general the local electoral principle was adhered to, even if some institutions were run by the nominees of directly elected representatives. So the Thames Conservancy Board (reconstituted 1894), the Metropolitan Water Board (1903), the Central Unemployed Body for London (1905), the Port of London Authority (1907) and the Local Pensions Committees (from 1911, to administer the Old Age Pensions Acts) were largely or entirely formed from the nominees of elected bodies, rather than government appointees. In 1900 Londoners in the County were electing some 2,350 representatives, around one for every 1,930 inhabitants; in 1999 there were 1,914 councillors in the whole of Greater London, one for every 3,500 people, governing far fewer functions than their predecessors a hundred years before. Of course, the franchise was narrower in 1900 and still weighted heavily towards the middle classes. But the electorate was wider for local elections than for parliamentary: 120,000 women had the local vote in London County, for instance, some 15 per cent of the electorate. Indeed, one of the ironic paradoxes of local democracy over the past hundred years, at its sharpest in London, was that the franchise widened to allow more and more people to vote for control over less and less.[5]

Even if London local government was more wide-ranging in 1900 than at any time after, it was still a mess of complicated, sometimes overlapping, functions, all an affront to the tidy mind:

The whole makes up a conglomerate which cannot be styled local government in any sense. There are so many ill-defined connections between the citizen and his representative that there ceases to be any effective connection at all. And London, the capital of the empire, with a glorious history, is under the heels of many interests, many cliques and parties, which play one against the other and never play for the community.[6]

That was Sir Laurence Gomme, historian, antiquarian, folklorist and chief clerk to the LCC, and by 'interests' and 'cliques' he meant local interests and the borough councils. For Gomme was a protagonist of big city government and the LCC was 'the greatest municipal authority in the world'. It never let Londoners forget it.

From 1889 to 1907 the LCC was under Progressive rule in an alliance on the council benches that spanned the class spectrum from aristocrat to working man – women could not stand for London councils until 1907, although two had been elected in 1889 until the courts forced them off. By any standards the LCC Progressives were a formidable group, including in the early years of the century figures like John Burns ('the best-known man in London'), Will Crooks, Sidney Webb, Sir John Williams Benn and many more. The Progressives were, by instinct, big spenders. They believed in state intervention and would push rates up to pay for it, raising long-term public loans on the security of London's vast rateable value for capital projects like tramway electrification, housing estates or a new County Hall. They favoured municipal enterprise over private competition, building up a large Works Department to take the profit element out of house-construction and civil engineering projects. And, in general, they took a class-based paternalistic and disapproving attitude to the people's pleasures – a nonconformist puritanism that expressed itself in the suppression of 'intoxicating drink', massage parlours, nudity on the stage and any public licentiousness brought to their notice or ferreted out. Not all Progressives pursued all these tendencies with the same vigour – the admirable Reverend Stewart Headlam, a Christian socialist from Bethnal Green elected to the Council in 1907, couldn't abide a puritan. But in the round, Progressive rule was noted for high spending, a boundless confidence in the ability of municipal enterprise to run everything for the greatest benefit of the greatest number, and an obsessive prudishness in policing public morals.[7]

At its most expansive, the Progressives' vision for London was an all-embracing welfare state forty years before the name was popularized:

the Council is becoming [1904] more and more the guardian – may I say 'the guardian angel' – of the citizen. Indeed, it now follows and guards him from the cradle to the grave. It looks after his health [inspecting common lodging houses, cowsheds and slaughterhouses, and registering midwives], personal safety [dangerous buildings and the London Fire Brigade] and afflicted relatives [in lunatic asylums]; it protects him from all sorts of public nuisances [from sewage disposal to indecent advertisements], it endeavours to see that he is decently housed, or itself houses him; it keeps an eye on his coal cellar and larder [weights and measures]; it endeavours to make his city more beautiful and convenient [street improvements], and provides electric motors [trams] and (presently) steam yachts for his convenience and pleasure; it looks after his municipal purse and corporate property, and treasures his historical memories [surveying ancient houses and running the blue plaque scheme from 1902]; it tends and enriches his broad acres and small open spaces and cheers him with music [the LCC bands played in the parks]; it sees that those he employs, directly or indirectly, enjoy tolerable wages and fair conditions; it speaks up for him in Parliament both as to what he wants and what he does not want, and . . . last and greatest of all it now looks after his children, good and bad, hoping, if it is possible, to make them better and wiser than their progenitors.[8]

This could lead, as Lord Salisbury, the Conservative prime minister who pushed through the London Government Act 1899, remarked, to 'megalomania'. Indeed, at various times the Progressive LCC sought control of London's water supply, its port, its telephones, its ambulances and its bulk electricity supply; and it opposed, as a threat to its position, the formation of a Traffic Board as recommended by the Royal Commission on London Traffic in 1905. It could be contemptuous of the new MBCs and local authorities on the County's edge – 'through-ticketing' trams run by the LCC and West Ham Corporation was opposed by the Council for years, to the clear detriment of Londoners. But the Progressives could also be adventurous in pushing forward the boundaries of municipal endeavour – inaugurating school meals for poor children in 1905 and within a year feeding 27,000 each week; or running a steamboat passenger service on the Thames through the summers of 1905–7.

A passion for collective enterprise developed in the boroughs too. Electricity generation for streetlighting branched out into domestic and industrial lighting and power – fifteen of the twenty-eight MBCs were producing all or most of their boroughs' supply needs by 1912. Camberwell had six public libraries, including one for children, and 'a magnificent Art Gallery' in 1902. Battersea was 'The Municipal Mecca', a monument to Progressivism and all its works – its Latchmere housing estate, opened 1903, was not 'tainted by off-licence or degraded by public house', to the satisfaction, no doubt, of the grateful tenants. Milk depots subsidizing pasteurized or sterilized milk for infants were opened in Battersea, Lambeth and elsewhere, despite uncertainty over boroughs' legal powers to do so. Disinfecting stations, tuberculosis dispensaries, baths and washhouses (including Russian vapour and Turkish baths), health visitors and women sanitary inspectors were all part and parcel of a thoroughly modern Metropolitan Borough.[9]

Not all borough councils pulled their weight. Paddington did not open its first public library until 1930, forty years after the most adventurous districts had established theirs. Only Southwark, Islington, Shoreditch, Stepney, Bermondsey and St Pancras attempted any slum clearance before the First World War, and that totalled just seven acres between them. Whereas St Marylebone could muster one sanitary inspector for every 8,400 residents, Wandsworth employed one for 24,000, and the LCC reported the inadequate level of sanitary inspection in Kensington and St Pancras to the Local Government Board in 1901. That, though, may have been more an act of political spite than concern for local citizens, for when Municipal Reform took over the LCC it similarly reported Progressive Bermondsey and Bethnal Green for too few sanitary inspectors in turn.

The main party political issue of these early years of the century, however, was spending and its effect on the rates. From the end of 1902, Conservatives in London, then known as Moderates, began to organize and campaign predominantly around the question of high rates caused by profligate 'socialistic' spending. They grew in members and support and remodelled their organization under the new name of Municipal Reform from March 1906. That was an especially promising year for them. Rates had risen steadily in London since the mid-1890s. They had jumped by 7 per cent when the municipalization of London's water supply led to the formation of the Metropolitan Water Board in 1903. Increased LCC expenditure on education pushed them up again in 1904 and 1905, not least because voluntary schools became chargeable to the rates. Then in 1906 the quinquennial revaluation caused a 9.3 per cent rise in the value of London property on which rates in the pound were charged. The rich paid the highest rates because they occupied the most expensive property and also because some of the cost of services in the poorest boroughs was borne by the wealthy through a limited 'equalization' mechanism. But the rich were best able to pay, and high rates bore even harder on the poor. Rates were often collected for councils by landlords as part of the worker's weekly rent. So they were a tangible burden on living costs and rising rates were resented by all classes. 'The cockney does not show much interest in municipal affairs,' reported the Progressive Percy Harris, 'But the rates he does talk of. Rates are never popular anywhere, but nowhere are they more disliked than in London.'[10]

There could, too, be some justifiable suspicion that not all rates were wisely spent. Corruption in building contracts made by the Mile End Union (Stepney) led to the prosecution of ten guardians after a scandal that broke in 1906. Public inquiries at Labour-Progressive Poplar and West Ham – not revealing corruption but questionable generosity in scales of out-relief and favouring 'local' contractors irrespective of price – took place that same year. In November 1906 Municipal Reform took control of twenty-two out of twenty-eight MBCs, compared with just eleven at the last elections in 1903.[11]

All this boded disastrously for the Progressives in the LCC election of March 1907. So it proved. This was one of the most astonishing local government elections of the century in London, hardly equalled in 1934, 1967–8 or even more than ninety years later by the contest for London's first directly elected mayor. Eighteen years of Progressive rule were brought to an end by a Conservative landslide, replacing a Progressive majority of forty-seven with a Municipal Reform majority of forty-two in a Council of 118 elected members. This was not the result of exhaustion by Progressive voters. They turned out in greater numbers than in the previous contest, despite many old favourites having been elected to Parliament in 1906 (thirty in all, including John Burns); despite the disaffection of Labour men, now with their own party in Parliament; and despite disgruntlement among the nonconformists, who continued to resent the Council as education authority supporting Rome and the Established Church 'on the rates'. The transformation was in the Municipal Reform vote, which rose by 81 per cent 'due to the polling of classes hitherto indifferent to municipal politics'. Above all this was a protest against the rates. It was whipped up by a brilliant campaign that fuelled fears of profligate socialism, municipal aggrandisement and business incompetence, all costing Londoners dear through the mounting 'debt of London' ('£110,000,000 or £146 per head'). The cost of tramway electrification and expansion, rates lost through long-empty sites at Kingsway and Aldwych, the new 'LCC ["Wastrels'"] palace' at County Hall, losses on the Thames steamboats (hit by poor summers and some managerial incompetence), the grab for bulk electricity supply in London, the allegedly rotten bricks coming out of the Norbury estate brickfields which the LCC had taken over with the land, the mud sticking to the Poplar workhouse, all used against the Progressives in a vituperative 'yellow press' campaign. Wagons filled with crumbling 'Norbury bricks' were hauled through the streets, 16 million copies of sixty-nine different leaflets were distributed, the wicked pen of George R. Sims ('Dagonet' of *The Referee*) was wielded in the Conservative cause, best of all a wonderful cartoon and poster campaign drawn by E. Huskinson, later editor of *Tatler*, brought devastating satire to bear against the Progressives. It was all to momentous – and lasting – effect. Despite a fright three years later when Progressives came within two seats of winning back the LCC, Municipal Reformers would rule at County Hall for the next twenty-seven years.[12]

From the beginning, theirs was an era of retrenchment and vigilant economy. For a time the spirit of Scrooge stalked London. The Thames steamboats, a laudable experiment that never recovered from being made an election laughing stock, were sold off (at a big loss) after three short seasons. The Works Department was shut down and 4,000 jobs were lost. Free school meals were cut on the basis that voluntary effort would provide, but it never did and they had to be reinstated after a year. Socialist Sunday Schools were banned from using LCC school premises and Mrs Gaskell's *Mary Barton* was banished from the schools for subversive tendencies.[13]

While parsimony ruled London, imperial ambition was allowed full play. The seeds of Flanders poppies were sown in the playgrounds of Waterloo – or Walworth or Wapping – in the seven years before 1914. When, just after the election of 1907, the *Daily Telegraph* provided twelve LCC schools with some union flags and flagstaffs, the Council responded by providing a flagpole at every school in London. Empire Day was first celebrated in

London's schools that May: 'Patriotic songs were sung, special lessons on British history were given, and a half-day holiday was given in the afternoon ... with the objective of bringing home to the minds of the children the greatness of their country and the duty of patriotism and loyalty.' In early 1908 the Council introduced a scheme to encourage its staff to join 'the Territorial Force'. Six years later the first of over 10,000 LCC staff went to war; 1,065 never came back.[14]

As in so much else, the First World War was a turning point in London politics and consequently in city self-government. It saw the true birth of a Labour Party in London and its swift displacement of Progressivism as the main representative party of the working class and the middle-class left.

This was a remarkable achievement. Before 1914 an Independent Labour movement in London had established a milieu of individuals, traditions and institutions that stretched far back into the struggle for democracy. But its hold on power, and its ability to influence the condition and life chances of London's working people, had been negligible. Only in West Ham and Woolwich had Labour won power with an outright majority on a borough council. Of these, West Ham's was the more virile tradition. West Ham South had sent Keir Hardie to Parliament in 1892–5, the first ever Independent Labour MP. From 1898 to 1900 the local Labour Party was 'the first in the country to control a town council'. In 1909 Labour was the largest party again but with no overall control and Will Thorne, the gas workers' leader, held Hardie's old seat for Labour from 1906. Even in West Ham, however, Labour control had been tenuous, and Municipal Reform ran the council from 1900 to 1909 and again from 1913. In Woolwich, Labour had a majority on the council only in 1903–6, though it sent Will Crooks to Parliament from 1903 to 1921, with a short break in 1910. Poplar had also established a strong but less successful tradition. The local Labour Party held the balance of power on the council from 1903 to 1906 and was heavily influential on the board of guardians; and George Lansbury was MP in Bow and Bromley in north Poplar from 1910 to 1912.[15]

Apart from West Ham, Woolwich and Poplar, Labour had succeeded in gaining merely small minority footholds on borough councils, usually quickly dislodged or dependent on Progressive or Liberal patronage. On the LCC there were only '1½ Labour members' out of 118 in 1913. And there were just three Labour MPs in London – Thorne, Crooks and C. W. Bowerman, the compositors' leader, at Deptford.[16]

A regrouping of Labour and socialist forces led to the formation of a London Labour Party (LLP) at Essex Hall, Strand, in May 1914. This helped foster local parties within the County and twenty-three had affiliated by that summer. But many were frail blooms and even boroughs like Stepney,

Bethnal Green and Camberwell had no Labour Party at all when war began.

That soon changed. There were many factors contributing to the wartime revolution in Labour's fortunes. Some were felt countrywide: pro-war Labour leaders were drafted into the Coalition Government from May 1915 and a few became national figures. Other elements had particular London effects. The growth of trade unionism, for instance, riding on the back of full employment and high wages, had a larger vacuum to fill in London – for long 'the Sphinx of Labour', according to Ben Tillett, the London dockers' leader – than in any other industrial area of the country. In east London by 1918 trade union membership grew by 80 per cent in four years, compared to 57 per cent nationally. It was among general unskilled labour, women and the low-paid that this rise had greatest impact. The National Union of General Workers' East End branches quadrupled their incomes during the war.[17]

Trade unions and political parties were also coopted into the burgeoning local bureaucracies that total war and its tightening central controls required. They took part in the local Prince of Wales Fund Relief Committees set up to assist widows; in the conscription tribunals and pensions committees; in the National Service and Food Control Committees. They set up their own organizations to put pressure on local government and to highlight abuses: like the London Food Vigilance Committee, formed by the LLP and London Cooperative Society, with thirty district committees to report profiteering and to campaign for rationing and the sale of commodities at cost.

All this experience of practical organization and the operation of the local state helped boost self-belief and sharpen class consciousness. The Russian Revolutions of 1917, the increasingly vocal and effective anti-war propaganda waged by the left wing of the Labour Party and the capital's 'rebel milieu' – that factious mix of socialists and anarchists who at last found some common ground in fighting the war – helped radicalize the political agenda in London. Swept along with the torrent, the Labour Party reformed its constitution in 1918. Its ambitious programme put housing as top priority for post-war reconstruction, a popular move in London especially. Then the Representation of the People Act 1918 gave the parliamentary vote for the first time to women, reward for wartime sacrifice and recognition of the new place they had won in civil society. This raised their proportion of London's local government electorate from 15 per cent to 50 per cent, almost doubling the County electorate in the process.[18]

Although these changes were in place by Armistice Day, Lloyd George's cut-and-run 'Khaki Election' of December 1918 threw Labour into confusion. Local parties were without organization or key supporters, the demobilization of men from the forces had barely begun and many working-class districts were without a local party altogether. Out of 394 Labour candidates nationally, just sixty were elected, a mere four from Greater London. Even so, just fighting it gave some nascent parties self-confidence, experience and a taste for blood. Major Clement Attlee, returning to Stepney after demobilization in early 1919, found, 'For the first time, the political Labour Movement was organized': there were active parties in Mile End, Limehouse, and Whitechapel and St George's.[19]

The next test was the long-postponed LCC election of March 1919. There had not been one for six years but despite this and the enlarged franchise, just one in six voters turned out in contested seats and twenty-seven out of sixty-one divisions returned unopposed candidates, mainly in middle-class areas. Yet the first signs of what Labour could do now became apparent. Campaigning on a platform of 'Home Rule for Greater London', rates abolition, more house-building and municipalization of coal, bread, meat and milk supplies as well as passenger transport, Labour nearly trebled its 1913 vote and won fifteen seats on the LCC. Next month, Labour scored more victories in the poor law guardians' elections, increasing its representation in the County from twenty-one to 135 seats out of 500 and gaining control of the Boards in Poplar and Woolwich.

From the spring and summer of 1919 the mood of London and the nation shifted. Anger and impatience for improved conditions showed itself in a number of unconnected incidents. Race riots flared up in Limehouse (May) and Poplar (June). A demonstration in May on behalf of unemployed ex-servicemen was broken up by police baton charges in Downing Street. Soldiers whose demobilization had been delayed rioted up and down the country in June and July. Industrial militancy brought the Metropolitan Police out on strike at the end of July, with some looting and rioting at King's Cross and the Elephant and Castle. Young men waged pitched battles with the police through July and a scorching August. Discontent over rising prices forced Parliament to rush through a Profiteering Act. There were demonstrations in September against evictions in the East End and a national rail strike proved 100 per cent solid in the capital. These were hectic times, with bayonets and revolvers common in London street fights, with tanks in Liverpool and gunboats on the Mersey, with talk of Bolshevik plots uncovered by police raids in west London. This was the revolutionary outpouring of discontent that the Armistice celebrations had temporarily deferred.

London Labour was the surprised beneficiary. Alive to the changing moment, the LLP launched a membership campaign in July. At a special party conference in September, Herbert Morrison, Secretary of the LLP since 1915, declared it would run 1,000 candidates for the 1,362 seats in contest at the MBC elections on 1 November. Housing was top of the agenda. George Lansbury in Poplar called for the replacement of the 'houseowners, jerry builders, and people interested in preserving slums' by 'our own men and women'. Dr Alfred Salter of Bermondsey demanded playgrounds, free gymnasia, recreation halls, public libraries and bathrooms in every working-class street. 'The Irish vote' was said to have been captured by Labour following the party's commitment to Home Rule in 1918, and Irish candidates were prominent in Battersea, Stepney, Fulham and elsewhere. The 'mass of East End Jewry' had switched to the Labour Party, who supported the Balfour Declaration's call for a Jewish homeland in Palestine. New council responsibilities under the Maternity and Child Welfare Act 1918, coupled with the expanded franchise, meant that 'Never did women show such an interest in municipal matters.'[20]

The result in many parts of London was a Labour landslide that would not be bettered for eighteen years. Labour won outright control of twelve of the twenty-eight MBCs and was the biggest party in two more. In the out-County districts it retained West Ham and won Enfield, London's second great armaments district after Woolwich. There were now Labour councillors everywhere in inner London except the City of Westminster. Virtually all of them had no experience whatsoever. The Greenwich Labour Party, now in power, had only been formed a year before. Stepney's Labour majority included just two ex-Liberals with any experience as councillors, and Southwark's none at all. The six Labour councillors elected in one north Wandsworth ward were the 'most astonished people in Clapham'.[21]

Amid all the celebrations Herbert Morrison sounded a cautious note in the LLP's monthly journal. Headlined 'A Grave Responsibility', he warned that Labour 'can no longer engage with complete freedom in criticism which is not associated with responsibility . . .' The 'gentleman who, on November 4, excitedly demanded to know from me "when your Borough Councils are to start the revolution" was talking through his hat . . .'[22] But on 4 November, and for some time after, the red flag flew over many of London's town halls. And Morrison found himself battling to restrain a tendency to adventurous and illegal direct action led by a Christian pacifist old enough to be his father.

George Lansbury – 'Good Old George' – was born in Halesworth, Suffolk, in 1859, the son of a railway-builders' clerk who travelled the country with his young family, settling in east London from 1866. His own working life was rich and varied – clerking, charcoal burning, coal heaving, emigrant life in Australia, running an inherited sawmill business, founding and editing the *Daily Herald*. His political mission was to 'enlist . . . one great army . . . to establish the Kingdom of Heaven on earth'. An unworldly radiance shone from his writings, his speeches moved audiences openly to tears, he inspired love and admiration in nearly all who met him. Lansbury's transcendental vision of 'the New Jerusalem' encompassed most spheres of human experience. Women would secure equality with men – he had been an active and self-sacrificing supporter of the pre-war suffragettes. The old Poplar would be swept away to be replaced by housing estates with their own theatres, parks with their own dance halls. Bodies would be rebuilt by sunbathing and swimming and sport cleansed of the cash nexus. 'Man-made evil' would be cast out. Lansbury was most comfortable on his chosen stage of east London rather than any national arena, even though Labour's misfortunes were to thrust him there. East London was his power base and he wished for no other. He was always more Poplar patriot than London leader. When it came to pursuing the interests of his people, he would take on the rest of London or the nation. His Christianity insulated him from cries of illegality or divisiveness. If the ends were right and the route to get there was non-violent and broke no moral law, then the means had to be right too.[23]

All this he showed in perhaps the most dramatic events in the modern history of London government. And, just like 1907, boring old rates were at the heart of the drama.

The post-war slump of 1920–21 hit the East End harder than any other part of London. The slump was one factor pushing rates up. The cost of poor relief increased as a consequence of unemployment, and to pay for this relief the Poplar Board of Guardians raised the poor rate that Poplar Borough Council had to collect on its behalf. But rates also rose because the new Labour council had increased the wages of its staff as one of its first acts on gaining power, and because it spent more to improve its health and other services. The council also had to collect the rates – or precepts – that other organizations like the LCC, the MAB and the Metropolitan Police required from all the boroughs of London, and these demands too were for more money than ever before. As Poplar Borough Council came to set its rate for 1921–22 it looked as though rates would have to rise from 15s 6d in the pound in 1919–20 (the figure inherited from Poplar's wartime Municipal Reform administration and already by far the highest in London) to 25s 6d. That would be an increase in two years of nearly 3s a week on the rent of an average working-class house. And that at a time when high unemployment meant that many were in no position to pay.

Alarmed at the prospect, partly of its own making, the council resolved in March 1921 not to levy the precepts of the LCC, MAB and Metropolitan Police. That action was unlawful but it cut Poplar's rates bill by more than a third. It also forcefully revived the old Progressive policy of 'rates equalization' for London: that Londoners should pay the same for local services wherever they lived in the capital, just as the citizens of Manchester or Birmingham would do.

Political pandemonium followed. In June 1921 the Municipal Reform-controlled LCC and MAB won orders of mandamus in the high court ordering Poplar Borough Council to collect and pay the precepts. The council refused to do so. Its appeal was substantially dismissed in July and the LCC and MAB issued committal proceedings. Thirty-six councillors and the town clerk were served with writs to appear at the High Court on 29 July 1921 to show why they should not go to prison for contempt of court.

The councillors and 2,000 supporters marched the five miles from Poplar town hall to the law courts under a famous banner:

POPLAR

BOROUGH COUNCIL

marching to the

HIGH COURT

and possibly to

PRISON

to secure

EQUALISATION OF RATES

for

POOR BOROUGHS

The Lord Chief Justice discharged four councillors and the town clerk but gave the remaining thirty-two councillors fourteen days in which to levy a rate. If they did not, they would go to prison. A special vacation hearing of the Court of Appeal extended the deadline to the end of August.

In the meantime, Sir Alfred Mond, the Coalition Minister of Health, gave some relief to Poplar. He ordered that better-off borough councils in London should make higher payments to the Metropolitan Common Poor Fund. These would then be passed on to the poorer boroughs. Poplar would benefit to the tune of 10d off the rates – compared to the 10s in the pound it was saving by not levying the precepts. This small but symbolic victory was not enough. On the night of the hearing in the Court of Appeal the council set its rate for the third quarter without the precepts. There would be no further debate on the issue within the deadline set by the court.

The first arrest by the sheriff's officers took place on 1 September, the last a week later. All five women councillors were arrested on 5 September and taken to Holloway gaol. Twenty-five men – thirty councillors in all were imprisoned – went to Brixton. The squalor and degradation of prison life caught most of them off their guard. One of the women was seven months pregnant and nine councillors were fifty or over, with Lansbury the oldest at sixty-two, and several were quickly removed to the prison infirmaries. But they soon established a routine which secured their self-respect in the face of considerable privation. They remained, after all, the duly elected burgesses of Poplar. Council business was conducted, in the presence of the hapless town clerk, in frequent sessions at Brixton prison. Concession after concession was screwed from the prison authorities, to the delight of the Labour press, until the Poplar councillors became an intolerable irritant to the Home Office. And to the leaders of the London Labour Party.

The councillors' unshakeable stand of 'release before negotiation' firmly stifled any discussions on the equalization issue until they were released from prison. This impasse was finally broken when Lloyd George set up a meeting between Morrison and Mond, who agreed to establish a conference on rates equalization in London. So that they could attend this conference, the Poplar councillors were released by the high court on 12 October, after some five or six weeks in prison. They made no fulsome apology to the court, merely regretting the disobedience that had been necessary to safeguard their community. They were freed to enthusiastic scenes in Poplar and an audible sigh of relief elsewhere.

The London conference on rates equalization was in broad terms a victory for Poplar. The subsidy for out-relief to the unemployed was increased and shared more equally among the boroughs. Fifteen MBCs were better off because they had to collect lower poor rates for their local guardians. Poplar benefited most, its rates cut by 5s 6d in the pound. Rates in the richer boroughs, including some run by Labour, had to rise to pay for the higher subsidy.[24]

So 'Poplarism' entered the language – and the intellectual heritage and mythology – of the British Labour movement. It stood for no-holds-barred direct action on behalf of the poor against an unjust system. But it had unintended consequences on London Labour politics and on the ever-awkward relationship between central and local government in the capital. Initially, the most significant impact was on Labour unity in London. Poplar polarized opinion within the LLP and among the Labour MBCs. The weight of opinion fell heavily against Lansbury and his comrades, who seemed not unduly worried as a result: they had never claimed a brief for London as a whole and had done little to take other boroughs with them. Only in next-door Bethnal Green did a council actively follow Poplar's lead, and the Bethnal Green leadership was openly Communist-dominated.

Stepney too had begun to move in support of Poplar. But outside the East End, Poplar provoked open criticism during March to August, and clandestine undermining, according to Lansbury, while the councillors were in gaol. Morrison, Mayor of Hackney at the time, was the lead tactician of the right and was able to take the LLP with him.[25]

Disunity damaged Labour in the run-up to the local elections of 1922. Labour seemed to be speaking with two voices in London, and Poplarism doubtless frightened off many potential middle-class supporters. But there were other sources of discontent. Despite a flurry of rate reductions in the half-year before the November 1922 MBC elections, rates in 1922–3 were on average 36 per cent higher in London than in 1919–20. The high wages of council staff under Labour, which these rates sustained, could be an affront to workers in low-paid or insecure employment. Trade union closed shops in Labour boroughs encouraged rumours of favouritism and petty corruption in the allocation of jobs and casual work. And central government policies and Municipal Reform control of the LCC left little scope for borough councils to make headway against unemployment and the housing question, the two great problems of the day and the party's main battleground of 1919.

These difficulties, as well as a secret pact between Municipal Reform and London Liberals to form a *de facto* anti-socialist alliance supported by most of the London press, all took their considerable toll on Labour's support. In November 1922 came electoral disaster at the MBC elections. Labour lost control of Camberwell, Greenwich, Islington, St Pancras, Stepney, Fulham, Hackney and Southwark; in the last three Labour lost every seat. It retained Battersea, Bermondsey (which had only gone Labour through by-elections in 1921), Deptford, Poplar and Woolwich; in Bethnal Green it was the largest party. In outer London, where it had less to lose, Edmonton, Enfield and Erith had all gone by 1922. London's revolutionary years were over.[26]

There were further defeats to come. A few Labour boards of guardians, Poplar prominent among them, insisted on paying relief at scales higher than the level qualifying for government subsidy. District auditors sought surcharges against individual guardians at Bermondsey and Poplar; then against Poplar councillors and councillors in Woolwich, Battersea and Bermondsey who refused to reduce their employees' £4 per week minimum wage, fixed at a time of high post-war inflation but now much above comparable London wage rates; then against the West Ham guardians, where Neville Chamberlain rushed through emergency powers in 1926, appointing commissioners to displace the elected board and impose government relief scales. Surcharges threatening the imprisonment and bankruptcy of nearly 100 London councillors and guardians, fought in legal actions up to the House of Lords, were eventually cancelled when wages and relief scales were forced down. Then, from 1930, boards of guardians were abolished altogether. This had been a reform advocated by many from the early years of the century, but one that government saw fit to tackle only after experiencing truculent Labour guardians, especially in London. The guardians' powers were given to the politically safer County and County Borough Councils, all of them Conservative-run in the capital apart from in West Ham.[27]

The defeat of organized labour in the General Strike of May 1926 was followed in London by bitter internecine struggles in local Labour parties to banish the pro-Communist left and assert an unimpeachable constitutionalism. The left was strongest and the struggles were most unforgiving in London. The 'atmosphere' at party meetings was 'savage with hate'. 'Unofficial Labour' left-wing candidates split the Labour vote at local elections in Bethnal Green, Battersea (where the Indian pro-Communist Shapurji Saklatvala was elected for Battersea North from 1922–3 and 1924–9), West Ham and many other places. By 1929 the Labour Party nationally had expelled fifteen London parties.[28]

Yet despite all these defeats the Labour Party slowly widened its appeal to London voters and deepened the affection and loyalty it inspired in many sections of the London working class. The housing record of Labour in power showed that it could with time deliver the goods on London's most pressing problem. Woolwich led the way with over 2,500 homes by 1931. Even little Hayes and Harlington – Labour through the unionized workforce of the Gramophone Company's huge works – had built 1,300 houses for a population of 24,000; while Municipal Reform Tottenham, with an enduring reputation as a slumlord-run authority from the early years of the century and a population six times bigger, had built just 815.

In demonstrating what could be done, Bermondsey was London Labour's showcase. 'If I were designing a coat of arms for the Borough of Bermondsey,' wrote a friendly reporter in 1928, 'I should suggest a healthy child in a green field with the motto, "It can be done".' Bermondsey's public health department was nationally renowned for its work on tuberculosis, its antenatal and baby clinics and health visiting service, its nurseries and dental clinics, its health education programme and hygiene films. In 1927 its new baths and public laundry provided 'Turkish, Russian, vapour and slipper baths equal to those of any London hotel, for we maintain that what is good for the West End is equally good for the workers of Bermondsey'. They were built by direct labour, designed by council architects and engineers, with the widest span of any reinforced concrete roof in the country, and powered by the council's own electricity. Perhaps Bermondsey was best known for the work of its Beautification Committee, led by Councillor Ada Salter, which

> aims at growing flowers in every vacant spot and planting trees in every street. The borough possesses no open spaces, so the Council has converted all the old churchyards into gardens . . . the people have joined in the work, and many-coloured blooms are to be seen in almost every front garden, while hardly a tenement is without a box on every window sill.

Council gardeners bred a new strain of dwarf dahlia which they proposed to name the 'Bermondsey Gem'. The achievements of these years were collectively commemorated as 'Bermondsey's Revolution'.[29]

In the great task of winning Londoners' votes, Labour's leaders sought especially to appeal to two elements: the middle classes and women. In fact there is not much evidence that Labour developed an appeal outside working-class London between the wars. It was when the middle classes left for the suburbs, concentrating workers ever more solidly in previously mixed areas, that inner London moved irresistibly into the Labour fold, taking first the central districts and slowly advancing outwards.[30]

But Labour had more success with women. Councils could do most for those domestic issues seen at the time as principally the woman's sphere. Two-thirds of London County's constituency parties had formed women's sections by June 1921. Where the London Cooperative Society was strong, in outer London in particular, Women's Cooperative Guilds replaced the sections as the focus of political work and education. International Women's Day was celebrated with marches, demonstrations and choral singing. On the Becontree estate the Coop issued a free monthly newspaper to 10,000 households. Prominent Labour women, Guild members like Annie Barnes of Stepney, found themselves oracles for their neighbours: 'People used to queue outside my door with their problems.' The final widening of the suffrage to give women electoral equality in 1928 reaped a reward for Labour in its general election victory a year later. As at West Fulham, with its slogan

> Women voters, choose your hero,
> Cast your vote for Dr Spero.

And yes, they did.[31]

The Morrison Years: London Government, 1934–64

In April 1915 the London Labour Party appointed Herbert Morrison as its secretary. He was then twenty-seven. His political mentor, Dr Alfred Salter of Bermondsey, fixed him up with a one-room office near Bricklayer's Arms goods station and it was from here that Morrison set out to build 'the most powerful local political organization ever to exist in this country'.[32]

Herbert Morrison was born in Brixton in 1888. In many ways he was a misfit. He had just one good eye – schoolfellows called him 'Ball of fat' because of his blank right eyeball. His father was a Tory policeman, a peculiar inheritance uncomfortably neither working nor middle class. An office worker all his life, Morrison rejected the workerist politics of the Labour left and Communist Party, going out of his way to stress the common interests of workers and the middle classes. Morrison was a rare and brilliant combination of administrator and visionary. If the administrator occupied the driving seat, the visionary looked over his shoulder, a conscience to guide the daily manoeuvring of practical politics. He was a thoroughbred workhorse with restless energy for detail, whether of electioneering or legislative reform or the financial management of giant undertakings. Admiring these skills in others predisposed him towards professionals and officials, and confirmed him in a framework of legality, of 'democratic constitutionalism', and of 'peaceful social transformation' rather than the 'chaos' that followed direct action. Within those boundaries he was a radical. 'I am all for speed', whether of municipalization, the public control of London Transport or practical building projects, from housing estates to hospitals to Thames bridges. 'Labour Gets Things Done!' was his triumphalist slogan of the late 1930s. He was a passionate centralist and state collectivist who believed that planning through big organizations 'in the communal interest' was the motor of socialism. Thinking big, he always took a London-wide view, often at odds with the interests of borough parties. Convinced that he and his planners knew best, he had the paternalist self-confidence to transform ideas into action and, in general, the skills to make them work.

Yet this arch-pragmatist nurtured a utopian soul. The Labour Party's purpose was 'to create a new social life, a more educated democracy, and an always improving type of youth, of manhood and womanhood'. He tried, and failed, to make the LLP a whole way of life, with Labour choral societies and symphony orchestras, theatre societies and football clubs. A talented ballroom dancer, he encouraged Labour town halls to institutionalize Saturday hops. An admirer of women, he took a patriarchal interest in their welfare and dreamed of virtually labour-free homes cleaned by vacuum-wielding council staff and municipal meals ordered by postcard the night before. A dreamer's vein of romance and sentimentality was most evident in his passion for his city: 'I love London; I love the Londoners.'[33] And, despite a glittering career in national politics, London was the object of Morrison's head and heart for the best years of his long public life.

By 1934 Morrison had been secretary of the LLP for nearly twenty years. In that time his own career had flourished. He was elected to the LCC in 1922, was MP for south Hackney in 1923–4 and 1929–31, and had been Minister of Transport when MacDonald's second government collapsed in 1931. There he just had time to begin the nationalization of London's buses, trams and tubes. But the LLP's main prize was a Labour LCC and these had been twenty largely unrewarding years as far as that was concerned.

Through the 1920s Labour had struggled to win 40 per cent of the LCC vote and its damaging political setback nationally in 1931 cost it dearly in London as elsewhere. Yet whereas Labour in the rest of the country still reeled from that shock until the outbreak of war, London Labour recovered with remarkable speed. Morrison, full-time at the LLP's Westminster Bridge Road headquarters, played a major part in that swift comeback. So too did demography, as the suburbanizing middle classes left central London increasingly to the workers. And so did the poor showing of Municipal Reform, now in power for twenty-seven years, especially in the capital's top political issue, housing.

It was Municipal Reform's housing record that Labour attacked head on in the dramatic LCC election of 1934. The LLP lost no opportunity to contrast the worn-out tawdry record of their geriatric opponents with the vigour, youth and energy of London Labour under Morrison's leadership. Labour's slogan – 'Up with the Houses! Down with the Slums!' – 'flashes from hoardings everywhere'. Some 15,000 copies of a penny handout for electors were sold, 26,000 bill posters distributed, 510,000 leaflets handed out and loudspeaker vans were deployed for the first time in a British election. There were special issues of *London News* (the party's monthly newsletter), a barrage (two or three a week) of *Election Notes* advising candidates and party workers on every aspect of the election, and press releases for 'Labour editors'. Labour's campaign was imaginative, relentless and brilliantly successful. The party reaped 51 per cent of the popular vote and polled more votes than any previous party at an LCC election. Labour now had sixty-nine councillors, thirty-four more than in 1931 and a majority of fourteen over Municipal Reform. Similar victories were achieved in the MBC elections of November 1934, where Labour captured fifteen out of twenty-eight councils.[34]

Despite enormous efforts in 1937 by a confident Municipal Reform to regain their lost hold on London, Labour improved on their position at both County and borough level: seventeen borough councils and seventy-five councillors out of 124 on the LCC in an unprecedentedly high poll of 43 per cent. This was a grip on inner London that remained inviolable from 1934 to 1968; and reasonably secure, with the odd wobble here and there, from 1971 till the end of the century. Similarly, in the older parts of outer London, Labour became the natural party of power during the 1930s: West Ham, East Ham, Barking, Dagenham, Leyton and Walthamstow in the east; Tottenham, Edmonton, Enfield in the north; but in the west and north-west only Willesden, Southall, Hayes and Harlington, and Uxbridge; and in the vast expanse of south London outside the County just Erith, far out on the riverside east of Woolwich. For the next sixty years outer London would broadly maintain this political geography of a Labour east and north and a Conservative south and west, though always in unstable equilibrium and each with enclaves in the enemy camp.[35]

The first five Morrison years saw Labour keep its promises to the people of London. Housing was the top political agenda item, but there were many other important concerns as well. The dithering over whether Waterloo Bridge should be replaced or repaired for restricted traffic only, which had haunted the Municipal Reform LCC for ten years, was ended in typical fashion when Labour pushed through a demolition scheme immediately on taking office. Eventually government was shamed into funding 60 per cent of Sir Giles Gilbert Scott's new structure – one masterpiece lost, another gained. 'Labour Gets Things Done!' was largely founded on this equivocal triumph. Then the Green Belt, a personal passion of Morrison, was begun with the acquisition of 565 acres in the first three years of office. Then education. The Labour LCC built five secondary schools and thirty new or enlarged elementary schools, providing new places for 21,000 children. Class sizes were reduced: 'Dark, drab classrooms, "open-trough sanitation", and flickering gas-jets gave place to wide, airy classrooms, hot- and cold-water services, medical inspection rooms and the provision of central assembly halls.'[36]

This attack on the Victorian legacy of London's public institutions was extended, too, to where it was needed most: in the hospitals and workhouses inherited from the poor law. These poor law establishments had been built and owned by local government but had come out of the hands of the guardians and Metropolitan Asylums Board only from April 1930. After that the 'public assistance' and public hospital authorities in Greater London were the LCC, the Middlesex, Surrey, Essex and Kent County Councils, and the County Borough Councils of West and East Ham and Croydon. Overnight the LCC had inherited from 'some 30 different authorities –

140 hospitals, schools [for pauper children, mainly orphans] and other institutions, 75,000 beds and about 180,000 people who are in receipt of relief', together with 26,000 extra staff.

The humanization of poor relief that this might have brought was held back, in the County at least, by the spending cuts which Municipal Reform felt duty-bound to impose after the 1931 economic crisis. Public assistance 'scales' became iron fetters preventing the humane consideration of individual circumstances. Within limits, much of this improved under Labour. Under the less than ringing slogan 'Humanity without Extravagance', relief was immediately extended to 11,000 people harshly refused it under Municipal Reform. Labour withdrew the most spiteful of the instructions to relieving officers – like calling at mealtimes to see if a neighbour was being treated to a cup of tea, in which case relief would be stopped. Among the long-term unemployed who had exhausted unemployment benefit and were on poor relief, married men were no longer separated from their families and sent for long periods to 'residential training centres' out of London; although the retention for 'exceptional cases' of three 'labour colonies' at Hollesley Bay, Suffolk, and elsewhere, brought the Labour LCC under Communist fire in 1934–5. The 'general mixed workhouse', the most punitive weapon in the poor law armoury, was abolished by the LCC. And institutions for the destitute elderly were humanized with curtains, 'chintz counterpanes in gay colours', wirelesses and less uniform attire.[37]

Finally, the hospitals. The great voluntary hospitals (like Bart's, the London, St Thomas's, Guy's and so on) were run as private charities. They had failed to keep up with technical advances and modern patient demand. In 1939 'a famous surgeon' writing in the *Lancet* complained they were 'years behind the times . . . with an equipment and in surroundings which would not be tolerated in a small provincial town in Sweden'. But until 1930 there was no real alternative to the voluntary hospitals, through waiting lists or 'paying beds', other than poor law 'infirmaries' which had grown out of provision for the 'sick poor'. These institutions provided 76 per cent of hospital beds in London County and all transferred to the LCC. Despite increasing use by people who were not receiving poor relief, '[o]ver them all hung the atmosphere of the Poor Law tradition', even after three years of Municipal Reform control.[38]

It was Labour who removed the poor law taint from the public hospitals. 'It was with some satisfaction that Herbert Morrison was able to inform the Council that the only way a relieving officer could enter a LCC hospital was by becoming a patient.' Big modernization programmes were implemented across London, specialisms were developed at individual sites for use by all Londoners, outpatient services introduced, scientific inquiry and innovation were fostered, staff hours were cut and salaries raised, 'maternity services were, literally, transformed beyond recognition', and the council's twenty-one mental hospitals with 34,000 in-patients had £1 million invested in them. This was the beginning of a revolution in London's hospital care. A vast amount was still to be done but a great start had been made.[39]

Lord Snell, first Labour chairman of the LCC in 1934, in his inaugural speech to the council had paid implicit tribute to the past twenty-seven years of Municipal Reform rule and the eighteen years of the Progressives before that: 'The breath of scandal has never touched [the Council]: its honour is very dear to all of us, and to the citizens of London.'[40] But that could not be said for all of London local government. If Progressives had been tarnished by the workhouse contract scandals of the early 1900s, and if Municipal Reform had never shaken off the mantle of the slum landlord, then Labour quickly built its own fiefdoms compromised by trade union power, nepotism and the petty purchase of influence.

The connection between municipal trade unionism and the Labour Party probably had some ill-effects from the beginning. This need not be exaggerated. Boroughs could still achieve mighty things for their communities while also creating jobs and protecting the living standards of those who filled them. But at worst it put political power into the hands of employees who had most to gain from secure and well-paid employment in easy conditions of labour; where jobs went not to people best equipped to fill them but to those best connected with councillors and trade union officials with influence at the town hall; and where scarce council houses could be allocated on the same warped criteria.

In inner London perhaps Stepney in the 1930s and early 1940s was the most notorious example. It was joked that 'SBC' (Stepney Borough Council) really stood for 'Sons, Brothers and Cousins'. And not far away in outer London, West Ham County Borough Council provoked similar resentment; it was said that in order to get a job with the council a man had to be a member of West Ham Football Club, the Labour Party and a Freemason. In 1937 Morrison and the LLP stepped in to stop Stepney filling jobs on unemployment relief schemes only on the personal recommendation of a councillor because of the enormous scope such a system would give to pelf. 'There has been a great deal of suggestion and criticism with regard to appointment to the public service in the East End which have been exploited by Fascists and other opponents of the Party.' Councillor Morry Davis, Labour leader of Stepney and long suspected of fondness for a backhander, eventually went to gaol in 1944 for trying to bribe a railway official who had caught him travelling without a ticket.[41]

Morry Davis was also the Air Raid Precautions (ARP) Controller for

Stepney. This was a typical East End appointment. In the rest of London, it was almost always town clerks or other officials who held this office. But in Stepney and West Ham the Labour Party only trusted its own. ARP had been an emerging priority for London local government since July 1935.[42] At that time the preparation of local schemes to protect the civilian population from air attack was voluntary. Many Labour authorities had traditions that espoused to some degree pacifism and war resistance – Salter of Bermondsey was a Quaker pacifist, Morrison had been a conscientious objector for political reasons during the First World War. So some boroughs refused to put schemes in place. Bermondsey, for instance, declined unanimously to establish an ARP committee as late as January 1937. However, the Air Raid Precautions Act 1937 made schemes compulsory in London from March 1938. Borough councils, the City and the LCC were instructed to put in place arrangements for recruiting air-raid wardens, rescue parties and auxiliary fire services, and for setting up casualty clearing stations, evacuation plans, gas detection and decontamination, and control and coordination measures.

That September the Munich crisis at last brought home the dangers of war to everyone. Forty million gas masks were distributed at council 'fitting centres' across the country. An epidemic of trench-digging broke out in the London parks in response to a Home Office instruction to provide trenches for 10 per cent of the population who might be caught in the open by bombing. In Hackney, short of municipal spades, a council appeal brought out hundreds of enthusiastic allotment-holders who dug in the parks and marshes enough trenches for 100,000 (about half the population) to fall into. They had to be guarded by night watchmen until eventually they were filled in again.[43]

Then, on 1 September 1939, the first great evacuation of children and mothers and hospital patients from London began. It was organized by the LCC, even for people outside the County. In three days over 600,000 were moved by rail and coach from the city 'without a single accident or casualty'. Moving out proved easier than moving in. Because fewer than expected had turned up for evacuation, and because trains were also needed to shift troops and essential personnel in and out of London, any train available was filled and moved out. In this way 'most' evacuees ended up in different areas from those originally intended for them. The ensuing administrative chaos tied up thousands of bureaucrats in the country reception areas and left the London exporting districts sorting out the mess for many months to come.[44]

London local government had planned precautions in the reasonable expectation that bombing would stretch them to the limit. But no one anticipated the onslaught that began with the terrible raid of 7 September

1940. For the next eight months Londoners and London government had to face the most furious bombardment of any civilian population in history to that time. At first they were overwhelmed. Later they recovered, in some places faster than others. And it was an unlucky fate that left the area least fit to cope confronting the worst of the raids. This was the East End, especially Stepney and West Ham.

Theirs was an ordeal by fire of utterly unprecedented ferocity.

By 8 p.m. on that first day of the London Blitz, the West Ham Fire Brigade had called for 500 more pumps; at 11 p.m. there were six extensive fires in and around the London Docks and six in the Surrey Commercial Docks area on a scale that were judged to call for over 1,000 pumps; the Royal Docks were heavily attacked and fires in the vicinity of the Royal Albert Dock and the George V Dock were completely out of hand. The heat from the fire at the Surrey Docks blistered paint on a fire boat 300 yards away. Sixty craft were sunk or destroyed on the river during this night, and blazing barges, their moorings having burnt through, drifted down river with the tide and threatened the riverside wharves. There were major fires at Woolwich Arsenal among stacked boxes of ammunition and crates of nitro-glycerine, and among the warehouse fires were pepper fires, rubber, paint, sugar, tea and grain fires, all with their own special difficulties and dangers.[45]

'In the main,' the official history of civil defence commented, 'the brigades stood up well to this great onslaught.' And in the main so did most of the other frontline services of London local government. The hospitals distinguished themselves. They were helped by the extra capacity – hutted wards, additional staff – granted them from 1938 to cope with the great numbers of casualties that bombing was expected to bring but never quite did. The air-raid warden and rescue services, with some exceptions as we have seen, worked to exhaustion with almost the dedication and heroism of the emergency fire service. There were, though, many problems early on with shelters. The government at first resisted using the tubes, which had proved popular if unauthorized shelters during the First World War. But Londoners forced the authorities to open them, sometimes smashing down gates and barriers to gain entry. The sanitary arrangements in large public shelters run by local authorities could at first be woefully inadequate, especi-ally in Stepney and the Silvertown area of West Ham, which had been virtually cut off from the rest of London by fire in the first bombing and where some evacuation had to be arranged by boat.

The second great problem was a lack of provision for the homeless. This was a failure of planning. Unaccountably, homelessness caused by bombing had been largely ignored by the government-directed ARP schemes. While casualties had been exaggerated, the huge destructive power of high-explosive bombs and the damage to house property that would be caused had been left out of the account. So had the problem of unexploded bombs, which rendered whole streets unusable until the bombs were defused. Some 'Rest Centres' were provided by the LCC in places and with equipment prescribed by government. But they were planned as poor law institutions because homeless people had always been thought of as paupers; and they were provisioned only for stays of a day or two, whereas people could be without homes for weeks on end. So there were too few centres and those there were had inadequate blankets, no spare clothing for hundreds bombed out in their night-clothes, no cooking facilities. There was tinned food but seldom a tin opener – one centre in Bethnal Green could muster 'two spoons and a blunt knife'. 'In the light of dimmed hurricane lamps' at a centre in Stepney, 'some 200 to 300 homeless people had the use of 10 pails and coal scuttles as lavatories'; situated near the door, people coming in trod the overflowing filth throughout the building. Some nineteen days after the first attack 25,000 homeless Londoners were living in conditions little better than these. In all, 1.4 million people in the London civil defence region – one in six of the Greater London population – were made homeless at some time during that first Blitz of September 1940 to May 1941.[46]

By February 1941 conditions had greatly improved in the shelters and rest centres. In disorganized Stepney and West Ham local voluntary organizations proved invaluable in putting things right, despite the resistance of local authorities who thought they could, or at least should, do everything. Indeed, councils had more to do than ever before: providing the Londoners' Meal Service at rest centres and shelters and mobile canteens in bomb-damaged streets and 'Civic Restaurants'; organizing salvage drives, savings and dig-for-victory campaigns and Forces' book collections; billeting foreign refugees and the homeless in requisitioned houses; managing greatly expanded ambulance and fire services (the London Fire Brigade grew from 2,500 pre-war to 25,000) until the latter were temporarily nationalized in the summer of 1941, after the main London Blitz had ended; arranging for the Home Tuition Service to teach returned evacuees or children who had never left; putting together concert parties and ballet, theatre and entertainment programmes in the parks, called 'holidays at home'; and planning for a future London once the war had ended – Abercrombie had been commissioned just after the first Blitz ended and the County of London Plan was published by the summer of 1943.[47]

In these so difficult years, Herbert Morrison remained an exemplar. From the moment war was declared he worked day and night at County Hall, sleeping on a camp bed next to his desk. Churchill brought him into government on 30 October 1940, three weeks or so after bombing began, as Minister for the Home Office and Home Security, specifically for his unique experience of London and Londoners. One of his first tasks was to replace Councillor Davis as Stepney's ARP Controller, eventually installing the town clerk of Islington in his place. In Morrison's trips out to the areas of worst damage he was almost as recognizable as Churchill: people 'crowded round, calling "Good old 'Erb!"' Ritchie Calder, one of the sternest critics of local government failures in the East End, thought Morrison's arrival saved 'a worsening situation'. There was not a loss of courage among the people but 'bitter *resentment* was growing . . . The very fact of Mr Morrison's appointment was a reassurance.'[48]

At the end of hostilities local government had learned to play a larger part in the lives of Londoners than ever before in history. Though not apparent in 1945, the war years were in fact the zenith of London self-government, at least as measured by the services it managed. For although the fire brigades were returned in April 1948 other, even more important, functions were taken away. The nationalization programme of the first Attlee government largely rested on removing institutions and staff from local government and running them centrally. First, the National Health Service vested the hospitals in the Minister of Health from July 1948. Morrison, Lord President of the Council and Deputy Prime Minister at the time, had unsuccessfully argued in Cabinet for the hospitals to be brought together under local government. Then, in quick succession, electricity was nationalized, taking away the plant and workers of some forty local authority enterprises in Greater London – and charging consumers in places like Bermondsey more in the process. And 'national assistance' replaced the public assistance previously administered by County and County Borough Councils.[49]

These were great losses to local government. But there were gains. Planning grew problematically, as we have seen, with the grand wartime schemes thankfully diluted by a post-war pragmatism that, on the other hand, involved many disastrous compromises with developers and the motor car. Huge housing programmes, as we have also seen, were carried out in London and the New Towns, again producing an equivocal legacy, time-limited by poor design, inferior technology and parsimonious government subsidy; and the homeless were little better served after the war than during it. The LCC retained some health service provision, especially for maternal and child health outside hospital. A programme of modern 'health centres' began, the first at Woodberry Down (Stoke Newington) in 1952; and the London Ambulance Service was greatly expanded and improved. Then the modernization of education in London was speeded up. The LCC led from the 1940s in the egalitarian shift from selection to comprehensive

schools. The first purpose-built comprehensive flagship for the post-war
world was opened at Kidbrooke (Greenwich) in September 1954: for 1,700
girls it had 'an assembly hall like an aircraft hangar'. The ex-LCC comprehensive school would, in time, become an uneven inheritance too.[50]

It was probably in leisure and the arts that London government built most
imaginatively on the wartime years. Victory celebrations in the parks in
1946 included a six-week run of *St Joan* at the Finsbury Park open-air
theatre, concerts and performances by the London Philharmonic Orchestra
and Sadler's Wells ballet, dance bands till midnight and open-air cinema for
children. The 1948 sculpture exhibition at Battersea Park, showing works
by Hepworth, Epstein, Moore and others, proved astonishingly popular.
The list of London parks was extended by the acquisition and fitting out of
Holland Park, Hurlingham Park and St George's Fields (Stepney), all in
1952, and others followed. The government-run – almost Morrison-run –
Festival of Britain of 1951, which brought Britain with a bang out of
despondency, could not have happened without the LCC's contribution.
Its Royal Festival Hall made the council's Architect's Department world-
famous overnight. 'Labour is giving London more fun' was one of the LLP's
slogans of the time.[51]

Morrison had ceased to be leader of the LCC in October 1940, but he
remained a member of the Council until 1945 and secretary of the LLP
until 1947. The two subsequent leaders of the LCC were much in Morrison's
pragmatic right-wing mould, though Charles (later Lord) Latham (leader
until 1947) and Sir Isaac Hayward (from then until 1964) lacked Morrison's
drive, vision, and charisma. In many ways they symbolized the sclerosis of
Labour rule in London that had begun to set in before the war in some areas
but by the 1950s had hardened the arteries at County Hall beyond reach of
the healer's art.[52]

It is difficult to pin down the roots of this morbidity. The Labour
Party's inherent tendency to schism and sectarian dispute – a legacy of both
nonconformism and the religion of Marxism – didn't help. Labour could be
a party of fratricides where those who won power clung on to it, not to do
anything positive with it but to stop opponents having their day. Career
path and personal wealth were eschewed for the party's sake. So advancement
within it could become the sole object of a life's ambition. In these circumstances politics were almost murderously personal. This was the climate in
which hardline party discipline was ruthlessly enforced against dissenters
within and the opposition without. When seventy-year-old Percy Harris
was re-elected as a Liberal to the LCC in 1946, the ruling Labour group
refused to give up a place on any committee to make room for him: 'The
Tories have many faults,' he reflected, 'but at least they have good manners.'

The tensions in the party, present from the beginning, between middle-class ideologues and working-class pragmatists and materialists, stoked up resentment as one or other element waxed or waned over time. This was an especially metropolitan factor. London was the largest agglomeration of the middle class in the country, its population was intensely mobile and its anonymity inevitably attracted every minority enthusiast and faddist under the sun. Then the private achievement of public goals made Labour a victim of its own success from the 1930s on by solving for individual workers the problems that had led them to join the Party in the first place. This also had its special London dimension, so that, for instance, the most energetic dockers of Silvertown, or the printers of south Islington and Finsbury, would move far away to a suburban LCC estate, leaving the party they had founded in the hands of teachers, welfare workers and bureaucrats living in Forest Gate or Upper Holloway. Where workers did not relinquish power in this way they could give rise to dynastic cliques. The Southwark party in the 1950s was apparently ruled by four families who 'froze out newcomers, and indeed discouraged membership!' By no means all of London's local Labour parties were in this state – Battersea, for instance, continued an active model of its kind until 1964 – and in every moribund party there were staunch and selfless spirits and undaunted activists. But more often than not the complexities of class, generation, geography and ideology – later compounded by race, gender and sexual preference – would render the Labour Party in London peculiarly prone to faction and bitter internal dissent.[53]

Few things were more expressive of ossification in the 1940s and 1950s than London Labour's attitude to Greater London government reform. This was an issue that had refused to go away. The settlement of 1900 had never been accepted by the Progressives, who went on agitating for a single council for London along the lines of a super-LCC. John Williams Benn, their most able leader, was still calling for the abolition of the MBCs on the eve of the First World War. And the failure to tackle the reality of Greater London perpetuated a County boundary that even by 1900 had been obsolete for twenty-five years or more. H. G. Wells (from the Fabian left) called in 1903 for a Greater London government for the built-up area and well beyond; Winston Churchill, then a Liberal, proposed a 'parliament' for Greater London; the Royal Commission on London Traffic in 1905 recommended a traffic board for an extensive metropolitan area; only Municipal Reform, in control of the LCC from 1907 and running almost all the borough councils, seemed predictably content with the status quo.[54]

The London government question was resurrected as soon as the First World War ended. The post-war housing crisis stimulated calls among

MBCs and others for a London-wide housing authority that could operate freely beyond the tight bounds of the County. The LCC responded by calling for an inquiry into Greater London government. In 1921 a Royal Commission was established under Lord Ullswater. It was an opportunity missed. Rather than make its own proposals for Greater London government – which its terms of reference certainly encouraged it to do – the Ullswater Commission merely exposed the LCC's vague ideas for a directly elected Greater London authority to its own sceptical scrutiny and the self-interested opposition of most of the outer London councils, which would be absorbed within any new arrangements. Having fostered disagreement on all sides, the Commission reported in 1923 and recommended no change – apart from an advisory committee on town-planning in London and the Home Counties. Two minority reports argued for a more radical approach on the lines of a Greater London council.[55]

Ullswater's damp squib settled nothing. There were calls right through the inter-war period for a Greater London government – not least from Morrison and the LLP under the banner of 'Home Rule for London' and an end to its 'status as a "municipal crown colony"'. The Greater London Regional Planning Committee, established to advise the Minister of Health by Neville Chamberlain in 1927, found itself utterly frustrated by its lack of teeth and called, in 1929, for a Greater London Regional Planning Authority with 'executive powers' for strategic planning. Ten years later a notable contribution to the debate was made by William Robson of the London School of Economics in *The Government and Misgovernment of London* (1939). Robson capitalized on all the collective anxiety of the time about the effects of London's hypergrowth on both the metropolis and the nation. He plainly showed that London government was a mess and always had been. But his solution – a Greater London Council covering an area nearly four times larger than the Metropolitan Police District, with sixty or so lower-tier authorities having populations of up to half a million – lacked appeal, if only because of its inhuman scale.[56]

Even during the war, dissatisfaction with the performance of parts of London government kept the reform issue simmering. The *Greater London Plan 1944*, despairing of local authorities agreeing over planning, recommended a 'Planning Board' with executive power; it would be made up of 'eminent men of affairs' appointed by a Minister. G. D. H. Cole, a socialist planner, proposed a London Regional Government in 1947, big enough to take in Staines, Watford and Thurrock.[57] In 1949 the London Planning Advisory Committee, set up by Lewis Silkin, a former LCC housing chairman and now Minister for Town and Country Planning, recommended an inquiry into Greater London government. But the Labour government did not respond. And by 1950 or thereabouts it was clear that a shift had taken place among those who were arguing for reform.

Until the end of the 1940s it had generally been the left who had most consistently argued for a Greater London authority of some sort. With the declining popularity of the Attlee government, however, abolishing Labour's London heartland at the LCC seemed an unattractive prospect. Labour had received a bad shock at the 1949 LCC elections when, at the nadir of the government's fortunes, it had come within one seat of losing the council to the Conservatives. Holding on to what it had was now paramount. And Labour's anti-reformers found a powerful ally in Morrison, whose enthusiasm for a Greater London Authority had waned as Labour's grip on the LCC had tightened from the late 1930s.

On the other hand, for Conservative Central Office its narrow defeat in 1949 seemed to prove that London would never be taken from Labour as long as 'London' was confined to the inner working-class districts. From the early 1950s London Conservatives, led by Enoch Powell, Director of the London Municipal Society from 1952 to 1956, worked on reorganization proposals which would abolish the LCC, strengthen the boroughs and create some sort of indirectly elected Greater London authority for metropolitan functions. Powell produced his plan in 1955. In the meantime, pressure for reform had built up from below. For more than thirty years areas like Ealing, Ilford and Bromley had agitated for County Borough status so they could run all services like education and personal health. But this had been resisted by successive governments reluctant to add to the complexities of London pending some root and branch reform. White papers on local government in 1956 and 1957 reaffirmed that nothing should be done about these claims until the whole question could be examined. And in July 1957 Henry Brooke – ex-LCC, ex-Hampstead Borough Council, now Minister of Housing and Local Government in Harold Macmillan's Conservative government – established the century's second Royal Commission on Local Government in Greater London, under Sir Edwin Herbert, a prominent solicitor.[58]

The Herbert Commission report of 1960 was a magnificent piece of work, 'one of the great state papers of recent years'. Its statement of the place of local self-government within a mature democracy remained an intellectual beacon even forty years on. Its grasp of the practical realities of power and party politics in London was no less sure. And its technical skill in proposing a rational and effective local government for Greater London which remained in touch with a population of over 7 million was exemplary.[59]

Herbert and his colleagues recommended that the 'primary unit of local government in the Greater London Area should be the borough', carrying all functions except those that were 'better performed' over a wider area. These would be the responsibility of a 'Council for Greater London', with boundaries roughly equivalent to the Metropolitan Police District. Functions would be 'as far as possible self-contained without overlapping or duplication and without the necessity for delegation from one to another'. Some fifty-two London borough councils would do everything except making a Greater London development plan, traffic management, house-building outside Greater London, cross-borough redevelopment schemes and standard-setting in education. Those functions would be the responsibility of a Greater London Council. This was all radical stuff except in one direction. The City Corporation was to be left alone – 'an institution of national importance' which did 'not cost the taxpayer or the ratepayer a penny piece'.[60]

Through all its work the Herbert Commission had to fight against the antediluvian opposition of the LLP and the Labour LCC, which clung to a senile defence of its position, out of date even since 1889. 'The LCC refused to discuss any question which did not relate directly to the Administrative County of London – an area which they insisted was still coterminous with "London".' Morrison was now the most vitriolic opponent of reform. 'I will stump London and we will fight in London to denounce the Government for this piece of political jobbery . . . this contemptible plot, I almost said a corrupt plot.' At one level Morrison had a point. The Herbert Commission had been established in part to secure a solution to the electorate's constitutional revulsion from Conservatism in London County. But the broad thrust of the Commission's proposals was unarguably right.

Herbert Morrison lost his battle to save a Labour LCC that he had fought fifty years to win and keep at all costs. He died on 6 March 1965. He was seventy-seven, had just lost the sight of his one eye but was otherwise in good health. 'He just died', his doctor thought, 'because he saw no further point in living.' Morrison's will asked that his ashes 'be scattered into the high tide of London's river from the terrace of County Hall where I was privileged to render several years of happy service to the people of London'. But the Thames was at low tide on the morning of his memorial service at Westminster Abbey and so his ashes were scattered on the water from an LCC fireboat, *Firebrace*, on 30 March 1965. A few hours later the Council's last ever meeting took place. The Morrison years were over.[61]

The GLC and After: Greater London Government, 1965–99

The London Government Act 1963 established a Greater London Council and thirty-two London Borough Councils while retaining the City Corporation. The new arrangements fell short of the Herbert Commission's wise injunction to avoid overlapping and duplication and of its aspiration for the boroughs to carry out all functions best discharged locally. The LCC's ghost would cast a dark shade for many years to come.

Planning was clear enough. The boroughs were responsible for deciding planning applications and producing local development plans; the GLC for producing a Greater London Development Plan with which local plans should be compatible. So was education, even if the Act put in place peculiar arrangements not envisaged by Herbert. The Commission had proposed the day-to-day running of schools by the boroughs, but standard-setting, policy, resourcing and inspection by the GLC. The Act provided for no GLC supervision at all in outer London, where the London boroughs were stand-alone education authorities. But in inner London the GLC (or the LCC resurrected) would do everything. There, education was to be run by an Inner London Education Authority, a statutory committee of the GLC with borough council representation.

Transportation was more muddled. Herbert had recommended that all road and traffic management should be given to the GLC. But the Act sandwiched the GLC between the Minister of Transport (responsible for trunk roads) and the boroughs (general road maintenance), while boroughs and the GLC would share parking responsibilities. Matters eventually became clearer. Public transport had been specifically excluded from Herbert's consideration. But this was rectified from 1970 when the GLC became Transport Planning Authority for London, with the task of integrating and improving public transport in the capital.

There was even greater confusion over housing. The GLC could buy land and build wherever it wanted. The enormous housing stock it inherited from the LCC (230,000 dwellings, including the suburban estates) would eventually be transferred to the boroughs, but on a timetable that took years to negotiate. When, in 1969 and 1974, councils were given power to encourage the improvement of areas of old housing rather than demolition, the GLC was given them, too. So the Act in effect put two housing authorities in every borough in London – one the borough council and the other the GLC.[62]

The London Government Act made one other change of lasting

significance to the recommendations of the Herbert Commission. This was to draw in the boundaries of Greater London, taking out some well-off suburban areas which had vociferously lobbied the government against inclusion. So Staines, Sunbury, Banstead, Esher, Epsom and Ewell, Walton and Weybridge and others were taken out of 'Greater London' in the west and south-west; Cheshunt and Chigwell in the north and east; and Caterham and Warlingham in the south. These changes, made at the behest of Conservative authorities, did the Tories' prospects in Greater London no favours. They helped put the GLC on a political knife-edge by balancing out suburb and inner city in what was virtually a microcosm of England. The new council would be much more susceptible to swings in the national political mood than the peculiar micro-climate of the old LCC had been.

This effect was felt from the beginning. Elections took place for shadow authorities in April 1964, to take over the new councils from 1 April 1965. To general surprise, and despite Morrison's anxieties about a contemptible Tory plot, Labour won overwhelming control of the GLC (sixty-four councillors to thirty-six) and nineteen of the thirty-two boroughs, including unlikely targets like Bexley and Hillingdon. The reason was clear enough. The elections had come at the fag-end of an unpopular and scandal-plagued government. The Greater London elections were the first opportunity for a nation that wanted a change to make its opinion felt.

An even more dramatic fluctuation the other way took place three and four years later. The deep unpopularity of the second Wilson government in mid-term, hit by an incompetently handled devaluation, was combined with a new element in London politics to be considered in a moment. The result was a landslide for the Conservatives in April 1967. They took control of the GLC with eighty-two seats out of 100. A year later, twenty-eight of the thirty-two London Borough Councils went Conservative too. Just Southwark, Tower Hamlets, Newham and Barking and Dagenham kept faith with Labour. The young Tory councillors in the majority at Islington, Hackney or Lambeth (twenty-five-year-old John Major among the latter) were as surprised as their Labour forerunners in the Metropolitan Boroughs had been in 1919. Such a landslide would not be repeated in London government for the rest of the century. But that pattern of Londoners voting in local elections largely in accordance with national preference produced a GLC that fluctuated in a gloomy double fugue, with political rule at County Hall often (for eleven years in twenty-one) out of kilter with the party in charge across the river at Westminster; and generally in conflict with half the London Borough Councils.

Maybe all this would not have mattered so badly had not the London Government Act shared so much power at local level between the boroughs and the GLC. Maybe, most of all, it would have mattered less had the times been more propitious. But the late 1960s and 1970s were years when there was fundamental disagreement over every element of change in London. There was no common ground – indeed, there was furious dispute – over roads versus communities, or redevelopment versus conservation, or the future of redundant industrial land. Getting things done in such a tempestuous climate proved noisy, bloody and endlessly protracted. So the Greater London Development Plan took seven years to be approved by the Secretary of State after Sir Frank Layfield's rewriting. So the exhausting débâcles over London's ringways and the future of Covent Garden. So the absence of a scheme capable of practical realization in Docklands. And so the war of attrition over housing in London.

From the beginning the GLC sought hegemony over London housing. It was allowed by government to delay handover of former LCC stock as a bargaining tool to get borough councils to do what it wanted, and to meet its own needs as a housing developer. But the first Labour GLC's big idea that 'London was one city' went down badly in a capital where local interests and popular loyalties were always stronger than any metropolitan world-view. For just as the old MBCs had successfully staked their claim against an overweening LCC, the London Borough Councils fiercely resented interference by the GLC as central authority in local affairs. Indeed, the boroughs had enough to do stifling the agitation of localists at home to tolerate attacks on their independence from outside. Integrating inward-looking Shoreditch into the new Hackney, or Conservative Hampstead into Labour Camden, was not achieved without robust jockeying for place, and in some cases resentment that lasted for years. It took Fulham more than a decade to regain independent recognition from Hammersmith by renaming the new borough Hammersmith and Fulham, for example.

It was not just parochial pride, though, that made boroughs bridle at the GLC trespassing on their interests. For politics raised its mischievous head. The Conservative boroughs of outer London suspected the GLC of reducing inner London's problems by exporting Labour-voting council tenants to the suburbs. Bromley and Redbridge were not alone in virtually refusing to cooperate with the GLC's efforts to rehouse Londoners in their areas; others were niggardly in their offers of help. When Conservatives captured the GLC and almost all the boroughs, housing policy switched drastically to council house sales and stock transfer to the boroughs, although both were at first curtailed by a Labour government until 1970 and reversed with Labour back at County Hall from 1973. In 1974 the GLC attempted to put together a housing strategy for London which tried hard not to alienate the outer boroughs. But their cautious agreement to negotiate was all set at nought by swingeing government cutbacks on housing capital from 1975.[63]

That failure, coming on top of ten years of housing strife and planning defeats, provoked the *Observer* to comment in May 1975 that 'regional housing strategy is the [GLC's] one claim to salvation. If it fails in that, what is it there for?' And that was a question many others were asking from the mid-1970s on. The boroughs had bedded down reasonably well – their travails were yet to come. But the GLC had not staked a satisfactory claim in London governance. There had been such wild swings in political control and policy direction. Policy had been blocked from above by government and below by the boroughs. The Council had lost functions like vehicle licensing to the Department of Transport in 1969, sewerage responsibilities to the water authorities in 1973, the London Ambulance Service to the NHS in 1974. True, it had gained the coordination of public transport in 1970, but here it was thwarted by chronic under-investment and poor management within London Transport (whose headquarters at 55 Broadway 'was known as the most affluent luncheon club in London'). So was the GLC necessary at all?[64]

Some thought not. In 1974 Geoffrey Finsberg, a former Hampstead Borough Councillor, Conservative leader of Camden Borough Council from 1968 to 1970, and then MP for Hampstead, produced *A Policy for London* which advocated stripping out the GLC's role and reviewing its purpose. This sparked off an even more radical movement for abolition within a section of the Conservative Party in London reminiscent (in reverse) of the Progressives' agitation for abolition of the Metropolitan Boroughs over sixty years before. In the new abolitionists' scheme 'a Minister for London would become the metropolitan authority' and self-government would be confined to the parts of London acting alone. At the GLC elections of 1977 'The Abolish the GLC Campaign' fought thirty-one out of ninety-two seats. They had little success. But London Conservatives, who won their third term at these elections, could hardly fail to take note.[65]

In their 1977 GLC manifesto, Horace Cutler, the Conservative leader, had undertaken to commission an 'independent inquiry into London government'. Bright-eyed, ebullient, with a cavalier beard and attitudes to match, Cutler was one of the two significant figures thrown up by the GLC in its troubled twenty-one year history. Born in 1912 at Tottenham, the son of a Metro-Land housebuilder who inherited his father's business, Cutler was elected to Harrow Borough Council in 1952 and Middlesex County Council in 1955, eventually leading both. Leader of the GLC from 1977 to 1981 he was knighted on the recommendation of a grateful Margaret Thatcher. He was witty, imaginative, forceful, a showman who could think big. He was an energetic advocate of local self-government and outspokenly hostile to central interference and restraint, even when that came from Conservative governments, as it certainly did from 1979. Cutler was the most impressive Conservative politician in the whole of that party's years of rule at County Hall. Yet such were the bleak prospects for lasting change during his time in power that his most enduring achievement was to get the GLC to pave the way for others to organize the annual London Marathon. The first race was held in August 1980.[66]

Cutler was an anti-abolitionist but also believed the GLC had taken on too much, especially with housing. He arranged for a fresh look at the council by commissioning Sir Frank Marshall, formerly the Conservative leader of Leeds, to review the GLC's role in London government. The Marshall Report of July 1978 concluded that a metropolitan authority continued to be necessary because 'The total interest of London as a whole transcends that of its constituent parts, their local needs and individual aspirations.' Marshall called for devolution from Whitehall to give the GLC a clearer and bigger strategic role. Government should pass to the GLC responsibility for trunk roads; for 'the complete public transport network in London, setting fares policies, approving investment plans and co-ordinating services', including contracting with British Rail; and, in 'the long run', the health service in London and the Metropolitan Police. Marshall also recommended that the GLC should let some services go to the boroughs, especially housing management and development. But he was notably less keen on devolution from County Hall to town hall than from Whitehall to the GLC. And, while suppressing for a few years the abolitionist war-cry by reaffirming the need for metropolitan government, his recommendations for more power to be given to it fell on stony ground. For in May 1979 a Conservative government was elected that proved more hostile to local government than any since the Attlee years of thirty years before.

One reason for its hostility was the increasing identification of local government with an adventurous and costly left-wing socialism. This was especially so in London. Something like a sea-change had gained momentum in London's local Labour parties ever since that seismic shock of the Conservative borough council election victories of May 1968. That landslide had not just been a response to the singular unpopularity of the Wilson government, although that was no doubt the main cause. Three weeks before polling day Enoch Powell made his 'rivers of blood' speech. It rudely thrust race relations on to the London electoral stage. According to John Major, Powell's speech 'turned a favourable Tory drift into an avalanche that changed the political landscape'. Some, but not all, Conservative candidates issued 'We Back Enoch' leaflets. In Lambeth the party won fifty-seven seats out of sixty.[67]

The popularity of Powell's views on race among white working-class Labour voters came as no surprise to the Labour Party in London. In September 1965 Bob Mellish, MP for Bermondsey and junior housing minister, had told the Labour Party conference he would not 'ask Lambeth to give precedence over its "own people" to coloured people', because to do so 'would be "asking Lambeth to create the most grievous racial disturbance we have ever seen in London"'. Delegates cheered him to the echo. Three years later and race had become a major factor in ejecting Labour from power.[68]

Race exacerbated those divisions already long present in the party in London between locals and newcomers, working-class materialists and middle-class ideologues. It intensified tendencies to isolationism within some borough parties already suffering from pressures imposed by amalgamation in the new borough structures, and by inner London gentrification. Ian Mikardo was selected by Poplar Labour Party to stand as MP not long before London government reorganization merged Poplar into Tower Hamlets. He found among party members 'more hostility to their new Labour colleagues and comrades from Bethnal Green and Stepney than they had ever shown to any Tories'. He also noted a 'racism which ran wider and deeper than I had expected'; 'I never saw a black face in any of the docks in my constituency or on any tug or barge or lighter. To the dockers, keeping out the "foreigners" was a part of the operation of a closed shop which excluded everybody who wasn't of their ilk . . .' Poplar Labour Party was just another closed shop. Neither was Poplar alone. Anti-Indian feeling ran high in the Southall Labour Party, for instance. And the new London Borough of Islington inherited much of its pre-1965 Metropolitan Borough parochialism which had been '"exclusionary", feared local activists and had a council leadership made up exclusively of older members who had lived in the borough all their lives'. In this climate, 'foreigner' could easily encompass the white middle classes as well as black newcomers.[69]

Race and gentrification were the key elements of change in the Labour Party, as in London as a whole, at the end of the 1960s. The Conservative landslide of 1968 helped dislodge many of the older party activists from their power base in the town halls. With the party flung into opposition, it became easier for middle-class newcomers to make a mark. Well educated, articulate, trained to argue, their self-confidence often honed by working in the media or in professions (like law or architecture) which brought special and useful knowledge to party discussions, the gentrifiers formed alliances dedicated to moving the party in new directions. For if the 'old guard' – a favourite phrase of the time – had been so good, why had they lost power in 1968? When they had held power, why had they done so little, most of all to improve housing conditions? And how could a 'socialist' council tolerate black people living in worse conditions than whites?

These tensions moved first and furthest in Islington. When Labour recovered from its three years in the wilderness – Islington was one of twenty-one London Labour boroughs in 1971 – a remarkably talented and forthright group of young councillors, many (but by no means all) middle-class and relatively new to the borough, began a virile assault on the capital's (and the nation's) worst living conditions. Nothing like it had been seen in London since Morrison's LCC in 1934. Not all the boroughs moved so fast. Hackney, Southwark, Tower Hamlets (overwhelmed by the housing problems of Bengali migrants in Spitalfields) and Newham lagged behind. But Lambeth, Camden and Brent were almost equally innovative. And everywhere the Labour Party began wrestling with new ideas and the new challenges emerging from a multicultural society.

The old guard did not give up easily. The 1970s were characterized in Labour parties throughout London by factionalism, shifting alliances and internecine strife. There was a bitterness that had not been seen since the anti-Communist struggles of the 1920s. Any number of elements were cast into this burning fiery furnace. Race grew in importance as minority groups gained in confidence, discovered the need for self-defence and found their way to a stake in civil society through party politics. It was less a question of choosing a party – that usually was Labour – than of choosing elements or groups to ally with inside it. Minorities found themselves jockeying for position and resources in competition with other minorities. So that in Hackney, for instance, Africans, West Indians, Asians (Muslim and non-Muslim) and the Orthodox Jews negotiated their separate allegiances to one or another faction on the basis less of ideology than of the practical benefits to be gained for their communities.

Ideas could, though, play a part through fashionable fancies like community development or decentralization. So could trade union power. Manual trade unions had much to lose from changes to working practices and much to gain (especially for women workers) from better wages. Getting their way often depended on pledging allegiance to old guard or new, depending on personalities, old debts or old scores. Indeed, it was frequently the manual trade unions that held the key to advancement within the local and London parties. Hardly a Labour council in London felt able to confront and resist its blue-collar workforce in the dreadful strikes of 1979's 'Winter of Discontent' because to do so would have meant losing power to the faction which *would* back the union.

Then gender and the politics of sexuality found a louder voice from the mid-1970s and after. So did countless single-issue 'pressure groups' that attached themselves to party or faction in a kaleidoscope of fragile and promiscuous unions: conservationists, environmentalists, squatters, anti-nuclear campaigners, roads protesters, lobbyists for single mothers or play-groups, protesters against abortion or kerb-crawling. All, at some time or another, actively engaged within local Labour parties or knocked importunately without. This excitement wove Shakespearian plots that were hard to follow. It all had little to do with the real lives of most London citizens – indeed, in the case of public-sector strikes, was directed against their interests. And the 'traditional Labour voter', the skilled worker in regular employment who had originally been the party's backbone but was now leaving inner London in droves for the suburbs and the New Towns, gave up trying to make sense of it.[70]

It was out of this feverish milieu that Ken Livingstone emerged to fill the London limelight on 7 May 1981. That night Labour won control of the GLC after four years' rule under Cutler. The question was, which Labour? Going into the elections, the GLC opposition was led by Andrew McIntosh, a moderate who had relied on right-wing support to take the leadership just a year before. He had beaten Livingstone by one vote with two abstentions. Yet it was Livingstone on whom Cutler concentrated his fire during the campaign and Livingstone to whom the television cameras turned on election night. And Livingstone who was to prove the most significant Labour Party figure of the post-Morrison years in London.

Born in Streatham in June 1945, Ken Livingstone grew up on the Tulse Hill Estate and then in suburban owner-occupation in West Norwood. He joined the local Lambeth Labour Party in 1968, that momentous year of change. In the dearth of eligible candidates, wiped out by the Tories' London landslide, he became a borough councillor in May 1971, after just three years' party membership. He remained on Lambeth Council until 1978. In 1973 he was elected a GLC councillor for Norwood, switching to a safer seat at Hackney North for the 1977 GLC elections when it became clear that the Conservatives were heading for victory. 'This was the first of Livingstone's frequent changes of constituency, which came to earn him a reputation as a carpetbagger.' He moved to Camden and in 1978 was elected to the local council, where he was chair of housing. By 1980 Livingstone had moved again, this time to Paddington, a GLC marginal which had to be won by Labour if, as appeared likely, Labour were to be in power at County Hall in 1981.[71]

At the end of the century the bright glare of the Livingstone years of 1981–6 obscured any cool assessment of his real worth to London politics and his real value to Londoners. History had perhaps proved unkind to him in pitting him against an opponent, in Margaret Thatcher, of apparently unlimited power and political ruthlessness. But then perhaps history might have been kinder had he played his hand less recklessly. There was no doubting Livingstone's charisma and its capacity to bloom in the public eye – his cheeky grin, his witty tongue, his mother, his newts, his cunning stunts all lapped up by a hungry press who knew a star when they saw one. And, in general, lapped up by Londoners too. Lansbury and Morrison, especially Morrison, had been showmen as well, gratefully conscious that personal popularity was half the battle in winning people over to their point of view. But they had many years to get their message across working on a stage – Poplar Borough Council, the LCC – which never disappeared from under them and on which they could build a sustainable legacy. Only time would tell whether the frail dowry of the Livingstone years was undermined by unfavourable force of circumstances or was meretricious from the outset.

It was Ken Livingstone who became the voice of the Labour left in London. Within twenty-four hours of the GLC victory he had engineered a party coup to oust McIntosh and to install himself as leader and his close allies as committee chairs. The left's victory at the heart of London government led to a redoubling of conflict, dissension and schism across the Labour parties of the capital. Things were hardly helped by Livingstone's *London Labour Briefing*, where personal attacks, laced with vitriol, anathematized Labour politicians of the right and centre.

There were splits everywhere. The formation of the Social Democratic Party in March 1981, after the Limehouse Declaration of two months previously, was largely a response to the increasingly ferocious intolerance of the Labour left in London. In June the new SDP-Liberal Alliance fomented a crop of defections from London Labour parties among a disaffected right which could argue that the Labour Party no longer looked after the interests of local people – especially (the barely spoken agenda) white people. Three councillors in Southwark joined the SDP in July, complaining that the local Labour Party had been seized by 'infiltrators'; by the end of the year fourteen more had joined them. In September sixteen Islington Labour councillors and a sitting MP defected, including the remnants of that party's 'old guard' who had been smarting and seething under a gentrified leadership for more than a decade. In Tower Hamlets and Hackney (especially Shoreditch) a cruder right-wing and half-covertly racist version of the Alliance centred around 'Liberal Focus', sometimes recruiting directly from far-right organizations like the National Front. In the 1982 London Borough Council elections Alliance councillors formed the largest opposition parties to Labour in Hackney, Newham and Tower Hamlets – where they would take control from 1986 to 1994. The old proletarian areas of inner London, which had given birth to Labour in the early years of the century, were the first to defect from a party that now seemed to offer nothing to the white working class. And for the left their departure was more a cause for rejoicing and bitter ostracism than any attempt to gather them back to the fold.

The most notable revulsion from Labour of these fissiparous early 1980s was the Bermondsey parliamentary by-election of February 1983. Labour's candidate, Peter Tatchell, seemed to symbolize everything that the Labour old guard and their supporters in London most resented. He was a newcomer (Australian, in Bermondsey since 1978), young (just thirty when selected), outspokenly gay, unrepentantly left-wing. On the other hand, for Tatchell and his supporters the Bermondsey Labour Party was a 'gerontocracy' (ageism had not yet entered the political lexicon), 'packed with right-wing Catholic dockers', led in Parliament by bullish Bob Mellish and on Southwark Council by similar Labour bosses in the old style. One of these, supported by Mellish, stood as Independent Labour and polled badly despite, perhaps because of, running a vile personal campaign against Tatchell. But Bermondsey's disaffection from Labour could hardly have been more dramatic, comprehensive or deeply felt; Simon Hughes won hands down for the Alliance, polling 17,000 votes against Peter Tatchell's 7,700.[72]

Bermondsey, of course, had been the jewel in London Labour's crown in the 1920s and 1930s. And it was significant that the 'infiltrator' Tatchell should claim that he was the true inheritor of that radical socialism which had once flourished in Bermondsey's soil but been allowed to wilt and atrophy by an old guard who had let down both the cause and the local people. Reclaiming the past to legitimize the present was a powerful motif in the war-torn Labour politics of the 1980s. During the rate-capping fiasco of 1984–5, when Labour parties across London (led, if that's the right word, by Lambeth, Hackney, Camden, Islington and Livingstone's GLC) competed to hold out longest against setting a legal rate – the ghostly shroud of Poplar, sixty years dead, was proudly waved once more. Although no one this time went to prison for their pains, councillors in Lambeth (and Liverpool) were surcharged and disqualified. When, in the wake of rate-capping and other bloody defeats, a new realism was espoused by Labour, a photograph of Herbert Morrison was dusted off, recovered from the basement of Hackney Town Hall and hung in the leader's office. Morrison may have been Mayor of Hackney in 1920–21 and an alderman till 1925, but 'Good Old 'Erb' had been a non-person in Hackney Labour Party for almost twenty years. Yet these were not fake symbols. They reinvented for modern times a London Labour heritage around which meanings could cluster and identities could be forged and recognized, even if there was much debate over just what were the 'true' traditions they represented.

Back at County Hall the GLC under Livingstone seemed fatally caught up in the quagmire of political rhetoric that had clogged Labour's arteries since at least the mid-1970s in most of inner London. The euphoria of the 1981 GLC election victory when, in a high turnout, voters came out in droves against a temporarily unpopular Conservative government, seemed to equip Livingstone to do battle with the dragon across the Thames. The whole agenda of the Livingstone GLC, in close alliance with so-called 'Loony Left' boroughs like Lambeth and Hackney, seemed set to provoke, challenge and defeat the Thatcher government. Any means would justify that end: ignoring the majority of Londoners in spending endless time and bottomless resources in pursuit of ideological purity on gender, sexuality and race – at the expense, so concluded the historian of Jewish participation in London political life, of a sixty-year attachment between Jewry and Labour; spending Londoners' taxes on recruiting comrades to an ever-enlarging payroll; funding grants for some 'community organizations' dedicated to little more than their own survival and the government's downfall; waging a publicity war against government on policies like 'troops out of Ireland'; confusing the boundary between GLC and the Labour Party when agitating at huge expense against rate-capping and other government initiatives; snubbing the royal family, always a mistake with cockney London. In all this Livingstone demonized those colleagues who departed from him along the way. It was all pretty dreadful stuff, even if it had considerable allure for many at the time.[73]

There were, though, some solid achievements and other good work was attempted. The Council's anti-racism agitation, carried by ILEA into every classroom in inner London, forced Londoners to think seriously about the implications of living in a multicultural society. And it changed behaviour for the better. The GLC's much-lambasted arts policy redirected subsidy for 'culture' away from the opera house and art gallery into more demotic and inclusive spheres embracing fashion, world music, fringe theatre and experimental art. The GLC tried to find a role in stemming the flood of jobs out of London. Its Greater London Enterprise Board exploited GLC land and capital to some positive ends into the early 1990s (for GLEB survived the abolition of its parent). Most of all, it tried valiantly to do something about London's transport and traffic problems. And for this, despite the eventual failure of 'Fares Fair', Londoners remained grateful to Livingstone's GLC even twenty years on.

The Labour Party manifesto for the 1981 GLC election, constructed under McIntosh's leadership, proposed a 25 per cent cut in London Transport fares followed by a freeze. The cost of this would be borne by ratepayers, estimated in the manifesto at a supplementary rate of 5p in the pound. But by the time Labour came to implement this pledge the government's punitive grant regime clawed back a pound subsidy for every pound a council spent beyond the government target. The actual cuts in fares made by the GLC averaged 32 per cent, but the cost to ratepayers was nearly 12p in the pound. This 'more than doubled Londoners' weekly outgoings to the GLC'.

It was both the cost and, more, the popularity of the fares cuts that enraged London Conservatives, especially in the run-up to the LBC elections of May 1982. And it was the enterprising leadership of Tory Bromley – old opponents of the Labour GLC in its early days of housing imperialism – who dreamed up the wheeze of challenging in the courts the GLC's decision to subsidize bus and tube fares from the rates at such a high level. They rationalized their challenge by arguing that Bromley would not benefit, because it did not have a tube, but would pay steeply through the GLC precept. The High Court at first instance rejected Bromley's claim: the GLC could subsidize London Transport and it was a matter of discretion how much that subsidy need cost. But Bromley appealed and the Appeal Court unanimously decided against the GLC on the basis that London Transport had a statutory duty to balance its books – fares covering costs – without the benefit of GLC subsidy. That was a decision upheld in the House of Lords. The government was hardly likely to alter London Transport's obligations, so Fares Fair was at an end. In January 1982 London Transport fares doubled. Livingstone voted against the increase, and for defiance of courts and government. He was in the minority. Perhaps, more than one opponent averred at the time, he knew the vote would be lost but that the gesture would be remembered.[74]

Livingstone's GLC, with the support of most Londoners, had fought to get a sensible funding regime for public transport in London and so ameliorate one of London's enduring disabilities. That it might well have worked was shown by an estimated 10 per cent increase in public transport during the three months' operation of Fares Fair, and a 6 per cent fall in cars entering London in the rush hour. It seemed preposterous that such a sensible strategy for Londoners should have been defeated in the courts: justice was with them but the law was against them.[75] The GLC did not give up entirely. A low-fare travelcard initiative ('Just the Ticket') followed in May 1983, again leading to very positive signs of increased public transport use and fewer cars. And a 'lorry ban' was implemented in central London from December 1984. By then, though, the government had taken responsibility for public transport in London away from the GLC and put it to a new London Regional Transport Board, appointed by ministers. Fares rose once more from January 1985. Even so, in the memories of a generation of Londoners from 1981 on, it was better to have tried and lost than never to have tried at all.[76]

Across the river in the Palace of Westminster, to have tried at all was treason most rare. Fares Fair, the travelcard and Ken Livingstone's charismatic leadership had made the Labour GLC both more recognizable and more popular, despite its risible extravagances of leftist gesture politics, than ever before in its brief history. It was, perhaps, typical of Margaret Thatcher that she chose to abolish the GLC at the moment it seemed most secure in the support of Londoners and when the abolition movement had been dormant for five years or so. The decision to do so was, it seems, very much hers. Although apparently mooted in secret for some time, it came as a thunderbolt to London Tories. Alan Greengross, their leader on the GLC, learned of it just three days before the commitment to abolish was made public in the Conservative general election manifesto of May 1983. When Margaret Thatcher won that second term she could claim a popular mandate for both scrapping the GLC and scuppering Ken Livingstone.[77]

A DoE white paper in October 1983 justified abolition of the GLC as a cost-effective attack on 'the "national overhead"'. When public transport was taken from the GLC it would have little to do. 'This generates a natural search for a "strategic" role which may have little basis in real needs' and might also 'conflict with national policies which are the responsibility of central government'. Abolition was needed in the interests of 'Streamlining the Cities'.[78]

These were weasel words and Londoners knew it. They saw the only organization prepared to do something to ease their transport problems being abolished because the government didn't like it spending money to do so and because it hated Livingstone and all his works. Opinion polls showed increasing, and soon overwhelming, support for retention of the GLC – 74 per cent against abolition in October 1984, for instance. Abolition was opposed by a significant band of Tory rebels in Parliament, led by Ted Heath, and in County Hall, led by Alan Greengross. *The Times*, the *Guardian*, the *Financial Times*, the London Chamber of Commerce, the Royal Town Planning Institute, the London School of Economics and almost everyone other than Conservative Central Office all raised their voices against abolition. Thousands of representations in response to the 1983 white paper flooded in, but the government refused to publish any, or even to say how many were in favour of its proposals. The GLC elections of 1985 were cancelled to ensure that the wishes of Londoners could not find expression at the ballot box. And with a monster firework party from the South Bank, London said goodbye to the GLC on 31 March 1986.

The GLC's passing was much lamented and with good cause. The whole process of its abolition had been greatly to the discredit of British parliamentary democracy, or parliamentary dictatorship as it seemed to have become. It was not a pleasant sight to see the destruction of a local democratic institution against the clear wishes of its electorate and largely to victimize the person selected to lead it. It was, to many even who had no love for Livingstone, a patent absurdity that a great city, alone of all the major capitals of the world, should have no city-wide government of its own. 'London' was now partitioned into thirty-two boroughs and the ancient City. For over 130 years, since 1855, there had been some organization, somehow locally accountable, which could take some sort of overview of London's concerns and needs. Now no more. On the other hand, the GLC had not been much more than a mitigated failure. Had it not been for the thwarted public transport experiments of 1981–4 probably few voices would have been raised to preserve it in its 1965 form. Yet to put nothing in its place seemed madness or worse.

The next five or six years were not a happy period in London government. The rate-capping wrangles of 1984–5 had left many local Labour parties in tatters. Political in-fighting scorched its mark on borough council administration, which in some places seemed barely able to cope with the tasks put upon it. The sluggish unresponsiveness of some inner London boroughs in the 1940s and 1950s had now been replaced by frenetic disorder as an endless succession of inexperienced politicians jockeyed for power, attaching to whichever faction or pressure group would have them. The burdens of inner London boroughs like Hackney and Lambeth seemed stretched to capitulation by the break-up of ILEA and the devolution of education in April 1990. That was also the first year of the poll tax, when serious rioting involving arson and looting broke out in London, starting in Hackney, then spreading to borough after borough as the first year's tax was set in each. It culminated in a riot in Trafalgar Square on 31 March 1990, the ferocity of which had not been seen in tourist London for decades. Then scandal after scandal broke: in Westminster over selling off graveyards, and later over council house sales allegedly devised to manipulate the political complexion of marginal wards; and in almost every borough in inner London over key-selling and other housing fraud (Hackney), children's services (Islington), direct labour organizations (Lambeth) and many more.

Beyond the troubled boroughs, the confusion of appointed boards and indirectly elected committees that had replaced the GLC proved almost impossible to navigate. London leadership was given to a Minister for London, a Minister for London Transport, a Cabinet Sub-Committee on London, one or more of which was responsible for a Government Office for London. Traffic management was divided between the Secretary of State for Transport, the thirty-two boroughs, the City, the Traffic Director for London, the Parking Director for London and the Traffic Control Systems Unit. Joint committees were set up to do things that the GLC had done, which could not be done without, but which government had no wish to do: the London Fire and Civil Defence Authority, the London Boroughs Grants Committee, the London Planning Advisory Committee, the London Research Centre Joint Committee, the London Waste Regional Authority, joint committees for transport, accessible transport, canals, ecology, joint committees without end. William Robson had written in 1939 of the misgovernment of London; but fifty years on this was the ungovernment of London, an incomprehensible, labyrinthine and costly jumble.[79]

Inevitably, the manner of the GLC's demise and the mess of post-abolition arrangements meant that some in London never stopped calling for something sensible to be put in the GLC's place. By 1992 the London Labour parties seemed to be getting over the worst of their self-destructive phase. A new realpolitik had taken root in most of the boroughs – even, for a time, Hackney and Lambeth – which allowed energy to be devoted to Londoners' needs and the prospects for London as a whole, especially its economic prospects in an employment downturn of unprecedented longevity. At the same time, Labour Party policy nationally was moving towards a new London government which, it was always plainly stated, would 'not recreate the GLC'. In this endeavour Labour had the wholehearted support of the *Evening Standard*, the capital's only city-wide daily newspaper, and the forthright advocacy of columnist Simon Jenkins, long versed in matters metropolitan. The stagnation of the Conservative government's initiatives for the capital, like Michael Heseltine's plans for 'Thames Gateway', the confusion and bickering over which city, and then which part of London, should host the Millennium Exhibition, and then over who was to pay for it, all served to reinforce the lack of leadership in London and the insufficiency of structures to allow leadership to flourish.

On the tenth anniversary of GLC abolition the Association of London Government, voice of the Labour boroughs, published its own proposals for a new London-wide authority. A couple of weeks later, in April 1996, Tony Blair publicly committed himself to establish a London Mayor if Labour won the next general election. He found unlikely support among Conservatives who had never approved of abolition or who now regretted having supported it (like Lord Howe and Lord Desmond Plummer, Tory GLC leader before Cutler). By the time of the May 1997 general election there was a clear choice facing Londoners between a party that promised to put London government back to the people and a party that promised nothing. In London the swing to Labour was markedly greater than in the rest of the country.[80]

In July 1997, just two months after taking office, the Blair government published a consultation paper on arrangements for electing a Greater London Authority comprising a Mayor and an 'Assembly'. And, maybe of even greater historic significance, for replacing the Home Secretary as police authority for London with an independent body made up substantially of Assembly members. A white paper in March 1998 fleshed out the very extensive functions it was now proposed to put into the hands of the Mayor, with the Assembly acting as 'a check and balance' against abuse of power. These proposals were put to Londoners in a referendum on 7 May 1998, the first-ever London-specific referendum in history. Some 34.6 per cent voted, and of those who did 72 per cent said yes to the new arrangements.

The Greater London Authority Act 1999 put in place the most radical experiment in English local democracy since the reforms of 1835 (Municipal Corporations) and 1888 (County Councils). A new Greater London Authority was formed of a directly elected Mayor and twenty-five Assembly Members, elected both for constituencies and on a party slate. There was no precedent at all for endowing an individual, rather than a council or committee, with such extensive executive powers as the London Mayor would now be given. The Mayor's financial responsibilities and personal patronage exceeded those of most secretaries of state and rivalled the prime minister's. Many lessons of the failed GLC had apparently been learned. Transport was this time the key function, including direct responsibility for trunk roads, London Transport and (after a critical decision had been made on private investment in the tube) London Underground. Second came economic development and regeneration, barely addressed by London government even during the GLC years. Third came the police, an entirely new function for London government, the Mayor setting the Met's budget and selecting Assembly members to sit on the new police authority for London. Fourth came planning, a primary GLC function of course and in the new arrangements largely inherited from the 1965–6 period. Fifth came the environment, with the Greater London Authority taking on a strategic role the GLC had never had in issues like pollution, noise and biodiversity. Sixth came culture, recognizing the lost opportunities of the ungovernment years and London's past failures to organize major cultural events (like the Olympic Games). These were formidable tasks, many of them entirely new. The desire not to re-create the GLC had been amply fulfilled. Except that Ken Livingstone was chosen by Londoners as their first directly elected Mayor in May 2000.

It was at best debatable whether these changes at the century's end would resolve the difficulties that had dogged London government since 1900 and even before. One question certainly had been satisfactorily resolved: the boundaries of Greater London had been put beyond dispute for all practical purposes by the London Government Act 1963. No one wished to reopen that question forty years on, and the 1999 Act at last brought the Metropolitan Police District into line with Greater London, shifting policing in the far-flung suburban areas to the Home Counties constabularies.

There was, though, no reason to believe that the Greater London Authority had resolved the old question of relations between the metropolitan authority and the London boroughs. Lessons had been learned; there was less overlapping or sharing of functions. But planning, environment and economic development impacted mightily on the boroughs, especially the last, where localities would be competing for inward investment and job creation. Then in some cases the Mayor had reserve powers to act where he considered a borough was defaulting on its duties. That was a sure recipe for conflict. Just how much would in practice result remained to be seen.

No conclusive settlement, either, had been struck in 1999 between the rights of Londoners to self-government and the rights of Whitehall to govern London for the nation. Executive power would certainly devolve from Whitehall to the Mayor. But the GLC and LCC had always had tax-raising powers while the Mayor and Assembly had none. How independent from government could the Mayor be when Whitehall held the purse strings? Would London government merely turn out to be the administration of London on behalf of the government of the day? Certainly the requirement for the Mayor to seek approval for his strategies from the relevant Secretaries of State offered much room for Whitehall manoeuvres behind the scenes. Responsibility for the health of Londoners remained firmly with the Secretary of State and not the Mayor, and the byzantine, unaccountable structures of appointed boards within the National Health Service left a democratic deficit that at some time would have to be faced. Neither was there any constitutional restraint which prevented Parliament taking away powers from the Greater London Authority if the mayoral experiment was adjudged somehow to have failed, maybe by refusing to do government's bidding. Perhaps this was an aspect of London government that could never be satisfactorily settled but would always be contingent on events, personalities and party politics.

London party politics, though, seemed as unattractively ugly at the end of the century as at any time in the previous hundred years and more. The job of London Mayor, as demanding as any in the British public service, called for a candidate of quite outstanding intellectual, political and ambassadorial abilities. But the processes of selecting both Conservative and Labour candidates in the run-up to the first mayoral contest of May 2000 were more reminiscent of a Whitehall farce than rational decision-making. There was no doubt that the resurrection of Ken Livingstone as the first London Mayor raised questions of the utmost political significance for Labour and for London. The extraordinary sight of Labour fighting with every trick in the book to keep out the candidate guaranteed to win the mayoralty for Labour had to be seen to be believed. Only time would tell whether the outcome proved right or wrong.

Afterword:
London in the Twenty-first Century

London is the prophet's graveyard. Trapped so much by its past, it shrugs off the efforts of utopians to reimagine it and planners to reshape it. Vast and unencompassable, it even soaked up the furious attempts of its greatest enemy to destroy it. Yet London still proved hugely susceptible to change in the twentieth century.

From the beginning, Ford Madox Ford had noted how 'London is being so rapidly and so constantly "made over" that to-day there are parts of the town about which it is difficult enough to find one's way'.[1] That was a trend that never ceased. But at the end of the century redevelopment had reached an accommodation with old London, so that it tended to be the already made-over parts of inner London that were constantly reinventing themselves every thirty years or so. In the process, London's skyline was restlessly on the move as great towers rose and fell in some fathomless slow-motion ballet. On the other hand, those parts of the pre-1900 inner areas that had escaped bulldozers and bombs remained relatively immune to change. So did the low-rise residential suburbs, largely the result of London doubling on the ground between the two world wars, which had not yet exhausted their first useful life by 1999. It seemed likely that this pattern of renewal and stability living side by side in London would remain intact through at least the first generation of the twenty-first century.

Change in the Londoner was even more revolutionary and far-reaching than change in London. The birth of a multiracial and multicultural society had burst on London almost from nowhere. With its traditional mistrust of strangers and 'foreigners', few communities were less prepared for such a revolution than London, especially its working-class districts. The shock waves were at first turbulent, sometimes violent. Surprisingly, things soon settled down. Within twenty years of the first mass arrivals most Londoners accepted that their city had changed for ever, and for good. Within another twenty, London was lauded as one of the most tolerant and successful of the world's multicultural societies. It had proved in part a melting pot, with an astonishing number of mixed-background relationships, but even more a great constellation of the world's people retaining their own identity in a single city. Learning to live with one another was a negotiation that involved both sharing and separateness. Respect for difference was a hard lesson to learn. It was eventually well learned in London.

Even so, the responsibility for constantly keeping that lesson in mind fell on all Londoners, blacks as well as whites. Racism had never mobilized significant numbers of Londoners politically and seemed unlikely to do so. But racism had not been obliterated from any of London's diverse communities at the dawn of the twenty-first century. Neither had its tragic consequences on London's streets, and in its council estates and schools.

Those same schools had now a major part to play in equipping Londoners for work in an economy that had been entirely transformed in the last forty years of the century. A new world had risen from the collapse of the city's industrial base in its long depression from the mid-1960s to the mid-1990s. Work was increasingly polarized between low-wage low-skill service-sector jobs and high-skilled office and professional work, with rewards in financial services satisfying Croesus at his most unquenchable.

The pre-1965 diversity of London's economy had greatly narrowed by 1999. The old had been based on myriad industries. That fact alone had largely protected it from the storm and stress of economic dislocation at home and abroad. Just how dangerous specialization in financial and business services, and tourism and cultural industries, would prove for London's long-term future prosperity was a moot point. But one consequence was already clear. There were far fewer opportunities for low-skilled Londoners to earn a decent living in the new economy than the old. Education and training seemed the way out of that conundrum. Yet an education that focused overwhelmingly on literacy and numeracy at school, and business studies afterwards, seemed capable of bringing its own contradictions. Educating the imagination and nurturing creative flare required sights to be set higher than spelling and grammar, fractions and decimals. And imagination and flare had never been more important to London if it were to succeed in its new globally competitive world-city role.

That role increasingly – unprecedentedly – was turned to satisfying the capacity for pleasure of its own citizens and the richest citizens of a global economy. It was a role for which London had undergone a long apprenticeship. Yet large components of pleasure in London had always contended with the law. So many London delights had been put beyond the pale and then made lawful in a century which had been uncertain how best to bolster an impermanent moral code. Alcohol, betting, gambling, nudity, even pornography had gradually won extensive legal sanction. Drugs had not, or not yet. For the consequences of criminalizing this particular pleasure were daily borne in on the Londoner. The everyday horror stories of crime (robbery with violence by addicts needing a fix, gun-law murder by dealers squabbling over territory) and police corruption (including wholesale drug dealing) showed no sign of abating at the century's end. All this was a national problem but it bore hardest on the capital. At some time debate would have to be had about whether the effects on society of criminalizing drug use could possibly be worse than the consequences of controlled legalization. When that time came the lessons of twentieth-century London would prove instructive.

Perhaps the office of Mayor, and the Greater London Assembly, would provide the means for the voice of Londoners to be heard over issues just like this, and for their ambitions to be realized. But here optimism had to be tempered with realism. From the very beginning of the new arrangements it was reasonably clear that they had not done away with the three great disabilities of London government. The abrasions between London's localities (the boroughs) and London as a whole (the Greater London Authority) were tangibly intact. 'Home Rule for London' would still have resonance as long as Whitehall and Westminster kept tight rein on the Mayor's (and the boroughs') purse strings. And the city's poisonous politics continued to elude an antidote.

At the end, it was to government and leadership that Londoners would need to look if progress were to be made with London's enduring challenges. Some of these had been left unresolved by the twentieth century; others had largely been created by it. Among the new challenges, like educating its people for a global economy, or racism in society and in the police, there were others – crime, litter, pollution – that had long persisted though taking new forms. Perhaps the most enduring of all was London's catatonic traffic congestion, still unsolved at the century's end as it had been time out of mind; but, in its extent and effects, worse than ever before. Whether a new local government and new leadership would make a difference remained to be seen. Even so, a broken 'voice for London' was better than no voice at all. And it would be up to Londoners just what they said with it.

So what a moment! A new millennium. And an old London struggling with its past, and with the legacy of a century, especially the last half-century, still very fresh in the mind.

There would surely be plenty of history in the making.

Notes

1. LONDON GROWING: 1900–1950

1. The accounts given are drawn from *The Times*, 19 and 21 May 1900; Shaw Desmond, *London Nights of Long Ago*, 1927, Ch. XII; Thomas Burke, *The Streets of London: Through the Centuries*, 1940, p. 136; W. Macqueen-Pope, '*Goodbye Piccadilly*', 1960, pp. 324–5.

2. There is little consensus over the interpretation of the 1801 Census figures for London. Edward Wedlake Brayley, *London and Middlesex [etc.]*, 1810, gives 865,623; Francis Sheppard, *London 1808–1870: The Infernal Wen*, 1971, gives 958,863; Roy Porter, *London: A Social History*, 1994, 'around a million'. I prefer to trust London County Council/LSS, *London Statistics*, meticulous up to 1938. It gives: Central Area *c.* 783,000; County 959,310; Greater London (Metropolitan Police District) 1,114,644.

3. See *Darlington's London and Environs*, 1902, p. 1; H. G. Wells, *Ann Veronica: A Modern Love Story*, 1909, pp. 96, 100; Ford Madox Hueffer, *The Soul of London: A Survey of a Modern City*, 1905, p. 16; James Dunn, *Modern London – Its Sins and Woes and the Sovereign Remedy*, 1906, pp. 2–3.

4. *Darlington's London and Environs*, 1902, p. 1 (preface to 3rd edn, *c.* 1900).

5. For a passionate argument in favour of the Victorians and their wholesome effect on twentieth-century London, see Donald J. Olsen, *The Growth of Victorian London*, 1976.

6. By 1988 London was the eighth largest city in the world, and New York was seventh, although London was still by far the largest city in Western Europe.

7. For the Greenwich foot tunnel, see London County Council, *Annual Report*, 1903, pp. 21–2, and 1904, pp. 20–21; for Vauxhall Bridge, see London County Council, *Annual Report*, 1903, p. 27, and 1907, p. 153.

8. For the history of County Hall, see Survey of London, *County Hall*, 1991.

9. On the Kingsway-Aldwych scheme, see Percy J. Edwards, *History of London Street Improvements, 1855–1897*, 1898; Charles Gordon, *Old Time Aldwych, Kingsway, and Neighbourhood*, 1903; London County Council, *Opening of Kingsway and Aldwych by His Majesty the King . . .*, 1905: these were all modernizers. For lamentation after the event, see Philip Norman, *London Vanished and Vanishing*, 1905, pp. 243–5; Walter Bell in Hanslip Fletcher (ed.), *London Passed and Passing: A Pictorial Record of Destroyed and Threatened Buildings, with Notes by Various Authors*, 1908, pp. 195–8; Malcolm C. Salaman and Charles Holme,

London Past and Present, 1916, pp. 9, 116; Arthur Machen, *Far Off Things*, 1922, pp. 126–7, and 1923, pp. 173–4; E. Beresford Chancellor, *Disappearing London*, 1927, pp. 4–5; G. K. Chesterton in A. St John Adcock (ed.), *Wonderful London*, Vol. III, n.d., p. 772. For a modern account, see Jonathan Schneer, *London 1900: The Imperial Metropolis*, 1999, Ch. 2.

10. On the architects and buildings of the Edwardian Baroque, see Edward Jones and Christopher Woodward, *A Guide to the Architecture of London*, 1983; Alistair Service, *The Architects of London: And Their Buildings from 1066 to the Present Day*, 1979; W. R. Dalzell, *The Shell Guide to the History of London*, 1981; Simon Bradley and Nikolaus Pevsner, *London I: The City of London*, 1997. The most useful survey of new building in this period, by an enthusiast for the new, remains Harold Clunn, *London Rebuilt, 1897–1927*, 1927. Indeed, Clunn's various studies of physical change in London from 1927 to 1947 are unsurpassed.

11. The term was Sir Edwin Lutyens's (1869–1944), architect of the British Medical Association building in Tavistock Square (1911–13), Hampstead Garden Suburb, the Cenotaph and New Delhi.

12. W. D. Howells, *London Films*, 1905, p. 11.

13. Carl Peters, *England and the English*, 1904, pp. 24–5.

14. On changes to the City, see James S. Ogilvy, *Relics and Memorials of London City*, n.d., p vi, and London County Council/LSS, *London Statistics*, Vol. 23, 1912–13, p. 55; on Saffron Hill, see London County Council, *Annual Report*, 1904, pp. 98–9, and 1905, p. 137; on Shoreditch and the East End, see Walter Besant and others, *The Fascination of London: Shoreditch and the East End*, 1908, pp. vii–viii; for Forster, see *Howards End*, 1910, pp. 42–3; Norman, *London Vanished and Vanishing*, pp. v–vi – the four-mile radius was measured from Charing Cross, the traditional centre of London, and governed the fares of Hackney carriages.

15. T. C. Barker and Michael Robbins, *A History of London Transport: Passenger Transport and the Development of the Metropolis: Vol. II, The Twentieth Century to 1970*, 1974. This is indispensable for a detailed understanding of the issues. Theodore Dreiser wrote a trilogy of novels based on Yerkes's life: *The Financier*, 1912, *The Titan*, 1914, and *The Stoic*, 1947 (published posthumously).

16. For Hampstead's resistance to trams on class grounds, see F. M. L. Thompson, *Hampstead: Building a Borough, 1650–1964*, 1974, p. 364; for Paddington's, see A. G. Gardiner, *John Benn and the Progressive Movement*, 1925, p. 512.

17. Thomas Burke, *London in My Time*, 1934, p. 78.

18. London County Council/LSS, *London Statistics*, Vol. 23, 1912–13, p. 466, and Vol. 25, 1914–15, p. 389; Clarence Rook, *London Side-Lights*, 1908, p. 301.

19. Hubert Llewellyn Smith (ed.), *The New Survey of London Life and Labour*, Vol. 1, 1930, p. 171.

20. On 1901–11, see London County Council/LSS, *London Statistics*, Vol. 23,

1912–13, p. 55; in the 1890s inner London had gained over 300,000 people, but if migration is taken into account that turned into a net loss outwards of 182,000: see Census 1901, *County of London*, p 61.

21. LMN, *London Municipal Notes*, Vol. 1, No. 5, May 1905, p. 121.
22. Charles Booth, *Life and Labour of the People in London*, Series 3, Vol. 1, 1902, p. 195.
23. The City as a wonder of the world is in Peters, *England and the English*, pp. 65, 67. For information on the City's day censuses, see City of London Corporation, *Ten Years' Growth of the City of London*, 1891. Figures for the 1911 day census come from London County Council/LSS, *London Statistics*, Vol. 23, 1912–13, p. 20n, and *The Year Book of Social Progress for 1912*, n.d., p. 169. Some of the walkers will, of course, have used public transport to get to London and then walked from railway station or tram terminus.
24. E. T. Cook, *Highways and Byways in London*, 1902, p. 247; Leonard Woolf, *Beginning Again: An Autobiography of the Years 1911–1918*, 1964, p. 21ff.
25. Cook, *Highways and Byways in London*, p. 287; Arthur Ransome, *Bohemia in London*, 1907, p. 110.
26. Ibid., pp. 38ff.; Forster, *Howards End*, p. 126; Cook, *Highways and Byways in London*, p. 232.
27. Henry James Forman, *London: An Intimate Picture*, 1913, pp. 187–8.
28. Ransome, *Bohemia in London*, pp. 234–5.
29. Rook, *London Side-Lights*, p. 7.
30. Cook, *Highways and Byways in London*, pp. 166, 6.
31. Ibid., pp. 211–12.
32. Booth, *Life and Labour of the People in London*, Series 3, Vol. 6, 1902, pp. 88, 105; Rook, *London Side-Lights*, p. 28.
33. George R. Sims, *Off the Track in London*, n.d., pp. 30 (Kensington) and 78 (Westminster).
34. Rook, *London Side-Lights*, pp. 15–16; Booth, *Life and Labour of the People in London*, Series 3, Vol. 2, 1902, p. 111.
35. Survey of London, *County Hall*, 1991, pp. 54–5.
36. Clunn, *London Rebuilt, 1897–1927*, p. 21.
37. Ibid., pp. 141–2.
38. Survey of London, Vol. XXXI, *The Parish of St James Westminster, Part II, North of Piccadilly*, 1963, p. 90. For a rare voice raised against improvement at the time, see Charles G. Harper, *London Yesterday, To-Day and To-Morrow*, 1925, Ch. IV.
39. Harold Clunn, *The Face of London: The Record of a Century's Changes and Developments*, 1934 (1951 edn, p. 12).
40. See London County Council, *Proposed Demolition of Nineteen City Churches*, 1920; London Society, *London's Squares and How to Save Them*, 1927; Royal

Commission on London Squares, 1928; and, for Edwardes Square, Survey of London, Vol. XLII, *Southern Kensington: Kensington Square to Earl's Court*, 1986, pp. 258–60. Protection was given by the London Squares Preservation Act 1931. For London and its past, see H. J. Massingham, *London Scene*, 1933, pp. 25–39.

41. Negley Harte, *The University of London, 1836–1986: An Illustrated History*, 1986, p. 225.

42. See the borough summaries for Finsbury, Holborn, Hackney and Westminster in Smith (ed.), *The New Survey of London Life and Labour*, Vol. III, 1932, and Vol. IV, 1934. For 1919, see *Daily Herald*, 2–8 September 1919.

43. See Registrar-General, *Statistical Review of England and Wales for the Year 1939*, Tables Part II, Civil, p. 25, for an estimate of the population mid-1939; Patrick Abercrombie, *Greater London Plan, 1944*, 1945, p. 27, gives the loss by migration from 1921 to January 1939 as 638,500.

44. On St Pancras, see M. Emily Cooke, *A Geographical Study of a London Borough: St Pancras*, 1932, pp. 56–7; on Stoke Newington, see Smith (ed.), *The New Survey of London Life and Labour*, Vol. III, 1932, p. 369; on Paddington, see ibid., Vol. VI, 1934, p. 431, and Michael Bonavia, *London Before I Forget*, 1990, pp. 133–4; on Brixton, see Sheila Patterson, *Dark Strangers: A Sociological Study of the Absorption of a Recent West Indian Migrant Group in Brixton, South London*, 1963, p. 54n; on Greene, see Norman Sherry, *The Life of Graham Greene: Vol. II, 1939–1955*, 1994, p. 22; on Highbury, information from the 1938 overcrowding survey in the Grosvenor Avenue area compared with the *New Survey*'s poverty map of 1930; on Hampstead, see Thompson, *Hampstead*, p. 428.

45. On Buckingham Palace Road, see *Daily Herald*, 1 July 1927; on Hampstead, see Smith (ed.), *The New Survey of London Life and Labour*, Vol. VI, 1934, p. 423; on Bloomsbury, see Paul Cohen-Portheim, *The Spirit of London*, 1935, pp. 27–8; on Chelsea, see H. G. Wells, *Christine Alberta's Father*, 1925, p. 51, and the *Star*, 22 September 1930, and Beatrice Curtis Brown, *Southwards from Swiss Cottage*, 1947, pp. 98–9, for similar scenes in the 1920s.

46. Jan and Cora Gordon, *The London Roundabout*, 1933, p. 68.

47. Rook, *London Side-Lights*, pp. 1–23; Hueffer, *The Soul of London: A Survey of a Modern City*, p. 36.

48. Ebenezer Howard, *Garden Cities of To-Morrow*, 1902; Samuel A. and Henrietta Barnett, *Practicable Socialism*, 1915, p. 264. The best survey of suburban London in the twentieth century remains Alan A. Jackson, *Semi-Detached London: Suburban Development, Life and Transport, 1900–39*, 1973 and subsequent editions; see also the very useful Paul Oliver et al. (eds.), *Dunroamin: The Suburban Semi and Its Enemies*, 1981, and Andrew Saint et al., *London Suburbs*, 1999.

49. Forster, *Howards End*, p. 319.

50. Census of England and Wales 1921, *County of London, Text*, 1923, p. 3.

51. Smith (ed.), *The New Survey of London Life and Labour*, Vol. I, 1930, p. 156.

52. The phrase is Patrick Abercrombie's in *Greater London Plan, 1944*, p. 2.

53. Clunn, *The Face of London: The Record of a Century's Changes and Developments*, p. 405.

54. M. C. Carr in F. M. L. Thompson (ed.), *The Rise of Suburbia*, 1982, p. 247.

55. Metropolitan Railway Co., *Metro-Land*, n.d.

56. On the shanty towns, see Dennis Hardy and Colin Ward, *Arcadia for All: The Legacy of a Makeshift Landscape*, 1984; on London-by-Sea, see Sue Farrant, 'London by the Sea: Resort Development on the South Coast of England, 1880–1939', *Journal of Contemporary History*, Vol. 22, No. 1, 1987. On Brighton novelists, I have in mind Graham Greene (*Brighton Rock*, 1938), Patrick Hamilton (*The West Pier*, 1951) and Julian Maclaren-Ross (*Of Love and Hunger*, 1947: more Bognor than Brighton, which none the less figures large).

57. Burke, *London in My Time*, 1934, p. 207.

58. J. B. Priestley, *English Journey*, 1934, p. 325.

59. At the Carreras tobacco factory in Mornington Crescent, 30 per cent of the 'cigarette girls' took more than an hour to get to work in 1936. New industries on the outskirts of London required a shorter commute. There is very little information about middle-class travel patterns in this period. See Kate K. Liepmann, *The Journey to Work: Its Significance for Industrial and Community Life*, 1944, and Harry W. Richardson and Derek H. Aldcroft, *Building in the British Economy between the Wars*, 1968, p. 315.

60. Barker and Robbins, *A History of London Transport: Passenger Transport and the Development of the Metropolis: Vol. II, The Twentieth Century to 1970*, p. 226.

61. On the origins of the LPTB, see ibid., Chs. X and XV; Herbert Morrison, *Socialisation and Transport: The Organisation of Socialised Industries with Particular Reference to the London Passenger Transport Bill*, 1933.

62. Priestley, *English Journey*, pp. 19–20.

63. Rupert Croft-Cooke, *The Sound of Revelry*, 1969, p. 57. On the numbers of cars licensed in London County, see London County Council/LSS, *London Statistics*, Vol. 41, 1936–8, p. 313.

64. All quotes from Metropolitan Railway Co., *Metro-Land*.

65. See V. S. Pritchett, *A Cab at the Door. An Autobiography: Early Years*, 1968; Louis Heren, *Growing Up Poor in London*, 1973; John Osborne, *A Better Class of Person: An Autobiography, 1929–1956*, 1981.

66. All from Clunn, *The Face of London: The Record of a Century's Changes and Developments*.

67. Sam Price Myers, *London South of the River*, 1949, p. 59.

68. Steen Eiler Rasmussen, *London: The Unique City*, 1934, p. 399.

69. C. F. G. Masterman, *The Condition of England*, 1909, Ch. III.

70. Gordon, *The London Roundabout*, p. 64.

71. Rachel Ferguson, *Passionate Kensington*, 1939, p. 25. For literary snobbery directed at suburbans, see the excellent study by John Carey, *The Intellectuals and the Masses: Pride and Prejudice among the Literary Intelligentsia*, 1992.

72. Rosamond Lehmann, *The Weather in the Streets*, 1936, pp. 24–5.

73. Age Exchange, *Just Like the Country: Memories of London Families Who Settled the New Cottage Estates, 1919–1939*, 1991, p. 39.

74. For snobbery against suburban council tenants and a rare photograph of the Wall, see ibid., pp. 53–4; see also Tom Jeffery in David Feldman and Gareth Stedman Jones (eds.), *Metropolis London: Histories and Representations since 1800*, 1989, p. 212.

75. See *3rd Report of the Commissioner for the Special Areas (England and Wales)*, 1936, and preface to the *Report* of the *Royal Commission on the Distribution of the Industrial Population*, 1940 (Barlow Report). See also Robert Sinclair, *Metropolitan Man: The Future of the English*, 1937, and S. Vere Pearson, *London's Overgrowth and the Causes of Swollen Towns*, 1939.

76. See *Town and Country Planning*, Vols. V–VII, 1937–9.

77. *Report* of the *Royal Commission on the Distribution of the Industrial Population*, pp. 200–202.

78. Philip Ziegler, *London at War, 1939–1945*, 1995, p. 11; London County Council, *The London Fire Brigade . . .*, 1925, p. 40ff.; W. T. Reay, *The Specials – How They Served London: The Story of the Metropolitan Special Constabulary*, 1920; for casualty figures for the 13 June 1917 raid, see William Nott-Bower, *Fifty-Two Years a Policeman*, 1926, p. 278. The best overall account is in Frank Morison, *War on Great Cities: A Study of the Facts*, 1937.

79. The most comprehensive account of the London Blitz is to be found in the three volumes of Winston G. Ramsey (ed.), *The Blitz: Then and Now*, 1987–9, eloquent testimony to the skill and dedication of amateur historical scholarship in Britain. See also Terence H. O'Brien, *Civil Defence*, 1955.

80. 'Mysterious Kôr' in Elizabeth Bowen, *The Demon Lover and Other Stories*, 1945, p. 173.

81. On the City, see City of London Corporation, *The City of London: A Record of Destruction and Survival*, 1951, pp. 186–7. The *Report of the Royal Commission on Housing in Greater London*, 1965, p. 11 (Milner Holland Report), seems to underestimate the number of houses that were slightly damaged in London: see C. M. Kohan, *Works and Buildings*, 1952, p. 225, and C. B. Purdom, *How Should We Rebuild London?*, 1945, p. 289. Outer London figures are for the London Civil Defence Region, somewhat larger than Greater London.

82. For Stepney, see D. L. Munby, *Industry and Planning in Stepney*, 1951, p. 85; for Croydon and Sutton and Cheam, see Ziegler, *London at War*, p. 303; for the location of V2 explosions, see Ramsey (ed.), *The Blitz: Then and Now*, Vol. 3.

83. See Anthony Aldgate and Jeffrey Richards, *Can Britain Take It: The British*

Cinema in the Second World War, 1986. The continuation after the war of anti-suburban feeling is displayed in Ronald Carton, *This Our London*, 1948, Ch. X, although Carton decries the prejudice.

84. The plans were: City of London Corporation, *Report on the Preliminary Draft Proposals for Post-War Reconstruction in the City of London*, 1944; City of London Corporation, *The City of London: A Record of Destruction and Survival* (this second, 1951, plan actually dated from 1947); J. H. Forshaw and Patrick Abercrombie, *County of London Plan*, 1943; Abercrombie, *Greater London Plan, 1944*.

85. On the fate of the plans, see Donald L. Foley, *Controlling London's Growth: Planning the Great Wen, 1940–1960*, 1963, and Stephen L. Elkin, *Politics and Land Use Planning: The London Experience*, 1974.

86. Kohan, *Works and Buildings*, pp. 225, 233.

87. G. D. H. Cole, *The Post-War Condition of Britain*, 1956, p. 372.

88. City of London Corporation, *The City of London: A Record of Destruction and Survival*, p. 42.

89. Oliver Marriott, *The Property Boom*, 1967, pp. 46–9; on Messina's house, see Marthe Watts, *The Men in My Life*, 1960, p. 181.

90. See Richard M. Titmuss, *Problems of Social History*, 1950.

91. Census of England and Wales 1951, *County Report: London*, 1953, p. xiii.

92. Nikolaus Pevsner, *London I: The Cities of London and Westminster*, 1957, pp. 102–3; Eric de Maré, *London's Riverside: Past, Present and Future*, 1958, pp. 160–61. The verdict on London as sordid and miserable is in V. S. Pritchett, *Midnight Oil*, 1971 p. 244; the City noticeboards are in Iris Murdoch, *Under the Net*, 1954, pp. 105–6.

2. LONDON REMADE: 1951–99

1. For the Festival of Britain, see Michael Frayn in Michael Sissons and Philip French (eds.), *Age of Austerity, 1945–51*, 1963; Harry Hopkins, *The New Look: A Social History of the Forties and Fifties in Britain*, 1963. The LCC's role in the Festival has, if anything, and untypically, been understated, even by its own historians.

2. For the best analysis of the office boom, see Oliver Marriott, *The Property Boom*, 1967, which is indispensably well informed; Simon Jenkins, *Landlords to London: The Story of a Capital and Its Growth*, 1975, and Shirley Green, *Who Owns London?*, 1986, which both borrow from Marriott while adding new emphases and later information; Lionel Esher, *A Broken Wave: The Rebuilding of England, 1940–1980*, 1981, for an insider's view of rebuilding London in these years. Peter Cowan and others, *The Office: A Facet of Urban Growth*, 1969, is also valuable.

3. For City floorspace destroyed in the Blitz, see City of London Corporation, *The City of London: A Record of Destruction and Survival*, 1951, pp. 42–3; D. F. Stevens in J. T. Coppock and Hugh C. Prince (eds.), *Greater London*, 1964, p. 179, shows the increasing proportion given to offices.

4. On the Church Commissioners, see Paddington, *The Church of England and Her Slum Ground Rents*, 1930; Paddington, *The Paddington Estate*, 1944; Green, *Who Owns London?*, pp. 19–21. On the aristocratic estates, see Jenkins, *Landlords to London*, p. 217.

5. See Simon Bradley and Nikolaus Pevsner, *London I: The City of London*, 1997, p. 128ff.

6. For the whole story, see Marriott, *The Property Boom*, pp. 157–66.

7. On Centre Point, see ibid., p. 110ff., and Stephen L. Elkin, *Politics and Land Use Planning: The London Experience*, 1974, pp. 54–73.

8. See Bradley and Pevsner, *London I: The City of London*, p. 131; Parliamentary Papers, *Piccadilly Circus: Report of the Working Party*, 1965; Peter G. Hall, *London 2000*, 1963.

9. See Greater London Council, *Greater London Development Plan Report of Studies*, 1969, map p. 265. For a celebration of the pre-war London skyline, see Charles G. Harper, *A Londoner's Own London*, 1927, pp. 233–51.

10. On nineteenth-century London's housing problem, see London County Council, *The Housing Question in London, 1855–1900*, 1900, Anthony S. Wohl, *The Eternal Slum: Housing and Social Policy in Victorian London*, 1977, and J. A. Yelling, *Slums and Slum Clearance in Victorian London*, 1986.

11. The old Nicol Street area of Bethnal Green was immortalized as the 'Jago' by novelist Arthur Morrison in 1894. It was cleared to make way for the Boundary Street Estate from 1893 to 1899. On Boundary Street, see London County Council, *The Housing Question in London, 1855–1900*, and Raphael Samuel, *East End Underworld: Chapters in the Life of Arthur Harding*, 1981. For a summary of housing developments up to the war, see London County Council, *London Housing*, 1937; Hugh Quigly and Ismay Goldie, *Housing and Slum Clearance in London*, 1934; J. A. Yelling, *Slums and Redevelopment: Policy and Practice in England, 1918–1945, with Particular Reference to London*, 1992.

12. London County Council/LSS, *London Statistics*, Vol. 41, 1936–8, pp. 142–68. On the suburban council estate, see Alan A. Jackson, *Semi-Detached London: Suburban Development, Life and Transport, 1900–39*, 1973.

13. On Highpoint, see Edward Jones and Christopher Woodward, *A Guide to the Architecture of London*, 1983, p. 344. For the influence of Europe on London's municipal architects, see CRHC, *Slum Clearance and Rehousing*, 1934, London County Council, *Housing: Working-class Housing on the Continent and the Application of Continental Ideas to the Housing Problem in the County of London*, 1936, and Elizabeth Denby, *Europe Re-Housed*, 1944.

14. The contemporary judgements are all from Hopkins, *The New Look*.

15. Ashley Smith, *The East-Enders*, 1961, p. 28.

16. On the LCC's role, see W. Eric Jackson, *Achievement: A Short History of the London County Council*, 1965, and London County Council, *Housing Service Handbook*, 1962. On high-rise and council building in general, see the indispensable Patrick Dunleavy, *The Politics of Mass Housing in Britain, 1945–1975: A Study of Corporate Power and Professional Influence in the Welfare State*, 1981, and Esher, *A Broken Wave*. On the Lansbury and Churchill Gardens Estates, see Ruth Glass et al., *London: Aspects of Change*, 1964.

17. Esher, *A Broken Wave*, p. 131. It is clear from Richard Crossman's diaries that he disliked high-rise housing while presiding over a massive building programme relying mainly on it: Crossman, *The Diaries of a Cabinet Minister: Vol. I, Minister of Housing, 1964–66*, 1975, p. 124.

18. The Ronan Point story is fully told in Dunleavy, *The Politics of Mass Housing in Britain, 1945–1975*, p. 242ff.

19. See Alex Henney, *Inside Local Government: A Case for Radical Reform*, 1984, pp. 194–5.

20. Figures for post-war council house-building from London County Council/ LSS, *London Statistics*, New Series, Vol. 1, 1945–54, p. 111, and Greater London Council/GLS, *Greater London Statistics*, Vol. 5, 1970, pp. 214–15.

21. What was to become from 1965 the London Borough of Havering showed a 28 per cent increase in population (54,000 people) between 1951 and 1961, by far the biggest in London. Next came Hillingdon (Feltham) with 18,000 (8.6 per cent).

22. On Thamesmead, see Greater London Council, *GLC Architecture 1965/70: The Work of the GLC's Department of Architecture and Civic Design*, n.d., and Esher, *A Broken Wave*, 1981.

23. See Marriott, *The Property Boom*, p. 185ff.

24. Greater London Council, *Greater London Development Plan Report of Studies*, 1969, p. 311; see also Peter G. Hall, *London 2001*, 1989, p. 23, for the population of New Towns in 1986.

25. See Peter Brimblecombe, *The Big Smoke: A History of Air Pollution in London since Medieval Times*, 1987; for the last serious fog in London, see Irma Kurtz, *Dear London: Notes from the Big City*, 1997, p. 174.

26. Hopkins, *The New Look*, p. 472.

27. The Edwardians republished many London classics, notably Kingsford's scholarly edition of Stow's *Survey of London* (1908) and Pierce Egan's 1821 book *Life in London* (1904) and its sequels. Works by Norman, Fletcher, Ogilvy, Bell, Bone and Chancellor have already been referred to in the notes to Chapter 1. For Gomme, see in particular his *London*, 1914. On Ashbee, see Hermione Hobhouse, *London Survey'd: The Work of the Survey of London*, 1994.

28. For an excellent introduction to the Survey of London, see ibid. On 17 Fleet Street, see London County Council, *No. 17 Fleet Street*, 1906.

29. See Harold Clunn, *The Face of London: The Record of a Century's Changes and Developments*, 1934, pp. 112–13, and, for the famous photo, Maurice Edelman, *Herbert Morrison: A Pictorial Biography*, 1948, p. 31. Clunn also has a photo of Morrison pulling on block and tackle to lift the first stone from the bridge.

30. Cecil Beaton, *History Under Fire: 52 Photographs of Air Raid Damage to London Buildings, 1940–41*, 1941; Sydney R. Jones, *London Triumphant*, 1941; Wanda Ostrowska and Viola G. Garvin, *London's Glory: Twenty Paintings of the City's Ruins . . .*, 1945; Joseph Bató and J. B. Priestley, *Defiant City*, 1942. See also William Kent, *The Lost Treasures of London*, 1947.

31. Stella Gibbons, *A Pink Front Door*, 1959, p. 21. On brightly coloured front doors, see also Hopkins, *The New Look*, p. 347, also writing of the 1950s, who mentions yellow as well as pink; he also uses the term 'frontiersmen' for the gentrifiers. A reference to Festival of Britain colours is in Ruth Glass, *Newcomers: The West Indians in London*, 1960, p. 48.

32. See *Report of the Royal Commission on Housing in Greater London*, 1965, pp. 422–5.

33. On the 1957–60 background, see John Greve, *London's Homeless*, 1964, pp. 16–18; *Report of the Royal Commission on Housing in Greater London*, 1965, pp. 180–81; Green, *Who Owns London?*, pp. 74–5. On Camden Town, see Tony Aldous, *The Illustrated London News Book of London's Villages*, 1980, pp. 5–6; Jonathan Raban, *Soft City*, 1974, p. 85. On Notting Hill, see Glass et al., *London: Aspects of Change*, pp. xviii–xix; Monica Dickens, *The Heart of London*, 1961, p. 49; Pearl Jephcott, *A Troubled Area: Notes on Notting Hill*, 1964, pp. 74–5. On Barnsbury, see Aldous, *The Illustrated London News Book of London's Villages*, p. 169; Sonia Roberts, *The Story of Islington*, 1975, p. 217ff. On Clapham see Aldous, *The Illustrated London News Book of London's Villages*, p. 60. On house prices, see Greve, *London's Homeless*, p. 58. On the joys of gentrification, see Jane Deverson and Katharine Lindsay, *Voices from the Middle Class: A Study of Families in Two London Suburbs*, 1975, p. 46ff.

34. (Glass et al., *London: Aspects of Change*, pp. xviii–xix.)

35. Bernard Levin, *The Pendulum Years: Britain and the Sixties*, 1970, p. 333. The Dales left Parkwood Hill in 1962 for the Outer Metropolitan Area, somewhere in East Anglia.

36. Not that the antiques stall was a new London phenomenon. For its inter-war counterpart, see Mary Benedetta, *The Street Markets of London*, 1936, with its fabulous photographs of Caledonian Market by Moholy-Nagy. And for life through the eyes of an antiques stall-holder, see Jane Brown, *I Had a Pitch on the Stones*, 1946. For the ramifications of 1960s retro-chic, see Raphael Samuel, *Theatres of Memory: Vol. I, Past and Present in Contemporary Culture*, 1994.

37. See Stephen Mullin in Judy Hillman (ed.), *Planning for London*, 1971, pp. 115–16; Raban, *Soft City*, p. 85ff.; Chris Hamnett and Peter Williams, 'Social Change in London: A Study of Gentrification', *London Journal*, Vol. 6, No. 1, 1980.

38. Michael Elliott, *Heartbeat London*, 1986, dubbed the gentrified arcs of inner London 'Brookstown'. Brooks was an estate agent who, rather than claiming too much for the houses he sold, deliberately extolled their vices, mercilessly listing the horrors that would have to be overcome if a house (or street) was to realize its full potential.

39. *Report of the Royal Commission on Housing in Greater London*, 1965, pp. 251–2. On later harassment caused by gentrification, see Holloway Tenant Co-operative, *A Better Place: The Story of the Holloway Tenant Co-operative Compiled from Records, Letters and Minutes of the Members*, 1974.

40. Crossman, *The Diaries of a Cabinet Minister*, 1975, pp. 324, 450–51, 456–7.

41. Ibid., p. 600; see also Henney, *Inside Local Government*, pp. 184–5.

42. See ibid., pp. 180–87, for the best account of this process.

43. Kathleen Denbigh, *Preserving London*, 1978, pp. 220–28.

44. On Covent Garden development, see especially Terry Christensen, *Neighbourhood Survival*, 1979 (the most thoughtful contemporary study); Brian Anson, *I'll Fight You for It! Behind the Struggle for Covent Garden*, 1981; Chuck Anderson and Ray Green, *Save the Jubilee Hall! The Battle to Preserve the 300-year-old Tradition of Street Market Trading in the Piazza of Covent Garden*, 1992; Esher, *A Broken Wave*, pp. 140–46. On Covent Garden and other places at risk, see Simon Jenkins, *A City at Risk: A Contemporary Look at London's Streets*, 1970.

45. On Bloomsbury and its 'disgusting' fate, see Richard Crossman, *The Diaries of a Cabinet Minister: Vol. II, Lord President of the Council and Leader of the House of Commons*, 1976, p. 496, and London Borough of Camden, *Bloomsbury: The Case against Destruction*, n.d. On Tolmers Square, see Nick Wates, *The Battle for Tolmers Square*, 1976, a brilliant memento of the hectic London property scene in the late 1960s and early 1970s.

46. See Jenkins, *Landlords to London*, p. 233.

47. See, for a very useful overview, Peter G. Hall, *Great Planning Disasters*, 1980, pp. 56–81.

48. For Islington, see Nicholas Deakin and Clare Ungerson, *Leaving London: Planned Mobility and the Inner City*, 1977, Ch. 6. That this was an inner London-wide phenomenon, see Graeme Shankland et al., *Inner London: Policies for Dispersal and Balance*, 1977, pp. 34–5, dealing with Stockwell (Lambeth).

49. Paul Harrison, *Inside the Inner City: Life under the Cutting Edge*, 1983, p. 230. See also Patrick Wright, *A Journey Through Ruins: The Last Days of London*, 1991, p. 68ff.

50. Aldous, *The Illustrated London News Book of London's Villages*, p. 79 (the most

informative of the London village guides). For others, see Nerina Shute, *London Villages*, 1977, and *More London Villages*, 1981; Peter Crookston (ed.), *Village London: The Observer's Guide to the Real London*, 1978; Denbigh, *Preserving London*; Glenys Roberts, *Metropolitan Myths*, 1982.

51. Judy Hillman, *A New Look for London*, 1988.

52. On the 1960s and 1970s, see John Pudney, *London's Docks*, 1975, pp. 178–86. On the 1982–92 period, see Survey of London, *Poplar, Blackwall and the Isle of Dogs: The Parish of All Saints,* Vol. XLIII, Ch. I, Vol. XLIV, Ch. XXIV, 1994, and Survey of London, *Docklands in the Making: The Redevelopment of the Isle of Dogs, 1981–1995,* 1995; on the earlier period, see Henney, *Inside Local Government*, pp. 246–50. For a detailed survey of the whole story, see Peter G. Hall, *Cities in Civilization: Culture, Innovation, and Urban Order*, 1998, Ch. 28.

53. See Susie Barson and Andrew Saint, *A Farewell to Fleet Street*, 1988. On the Goldman Sachs building, see Andreas C. Papadakis (ed.), *Post-Modern Triumphs in London*, 1991, p. 45; Bradley and Pevsner, *London I: The City of London*, p. 500.

54. Ibid., pp. 142–3.

55. The claim was a forecast in *The Times*, 20 May 1992, quoted in Survey of London, *Poplar, Blackwall and the Isle of Dogs: The Parish of All Saints*, Vol. XLIV, 1994, p. 706, and Bradley and Pevsner, *London I: The City of London*, p. 141. On Broadgate, see Papadakis (ed.), *Post-Modern Triumphs in London*, pp. 46–7; Bradley and Pevsner, *London I: The City of London*; Broadgate, *Broadgate and Liverpool Street Station*, 1991. Broadgate literally moved the City into Shoreditch: the City's historic boundaries were moved north to take in the new development around 1992–3, the rateable value of Hackney reducing accordingly.

56. The judgement on Farrell is Kenneth Powell's in Papadakis (ed.), *Post-Modern Triumphs in London*, p. 7.

57. See Tim Butler, '"People Like Us": The Gentrification of Hackney in the 1980s', in Tim Butler and Michael Rustin (eds.), *Rising in the East? The Regeneration of East London*, 1996, pp. 81–107.

58. I. Bristow et al., *The Saving of Spitalfields*, 1989.

59. Ibid., p. 170.

60. *The Times*, 28 March 1998.

61. *The Times*, 21 March 1998.

62. Henney, *Inside Local Government*, p. 190.

63. On late-century population figures and projections, see London Research Centre, *London 98*, 1998, pp. 18–20.

64. See also Jerry White and Michael Young, *Governing London*, 1996.

65. Greater London Council/GLS, *Greater London Statistics*, Vol. 2, 1967, p. 61; London Research Centre, *London 98*, 1998, p. 109.

66. *The Times*, 11 December 1996.

67. Angela Carter, *Wise Children*, 1991, p. 1.

68. Each of London's town centres is given a dot or other symbol in a map on p. 25 of London Planning Advisory Committee, *1994 Advice on Strategic Planning Guidance for London*, 1994. In an idle moment I counted 169.

3. LONDONERS: 1900–1947

1. Arnold Bennett, *A Man from the North*, 1898, pp. 1–2.
2. Ethel Mannin, *Sounding Brass*, 1925.
3. Ritchie Calder, *The Lesson of London*, 1941, pp. 62–3.
4. Anon., *Tempted London: Young Men*, 1888, p. 1.
5. For Elizabeth Bowen's memoir, see John Lehmann (ed.), *Coming to London*, 1957, p. 74ff.; Sam Price Myers, *London South of the River*, 1949, p. 7; Glyn Roberts, *I Take This City*, 1933, p. 13; J. B. Priestley in A. St John Adcock (ed.), *Wonderful London*, Vol. II, n.d., p. 729; David Low, *Low's Autobiography*, 1956, p. 84.
6. H. G. Wells, *Tono-Bungay*, 1909, p. 75.
7. Stephen Hobhouse, *Forty Years and an Epilogue: An Autobiography (1881–1951)*, 1951, p. 82; Harry Pollitt, *Serving My Time*, 1940, pp. 90–91; J. T. Murphy, *New Horizons*, 1941, pp. 179, 289.
8. Dolly Davey, *A Sense of Adventure*, 1980, pp. 10–11; on Bill Rounce, see Gavin Weightman and Steve Humphries, *The Making of Modern London, 1914–1939*, 1984, pp. 50–51; 'rural idiocy' is Karl Marx, of course.
9. George Orwell, 'Autobiographical Note', April 1940, in *My Country Right or Left and Other Selected Essays and Journalism*, 1998, p. 1; Tom Hopkinson, *Of This Our Time: A Journalist's Story, 1905–50*, 1982, p. 139; Storm Jameson, *Journey from the North: Autobiography of Storm Jameson*, Vol. I, 1969, p. 140.
10. Figures from Hubert Llewellyn Smith (ed.), *The New Survey of London Life and Labour*, 1930–35, Vol. I, p. 83, and Vol. VI, p. 262, giving data not available in the published Census reports. 'London-born' here means 'County of London-born'. No comparative figures are available for Greater London.
11. See A. M. Carr-Saunders and D. Caradog Jones, *A Survey of the Social Structure of England and Wales: As Illustrated by Statistics*, 1937, p. 4, and Census of England and Wales 1931, *General Tables*, 1935, pp. 179, 199.
12. See, for example, John A. Jackson in Ruth Glass et al., *London: Aspects of Change*, 1964, p. 296ff.
13. Figures calculated from Census of England and Wales 1901, *County of London*, p. 155; 1911, *Summary Tables*, p. 219; 1921, *County of London, Tables*, 1922, Part II, p. 112; 1931, *General Tables*, p. 179; 1951, *Report on Greater London and 5 Other Conurbations*, 1956, p. 62.
14. It is possible to compare reasonably precisely the origins of provincial-born

Londoners in 1901 and 1951. Using the 1901 categories, migrants from the North Midlands, North-Western Counties, Yorkshire and the Northern Counties totalled 142,000 in the County of London in 1901, 12.4 per cent of the provincial-born; in 1951 they totalled 178,500, or 23 per cent: Census of England and Wales 1901, *County of London*, p. 155; 1951, *County Report: London*, 1953, pp. 62–3.

15. Smith (ed.), *The New Survey of London Life and Labour*, Vol. II, p. 462, noted anti-Irish prejudice among employers of office cleaners around 1930.

16. Roberts, *I Take This City*, p. 105.

17. On newcomers to outer London, see Smith (ed.), *The New Survey of London Life and Labour*, Vol. VI, p. 253.

18. See George R. Sims (ed.), *Living London*, n.d., Vol. II, pp. 267–73; A. St John Adcock (ed.), *Wonderful London*, n.d., Vol. II, pp. 664–75.

19. Sims (ed.), *Living London*, Vol. II, pp. 270–71. For the Victorian background, see Lynn Holden Lees, *Exiles of Erin: Irish Migrants in Victorian London*, 1979. For Irish politics in London around 1900, see Jonathan Schneer, *London 1900: The Imperial Metropolis*, 1999, p. 171ff.

20. See H. Wilson Harris and Margaret Bryant, *The Churches and London (an Outline Survey of Religious Work in the Metropolitan Area)*, n.d., pp. 307–8, for the effects of the Welsh revival in London. For an overview of religious life in London around that time, see Richard Mudie-Smith, *The Religious Life of London*, 1904. On the clannishness of the Welsh, see James A. Jones, *London's Eight Millions*, 1935, p. 292.

21. Ford Madox Hueffer, *The Soul of London: A Survey of a Modern City*, 1905, pp. 147–8.

22. Jones, *London's Eight Millions*, pp. 293–4; on 1900, see Arthur W. A Beckett, *London at the End of the Century: A Book of Gossip*, 1900, pp. 18–19.

23. Robert Sinclair, *Metropolitan Man: The Future of the English*, 1937, p. 103.

24. See Smith (ed.), *The New Survey of London Life and Labour*, Vol. VI, p. 65.

25. In John Lehmann (ed.), *Coming to London*, 1957, p. 17.

26. Wells, *Tono-Bungay*, pp. 109–10.

27. Davey, *A Sense of Adventure*, p. 11.

28. Clarence Rook, *London Side-Lights*, 1908, pp. 28–9; Pollitt, *Serving My Time*, p. 91; H. V. Morton, *London*, 1940, p. vii; Michael Young and Peter Willmott, *Family and Kinship in East London*, 1957, p. 88.

29. On the slur, see Roberts, *I Take This City*, p. 122. On the pariah among dialects, see William Matthews, *Cockney Past and Present: A Short History of the Dialect of London*, 1938, p. xii. On the gums, see Sinclair, *Metropolitan Man*, pp. 26, 28. On the construction of 'the Cockney' in the popular imagination, see Gareth Stedman Jones in David Feldman and Gareth Stedman Jones (eds.), *Metropolis London: Histories and Representations since 1800*, 1988, Ch. 11.

30. See Basil Woon, *Hell Came to London: A Reportage of the Blitz during 14 Days*, 1941.
31. Calder, *The Lesson of London*, p. 63.
32. Harold Bellman, *Cornish Cockney: Reminiscences and Reflections*, 1947, p. 8.
33. For the changes over time, see Smith (ed.), *The New Survey of London Life and Labour*, Vol. I, p. 82.
34. Bernard Gainer, *The Alien Invasion: The Origins of the Aliens Act of 1905*, 1972, p. 210. On post-First World War restrictions, see Adcock (ed.), *Wonderful London*, Vol. III, pp. 1011–23. On Jewish assimilation after 1914, see V. D. Lipman, *Social History of the Jews in England, 1850–1950*, 1954.
35. Cyril Foster Garbett, *In the Heart of South London*, 1931, p. 7.
36. Count Armfelt in Sims (ed.), *Living London*, Vol. I, p. 241 (see also Arthur Sherwell, *Life in West London: A Study and a Contrast*, 1897, p. 172); Alec Waugh in Adcock (ed.), *Wonderful London*, Vol. I, pp. 129–30; Thomas Burke, *Nights in Town: A London Autobiography*, 1915, p. 253. On the early history of foreigners in Soho, see E. F. Rimbault, *Soho and Its Associations: Historical, Literary, and Artistic*, 1895; Survey of London, Vol. XXXIII, *The Parish of St Anne Soho*, 1966, Ch. 1. However, there is a great disparity between the latter's quoted estimate of Soho's two-thirds' foreign population in 1903 and Arthur Sherwell's 1897 estimate of 11 per cent. Sherwell's is more like it.
37. The 25,000 estimate for French people in Greater London around 1911 is from Harris and Bryant, *The Churches and London*; other population figures are from Census of England and Wales 1911, *Vol. IX, Birthplaces*, and 1931, *General Tables*. On the London French generally, see Sims (ed.), *Living London*, Vol. II, pp. 133–8; see Thomas Burke, *City of Encounters: A London Divertissement*, 1932, p. 26, for Old Compton Street, and George R. Sims, *Off the Track in London*, n.d., p. 117ff. for the snails. On Soames Forsyte's Soho adventures around 1899–1900, see John Galsworthy, *In Chancery*, 1920, pp. 473–5, 721.
38. On pre-1914 German London see Sims (ed.), *Living London*, Vol. III, pp. 57–62 (the description of Leman Street is from p. 60), and Adcock (ed.), *Wonderful London*, Vol. III, p. 1017. The description of the German churches comes from Harris and Bryant, *The Churches and London*, pp. 299–300, and Edward G. Howarth and Mona Wilson, *West Ham: A Study in Sociological and Industrial Problems*, 1907, pp. 59, 143, give details of the glassblowers in West Ham. See Elizabeth McKellar, *The German Hospital in Hackney: A Social and Architectural History*, 1991; Mark Grossek, *First Movement*, 1937, on Ratschüler's and much else; Panikos Panayi, *German Immigrants to Britain during the Nineteenth Century, 1815–1914*, 1995.
39. On the effects of the First World War on the German community, Panikos Panayi (ed.), *Racial Violence in Britain in the Nineteenth and Twentieth Centuries*, 1996, Ch. 4, gives details of the riots; Louis Bamberger, *Bow Bell Memories*, 1931, p. 17, and Osbert Lancaster, *All Done from Memory*, 1963, Ch. 2, write of

the disappearance of the German bands. Rudolf Rocker, *The London Years*, 1956, gives an inside view of internment. See also Michael MacDonagh, *In London during the Great War: The Diary of a Journalist*, 1935.

40. See Horace Wyndham and Dorothea St J. George, *Nights in London: Where Mayfair Makes Merry*, 1926, p. 80, for the reappearance of German restaurants, and Nick Merriman (ed.), *The Peopling of London: Fifteen Thousand Years of Settlement from Overseas*, 1993, p. 114, for the refugees from Nazism and generally.

41. Paul Morand, *A Frenchman's London*, 1934, p. 188. On the Italian quarter generally, see Lucio Sponza, *Italian Immigrants in Nineteenth-Century Britain: Realities and Images*, 1988; Terri Colpi, *The Italian Factor: The Italian Community in Great Britain*, 1991; Sims (ed.), *Living London*, Vol. I, pp. 183–9; Sims, *Off the Track in London*, pp. 146–62; Adcock (ed.), *Wonderful London*, Vol. III, p. 1018; Harris and Bryant, *The Churches and London*, p. 305; James A. Jones, *Wonderful London Today*, 1934, pp. 134–5. On the July procession, see *Daily Herald*, 19 July 1926; on the Italian restaurant see Joseph Conrad, *The Secret Agent: A Simple Tale*, 1907, p. 149; on Soho as the Italian quarter, see Harold Clunn, *The Face of London: The Record of a Century's Changes and Developments*, 1934, p. 153; and on anti-Italian riots in Soho during the war, see Judith Summers, *Soho: A History of London's Most Colourful Neighbourhood*, 1989, pp. 181–9, and Panayi (ed.), *Racial Violence in Britain in the Nineteenth and Twentieth Centuries*, 1996, Ch. 7.

42. See the appendix to Thomas Burke, *Dinner Is Served!*, 1937. Trouble between Italians and Cypriots is mentioned in Jones, *Wonderful London Today*, 1934, pp. 134–5.

43. Chaim Lewis, *A Soho Address*, 1965. Ever since William Goldman's *East End My Cradle*, 1940, the Jewish autobiographical literary tradition has been the strongest in London. Chaim Lewis's memoirs form one of the significant texts. There are many more, but I would single out Bernard Kops, *The World is a Wedding*, 1963; Emanuel Litvinoff, *Journey through a Small Planet*, 1972; Joe Jacobs, *Out of the Ghetto: My Youth in the East End, Communism and Fascism, 1913–1939*, 1978; Charles Poulsen, *Scenes from a Stepney Youth*, 1988; Arnold Wesker, *As Much As I Dare: An Autobiography (1932–1959)*, 1994; Morris Beckman, *The Hackney Crucible*, 1996.

44. For estimates of the population of London Jewry before 1914, see V. D. Lipman, *Social History of the Jews in England*, 1954, pp. 99–100. He gives 140–150,000 around 1900 and 180,000 by 1914. This includes non-immigrant Anglo-Jewry and many who had already dispersed from the East End. The 1911 Census gives nearly 47,000 Russians and Russian Poles living in Stepney, but not all these were Jews, and migrants' children born in London are excluded from the figures. The gender balance within the 47,000 was markedly even: 23,641 were

men. The estimate of 234,000 in Greater London in 1933 is given in Maurice Freedman (ed.), *A Minority in Britain: Social Studies of the Anglo-Jewish Community*, 1955, p. 68.

45. On the community generally, see C. Russell and H. S. Lewis, *The Jews in London (a Study of Racial Character and Present-day Conditions)*, 1900; Lipman, *Social History of the Jews in England*, and *A Century of Social Service, 1869–1959: The Jewish Board of Guardians*, 1959; Lloyd P. Gartner, *The Jewish Immigrant in England, 1870–1914*, 1973; Chaim Bermant, *Point of Arrival: A Study of London's East End*, 1975; William J. Fishman, *East End Jewish Radicals, 1875–1914*, 1975, and *East End 1888: A Year in a London Borough among the Labouring Poor*, 1988; Jerry White, *Rothschild Buildings: Life in an East End Tenement Block, 1887–1920*, 1980.

46. Charles Booth, *Life and Labour of the People in London*, Series 3, Vol. I, 1902, p. 152. See also Andrew Godley in Anne J. Kershen (ed.), *London: The Promised Land? The Migrant Experience in a Capital City*, 1997, pp. 56–62.

47. Roberts, *I Take This City*, p. 120.

48. Beatrice Ali, *The Good Deeds of a Good Woman*, 1976; Caroline Adams, *Across Seven Seas and Thirteen Rivers: Life Stories of Pioneer Sylhetti Settlers in Britain*, 1987.

49. E. T. Cook, *Highways and Byways in London*, 1902, p. 295.

50. See Ras Prince Monolulu, *I Gotta Horse*, n.d.; Michael Banton, *The Coloured Quarter: Negro Immigrants in an English City*, 1955; Peter Fryer, *Staying Power: Black People in Britain since 1504*, 1984; Rozina Visram, *Ayahs, Lascars and Princes: Indians in Britain, 1700–1947*, 1986; Ron Ramdin, *The Making of the Black Working Class in Britain*, 1987.

51. Leon Trotsky, *My Life: The Rise and Fall of a Dictator*, 1930, Ch. XI.

52. See Sheila Patterson in Glass et al., *London: Aspects of Change*.

53. The Survey of London, Vol. XLIII, *Poplar, Blackwall and the Isle of Dogs: The Parish of All Saints*, 1994, p. 113, gives 5,000 at its peak in the 1930s, but I can find no justification for that in any source and the Survey gives none; it may be a misprint. According to the local rector, in 1930 the population had declined from its peak in the First World War and he put its 'normal' population pre-1914 as 'under 300' (J. G. Birch, *Limehouse through Five Centuries*, 1930, p. 144). The 1930s seem to have been marked more by decline than by any special influx: a survey of 1935 quoted by Banton, *The Coloured Quarter*, p. 37, gives just 100 Chinese in Limehouse, stating that they 'have decreased in numbers very considerably'. Census figures for Chinese in Britain and London are given in Ng Kwee Choo, *The Chinese in London*, 1968, but these probably underestimate the real numbers. On Billie Carleton, see *The Times*, 4, 13, 14 and 21 December 1918, 3, 17 and 24 January 1919 and 5 and 8 April 1919, and S. Ingleby Oddie, *Inquest*, 1941, Ch. 11.

54. For an insider's story, rare enough in this secretive community, see Annie Lai, Bob Little and Pippa Little in *Oral History*, Vol. 14, No. 1, 1986, pp. 18–30. For the forty-nine arrests, see *Evening Standard*, 2 February 1920. See also Virginia Berridge, 'East End Opium Dens and Narcotic Use in Britain', *London Journal*, Vol. 4, No. 1, 1978.

55. Birch, *Limehouse through Five Centuries*, pp. 144–5. On the Limehouse novels etc., see Thomas Burke, *Limehouse Nights: Tales of Chinatown*, 1916, *The Song Book of Quong Lee of Limehouse*, 1920, *Whispering Windows: Tales of the Waterside*, 1921, *More Limehouse Nights*, 1921, *East of Mansion House*, 1926, and *The Pleasantries of Old Quong*, 1931.

56. Thomas Burke, *Out and About: A Note-book of London in War-Time*, 1919, p. 12.

57. On the Polish community generally, see Jerzy Zubrzycki, *Polish Immigrants in Britain: A Study of Adjustment*, 1956; Patterson in Glass et al., *London: Aspects of Change*; Elspeth Huxley, *Back Street New Worlds: A Look at Immigrants in Britain*, 1964, Ch. 3.

58. See Geoff Dench, *Maltese in London: A Case-study in the Erosion of Ethnic Consciousness*, 1975, p. 32.

59. See H. M. D. Parker, *Manpower: A Study of War-time Policy and Administration*, 1957, pp. 342–3, 423, for the wartime importation of labour; see Banton, *The Coloured Quarter*, p. 79, for the effects on Stepney; and for the effects of the war on immigration generally, see Ian R. G. Spencer, *British Immigration Policy since 1939: The Making of Multi-racial Britain*, 1997, pp. 14–18.

60. Wells, *Tono-Bungay*, pp. 204–5.

61. M. Vivian Hughes, *A London Family 1870–1900*, 1946, p. 77; Ian Niall, *A London Boyhood*, 1974, p. 33; Gerald Kersh, 'The Extraordinarily Horrible Dummy', *Penguin Parade*, 6 April 1939, p. 139.

62. I've not tried to track down the original but it is quoted in one of the prefatory pages of Francis Miltoun, *Dickens' London*, 1904.

63. London County Council, *Housing . . .* , 1924, pp. 17–19. See also London County Council, *Housing: With Particular Reference to Post-war Housing Schemes*, 1928, pp. 111–16; Walter Besant, *London South of the Thames*, 1912, pp. 68–9, 114–15; Survey of London, Vol. XXV, *The Parishes of St George the Martyr, Southwark and St Mary, Newington*, 1955, p. 121, which wrongly gives the date of clearance as 1910. Limited clearance did take place by 1915 but most of the area was not demolished until after the war. An Alsatia was a sanctuary for thieves and debtors; the Mint, Southwark's ancient Alsatia, was very close to Tabard Street and cleared in 1887.

64. Booth, *Life and Labour of the People in London*, Series 3, Vol. I, pp. 50–51; Survey of London, Vol. XLIV, *Poplar, Blackwall and the Isle of Dogs: The Parish of All Saints*, 1994, Ch. XXIII; Jones, *Wonderful London Today*, pp. 24–8. The 'Down Town' area of Rotherhithe along Rotherhithe Street seems to have been similar

to Bow Creek: see A. G. Linney, *The Peepshow of the Port of London*, n.d., pp. 149–52.

65. For Violet Kray's reminiscence, see John Pearson, *The Profession of Violence: The Rise and Fall of the Kray Twins*, 1995, p. 21. For Bethnal Green generally, see Young and Willmott, *Family and Kinship in East London*, p. 82.

66. See Jerry White, *The Worst Street in North London: Campbell Bunk, Islington, between the Wars*, 1986.

67. The quote is from Mary Cook in North Kensington Local History Project, *Our Homes, Our Streets*, 1987, p. 6. On Notting Dale generally, see Kensington Borough Council, *MOH Annual Report*, 1907, No. VII, p. 129ff.; Survey of London, Vol. XXXVII, *Northern Kensington*, 1973, Ch. XIV; Florence M. Gladstone, *Notting Dale in Bygone Days*, 1924, Ch. VII; George R. Sims, *The Mysteries of Modern London*, 1906, Ch. XV; Sims, *Off the Track in London*, Ch. II; Mrs Cecil Chesterton, *I Lived in a Slum*, 1936, Chs. I–III. On the Metropolitan Gypsyries, see George Borrow, *Romano Lavo-Lil: Word-book of the Romany or, English Gypsy Language*, 1874.

68. Marie Paneth, *Branch Street: A Sociological Study*, 1944; B. M. Spinley, *The Deprived and the Privileged: Personality Development in English Society*, 1953.

69. See *Hendon Gazette*, 12 June 1931.

70. On Becontree, see Terence Young, *Becontree and Dagenham: A Report Made for the Pilgrim Trust*, 1934, p. 166, and Andrzej Olechnowicz, *Working-Class Housing in England Between the Wars: The Becontree Estate*, 1997; on Honor Oak (anonymized), see L. E. White, *Tenement Town*, 1946, p. 17.

71. Ruth Durant, *Watling: A Survey of Social Life on a New Housing Estate*, 1939, Ch. IV.

72. Doris Bailey, *Children of the Green: A True Story of Childhood in Bethnal Green, 1922–1937*, 1981, p. 71; Hugh Massingham, *I Took Off My Tie*, 1936, p. 223.

73. Ted Willis, *Whatever Happened to Tom Mix?*, 1970, p. 112.

74. Barbara Nixon, *Raiders Overhead: A Diary of the London Blitz*, 1943, p. 62; see also E. Doreen Idle, *War over West Ham: A Study of Community Adjustment*, 1943, p. 51. See *The Island: The Life and Death of an East London Community, 1870–1970*, 1979. On neighbouring in north Lambeth, see Mass-Observation, *Britain*, 1939, and Mary Chamberlain, *Growing Up in Lambeth*, 1989, Ch. 2.

75. A. S. Jasper, *A Hoxton Childhood*, 1969; John Osborne, *A Better Class of Person: An Autobiography, 1929–1956*, 1981.

76. The area of study was the Oswald Street/Pedro Street/Overbury Street area east of Glyn Road and south of Millfields Road and I compared the electoral registers at fixed points between 1923 and 1939. On patterns of movement in the very rough Campbell Road, Finsbury Park, which tend to support the picture that emerges from the Hackney study, see White, *The Worst Street in North London*, p. 263.

77. Durant, *Watling*, pp. 16–17.

78. Maurice Gorham, *Londoners*, 1951, p. 2.

79. On the Tucks and the Kings, see *Daily Herald*, 23 June 1930, and *South London Press*, 4 July, 18 July and 1 August 1930. For the reference to terrorism, see Smith (ed.), *The New Survey of London Life and Labour*, Vol. VI, p. 184; generally, see White, *The Worst Street in North London*, pp. 90–101.

80. John Holloway, *A London Childhood*, 1966, pp. 10–11; Goldman, *East End My Cradle*, p. 137.

81. Davey, *A Sense of Adventure*, p. 21; Horace Thorogood, *East of Aldgate*, 1935, p. 17.

82. Maud Pember Reeves, *Round about a Pound a Week*, 1913, pp. 2–3; Massingham, *I Took Off My Tie*, p. 226.

83. Ibid., p. 130.

84. Elizabeth Bowen, *The Heat of the Day*, 1949, pp. 85–7.

85. On Hoxton, see Robert R. Hyde, *Industry Was My Parish*, 1968, p. 18; on Greenwich, see E. Wight Bakke, *The Unemployed Man: A Social Study*, 1933, pp. 7–8; on England, see George Orwell, *The Collected Essays, Journalism and Letters of George Orwell*, edited by Sonia Orwell and Ian Angus, 1968, Vol. III, p. 16 (*The English People*, 1944).

86. Gainer, *The Alien Invasion*, p. 58.

87. From a very extensive literature I would select: on the pre-1914 period, ibid.; on the BUF in east London in the 1930s, Thomas P. Linehan, *East London for Mosley: The British Union of Fascists in East London and South-West Essex*, 1996; on the 1940s, Morris Beckman, *The 43 Group*, 1992. Fears of a pogrom in the Blitz are recounted in Calder, *The Lesson of London*, pp. 72–3; see also L. R. Dunne, *Report on an Inquiry into the Accident at Bethnal Green Tube Station Shelter*, 1943, and Winston G. Ramsey (ed.), *The Blitz: Then and Now*, Vol. III, 1989, pp. 220–29. The Bethnal Green psychological survey is J. H. Robb, *Working-Class Anti-Semite*, 1954. For a wider discussion of attitudes to foreigners, especially among London children, see Anna Davin, *Growing Up Poor: Home, School and Street in London, 1870–1914*, 1996, p. 199ff.

88. On the East End race riots of 1919, see *The Times*, 17 June and 1 July 1919, *Evening Standard*, 11 August 1919, Fryer, *Staying Power*, p. 310, and Panayi (ed.), *Racial Violence in Britain in the Nineteenth and Twentieth Centuries*, Ch. 5. On the colour bar, see Mary Trevelyan, *From the Ends of the Earth*, 1942, p. 50; K. L. Little, *Negroes in Britain: A Study of Racial Relations in English Society*, 1947; Monolulu, *I Gotta Horse*, p. 173ff.; Learie Constantine, *Colour Bar*, 1954; Fryer, *Staying Power*, p. 356ff. Louis Gillain's extraordinary memoir is *The Pavement My Pillow*, 1954 (p. 65).

89. Little, *Negroes in Britain*, p. 271ff.

4. THE REMAKING OF THE LONDONER: 1948–99

1. Sheila Patterson, *Dark Strangers: A Sociological Study of the Absorption of a Recent West Indian Migrant Group in Brixton, South London*, 1963, p. 3.

2. Census of England and Wales 1951, *Report on Greater London and 5 Other Conurbations*, 1956, pp. 56–7. These figures are for Greater London. The numbers given in the Census as born in India and Pakistan totalled nearly 40,000 but the large majority of these were whites born abroad.

3. London Research Centre, *London 95*, 1995, pp. 50–52; Census of England and Wales 1951, *Report on Greater London and 5 Other Conurbations*, pp. 52–7; 1981, *Country of Birth: Great Britain*, 1983, pp. 28–9. The list of foreign countries excludes Eire. The 2001 projection is in London Research Centre, *Cosmopolitan London: Past, Present and Future*, 1997, p. iii. On the 307 languages, see *The Times*, 22 January 2000.

4. George Lamming, *The Emigrants*, 1954, p. 37.

5. See Mike Phillips and Trevor Phillips, *Windrush: The Irresistible Rise of Multi-racial Britain*, 1998, p. 66 for Lord Kitchener; Donald Hinds, *Journey to an Illusion: The West Indian in Britain*, 1966, p. 200; Eric Ferron, *'Man, You've Mixed': A Jamaican Comes to Britain*, 1995, p. 19.

6. Sam Selvon, *The Lonely Londoners*, 1956, pp. 121–2.

7. On the early years, see Clarence Senior and Douglas Manley, *A Report on Jamaican Migration to Great Britain*, n.d.; on under-enumeration in the 1961 Census, see Clifford S. Hill, *West Indian Migrants and the London Churches*, 1963, Appendix 1. On London Transport recruitment, see Dennis Brooks, *Race and Labour in London Transport*, 1975, pp. 256–63; on later numbers, see Ian R. G. Spencer, *British Immigration Policy since 1939: The Making of Multi-racial Britain*, 1997, an authoritative review of immigration policy and practice.

8. On West Indian women migrants, see especially Nancy Foner, *Jamaica Farewell: Jamaican Migrants in London*, 1979, and Beverley Bryan et al., *The Heart of Race: Black Women's Lives in Britain*, 1985.

9. Sam Selvon, *The Housing Lark*, 1965, p. 17; Lamming, *The Emigrants*, p. 39; Patterson, *Dark Strangers*, p. 376, and Hinds, *Journey to an Illusion*, p. 38 for the stereotypes; Stuart B. Philpott in James L. Watson (ed.), *Between Two Cultures: Migrants and Minorities in Britain*, 1977, p. 109 for the Montserratians; and Hinds, *Journey to an Illusion*, for the aspirations of West Indian nationalism.

10. This railroad determinism is most firmly (though hardly persuasively) stated in Michael Young and Peter Willmott, *The Symmetrical Family: A Study of Work and Leisure in the London Region*, 1973, pp. 58–9.

11. Joyce Egginton, *They Seek a Living*, 1957, pp. 62–6.

12. On Massa Johnson, see Patterson, *Dark Strangers*, p. 53; on black troops in Brixton in 1944, see Fred Narborough, *Murder on My Mind*, 1959, p. 74; on Geneva and Somerleyton Roads, see Elizabeth Burney, *Housing on Trial: A Study of Immigrants and Local Government*, 1967; for London Harlem, see Colin MacInnes, *City of Spades*, 1957, p. 159.

13. See Michael Abdul Malik, *From Michael de Freitas to Michael X*, 1968.

14. On the dispersal of West Indian migrants compared to the Irish, see Ceri Peach, *West Indian Migration to Britain: A Social Geography*, 1968, pp. 86–7.

15. See Ruth Glass, *Newcomers: The West Indians in London*, 1960, p. 48.

16. There are many excellent studies of the West Indian migration to London, especially in the early years. I have found most useful Michael Banton, *The Coloured Quarter: Negro Immigrants in an English City*, 1955; Senior and Manley, *A Report on Jamaican Migration to Great Britain*; Egginton, *They Seek a Living*; Glass, *Newcomers*; S. K. Ruck (ed.), *The West Indian Comes to England: A Report Prepared for the Trustees of the London Parochial Charities by the Family Welfare Association*, 1960; Patterson, *Dark Strangers*; Hill, *West Indian Migrants and the London Churches*; R. B. Davison, *Black British: Immigrants to England*, 1966; Hinds, *Journey to an Illusion*; Peach, *West Indian Migration to Britain*, 1968. For a fine oral history of the West Indian in Britain, and most information on the *Empire Windrush*, see Phillips and Phillips, *Windrush*.

17. 'A Short Guide for Jumbles', *Twentieth Century*, March 1956, quoted in Colin MacInnes, *England, Half English*, 1961, p. 19ff, where he apologized for using 'the odious word "half-caste"'. Clive James, *Falling Towards England*, 1985, pp. 20–21. Hunter Davies (ed.), *The New London Spy: A Discreet Guide to the City's Pleasures*, 1966, p. 249 (in original the extract is in italics).

18. See Geoff Dench, *Maltese in London: A Case-study in the Erosion of Ethnic Consciousness*, 1975.

19. See Robin Oakley in Verity Saifullah Khan (ed.), *Minority Families in Britain: Support and Stress*, 1979.

20. See James Watson in Watson (ed.), *Between Two Cultures*; Ng Kwee Choo, *The Chinese in London*, 1968; Home Affairs Committee, *Chinese Community in Britain*, 1985; Judith Summers, *Soho: A History of London's Most Colourful Neighbourhood*, 1989.

21. Spencer, *British Immigration Policy since 1939*, pp. 118–19.

22. See Ashley Smith, *The East-Enders*, 1961, pp. 66–7; Caroline Adams, *Across Seven Seas and Thirteen Rivers: Life Stories of Pioneer Sylhetti Settlers in Britain*, 1987; Anne Kershen in Anne J. Kershen (ed.), *London: The Promised Land? The Migrant Experience in a Capital City*, 1997.

23. Campaign Against Racism and Fascism/Southall Rights, *Southall: The Birth of a Black Community*, 1981, pp. 30–31; see also Nicholas Deakin and others, *Colour, Citizenship and British Society*, 1970, p. 301; Parminder Bhachu, *Twice*

Migrants: East African Sikh Settlers in Britain, 1985; Dilip Hiro, *Black British, White British*, 1973.

24. See, for the earlier period, Anna Craven, *West Africans in London*, 1968.

25. See Census of England and Wales 1971, *County Report: Greater London*, 1973, Part I, p. 70; 1981, *Country of Birth: Great Britain*, 1983, p. 28; William G. Kuepper et al., *Ugandan Asians in Great Britain: Forced Migration and Social Absorption*, 1975.

26. See Harald Tambs-Lyche, *London Patidars: A Case Study in Urban Ethnicity*, 1980; Bhachu, *Twice Migrants*, on the 'Victorian Sikhs'; Shirley Green, *Who Owns London?*, 1986, pp. 183–4, on the rich migrants.

27. London Research Centre, *Cosmopolitan London*, p. 10; London Research Centre, *London 95*, p. 51.

28. Michael Binyon in *The Times*, 7 July 1996; see also Nick Merriman (ed.), *The Peopling of London: Fifteen Thousand Years of Settlement from Overseas*, 1993, pp. 72–9.

29. See Jonathon Green, *Them: Voices from the Immigrant Community in Contemporary Britain*, 1990, pp. 279, 294–5. Maureen Duffy, *Londoners*, 1983, p. 78.

30. Colin MacInnes, *London: City of Any Dream*, 1962, p. xxxi.

31. V. S. Naipaul, *The Enigma of Arrival: A Novel in Five Sections*, 1987, pp. 122–3; Andrew Salkey, *Escape to an Autumn Pavement*, 1960, p. 206; Patterson, *Dark Strangers*, p. 5.

32. For Mervyn Morris, see Henri Tajfel and John L. Dawson (eds.), *Disappointed Guests: Essays by African, Asian and West Indian Students*, 1965, p. 7; Ferron, 'Man, You've Mixed', p. 14ff.; for the bus conductor, see Hinds, *Journey to an Illusion*, p. 73; Lynne Reid Banks, *The L-Shaped Room*, 1960, pp. 59, 291 (for example); Nell Dunn, *Up the Junction*, 1963, pp. 93–4; the Jamaican is quoted in Foner, *Jamaica Farewell*, p. 41.

33. Tajfel and Dawson (eds.), *Disappointed Guests*, p. 120; Ferron, 'Man, You've Mixed', pp. 27, 38–9.

34. On early troubles, see Glass, *Newcomers*, p. 128ff.; on Camden Town, see *St Pancras Chronicle*, 20 August 1954; on Cable Street, see David M. Downes, *The Delinquent Solution: A Study in Subcultural Theory*, 1966, p. 212, Banton, *The Coloured Quarter*, and Joseph Williamson, *Father Joe: The Autobiography of Joseph Williamson of Poplar and Stepney*, 1963.

35. Senior and Manley, *A Report on Jamaican Migration to Great Britain*, p. 26.

36. On the post-war London housing problem, see Census of England and Wales 1951, *County Report*, 1953; Senior and Manley, *A Report on Jamaican Migration to Great Britain*; *Report of the Royal Commission on Housing in Greater London*, 1965; John Greve, *London's Homeless*, 1964; Shirley Green, *Rachman*, 1979.

37. The landladies' survey is quoted in Senior and Manley, *A Report on Jamaican Migration to Great Britain*; on colour bar adverts, see Glass, *Newcomers*, and

Patterson, *Dark Strangers*; on Southall property values, see Elspeth Huxley, *Back Streets New Worlds: A Look at Immigrants in Britain*, 1964, pp. 88–91.

38. See Senior and Manley, *A Report on Jamaican Migration to Great Britain*; Egginton, *They Seek a Living*, 1957; Glass, *Newcomers*.

39. On the difficulties of West Indian Christians in London, see Hill, *West Indian Migrants and the London Churches*. For the charge that migrants had 'lowered' Notting Dale, see Pearl Jephcott, *A Troubled Area: Notes on Notting Hill*, 1964, p. 30.

40. For a convincingly revisionist view, see Green, *Rachman*.

41. See Glass, *Newcomers*, Map 2.

42. Jephcott, *A Troubled Area*, pp. 33–4.

43. See Malik, *From Michael de Freitas to Michael X*.

44. See T. R. Fyvel, *The Insecure Offenders: Rebellious Youth in the Welfare State*, 1961.

45. See Morris Beckman, *The 43 Group*, Appendices A–C.

46. *Manchester Guardian*, 2 September 1958, quoted in Glass, *Newcomers*, pp. 138–9; see also Fyvel, *The Insecure Offenders*; Majbritt Morrison, *Jungle West 11*, 1964, pp. 26–30; Hiro, *Black British, White British*; Ron Ramdin, *The Making of the Black Working Class in Britain*, 1987; Edward Pilkington in Panikos Panayi (ed.), *Racial Violence in Britain in the Nineteenth and Twentieth Centuries*, 1996, Ch. 9; Phillips and Phillips, *Windrush*.

47. See Tajfel and Dawson, *Disappointed Guests*, p. 52; Hinds, *Journey to an Illusion*, pp. 140–41; Malik, *From Michael de Freitas to Michael X*, p. 77.

48. See Glass, *Newcomers*, p. 164ff.; Phillips and Phillips, *Windrush*, p. 181ff.

49. Davison, *Black British*, p. 127.

50. W. W. Daniel, *Racial Discrimination in England: Based on the PEP Report*, 1968, pp. 155–9.

51. Prafulla Mohanti, *Through Brown Eyes*, 1985, pp. 158–61; see also Gus John and Derek Humphry, *Because They're Black*, 1971, p. 67; Peter Fryer, *Staying Power: Black People in Britain since 1504*, 1984, p. 384.

52. See John and Humphry, *Because They're Black*, pp. 48–52; Chaim Bermant, *Point of Arrival: A Study of London's East End*, 1975, p. 249ff. On the skinheads, see Nick Knight, *Skinhead*, 1982.

53. Bethnal Green and Stepney Trades Council, *Blood on the Streets: A Report on . . . Racial Attacks in East London*, 1978, pp. 3–5; see also Kuepper et al., *Ugandan Asians in Great Britain*; Campaign Against Racism and Fascism/Southall Rights, *Southall*; Fryer, *Staying Power*, pp. 395–6; Panayi (ed.), *Racial Violence in Britain in the Nineteenth and Twentieth Centuries*, Ch. 10.

54. Linton Kwesi Johnson is quoted in Phillips and Phillips, *Windrush*, p. 325. See Arthur Wesley Helweg, *Sikhs in England*, 1986, pp. 196–7, for Southall; on 'The Uprising', see Ferdinand Dennis, *Behind the Frontlines: Journey into Afro-Britain*, 1988, pp. 197–8.

55. Huxley, *Back Streets New Worlds*, p. 81.

56. Calculated from Greater London Council/GLS, *Greater London Statistics*, Vol. 7, 1972, pp. 222, 226–7.

57. Graeme Shankland et al., *Inner London: Policies for Dispersal and Balance*, 1977, pp. 49–50.

58. Jonathan Raban, *Soft City*, 1974, pp. 187–9.

59. Shankland et al., *Inner London*, pp. 123–4.

60. For the Thames TV survey, see David Wilcox and David Richards, *London: The Heartless City*, 1977, p. 11. Paul Harrison, *Inside the Inner City: Life under the Cutting Edge*, 1983, p. 204.

61. On Bethnal Green, see Peter Townsend, *The Family Life of Old People*, 1957, pp. 46, 216; on Stepney, see Smith, *The East-Enders*, p. 15; Downes, *The Delinquent Solution*, pp. 224–5.

62. On Kentish Town, see Gillian Tindall, *The Fields Beneath: The History of One London Village*, 1977, p. 226. Susan Fainstein et al. (eds.), *Divided Cities: New York and London in the Contemporary World*, 1992, p. 159.

63. Smith, *The East-Enders*, p. 156.

64. Peter Willmott and Michael Young, *Family and Class in a London Suburb*, 1960, p. 7.

65. Michael Young and Peter Willmott, *Family and Kinship in East London*, 1957.

66. Raymond Firth (ed.), *Two Studies of Kinship in London*, 1956.

67. Hannah Gavron, *The Captive Wife: Conflicts of Housebound Mothers*, 1966.

68. On Dagenham in the 1950s, see Peter Willmott, *The Evolution of a Community: A Study of Dagenham after 40 Years*, 1963; on Dagenham in the 1990s, see Margaret O'Brien and Deborah Jones in Tim Butler and Michael Rustin (eds.), *Rising in the East? The Regeneration of East London*, 1996, p. 72; on South Oxhey, see Margot Jefferys in Ruth Glass et al., *London: Aspects of Change*, 1964.

69. On Woodford, see Willmott and Young, *Family and Class in a London Suburb*; on 'Greenbanks', see Raymond Firth et al., *Families and Their Relatives: Kinship in a Middle-class Sector of London. An Anthropological Study*, 1969; on the others, see Jane Deverson and Katharine Lindsay, *Voices from the Middle Class: A Study of Families in Two London Suburbs*, 1975; see also Ruth M. Crichton, *Commuters' Village: A Study of Community and Commuters in the Berkshire Village of Stratfield Mortimer*, 1964 (study undertaken in 1962).

70. Anthea Holme, *Housing and Young Families in East London*, 1985.

71. Craven, *West Africans in London*, p. 75 for the West Hampstead house. Buchi Emecheta, *Head above Water*, 1986, pp. 41–2.

72. Dennis, *Behind the Frontlines*, p. 191.

73. Mohanti, *Through Brown Eyes*, p. 169; Shankland et al., *Inner London*, p. 42.

74. Monica Dickens, *The Heart of London*, 1961, p. 48.

75. David Thomson, *In Camden Town*, 1983, p. 31ff.

76. Tindall, *The Fields Beneath*, p. 230.

77. On Ealing, see Campaign Against Racism and Fascism/Southall Rights, *Southall*, pp. 31–4; Deakin and others, *Colour, Citizenship and British Society*, p. 176; Emecheta, *Head above Water*, p. 46.

78. On the positive role of the LCC, GLC and Lambeth Borough Council in home ownership, see Burney, *Housing on Trial*, pp. 51–4, 124; on the Jamaican survey, see Foner, *Jamaica Farewell*, p. 46; on the Mauritians, see A. R. Mannick, *Mauritians in London*, 1987, p. 16; on the Sikhs, see Bhachu, *Twice Migrants*, p. 61; on the suburban profile, see Colin Brown, *Black and White Britain: The Third PSI Survey*, 1984, p. 98.

79. On the Loughborough Estate, see Burney, *Housing on Trial*, p. 134; on the Ugandan Asians, see Kuepper et al., *Ugandan Asians in Great Britain*, p. 81.

80. The list of estates comes from George Tremlett, *Living Cities*, 1979, p. 87; the figures for Holly Street are from Harrison, *Inside the Inner City*, p. 229, and for Broadwater Farm from *The Broadwater Farm Inquiry: Report of the Independent Inquiry into Disturbances of October 1985 at the Broadwater Farm Estate, Tottenham*, 1986. For a sophisticated overview, see David Smith and Anne Whalley, *Racial Minorities and Public Housing*, 1975. See also Shankland et al., *Inner London*, 1977.

81. For the East End, see Bethnal Green and Stepney Trades Council, *Blood on the Streets*; for Holly Street, see Harrison, *Inside the Inner City*, p. 382.

82. *The Broadwater Farm Inquiry*, pp. 24–9; see also Michael Elliott, *Heartbeat London*, 1986, pp. 54–5. On 'Parkview', see C. Lesley Andrews, *Tenants and Town Hall*, 1979, pp. 53, 59.

83. Tony Parker, *The People of Providence: A Housing Estate and Some of Its Inhabitants*, 1983.

84. For deterioration during the 1980s, see London Research Centre, *The Capital Divided: Mapping Poverty and Social Exclusion in London*, 1996, pp. 72–3; Anne Power and Rebecca Tunstall, *Swimming against the Tide: Polarisation or Progress on 20 Unpopular Council Estates, 1980–1995*, 1995, pp. 25–6.

85. On Holly Street, see London Borough of Hackney, *'Just What the Doctor Ordered': A Study of Housing, Health and Community Safety in Holly Street, Hackney, June 1996*, 1996, p. 19, and *Upwardly Mobile: Holly Street 1998*, 1998, p. 14; on Clapton Park, see London Borough of Hackney, *MORI: Residents' Survey. Final Report*, 1997, p. 6. On the country's 'unpopular places', see Roger Burrows and David Rhodes, *Unpopular Places? Area Disadvantage and the Geography of Misery in England*, 1998, pp. 23–6, 30.

86. Dennis, *Behind the Frontlines*, p. 207.

87. Terri Colpi, *The Italian Factor: The Italian Community in Great Britain*, 1991, pp. 195–6.

88. Hanif Kureishi, *The Black Album*, 1995, pp. 133–4.

89. For 1959, see Ramdin, *The Making of the Black Working Class in Britain*, p. 225;

for 1961–2, see Larry Ford, quoted in Phillips and Phillips, *Windrush*, pp. 274–5; for 1966, see Cecil Gutzmore in Winston James and Clive Harris (eds.), *Inside Babylon: The Caribbean Diaspora in Britain*, 1993, p. 215. On the older tradition, I know I've read it somewhere but I can't trace the source.

90. On the Louis Armstrong incident, see Tajfel and Dawson (eds.), *Disappointed Guests*, pp. 18–19.
91. Banks, *The L-Shaped Room*, pp. 166–7.

5. CAPITAL AND LABOUR

1. On the port, see Joseph G. Broodbank, *History of the Port of London*, 1921, who carries the most intimate narrative of the origins of the Port of London Act 1908; on the PLA, see D. J. Owen, *The Port of London Yesterday and Today*, 1927, and Alan Bell, *Port of London, 1909–1934*, 1934; see also John Pudney, *London's Docks*, 1975, for what was almost a valediction.
2. On London dock labour before the First World War, see H. A. Mess, *Casual Labour at the Docks*, 1916, and for the late nineteenth century, see Charles Booth, *Life and Labour of the People in London*, Vol. 7, 1896, and Gareth Stedman Jones, *Outcast London: A Study of the Relationship between Classes in Victorian Society*, 1971. On the 1937 incident, see London District Communist Party, *Sixteen Bob a Day for Dockers: Abolish Casual Labour*, n.d., p. 12.
3. See Raymond Smith, *Sea-Coal for London: History of the Coal Factors in the London Market*, 1961, pp. 339, 348. After the First World War the proportion of rail-borne coal fell to around one-third of the total, mainly due to electric power stations operating along the riverside and so obtaining coal by barge.
4. For the proportions of horse-drawn and motor vehicles in the early years, see the various annual traffic censuses carried out by the LCC and reported in *London Statistics*. For Watney Combe Reid, see Hurford Janes, *The Red Barrel: A History of Watney Mann*, 1963, pp. 188–9.
5. Robert R. Hyde, *Industry Was My Parish*, 1968, pp. 11–12.
6. For the ivory, see A. G. Linney, *The Peepshow of the Port of London*, n.d.; for the Crude Drug Department, see George R. Sims (ed.), *Living London*, n.d., Vol. III, p. 286; for the hair, see W. J. Passingham, *London's Markets: Their Origin and History*, n.d., p. 231; see also, generally, S. W. Dowling, *The Exchanges of London*, 1929, and Passingham, *London's Markets*.
7. David Kynaston's monumental and brilliant study of the internal workings of the City of London is indispensable. For an overview of the City in the nation's finances in these years, see William Ashworth, *An Economic History of England, 1870–1939*, 1960, p. 168ff., and Sidney Pollard, *The Development of the British Economy*, 1962, p. 14ff.

8. All these and many more were listed in City of London Corporation, *Ten Years' Growth of the City of London*, 1891, p. 101ff.; on the larger factories, see the Royal Commission on London Traffic, 1905–6, Vol. V, *Maps and Diagrams*, Plan F.

9. Walter Besant and others, *The Fascination of London: Shoreditch and the East End*, 1908, pp. 34–5. On Poplar, see François Bédarida, 'Urban Growth and Social Structure in Nineteenth-Century Poplar', *London Journal*, Vol. 1, No. 2, 1975.

10. On West Ham, see Arthur Philip Crouch, *Silvertown and Neighbourhood (Including East and West Ham): A Retrospect*, 1900, Edward G. Howarth and Mona Wilson, *West Ham: A Study in Social and Industrial Problems*, 1907, and John Marriott, '"West Ham: London's Industrial Centre and Gateway to the World". 1. Industrialization, 1840–1910', *London Journal*, Vol. 13, No. 2, 1987–8, and '"West Ham: London's Industrial Centre and Gateway to the World". 2. Stabilization and Decline, 1910–1939', *London Journal*, Vol. 14, No. 1, 1989; on Beckton, see Alfred Stokes, *East Ham: From Village to County Borough*, 1933, pp. 262–5.

11. Clementina Black, 'London's Tailoresses', *Economic Journal*, Vol. XIV, 1904, p. 559.

12. R. H. Tawney, *The Establishment of Minimum Rates in the Tailoring Industry under the Trades Board Act of 1909*, 1915, p. 6.

13. See Booth, *Life and Labour of the People in London*, Vol. 4, 1893; Black, 'London's Tailoresses'; Tawney, *The Establishment of Minimum Rates in the Tailoring Industry under the Trades Board Act of 1909*; on productivity, see Andrew Godley, 'Immigrant Entrepreneurs and the Emergence of London's East End as an Industrial District', *London Journal*, Vol. 21, No. 1, 1996, pp. 40–41.

14. On the east London furniture trade, see Booth, *Life and Labour of the People in London*, Vol. 4, 1893; Peter G. Hall, *The Industries of London since 1861*, 1962; J. E. Martin, *Greater London: An Industrial Geography*, 1966; J. L. Oliver, *The Development and Structure of the Furniture Industry*, 1966.

15. Booth, *Life and Labour of the People in London*, Vol. 6, 1895, p. 126.

16. Ibid., p. 25ff.

17. Ibid., pp. 8–10.

18. James A. Jones, *Wonderful London Today*, p. 22.

19. R. M. Fox, *Smoky Crusade*, 1937, pp. 49–50.

20. W. F. Watson, *Machines and Men: An Autobiography of an Itinerant Mechanic*, 1935, p. 70.

21. On the inventive role of Hatton Garden, see H. Marryat and Una Broadbent, *The Romance of Hatton Garden*, 1930.

22. Martin, *Greater London*, pp. 35–9.

23. *Darlington's London and Environs*, 1902, p. 236. An 'aërated' was a restaurant of the Aërated Bread Co. (ABC) chain.

24. Census of England and Wales 1901, *County of London*, p. 76ff.

25. London County Council/LSS, *London Statistics*, Vol. 23, 1913–14, pp. 72–7.

26. Booth, *Life and Labour of the People in London*, Series 2, Vol. 5, 1902, p. 84.

27. See Douglas H. Smith, *The Industries of Greater London: Being a Survey of the Recent Industrialization of the Northern and Western Sectors of Greater London*, 1933, and Martin, *Greater London*, for the larger impact of war production, especially in west London; and Jerry White, *Rothschild Buildings: Life in an East End Tenement Block, 1887–1920*, 1980, and Julia Bush, *Behind the Lines: East London Labour, 1914–1919*, 1984, for some effects on the East End and Jewish workers in particular.

28. On wartime munitions workers (skilled engineers) see James Hinton, *The First Shop Stewards' Movement*, 1973; for workers' experiences, see Watson, *Machines and Men*, Fox, *Smoky Crusade*, and H. J. Bennett, *I Was a Walworth Boy*, 1980; for unemployment in the building industry and generally, see London County Council/LSS, *London Statistics*, Vol. 26, 1915–20, pp. 85–7; and for the docks, see Broodbank, *History of the Port of London*, Vol. 2, and Bush, *Behind the Lines*.

29. On Victoria Station, see C. Sheridan Jones, *London in War-Time*, 1917, p. 25; on the musicians, see Michael MacDonagh, *In London during the Great War: The Diary of a Journalist*, 1935, p. 121 – we've already noted the German bands in Ch. 3; on the old men, see Mess, *Casual Labour at the Docks*, p. 137, and E. J. Lidbetter, *Heredity and the Social Problem Group*, 1933, p. 13; on the prisons, see Basil Thomson, *The Criminal*, 1925, p. 210ff., Wallace Blake, *Quod*, n.d., p. 158, and Hermann Mannheim, *Social Aspects of Crime in England between the Wars*, 1941, p. 100; and for the statistics, see London County Council/LSS, *London Statistics*, Vol. 26, 1915–20, pp. 74–5, 79, 152. The decline in 'lunatics' seems not to be explained by the use of the LCC mental hospitals for war casualties, because those mentally ill who were moved to other institutions were included in the figures.

30. For the general picture, see Arthur Marwick, *The Deluge: British Society and the First World War*, 1965, p. 125; and for the summonses, see London County Council/LSS, *London Statistics*, Vol. 26, 1915–20, p. 240. R. D. Blumenfeld, *All in a Lifetime*, 1931, pp. 59–60.

31. The national statistics are in A. L. Bowley, *Prices and Wages in the United Kingdom, 1914–1920*, 1921, p. 184ff. On the London effects, see London County Council, *The London Ambulance Service*, 1925, MacDonagh, *In London during the Great War*, and Bush, *Behind the Lines*.

32. The Hammersmith policeman was Harry Daley, *This Small Cloud: A Personal Memoir*, 1986, pp. 136–7. The classic text on the inter-war lure of London is the *Royal Commission on the Distribution of the Industrial Population*, 1940, especially Ch. XIV. See also Smith, *The Industries of Greater London*; Alfred Plummer, *New British Industries in the Twentieth Century: A Survey of Development and*

Structure, 1937; Political and Economic Planning, *Report on the Location of Industry*, 1939; the *Annual Reports* of His Majesty's Inspector of Factories, 1919–39; William H. Beveridge, *Full Employment in a Free Society*, 1944; Patrick Abercrombie, *Greater London Plan, 1944*, 1945; M. P. Fogarty, *Prospects of the Industrial Areas of Great Britain*, 1945; Hall, *The Industries of London since 1861*; Martin, *Greater London*.

33. See Political and Economic Planning, *Report on the Location of Industry*, 1939, p. 262ff. – its figures are from the 1931 Census. On the size of enterprises, see Ashworth, *An Economic History of England, 1870–1939*, p. 358. For 1931, see His Majesty's Inspector of Factories, *Annual Report*, 1931, pp. 9–10, and for Acton to Slough, see ibid., 1928, pp. 6–7. On west London generally, see Smith, *The Industries of Greater London*, Ch. V; London Passenger Transport Board, 1937, p. 24ff.; Abercrombie, *Greater London Plan, 1944*, pp. 201–2; Martin, *Greater London*, Ch. 2; John Armstrong, 'The Development of the Park Royal Industrial Estate in the Interwar Period: A Re-examination of the Aldcroft/Richardson Thesis', *London Journal*, Vol. 21, No. 1, 1996.

34. J. H. Forshaw and Patrick Abercrombie, *County of London Plan*, 1943, p. 90.

35. For employment figures in insured trades, see London County Council/LSS, *London Statistics*, Vol. 41, 1936–8, p. 59. For beer, see Hubert Llewellyn Smith (ed.), *The New Survey of London Life and Labour*, Vol. II, 1931, pp. 238–41. On Bermondsey and Clerkenwell, see ibid., Vol. V, 1933, p. 310, and Vol. VIII, 1934, p. 163.

36. Fogarty, *Prospects of the Industrial Areas of Great Britain*, p. 422. On the expanding and contracting industries between the wars, see Beveridge, *Full Employment in a Free Society*, pp. 316–20. And on their London significance, see Political and Economic Planning, *Report on the Location of Industry*, 1939, pp. 262–77.

37. The Islington figures are from the *Annual Reports* of the Islington Medical Officer of Health, 1914–38. Forshaw and Abercrombie, *County of London Plan*, gives 1,998 workshops in 1938. Metropolitan Borough of Camberwell, *Official Guide*, n.d., p. 82.

38. Forshaw and Abercrombie, *County of London Plan*, pp. 88–9.

39. Fogarty, *Prospects of the Industrial Areas of Great Britain*, pp. 418–20.

40. See Raphael Samuel, *Island Stories: Unravelling Britain. Theatres of Memory: Vol. II*, 1998, p. 88.

41. For the clerks, see NUCAW, *From 9 to 5.30*, 1936, pp. 3–4. For Hutt see Allen Hutt, *The Condition of the Working-Class in Britain*, 1933, p. 168. For the rest, see Smith (ed.), *The New Survey of London Life and Labour*, 1930–35, Vol. II, pp. 220–21, 224–5; Vol. V, pp. 28, 36–7, 98, 292–3; Vol. VIII, pp. 167, 170–72.

42. On the carman, see ibid., Vol. VIII, 1934, p. 39; on the London bus disputes of the 1930s, see Ken Fuller, *Radical Aristocrats: London Busworkers from the 1880s to the 1980s*, 1985.

43. Max Cohen, *What Nobody Told the Foreman*, 1953, pp. 34–5; the car-maker was William Ferrie, *The Banned Broadcast of William Ferrie*, 1934, pp. 6–7.

44. *Daily Worker*, 15 February 1937.

45. *Daily Worker*, 16 April 1932, letter from 'Chemical Worker, Hackney'; Doris Bailey, *Children of the Green: A True Story of Childhood in Bethnal Green, 1922–1937*, 1981, p. 106.

46. Female participation rates are in A. H. Halsey (ed.), *British Social Trends since 1900: A Guide to the Changing Social Structure of Britain*, 1988, p. 172. For the general picture, see D. Gittins, *Fair Sex: Family Size and Structure, 1900–39*, 1982, and Jane Lewis, *Women in England, 1870–1950: Sexual Divisions and Social Change*, 1984.

47. Calculated from figures in the Census of England and Wales 1911, *Occupations and Industries*; 1921, *County of London, Tables*, Part II, 1922; 1931, *Occupation Tables*, 1934; Smith (ed.), *The New Survey of London Life and Labour*, Vol. I, 1930, pp. 424–7; London County Council/LSS, *London Statistics*, Vol. 41, 1936–8, p. 59.

48. Edith Hall, *Canary Girls and Stockpots*, 1977, p. 29; the provincial-born figures come from *New Survey*, Vol. I, 1930, p. 467. See also S. Vere Pearson, *London's Overgrowth and the Causes of Swollen Towns*, 1939, p. 16.

49. On the protection movement and help for runaways, see *Daily Herald*, 12 November 1926 and 10 October 1927; and for Annie Hatton, see *Daily Herald* 19, 23 and 26 November and 3 December 1928.

50. For Ethel Waite, see *Daily Herald*, 9 June 1928. *Daily Herald*, 10 September 1927.

51. *Daily Worker*, 29 February 1932. On the Bedaux system, see Geoff Brown, *Sabotage: A Study in Industrial Conflict*, 1977. The full-blown Bedaux system was installed, or attempts were made to install it, at Peak Frean's Biscuits, Bermondsey (1931), Nestlé's Chocolates, Hayes (1931), Rogers' shirt manufacturers, Bermondsey (1932), Briggs' Motor Bodies, Dagenham (1933), Venesta Plywood, West Ham (1933), Elliott Brothers' electrical engineers, Lewisham (1933), Mullard's radio factory, Mitcham (1934), Rego Clothiers, Edmonton (1934) and doubtless more.

52. Smith (ed.), *The New Survey of London Life and Labour*, Vol. V, 1933, pp. 192–3; on Woolworth's wages, see *Daily Herald*, 11 May 1928.

53. Winifred Holtby, *South Riding: An English Landscape*, 1936, p. 396.

54. For bomb damage to the port in the First World War, see Broodbank, *History of the Port of London*, Vol. II, p. 470; for the Second World War, see Arthur Bryant, *Liquid History: To Commemorate Fifty Years of the Port of London Authority, 1909–1959*, 1960, p. 57.

55. See C. M. Kohan, *Works and Buildings*, 1952, pp. 318ff., 328ff.

56. See Mark Benney, *Over to Bombers*, 1943; Abercrombie, *Greater London Plan,*

1944, pp. 44–7; C. B. Purdom, *How Should We Rebuild London?*, 1945, pp. 57–65; and Philip Ziegler, *London at War, 1939–1945*, 1995, pp. 160–61, 260–61. I can find no evidence to support Ziegler's statement that 'there was more industry in Greater London in 1943 than before the war'; it contradicts Abercrombie and Purdom, who had an interest in such matters, and the drop in population makes it inherently unlikely.

57. Ibid., p. 124.

58. Winston G. Ramsey (ed.), *The Blitz: Then and Now*, 1987–9, Vol. 2, pp. 396–9.

59. Abercrombie, *Greater London Plan, 1944*, p. 47.

60. See Hall, *The Industries of London since 1861*, p. 21, for 1951 and Abercrombie, *Greater London Plan, 1944*, p. 203, for 1931.

61. For 1938, see Forshaw and Abercrombie, *County of London Plan*, pp. 88–9, and for 1947, see London County Council, *Administrative County of London Development Plan: Analysis*, 1951, p. 71. In concluding (ibid., p. 70) that the job losses over the period amounted to 18 per cent, the City seems to have been included in the 1947 figures but excluded from 1938, thus understating the loss. If the City is included in both years the loss is 22 per cent. On the East End furniture industry, see Oliver, *The Development and Structure of the Furniture Industry*, p. 77. On changes in central London's industrial profile, see D. F. Stevens in J. T. Coppock and Hugh C. Prince (eds.), *Greater London*, 1964, p. 186.

62. Hall, *The Industries of London since 1861*, p. 126ff.; Martin, *Greater London*, p. 217.

63. See James Bird, *The Geography of the Port of London*, 1957; Bryant, *Liquid History*; James Bird in Coppock and Prince (eds.), *Greater London*.

64. On the origins of the London airports, see Peter G. Hall, *Great Planning Disasters*, 1980; though Spike Mays, *Last Post*, 1974, p. 42ff., who worked at Heathrow in the early years, gives a different date for the Fairey runway. Airport statistics are in London County Council/LSS, *London Statistics*, New Series, Vol. III, 1947–56, pp. 178–9; and Greater London Council, *Greater London Statistics*, Vol. 1, 1966, p. 44.

65. Peter G. Hall, *Cities in Civilization: Culture, Innovation and Urban Order*, 1998, p. 897. For floorspace figures see D. F. Stevens in Coppock and Prince (eds.), *Greater London*, p. 179.

66. Greater London Council, *Greater London Development Plan Report of Studies*, 1969, p. 46, Table 3.19.

67. Greater London Council, *The London Industrial Strategy*, 1985, p. 333ff.; earlier calculations from Greater London Council, *Greater London Development Plan Report of Studies*, p. 46ff.

68. Michael Bonavia, *London Before I Forget*, 1990, p. 109; J. B. Priestley, *Angel Pavement*, 1930, p. 97.

69. Political and Economic Planning, *Report on the Location of Industry*, 1939, p. 68.

70. Ruth Glass et al., *London: Aspects of Change*, 1964, p. xvi.

71. Census of England and Wales 1931, *Occupation Tables*, 1934, p. 251ff.; 1951, *Report on Greater London and 5 Other Conurbations*, 1956, p. 233ff.

72. Purdom, *How Should We Rebuild London?*, pp. 52–3.

73. W. W. Daniel, *Racial Discrimination in England: Based on the PEP Report*, 1968, pp. 61–2. On Selfridge's, see Jonathon Green, *Them: Voices from the Immigrant Community in Contemporary Britain*, 1990, pp. 197–8.

74. See Clifford S. Hill, *West Indian Migrants and the London Churches*, 1963; Rashmi Desai, *Indian Immigrants to Britain*, 1963; James L. Watson (ed.), *Between Two Cultures: Migrants and Minorities in Britain*, 1977, for Chinese restaurants, and all the early commentators in London's immigrant communities cited in Ch. 4.

75. See, for example, Donald L. Foley, *Controlling London's Growth: Planning the Great Wen, 1940–1960*, 1963, p. 91; and Peter Cowan and others, *The Office: A Facet of Urban Growth*, 1969, pp. 189–91.

76. See D. E. Keeble, *Industrial Decentralization and the Metropolis: The North-West London Case*, 1968.

77. See C. D. Foster and Ray Richardson in David V. Donnison and David Eversley (eds.), *London: Urban Patterns, Problems, and Policies*, 1973, pp. 104–7.

78. See Bird, *The Geography of the Port of London*; Nigel Spearing, 'London's Docks: Up or Down the River?', *London Journal*, Vol. 4, No. 2, 1978; Alan Palmer, *The East End: Four Centuries of London Life*, 1989.

79. Hall revisited the 1963 prophecies in Peter G. Hall, *London 2001*, 1989, p. 50ff.; John Greve, *London's Homeless*, 1964, pp. 34, 35–6; on record tonnages, see Port of London Authority, *Annual Report*, 1963–4, p. 2; James Bird in Coppock and Prince (eds.), *Greater London*, p. 222.

80. Information from Port of London Authority, *Annual Reports*, 1962–3–1981. The daily press is another useful, if dispiriting, source.

81. On the dock closures, see ibid.; Spearing, 'London's Docks' (still optimistic about the future of the upper port); Alice Coleman, 'The Death of the Inner City: Cause and Cure', *London Journal*, Vol. 6, No. 1, 1980, pp. 17–18; Palmer, *The East End*; Hall, *Cities in Civilization*, p. 891ff.

82. Greater London Council, *The London Industrial Strategy*, p. 6; on Tower Hamlets, see Coleman, 'The Death of the Inner City', p. 5.

83. For the various figures, see Nick Buck et al., *The London Employment Problem*, 1986, p. 68; Andy C. Pratt in James Simmie (ed.), *Planning London*, 1994, p. 21; London Research Centre, *London 98*, 1998, p. 64, and *London at Work*, 1998.

84. Donnison and Eversley (eds.), *London*, pp. 24–5.

85. Anne Lapping, 'London's Burning! London's Burning! A Survey', *The Economist*, 1 January 1977, p. 22.

86. On the LOB-inspired moves, see Gerald Manners in Hugh Clout (ed.),

Changing London, 1978, p. 5; on the Bristol effect and the insurance industry, see M. Boddy et al., *Sunbelt City? A Study of Economic Change in Britain's M4 Growth Corridor*, 1986, p. 101ff.; on the MoD Procurement Agency, see *The Times*, 18 December 1995.

87. London Research Centre, *London at Work*, p. 2.

88. See Hamish McCrae and Frances Cairncross, *Capital City: London as a Financial Centre*, 1984, pp. 15–6; City of London Corporation, *International Banking Developments and London's Position as an International Banking Centre*, 1994; on the number of American banks, see Jerry Coakley in Leslie Budd and Sam Whimster (eds.), *Global Finance and Urban Living: A Study of Metropolitan Change*, 1992, p. 57.

89. McCrae and Cairncross, *Capital City*, p. 18; see also City of London Corporation, *International Banking Developments and London's Position as an International Banking Centre*; John Plender and Paul Wallace, *The Square Mile: A Guide to the New City of London*, 1985.

90. City of London Corporation, *International Banking Developments and London's Position as an International Banking Centre*, p. 41.

91. Greater London Council/GLS, *Greater London Statistics*, Vol. 1, 1966, p. 27, Vol. 16, 1983–4, p. 53.

92. On Big Bang and the run-up, see McCrae and Cairncross, *Capital City*; Plender and Wallace, *The Square Mile*; Adrian Hamilton, *The Financial Revolution: The Big Bang Worldwide*, 1986; Derek Diamond in Keith Hoggart and David Green (eds.), *A New Metropolitan Geography*, 1991.

93. Employment figures for 1989 and 1991 are in City of London Corporation, *The Competitive Position of London's Financial Services: Final Report*, 1995, Ch. 2, p. 4; the 1998 figure is in NOMIS Labour Force Survey, Region 81 (London), June 1998. The proportion of GDP is in London Research Centre, *London 98*, 1998, p. 52. On commuting see Andy Coupland in Andy Thornley (ed.), *The Crisis of London*, 1992, p. 32.

94. Andrew Church and Martin Frost, 'The Employment Focus of Canary Wharf and the Isle of Dogs: A Labour Market Perspective', *London Journal*, Vol. 17, No. 2, 1992, p. 135. On City employment in 1991, see London Research Centre, *London 95*, 1995, p. 122.

95. See especially Saskia Sassen, *The Global City: New York, London, Tokyo*, 1991; see also Anthony D. King, *Global Cities: Post-imperialism and the Internationalization of London*, 1990; Susan S. Fainstein et al., *Divided Cities: New York and London in the Contemporary World*, 1992; Susan S. Fainstein, *The City Builders: Property, Politics, and Planning in London and New York*, 1994; Hall, *Cities in Civilization*.

96. The quotation is from *Darlington's London and Environs*, p. 6, and was probably written in 1896. See also Sims (ed.), *Living London*, Vol. II, p. 236ff. It's hard to agree in this instance with David Eversley ('The Ganglion of Tourism: An

Unresolvable Problem for London', *London Journal*, Vol. 3, No. 2, 1977, pp. 188—9) that 'Tourism in London is an entirely new phenomenon . . .' On the location of London hotels and which class of visitor would be most at home in which, see K. Baedeker, *London and Its Environs*, 1911.

97. See D. F. Stevens in Coppock and Prince (eds.), *Greater London*, pp. 192—4; Clout (ed.), *Changing London*, p. 51; Eversley, 'The Ganglion of Tourism', pp. 189—90; figures on tourist numbers from 1975 supplied by LTB.

98. Greater London Council, *The London Industrial Strategy*, p. 593.

99. Visitor attraction statistics are in London Research Centre, *London 98*, p. 99, and available annually from the LTB. For the breakdown of GDP, see ibid., p. 52.

100. Greater London Council, *The London Industrial Strategy*, p. 465.

101. See, for example, F. E. Ian Hamilton in Hoggart and Green (eds.), *A New Metropolitan Geography*, p. 73.

102. London Planning Advisory Committee and Others, *London: World City Moving into the 21st Century, a Research Project*, 1991, p. 45.

103. On Hoxton, and more generally, see Michael Hebbert, *London: More by Fortune Than Design*, 1998, p. 157.

104. See, for example, the piece by Fay Maschler on 'Boom Town London' in *Evening Standard*, 2 September 1997.

105. London TEC Council, *London's Employer Survey, 1997—1998*, 1998, p. 12ff.

106. Andy Coupland in Thornley (ed.), *The Crisis of London*, p. 29.

107. See, for instance, Michael Hebbert's excellent overview in Hebbert, *London*.

6. RICHER AND POORER

1. For the East End lone parent, see Peter Townsend et al., *Poverty and Labour in London: Interim Report of a Centenary Study*, 1987, pp. 56—7; for Terry, the Calane family and their better-off neighbours, see Paul Harrison, *Inside the Inner City: Life under the Cutting Edge*, 1983, pp. 151—4, 160—61.

2. Mrs C. Chesterton, *I Lived in a Slum*, 1936, pp. 36—43 (Notting Dale).

3. Hugh Quigley and Ismay Goldie, *Housing and Slum Clearance*, 1934, pp. 214—15 (Hammersmith).

4. Maud Pember Reeves, *Round about a Pound a Week*, 1913, pp. 129—31, 110—11.

5. Ibid., p. 2.

6. On the background to the Booth Survey, see Henry Mayers Hyndman, *The Record of an Adventurous Life*, 1911, pp. 330—32; T. S. and M. B. Simey, *Charles Booth: Social Scientist*, 1960, Ch. 3; the findings are summarized in Charles Booth,

Life and Labour of the People in London, 1902, Vol. 17, p. 9; for the descriptions of poverty, see ibid., 1892, Series I, Vol. 1, p. 131.

7. The figures for pauperism and pensions (but not unemployment benefit) can reliably be traced in London County Council/LSS, *London Statistics*, at least until 1938.

8. A. L. Bowley, *Wages and Incomes in the United Kingdom since 1860*, 1937, p. 64.

9. Ibid., p. 61.

10. R. F. George, 'A New Calculation of the Poverty Line', *Journal of the Royal Statistical Society*, 1937; B. Seebohm Rowntree, *The Human Needs of Labour*, 1937, pp. 11–12.

11. For the estimate of poverty, see Hubert Llewellyn Smith (ed.), *The New Survey of London Life and Labour*, Vol. VI, 1934, p. 89. The *New Survey*'s 'London' was bigger than Booth's, taking in some of the late-Victorian and Edwardian out-County suburbs like West Ham, East Ham, Willesden, Hornsey, etc. Bowley's view on changes in poverty over the generations is in Vol. III, 1932, p. 72. The reworking of the *New Survey* estimates in the light of both George and Rowntree is mine. The estimate of those living below the George standard includes those in the *New Survey* area living at less than 5s above the poverty line. That, at 44s, is lower than the George figure of 47s 4d. But the average working-class household in the survey area contained only 3.48 persons and for a family of husband, wife and one child of ten George proposed a poverty line of 42s 7d. The 23 per cent of all Londoners would equate to 34 per cent of working-class Londoners, and that falls in line with G. D. H. and Margaret Cole's 1937 estimate that a third of working-class families in Britain lived below the Rowntree standard (*The Condition of Britain*, 1937, pp. 260–61).

12. Numbers in receipt of supplementary benefit (and later income support) in London are given in Greater London Council/GLS, *Greater London Statistics*, and (from 1986–7) the London Research Centre's annual London statistics. On London as the least poor region, see Peter Townsend, *Poverty in the United Kingdom: A Survey of Household Resources and Standard of Living*, 1979, p. 284.

13. On the strike and its effects in Hackney, see Harrison, *Inside the Inner City*, p. 145ff.; the 1994 figures are given in London Research Centre, *The Capital Divided: Mapping Poverty and Social Exclusion in London*, 1996, p. 147; the comparative figures nationally are in London Research Centre, *London 98*, 1998, p. 85.

14. The 1983 picture is in Townsend et al., *Poverty and Labour in London*, p. 47; that for 1996 is in London Research Centre, *The Capital Divided*, Ch. 2.

15. Ibid., p. 29.

16. Figures calculated from Census 1991, *Key Statistics for Urban and Rural Areas: The South East*, 1998, pp. 133–5.

17. See Richard M. and Kathleen Titmuss, *Parents Revolt: A Study of the Declining*

Birth-rate in the Acquisitive Societies, 1942. On the numbers of London men killed in the First World War, see Census of England and Wales 1931, *County of London*, 1932, p. vii.

18. Smith (ed.), *The New Survey of London Life and Labour*, Vol. I, 1930, p. 5.
19. On pre- and post-war wage rates, see A. L. Bowley, *Prices and Wages in the United Kingdom, 1914–1920*, 1921, and *Some Economic Consequences of the War*, 1930; and Labour Research Department, *Wages, Prices and Profits*, 1921, p. 48ff. On women's work in particular, see Irene Osgood Andrews, *Economic Effects of the War upon Women and Children in Great Britain*, 1918.
20. *East London Advertiser*, 24 February 1917.
21. For the pianos, see R. D. Blumenfeld, *All in a Lifetime*, 1931, p. 61; Florence Roberts, *The Ups and Downs of Florrie Roberts*, 1980, p. 5ff.; Dorothy Scannell, *Mother Knew Best: An East End Childhood*, 1974, p. 66; there are other examples in Jerry White, *Rothschild Buildings: Life in an East End Tenement Block, 1887–1920*, 1980, pp. 34–7.
22. 24 January 1919.
23. Thomas Burke, *London in My Time*, 1934, pp. 17, 29. On pre-war poverty as it affected children, see Anna Davin, *Growing Up Poor: Home, School and Street in London, 1870–1914*, 1996; on the sufferings of the London unemployed between the wars, see Jerry White in Geoffrey Alderman and Colin Holmes (eds.), *Outsiders and Outcasts: Essays in Honour of William J. Fishman*, 1993.
24. The expenditure on inessentials is given in Sidney Pollard, *The Development of the British Economy, 1914–1950*, 1962, p. 177; Louis Heren, *Growing Up Poor in London*, 1973, p. 40, deals with the compositors; and Robert Graves and Alan Hodge, *The Long Week-end: A Social History of Great Britain, 1918–1939*, 1941, p. 175, covers the women.
25. See the remarkable contrast at Webb Street School, Bermondsey, in Barclay Baron, *The Doctor: The Story of John Stansfield of Oxford and Bermondsey*, 1952, facing p. 214.
26. See Cyril Burt (the LCC's controversial child psychologist), *The Backward Child*, 1937, p. 123; Horace Thorogood, *East of Aldgate*, 1935, pp. 38–9; Thomas Okey, *A Basketful of Memories: An Autobiographical Sketch*, 1930, pp. 143–9 makes similar points. Heren, *Growing Up Poor in London*, p. 194.
27. See, for instance, Women's Group on Public Welfare, *Our Towns: A Close-up*, 1943, Ch.1.
28. Smith (ed.), *The New Survey of London Life and Labour*, Vol. I, 1930, p. 192. On the lipsticks, see Graves and Hodge, *The Long Week-end*, p. 278.
29. Burke, *London in My Time*, p. 29.
30. On the yuppie and his cognates, see Sam Whimster's delightful essay in Leslie Budd and Sam Whimster (eds.), *Global Finance and Urban Living: A Study of Metropolitan Change*, 1992.

31. John Galsworthy, *The Man of Property*, 1906, Part 1, Ch. I – the Saga opens *c.* 1886.

32. *The Times*, 10 February 1999.

33. The results of the postcode survey are given in the *Evening Standard*, 16 September 1996; Booth's list is in Booth, *Life and Labour of the People in London*, Vol. 17, 1902, p. 17. On suburban poverty between the wars, see R. M. Noordin, *Through a Workhouse Window: Being a Brief Summary of Three Years Spent by the Youngest Member of a Board of Guardians in the Course of His Duties*, 1929, p. 90ff. (Becontree); and the sad case of Minnie Weaving (a housewife on the Downham Estate who starved to death in the struggle to pay the rent and feed her family) was reported in the *Daily Worker*, 30 January 1933, and covered in Allen Hutt, *The Condition of the Working-Class in Britain*, 1933, p. 153. For the late-century rediscovery, see *Sunday Times*, 21 March 1999.

34. Census 1991, *Key Statistics for Urban and Rural Areas*, calculated from Tables 6 and 10.

35. For the evidence of widening inequality see Townsend et al., *Poverty and Labour in London*, p. 45; London Research Centre, *The Capital Divided*, pp. 3, 24, and *Focus on London 99*, 1999, p. 92.

36. For London's vital statistics, often compared with the nation's, see the annual volumes of London County Council/LSS, *London Statistics*; Greater London Council/GLS, *Greater London Statistics*; and London Research Centre, *London 95*, etc.; for the 1980s and 1990s, see London Research Centre, *The Capital Divided*, and Health of Londoners Project, *The Health of Londoners: a Public Health Report, 1998*.

37. Quoted in G. C. M. M'Gonigle and J. Kirby, *Poverty and Public Health*, 1936, pp. 33–5.

38. Royal Borough of Kensington, *Annual Reports of Medical Officer of Health*, 1932–4.

39. See London County Council, *Annual Report*, 1910, pp. 30–43, and London County Council/LSS, *London Statistics*, Vol. 41, 1936–8, p. 43. On diphtheria as a London disease, see J. A. H. Brincker, 'The Case for Diphtheria Immunisation', *Public Health*, August 1927.

40. John Holloway, *A London Childhood*, 1966, p. 26ff; Grace Foakes, *My Part of the River*, 1976, pp. 76–7; George Cook, *A Hackney Memory Chest*, 1983; Rose Gamble, *Chelsea Child*, 1979, p. 97ff; Robert Barltrop, *My Mother's Calling Me: Part I, Growing up in North East London between the Wars*, 1984, p. 13. See also Bella Aronovitch, *Give It Time: An Experience of Hospital, 1928–32*, 1974.

41. For a full report of the Inquiry findings into the outbreak, see *Public Health*, Vol. LI, No. 6, March 1938.

42. On the cancer study, see Sidney Davies, 'A Note on Cancer Occurrence in Hampstead and Shoreditch', *Public Health*, March 1924; on heart disease, see

London County Council/LSS; and on the 1990s, see Health of Londoners Project, *The Health of Londoners*, p. 16.

43. See Daniel Dorling, *Death in Britain: How Local Mortality Rates Have Changed, 1950-1990s*, 1997; Health of Londoners Project, *The Health of Londoners*, pp. 20–2; London Research Centre, *The Capital Divided*, p. 162. See also David Widgery, *Some Lives! A GP's East End*, 1991.

44. Quoted in George Orwell, *The Road to Wigan Pier*, 1937, p. 117. Orwell compliments Maugham on his frankness.

45. Census of England and Wales 1971, *County Reports: Greater London*, 1973, Part III, Table 25.

46. On laundry, see Fabian Society, Tract No. 190, *Metropolitan Borough Councils*, 1947, pp. 6–7; on Southam Street, see Royal Borough of Kensington, *Annual Reports of Medical Officer of Health*, 1934, p. 42.

47. Reeves, *Round about a Pound a Week*, pp. 36–7; Chris Massie, *The Confessions of a Vagabond*, n.d., pp. 90–91; Irene T. Barclay and Evelyn E. Perry, *Report on the Survey on Housing Conditions in Ward 2 of the Metropolitan Borough of St Pancras*, 1933, pp. 8, 14.

48. For Shoreditch and the County, see Quigley and Goldie, *Housing and Slum Clearance*, pp. 91–4. *Architects' Journal*, 26 October 1933, p. 524 (emphasis in original).

49. *Daily Herald*, 9–10 January 1928; see also S. Ingleby Oddie, *Inquest*, 1941, Ch. XIV, for an account of the events and the subsequent Westminster inquest.

50. See Parliamentary Papers, Ministry of Health, *Housing Act 1935: Report on the Overcrowding Survey in England and Wales*, 1936, pp. xvi–xviii.

51. See *Report of the Royal Commission on Housing in Greater London*, 1965, pp. 73, 84; Census of England and Wales 1961, *County Report: London*, 1963, p. xix.

52. This is the figure for 'household spaces'; local authorities owned 25 per cent of the County's 'structurally separate dwellings', but that ignored the dwellings not structurally separated from each other in houses in multiple occupation.

53. Calculated from Census 1991, *Key Statistics for Urban and Rural Areas*, pp. 82–110.

54. Greater London Council/GLS, *Greater London Statistics*, Vol. 24, 1991–2, p. 226.

55. Orwell, *The Road to Wigan Pier*, p. 71.

56. For the pre-First World War figures, see London County Council/LSS, *London Statistics*, Vol. 25, p. 85. The numbers in casual wards fluctuated considerably during the year and between years.

57. John Newsom, '*On the Other Side . . .*', 1930, p. 20ff. There is a very extensive literature of London vagrant and common lodging-house life in the twentieth century, including Jack London, *The People of the Abyss*, 1903; Mary Higgs, *Glimpses into the Abyss*, 1906; W. H. Davies, *The Autobiography of a Super-Tramp*,

1908, and *The Adventures of Johnny Walker, Tramp*, 1926; Frank L. Jennings, *In London's Shadows*, 1926, and *Men of the Lanes: The Autobiography of the Tramps' Parson*, 1958; Chesterton, *I Lived in a Slum*; Newsom, '*On the Other Side . . .*'; Frank Gray, *The Tramp: His Meaning and Being*, 1931; Terence Horsley, *The Odyssey of an Out-of-Work*, 1931; George Orwell, *Down and Out in Paris and London*, 1933; John Brown, *I Was a Tramp*, n.d.; W. A. Gape, *Half a Million Tramps*, 1936; Louis Gillain, *The Pavement My Pillow*, 1954; Jeremy Sandford, *Down and Out in Britain*, 1971; Robin Page, *Down among the Dossers*, 1973; Thomas Callaghan, *Tramp's Chronicle*, 1983.

58. I am thinking (for the 1990s) of Nick Danziger, *Danziger's Britain: A Journey to the Edge*, 1996, and his extraordinary photograph of Ian, a south London vagrant, facing p. 52; and, for instance, the vagrant outside the Drury Lane cookshop called 'A Convicts' Home', or the woman vagrant in Short's Gardens ('The "Crawlers"') in John Thomson and Adolphe Smith, *Street Life in London*, 1877.

59. Callaghan, *Tramp's Chronicle*, p. 202, recalls the post-war years; Page, *Down among the Dossers*, p. 109, makes the comparison with the 1920s.

60. On young rough sleepers, see the 'Special Report' on 'Secret London' in the *Big Issue*, 31 March–6 April 1997, pp. 12–26; on the numbers, see London Research Centre, *The Capital Divided*, p. 86.

61. The desires of ex-servicemen were noted by Dan Rider, *Ten Years' Adventures among Landlords and Tenants: The Story of the Rent Acts*, 1927, p. 203, who also gives the best account of the wartime and post-war housing situation in London; the hoax was reported in the *Evening Standard*, 6 December 1919; and reports of squatting can be found in *Daily Herald*, 26 November 1920, 12 July 1921, 15 April and 1 September 1922. See also David Englander, *Landlord and Tenant in Urban Britain, 1838–1918*, 1983.

62. See London District Communist Party, *Bramley's Speech at the Old Bailey: The Trial of the London Communists Arrested for Action on Behalf of London's Homeless, September, 1946*, 1946; and James Hinton, 'Self-help and Socialism: The Squatters' Movement of 1946', *History Workshop Journal*, Issue 25, 1988.

63. See John Greve, *London's Homeless*, 1964, pp. 16–18; on Sandford's intervention, see Stanley Alderson, *Britain in the Sixties: Housing*, 1962, pp. 110–12. For developments in the later 1960s, see John Greve et al., *Homelessness in London*, 1971.

64. The numbers of squatters in 1976 is taken from Stephen Platt in Stuart Henry (ed.), *Can I Have It in Cash? A Study of Informal Institutions and Unorthodox Ways of Doing Things*, 1981, p. 108ff. Figures for families in temporary accommodation are in London Research Centre, *London 95*, p. 99, and *Focus on London 99*, p. 48.

65. On the use of 'spiv' from the 1890s, see Eric Partridge's *A Dictionary of Historical Slang*, 1972; George 'Jack' Frost, *Flying Squad*, 1950, p. 68, writes of everyone's bemusement at Worby's use of the word in the late 1930s and the 'always with

us' quote which he attributes to ex-Superintendent John Sands of Scotland Yard; the best review of the 1940s spiv remains David Hughes's essay in Michael Sissons and Philip French (eds.), *Age of Austerity, 1945–51,* 1963, p. 86ff., from which the long quote comes; on Ally Sloper, the cartoon Cockney wide-boy who appeared in various guises from 1867 to 1923, see Peter Bailey's brilliant article, '"Ally Sloper's Half-Holiday", Comic Art in the 1880s', *History Workshop Journal,* Issue 16, 1983.

66. Michael Hebbert, *London: More by Fortune Than Design,* 1998, p. 179; Dick Hobbs, *Doing the Business: Entrepreneurship, the Working Class, and Detectives in the East End of London,* 1988, pp. 3–8. See also Janet Foster, *Villains: Crime and Community in the Inner City,* 1990.

67. All the examples listed here came out of interviews with elderly Islington residents (although their childhood memories covered a wider area of north London) carried out by Fran Bennett in the autumn of 1978. I am grateful to her for allowing me to use the material she gathered.

68. On the roughly equal numbers of men and women street sellers at the turn of the century, see Census of England and Wales 1901, *County of London,* pp. 90–91; on the Victoria paper stall, see Hunter Davies, *The Other Half,* 1966, p. 97ff.; on the flower girls and their tricks, see Olive Christian Malvery, *The Soul Market (with which is included 'The Heart of Things'),* 1906, p. 15; on the perils of street singing, see Jennings, *In London's Shadows,* p. 95.

69. Harold Hardy's statement is in Booth, *Life and Labour of the People in London,* Vol. VII, 1896, p. 260; the estimate of 30,000 street sellers is in Smith (ed.), *The New Survey of London Life and Labour,* Vol. III, 1932, p. 290; and 106 is in Parliamentary Papers, Ministry of Agriculture and Fisheries, *Markets and Fairs in England and Wales,* 1930, p. 137.

70. On the 1927 reforms and bribery of the police, see S. K. Ruck in Smith (ed.), *The New Survey of London Life and Labour,* Vol. III, 1932, pp. 298–9; on the survival of Notting Dale's Rag Fair, see Chesterton, *I Lived in a Slum,* pp. 58–9; James Curtis, *What Immortal Hand,* 1939, p. 96.

71. Harry Williams, *South London,* 1949, pp. 330–32.

72. On the revival of East Street, see Alex Forshaw and Theo Bergström, *The Markets of London,* 1983, p. 58.

73. Those who detected a falling off included Edwin Pugh in A. St J. Adcock (ed.), *Wonderful London,* n.d., Vol. I, p. 220; Alfred Rosling Bennett, *London and Londoners in the Eighteen-Fifties and Sixties,* 1924, pp. 47, 60, 68–9; R. Thurston Hopkins, *London Pilgrimages,* 1928, p. 39; Compton Mackenzie, *Our Street,* 1931, pp. 71–2, 89, 186–92; and Burke, *London in My Time,* pp. 48–51.

74. James A. Jones, *Wonderful London Today,* 1934, pp. 66–72; on cheap-jackery, see Philip Allingham, *Cheapjack,* 1934; on the rat-catcher see Mackenzie, *Our Street,* pp. 186–7.

75. John C. Goodwin, *One of the Crowd*, 1936, pp. 46, 211ff.; see also the same author's *Queer Fish*, n.d. (*c.* 1925).
76. Orwell, *Down and Out in Paris and London*, p. 162ff.
77. On the buskers see Booth, *Life and Labour of the People in London*, 1896, Series I, Vol. IV, p. 143 (numbers of Italian organ grinders); George R. Sims (ed.), *Living London*, n.d., Vol. III, p. 63ff.; Thomas Burke, *The London Spy: A Book of Town Travels*, 1922, p. 33, for the Jewish bagpipers and others; Jones, *Wonderful London Today*, pp. 37–43; for inside views of the busking life, see Bonar Thompson, *Hyde Park Orator*, 1933, and Gillain, *The Pavement My Pillow*; and for the early 1950s, see Julian Franklyn, *The Cockney: A Survey of London Life and Language*, 1953, pp. 58–61.
78. On second-hand women's clothing in the 1930s, see Melanie Tebbutt, *Making Ends Meet: Pawnbroking and Working-class Credit*, 1983, p. 157; on the paucity of shops selling new books compared to second-hand, see E. T. Cook, *Highways and Byways in London*, 1902, p. 303; on scrap metal see Gilbert Kelland, *Crime in London*, 1986, p. 30; Charlie Richardson, *My Manor*, 1991, p. 47.
79. On the numbers of stalls, see Smith (ed.), *The New Survey of London Life and Labour*, Vol. III, 1932, p. 293; Mayfair came to the Cally in Burke, *The London Spy*, p. 158; and the early-morning rush is described in typescript dated 27 April 1932, Parcel 8/3, Islington Summary, *New Survey of Life and Labour in London* archive, British Library of Political Science, London School of Economics. On the market generally, see Mary Benedetta, *The Street Markets of London*, 1936; for a stall-holder's experience see Jane Brown, *I Had a Pitch on the Stones*, 1946; and from the collector's point of view, see Jan and Cora Gordon, *The London Roundabout*, 1933.
80. Benedetta, *The Street Markets of London*, p. 156; the story of the necklace is in W. J. Passingham, *London's Markets: Their Origin and History*, n.d., pp. 31–2.
81. Forshaw and Bergström, *The Markets of London*, say antiques had not been heard of in Portobello Road until the late 1950s, but Monica Dickens, who lived nearby, recalled a 'flea market' there in the 1920s and after (*An Open Book*, 1978, p. 104); and Ronald Searle and Kaye Webb, *Looking at London: And People Worth Meeting*, 1953, pp. 45–6, show it was well known for antiques and curios by the early 1950s.
82. Booth, *Life and Labour of the People in London*, Vol. VII, 1896, p. 289ff.; Herbert Hodge, *I Drive a Taxi*, 1939, p. 63, gives the number of cabs in 1937 and tells it from the driver's point of view (see also his *Cab Sir?*, 1939); and the estimate of minicab drivers in London is from *Evening Standard*, 9 October 1996.
83. See Stuart Henry (ed.), *Can I Have It in Cash? A Study of Informal Institutions and Unorthodox Ways of Doing Things*, 1981, p. 12. On the used-car dealers of Notting Dale, see *The Times*, 3 September 1958.

84. Ferdynand Zweig, *Labour, Life and Poverty*, 1949, pp. 8–9; Harrison, *Inside the Inner City*, p. 134. For confirmatory evidence on London lorry drivers around 1946, see Freddie Foreman, *Respect: Autobiography of Freddie Foreman – Managing Director of British Crime*, 1996, p. 35.

85. The figures for each year are in London County Council/LSS.

86. Arthur R. L. Gardner, *Prisoner at the Bar*, 1931, pp. 71–3, for the begging wheezes and hiring children; on the latter, see also Gray, *The Tramp;* Jennings, *In London's Shadows*, pp. 98–9.

87. John Worby, *Spiv's Progress*, 1939, p. 65.

88. Gillain, *The Pavement My Pillow*, p. 95.

89. Orwell, *The Road to Wigan Pier*, p. 70. On Greenwich, see E. Wight Bakke, *The Unemployed Man: A Social Study*, 1933, pp. 93–6.

90. The advantages of Deptford and the UAB investigation are in Pilgrim Trust, *Men without Work: A Report Made to the Pilgrim Trust*, 1938, pp. 62–3; George Leslie Tiley, 'Memories of Islington Between the Wars', MS, 1975, pp. 19–20.

91. On the SPGBer see Robert Barltrop, *The Monument: The Story of the Socialist Party of Great Britain*, 1975, pp. 70–71; Cecil Chapman, *The Poor Man's Court of Justice: 25 Years as a Metropolitan Police Magistrate*, 1925, p. 129.

92. Harrison, *Inside the Inner City*, p. 148.

93. *Evening Standard*, 14 November 1996.

94. Danziger, *Danziger's Britain*, pp. 14–5.

7. CITY OF DREADFUL NIGHT

1. Harding's recollections, sixty years on, were recorded by Raphael Samuel in *East End Underworld: Chapters in the Life of Arthur Harding*, 1981, Ch. 12; the magistrate's in Chartres Biron, *Without Prejudice: Impressions of Life and Law*, 1936, p. 252ff.; and the policeman's in Frederick Porter Wensley, *Detective Days: The Record of 42 Years' Service in the Criminal Investigation Department*, 1931, Ch. XII.

2. The practice features in a fine London novel of the 1920s, Thomas Burke, *The Bloomsbury Wonder*, 1929, pp. 35–6.

3. On the racecourse gangs, James Morton, *Gangland: London's Underworld*, 1992, Ch. 1, gives a useful overview. See also Billy Hill, *Boss of Britain's Underworld*, 1955; Tom Divall, *Scoundrels and Scallywags (and Some Honest Men)*, 1929; James Berrett, *When I Was at Scotland Yard*, 1932; F. D. 'Nutty' Sharpe, *Sharpe of the Flying Squad*, 1938; Edward Greeno, *War on the Underworld*, 1960. The end of the gangs was forecast in Walter Hambrook, *Hambrook of the Yard*, 1937, p. 189.

4. Wensley, *Detective Days*, 1931, p. 107ff.

5. On the German gangs, see ibid., p. 40, and Hambrook, *Hambrook of the Yard*,

pp. 36–7. On the pearls, see Christmas Humphreys, *The Great Pearl Robbery of 1913: A Record of Fact*, 1929.

6. See Donald Rumbelow, *The Houndsditch Murders: And the Siege of Sidney Street*, 1973; William Nott-Bower, *Fifty-Two Years a Policeman*, 1926; Wensley, *Detective Days*; B. Leeson, *Lost London: The Memoirs of an East End Detective*, 1930.

7. On Cockney thieves, see Wensley, *Detective Days*, p. 137; on Delaney, see Robert Fabian, *Fabian of the Yard*, 1950, p. 33ff.; on celluloid and housebreaking, see Robert Higgins, *In the Name of the Law*, 1958, pp. 33, 25.

8. On Hoxton and its dips, see Charles Booth, *Life and Labour of the People in London*, Series 3, Vol. II, 1902, p. 111; Charles Leach, *On Top of the Underworld*, 1933, p. 88ff.; Hambrook, *Hambrook of the Yard*, p. 55ff.; Greeno, *War on the Underworld*, p. 21; Tony Parker and Robert Allerton, *The Courage of His Convictions*, 1962, p. 27ff.; Robert R. Hyde, *Industry Was My Parish*, 1968, p. 40. On the Nile Mob at Goodwood, see Higgins, *In the Name of the Law*, pp. 42–3. And K. Baedeker, *London and Its Environs*, 1911, p. 63.

9. On the Shoreditch incident, see Sharpe, *Sharpe of the Flying Squad*, p. 22ff. For the view that stealing from the poor is a post-war phenomenon, see Robert Barltrop and Jim Wolveridge, *The Muvver Tongue*, 1980, p. 55. On criminality in the poorest streets, see Jerry White, *The Worst Street in London: Campbell Bunk, Islington between the Wars*, 1986, pp. 47, 100–101.

10. Sharpe, *Sharpe of the Flying Squad*, pp. 154–5.

11. See ibid., p. 40; Ruby Sparks, *Burglar to the Nobility*, 1961.

12. See Netley Lucas, *London and Its Criminals*, 1924, pp. 99–104; Sharpe, *Sharpe of the Flying Squad*, p. 144ff.

13. Wensley, *Detective Days*, p. 84.

14. Ibid., pp. 300–301. On drunkenness, see Hubert Llewellyn Smith (ed.), *The New Survey of London Life and Labour*, Vol. IX, 1935, p. 249, and Vol. I, 1930, pp. 35–6; E. Roy and Theodora Calvert, *The Lawbreaker: A Critical Study of the Modern Treatment of Crime*, 1933, pp. 33–5; and Hermann Mannheim, *Social Aspects of Crime in England between the Wars*, 1940, for the most comprehensive overview of trends nationwide. In 1998 there were 39,000 arrests for drunkenness by the Metropolitan Police.

15. Figures for 1903 and 1928 from Smith (ed.), *The New Survey of London Life and Labour*, Vol. I, 1930, p. 400; and for 1933–9 from the *Annual Reports* of the Commissioner of Police of the Metropolis for the years 1933 (p. 49) and 1939 (p. 48).

16. Fabian, *Fabian of the Yard*, p. 93; see also Harold Scott, *Scotland Yard*, 1954, Ch. 7; Higgins, *In the Name of the Law*, Ch. 10.

17. See Clarence Rook, *The Hooligan Nights: Being the Life and Opinions of a Young and Impertinent Criminal Recounted by Himself . . .*, 1899; S. F. Hatton, *London's*

Bad Boys, 1931; L. Le Mesurier, *Boys in Trouble: A Study of Adolescent Crime and Its Treatment*, 1931; Smith (ed.), *The New Survey of London Life and Labour*, Vol. IX, 1935, p. 354; A. E. Morgan, *The Needs of Youth: A Report Made to King George's Jubilee Trust Fund*, 1939, p. 164ff.; A. M. Carr-Saunders et al., *Young Offenders: An Enquiry into Juvenile Delinquency*, 1943, pp. vii–viii.

18. Of 1,200 LCC schools, 290 were destroyed or seriously damaged by bombing or rockets, and a further 310 extensively damaged; just fifty escaped unscathed. See Stuart Maclure, *One Hundred Years of London Education, 1870–1970*, 1970, p. 138.

19. On the rise in juvenile arrests, see London County Council/LSS, *London Statistics*, New Series, Vol. I, 1945–54, p. 132. On the Elephant Boys, see Harry Hopkins, *The New Look: A Social History of the Forties and Fifties in Britain*, 1963, pp. 207–8; on the weaponry, see Robert Fabian, *London after Dark: An Intimate Record of Night Life in London, and a Selection of Crime Stories from the Case Book of Robert Fabian*, 1954, p. 101ff.; and on Michael Davies, see Tony Parker, *The Plough Boy*, 1965.

20. H. Montgomery Hyde (ed.), *Trial of Christopher Craig and Derek William Bentley*, 1954, p. 1. See also William Bentley, *My Son's Execution*, 1957; Christopher Berry-Dee and Robin Odell, *Dad, Help Me Please*, 1990.

21. On the prostitute murders of the 1930s, see Sharpe, *Sharpe of the Flying Squad*; John Du Rose, *Murder Was My Business*, 1971, p. 92, claimed to know the identity of Jack the Stripper and said he eluded justice by committing suicide; a similar theory attaches to Jack the Ripper.

22. The best account is in Higgins, *In the Name of the Law*, Ch. 4; see also Greeno, *War on the Underworld*, p. 116ff.

23. George Orwell, 'Decline of the English Murder', *Tribune*, February 1946.

24. See Macdonald Critchley (ed.), *The Trial of Neville George Clevely Heath*, 1951.

25. See Lord Dunboyne (ed.), *The Trial of John George Haigh (the Acid Bath Murder)*, 1953.

26. The magnificent account in Ludovic Kennedy, *Ten Rillington Place*, 1961, remains definitive, but see also Michael Eddowes, *The Man on Your Conscience: An Investigation of the Evans Murder Trial*, 1955, F. Tennyson Jesse (ed.), *Trials of Timothy John Evans and John Reginald Halliday Christie*, 1957, and Daniel Brabin, *Rillington Place*, 1966; for Nilsen, see Brian Masters, *Killing for Company*, 1985.

27. These are figures for the Metropolitan Police District and the City combined. See London County Council/LSS, *London Statistics*, Vol. I, 1945–54, p. 130. On crime in the Second World War, with a special focus on London, see Edward Smithies, *Crime in Wartime: A Social History of Crime in World War II*, 1982.

28. Wally Thompson, *Time off My Life*, 1956, p. 140; on handbag snatching, see Peter Beveridge, *Inside the CID*, 1957, p. 74.

29. Frankie Fraser, *Mad Frank: Memoirs of a Life of Crime*, 1994, pp. 26–7; Beveridge, *Inside the CID*, pp. 73–4; on metals and the Korean War, see London County Council/LSS, *London Statistics*, New Series, Vol. I, 1945–54, p. 131.

30. Barbara Nixon, *Raiders Overhead: A Diary of the London Blitz*, 1943, p. 82; Thompson, *Time off My Life*, 1956, p. 140.

31. See Fred Narborough, *Murder on My Mind*, 1959, pp. 71–2, for the guns; Claud Mullins, *Fifteen Years' Hard Labour*, 1948, pp. 46–7, 73, for the costermongers; on deserters in Soho, see Andrew Sinclair, *War Like a Wasp: The Lost Decade of the 'Forties*, 1989, p. 51; and Alfie Hinds's explanation is in Alfred Hinds, *Contempt of Court*, 1966, p. 9. Maybe he didn't need much encouragement: 'My mother . . . was well known in the London underworld as a hoister . . .'

32. Fabian, *London After Dark*, pp. 93–4.

33. Ernest Millen, *Specialist in Crime*, 1972, p. 243; Du Rose, *Murder Was My Business*, p. 18.

34. See Hill, *Boss of Britain's Underworld*, and Morton, *Gangland*, Ch. 2, for the background; see Narborough, *Murder on My Mind*, p. 86ff., for the Corner Mob, and Hill, *Boss of Britain's Underworld*, pp. 6–7, for the mobs of post-war London and their topography.

35. On the chiv, see ibid., p. 8, and p. 101 for the torture.

36. On the Treacle Plaster Robbery, see Francis Carlin, *Reminiscences of an Ex-Detective*, 1925, Ch. V; Cecil Chapman, *The Poor Man's Court of Justice: 25 Years as a Metropolitan Police Magistrate*, 1925, p. 209ff.

37. Hill, *Boss of Britain's Underworld*, pp. 162–8. The assessment of Eastcastle Street as the opening of a new era was by a policeman, Richard Jackson, in his *Occupied with Crime*, 1967, p. 129.

38. On the KLM raid, see Hill, *Boss of Britain's Underworld*, Ch. 16; Fraser, *Mad Frank*, p. 108.

39. On robbery generally in the 1950s, see F. H. McClintock and Evelyn Gibson, *Robbery in London*, 1961; Jackson, *Occupied with Crime*, pp. 203–4.

40. See, among a large collection, Piers Paul Read, *The Train Robbers*, 1978; Ronnie Biggs, *His Own Story*, 1981, and *Odd Man Out: My Life on the Loose and the Truth about the Great Train Robbery*, 1994; Jack Slipper, *Slipper of the Yard*, 1981.

41. On the Richardsons, see Robert Parker, *Rough Justice*, 1981; Charlie Richardson, *My Manor*, 1991; Morton, *Gangland*; Fraser, *Mad Frank*.

42. John Pearson, *The Profession of Violence: The Rise and Fall of the Kray Twins*, 1973, and its many subsequent editions remains the best overview in a growing library of Kray memorabilia, including the twins' own and their older brother Charlie's autobiographies. 'Truth', of course, remains hard to pin down. See also Leonard Read, *Nipper: The Story of Leonard 'Nipper' Read*, 1991, for the

policeman's view. For some of the contemporary context, see Gerald Sparrow, *Gang-Warfare: A Probe into the Changing Pattern of British Crime*, 1968, especially pp. 50–51, for his estimate of gaming houses paying protection.

43. Crime figures are published in the *Annual Reports* of the Commissioner of Police of the Metropolis. National figures are in Criminal Statistics, England and Wales, published annually.

44. On the rise in crime of the 1960s and 1970s, see Leon Radzinowicz and Joan King, *The Growth of Crime: The International Experience*, 1977; Ben Whitaker, *The Police in Society*, 1979, p. 266; F. H. McClintock and N. Howard Avison, *Crime in England and Wales*, 1968; Peter Laurie, *Scotland Yard: A Personal Inquiry*, 1970; John Ball et al., *Cops and Robbers: An Investigation into Armed Bank Robbery*, 1978; Richard Kinsey et al., *Losing the Fight against Crime*, 1986.

45. Norman Shrapnel, *The Seventies: Britain's Inward March*, 1980, p. 142.

46. On the 1920s, see J. Kenneth Ferrier, *Crooks and Crime*, 1928, p. 199ff.; and James Berrett, *When I Was at Scotland Yard*, 1932, p. 167ff.; on 1939, see Fabian, *Fabian of the Yard*, p. 64ff.; and on 1954–5, see Leonard Burt, *Commander Burt of Scotland Yard*, 1959, pp. 120–23.

47. For the main events of the 1973–82 campaigns, see Robert Mark, *In the Office of Constable*, 1978, and David McNee, *McNee's Law*, 1983.

48. John Camden Hotten, *The Slang Dictionary*, 1865, p. 183. He gives the primary use of mug as 'to strike in the face, or fight. Also, to rob by the garrote.'

49. On mugging as a moral panic of the 1970s, see Stuart Hall et al., *Policing the Crisis: Mugging, the State, and Law and Order*, 1978.

50. On the 1970s, see Michael Pratt, *Mugging as a Social Problem*, 1980.

51. The *British Crime Survey*, 1988, pp. 19–20, showed increasing propensity to report and record crime over the years. It estimated 59 per cent of burglary with loss was recorded by police in 1972 and 85 per cent in 1987; the figures for the percentage reported were 78 per cent and 90 per cent respectively.

52. London Research Centre, *Focus on London 99*, 1999, pp. 96–8. The Islington data come from Trevor Jones et al., *The Islington Crime Survey: Crime, Victimization and Policing in Inner-city London*, 1986.

53. *Sunday Times Magazine*, 15 August 1999, p. 23.

54. Royal Commission upon the Duties of the Metropolitan Police, *Report Together with Appendices*, 1908, Vol. I, pp. 388–409.

55. *The Times*, 24 December 1908.

56. Royal Commission upon the Duties of the Metropolitan Police, *Report Together with Appendices*, 1908, Vol. I, p. 66; Arthur Thorp, *Calling Scotland Yard: Being the Casebook of Chief Superintendent Arthur Thorp*, 1954, pp. 26–7.

57. John Capstick, *Given in Evidence*, 1960, p. 37.

58. For Enfield, see *Tottenham and Edmonton Weekly Herald*, 18 July 1919; for Greenwich, see *The Times*, 8 July 1919; for Wood Green, see *Tottenham and*

Edmonton Weekly Herald, 15 August 1919; for Brixton, see *The Times*, 5 August 1919; for Tottenham, see *Tottenham and Edmonton Weekly Herald*, 19 September 1919; for Kilburn, see *Daily Herald*, 2 September 1919; the north London magistrate is quoted in *Islington Gazette*, 11 August 1919; Gervais Rentoul, *Sometimes I Think: Random Reflections and Recollections*, 1940, p. 81. For a more recent study of hostile crowds, see Phil Cohen, 'Policing the Working-class City', in National Deviancy Conference/Conference of Socialist Economists, *Capitalism and the Rule of Law: From Deviancy Theory to Marxism*, 1979, p. 121ff. See also White, *The Worst Street in North London*, Ch. 4.

59. Booth, *Life and Labour of the People in London*, 1902, Series 2, Vol. 5, p. 29.

60. On sus in the 1930s, see Ronald Kidd, *British Liberty in Danger: An Introduction to the Study of Civil Rights*, 1940, p. 107ff.; on police station and other beatings, see Graham Grant, *The Diary of a Police Surgeon*, 1920, pp. 15–16, Chapman, *The Poor Man's Court of Justice*, pp. 149–52, Albert Lieck, *Bow Street World*, 1938, pp. 51–2; on obscene remarks in the streets, see Hugh R. P. Gamon, *The London Police Court To-Day and To-Morrow*, 1907, p. 26; on Helen Adele, see the daily press for August 1928; on the virgin prostitute, see *Daily Herald*, 28 May 1928.

61. Louis Heren, *Growing Up Poor in London*, 1973, p. 79; Desmond Morse-Boycott, *Ten Years in a London Slum: Being the Adventures of a Clerical Micawber*, 1931, pp. 18–19; Victor Meek, *Cops and Robbers*, 1962, p. 14.

62. On Trenchard, see Andrew Boyle, *Trenchard*, 1962, pp. 637–8. On Limehouse, see Cecil Bishop, *From Information Received*, 1932, pp. 18–19. The practice of giving beer probably declined after the First World War but remained common enough; it was certainly rife in the West End around 1970, as the author can testify. Harry Daley, *This Small Cloud: A Personal Memoir*, 1986, pp. 92–109.

63. Gilbert Kelland, *Crime in London*, 1986, pp. 32–5.

64. Greeno, *War on the Underworld*, p. 19.

65. On Goddard, see the daily press for 22–30 January 1929; K. Meyrick, *Secrets of the 43: Reminiscences by Mrs Meyrick*, 1933; Douglas G. Browne, *The Rise of Scotland Yard: A History of the Metropolitan Police*, 1956, p. 333ff.; and Morton, *Gangland*.

66. On Trenchard's view of the CID, see Boyle, *Trenchard*, p. 609; Narborough, *Murder on My Mind*, p. 86; Kelland, *Crime in London*, pp. 39–40.

67. Daley, *This Small Cloud*, p. 201; William Rawlings, *A Case for the Yard*, 1961, p. 33.

68. On the failure of Sir Basil Thomson's appeal against conviction, see *Daily Herald*, 6 February 1926. On the Money-Savidge case, see S. Fowler Wright, *Police and Public*, 1929; Lieck, *Bow Street World*; Lilian Wyles, *A Woman at Scotland Yard: Reflections on the Struggles and Achievements of 30 Years in the Metropolitan Police*, 1952; and the daily press of May 1928. On the motorist and

the police, see Maurice Tomlin, *Police and Public*, 1936, pp. 110–11; and T. A. Critchley, *A History of the Police in England and Wales, 900–1966*, 1967, pp. 176–7, 273–4.

69. *Dixon of Dock Green* was not the first of the enormous run of London police series that filled so much of British TV in the second half of the century. That honour seems to have gone to *Fabian of the Yard*, 1954; *Colonel March of Scotland Yard* was also shown in the same year as *Dixon*.

70. On the telephone, see Hambrook, *Hambrook of the Yard*, pp. 40–43; on Bungo, see H. M. Howgrave-Graham, *Light and Shade at Scotland Yard*, 1947, pp. 9–10; on superintendents on horseback, see Nevil Macready, *Annals of an Active Life*, 1924, Vol. I, p. 316; on the numbers of women in the Met, see Greater London Council/GLS, *Greater London Statistics*, Vol. 1, 1966, p. 188.

71. On Syme, see Gerald W. Reynolds and Anthony Judge, *The Night the Police Went on Strike*, 1968, p. 6ff. On the culture of secrecy, see Iain Adamson, *The Great Detective: A Life of Deputy Commander Reginald Spooner of Scotland Yard*, 1966, p. 272. On the tie, see Beveridge, *Inside the CID*, p. 41. Read, *Nipper*, pp. 49–50.

72. Parliamentary Papers, *The Stephen Lawrence Inquiry: Report of an Inquiry by Sir William Macpherson of Cluny*, 1999.

73. Glyn Roberts, *I Take This City*, 1933, p. 128; 'nigger' crops up nonchalantly in W. C. Gough, *From Kew Observatory to Scotland Yard: Being Experiences and Travels in 28 Years of Crime Investigation*, 1925, and Sharpe, *Sharpe of the Flying Squad*, for example.

74. Quoted in Donald Hinds, *Journey to an Illusion: The West Indian in Britain*, 1966, pp. 140–41. See also Ruth Glass, *Newcomers: The West Indians in London*, 1960, pp. 168–9; Michael Abdul Malik, *From Michael de Freitas to Michael X*, 1968, Ch. 9.

75. On Joe Hunte's pamphlet, see Paul Gordon, *White Law: Racism in the Police, Courts and Prisons*, 1983, p. 24ff.

76. On Ifill, see Gus John and Derek Humphry, *Because They're Black*, 1971, p. 119ff.; on Gomwalk, see Derek Humphry, *Police Power and Black People*, 1972, p. 68ff.

77. On the Mangrove march, see Darcus Howe, *From Bobby to Babylon: Blacks and British Police*, 1988, p. 38ff., for the liveliest account. See also Gordon, *White Law*, 1983, pp. 39ff., 97–8; and Michael Keith, *Race, Riots and Policing: Lore and Disorder in a Multi-racist Society*, 1993, for background and subsequent events.

78. Parliamentary Papers, *The Brixton Disorders: Report of an Inquiry by the Rt. Hon. The Lord Scarman, OBE*, 1981, p. 34.

79. Ibid. The most thorough analysis of the 1981 riots as a whole is in Keith, *Race, Riots and Policing*, see also John Benyon (ed.), *Scarman and After: Essays Reflecting*

Lord Scarman's Report, the Riots and their Aftermath, 1984, and John Benyon, *A Tale of Failure: Race and Policing*, 1986.

80. Melissa Benn and Ken Worpole, *Death in the City: An Examination of Police-related Deaths in London*, 1986, p. 64.

81. *Broadwater Farm Revisited: Second Report of the Independent Inquiry into Disturbances of October 1985 at the Broadwater Farm Estate, Tottenham*, 1989, pp. 41–3.

82. Mark, *In the Office of Constable*, is commendably honest in this as in other matters; but honesty did not make him right.

83. Ibid., p. 286; Marshall is quoted approvingly in Whitaker, *The Police in Society*, p. 235.

84. McNee, *McNee's Law*, p. 121ff; Kelland, *Crime in London*, pp. 282–85.

85. David J. Smith et al., *Police and People in London*, 1983, Vol. IV: *The Police in Action*, pp. 113, 116.

86. Benyon, *A Tale of Failure*, p. 40.

87. Parliamentary Papers, *The Stephen Lawrence Inquiry: Report of an Inquiry by Sir William Macpherson of Cluny*, 1999, Vol. I, para 6.45 (d).

88. Sheila Patterson, *Dark Strangers: A Sociological Study of the Absorption of a Recent West Indian Migrant Group in Brixton, South London*, 1963, pp. 88–9; Simon Holdaway and Anne-Marie Barron, *Resigners? The Experience of Black and Asian Police Officers*, 1997, pp. 196–8, for Sir Paul Condon's difficulties with the Black Police Association.

89. See Mary Grigg, *The Challenor Case*, 1965; Morton, *Gangland*.

90. Quoted in David Ascoli, *The Queen's Peace: The Origins and Developments of the Metropolitan Police, 1829–1979*, 1979, pp. 308–9.

91. Williamson is quoted in Morton, *Gangland*, p. 134. See also B. Cox et al., *The Fall of Scotland Yard*, 1977.

92. Mark, *In the Office of Constable*, pp. 124, 127–31, 164–5, 199, 226. See also Cox et al., *The Fall of Scotland Yard*.

93. On DCS Lundy, see Andrew Jennings et al., *Scotland Yard's Cocaine Connection*, 1990. The Robbery Squad officer was the late DCI Eist, on whom see Freddie Foreman, *Respect: Autobiography of Freddie Foreman – Managing Director of British Crime*, 1996, pp. 206–7; Jennings et al., *Scotland Yard's Cocaine Connection*, p. 19; Morton, *Gangland*. Eist was prosecuted for corruption but acquitted. For a broader cultural analysis of the detective, see Dick Hobbs, *Doing the Business: Entrepreneurship, the Working Class, and Detectives in the East End of London*, 1988.

94. On Operation Countryman and the Met's defence, see McNee, *McNee's Law*, Ch. 9, and Kelland, *Crime in London*, p. 303ff. The journalists were Jennings et al., *Scotland Yard's Cocaine Connection*, pp. 187–8.

95. *The Times*, 16 May 1998; see also 15 October 1998.

8. THE SWINGING CITY

1. R. M. Fox, *Smoky Crusade*, 1937, p. 30ff. He talks of the 'Monkeys' Parade' but the maybe less grammatical version of Monkey Parade was most commonly met with.

2. On the City Imperial Volunteers, see Henry Smith, *From Constable to Commissioner: The Story of Sixty Years, Most of Them Misspent*, 1910, pp. 209–14, and R. D. Blumenfeld, *R.D.B.'s Diary, 1887–1914*, 1930, p. 117; on pageants, see J. B. Booth, '*A Pink 'Un' Remembers*, 1937, p. 4; Sidney Lee, *King Edward VII: A Biography*, 1927, Vol. II, for the events of 1901–10, and Harold Nicholson, *King George the Fifth: His Life and Reign*, 1952, for 1911; see Percy Armytage, *By the Clock of St James's*, 1927, for an insider's view of these events.

3. On Earls Court and the Great Wheel, see George R. Sims (ed.), *Living London*, n.d., Vol. 3, pp. 161, 341ff; *Darlington's London and Environs*, 1902, p. 355; J. B. Booth, *London Town*, 1929, p. 178ff.; Harold Clunn, *The Face of London: The Record of a Century's Changes and Developments*, 1934, pp. 357–8; Claude Langdon, *Earls Court*, 1953, p. 20ff. On White City, see Clunn, *The Face of London*, pp. 377–8; M. Willson Disher, *Pleasures of London*, 1950, pp. 280–81; Langdon, *Earls Court*, p. 22. For the gaudy girls, see Betty May, *Tiger-Woman: My Story*, 1929, p. 18 – she is recalling the Limehouse of her youth. On Ally Pally, see Ron Carrington, *Alexandra Park and Palace: A History*, 1975.

4. See Ralph Nevill, *Night Life: London and Paris – Past and Present*, 1926, p. 68, for his recollections of the 1880s and 1890s, and *Mayfair and Montmartre*, 1921, pp. 71–2, for pre-1914 luxury. On the lights, see Robert Machray, *The Night Side of London*, 1902, p. 4, and W. J. Loftie, *The Colour of London: Historic, Personal, and Local*, 1907, p. 151.

5. Machray, *The Night Side of London*, pp. 10–21.

6. On Piccadilly virgins, see Booth, *London Town*, p. 131; on prostitution in 1906, see Royal Commission upon the Duties of the Metropolitan Police, *Report Together with Appendices*, 1908, Vol. I, pp. 85, 216; on the brothels, see Cecil Chapman, *The Poor Man's Court of Justice: 25 Years as a Metropolitan Police Magistrate*, 1925, p. 94. Thomas Burke, *Nights in Town: A London Autobiography*, 1915, p. 86.

7. For Swan and Edgar, see Royal Commission upon the Duties of the Metropolitan Police, *Report Together with Appendices*, 1908, Vol. I, p. 119; George Gissing, *The Crown of Life*, 1899, p. 182; H. G. Wells, *Anne Veronica: A Modern Love Story*, 1909, pp. 100–106.

8. W. H. Davies in A. St John Adcock (ed.), *Wonderful London*, n.d., Vol. 3, p. 970; William Margrie, *The Diary of a London Explorer: Forty Years of Vital*

London Life, 1934, p. 6; Eileen Baillie, *The Shabby Paradise: The Autobiography of a Decade*, 1958, p. 17ff.

9. Henry Green, *Caught*, 1943, p. 119; see Chartres Biron, *Without Prejudice: Impressions of Life and Law*, 1936, p. 285, for the work of the courts; Lilian Wyles, *A Woman at Scotland Yard: Reflections on the Struggles and Achievements of 30 Years in the Metropolitan Police*, 1952, p. 14, for the girls flocking to London; George Riley Scott, *A History of Prostitution: From Antiquity to the Present Day*, 1936, p. 124, and Hubert Llewellyn Smith (ed.), *The New Survey of London Life and Labour*, Vol. IX, 1935, p. 293, for the increase in prostitution; and London County Council/LSS, *London Statistics*, Vol. 26, 1915–20, p. 214–15, for figures of prosecutions. See Sheila Cousins, *To Beg I Am Ashamed*, 1938, for an informative prostitute's memoir of the time. On Wardour Street, see Patrick Hamilton, *The Midnight Bell*, 1929, pp. 49, 70; on Villiers Street, see Lewis Melville, *The London Scene*, 1926, pp. 88–90.

10. On the wartime darkness, see John F. Macdonald, *Two Towns – One City: Paris – London*, 1917, p. 172ff.; A. Ludovici, *An Artist's Life in London and Paris, 1870–1925*, 1926, p. 188; Thomas Burke, *London in My Time*, 1934, p. 125ff.; on the uniforms, see ibid., pp. 121–2.

11. C. Sheridan Jones, *London in War-Time*, 1917, pp. 26–7.

12. Ethel Mannin, *Sounding Brass*, 1925, p. 82.

13. Armistice Day and Night are recalled in Michael MacDonagh, *In London during the Great War: The Diary of a Journalist*, 1935, pp. 329–30 (who considered it more abandoned than Mafeking Night), Burke, *London in My Time*, p. 124 (who thought it more restrained, but who was only a child at the time), and Paul Hogarth and Malcolm Muggeridge, *London à la Mode*, 1966, p. 8 (though Muggeridge was at a shockable age, just fifteen or so). For Peace Day street parties, see Clara E. Grant, *From 'Me' to 'We' (Forty Years on Bow Common)*, n.d., pp. 149–50. On the declining Monkey Parade, see E. Wight Bakke, *The Unemployed Man: A Social Study*, 1933, p. 184, Thomas Burke, *The Wind and the Rain: A Book of Confessions*, 1924, pp. 45–6, and Burke, *London in My Time*, p. 150; on declining street games, see Norman Douglas, *London Street Games*, 1931, p. xi, Margrie, *The Diary of a London Explorer*, p. 6, and William Matthews, *Cockney Past and Present: A Short History of the Dialect of London*, 1938, p. 103; Derby Night is recalled in Burke, *The Wind and the Rain*, 1924, pp. 50–51.

14. On flashing, see Taylor Croft, *The Cloven Hoof: A Study of Contemporary London Vices*, 1932, pp. 98–9; on bonfires, see S. F. Hatton, *London's Bad Boys*, 1931, p. 26; on Will Crooks's funeral, see *Daily Herald*, 10 June 1921.

15. For the ghosts, see *Daily Herald*, 23 January and 26 March 1928. On the Bedford Row attempted murder, see *Daily Herald*, 4 September 1922; for the Holloway suicide, see *Islington Gazette*, 30 January 1924; and for Somers Town, see Desmond Morse-Boycott, *Ten Years in a London Slum: Being the Adventures of a*

Clerical Micawber, n.d., pp. 35–6. On the problems of Highbury Corner and Highbury Station Road, see *Islington Gazette*, 29 September 1926, 6 September 1927 and 23 June 1928.

16. Figures from Jake Rollin, *Rothmans Book of Football Records*, 1998. I am grateful to Tony Mason for help with this point.

17. For the speedway crowds, see *Daily Herald*, 6 April 1932, and *Daily Worker*, 4 January 1933, 16 May 1938 and 1 May 1939. On the prominence of sport in London in these years, see Paul Morand, *A Frenchman's London*, 1934, p. 138ff.; Smith (ed.), *The New Survey of London Life and Labour*, Vol. IX, 1935, Ch. III; Charles Graves, *The Price of Pleasure*, 1935; Donald McDougall, *Fifty Years a Borough, 1886–1936: The Story of West Ham*, 1936, p. 216ff.; A. E. Morgan, *The Needs of Youth: A Report Made to King George's Jubilee Trust Fund*, 1939; Langdon, *Earls Court*.

18. Parks acreage calculated from London County Council/LSS, *London Statistics*, Vol. 31, 1925–6, p. 137, and Vol. 41, 1936–8, p. 187ff.; rising use of facilities from Smith (ed.), *The New Survey of London Life and Labour*, Vol. IX, 1935, p. 58.

19. On this aspect of Lansbury's career, see Edgar Lansbury, *George Lansbury, My Father*, n.d., pp. 60–61; Raymond Postgate, *The Life of George Lansbury*, 1951, p. 247ff. See *The Times*'s leaders of 7 and 11 February 1930.

20. Hubback is remembered in Diana Hopkinson, *Family Inheritance: A Life of Eva Hubback*, 1954, p. 67; Markino is writing in Loftie, *The Colour of London*, pp. xxxv–vi; and Gallipoli is recalled in Mass-Observation, *Britain*, 1939, p. 166.

21. Ibid., pp. 177–80.

22. Disher, *Pleasures of London*, pp. 178–9; see also Terence H. O'Brien, *Civil Defence*, 1955, p. 518ff., and Tom Harrisson, *Living through the Blitz*, 1976, pp. 110–25.

23. Anthony Powell, *The Soldier's Art*, 1966, pp. 399–400; W. Macqueen-Pope, '*Goodbye Piccadilly*', 1960, p. 182, for the ghastly girls.

24. On wartime Paddington, see Paddington, *The Paddington Estate*, 1944, pp. 17–18. On the perceived extension of the prostitute area, see Peter Beveridge, *Inside the CID*, 1957, p. 171. An old Soho resident is quoted in Tony Aldous, *The Illustrated London News Book of London's Villages*, 1980, p. 242.

25. On estimates of numbers, see Royal Commission upon the Duties of the Metropolitan Police, *Report Together with Appendices*, 1908, Vol. I, p. 85; John Gosling and Douglas Warner, *The Shame of a City: An Inquiry into the Vice of London*, 1960, p. 17ff. (for the 1958 estimate of 3,000), and Gerald Sparrow, *Gang-Warfare: A Probe into the Changing Pattern of British Crime*, 1968, p. 76. The 1949 study is in C. H. Rolph (ed.), *Women of the Streets: A Sociological Study of the Common Prostitute*, 1955, pp. 52–4.

26. *Report of the Committee on Homosexual Offences and Prostitution*, 1957, p. 81. On the Messinas, see Rhoda Lee Finmore, *Immoral Earnings: Or Mr Martin's Profession*, 1951; Marthe Watts, *The Men in My Life*, 1960; John Du Rose, *Murder Was My Business*, 1971, p. 35ff.; Gilbert Kelland, *Crime in London*, 1986, p. 59ff. On Stepney, see Joseph Williamson, *Father Joe: The Autobiography of Joseph Williamson of Poplar and Stepney*, 1963, and the much more considered David M. Downes, *The Delinquent Solution: A Study in Subcultural Theory*, 1966. On black pimps and white prostitutes, see, from the prostitute's view, Majbritt Morrison, *Jungle West 11*, 1964.

27. Clarence Rook, *The Hooligan Nights: Being the Life and Opinions of a Young and Impertinent Criminal Recounted by Himself . . .* , 1899, p. 20. On this early period, see also Stephen Humphries, *Hooligans or Rebels? An Oral History of Working-class Childhood and Youth, 1889–1939*, 1981, and Geoffrey Pearson, *Hooligan: A History of Respectable Fears*, 1983.

28. Mass-Observation, *Report on Juvenile Delinquency*, 1949, pp. 40–41, 49.

29. The south London Edwardian connection is given in Colin MacInnes, *England, Half English*, 1961, pp. 149–50, Tony Parker, *The Plough Boy*, 1965, and T. R. Fyvel, *The Insecure Offenders: Rebellious Youth in the Welfare State*, 1961, which remains the best study of this controversial phenomenon. But Bill Osgerby, *Youth in Britain since 1945*, 1998, seems nearer the mark in focusing on the American influences which had played such an important part in British youth culture since 1930 if not before.

30. Twiggy Lawson, *Twiggy: In Black and White*, 1997, pp. 27–9.

31. Booth, *London Town*, pp. 168–9.

32. For a Londoner's view of Parisian charms at the turn of the century, see Arthur W. A. Beckett, *London at the End of the Century: A Book of Gossip*, 1900, Chs. XXXII, XXXIV, XXXVI. Sydney A. Moseley, *The Night Haunts of London*, 1920, p. 31; Compton Mackenzie, *Carnival*, 1912, p. 307.

33. Compton Mackenzie, *Sinister Street*, 1913–14, pp. 698–99. For some of the background to *Sinister Street*, see Compton Mackenzie, *My Life and Times: Octave Three, 1900–1907*, 1964, pp. 235–6, and *My Life and Times: Octave Four, 1907–1915*, 1965, pp. 124, 153–5. The 'Café d'Orange' was probably the Café de l'Europe, Leicester Square.

34. On the *cabinet particulier*, see 'Chicago May', *Chicago May: Her Story*, 1929, p. 99, writing of a Shaftesbury Avenue 'wine room' around 1900; Wells, *Anne Veronica*, 1909, p. 197ff.; Arthur Sherwell, *Life in West London: A Study and a Contrast*, 1897, pp. 141–3. See ibid. generally for the pubs, clubs and vices of Soho and the Fitzroy Square area. On the French pub, see any Soho memoir and also the obituary of Gaston Berlemont in *The Times*, 3 November 1999. On Madame Strindberg, see Nina Hamnett, *Laughing Torso: Reminiscences of Nina Hamnett*, 1932, p. 47; on Murray's and the tango, see Moseley, *The Night Haunts of London*,

p. 15; on the nightclub 'boom' from 1911, see Horace Wyndham and Dorothea St J. George, *Nights in London: Where Mayfair Makes Merry*, 1926, p. 15ff.

35. Charles Booth, *Life and Labour of the People in London*, Vol. 17, 1902, p. 133; Sherwell, *Life in West London*, p. 133.

36. For Hubback, see Hopkinson, *Family Inheritance*, p. 73. On the LCC's puritan policy, see the highly informative Susan D. Pennybacker, *A Vision for London, 1889–1914: Labour, Everyday Life and the LCC Experiment*, 1995, p. 210ff. Mackenzie, *Carnival*, p. 136. That 'the Orient' was the Alhambra, see Mackenzie, *My Life and Times: Octave Four* (reminiscences for 1911).

37. Figures for cinematograph licences are in the annual volumes of London County Council/LSS, *London Statistics*. For the early days of the cinema in London, see H. G. Hibbert, *Fifty Years of a Londoner's Life*, 1916, p. 266ff.; Graves, *The Price of Pleasure*, p. 40ff.; Political and Economic Planning, *The British Film Industry*, 1952, Ch. II; Colin Sorensen, *London on Film: 100 Years of Filmmaking in London*, 1996, p. 13ff.

38. Thomas Burke, *Will Someone Lead Me to a Pub?*, 1936, pp. 49–50.

39. Jones, *London in War-Time*, p. 5, for both gambling and secret rendezvous, and pp. 36–7 for shebeens; Sidney Theodore Felstead, *The Underworld of London*, 1923, pp. 4–5, for prospering nightclubs; R. L. Dearden and Netley Lucas, *The Autobiography of a Crook*, 1924, p. 30, for crazy war-days.

40. Moseley, *The Night Haunts of London*, pp. 40–41; Felstead, *The Underworld of London*, pp. 24, 264ff.; see also Virginia Berridge, *Opium and the People: Opiate Use and Drug Control Policy in Nineteenth and Early Twentieth Century England*, 1999.

41. Nevill, *Mayfair and Montmartre*, p. 116, and *Yesterday and To-Day*, 1922, pp. 180, 200; Booth, *London Town*, p. 24. On the history of the licensing laws, see Parliamentary Papers, *Report of the Departmental Committee on Liquor Licensing*, 1972, p. 297ff.

42. For Murray's, see Moseley, *The Night Haunts of London*, pp. 17–18; Charles Graves, *Champagne and Chandeliers: The Story of the Café de Paris*, 1958, p. 10; Jack Glicco, *Madness after Midnight*, 1952, p. 131, for the Nest; Richard Carlish, *King of Clubs*, 1962, pp. 26–7.

43. For the Café de Paris and the Prince of Wales, see Graves, *Champagne and Chandeliers*, p. 10; on Lambs Club and black men's clubs, see Robert Fabian, *London after Dark: An Intimate Record of Night Life in London, and a Selection of Crime Stories from the Case Book of Robert Fabian*, 1954, pp. 16–18; Glicco, *Madness after Midnight*, pp. 16–17, for the Morgue; Kenneth Hare, *London's Latin Quarter*, 1926, pp. 72–4, for the Bullfrogs Club; on the Gargoyle, see ibid., pp. 79–82, and Eric St Johnston, *One Policeman's Story*, 1978, p. 47, for the Matisse; K. Meyrick, *Secrets of the 43: Reminiscences by Mrs Meyrick*, 1933, p. 158, for the Silver Slipper; Croft, *The Cloven Hoof*, p. 62ff., for gay men's haunts, and Mark Benney, *What Rough Beast? A Biographical Fantasia on the Life*

of Professor J. R. Neave, Otherwise Known as Ironfoot Jack, 1939, p. 312ff., for the Caravan Club, which is likely a pseudonym.

44. See Wyndham and George, *Nights in London*, p. 51, for the Embassy Club; Carlish, *King of Clubs*, for the 43 Club's chocolates.

45. Croft, *The Cloven Hoof*, p. 20; see Stanley Scott, *Tales of Bohemia, Taverns and the Underworld: Stories and Sketches of People Famous, Infamous, and Obscure*, n.d., p. 83ff., for smuggling, and Felstead, *The Underworld of London*, pp. 268–9, for street prices. On Chang, see *The Times*, 11 April 1924.

46. Anthony Powell, *The Acceptance World*, 1955, p. 656ff.; Russian billiards was a sort of pool played with five balls. Wally Thompson, *Time off My Life*, 1956, pp. 66–7.

47. On the Rising Sun, see Basil Hogarth (ed.), *Trial of Robert Wood (the Camden Town Case)*, 1936, pp. 138–9, 155; on the early days of the café bar, see Stephen Graham, *London Nights (a Series of Studies and Sketches of London at Night)*, 1925, p. 167; George Scott Moncrieff, *Café Bar*, 1932, p. 4.

48. Mass-Observation, *Report on Juvenile Delinquency*, Ch. IV. On the London supercinemas, see Jeffrey Richards, *The Age of the Dream Palace: Cinema and Society in Britain, 1930–1939*, 1984, Ch.1.

49. *Islington and Holloway Press*, 7 April 1934.

50. For the destruction of the Café de Paris, see Graves, *Champagne and Chandeliers*, pp. 115–25.

51. Green, *Caught*, p. 49; on the Americans, see Andrew Sinclair, *War Like a Wasp: The Lost Decade of the 'Forties*, 1989, p. 167; Sinclair's is a brilliant chronicle of Soho and Fitzrovian literary and bohemian life in the 1940s.

52. On the Colony Room, see, for example, MacInnes, *England, Half English*, 1961, p. 64ff. where Muriel's is thinly disguised as 'Mabel's'; Frank Norman and Jeffrey Bernard, *Soho Night and Day*, 1966, p. 66ff.; Frank Norman, *Norman's London*, 1969, p. 186ff.; Daniel Farson, *Never a Normal Man: An Autobiography*, 1997, p. 118ff. Muriel Spark, *The Girls of Slender Means*, 1963, p. 35, for the Schiaparelli dress. Francis Marshall, *The London Book*, n.d., pp. 137–8. For the chaperone and a critical eye on the 1950s season, see Andrew Sinclair, *The Breaking of Bumbo*, 1959.

53. On 'the biggest brothel in Europe', see Morrison, *Jungle West 11*, p. 9; on the shebeens, see Kelland, *Crime in London*, pp. 81–7. See Jonathon Green, *Days in the Life: Voices from the English Underground, 1961–1971*, 1988, and Mike Phillips and Trevor Phillips, *Windrush: The Irresistible Rise of Multi-racial Britain*, 1998, for the early connections between Notting Hill and the 1960s underground.

54. On the 1950s Soho cafés, see Norman, *Norman's London*, p. 18, reprinting a piece from 1958; for the 2i's, see Norman and Bernard, *Soho Night and Day*, p. 16ff.; and for a rough guide to Soho and rock, see *Rock and Pop (London)*, 1997.

55. MacInnes, *England, Half English*, pp. 58–9.

56. On the early coverage, see Christopher Booker, *The Neophiliacs: A Study of the Revolution in English Life in the Fifties and Sixties*, 1969, p. 18, and Arthur Marwick, *The Sixties: Cultural Revolution in Britain, France, Italy, and the United States, c. 1958–c. 1974*, 1998, pp. 396, 456.

57. John Major, *The Autobiography*, 1999, p. 41. 'Petronius', *London Unexpurgated*, 1969, p. 18.

58. *Time*, 15 April 1966, p. 30ff. Halasz had known London since 1949.

59. For the judgement on Abbey Road, see *Rock and Pop (London)*, 1997, p. 109. George Melly, *Revolt into Style: The Pop Arts in Britain*, 1970, p. 73.

60. Marwick, *The Sixties*, p. 468.

61. Glicco, *Madness after Midnight*, pp. 133–4; on the London Casino, see Hunter Davies, *The Other Half*, 1966, p. 131ff.

62. Edward Greeno, *War on the Underworld*, 1960, pp. 84–6. Fabian, *London after Dark*, p. 71, for the 'French Circus'. Nigel Balchin, *Darkness Falls from the Air*, 1942, pp. 143–5.

63. Croft, *The Cloven Hoof*, pp. 138–46.

64. On the rapid rise of the Soho strip club from August 1959, see Norman, *Norman's London*, p. 141, written in 1963; and on the clip joint see Kelland, *Crime in London*, p. 101ff.

65. This point is made, as a defining moment for Swinging London, in Michael Moorcock, *Mother London: A Novel*, 1988, pp. 96–7.

66. Some key texts for this period of life in London are Len Deighton (ed.), *Len Deighton's London Dossier*, 1967; 'Petronius', *London Unexpurgated*; Booker, *The Neophiliacs*; Melly, *Revolt into Style*; Nicholas Saunders, *Alternative London*, 1970; *Time Out*, 1972; Jonathan Raban, *Soft City*, 1974; Richard Neville, *Hippie Hippie Shake: The Dreams, the Trips, the Trials, the Love-ins, the Screw-ups . . . the Sixties*, 1995; Marwick, *The Sixties*.

67. An interesting survey of changing fashion in London between 1850 and 1950 is given in Barbara Worsley-Gough, *Fashions in London*, 1952.

68. Melly, *Revolt into Style*, p. 63ff., for the Saddle Room.

69. Ibid., p. 94ff., for the Ad-Lib (written 1965); Hunter Davies (ed.), *The New London Spy: A Discreet Guide to the City's Pleasures*, 1966, p. 170ff., and Deighton (ed.), *Len Deighton's London Dossier*, p. 19ff.; and Green, *Days in the Life*, generally.

70. For Camden Town, see Ann Scanlon, *Those Tourists Are Money: The Rock'n'Roll Guide to Camden*, 1997, p. 3; Michael Elliott, *Heartbeat London*, 1986, pp. 157–9.

71. The Stringfellow point was made ibid., p. 158; and see Osgerby, *Youth in Britain since 1945*, pp. 176–8, 201–2, for acid-house and jungle.

72. Moorcock, *Mother London*, p. 127.

73. On the shifting fortunes of the Soho sex industry from 1959 to 1989, see

Kelland, *Crime in London*, p. 101ff., and Judith Summers, *Soho: A History of London's Most Colourful Neighbourhood*, 1989, pp. 212–23.

74. On the 'new cocaine epidemic', see *Evening Standard*, 4 September 1995; the British Crime Survey is reported in London Research Centre, *Focus on London 99*, 1999, p. 95.

75. The communal houses of Notting Hill are in Green, *Days in the Life*, p. 14, and the trendy Arts Lab ibid., p. 169ff.

76. *Newsweek*, 4 November 1996 – Michael Elliott was one of the authors. The parallels with the 1960s were well brought out by a feature in *Vanity Fair*, March 1997.

9. GOVERNING THE UNGOVERNABLE

1. H. O. Arnold-Forster, *Our Great City, or London the Heart of the Empire*, 1900, p. 217.

2. From a large choice of texts, David Owen, *The Government of Victorian London, 1855–1889: The Metropolitan Board of Works, the Vestries, and the City Corporation*, 1982, remains the best overview for this period of London government up to 1889. The boundaries of London county were effectively put in place by the Registrar General in 1846; see Census of Great Britain 1851, *Population Tables*, Vol. 1, Division 1, p. 45.

3. The best account of the formation of the Metropolitan Borough Councils is John Davis, *Reforming London: The London Government Problem*, 1988.

4. On the School Board for London, see Hugh B. Philpott, *London at School: The Story of the School Board, 1870–1904*, 1904. On the vexed question of transfer, see Beatrice Webb, *The Diary of Beatrice Webb: Vol. II, 1892–1905: 'All the good things of life'*, edited by Norman and Jean MacKenzie, 1983; Gwilym Gibbon and Reginald W. Bell, *History of the London County Council, 1889–1939*, 1939; Stuart Maclure, *One Hundred Years of London Education, 1870–1970*, 1970.

5. Details of the franchise, electorate, constitution and functions of the various local government bodies in London are to be found fully set out in any of the annual volumes of London County Council/LSS, *London Statistics*, up to 1938.

6. Sir G. Laurence Gomme, *London*, 1914, pp. 328–9.

7. On the Progressives, see Sidney Webb, *The London Programme*, 1895; Percy A. Harris, *London and Its Government*, 1913 and 1931, and *Forty Years in and out of Parliament*, 1947; A. G. Gardiner, *John Benn and the Progressive Movement*, 1925; J. Scott Lidgett, *My Guided Life*, 1936; William Kent, *John Burns: Labour's Lost Leader*, 1950 (where the description of Burns is to be found on pp. 175–6); Davis, *Reforming London*; Andrew Saint (ed.), *Politics and the People of London: The London County Council, 1889–1965*, 1989. On Headlam, see Susan D.

Pennybacker, *A Vision for London, 1889–1914: Labour, Everyday Life and the LCC Experiment*, 1995.

8. J. Williams Benn, LCC Chairman, in London County Council, *Annual Report*, 1904, p. 3.

9. John Burns's speech opening the Latchmere estate is in Kent, *John Burns*, p. 127.

10. Harris, *London and Its Government*, p. 103. The trajectory of London rates is fully described in London County Council/LSS, *London Statistics*, Vol. 25, 1914–15, Chs. XLIII–XLVI.

11. On the Mile End guardians, see Albert Lieck, *Bow Street World*, 1938, pp. 104–6; the prosecution, which led to the imprisonment and disqualification of several guardians, was in 1908. On the Poplar guardians, see the note of Beatrice Webb's revealing visit of 19 March 1906 in Webb, *The Diary of Beatrice Webb: Vol. III, 1905–1924: 'The power to alter things'*, edited by Norman and Jean MacKenzie, 1984, pp. 33–4.

12. On the 1907 election, see *The Times* 1907; LMN, *London Municipal Notes*, Vols. 3–4 (July 1906–June 1907); Webb, *The Diary of Beatrice Webb: Vol. III*, 1984; Gardiner, *John Benn and the Progressive Movement*, p. 329ff.; Ken Young, *Local Politics and the Rise of Party: The London Municipal Society and the Conservative Intervention in Local Elections, 1894–1963*, 1975, p. 93ff.; Pennybacker, *A Vision for London, 1889–1914*, is the best modern study. On Huskinson, see H. Simonis, *The Street of Ink: An Intimate History of Journalism*, 1917, pp. 255–6; a volume of his *LCC Election Cartoons* was published after the election.

13. On the banning of Mrs Gaskell, see *The Reformers' Year Book 1908*, p. 89.

14. On imperialism in the schools, see LMN, *London Municipal Notes*, Vol. 5, No. 31, September 1907, p. 535; London County Council, *Annual Report*, 1908, pp. 57, 69; 1909, p. 3; (on the Territorials) 1909, p. 3. On the LCC's war casualties, see London County Council, *Annual Report*, 1922, p. 197.

15. Paul Thompson, *Socialists, Liberals and Labour: The Struggle for London, 1885–1914*, 1967, remains the main introduction to London politics and the rise of Labour before 1914. On West Ham and Labour, see Will Thorne, *My Life's Battles*, 1925, Jack Jones, *My Lively Life*, 1929, and John Marriott, *The Culture of Labourism: The East End between the Wars*, 1991. See W. Barefoot, *Twenty-Five Years' History of the Woolwich Labour Party, 1903–1928*, 1928.

16. One and a half Labour members was Herbert Morrison's quip in *An Autobiography*, 1960, p. 73. The one was Susan Lawrence, Poplar South, a defector from Municipal Reform, and the half was Harry Gosling, Whitechapel and St George's-in-the-East, still sailing under a Progressive flag though he later joined the Labour Party; see Harry Gosling, *Up and Down Stream*, 1927.

17. On the rise of trade unionism in the East End during the First World War, see Julia Bush, *Behind the Lines: East London Labour, 1914–1919*, 1984. On east London labour in the early years of the war, see E. Sylvia Pankhurst, *The Home*

Front: A Mirror to Life in England during the First World War, 1932. See also Ken Weller, *'Don't be a soldier!' The Radical Anti-war Movement in North London, 1914–1918*, 1985; London Trades Council, *London Trades Council, 1860–1950: A History*, 1950.

18. For details of the London electorate, see London County Council/LSS, *London Statistics*, Vol. 25, 1914–15, p. 24, and Vol. 26, 1915–20, p. 18. For the 'rebel milieu', see Weller, *'Don't be a soldier!'*.

19. On Stepney, see C. R. Attlee, *As It Happened*, 1954, p. 54, and Kenneth Harris, *Attlee*, 1982, p. 42ff.

20. On the LLP special party conference and the ensuing campaign, see *Daily Herald*, 10 September, 24 and 28 October 1919. On the Jewish vote, see Geoffrey Alderman, *London Jewry and London Politics, 1889–1986*, 1989, pp. 77–8. On women voters, see *Evening Standard*, 17 October 1919.

21. On Greenwich, see *Daily Herald*, 15 October 1919; on Stepney see Attlee, *As It Happened*, pp. 47–8, and Harris, *Attlee*, pp. 45–6; on Southwark, see G. G. Eastwood, *George Isaacs: Printer, Trade Union Leader, Cabinet Minister*, n.d., p. 124; on Wandsworth, see Arthur Peacock, *Yours Fraternally*, 1945, p. 13, and Alfred James Hurley, *Days That Are Gone: Milestones I Have Passed in South-West London*, 1947, pp. 57–8.

22. London Labour Party, *The London Labour Chronicle*, December 1919, p. 1.

23. On Lansbury, see George Lansbury, *My Life*, 1928, and *Looking Backwards – and Forwards*, 1935; Edgar Lansbury, *George Lansbury, My Father*, 1933; Raymond Postgate, *The Life of George Lansbury*, 1951 (the best account); Bob Holman, *Good Old George: The Life of George Lansbury*, 1990. See also George Lansbury, *Your Part in Poverty*, 1917, *These Things Shall Be*, 1920, and *My England*, 1934, for his characteristic catechism.

24. On Poplarism, see Noreen Branson, *Poplarism, 1919–1925: George Lansbury and the Councillors' Revolt*, 1979, and Jim Gillespie in David Feldman and Gareth Stedman Jones (ed.), *Metropolis London: Histories and Representations since 1800*, 1989, pp. 163–88.

25. For Morrison's analysis of Poplarism, see London Labour Party, *The London Labour Chronicle*, November 1921.

26. On the anti-socialist alliance, see Young, *Local Politics and the Rise of Party*, p. 121ff.

27. On the extraordinary story of the West Ham guardians, see Marriott, *The Culture of Labourism*, 1991.

28. For the savage with hate remark, concerning Lewisham, see Leslie Paul, *Angry Young Man*, 1951, p. 83. See Mike Squires, *Saklatvala: A Political Biography*, 1990.

29. See *Daily Herald*, 9 March 1928 (the motto), 26 September 1927 (the baths), 9 September 1927 (the flowers). On the public health department, see D. M. Connan, *A History of the Public Health Department in Bermondsey*, 1935. On

Bermondsey's Revolution, see Fenner Brockway, *Bermondsey Story: The Life of Alfred Salter*, 1949, Ch. VIII.

30. On the elusive middle-class vote in Lewisham, see Tom Jeffery in Feldman and Jones (ed.), *Metropolis London*, pp. 189–218.

31. On Becontree, see Terence Young, *Becontree and Dagenham: A Report Made for the Pilgrim Trust*, 1934, p. 192. On Stepney, see Annie Barnes, *Tough Annie: From Suffragette to Stepney Councillor*, 1980, p. 35. For Dr Spero, who was disqualified as an MP through bankruptcy, see *Daily Herald*, 24 May 1929; and for Fulham Labour Party a few years later, see Michael Stewart, *Life and Labour: An Autobiography*, 1980, p. 40ff.

32. Bernard Donoughue and G. W. Jones, *Herbert Morrison: Portrait of a Politician*, 1973, is the definitive life and the quote is from pp. 38–9. See also Maurice Edelman, *A Pictorial Biography*, 1948, and Morrison, *An Autobiography*.

33. Herbert Morrison, *How Greater London is Governed*, 1935, p. 9.

34. On the internal workings of the LLP campaign, see London Labour Party, *The Work of the London Labour Party*, 1933–4, and London Labour Party Executive Committee papers, 1933–4 (Greater London Record Office).

35. I am indebted to Dan Weinbren for energetic work in charting the rise of Labour in outer London between the wars.

36. Brian Barker, *Labour in London: A Study in Municipal Achievement*, 1946, p. 157. See also London Labour Party, *What Labour Has Done for London: The Work of the Labour LCC, 1934–1945*, 1945.

37. See Barker, *Labour in London*, p. 122ff. On Hollesley Bay, see London Labour Party, *'What about Belmont?' The Facts about Residential Training Centres under the Labour LCC*, 1935. On the workhouse, see London County Council, *'The House': London's Public Assistance Institutions*, 1939.

38. The doctor is quoted in Barker, *Labour in London*, p. 135.

39. Morrison and the maternity services are ibid., p. 137ff.; see also London County Council, *The LCC Hospitals: A Retrospect*, 1949.

40. Harry Snell, *Men, Movements, and Myself*, 1936, pp. 262–3.

41. On Morrison's intervention in Stepney, see London Labour Party Executive Committee papers, 1936–7, pp. 7222–5. On Davis, see Alderman, *London Jewry and London Politics, 1889–1986*, and Henry Felix Srebrnik, *London Jews and British Communism, 1939–1945*, 1995. For the early history of municipal blue-collar trade unionism, especially in London, see Bernard Dix and Stephen Williams, *Serving the Public – Building the Union: The History of the National Union of Public Employees: Vol. I, The Forerunners, 1889–1928*, 1987.

42. For a full account of ARP, see Terence O'Brien, *Civil Defence*, 1955.

43. See Jennifer Golden, *Hackney at War*, 1995, pp. 21–2.

44. See Richard M. Titmuss, *Problems of Social History*, 1950, for the most complete account of evacuation. See also Richard Padley and Margaret Cole, *Evacuation*

Survey: A Report to the Fabian Society, 1940; Susan Isaacs (ed.), *The Cambridge Evacuation Survey: A Wartime Study in Social Welfare and Education*, 1941; Women's Group on Public Welfare, *Our Towns: A Close-up*, 1943; and, on the work of the LCC, W. Eric Jackson, *Achievement: A Short History of the London County Council*, 1965, p. 33ff.

45. O'Brien, *Civil Defence*, pp. 454–5.

46. See Titmuss, *Problems of Social Policy*, p. 251ff. See also Ritchie Calder, *The Lesson of London*, 1941; Negley Farson, *Bomber's Moon*, 1941; E. Doreen Idle, *War over West Ham: A Study of Community Adjustment*, 1943; Barbara Nixon, *Raiders Overhead: A Diary of the London Blitz*, 1943; William Sansom, *Westminster in War*, 1947.

47. See Jackson, *Achievement*, for the LCC's role in this wartime growth in local government services.

48. For the removal of Davis, see Titmuss, *Problems of Social Policy*, p. 295; Alderman, *London Jewry and London Politics, 1889–1986*, pp. 85–6; Srebrnik, *London Jews and British Communism, 1939–1945*, p. 45. On Morrison's reception by Londoners, see Frank R. Lewey, *Cockney Campaign*, n.d., p. 46. Calder, *The Lesson of London*, p. 93.

49. On Morrison's battle to keep the hospitals, see Kenneth O. Morgan, *Labour in Power, 1945–1951*, 1984, pp. 154–5. The electricity undertakings nationalized were listed in schedule II of the Electricity Act 1947; on the effects in Bermondsey, see Sue Goss, *Local Labour and Local Government: A Study of Changing Interests, Politics and Policy in Southwark from 1919 to 1982*, 1988, p. 51.

50. On Kidbrooke, see Harry Hopkins, *The New Look: A Social History of the Forties and Fifties in Britain*, 1963, p. 152.

51. London Labour Party, *Labour Keeps Faith with London: The Work of the Labour LCC, 1946–48*, n.d., n.p. See also Jackson, *Achievement*; S. K. Ruck, *Municipal Entertainment and the Arts: In Greater London*, 1965; Saint (ed.), *Politics and the People of London*.

52. On Latham and Hayward, see John Mason, ibid.

53. For poor old Percy, see Harris, *Forty Years in and out of Parliament*, pp. 194–6. On West Ham in the late 1930s and early 1940s, see Idle, *War over West Ham*, pp. 30–32; on Finsbury, see Nixon, *Raiders Overhead*, Ch. 11; on Southwark, see Goss, *Local Labour and Local Government*, p. 45; on Battersea, see Douglas Jay, *Change and Fortune: A Political Record*, 1980, pp. 157–8; on Poplar Labour Party in 1962 – 'appallingly inferior to Reading' – see Ian Mikardo, *Back-Bencher*, 1988, p. 171.

54. The best study of proposals for London government reform from 1900 to 1960 is Ken Young and Patricia L. Garside, *Metropolitan London: Politics and Urban Change, 1837–1981*, 1982. See also H. G. Wells, *Mankind in the Making*, 1903, Appendix 1; LMN, *London Municipal Notes*, 1906–14.

55. See *Report of the Commissioners Appointed to Inquire into the Local Government of Greater London*, 1923.

56. William A. Robson, *The Government and Misgovernment of London*, 1939, Part III. On the LLP's position, see Donoughue and Jones, *Herbert Morrison*, p. 115; on the GLRPC, see Gwilym Gibbon, *Reconstruction and Town and Country Planning: With an Examination of the Uthwatt and Scott Reports*, 1943, and for its governmental proposals, see Greater London Regional Planning Committee, *First Report*, 1929, p. 7.

57. Patrick Abercrombie, *Greater London Plan, 1944*, 1945, p. 183; G. D. H. Cole, *Local and Regional Government*, 1947, p. 189ff.

58. On the origins of the Herbert Commission, see Frank Smallwood, *Greater London: The Politics of Metropolitan Reform*, 1965; Gerald Rhodes, *The Government of London: The Struggle for Reform*, 1970; S. K. Ruck and Gerald Rhodes, *The Government of Greater London*, 1970; Young, *Local Politics and the Rise of Party*; Young and Garside, *Metropolitan London*.

59. *Report of the Royal Commission on Local Government in Greater London, 1957–60*, 1960; the judgement was David Donnison's in his *Health, Wealth and Democracy in Greater London*, 1962, p. 5.

60. *Report of the Royal Commission on Local Government in Greater London, 1957–60*, pp. 200–237. On the Commission's report and the London Government Act 1963, see Smallwood, *Greater London*; Rhodes, *The Government of London*; Ruck and Rhodes, *The Government of Greater London*; Young, *Local Politics and the Rise of Party*; Young and Garside, *Metropolitan London*.

61. Donoughue and Jones, *Herbert Morrison*, pp. 560–61.

62. On the differences between the Herbert Commission recommendations and the Act, and how they came about, see Smallwood, *Greater London*; Gerald Rhodes, *The Government of London: The Struggle for Reform*, 1970; Ruck and Rhodes, *The Government of Greater London*; and Frank Marshall, *The Marshall Inquiry on Greater London: Report to the Greater London Council*, 1978.

63. See Ken Young and John Kramer, *Strategy and Conflict in Metropolitan Housing: Suburbia versus the Greater London Council, 1965–75*, 1978, for a brilliant analysis of the 1964–77 period of GLC–borough relations on the housing question.

64. The *Observer* is quoted ibid., p. 180; the luncheon-club quip is in Horace Cutler, *The Cutler Files*, 1982, p. 150.

65. See Young and Kramer, *Strategy and Conflict in Metropolitan Housing*, pp. 210–11; Cutler, *The Cutler Files*, p. 177.

66. On Cutler, see ibid.; *The Times*, 3 March 1997.

67. John Major, *The Autobiography*, pp. 39–40.

68. Mellish is quoted in Dilip Hiro, *Black British, White British*, 1973, p. 271.

69. Mikardo, *Back-Bencher*, pp. 167–8, 173; Campaign against Racism and Fascism/Southall Rights, *Southall: The Birth of a Black Community*, 1981, pp. 25ff., 39ff.;

for Islington, see Andrew D. Glassberg, *Representation and Community*, 1981, p. 50.

70. For some of the tensions of this period in Lambeth, see Cynthia Cockburn, *The Local State: Management of Cities and People*, 1977; in Southwark, see Peter Tatchell, *The Battle for Bermondsey*, 1983, and Goss, *Local Labour and Local Government*.

71. The carpetbagger tag is in John Carvel, *Citizen Ken*, 1984, p. 62.

72. See Tatchell, *The Battle for Bermondsey*, and Goss, *Local Labour and Local Government*; and, more generally on the travails of the times, see Alex Henney, *Inside Local Government: A Case for Radical Reform*, 1984.

73. On London Jewry in these years, see *London Jewry and London Politics, 1889–1986*, pp. 127ff. And on the period generally, see Carvel, *Citizen Ken*, Andrew Forrester et al., *Beyond Our Ken: A Guide to the Battle for London*, 1985, and Francis Wheen, *The Battle for London*, 1985.

74. See Carvel, *Citizen Ken*; Forrester et al., *Beyond Our Ken*; Wheen, *The Battle for London*; Norman Flynn et al., *Abolition or Reform? The GLC and the Metropolitan Counties*, 1985.

75. This tag is from Thomas Love Peacock but I've lost the reference.

76. Estimates of increased public transport use are in Wheen, *The Battle for London*, p. 44.

77. On the decision to abolish the GLC, see Margaret Thatcher, *The Downing Street Years*, 1993, pp. 284, 305; Geoffrey Howe, *Conflict of Loyalty*, 1994, pp. 287, 460; Kenneth Baker, *The Turbulent Years: My Life in Politics*, 1993, p. 97ff.; Forrester et al., *Beyond Our Ken*; Wheen, *The Battle for London*; Flynn et al., *Abolition or Reform?*.

78. Department of the Environment, *Streamlining the Cities: Government Proposals for Reorganizing Local Government in Greater London and the Metropolitan Counties*, 1983, pp. 2–3.

79. On the mess that followed the GLC, see Tony Travers and George Jones, *The New Government of London*, 1991 and 1997; Roy Porter, *London: A Social History*, 1994, pp. 1–8, 382–9; Jerry White and Michael Young, *Governing London*, 1996.

80. In England the swing from Conservatives to Labour was 10.7 per cent; in inner London 11 per cent; in outer London 14.3 per cent.

AFTERWORD: LONDON IN THE TWENTY-FIRST CENTURY

1. In his chapter on the future of London at the end of W. W. Hutchings, *London Town Past and Present*, 1909, p. 1094.

Bibliography

Unless stated otherwise, all books, journals and pamphlets listed were published in London and the first editions have been used. Parliamentary Papers and Royal Commission reports are listed under those headings within the Bibliography.

A Beckett, Arthur W., *London at the End of the Century: A Book of Gossip*, 1900

Abercrombie, Patrick, *Greater London Plan, 1944*, 1945

Adams, Caroline, *Across Seven Seas and Thirteen Rivers: Life Stories of Pioneer Sylhetti Settlers in Britain*, 1987

Adamson, Iain, *The Great Detective: A Life of Deputy Commander Reginald Spooner of Scotland Yard*, 1966

Adcock, A. St John (ed.), *Wonderful London*, 3 vols., n.d. (1926–7)

Age Exchange (Antonia Rubinstein, ed.), *Just Like the Country: Memories of London Families Who Settled the New Cottage Estates, 1919–1939*, 1991

Alderman, Geoffrey, *London Jewry and London Politics, 1889–1986*, 1989

Alderman, Geoffrey, and Holmes, Colin (eds.), *Outsiders and Outcasts: Essays in Honour of William J. Fishman*, 1993

Alderson, Stanley, *Britain in the Sixties: Housing*, 1962

Aldgate, Anthony, and Richards, Jeffrey, *Britain Can Take It: The British Cinema in the Second World War*, 1986

Aldous, Tony, *The Illustrated London News Book of London's Villages*, 1980

Ali, Beatrice, *The Good Deeds of a Good Woman*, 1976

Allingham, Philip, *Cheapjack*, 1934

Amis, Martin, *London Fields*, 1989

Anderson, Chuck, and Green, Ray, *Save the Jubilee Hall! The Battle to Preserve the 300-year-old Tradition of Street Market Trading in the Piazza of Covent Garden*, 1992

Andrews, C. Lesley, *Tenants and Town Hall*, 1979

Andrews, Irene Osgood, *Economic Effects of the War upon Women and Children in Great Britain*, New York, 1918

Anon. (Margaret Harkness?), *Tempted London: Young Men*, 1888

Anson, Brian, *I'll Fight You for It! Behind the Struggle for Covent Garden*, 1981

Armstrong, John, 'The Development of the Park Royal Industrial Estate in the Interwar Period: A Re-examination of the Aldcroft/Richardson Thesis', *London Journal*, Vol. 21, No. 1, 1996

Armytage, Percy, *By the Clock of St James's*, 1927

Arnold-Forster, H. O., *Our Great City, or London the Heart of the Empire*, 1900

Aronovitch, Bella, *Give It Time: An Experience of Hospital, 1928–32*, 1974

Ascoli, David, *The Queen's Peace: The Origins and Development of the Metropolitan Police, 1829–1979*, 1979

Ashworth, William, *An Economic History of England, 1870–1939*, 1960

Attlee, C. R., *As It Happened*, 1954

Baedeker, K., *London and Its Environs*, 1911

Bailey, Doris, *Children of the Green: A True Story of Childhood in Bethnal Green, 1922–1937*, 1981

Bailey, Peter, '"Ally Sloper's Half-Holiday", Comic Art in the 1880s', *History Workshop Journal*, Issue 16, 1983

Baillie, Eileen, *The Shabby Paradise: The Autobiography of a Decade*, 1958 (1959 Reader's Union edn)

Baker, Kenneth, *The Turbulent Years: My Life in Politics*, 1993

Bakke, E. Wight, *The Unemployed Man: A Social Study*, 1933

Balchin, Nigel, *Darkness Falls from the Air*, 1942

Ball, John, et al., *Cops and Robbers: An Investigation into Armed Bank Robbery*, 1978

Bamberger, Louis, *Bow Bell Memories*, 1931

Banks, Lynne Reid, *The L-Shaped Room*, 1960

Banton, Michael, *The Coloured Quarter: Negro Immigrants in an English City*, 1955

Barclay, Irene T., and Perry, Evelyn E. *Report on the Survey on Housing Conditions in Ward 2 of the Metropolitan Borough of St Pancras*, 1933

Barefoot, W., *Twenty-Five Years' History of the Woolwich Labour Party, 1903–1928*, 1928

Barker, Brian, *Labour in London: A Study in Municipal Achievement*, 1946

Barker, T. C., and Robbins, Michael, *A History of London Transport: Passenger Transport and the Development of the Metropolis: Vol. II, the Twentieth Century to 1970*, 1974

Barltrop, Robert, *The Monument: The Story of the Socialist Party of Great Britain*, 1975

– *My Mother's Calling Me: Part I, Growing up in North East London between the Wars*, 1984

Barltrop, Robert, and Wolveridge, Jim, *The Muvver Tongue*, 1980

Barnes, Annie, *Tough Annie: From Suffragette to Stepney Councillor*, 1980

Barnett, Samuel A. and Mrs Henrietta, *Practicable Socialism* (new series), 1915

Baron, Barclay, *The Doctor: The Story of John Stansfeld of Oxford and Bermondsey*, 1952

Barson, Susie, and Saint, Andrew, *A Farewell to Fleet Street*, 1988

Bató, Joseph, and Priestley, J. B. *Defiant City*, 1942

Beaton, Cecil, *History Under Fire: 52 Photographs of Air Raid Damage to London Buildings, 1940–41*, 1941

Beckman, Morris, *The 43 Group*, 1992

– *The Hackney Crucible*, 1996

Béderida, François, 'Urban Growth and Social Structure in Nineteenth-Century Poplar', *London Journal*, Vol. I, No. 2, 1975

Bell, Alan, *Port of London, 1909–1934*, 1934

Bellman, Sir Harold, *Cornish Cockney: Reminiscences and Reflections*, 1947

Benedetta, Mary, *The Street Markets of London*, 1936

Benn, Melissa, and Worpole, Ken, *Death in the City: An Examination of Police-related Deaths in London*, 1986

Bennett, Alfred Rosling, *London and Londoners in the Eighteen-Fifties and Sixties*, 1924

Bennett, Arnold, *A Man from the North*, 1898 (1914 edn)

Bennett, H. J., *I Was a Walworth Boy*, 1980

Benney, Mark, *Low Company: Describing the Evolution of a Burglar*, 1936

– *What Rough Beast? A Biographical Fantasia on the Life of Professor J. R. Neave, Otherwise Known as Ironfoot Jack*, 1939

– *Over to Bombers*, 1943

– *Almost a Gentleman*, 1966

Bentley, William George, *My Son's Execution*, 1957

Benyon, John, *A Tale of Failure: Race and Policing*, Coventry, 1986

Benyon, John (ed.), *Scarman and After: Essays Reflecting on Lord Scarman's Report, the Riots and their Aftermath*, 1984

Bermant, Chaim, *Point of Arrival: A Study of London's East End*, 1975

Berrett, James, *When I Was at Scotland Yard*, 1932

Berridge, Virginia, 'East End Opium Dens and Narcotic Use in Britain', *London Journal*, Vol. 4, No. 1, 1978

– *Opium and the People: Opiate Use and Drug Control Policy in Nineteenth and Early Twentieth Century England*, 1999

Berry-Dee, Christopher, and Odell, Robin, *Dad, Help Me Please*, 1990

Besant, Walter, *London South of the Thames*, 1912

Besant, Walter, and others, *The Fascination of London: Shoreditch and the East End*, 1908

Bethnal Green and Stepney Trades Council, *Blood on the Streets: A Report . . . on Racial Attacks in East London*, 1978

Beveridge, Peter, *Inside the CID*, 1957

Beveridge, William H., *Full Employment in a Free Society*, 1944

Bhachu, Parminder, *Twice Migrants: East African Sikh Settlers in Britain*, 1985

Biggs, Ronnie, *His Own Story*, 1981

– *Odd Man Out: My Life on the Loose and the Truth about the Great Train Robbery*, 1994

Birch, J. G., *Limehouse through Five Centuries*, 1930

Bird, James, *The Geography of the Port of London*, 1957

Biron, Sir Chartres, *Without Prejudice: Impressions of Life and Law*, 1936

Bishop, Cecil, *From Information Received*, 1932

Black, Clementina, 'London's Tailoresses', *Economic Journal*, Vol. XIV, 1904

Blake, Wallace, *Quod*, n.d. (*c.* 1928)

Blumenfeld, R. D., *R.D.B.'s Diary, 1887–1914*, 1930

– *All in a Lifetime*, 1931

Boddy, M., et al., *Sunbelt City? A Study of Economic Change in Britain's M4 Growth Corridor*, Oxford, 1986

Bonavia, Michael, *London Before I Forget*, Worcester, 1990

Booker, Christopher, *The Neophiliacs: A Study of the Revolution in English Life in the Fifties and Sixties*, 1969

Booth, Charles, *Life and Labour of the People in London*, 17 vols., 1892–1902

Booth, J. B., *London Town*, 1929

– *A 'Pink 'Un' Remembers*, 1937

Borrow, George, *Romano Lavo-Lil: Word-book of the Romany or, English Gypsy Language*, 1874 (1923 edn)

Bowen, Elizabeth, *The Demon Lover and Other Stories*, 1945

– *The Heat of the Day*, 1949 (1950 edn)

Bowley, A. L., *Prices and Wages in the United Kingdom, 1914–1920*, Oxford, 1921

– *Some Economic Consequences of the War*, 1930

– *Wages and Income in the United Kingdom since 1860*, Cambridge, 1937

Boyle, Andrew, *Trenchard*, 1962

Brabin, Daniel, *Rillington Place*, 1966 (1999 edn)

Bradley, Simon, and Pevsner, Nikolaus, *London I: The City of London*, 1997

Bragg, Melvyn, *Crystal Rooms*, 1992

Braine, John, *The Crying Game*, 1968 (1972 edn)

Branson, Noreen, *Poplarism, 1919–1925: George Lansbury and the Councillors' revolt*, 1979

Brayley, Edward Wedlake, *London and Middlesex [etc.]*, 5 vols., 1810–16

Brimblecombe, Peter, *The Big Smoke: A History of Air Pollution in London since Medieval Times*, 1987

Brincker, J. A. H., 'The Case for Diphtheria Immunisation', *Public Health*, August 1927

Bristow, I., et al., *The Saving of Spitalfields*, 1989

Broadgate (Rosehaugh Stanhope Developments plc and British Railways Board), *Broadgate and Liverpool Street Station*, 1991

The Broadwater Farm Inquiry: Report of the Independent Inquiry into Disturbances of October 1985 at the Broadwater Farm Estate, Tottenham, 1986

Broadwater Farm Revisited: Second Report of the Independent Inquiry into Disturbances of October 1985 at the Broadwater Farm Estate, Tottenham, 1989

Brockway, Fenner, *Bermondsey Story: The Life of Alfred Salter*, 1949

Brome, Vincent, *J. B. Priestley*, 1988

Broodbank, Joseph G., *History of the Port of London*, 2 vols., 1921

Brooks, Dennis, *Race and Labour in London Transport*, 1975

Brown, Beatrice Curtis, *Southwards from Swiss Cottage*, 1947

Brown, Colin, *Black and White Britain: The Third PSI Survey*, 1984

Brown, Geoff, *Sabotage: A Study in Industrial Conflict*, Nottingham, 1977

Brown, Jane, *I Had a Pitch on the Stones*, 1946

Brown, John, *I Was a Tramp*, n.d. (*c.* 1935)

Browne, Douglas G., *The Rise of Scotland Yard: A History of the Metropolitan Police*, 1956

Bryan, Beverley, et al., *The Heart of the Race: Black Women's Lives in Britain*, 1985

Bryant, Arthur, *Liquid History: To Commemorate Fifty Years of the Port of London Authority, 1909–1959*, 1960

Buck, Nick, et al., *The London Employment Problem*, 1986

Budd, Leslie, and Whimster, Sam (eds.), *Global Finance and Urban Living: A Study of Metropolitan Change*, 1992

Burke, Thomas, *Nights in Town: A London Autobiography*, 1915

– *Limehouse Nights: Tales of Chinatown*, 1916

– *Out and About: A Note-book of London in War-Time*, 1919

– *The Song Book of Quong Lee of Limehouse*, 1920

– *Whispering Windows: Tales of the Waterside*, 1921

– *More Limehouse Nights*, 1921

– *The London Spy: A Book of Town Travels*, 1922

– *The Wind and the Rain: A Book of Confessions*, 1924

– *East of Mansion House*, 1926

– *The Sun in Splendour*, 1927

– *The Bloomsbury Wonder*, 1929

– *The Pleasantries of Old Quong*, 1931

– *City of Encounters: A London Divertissement*, 1932

– *London in My Time*, 1934

– *Will Someone Lead Me to a Pub?*, 1936

– *Dinner Is Served!*, 1937

– *The Streets of London: Through the Centuries*, 1940

Burney, Elizabeth, *Housing on Trial: A Study of Immigrants and Local Government*, 1967

Burrows, Roger, and Rhodes, David, *Unpopular Places? Area Disadvantage and the Geography of Misery in England*, Bristol, 1998

Burt, Cyril, *The Backward Child*, 1937 (4th edn, 1958)

Burt, Leonard, *Commander Burt of Scotland Yard*, 1959

Bush, Julia, *Behind the Lines: East London Labour, 1914–1919*, 1984

Butler, Tim, and Rustin, Michael (eds.), *Rising in the East? The Regeneration of East London*, 1996

Calder, Ritchie, *The Lesson of London*, 1941

Callaghan, Thomas, *Tramp's Chronicle*, 1983

Calvert, E. Roy and Theodora, *The Lawbreaker: A Critical Study of the Modern Treatment of Crime*, 1933

Camberwell, Metropolitan Borough of, *Official Guide*, n.d. (5th edn, *c.* 1936)

Camden, London Borough of, *Bloomsbury: The Case against Destruction*, n.d. (*c.* 1974)

Campaign against Racism and Fascism/Southall Rights, *Southall: The Birth of a Black Community*, 1981

Capstick, John, with Jack Thomas, *Given in Evidence*, 1960

Carey, John, *The Intellectuals and the Masses: Pride and Prejudice among the Literary Intelligentsia, 1880–1939*, 1992

Carlin, Francis, *Reminiscences of an Ex-Detective*, 1925

Carlish, Richard, *King of Clubs*, 1962

Carrington, Ron, *Alexandra Park and Palace: A History*, 1975

Carr-Saunders, A. M., and Jones, D. Caradog, *A Survey of the Social Structure of England and Wales: As Illustrated by Statistics*, Oxford 1937, (2nd edn)

Carr-Saunders, A. M., et al., *Young Offenders: An Enquiry into Juvenile Delinquency*, Cambridge, 1943

Carter, Angela, *Wise Children*, 1991 (1992 pb edn)

Carton, Ronald, *This Our London*, 1948

Carvel, John, *Citizen Ken*, 1984

Census of Great Britain, 1851, *Population Tables: Vols. I and II*, 1852

Census of England and Wales 1901, *County of London*, Cd. 875

Census of England and Wales 1911, *Vol. IX, Birthplaces*, Cd. 7017

Census of England and Wales 1911, *Occupations and Industries, Part II*, Cd. 7019

Census of England and Wales 1911, *Summary Tables* Cd. 7929

Census of England and Wales 1921, *County of London, Tables*, 1922

Census of England and Wales 1921, *County of London, Text*, 1923

Census of England and Wales 1931, *County of London*, 1932

Census of England and Wales 1931, *Occupation Tables*, 1934

Census of England and Wales 1931, *General Tables*, 1935

Census of England and Wales 1951, *County Report: London*, 1953

Census of England and Wales 1951, *Housing Report*, 1956

Census of England and Wales 1951, *Report on Greater London and 5 Other Conurbations*, 1956

Census of England and Wales 1961, *County Report: London*, 1963

Census of England and Wales 1971, *County Report: Greater London*, Parts I–III, 1973

Census 1981, *Country of Birth: Great Britain*, 1983

Census 1991, *Key Statistics for Urban and Rural Areas: The South East*, 1998

Chamberlain, Mary, *Growing Up in Lambeth*, 1989

Chancellor, E. Beresford, *Disappearing London*, 1927

Chapman, Cecil, *The Poor Man's Court of Justice: 25 Years as a Metropolitan Police Magistrate*, 1925

Chesterton, Mrs Cecil, *In Darkest London*, 1926 (2nd edn, 1930)

– *I Lived in a Slum*, 1936

'Chicago May' (May Churchill Sharpe), *Chicago May: Her Story*, 1929

Choo, Ng Kwee, *The Chinese in London*, 1968

Christensen, Terry, *Neighbourhood Survival*, 1979

Church, Andrew, and Frost, Martin, 'The Employment Focus of Canary Wharf and the Isle of Dogs: A Labour Market Perspective', *London Journal*, Vol. 17, No. 2, 1992

City of London Corporation, *Ten Years' Growth of the City of London*, 1891

– *Report on the Preliminary Draft Proposals for Post-War Reconstruction in the City of London*, 1944

– *The City of London: A Record of Destruction and Survival*, 1951

– *International Banking Developments and London's Position as an International Banking Centre*, 1994

– *The Competitive Position of London's Financial Services: Final Report*, 1995

Clout, Hugh (ed.), *Changing London*, 1978

Clunn, Harold, *London Rebuilt, 1897–1927*, 1927

– *The Face of London: The Record of a Century's Changes and Developments*, 1934 (1st edn, 1932)

Cockburn, Cynthia, *The Local State: Management of Cities and People*, 1977

Cohen, Max, *What Nobody Told the Foreman*, 1953

Cohen, Phil, 'Policing the Working-class City', in National Deviancy Conference/Conference of Socialist Economists, *Capitalism and the Rule of Law: From Deviancy Theory to Marxism*, 1979

Cohen-Portheim, Paul, *The Spirit of London*, 1935

Cole, G. D. H., *Local and Regional Government*, 1947

– *The Post-War Condition of Britain*, 1956

Cole, G. D. H. and M. I., *The Condition of Britain*, 1937

Coleman, Alice, 'The Death of the Inner City: Cause and Cure', *London Journal*, Vol. 6, No. 1, 1980

Colpi, Terri, *The Italian Factor: The Italian Community in Great Britain*, 1991

Commissioner of Police of the Metropolis, *Annual Reports* (various years)

Connan, D. M., *A History of the Public Health Department in Bermondsey*, 1935

Conrad, Joseph, *The Secret Agent: A Simple Tale*, 1907 (1923 edn)

Constantine, Learie, *Colour Bar*, 1954

Cook, Mrs E. T., *Highways and Byways in London*, 1902

Cook, George, *A Hackney Memory Chest*, 1983

Cooke, M. Emily, *A Geographical Study of a London Borough: St Pancras*, 1932

Copeman, Fred, *Reason in Revolt*, 1948

Coppock, J. T., and Prince, Hugh C. (eds.), *Greater London*, 1964

Cousins, Sheila, *To Beg I Am Ashamed*, New York, 1938

Cowan, Peter, and others, *The Office: A Facet of Urban Growth*, 1969

Cox, B., et al., *The Fall of Scotland Yard*, Hardmondsworth, 1977

Craven, Anna, *West Africans in London*, 1968

CRHC (Council for Research on Housing Construction), *Slum Clearance and Rehousing*, 1934

Crichton, Ruth M., *Commuters' Village: A Study of Community and Commuters in the Berkshire Village of Stratfield Mortimer*, 1964

Critchley, Macdonald (ed.), *The Trial of Neville George Clevely Heath*, 1951

Critchley, T. A., *A History of Police in England and Wales, 900–1966*, 1967

Croft, Taylor, *The Cloven Hoof: A Study of Contemporary London Vices*, 1932

Croft-Cooke, Rupert, *The Sound of Revelry*, 1969

Crookston, Peter (ed.), *Village London:* The Observer*'s Guide to the Real London*, 1978

Crossman, Richard, *The Diaries of a Cabinet Minister: Vol. I, Minister of Housing, 1964–66*, 1975

– *The Diaries of a Cabinet Minister: Vol. II, Lord President of the Council and Leader of the House of Commons*, 1976

Crouch, Arthur Philip, *Silvertown and Neighbourhood (Including East and West Ham): A Retrospect*, 1900

Curtis, James *The Gilt Kid*, 1936

– *They Drive by Night*, 1938

– *What Immortal Hand*, 1939

Cutler, Horace, *The Cutler Files*, 1982

Daley, Harry, *This Small Cloud: A Personal Memoir*, 1986

Dalzell, W. R., *The Shell Guide to the History of London*, 1981

Daniel, W. W., *Racial Discrimination in England: Based on the PEP Report*, Harmondsworth, 1968

Danziger, Nick, *Danziger's Britain: A Journey to the Edge*, 1996

Darlington's London and Environs, 1902 (4th edn)

Davey, Dolly, *A Sense of Adventure*, 1980

Davies, Hunter, *The Other Half*, 1966

Davies, Hunter (ed.), *The New London Spy: A Discreet Guide to the City's Pleasures*, 1966

Davies, Sidney, 'A Note on Cancer Occurrence in Hampstead and Shoreditch', *Public Health*, March 1924

Davies, W. H., *The Autobiography of a Super-Tramp*, 1908 (1942 edn)

– *The Adventures of Johnny Walker, Tramp*, 1926 (1932 edn)

Davin, Anna, *Growing Up Poor: Home, School and Street in London, 1870–1914*, 1996

Davis, John, *Reforming London: The London Government Problem*, Oxford, 1988

Davison, R. B., *Black British: Immigrants to England*, 1966

Deakin, Nicholas and Ungerson, Clare, *Leaving London: Planned Mobility and the Inner City*, 1977

Deakin, Nicholas, and others, *Colour, Citizenship and British Society*, 1970

Dearden, R. L., and Lucas, Netley, *The Autobiography of a Crook*, 1924

Deighton, Len (ed.), *Len Deighton's London Dossier*, 1967

De Maré, Eric, *London's Riverside: Past, Present and Future*, 1958.

Denbigh, Kathleen, *Preserving London*, 1978

Denby, Elizabeth, *Europe Re-Housed*, 1944 (1st edn, 1938)

Dench, Geoff, *Maltese in London: A Case-study in the Erosion of Ethnic Consciousness*, 1975

Dennis, Ferdinand, *Behind the Frontlines: Journey into Afro-Britain*, 1988

Department of the Environment, *Streamlining the Cities: Government Proposals for Reorganizing Local Government in Greater London and the Metropolitan Counties*, Cd. 9063, 1983

Desai, Rashmi, *Indian Immigrants to Britain*, 1963

Desmond, Shaw, *London Nights of Long Ago*, 1927

Deverson, Jane, and Lindsay, Katharine, *Voices from the Middle Class: A Study of Families in Two London Suburbs*, 1975

Dickens, Monica, *The Heart of London*, 1961 (Book Club edn)

– *An Open Book*, 1978

Disher, M. Willson, *Pleasures of London*, 1950

Divall, Tom, *Scoundrels and Scallywags (and Some Honest Men)*, 1929

Dix, Bernard, and Williams, Stephen, *Serving the Public – Building the Union: The History of the National Union of Public Employees: Vol. I, The Forerunners, 1889–1928*, 1987

Donnison, D. V., *Health, Welfare and Democracy in Greater London*, LSE Greater London Papers No. 5, 1962

Donnison, David V. and Eversley, David (eds.), *London: Urban Patterns, Problems, and Policies*, 1973

Donoughue, Bernard, and Jones, G. W., *Herbert Morrison: Portrait of a Politician*, 1973

Dorling, Daniel, *Death in Britain: How Local Mortality Rates Have Changed, 1950s–1990s*, York, 1997

Douglas, Norman, *London Street Games*, 1931 (1st edn, 1916)

Dowling, S. W., *The Exchanges of London*, 1929

Downes, David M., *The Delinquent Solution: A Study in Subcultural Theory*, 1966

Drabble, Margaret, *Arnold Bennett*, 1974

Duffy, Maureen, *Londoners*, 1983

Dunboyne, Lord (ed.), *The Trial of John George Haigh (the Acid Bath Murder)*, 1953

Dunleavy, Patrick, *The Politics of Mass Housing in Britain, 1945–1975: A Study of Corporate Power and Professional Influence in the Welfare State*, Oxford, 1981

Dunn, James, *Modern London – Its Sins and Woes and the Sovereign Remedy*, 1906

Dunn, Nell, *Up the Junction*, 1963

Dunne, L. R., *Report on an Inquiry into the Accident at Bethnal Green Tube Station Shelter*, 1943 (1999 edn)

Durant, Ruth, *Watling: A Survey of Social Life on a New Housing Estate*, 1939

Du Rose, John, *Murder Was My Business*, 1971

Eastwood, G. G., *George Isaacs: Printer, Trade Union Leader, Cabinet Minister*, n.d. (*c.* 1952)

Eddowes, Michael, *The Man on Your Conscience: An Investigation of the Evans Murder Trial*, 1955

Edelman, Maurice, *Herbert Morrison: A Pictorial Biography*, 1948

Edwards, Percy J., *History of London Street Improvements, 1855–1897*, 1898

Egginton, Joyce, *They Seek a Living*, 1957

Elkin, Stephen L., *Politics and Land Use Planning: The London Experience*, 1974

Elliott, Michael, *Heartbeat London*, 1986

Emecheta, Buchi, *Head above Water*, 1986

Englander, David, *Landlord and Tenant in Urban Britain, 1838–1918*, Oxford, 1983

Esher, Lionel, *A Broken Wave: The Rebuilding of England, 1940–1980*, 1981

Eversley, David, 'The Ganglion of Tourism: An Unresolvable Problem for London?', *London Journal*, Vol. 3, No. 2, 1977

Fabian, Robert, *Fabian of the Yard: An Intimate Record*, 1950

– *London after Dark: An Intimate Record of Night Life in London, and a Selection of Crime Stories from the Case Book of Robert Fabian*, 1954

Fabian Society, Tract No. 190 (J. E. MacColl), *Metropolitan Borough Councils*, 1947

Fainstein, Susan S., *The City Builders: Property, Politics, and Planning in London and New York*, Oxford, 1994

Fainstein, Susan S., et al. (eds.), *Divided Cities: New York and London in the Contemporary World*, Oxford, 1992

Farrant, Sue, 'London by the Sea: Resort Development on the South Coast of England, 1880–1939', *Journal of Contemporary History*, Vol. 22, No. 1, 1987

Farson, Daniel, *Never a Normal Man: An Autobiography*, 1997

Farson, Negley, *Bomber's Moon*, 1941

Feldman, David, and Jones, Gareth Stedman (eds.), *Metropolis London: Histories and Representations since 1800*, 1989

Felstead, Sidney Theodore, *The Underworld of London*, 1923

Ferguson, Rachel, *Passionate Kensington*, 1939

Ferrie, William, *The Banned Broadcast of William Ferrie*, 1934

Ferrier, J. Kenneth, *Crooks and Crime*, 1928 (2nd edn)

Ferron, Eric, '*Man, You've Mixed*': *A Jamaican Comes to Britain*, 1995

Finmore, Rhoda Lee, *Immoral Earnings: Or Mr Martin's Profession*, 1951

Firth, Raymond (ed.), *Two Studies of Kinship in London*, 1956

Firth, Raymond, et al., *Families and Their Relatives: Kinship in a Middle-class Sector of London. An Anthropological Study*, 1969

Fishman, William J., *East End Jewish Radicals, 1875–1914*, 1975

– *East End 1888: A Year in a London Borough among the Labouring Poor*, 1988

Fletcher, Hanslip (ed.), *London Passed and Passing: A Pictorial Record of Destroyed and Threatened Buildings, with Notes by Various Authors*, 1908

Flynn, Norman, et al., *Abolition or Reform? The GLC and the Metropolitan Counties*, 1985

Foakes, Grace, *My Part of the River*, 1976

Fogarty, M. P., *Prospects of the Industrial Areas of Great Britain*, 1945

Foley, Donald L., *Controlling London's Growth: Planning the Great Wen, 1940–1960*, Berkeley, CA, 1963

Foner, Nancy, *Jamaica Farewell: Jamaican Migrants in London*, 1979

Foreman, Freddie, *Respect: Autobiography of Freddie Foreman – Managing Director of British Crime*, 1996 (1997 pb edn)

Forman, Henry James, *London: An Intimate Picture*, New York, 1913

Forrester, Andrew, et al., *Beyond Our Ken: A Guide to the Battle for London*, 1985

Forshaw, Alec, and Bergström, Theo, *The Markets of London*, Harmondsworth, 1983

Forshaw, J. H., and Abercrombie, Patrick, *County of London Plan*, 1943

Forster, E. M., *Howards End*, 1910 (1996 Folio Society edn)

Foster, Janet, *Villains: Crime and Community in the Inner City*, 1990

Fowler Wright, S., *Police and Public*, 1929

Fox, R. M., *Smoky Crusade*, 1937

Franklyn, Julian, *The Cockney: A Survey of London Life and Language*, 1953

Fraser, Frankie, *Mad Frank: Memoirs of a Life of Crime*, 1994

Freedman, Maurice (ed.), *A Minority in Britain: Social Studies of the Anglo-Jewish Community*, 1955

French, Sean, *Patrick Hamilton: A Life*, 1993

Frost, George 'Jack', *Flying Squad*, 1950

Fryer, Peter, *Staying Power: Black People in Britain since 1504*, New Jersey, 1984

Fuller, Ken, *Radical Aristocrats: London Busworkers from the 1880s to the 1980s*, 1985

Fyvel, T. R., *The Insecure Offenders: Rebellious Youth in the Welfare State*, 1961

Gainer, Bernard, *The Alien Invasion: The Origins of the Aliens Act of 1905*, 1972

Galsworthy, John, *The Man of Property*, 1906 (*The Forsyte Saga*, 1929 edn)

– *In Chancery*, 1920 (*The Forsyte Saga*, 1929 edn)

Gamble, Rose, *Chelsea Child*, 1979

Gamon, Hugh R. P., *The London Police Court To-Day and To-Morrow*, 1907

Gape, W. A., *Half a Million Tramps*, 1936

Garbett, Cyril Forster, *In the Heart of South London*, 1931

Gardiner, A. G., *John Benn and the Progressive Movement*, 1925

Gardner, Arthur R. L., *Prisoner at the Bar*, 1931

Gartner, Lloyd P., *The Jewish Immigrant in England, 1870–1914*, 1973, (2nd edn)

Gavron, Hannah, *The Captive Wife: Conflicts of Housebound Mothers*, 1966 (1983 edn)

George, R. F., 'A New Calculation of the Poverty Line', *Journal of the Royal Statistical Society*, 1937

Gibbon, Sir Gwilym, *Reconstruction and Town and Country Planning: With an Examination of the Uthwatt and Scott Reports*, 1943

Gibbon, Sir Gwilym, and Bell, Reginald W., *History of the London County Council, 1889–1939*, 1939

Gibbons, Stella, *A Pink Front Door*, 1959

Gillain, Louis, *The Pavement My Pillow*, 1954

Gissing, George, *The Crown of Life*, 1899

Gittins, D., *Fair Sex: Family Size and Structure, 1900–39*, 1982

Gladstone, Florence M., *Notting Hill in Bygone Days*, 1924

Glass, Ruth, *Newcomers: The West Indians in London*, 1960

Glass, Ruth, et al., *London: Aspects of Change*, 1964

Glassberg, Andrew D., *Representation and Community*, 1981

Glicco, Jack, *Madness after Midnight*, 1952

Godley, Andrew, 'Immigrant Entrepreneurs and the Emergence of London's East End as an Industrial District', *London Journal*, Vol. 21, No. 1, 1996

Golden, Jennifer, *Hackney at War*, 1995

Goldman, Willy, *East End My Cradle*, 1940 (1947 edn)

Gomme, Sir G. Laurence, *London*, 1914

Goodwin, John C., *One of the Crowd*, 1936

Gordon, Charles [James Ashton], *Old Time Aldwych, Kingsway, and Neighbourhood*, 1903

Gordon, Jan and Cora, *The London Roundabout*, 1933

Gordon, Paul, *White Law: Racism in the Police, Courts and Prisons*, 1983

Gorham, Maurice, *Londoners*, 1951

Gosling, Harry, *Up and Down Stream*, 1927

Gosling, John, and Warner, Douglas, *The Shame of a City: An Inquiry into the Vice of London*, 1960 (1963 pb edn)

Goss, Sue, *Local Labour and Local Government: A Study of Changing Interests, Politics and Policy in Southwark from 1919 to 1982*, Edinburgh, 1988

Gough, W. C., *From Kew Observatory to Scotland Yard: Being Experiences and Travels in 28 Years of Crime Investigation*, 1925

Gould, Tony, *Inside Outsider: The Life and Times of Colin MacInnes*, 1983 (1993 pb edn)

Graham, Stephen, *London Nights (a Series of Studies and Sketches of London at Night)*, 1925

Grant, Clara E., *From 'Me' to 'We' (Forty Years on Bow Common)*, n.d. (*c.* 1940)

Grant, Graham, *The Diary of a Police Surgeon*, 1920

Graves, Charles, *The Price of Pleasure*, 1935

– *Champagne and Chandeliers: The Story of the Café de Paris*, 1958

Graves, Robert, and Hodge, Alan, *The Long Week-end: A Social History of Great Britain, 1918–1939*, 1941

Gray, Frank, *The Tramp: His Meaning and Being*, 1931

Greater London Council, *Greater London Development Plan Report of Studies*, 1969

– *GLC Architecture 1965/70: The Work of the GLC's Department of Architecture and Civic Design*, n.d. (*c.* 1970)

– *The London Industrial Strategy*, 1985

– GLS, *Greater London Statistics* (various years, continued by London Research Centre from 1986–7 to 1994–5)

Greater London Regional Planning Committee, *First Report*, 1929

Green, Henry, *Caught*, 1943

Green, Jonathon, *Days in the Life: Voices from the English Underground, 1961–1971*, 1988

– *Them: Voices from the Immigrant Community in Contemporary Britain*, 1990

Green, Shirley, *Rachman*, 1979

– *Who Owns London?*, 1986

Greeno, Edward, *War on the Underworld*, 1960

Greve, John, *London's Homeless*, 1964

Greve, John, et al., *Homelessness in London*, Edinburgh, 1971

Grigg, Mary, *The Challenor Case*, Harmondsworth, 1965

Grossek, Mark, *First Movement*, 1937

Hackney, London Borough of, *'Just What the Doctor Ordered': A Study of Housing, Health and Community Safety in Holly Street, Hackney, June 1996*, 1996

– *MORI: Residents' Survey. Final Report*, 1997

– *Upwardly Mobile: Holly Street 1998*, 1998

Hall, Edith, *Canary Girls and Stockpots*, Luton, 1977

Hall, Peter G., *The Industries of London since 1861*, 1962

– *London 2000*, 1963

– *Great Planning Disasters*, 1980

– *London 2001*, 1989

– *Cities in Civilization: Culture, Innovation, and Urban Order*, 1998

Hall, Radclyffe, *Adam's Breed*, 1924

Hall, Stuart, et al., *Policing the Crisis: Mugging, the State, and Law and Order*, 1978

Halsey, A. H. (ed.), *British Social Trends since 1900: A Guide to the Changing Social Structure of Britain*, 1988

Hambrook, Walter, *Hambrook of the Yard*, 1937

Hamilton, Adrian, *The Financial Revolution: The Big Bang Worldwide*, 1986

Hamilton, Patrick, *The Midnight Bell*, 1929 (1987 trilogy edn)

– *The Plains of Cement*, 1934 (1987 trilogy edn)

– *Hangover Square: A Story of Darkest Earl's Court*, 1941 (1985 Penguin edn)

Hamnett, Chris, and Williams, Peter, 'Social Change in London: A Study of Gentrification', *London Journal*, Vol. 6, No. 1, 1980

Hamnett, Nina, *Laughing Torso: Reminiscences of Nina Hamnett*, 1932

Hardy, Dennis, and Ward, Colin, *Arcadia for All: The Legacy of a Makeshift Landscape*, 1984

Hare, Kenneth, *London's Latin Quarter*, 1926

Harper, Charles G., *London Yesterday, To-Day and To-Morrow*, 1925

– *A Londoner's Own London*, 1927

Harris, H. Wilson, and Bryant, Margaret, *The Churches and London (an Outline Survey of Religious Work in the Metropolitan Area)*, n.d.(*c.* 1913)

Harris, Kenneth, *Attlee*, 1982

Harris, Percy A., *London and Its Government*, 1913

– *London and Its Government*, 1931

Harris, Sir Percy A., *Forty Years in and out of Parliament*, 1947

Harrison, Paul, *Inside the Inner City: Life under the Cutting Edge*, 1983

Harrisson, Tom, *Living through the Blitz*, 1976 (1978 Penguin edn)

Harte, Negley, *The University of London, 1836–1986: An Illustrated History*, 1986

Hatton, S. F., *London's Bad Boys*, 1931

Health of Londoners Project, *The Health of Londoners: A Public Health Report for Londoners*, 1998

Hebbert, Michael, *London: More by Fortune Than Design*, 1998

Helweg, Arthur Wesley, *Sikhs in England*, Delhi, 1986 (2nd edn)

Henney, Alex, *Inside Local Government: A Case for Radical Reform*, 1984

Henry, Stuart (ed.), *Can I Have It in Cash? A Study of Informal Institutions and Unorthodox Ways of Doing Things*, 1981

Heren, Louis, *Growing Up Poor in London*, 1973

Hibbert, H. G., *Fifty Years of a Londoner's Life*, 1916

Higgins, Robert, *In the Name of the Law*, 1958

Higgs, Mary, *Glimpses into the Abyss*, 1906

Hill, Billy, *Boss of Britain's Underworld*, 1955

Hill, Clifford S., *West Indian Migrants and the London Churches*, 1963

Hillman, Judy, *A New Look for London*, 1988

Hillman, Judy (ed.), *Planning for London*, Harmondsworth, 1971

Hinds, Alfred, *Contempt of Court*, 1966

Hinds, Donald, *Journey to an Illusion: The West Indian in Britain*, 1966

Hinton, James, *The First Shop Stewards' Movement*, 1973

– 'Self-help and Socialism: The Squatters' Movement of 1946', *History Workshop Journal*, Issue 25, 1988

Hiro, Dilip, *Black British, White British*, 1973 (revised edn)

[HMFI] His Majesty's Inspector of Factories, *Annual Reports*, 1919–39

Hobbs, Dick, *Doing the Business: Entrepreneurship, the Working Class, and Detectives in the East End of London*, 1988

Hobhouse, Hermione, *London Survey'd: The Work of the Survey of London*, 1994

Hobhouse, Stephen, *Forty Years and an Epilogue: An Autobiography (1881–1951)*, 1951

Hodge, Herbert, *I Drive a Taxi*, 1939

Hogarth, Basil (ed.), *Trial of Robert Wood (the Camden Town Case)*, 1936

Hogarth, Paul, and Muggeridge, Malcolm, *London à la Mode*, 1966

Hoggart, Keith, and Green, David (eds.), *A New Metropolitan Geography*, 1991

Holdaway, Simon, and Barron, Anne-Marie, *Resigners? The Experience of Black and Asian Police Officers*, 1997

Holloway, John, *A London Childhood*, 1966

Holloway Tenant Co-operative, *A Better Place: The Story of the Holloway Tenant Co-operative Compiled from Records, Letters and Minutes of the Members*, 1974

Holman, Bob, *Good Old George: The Life of George Lansbury*, 1990

Holme, Anthea, *Housing and Young Families in East London*, 1985

Holtby, Winifred, *South Riding: An English Landscape*, 1936

Home Affairs Committee, *Chinese Community in Britain*, 1985 (2nd report)

Hopkins, Harry, *The New Look: A Social History of the Forties and Fifties in Britain*, 1963 (1964 Reader's Union edn)

Hopkins, R. Thurston, *London Pilgrimages*, 1928

Hopkinson, Diana, *Family Inheritance: A Life of Eva Hubback*, 1954

Hopkinson, Tom, *Of This Our Time: A Journalist's Story, 1905–50*, 1982

Horsley, Terence, *The Odyssey of an Out-of-Work*, 1931

Hotten, John Camden, *The Slang Dictionary*, 1865

Howard, Ebenezer, *Garden Cities of To-Morrow*, 1902

Howarth, Edward G. and Wilson, Mona, *West Ham: A Study in Social and Industrial Problems*, 1907

Howe, Darcus, *From Bobby to Babylon: Blacks and British Police*, 1988

Howe, Geoffrey, *Conflict of Loyalty*, 1994

Howells, W. D., *London Films*, 1905

Howgrave-Graham, H. M., *Light and Shade at Scotland Yard*, 1947

Hueffer, Ford Madox, *The Soul of London: A Survey of a Modern City*, 1905 (1911 edn)

Hughes, M. Vivian, *A London Family between the Wars*, 1940

– *A London Family 1870–1900*, 1946

Humphreys, Christmas, *The Great Pearl Robbery of 1913: A Record of Fact*, 1929

Humphries, Stephen, *Hooligans or Rebels? An Oral History of Working-class Childhood and Youth, 1889–1939*, 1981

Humphry, Derek, *Police Power and Black People*, 1972

Hurley, Alfred James, *Days That Are Gone: Milestones I Have Passed in South-West London*, 1947

Hutchings, W. W., *London Town Past and Present*, 2 vols., 1909

Hutt, Allen, *The Condition of the Working-Class in Britain*, 1933

Huxley, Elspeth, *Back Streets New Worlds: A Look at Immigrants in Britain*, 1964

Hyde, H. Montgomery (ed.), *Trial of Christopher Craig and Derek William Bentley*, 1954

Hyde, Robert R., *Industry Was My Parish*, 1968

Hyndman, Henry Mayers, *The Record of an Adventurous Life*, 1911

Idle, E. Doreen, *War over West Ham: A Study of Community Adjustment*, 1943

Inwood, Stephen, *A History of London*, 1998

Isaacs, Susan (ed.), *The Cambridge Evacuation Survey: A Wartime Study in Social Welfare and Education*, 1941

The Island: The Life and Death of an East London Community, 1870–1970, 1979

Jackson, Alan A., *Semi-Detached London: Suburban Development, Life and Transport, 1900–39*, 1973

Jackson, Sir Richard, *Occupied with Crime*, 1967

Jackson, W. Eric, *Achievement: A Short History of the London County Council*, 1965

Jacobs, Joe, *Out of the Ghetto: My Youth in the East End, Communism and Fascism, 1913–1939*, 1978

James, Clive, *Falling towards England*, 1985 (1986 pb edn)

James, Winston, and Harris, Clive (eds.), *Inside Babylon: The Caribbean Diaspora in Britain*, 1993

Jameson, Storm, *Journey from the North: Autobiography of Storm Jameson*, 2 vols., 1969–70

Janes, Hurford, *The Red Barrel: A History of Watney Mann*, 1963

Jasper, A. S., *A Hoxton Childhood*, 1969

Jay, Douglas, *Change and Fortune: A Political Record*, 1980

Jenkins, Simon, *A City at Risk: A Contemporary Look at London's Streets*, 1970

– *Landlords to London: The Story of a Capital and Its Growth*, 1975

Jennings, Andrew, et al., *Scotland Yard's Cocaine Connection*, 1990

Jennings, Frank L., *In London's Shadows*, 1926

– *Men of the Lanes: The Autobiography of the Tramps' Parson*, 1958

Jephcott, Pearl, *A Troubled Area: Notes on Notting Hill*, 1964

Jesse, F. Tennyson (ed.), *Trials of Timothy John Evans and John Reginald Halliday Christie*, 1957

John, Gus, and Humphry, Derek, *Because They're Black*, Harmondsworth, 1971

Johnson, Pamela Hansford, *This Bed Thy Centre*, 1935 (1963 edn)

– *The Monument*, 1938

Jones, C. Sheridan, *London in War-Time*, 1917

Jones, Edward, and Woodward, Christopher, *A Guide to the Architecture of London*, 1983

Jones, Gareth Stedman, *Outcast London: A Study in the Relationship between Classes in Victorian Society*, Oxford, 1971

Jones, Jack, *My Lively Life*, 1929

Jones, James A., *Wonderful London Today*, 1934

– *London's Eight Millions*, 1935

Jones, Sydney R., *London Triumphant*, 1941

Jones, Trevor, et al., *The Islington Crime Survey: Crime, Victimization and Policing in Inner-city London*, 1986

Keeble, D. E., *Industrial Decentralization and the Metropolis: The North-West London Case*, 1968

Keith, Michael, *Race, Riots and Policing: Lore and Disorder in a Multi-racist Society*, 1993

Kelland, Gilbert, *Crime in London*, 1986 (1996 pb edn)

Kennedy, Ludovic, *Ten Rillington Place*, 1961

Kent, William, *The Lost Treasures of London*, 1947

– *John Burns: Labour's Lost Leader*, 1950

Kersh, Gerald, 'The Extraordinarily Horrible Dummy', *Penguin Parade*, 6 April 1939

Kershen, Anne J. (ed.), *London: The Promised Land? The Migrant Experience in a Capital City*, Aldershot, 1997

Khan, Verity Saifullah (ed.), *Minority Families in Britain: Support and Stress*, 1979

Kidd, Ronald, *British Liberty in Danger: An Introduction to the Study of Civil Rights*, 1940

King, Anthony D., *Global Cities: Post-imperialism and the Internationalization of London*, 1990

Kinsey, Richard, et al., *Losing the Fight against Crime*, 1986

Knight, Nick, *Skinhead*, 1982

Kohan, C. M., *Works and Buildings*, 1952 (Civil History of the Second World War)

Kops, Bernard, *The World is a Wedding*, 1963

Kuepper, William G., et al., *Ugandan Asians in Great Britain: Forced Migration and Social Absorption*, 1975

Kureishi, Hanif, *The Buddha of Suburbia*, 1990 (pb edn)

– *The Black Album*, 1995 (1996 edn)

Kurtz, Irma, *Dear London: Notes from the Big City*, 1997

Kynaston, David, *The City of London, 1815–1945*, 3 vols., 1994–9

Labour Research Department, *Wages, Prices and Profits*, 1921

Lamming, George, *The Emigrants*, 1954

Lancaster, Osbert, *All Done from Memory*, 1963

Langdon, Claude, *Earls Court*, 1953

Lansbury, Edgar, *George Lansbury, My Father*, n.d. (*c.* 1933)

Lansbury, George, *Your Part in Poverty*, 1917

– *These Things Shall Be*, 1920

– *My Life*, 1928

– *My England*, 1934

– *Looking Backwards – and Forwards*, 1935

Lapping, Anne, 'London's Burning! London's Burning! A Survey', *The Economist*,
  1 January 1977

Laurie, Peter, *Scotland Yard: A Personal Inquiry*, 1970

Lawson, Twiggy, *Twiggy: In Black and White*, 1997

Leach, Charles, *On Top of the Underworld*, 1933

Lee, Sir Sidney, *King Edward VII: A Biography*, 2 vols., 1925–7

Lees, Lynn Holden, *Exiles of Erin: Irish Migrants in Victorian London*, Manchester,
  1979

Leeson, B., *Lost London: The Memoirs of an East End Detective*, 1930

Lehmann, John (ed.), *Coming to London*, 1957

Lehmann, Rosamond, *The Weather in the Streets*, 1936 (1981 pb edn)

Le Mesurier, Mrs L., *Boys in Trouble: A Study of Adolescent Crime and Its Treatment*,
  1931

Levin, Bernard, *The Pendulum Years: Britain and the Sixties*, 1970

Lewey, Frank R., *Cockney Campaign*, n.d. (*c.* 1943)

Lewis, Chaim, *A Soho Address*, 1965

Lewis, Jane, *Women in England, 1870–1950: Sexual Divisions and Social Change*, 1984

Lidbetter, E. J., *Heredity and the Social Problem Group*, Vol. I, 1933

Lidgett, J. Scott, *My Guided Life*, 1936

Lieck, Albert, *Bow Street World*, 1938

Liepmann, Kate K., *The Journey to Work: Its Significance for Industrial and Community
  Life*, 1944

Linehan, Thomas P., *East London for Mosley: The British Union of Fascists in East
  London and South-West Essex, 1933–40*, 1996

Linney, A. G., *The Peepshow of the Port of London*, n.d. (*c.* 1929)

Lipman, V. D., *Social History of the Jews in England, 1850–1950*, 1954

– *A Century of Social Service, 1869–1959: The Jewish Board of Guardians*, 1959

Little, K. L., *Negroes in Britain: A Study of Racial Relations in English Society*, 1947

Litvinoff, Emanuel, *Journey through a Small Planet*, 1972

Loftie, W. J., *The Colour of London: Historic, Personal, and Local*, 1907

LMN (London Municipal Society), *London Municipal Notes* (various years)

London, Jack, *People of the Abyss*, 1903 (1977 edn)

London County Council, *Annual Report* (various years)

– *The Housing Question in London, 1855–1900,* 1900

– *Opening of Kingsway and Aldwych by His Majesty the King . . .,* 1905

– *No. 17 Fleet Street,* 1906

– *Proposed Demolition of Nineteen City Churches,* 1920

– *Record of Service in the Great War 1914–18 by Members of the Council's Staff,* 1922

– *Housing . . .,* 1924

– *The London Ambulance Service . . .,* 1925

– *The London Fire Brigade . . .,* 1925

– *Housing: With Particular Reference to Post-war Housing Schemes,* 1928

– *Housing: Working-class Housing on the Continent and the Application of Continental Ideas to the Housing Problem in the County of London,* 1936

– *London Housing,* 1937

– (Public Assistance Department), '*The House': London's Public Assistance Institutions,* 1939

– *The LCC Hospitals: A Retrospect,* 1949

– *Administrative County of London Development Plan 1951: Analysis,* 1951

– *Housing Service Handbook,* 1962

– /LSS, *London Statistics* (various years)

London District Communist Party, *Sixteen Bob a Day for Dockers: Abolish Casual Labour,* n.d. (*c.* 1937)

– *Bramley's Speech at the Old Bailey: The Trial of the London Communists Arrested for Action on Behalf of London's Homeless, September, 1946,* 1946

London Labour Party, *'What about Belmont?' The Facts about Residential Training Centres under the Labour LCC,* 1935

– *What Labour Has Done for London: The Work of the Labour LCC, 1934–1945,* 1945

– *Labour Keeps Faith with London: The Work of the Labour LCC, 1946–48,* (n.d. 1948)

– *The London Labour Chronicle* (various years)

– *The Work of the London Labour Party* (annual report, various years)

London Passenger Transport Board, *4th Annual Report and Accounts Year Ended 30 June 1937,* 1937

London Planning Advisory Committee and others, *London: World City Moving into the 21st Century, a Research Project,* 1991

– *1994 Advice on Strategic Planning Guidance for London,* 1994

London Research Centre, *London 95,* 1995

– (Edwards, Phillip, and Flatley, John [eds.]), *The Capital Divided: Mapping Poverty and Social Exclusion in London,* 1996

– (Storkey, Marian, et al.), *Cosmopolitan London: Past, Present and Future,* 1997

– *London at Work,* 1998

– (Pullinger, John, and Holding, Alison [eds.]), *London 98,* 1998

– *Focus on London 99,* 1999

London Society, *London's Squares and How to Save Them*, 1927

London TEC Council, *London's Employer Survey, 1997–1998*, 1998

London Trades Council, *London Trades Council, 1860–1950: A History*, 1950

Low, David, *Low's Autobiography*, 1956

Lucas, Netley, *London and Its Criminals*, 1926

Ludovici, A., *An Artist's Life in London and Paris, 1870–1925*, 1926

Macaulay, Rose, *The World My Wilderness*, Boston, Mass., 1950

McClintock, F. H., and Avison, N. Howard, *Crime in England and Wales*, 1968

McClintock, F. H., and Gibson, Evelyn, *Robbery in London*, 1961

McCrae, Hamish, and Cairncross, Frances, *Capital City: London as a Financial Centre*, 1984

MacDonagh, Michael, *In London during the Great War: The Diary of a Journalist*, 1935

Macdonald, John F., *Two Towns – One City: Paris – London*, 1917

McDougall, Donald, *Fifty Years a Borough, 1886–1936: The Story of West Ham*, 1936

Machen, Arthur, *Far Off Things*, 1922 (1974 edn)

– *Things Far and Near*, 1923 (1974 edn)

Machray, Robert, *The Night Side of London*, 1902

MacInnes, Colin, *City of Spades*, 1957 (1969 one-vol. London Trilogy edn)

– *Absolute Beginners*, 1959 (1969 one-vol. London Trilogy edn)

– *England, Half English*, 1961

– *London: City of Any Dream*, 1962

McKellar, Elizabeth, *The German Hospital in Hackney: A Social and Architectural History*, 1991

Mackenzie, Compton, *Carnival*, 1912 (*c.* 1936 Nash's Famous Fiction Library edn)

– *Sinister Street*, 1913–14

– *Our Street*, 1931

– *My Life and Times: Octave Three, 1900–1907*, 1964

– *My Life and Times: Octave Four, 1907–1915*, 1965

Maclure, Stuart, *One Hundred Years of London Education, 1870–1970*, 1970

McNee, Sir David, *McNee's Law*, 1983

Macqueen-Pope, W., '*Goodbye Piccadilly*', 1960

Macready, Sir Nevil, *Annals of an Active Life*, 2 vols., 1924

Major, John, *The Autobiography*, 1999

Malik, Michael Abdul, *From Michael de Freitas to Michael X*, 1968

Malvery, Olive Christian, *The Soul Market (with which is included 'The Heart of Things')*, 1906

Mannheim, Hermann, *Social Aspects of Crime in England between the Wars*, 1940

– *War and Crime*, 1941

Mannick, A. R. *Mauritians in London*, Mayfield, Sussex, 1987

Mannin, Ethel, *Sounding Brass*, 1925

Margrie, William, *The Diary of a London Explorer: Forty Years of Vital London Life*, 1934

Mark, Sir Robert, *In the Office of Constable*, 1978

Marriott, John, ' "West Ham: London's Industrial Centre and Gateway to the World".1. Industrialization, 1840–1910', *London Journal*, Vol. 13, No. 2, 1987–8

– ' "West Ham: London's Industrial Centre and Gateway to the World". 2. Stabilization and Decline, 1910–1939', *London Journal*, Vol. 14, No. 1, 1989

– *The Culture of Labourism: The East End between the Wars*, Edinburgh, 1991

Marriott, Oliver, *The Property Boom*, 1967

Marryat, H. and Broadbent, Una, *The Romance of Hatton Garden*, 1930

Marshall, Francis, *The London Book*, n.d. (1951)

Marshall, Sir Frank, *The Marshall Inquiry on Greater London: Report to the Greater London Council*, 1978

Martin, J. E., *Greater London: An Industrial Geography*, 1966

Marwick, Arthur, *The Deluge: British Society and the First World War*, 1965 (1967 pb edn)

– *The Sixties: Cultural Revolution in Britain, France, Italy, and the United States, c. 1958–c. 1974*, Oxford, 1998

Mason, George, *George Mason, Councillor*, 1983

Massie, Chris, *The Confessions of a Vagabond*, n.d. (*c.* 1932)

Massingham, H. J., *London Scene*, 1933

Massingham, Hugh, *I Took Off My Tie*, 1936

Mass-Observation, *Britain*, Harmondsworth, 1939

– (Willcock, H. D.), *Report on Juvenile Delinquency*, 1949

Masterman, C. F. G., *The Condition of England*, 1909

Masters, Brian, *Killing for Company*, 1985 (1995 pb edn)

Matthews, William, *Cockney Past and Present: A Short History of the Dialect of London*, 1938 (1972 edn)

May, Betty, *Tiger-Woman: My Story*, 1929

Mays, Spike, *Last Post*, 1974

Meek, Victor, *Cops and Robbers*, 1962

Melly, George, *Revolt into Style: The Pop Arts in Britain*, 1970 (1972 pb edn)

Melville, Lewis, *The London Scene*, 1926

Merriman, Nick (ed.), *The Peopling of London: Fifteen Thousand Years of Settlement from Overseas*, 1993

Mess, H. A., *Casual Labour at the Docks*, 1916

Metropolitan Borough of Islington, *Annual Reports of Medical Officer of Health*, 1914–38

Metropolitan Railway Co., *Metro-Land*, n.d. (*c.* 1925)

Meyrick, Mrs K., *Secrets of the 43: Reminiscences by Mrs Meyrick*, 1933

M'Gonigle, G. C. M., and Kirby, J., *Poverty and Public Health*, 1936

Mikardo, Ian, *Back-Bencher*, 1988

Millen, Ernest, *Specialist in Crime*, 1972

Miltoun, Francis, *Dickens' London*, 1904

Mohanti, Prafulla, *Through Brown Eyes*, Oxford, 1985

Monolulu, Ras Prince, *I Gotta Horse*, n.d. (*c.* 1950)

Moorcock, Michael, *Mother London: A Novel*, 1988

Morand, Paul, *A Frenchman's London*, 1934

Morgan, A. E., *The Needs of Youth: A Report Made to King George's Jubilee Trust Fund*, 1939

Morgan, Kenneth O., *Labour in Power, 1945–1951*, 1984

Morison, Frank, *War on Great Cities: A Study of the Facts*, 1937

Morrison, Arthur, *The Hole in the Wall*, 1902

Morrison, Herbert, *Socialisation and Transport: The Organisation of Socialised Industries with Particular Reference to the London Passenger Transport Bill*, 1933

– *How Greater London is Governed*, 1935

– *An Autobiography*, 1960

Morrison, Majbritt, *Jungle West 11*, 1964

Morse-Boycott, Desmond, *Ten Years in a London Slum: Being the Adventures of a Clerical Micawber*, n.d. (*c.* 1930)

– *We Do See Life! Faith, Hope and Comedy in the 'Underworld' of London*, n.d. (*c.* 1931)

Morton, H. V., *Our Fellow Men*, 1936

– *London*, 1940 (7th edn, 1942)

Morton, James, *Gangland: London's Underworld*, 1992 (1993 pb edn)

– *Bent Coppers: A Survey of Police Corruption*, 1993 (1994 pb edn)

Moseley, Sydney A., *The Night Haunts of London*, 1920

Mudie-Smith, Richard, *The Religious Life of London*, 1904

Mullins, Claud, *Fifteen Years' Hard Labour*, 1948

Munby, D. L., *Industry and Planning in Stepney*, 1951

Murdoch, Iris, *Under the Net*, 1954 (1999 pb edn)

Murphy, J. T., *New Horizons*, 1941

Myers, Sam Price, *London South of the River*, 1949

Naipaul, V. S., *The Enigma of Arrival: A Novel in Five Sections*, 1987

Narborough, Fred, *Murder on My Mind*, 1959

Nevill, Ralph, *Mayfair and Montmartre*, 1921

– *Yesterday and To-Day*, 1922

– *Night Life: London and Paris – Past and Present*, 1926

Neville, Richard, *Hippie Hippie Shake: The Dreams, the Trips, the Trials, the Love-ins, the Screw-ups . . . the Sixties*, 1995 (1996 pb edn)

Newsom, John, '*On the Other Side . . .*', Oxford, 1930

Niall, Ian, *A London Boyhood*, 1974

Nicholson, Harold, *King George the Fifth: His Life and Reign*, 1952 (1967 pb edn)

Nixon, Barbara, *Raiders Overhead: A Diary of the London Blitz*, 1943 (1980 edn)

Noordin, R. M., *Through a Workhouse Window: Being a Brief Summary of Three Years Spent by the Youngest Member of a Board of Guardians in the Course of His Duties*, 1929

Norman, Frank, *Norman's London*, 1969

Norman, Frank, and Bernard, Jeffrey, *Soho Night and Day*, 1966

Norman, Philip, *London Vanished and Vanishing*, 1905

North Kensington Local History Project, *Our Homes, Our Streets*, 1987

Nott-Bower, Sir William, *Fifty-Two Years a Policeman*, 1926

NUCAW (National Union of Clerks and Administrative Workers), *From 9 to 5.30*, n.d. (*c.* 1936)

O'Brien, Terence H., *Civil Defence*, 1955 (Civil History of Second World War)

Oddie, S. Ingleby, *Inquest*, 1941

Ogilvy, James S., *Relics and Memorials of London City*, n.d. (*c.* 1910)

Okey, Thomas, *A Basketful of Memories: An Autobiographical Sketch*, 1930

Olechnowicz, Andrzej, *Working-Class Housing in England Between the Wars: The Becontree Estate*, Oxford, 1997

Oliver, J. L., *The Development and Structure of the Furniture Industry*, 1966

Oliver, Paul, et al. (eds.), *Dunroamin: The Suburban Semi and Its Enemies*, 1981

Olsen, Donald J., *The Growth of Victorian London*, 1976 (1979 pb edn)

Orwell, George, *Down and Out in Paris and London*, 1933 (1998 Folio Society edn)

– *The Road to Wigan Pier*, 1937 (1998 Folio Society edn)

– *My Country Right or Left and Other Selected Essays and Journalism* (1998 Folio Society edn)

– *The Collected Essays, Journalism and Letters of George Orwell*, edited by Sonia Orwell and Ian Angus, 4 vols., 1968 (1970 Penguin edn)

Osborne, John, *A Better Class of Person: An Autobiography, 1929–1956*, 1981 (1982 pb edn)

Osgerby, Bill, *Youth in Britain since 1945*, Oxford, 1998

Ostrowska, Wanda, and Garvin, Viola G., *London's Glory: Twenty Paintings of the City's Ruins . . .* , 1945

Owen, David, *The Government of Victorian London, 1855–1889: The Metropolitan Board of Works, the Vestries, and the City Corporation*, Cambridge, Mass., 1982

Owen, D. J., *The Port of London Yesterday and Today*, 1927

Paddington (Church of England), *The Church of England and Her Slum Ground Rents*, 1930

– (London Diocesan Conference), *The Paddington Estate*, 1944

Padley, Richard, and Cole, Margaret, *Evacuation Survey: A Report to the Fabian Society*, 1940

Page, Robin, *Down among the Dossers*, 1973

Palmer, Alan, *The East End: Four Centuries of London Life*, 1989

Panayi, Panikos, *German Immigrants in Britain during the Nineteenth Century, 1815– 1914*, Oxford, 1995

Panayi, Panikos (ed.), *Racial Violence in Britain in the Nineteenth and Twentieth Centuries*, 1996 (revised edn)

Paneth, Marie, *Branch Street: A Sociological Study*, 1944

Pankhurst, E. Sylvia, *The Home Front: A Mirror to Life in England during the First World War*, 1932 (1987 edn)

Papadakis, Andreas C. (ed.), *Post-Modern Triumphs in London*, 1991

Parker, H. M. D., *Manpower: A Study of War-time Policy and Administration*, 1957 (Civil History of Second World War)

Parker, Robert, *Rough Justice*, 1981

Parker, Tony, *The Plough Boy*, 1965

– *The People of Providence: A Housing Estate and Some of Its Inhabitants*, 1983

Parker, Tony, and Allerton, Robert, *The Courage of His Convictions*, 1962

Parliamentary Papers excluding Royal Commissions and Censuses

>   Ministry of Agriculture and Fisheries, *Markets and Fairs in England and Wales*, 1930

>   Ministry of Health, *Housing Act 1935: Report on the Overcrowding Survey in England and Wales*, 1936

>   *Report of the Committee on Homosexual Offences and Prostitution*, Cd. 247, 1957

>   Ministry of Housing and Local Government, Ministry of Transport, *Piccadilly Circus: Report of the Working Party*, 1965

>   *Report of the Departmental Committee on Liquor Licensing*, Cd. 5154, 1972

>   *The Brixton Disorders: Report of an Inquiry by the Rt. Hon. The Lord Scarman, OBE*, Cd. 8427, 1981

>   *The Stephen Lawrence Inquiry: Report of an Inquiry by Sir William Macpherson of Cluny*, 2 vols., Cd. 4262, 1999

Passingham, W. J., *London's Markets: Their Origin and History*, n.d. (*c.* 1934)

Patterson, Sheila, *Dark Strangers: A Sociological Study of the Absorption of a Recent West Indian Migrant Group in Brixton, South London*, 1963

Paul, Leslie, *Angry Young Man*, 1951

Peach, Ceri, *West Indian Migration to Britain: A Social Geography*, 1968

Peacock, Arthur, *Yours Fraternally*, 1945

Pearson, Geoffrey, *Hooligan: A History of Respectable Fears*, 1983

Pearson, John, *The Profession of Violence: The Rise and Fall of the Kray Twins*, 1995 (4th edn)

Pearson, S. Vere, *London's Overgrowth and the Causes of Swollen Towns*, 1939

Pennybacker, Susan D., *A Vision for London, 1889–1914: Labour, Everyday Life and the LCC Experiment*, 1995

Peters, Carl, *England and the English*, 1904

'Petronius', *London Unexpurgated*, 1969

Pevsner, Nikolaus, *London I: The Cities of London and Westminster*, 1957

Phillips, Mike, and Phillips, Trevor, *Windrush: The Irresistible Rise of Multi-racial Britian*, 1998

Philpott, Hugh B., *London at School: The Story of the School Board, 1870–1904*, 1904

Pilgrim Trust, *Men without Work: A Report Made to the Pilgrim Trust*, Cambridge, 1938

Plender, John, and Wallace, Paul, *The Square Mile: A Guide to the New City of London*, 1985

Plummer, Alfred, *New British Industries in the Twentieth Century: A Survey of Development and Structure*, 1937

Political and Economic Planning, *Report on the Location of Industry*, 1939

– *The British Film Industry*, 1952

Pollard, Sidney, *The Development of the British Economy, 1914–1950*, 1962

Pollitt, Harry, *Serving My Time*, 1940

Porter, Roy, *London: A Social History*, 1994

Port of London Authority, *Annual Reports*, 1962–81

Postgate, Raymond, *The Life of George Lansbury*, 1951

Poulsen, Charles, *Scenes from a Stepney Youth*, 1988

Powell, Anthony, *The Acceptance World*, 1955 (1997 Mandarin edn)

– *The Soldier's Art*, 1966 (1997 Mandarin edn)

Power, Anne, and Tunstall, Rebecca, *Swimming against the Tide: Polarisation or Progress on 20 Unpopular Council Estates, 1980–1995*, York, 1995

Pratt, Michael, *Mugging as a Social Problem*, 1980

Priestley, J. B., *Angel Pavement*, 1930 (1935 edn)

– *Wonder Hero*, 1933

– *English Journey*, 1934 (1949 edn)

– *They Walk in the City*, 1936

Pritchett, V. S., *A Cab at the Door. An Autobiography: Early Years*, 1968

– *Midnight Oil*, 1971

Pudney, John, *London's Docks*, 1975

Purdom, C. B., *How Should We Rebuild London?*, 1945

Quigley, Hugh, and Goldie, Ismay, *Housing and Slum Clearance in London*, 1934

Raban, Jonathan, *Soft City*, 1974 (1988 edn)

Radzinowicz, Sir Leon, and King, Joan, *The Growth of Crime: The International Experience*, 1977 (1979 pb edn)

Ramdin, Ron, *The Making of the Black Working Class in Britain*, Aldershot, 1987

Ramsey, Winston G. (ed.), *The Blitz: Then and Now*, 3 vols., 1987–9

Ransome, Arthur, *Bohemia in London*, 1907 (1st US edn)

Rasmussen, Steen Eiler, *London: The Unique City*, 1934 (1st English edn, 1937)

Rawlings, William, *A Case for the Yard*, 1961

Read, Leonard, *Nipper: The Story of Leonard 'Nipper' Read*, 1991 (1992 pb edn)

Read, Piers Paul, *The Train Robbers*, 1978

Reay, W. T., *The Specials – How They Served London: The Story of the Metropolitan Special Constabulary*, 1920

Reeves, Maud Pember, *Round about a Pound a Week*, 1913 (1979 edn)

Registrar-General, *Statistical Review of England and Wales for the Year 1939: Tables, Part I, Medical*, 1939

Rentoul, Sir Gervais, *Sometimes I Think: Random Reflections and Recollections*, 1940

Reynolds, Gerald W., and Judge, Anthony, *The Night the Police Went on Strike*, 1968

Rhodes, Gerald, *The Government of London: The Struggle for Reform*, 1970

Rhodes, Gerald (ed.), *The New Government of London: The First Five Years*, 1972

Richards, Jeffrey, *The Age of the Dream Palace: Cinema and Society in Britain, 1930–1939*, 1984

Richardson, Charlie, *My Manor*, 1991 (1992 pb edn)

Richardson, Harry W., and Aldcroft, Derek H., *Building in the British Economy between the Wars*, 1968

Rider, Dan, *Ten Years' Adventures among Landlords and Tenants: The Story of the Rent Acts*, 1927.

Rimbault, E. F., *Soho and Its Associations: Historical, Literary, and Artistic*, 1895

Robb, J. H., *Working-Class Anti-Semite*, 1954

Roberts, Florence, *The Ups and Downs of Florrie Roberts*, 1980

Roberts, Glenys, *Metropolitan Myths*, 1982

Roberts, Glyn, *I Take This City*, 1933

Roberts, Sonia, *The Story of Islington*, 1975

Robson, William A., *The Government and Misgovernment of London*, 1939

Rocker, Rudolf, *The London Years*, 1956

Rollin, Jake, *Rothmans Book of Football Records*, 1998

Rolph, C. H. (ed.), *Women of the Streets: a Sociological Study of the Common Prostitute*, 1955 (1961 pb edn)

Rook, Clarence, *The Hooligan Nights: Being the Life and Opinions of a Young and Impertinent Criminal Recounted by Himself . . .* , 1899 (Oxford, 1979 edn)

– *London Side-Lights*, 1908

Rowntree, B. Seebohm, *The Human Needs of Labour*, 1937

Royal Borough of Kensington, *Annual Reports of Medical Officer of Health*, 1932–4

Royal Commissions

    Royal Commission on London Traffic: Vol. I, *Report*; Vol. V, *Maps and Diagrams*, Cd. 2597, 1905–6

    Royal Commission upon the Duties of the Metropolitan Police, *Report Together with Appendices*, 3 vols., Cd. 4156, 4260, 4261, 1908 (Commission established 1906)

Report of the Commissioners Appointed to Inquire into the Local Government of Greater London, Cd. 1830, 1923 (Ullswater Commission)

Report of the Royal Commission on London Squares, Cd. 3196, 1928

Royal Commission on the Distribution of the Industrial Population: Report, Cd. 6153, 1940 (Barlow Report)

Report of the Royal Commission on Local Government in Greater London, 1957–60, 1960 (Herbert Commission)

Report of the Royal Commission on Housing in Greater London, Cd. 2605, 1965 (Milner Holland Report)

Ruck, S. K., *Municipal Entertainment and the Arts: In Greater London*, 1965

Ruck, S. K. (ed.), *The West Indian Comes to England: A Report Prepared for the Trustees of the London Parochial Charities by the Family Welfare Association*, 1960

Ruck, S. K., and Rhodes, Gerald, *The Government of Greater London*, 1970

Rumbelow, Donald, *The Houndsditch Murders: And the Siege of Sidney Street*, 1973

Russell, C., and Lewis, H. S., *The Jew in London (a Study of Racial Character and Present-day Conditions)*, 1900

Saint, Andrew (ed.), *Politics and the People of London: The London County Council, 1889–1965*, 1989

Saint, Andrew, et al., *London Suburbs*, 1999

St Johnston, Eric, *One Policeman's Story*, 1978

Salaman, Malcolm C. and Holme, Charles, *London Past and Present*, 1916

Salkey, Andrew, *Escape to an Autumn Pavement*, 1960

Samuel, Raphael, *East End Underworld: Chapters in the Life of Arthur Harding*, 1981

– *Theatres of Memory: Vol. I, Past and Present in Contemporary Culture*, 1994

– *Island Stories: Unravelling Britain. Theatres of Memory: Vol. II*, 1998

Sandford, Jeremy, *Down and Out in Britain*, 1971 (1972 revised pb edn)

Sansom, William, *Westminster in War*, 1947

Sassen, Saskia, *The Global City: New York, London, Tokyo*, Princeton, NJ, 1991

Saunders, Nicholas, *Alternative London*, 1970

Scanlon, Ann, *Those Tourists Are Money: The Rock 'n' Roll Guide to Camden*, 1997

Scannell, Dorothy, *Mother Knew Best: An East End Childhood*, 1974

Schneer, Jonathan, *London 1900: The Imperial Metropolis*, New Haven, Conn., 1999

Scott, George Riley, *A History of Prostitution: From Antiquity to the Present Day*, 1936

Scott, Sir Harold, *Scotland Yard*, 1954 (1957 pb edn)

Scott, J. D., *Siemens Brothers 1858–1958: An Essay in the History of Industry*, 1958

Scott, Stanley, *Tales of Bohemia, Taverns and the Underworld: Stories and Sketches of People Famous, Infamous, and Obscure*, n.d. (c. 1925)

Scott Moncrieff, George, *Café Bar*, 1932

Searle, Ronald, and Webb, Kaye, *Looking at London: And People Worth Meeting*, 1953

Selvon, Sam, *The Lonely Londoners*, 1956 (1985 edn)

– *The Housing Lark*, 1965 (1st US edn, 1990)

Senior, Clarence, and Manley, Douglas, *A Report on Jamaican Migration to Great Britain*, Kingston, Jamaica, n.d. (1955)

Service, Alistair, *The Architects of London: And Their Buildings from 1066 to the Present Day*, 1979

Shankland, Graeme, et al., *Inner London: Policies for Dispersal and Balance*, 1977

Sharpe, F. D. ('Nutty'), *Sharpe of the Flying Squad*, 1938

Sheppard, Francis, *London 1808–1870: The Infernal Wen*, 1971

– *London: A History*, Oxford, 1997

Sherry, Norman, *The Life of Graham Greene: Vol. II, 1939–1955*, 1994

Sherwell, Arthur, *Life in West London: A Study and A Contrast*, 1897

Shrapnel, Norman, *The Seventies: Britain's Inward March*, 1980

Shute, Nerina, *London Villages*, 1977

– *More London Villages*, 1981

Simey, T. S. and M. B., *Charles Booth: Social Scientist*, Oxford, 1960

Simmie, James (ed.), *Planning London*, 1994

Simonis, H., *The Street of Ink: An Intimate History of Journalism*, 1917

Sims, George R., *The Mysteries of Modern London*, 1906

– *Off the Track in London*, n.d. (c. 1911)

Sims, George R. (ed.), *Living London*, 3 vols., n.d. (1902–3)

Sinclair, Andrew, *The Breaking of Bumbo*, 1959

– *War Like a Wasp: The Lost Decade of the 'Forties*, 1989

Sinclair, Robert, *Metropolitan Man: The Future of the English*, 1937

Sissons, Michael, and French, Philip (eds.), *Age of Austerity, 1945–51*, 1963 (1964 Penguin edn)

Slipper, Jack, *Slipper of the Yard*, 1981

Smallwood, Frank, *Greater London: The Politics of Metropolitan Reform*, 1965

Smith, Ashley, *The East-Enders*, 1961

Smith, David, and Whalley, Anne, *Racial Minorities and Public Housing*, 1975

Smith, David J., et al., *Police and People in London*, 4 vols., 1983

Smith, Douglas H., *The Industries of Greater London: Being a Survey of the Recent Industrialisation of the Northern and Western Sectors of Greater London*, 1933

Smith, Sir Henry, *From Constable to Commissioner: The Story of Sixty Years, Most of Them Misspent*, 1910

Smith, Sir Hubert Llewellyn (ed.), *The New Survey of London Life and Labour*, 9 vols., 1930–35

Smith, Raymond, *Sea-Coal for London: History of the Coal Factors in the London Market*, 1961

Smithies, Edward, *Crime in Wartime: A Social History of Crime in World War II*, 1982

Snell, Lord (Harry), *Men, Movements, and Myself*, 1936 (1938 edn)

Sorensen, Colin, *London on Film: 100 Years of Filmmaking in London*, 1996

Southgate, Walter, *That's the Way It Was: A Working-class Autobiography, 1890–1950*, 1982

Spark, Muriel, *The Girls of Slender Means*, 1963 (Penguin edn)

Sparks, Ruby, *Burglar to the Nobility*, 1961

Sparrow, Gerald, *Gang-Warfare: A Probe into the Changing Pattern of British Crime*, 1968

Spearing, Nigel, 'London's Docks: Up or Down the River?', *London Journal*, Vol. 4, No. 2, 1978

Spencer, Ian R. G., *British Immigration Policy since 1939: The Making of Multi-racial Britain*, 1997

Spinley, B. M., *The Deprived and the Privileged: Personality Development in English Society*, 1953

Sponza, Lucio, *Italian Immigrants in Nineteenth-Century Britain: Realities and Images*, Leicester, 1988

Squires, Mike, *Saklatvala: A Political Biography*, 1990

Srebrnik, Henry Felix, *London Jews and British Communism, 1939–1945*, 1995

Stewart, Michael, *Life and Labour: An Autobiography*, 1980

Stokes, Alfred, *East Ham: From Village to County Borough*, 1933

Storey, David, *Flight into Camden*, 1960 (1st US edn, 1961)

Summers, Judith, *Soho: A History of London's most Colourful Neighbourhood*, 1989

Survey of London, Vol. XXV, *The Parishes of St George the Martyr, Southwark and St Mary, Newington*, 1955

– Vols. XXXI–II, *The Parish of St James Westminster, Part II, North of Piccadilly*, 1963

– Vols. XXXIII–IV, *The Parish of St Anne Soho*, 1966

– Vol. XXXVII, *Northern Kensington*, 1973

– Vol. XLII, *Southern Kensington: Kensington Square to Earl's Court*, 1986

– (monograph No. 17), *County Hall*, 1991

– Vols. XLIII–IV *Poplar, Blackwall and the Isle of Dogs: The Parish of All Saints*, 1994

– (Cox, Alan), *Docklands in the Making: The Redevelopment of the Isle of Dogs, 1981–1995*, 1995

Swift, Graham, *Last Orders*, 1996.

Tajfel, Henri and Dawson, John L. (eds.), *Disappointed Guests: Essays by African, Asian and West Indian Students*, 1965

Tambs-Lyche, Harald, *London Patidars: A Case Study in Urban Ethnicity*, 1980

Tatchell, Peter, *The Battle for Bermondsey*, 1983

Tawney, R. H., *The Establishment of Minimum Rates in the Tailoring Industry under the Trades Board Act of 1909*, 1915

Tebbutt, Melanie, *Making Ends Meet: Pawnbroking and Working-Class Credit*, Leicester, 1986

Thatcher, Margaret, *The Downing Street Years*, 1993

Thompson, Bonar, *Hyde Park Orator*, 1933 (1936 edn)

Thompson, F. M. L., *Hampstead: Building a Borough, 1650–1964*, 1974

Thompson, F. M. L. (ed.), *The Rise of Suburbia*, Leicester, 1982

Thompson, Paul, *Socialists, Liberals and Labour: The Struggle for London, 1885–1914*, 1967

Thompson, Wally, *Time off My Life*, 1956

Thomson, Basil, *The Criminal*, 1925

Thomson, David, *In Camden Town*, 1983 (1985 Penguin edn)

Thorne, Will, *My Life's Battles*, 1925

Thornley, Andy (ed.), *The Crisis of London*, 1992

Thorogood, Horace, *East of Aldgate*, 1935

Thorp, Arthur, *Calling Scotland Yard: Being the Casebook of Chief Superintendent Arthur Thorp*, 1954

Thurtle, Ernest, *Time's Winged Chariot: Memories and Comments*, 1945

Tiley, George Leslie, 'Memories of Islington Between the Wars', MS 1975 (reprinted in *The Illustrated Islington History Journal*, Nos. 13–14, 1987)

Time Out's Book of London, 1970

The Times, The Story of the London County Council, 1907

Tindall, Gillian, *The Fields Beneath: The History of One London Village*, 1977 (1980 pb edn)

Titmuss, Richard M., *Problems of Social Policy*, 1950 (Civil History of Second World War)

Titmuss, Richard M. and Kathleen, *Parents Revolt: A Study of the Declining Birth-rate in the Acquisitive Societies*, 1942

Tomlin, Maurice, *Police and Public*, 1936

Townsend, Peter, *The Family Life of Old People*, 1957 (1963 Penguin edn)

– *Poverty in the United Kingdom: A Survey of Household Resources and Standard of Living*, 1979

Townsend, Peter, et al., *Poverty and Labour in London: Interim Report of a Centenary Study*, 1987

Travers, Tony, and Jones, George, *The New Government of London*, 1991

– *The New Government of London*, 1997

Tremlett, George, *Living Cities*, 1979

Trevelyan, Mary, *From the Ends of the Earth*, 1942

Trotsky, Leon, *My Life: The Rise and Fall of a Dictator*, 1930

Visram, Rozina, *Ayahs, Lascars and Princes: Indians in Britain, 1700–1947*, 1986

Wallman, Sandra and associates, *Living in South London: Perspectives on Battersea, 1871–1981*, 1982

Waltham Forest Oral History Workshop, *Touch Yer Collar Never Swaller: Memories of Childhood Illness before the Health Service*, 1984

Wates, Nick, *The Battle for Tolmers Square*, 1976

Watson, James L. (ed.), *Between Two Cultures: Migrants and Minorities in Britain*, Oxford, 1977

Watson, W. F., *Machines and Men: An Autobiography of an Itinerant Mechanic*, 1935

Watts, Marthe, *The Men in My Life*, 1960

Webb, Beatrice, *The Diary of Beatrice Webb: Vol. II, 1892–1905. 'All the good things of life'*, edited by Norman and Jean Mackenzie, 1983

– *The Diary of Beatrice Webb: Vol. III, 1905–1924. 'The power to alter things'*, edited by Norman and Jean Mackenzie, 1984

Webb, Sidney, *The London Programme*, 1895 (revised edn)

Weightman, Gavin, and Humphries, Steve, *The Making of Modern London, 1914–1939*, 1984

Weller, Ken, *'Don't be a Soldier!' The Radical Anti-war Movement in North London, 1914–1918*, 1985

Wells, H. G., *Mankind in the Making*, 1903

– *Ann Veronica: A Modern Love Story*, 1909

– *Tono-Bungay*, 1909 (1926 Essex edn)

– *Christine Alberta's Father*, 1925

Wensley, Frederick Porter, *Detective Days: The Record of 42 Years' Service in the Criminal Investigation Department*, 1931

Wesker, Arnold, *As Much As I Dare: An Autobiography (1932–1959)*, 1994

Wheen, Francis, *The Battle for London*, 1985

Whitaker, Ben, *The Police in Society*, 1979

White, Jerry, *Rothschild Buildings: Life in an East End Tenement Block, 1887–1920*, 1980

– *The Worst Street in North London: Campbell Bunk, Islington, between the Wars*, 1986

White, Jerry, and Young, Michael, *Governing London*, 1996

White, L. E., *Tenement Town*, 1946

Widgery, David, *Some Lives! A GP's East End*, 1991 (1993 pb edn)

Wilcox, David, and Richards, David, *London: The Heartless City*, 1977

Williams, Harry, *South London*, 1949

Williamson, Joseph, *Father Joe: The Autobiography of Joseph Williamson of Poplar and Stepney*, 1963

Willis, Ted, *Whatever Happened to Tom Mix?*, 1970

Willmott, Peter, *The Evolution of a Community: A Study of Dagenham after 40 Years*, 1963

Willmott, Peter, and Young, Michael, *Family and Class in a London Suburb*, 1960 (1976 edn)

Wilson, Colin, *Adrift in Soho*, 1961

Wohl, Anthony S., *The Eternal Slum: Housing and Social Policy in Victorian London*, 1977

Women's Group on Public Welfare, *Our Towns: A Close-up*, 1943

Woolf, Leonard, *Beginning Again: An Autobiography of the Years 1911–1918*, 1964

Woolf, Virginia, *The Years*, 1937

Woon, Basil, *Hell Came to London: A Reportage of the Blitz during 14 Days*, 1941

Worby, John, *The Other Half: The Autobiography of a Spiv*, 1937

– *Spiv's Progress*, 1939

Worpole, Ken, *Dockers and Detectives: Popular Reading, Popular Writing*, 1983

Worsley-Gough, Barbara, *Fashions in London*, 1952

Wright, Patrick, *A Journey through Ruins: The Last Days of London*, 1991

Wyles, Lilian, *A Woman at Scotland Yard: Reflections on the Struggles and Achievements of 30 Years in the Metropolitan Police*, 1952

Wyndham, Horace, and George, Dorothea St J., *Nights in London: Where Mayfair Makes Merry*, 1926

Yelling, J. A., *Slums and Slum Clearance in Victorian London*, 1986

– *Slums and Redevelopment: Policy and Practice in England, 1918–1945, with Particular Reference to London*, 1992

Young, Ken, *Local Politics and the Rise of Party: The London Municipal Society and the Conservative Intervention in Local Elections, 1894–1963*, 1975

Young, Ken, and Garside, Patricia L., *Metropolitan London: Politics and Urban Change, 1837–1981*, 1982

Young, Ken, and Kramer, John, *Strategy and Conflict in Metropolitan Housing: Suburbia versus the Greater London Council, 1965–75*, 1978

Young, Michael, and Willmott, Peter, *Family and Kinship in East London*, 1957

– *The Symmetrical Family: A Study of Work and Leisure in the London Region*, 1973

Young, Terence, *Becontree and Dagenham: A Report Made for the Pilgrim Trust*, 1934

Ziegler, Philip, *London at War, 1939–1945*, 1995 (1996 pb edn)

Zubrzycki, Jerzy, *Polish Immigrants in Britain: A Study of Adjustment*, The Hague, 1956

Zweig, Ferdynand, *Labour, Life and Poverty*, 1949 (1975 edn)

Index

Mosley, Sir Oswald (fascist) 127–8, 150
motor car 20, 29, 32, 51–2, 84, 156, 181–2, 201, 226, 227, 228, 247, 253, 264–5, 292, 325
Mottingham Estate (Bromley) 36, 54
Moya, John Hidalgo (architect) 46, 54
mud 14
Muggeridge, Malcolm (journalist) 315
Municipal Reform 361–3, 370, 371, 374–7, 383
Murdoch, Rupert (entrepreneur) 79
Murphy, John T. (Communist) 93
Murray, Dalton (club owner) 333
Murrow, Ed (journalist) 116
Museum of London 79
music 167, 181, 213–14, 249–50, 325–6, 328, 330, 333, 335, 338–42, 344–5, 346–51, 357, 373
music hall 246, 249, 263, 311, 327, 330–31, 343
Muswell Hill (Hornsey) 24, 271, 342
Myers, Sam (writer) 92

Nabarro, Gerald (Conservative politician) 60
Naipaul, V. S. (novelist) 144
Nairn, Ian (writer) 68
Narborough, Fred (policeman) 274, 291
Nash, John (architect) 19–20
National Front 151–2, 395
National Gallery 213
National Lottery 85
National Trust 61, 213
NatWest Tower (City) 53
Neal's Yard (Covent Garden) 287
Neasden (Willesden) 326, 342
Neave, Jack 'Ironfoot' (Soho character) 334
neighbouring 116–26, 157–61
Nevill, Ralph (writer) 311, 327, 333
Neville, Richard (writer) 345
New Court (City) 200
New Cross (Deptford) 75, 274, 298
New North Road (Hoxton) 122
New Towns 42, 59–60, 72, 77, 155, 163, 203, 394; *see also* individual towns
New York 11, 46, 47, 141, 142, 209, 210, 211, 284, 341, 342, 345, 350, 409
Newham 59, 77, 83, 84, 143, 152, 154, 206, 234, 235, 245–6, 388, 393, 395; *see also* East Ham, Stratford, West Ham
Newington (Southwark) 316
Niall, Ian (writer) 116
nightclubs 101,116, 211, 228, 277, 278, 290,

296, 316, 327, 329, 331–5, 338, 343–4, 346–51
Nile Street (Hoxton) 263
Nilsen, Dennis (murderer) 271
Nixon, Barbara (writer) 122, 273
noise 14
Norbury Estate (Croydon) 362
Norman, Frank (writer) 339
Norman, Philip (artist and historian) 12, 61
North Circular Road 32, 41, 71
Northampton 59, 270
Northampton, Marquess of 64
Norwood (Lambeth and Croydon) 26, 124, 233, 394
Notting Dale (Kensington) 18, 108, 118–19, 149–50, 232, 248, 253, 271, 286, 339
Notting Hill (Kensington) 64, 83, 135–6, 147–50,161, 270, 274, 279, 296, 297, 322, 323, 325, 339–40, 345, 349–51
Notting Hill Carnival 167, 297, 298, 326, 350
Notting Hill Gate 52, 131
Nottingham 38, 149, 196

office development 20, 42–3, 47–53, 58–9, 78–81, 82, 199, 202–3, 207–8, 211; *see also* City of London
office work 34, 184, 187, 188, 191, 196, 198, 199–201, 202, 373
Ogilvy, James (artist and historian) 61
Old Bailey (City) 10, 259, 267, 270, 280, 290, 323
Old Compton Street (Soho) 105, 329, 340, 343
Old Kent Road (Southwark) 313
Old Street (Shoreditch) 180, 229, 259
Olympia (Kensington) 107, 289, 310
Olympia and York (property developers) 78–9
Olympic Games 310, 323, 402
O'Mahoney, Maurice (criminal) 279
Orchard Place (Bow) 117–18
Orpington 57
Orwell, George (writer) 63, 94, 127, 227, 239, 249, 255, 270
Osborne, John (playwright) 33, 122
Osterley (Heston) 189
Ostrowska, Wanda (artist) 62
Ove, Horace (writer) 350
Owen, David (Labour and Social/Liberal Democratic politician) 74
Oxford Gardens (Notting Hill) 149

Powell, Anthony (novelist) 321, 335, 337
Powell, Enoch (Conservative politician) 151–2, 296, 361, 385, 391–2
Powell, Philip (architect) 46, 54
Pretty Things, The (band) 342
Priestley, J. B. (writer) 30, 32, 37, 92, 93, 195, 200
Prince's Gardens (Brompton) 229
Pritchett, V. S. (writer) 33
Progressives 356–63, 383, 390
Proms 213
prostitution 18, 22, 49, 66, 74, 81, 105–6, 145, 148, 149, 161, 193–4, 227, 260, 269–70, 271, 288, 289, 296, 311–14, 316, 321–3, 327–9, 331, 332, 335–6, 339, 343–4, 349
Prowse Place (Camden Town) 145
Prudential Assurance Co. 10, 69
pubs 99, 100, 151, 185, 260, 289, 313, 329–30, 337–8, 341, 347, 348
punks 326, 331
Purdom, C. B. (town planner) 201
Purfleet 189–90
Putney (Wandsworth) 229, 248, 276, 292

Quant, Mary (fashion designer) 343
Queen Anne's Gate (Westminster) 83, 337
Queen Square (Holborn) 108
Queen Victoria Street (City) 49, 197
Queens Park Rangers Football Club 297
Queensway (Bayswater) 140
queuing 225, 263, 321

Raban, Jonathan (writer) 154
Rachman, Peter (landlord) 66, 147, 148
radio 125, 225, 227, 244, 250, 316
Raft, George (actor) 278
Ragged School Museum (Tower Hamlets) 213
Railton Road (Brixton) 67, 299
Ransome, Arthur (writer) 17
Rasmussen, Steen Eiler (architect and historian) 34
Ratcliff (Stepney) 112
rats 236–7
Ravensbourne River 171
Rawlings, William (policeman) 291
Raymond, Paul (club owner) 344
Rayne, Max (property developer) 48
Read, Leonard 'Nipper' (policeman) 294
Red Lion Square (Holborn) 152
Redbridge 389; *see also* individual districts

Reeves, Maud Pember (sociologist) 125, 219, 223, 236
Regent Palace Hotel (Piccadilly Circus) 10
Regent Street (Westminster) 6, 19–20, 109, 312, 328, 334, 337, 338
Regent's Park 64, 106, 140, 280, 320
Reichmann Brothers (property developers) 78–9
Reigate 293
religious life 98–9, 105, 106, 107–8, 109, 111, 112, 115, 116, 134, 140, 147, 193–4
Rennie, John (architect and engineer) 62
Rentoul, Sir Gervais (magistrate) 287
restaurants 16, 20, 105, 106, 107, 108, 113, 114, 115, 128–9, 137, 201–2, 213, 228, 311, 327–9, 334, 338, 350–51
Reynolds, Bruce (criminal) 276–7
Ribuffi, Luigi (club owner) 290
Rice-Davies, Mandy (model) 142
Richard, Cliff (singer) 340
Richardson brothers (criminals) 251, 275, 277
Richmond 25, 74, 238
Rillington Place (Notting Dale) 271
ring roads 41, 49, 68–9, 71–2, 389
riots 21, 76, 107, 108, 111, 128, 136, 145, 148–50, 152–3, 221, 287, 296, 297, 298–300, 325, 365, 400
Ripper, Jack the (murderer) 18, 21, 269, 270, 348
Rippon, Geoffrey (Conservative politician) 70, 72
Ritz Hotel (Piccadilly) 10
Rix, Brian (actor) 292
Roberts, Florrie (housewife) 225
Roberts, Glyn (journalist) 92, 102
Robinson, Chief Superintendent 299
Robson, William (social scientist) 384, 401
Rock Against Racism 152
Rockers 326
Roding River 171
Roehampton (Wandsworth) 54, 229
Rogers, Lord Richard (architect) 80, 81
Rolling Stones (band) 341, 342, 347
Rolt, Terry (criminal) 267
Romford 24, 43, 155, 207
Ronan Point (Newham) 56, 83
Rook, Clarence (journalist) 17, 24, 101, 268, 324
Rope Yard Rails (Woolwich) 118
Rosehaugh Stanhope Developments (property developers) 80